Benchmark ADVANCE

English Language Development

TEACHER'S RESOURCE SYSTEM

Create engaged learners who effectively

- develop language
- build knowledge
- express understanding

to gain a solid foundation of language and literacy.

English Language Development

TEACHER'S RESOURCE SYSTEM

Development Team

Authors
Peter Afflerbach, Ph.D., University of Maryland
Silvia Dorta-Duque de Reyes, M.A.,
    Benchmark Education Company
Queta Fernandez, Spanish Literacy Consultant
Linda Hoyt, M.A., Author and Literacy Consultant
Adria Klein, Ph.D., California State University, San Bernardino
Carrie Smith, M.S., Benchmark Education Company

Contributing Authors
Farah Assiraj, M.A., Boston Public Schools
Jorge Cuevas Antillón, M.A., San Diego County
    Office of Education
Erin Bostick Mason, M.A. Ed., California State University,
    San Bernardino
Marjorie McCabe, Ph.D., California State University,
    San Bernardino
Jill Kerper Mora, Ph.D., San Diego State University
Jeff Zwiers, Ed.D., Stanford University

Linguistic Consultants
Sandra Ceja, InterLingual SoLutions, Carlsbad, California
Youniss El Cheddadi, Arabic Department, San Diego
    State University
Lilly Cheng, Ph.D., University of California, San Diego

Benchmark *ADVANCE*™

BENCHMARK EDUCATION COMPANY
145 Huguenot Street • New Rochelle, NY 10801

For ordering information, call Toll-Free 1-877-236-2465 or visit our website at www.benchmarkeducation.com.

ISBN: 978-1-5125-3344-6

Table of Contents

ELD in tandem with ELA Instruction

Accelerate English Learners with amplified ELD instruction that ensures success!

The focused English language development in *Benchmark Advance* has a unique architecture that supports core ELA goals. ELD instruction ensures that English Learners participate meaningfully in cognitively demanding core lessons as they learn how English works.

Using English Purposefully — Build English language skills using the core ELA content.

Meaningful Interaction — Provide engaging opportunities for language production through structured academic conversations.

Knowledge of English — Learn how English works through explicit instruction and purposeful, engaging practice.

Scaffold students to access complex texts.

English Learners read complex core texts amplified with visual support and scaffolded with language development instruction.

Rather than lower the cognitive demands on English Learners, Advance supports them in acquiring grade-level concepts and skills. *Texts for English Language Development* include complex core texts with added graphic elements and organization to support comprehension, vocabulary development, and text analysis.

Differentiate instruction at three intensity levels based on ongoing assessment.

Every lesson has three levels of differentiated support with a built-in acceleration plan to ensure that ELs advance.

Fifteen explicit lessons per unit (one per day) ensure that students:

- Access complex texts
- Build academic vocabulary
- Learn English syntax and structures
- Engage in purposeful collaborative conversation
- Develop strong English writing skills

Every lesson supports differentiated language instruction at three intensity levels–substantial, moderate, and light– enabling teachers to adjust instruction as needed based on their observations.

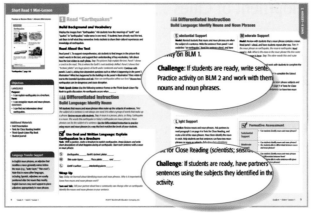

ELs at all levels are challenged to increase their proficiency.

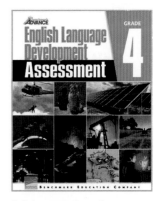

Rubrics support ongoing assessment opportunities built into the lessons.

Explicitly teach and practice how English language works.

Use rich examples from the text along with explicit modeling and practice to build English grammar and syntax.

Lessons in how language works come directly from the core texts. **Sustained and consistent practice** is provided for every language lesson at three intensity levels that ensure both **teacher-to-student interaction** and **student-to-student interaction**.

Explicit language instruction that comes out of core texts

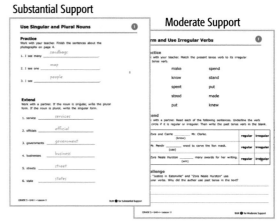

Meaningful practice at differentiated intensity levels

Provide meaningful language production opportunities.

Hands-on tools support students to engage in purposeful academic conversations.

Through the lessons students learn a range of academic sentence frames that support key building blocks of collaborative conversation:

- asking questions
- explaining ideas
- building on the ideas of others
- expressing and supporting opinions

Hands-on student tools support listening and speaking for a range of academic purposes.

Grades K–1

Grades 2–6

Accelerate foundational skills.

Accelerated lessons support ELs in Grades 3–6 who need explicit foundational skills instruction.

Lessons support

- Print Concepts
- Phonological Awareness
- Phonics
- Fluency

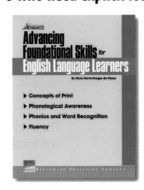

Lesson Overview

Each lesson includes whole-group and differentiated instruction at three intensity levels.

Lessons use grade-level content from *Texts for English Language Development.*

Teacher-talk and question prompts support students' comprehension and vocabulary acquisition.

Objectives are expressed in **student-friendly "can do" statements.**

Every lesson has a **language skill based on examples from the text.**

The culminating activity in every lesson provides an **opportunity to assess language.** The three red-checked activities in each unit have supporting rubrics in *English Language Development Assessment.*

Sidebar tips alert teacher to grammar and syntax skills that present potential challenges for students of certain language groups.

The whole-group **Wrap Up** promotes skill transfer to other content areas.

Mentor Read 1 Mini-Lesson

Preview or Review Week 1 ELA Mini-Lessons

Hello, Community Garden!

① Between the city buildings, one plot of land was a problem.

② Some neighbors decided to turn the lot into a vegetable garden.

③ The plants grew big and healthy.

④ Soon there were delicious carrots, tomatoes, and beans for everyone to share.

ThinkSpeakListen
Tell the kinds of plants you see on this page.

"Hello, Community Garden!" p. 4

Student Objectives

LANGUAGE
Purpose:
• I can talk about vegetables in a garden.
Form:
• I can identify nouns.
CONTENT
• I can use domain-specific vocabulary related to gardening.

Additional Materials
• Unit Presentation
• Think-Speak-Listen Bookmark
• Student journals

Language Transfer Support

Speakers of Chinese, Hmong, and Vietnamese may need additional support to use the plural form of nouns. There is no plural form in their languages. Also, in Haitian Creole, the plural form is often omitted.

---

1 Read "Hello, Community Garden!"

Build Background and Vocabulary

Display the images with text. Read the title aloud and Invite students to share their cultural knowledge and experiences about community gardens. If students have already read the text, ask them to tell what they remember. Then point to each panel and ask students to tell you what they see. Use the visuals to teach key words, such as *land, neighbors,* and *lot.*

Differentiated Instruction
Read Aloud the Text

Read aloud panel 1. Point out the images of words in the text and Mentor Read (*land, garden, vegetable,* etc.). Ask questions: *What is growing on the land? Why is it a problem?* Help students answer. Explain that weeds are plants we don't want. Continue with panels 2–4. In panel 2, explain that a *lot* is unused space. For panel 4, **ask:** *What did the neighbors get from their garden?* Make sure students understand *turn into, grew,* and *delicious.* Afterward, ask the Essential Question: *Why do people get involved in their communities?* Model thinking through the answer.

Use the Differentiated Instruction to continue building comprehension and language in a way that best matches the levels of your students.

Think-Speak-Listen: Use the following sentence frame or the Think-Speak-Listen Bookmark for discussion: *I see _____ on this page.*

Build Language: Use Nouns to Name Things

Point out examples of nouns that are things in the panels. Say: *(A garden) is a noun.* Explain that a noun is a word that names a thing. Point out objects in the classroom and say the noun that identifies them. Have students repeat after you. Then invite students to name other nouns.

☑ Use Oral and Written Language: Talk About Vegetables in a Garden

Task: *Work with a group to create a vegetable garden. Draw a vegetable to add to your garden. Present your garden to the class and tell what you know about your vegetable.*

Use this opportunity to assess students using the rubric in *English Language Assessment.*

Sample sentences:
Ⓢ *This is a tomato. I like/don't like tomatoes.*
Ⓜ *This is a carrot. Carrots grow in the ground. I like/don't like to eat carrots.*
Ⓛ *This is a green bean. Green beans are vegetables. They grow in the ground. They taste good/don't taste good.*

🔄 Wrap Up

Say: *Nouns name things. What are some nouns that you remember about gardens?*

Turn and Talk: *Tell your partner two nouns that you see on the playground.*

©2018 Benchmark Education Company, LLC

Differentiated Instruction amplifies one section of a lesson.

👥 Differentiated Instruction
Read Aloud the Text

ⓈSubstantial Support

Model: Read panel 1. Have students echo-read the panel. Gesture and point as you **say:** *The text says the land is a problem. Let's look at the picture. I see weeds. Weeds are not pretty. I think the weeds are a problem.*

Practice: Read panel 2. Have students echo-read the panel. Help students understand the land has turned into a garden. **Say:** *The land is different. Where are the weeds now? What is this? Who helped?* Help students answer. Point to panel 3. Have students pretend to be growing plants, crouching down and standing up with arms stretched. Point to panel 4. Say the names of vegetables with students and ask them to tell which ones they like and don't like.

Extend: Have pairs take turns pointing to a picture and saying a word or phrase about it.

Challenge: Ask: *Who made the garden?*

Ⓜoderate Support

Model: Point to panel 1. Have students echo-read the panel. **Say:** *I read and learned that this land is in the city, and the land is a problem. I see ugly weeds, so I think the weeds are the problem.*

Practice: Point to panel 2. Have students echo-read the panel. Have students tell you what they see. **Ask:** *What happened to the land and the ugly weeds? Who made the garden?* Help students answer. Point to panel 3. Have students act out being healthy growing plants. Point to panel 4. Say the names of vegetables with students and ask them to tell which ones they like and don't like.

Extend: Have pairs take turns pointing to a panel and saying a sentence about it.

Challenge: Ask: *What will happen to the vegetables in the garden?*

Ⓛight Support

Model: Point to panel 1. Have students echo-read the panel. **Say:** *The title tells me this story is about a community garden, but the picture doesn't look like a garden. I see land with weeds on it. I learn it is in the city and it's a problem. The weeds are ugly, so I think the weeds are a problem.*

Practice: Point to panel 2. Have students echo-read the panel. **Ask:** *What happened to the land and ugly weeds?* Help students answer. Point to panel 3. Have students act out being healthy growing plants and then unhealthy plants. Point to panel 4. Have students name the vegetables and tell why they like or don't like them.

Extend: Have pairs take turns pointing to a panel and saying two things they learned in the picture and text.

Challenge: Ask: *Why do people make community gardens?*

☑ Formative Assessment

Substantial Support	• Can students use words about gardens, including *land, plants, garden,* and the names of vegetables, to name items in the picture?
Moderate Support	• Can students use words about gardens, including *land, weeds, neighbors, garden,* and the names of vegetables, to say phrases or sentences about each picture?
Light Support	• Can students use words about gardens, including *land, weeds, neighbors, garden,* and the names of vegetables, to say two sentences about each picture?

The Differentiated Instruction has a built-in acceleration plan **AT EVERY INTENSITY LEVEL:** *Model, Practice, Extend, Challenge*

- Instruction at the **Substantial Support** level accelerates students toward moderate level expectations.

- Instruction at the **Moderate Support** level accelerates students toward light support expectations.

- Instruction at the **Light Support** level bridges students to on-level language expectations. In Grades 2–6, students use the *ELA Texts for Close Reading* booklet as the basis for instruction.

Academic Writing Instruction

Students in Grades 2-6 read like writers to develop their own writing skills.

Through careful analysis of mentor texts, students learn the language structures and word choices writers use across text types.

Introduction Lesson

The Introduction lesson is targeted for students at ALL levels of support. Students analyze the challenging on-level ELA mentor text to learn basic writing frames to talk about sources and explain ideas.

Light Support

Students analyze the same **on-level ELA mentor text** to learn more complex structures to explain and support ideas.

Extend and Scaffold Academic Language for Writing

Analyze the Mentor Text: Language Purpose and Structure

Introduction — All Levels of Support

Materials List
- **Mentor Text L** BLM X Light Support
- **Writing Frames Teacher Page** BLM Y
- **Writing Frames Student Page** BLM Z

- Have a copy of BLM Y to refer to during the lesson.

- Distribute BLMs X and Z to each student.

- Read aloud the writing prompt on BLM X. Explain that students will read and analyze the language one writer used to respond to this prompt.

- Have students follow along as you read aloud paragraph 1 of "Emperor Penguins of Antarctica."

- Point out the sentence *The penguin has adapted so that it can live there.* **Ask:** *Why did the author use this language? What is its purpose?* Help students understand that the author uses the frame *From reading ___ I learned that ___* to support students' opinions in "Emperor Penguins of Antarctica."

- Have students write this frame into the "Cause and Effect" row of their Academic Writing Frames tool (BLM Z). Tell students this is one frame they can use in their writing to show the relationship between cause and effect.

- Analyze other bold phrases in paragraph 1. Explain their purpose and help students add the frames to BLM Z.

- Follow these steps as you read additional paragraphs.

- Read aloud the writing prompt on BLM Z. Work with students to generate additional frames they could use as they write a response to this prompt. Refer to BLM Y for examples.

Based on students' needs, conduct additional lessons using the differentiated instruction and tools provided.

Light Support — Differentiated Instruction

Materials List
- **Mentor Text L** BLM X Light Support
- **Writing Frames Teacher Page** BLM Y
- **Writing Frames Student Page** BLM Z

Students will need their copies of BLMs X and Z from the initial lesson. Refer to the chart below and your copy of BLM Y during the lesson.

- Explain that students will reread "Emperor Penguins of Antarctica" to analyze more phrases and sentences that the writer used.

- Reread the text with students one paragraph at a time.

- Ask individuals or partners to find and underline each phrase in the chart below, read the sentence it appears in, and try to determine the sentence's purpose in the text.

- Provide explanation as necessary, then have students add the frames to the "Other Academic Phrases and Sentences" column of BLM Z.

- Encourage students to generate related frames and add them to their chart.

LIGHT SUPPORT		
Purpose	**Phrase/Sentence (Paragraph)**	**Frame**
Cause/ Effect	It has adapted in interesting ways so that it can live there (para. 1).	It has _____ so _____.
Cite sources from text	In "Adapting to Survive," I saw and heard that penguins are the only animals "to live on the Antarctic all year round" and other birds leave when winter comes (para. 2).	In _____, I saw and heard that _____.
Add	I read that huddling close together also helps emperor penguins stay warm (para. 4).	I read that _____ also _____.
Compare and Contrast	Winter in Antarctica is harsh, but emperor penguins don't think so (para. 5).	_____ but _____.
Time	The long, dark days are soon over, and all the penguins return to the sea together (para. 5).	The _____ soon.

During differentiated instruction lessons, students deconstruct complex sentences in mentor texts with varying levels of support.

Moderate Support

Students analyze a mentor text at the **moderate support level** to learn writing frames that help them cite sources, give reasons, and compare and contrast ideas, among others.

Substantial Support

Students analyze a mentor text written at the **substantial support level** to learn writing frames that help them organize and explain their ideas.

Moderate Support — Differentiated Instruction

Materials List
- **Mentor Text M** BLM A Moderate Support
- **Writing Frames Teacher Page** BLM Y
- **Writing Frames Student Page** BLM Z

Use BLM A and the phrases and sentences appropriate for the support level you are targeting.

- Distribute BLM A. Students will also need their copy of BLM Z.

- Read aloud BLM A as students follow along.

- Then reread the text one paragraph at a time, stopping after each paragraph to focus on the bold and underlined phrases and sentences. Work with students to understand the purpose of each phrase within the text. Have students write the corresponding sentence frame in the "Other Academic Phrases and Sentences" column of BLM Z.

- Have partners practice using one or more of these sentence frames to expand an idea in the essay they are writing. Have students share their examples with other members of the group.

MODERATE SUPPORT

Purpose	Phrase/Sentence	Frame
Cause/Effect	The penguin has adapted so that it can live there (para. 1).	_____ so _____.
Cite sources from text	I read in the text that a "layer of blubber, or fat" keeps the penguin warm (para. 3).	I read in _____ that _____.
Add Information	Penguins also huddle to stay warm (para. 4).	_____ also _____.
Compare/Contrast	Winter in Antarctica is cold, but emperor penguins stay warm (para. 5).	_____ but _____.
Time	After two months, the eggs hatch (para. 5).	After _____, _____.

Substantial Support — Differentiated Instruction

Materials List
- **Mentor Text S** BLM B Substantial Support
- **Writing Frames Teacher Page** BLM Y
- **Writing Frames Student Page** BLM Z

Students will need their copy of BLM Z from the initial lesson.

- Distribute BLM B.

- Follow the procedure explained in the Moderate Support lesson.

SUBSTANTIAL SUPPORT

Purpose	Phrase/Sentence	Frame
Cause/Effect	The penguin lives there because it has adapted to the cold (para. 1).	_____ because _____.
Cite sources from text	I read in the text that a "layer of blubber, or fat" keeps the penguin warm (para. 3).	I read in _____ that _____.
Add	Penguins also huddle to stay warm (para. 4).	_____ also _____.
Compare/Contrast	The winter is cold, but emperor penguins stay warm (para. 5).	_____ but _____.
Time	After two months, the eggs hatch (para. 5).	After _____, _____.

The U.S. Constitution: Then and Now

Essential Question

Why do laws continue to evolve?

In this unit, students read and compare selections about the development of laws and about people who have fought to change unfair laws to analyze why laws evolve.

Unit 1 Lessons at a Glance

Language Skills

Week 1
- Use Simple Past and Past Perfect Verb Tenses
- Understand the Language of Chronology
- Narrative Writing to Sources
- Understand Modal Auxiliaries
- Use Facts and Examples to Explore Word Meaning

Week 2
- Understand Pronoun-Antecedent Agreement
- Use Appositives
- Use Irregular Verbs
- Use Past and Past Perfect Verb Tenses
- Use Prefixes and Suffixes

Week 3
- Use Subordinating Conjunctions
- Condense Ideas
- Combine Sentences to Connect Ideas
- Analyze Verbs and Verb Phrases
- Use Regular and Irregular Verbs

Lessons

Preview or Review Week 1 ELA Mini-Lessons

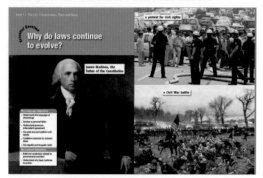

"Essential Question," pages 2–3

Student Objectives

LANGUAGE
Purpose:
• I can understand the Essential Question.
CONTENT
• I can understand the topic of the unit.

Additional Materials
• Unit Presentation
• Think-Speak-Listen Flip Book
• *Texts for Close Reading* booklet
• Student journals

Introduce Unit 1:
The U.S. Constitution: Then and Now

Use the short lesson below to introduce the topic of the unit and help students understand the Essential Question.

Build Background and Vocabulary

Draw students' attention to the pictures on pp. 2–3.

Say: *The topic of this unit is "The U.S. Constitution: Then and Now." These pictures introduce the ideas that we will read about.*

Create a three-column chart as shown below. Write: *James Madison, the father of the Constitution.* Read it aloud with students. Explain that the U.S. Constitution, created in 1787, describes the government and laws of the United States. Many of its ideas came from James Madison, the fourth president, so he is considered to be the **father** of the **Constitution**. Write the words *father* and *Constitution* and explain them. Continue in this way with the other pictures.

James Madison, the Father of the Constitution	A Protest for Civil Rights	A Civil War Battle
father Constitution – 1787	1960s protest protester inequality civil rights police	Civil War–1861-1865 battle flag soldiers army

👤👤👤 Differentiated Instruction
Explain the Essential Question

Read aloud the Essential Question: *Why do laws continue to evolve?* Explain key words by definition and examples: **evolve, laws, over time**. Encourage students to give examples, for instance of things that evolve (telephones, cars, etc.).

Use the Differentiated Instruction to help students at all levels understand the Essential Question.

Display or invite students to access the Unit 1 video. After the video **Ask:** *How does the video help you answer the Essential Question?*

Then proceed to Lesson 1.

Differentiated Instruction
Explain the Essential Question

Substantial Support

Point to the picture of the U.S. Constitution.

Write: *The U.S. Constitution describes the laws of the country* Have students say the sentence with you. Explain that laws are like rules. Give examples of laws. Point to the picture of the civil rights protest.

Gesture and say: *Sometimes people do not like the laws. The people get angry. They protest. In the 1960s African Americans were not free. People told the government to change the laws. What happened? The laws changed. The laws about African Americans changed, or evolved, over time.*

Say: *In this unit we will learn about our country's rules and why the rules sometimes change.*

Moderate Support

Say: *The U.S. Constitution describes the laws and our rights.*

Point to the picture of the civil rights protest.

Say: *The Civil Rights Movement changed the laws in our Constitution.*

Write: *Women were not able to vote until the year 1820/1920.* Read the sentence aloud and have students repeat. Elicit the correct year.

Write: *Eighteen-year-olds were not able to vote until 1871/1971.* Elicit the correct answer.

Say: *The laws about voting changed, or evolved, over time. Why? In this unit we will learn about our country's rules and why they change over time.*

Light Support

Say: *The U.S. Constitution describes the laws and our freedoms.*

Elicit examples of freedoms and help as necessary. Point to the picture of the civil rights protest.

Say: *The Civil Rights Movement changed the laws of our Constitution.*

Write: *Women were not able to vote until the year 1820/1920.* Say the sentence with students. Elicit the correct year.

Write: *Eighteen-year-olds were not able to vote until 1871/1971.* Elicit the correct year.

Say: *Some laws have changed, or evolved, over time. Why? In this unit we will learn about our country's rules and why they change over time.*

✓ Formative Assessment

Substantial Support	• Can students say what the Constitution is with help? • Can students show understanding of key words such as **law** and **protest** with help?
Moderate Support	• Can students say what the Constitution is? • Can students explain the words **law** and **protest** with a little help? • Can students give an example of a law evolving over time?
Light Support	• Can students say what the Constitution is? • Can students explain the words **law, protest** and **rights**? • Can students give an example of a law evolving over time?

Preview or Review Week 1 ELA Mini-Lessons

"Creating the Constitution," page 4

Student Objectives

LANGUAGE
Purpose:
• I can write a magazine article.
Form:
• I can use simple past and past perfect verb tenses.
CONTENT
• I can use domain-specific vocabulary related to historical events.

Additional Materials
• Unit Presentation
• *Texts for Close Reading* booklet
• Think-Speak-Listen Flip Book
• Student journal

Language Transfer Support

Note that speakers of Chinese, Haitian Creole, Thai, Hmong, or Vietnamese may need additional support to distinguish between simple past and past perfect verb tenses. These languages do not use tense inflections, and often use context or expressions of time such as before now with the present tense to indicate past actions that occurred before other past actions.

1 Read "Creating the Constitution"

Build Background and Vocabulary

Display the images and explain their importance in the text. If students have already read the text, ask them what they remember. Invite students to share their cultural experiences and knowledge of the creation of the Constitution.

Read Aloud the Text

Read panel 1. To support comprehension, ask students to find images in the picture that match words in the text (delegates, government, etc.) and ask *wh-* questions, such as *Who are these people?* Repeat with panels 2 - 4. After reading, **ask:** *Why did Madison become the principle writer of the constitution?* Have students answer using this sentence frame: I think he became the principle writer because _____. Refer to the Essential Question. **Say:** *This type of text is called informational social studies.*

Think-Speak-Listen: Use the following sentence frame or the Think-Speak-Listen Flip Book to guide the discussion: *James Madison thought it was important to create a stronger central government because _____ and _____.*

👥👥 Differentiated Instruction
Build Language: Use Simple Past and Past Perfect Verb Tenses

Write: *Madison argued for a strong central government. Madison had previously created the state constitution for Virginia.* Explain that the first sentence is in the simple past tense and the second is in the past perfect tense. **Say:** *When we describe an action in the past that happened before another action, we use the past perfect tense.* Use the Differentiated Instruction to practice using simple past and past perfect verb tenses in a way that best matches the levels of your students.

✓ Use Oral and Written Language Expression: Write a Magazine Article

Task: *With a partner, pretend you are writing a magazine article about James Madison that explains how he helped create the Constitution. Collaborate with your peers to write complete sentences that use simple past tense and past perfect tense verbs.*

Ⓢ *James Madison _____ to Philadelphia in 1787. He _____ one of the delegates.*

Ⓜ *In 1787, James Madison _____ one of a group of delegates. Their goal _____ to the government.*

Ⓛ *When James Madison _____, he and fifty-six other delegates _____.*

🔄 Wrap Up

Why is it important to use verb tenses correctly in a text?

Turn and Talk: *Use simple past and past perfect tenses to describe what you've learned about the making of the Constitution.*

👪 Differentiated Instruction
Build Language: Use Simple Past and Past Perfect Verb Tenses

ⓢubstantial Support

Model: Read the first sentence of panel 3. Point out the verb *argued*. **Say:** *I know that verbs can tell me when something happens as well as the action.* Circle the *-ed* ending. **Say:** *I see that the verb argued ends in -ed. This tells me the action happened in the past.*

Practice: Display panel 4 and point out *the delegates decided on a final document.* Point to the verb *decided*. **Ask:** *How do we know the verb decided tells us about an action that happened in the past?* Elicit answers. Distribute BLM 1. Help students complete the chart with simple past tense form of the verbs from the text.

Extend: Have students work with a partner to complete the sentences with simple past tense verbs from the chart in the **Practice** activity.

Challenge: If students are ready, have them write an original sentence using the simple past tense form of one of the verbs in the chart.

ⓜoderate Support

Model: Write: *Madison had created the state constitution for Virginia.* **Say:** *I know that created ends in -ed so it is a past tense verb. This sentence tells us that Madison created the state constitution for Virginia before he created the constitution.* Circle *had created.* *The verb phrase had created tells me the action happened in the past, before another action. This tense is called the past perfect.*

Practice: Distribute BLM 2. Help students complete the chart with verbs in the simple past and past perfect tenses.

Extend: Have students work with a partner to complete the sentences on the BLM.

Challenge: If students are ready, help them write two original sentences using verbs in the simple past and past perfect tenses.

ⓛight Support

Use the text on pp. 4–5 in the *Texts for Close Reading* to complete the following activities.

Practice: Have pairs list the verbs they find in the simple past tense in the text. **Say:** *Most historical text is written in the past tense. Verbs in the simple past tense show action that has happened.* Write the first sentence in the second paragraph. Highlight had and created. **Say:** *Verbs in the past perfect tense use had with a main verb to describe an action in the past that happened before another action in the past.*

Extend: Have partners summarize the events that led to the creation of the constitution. Instruct them to use a verb in the simple past tense and one in the past perfect tense to show two past actions in each sentence.

Challenge: Have partners read their sentences aloud and explain the order of events.

☑ Formative Assessment

Substantial Support	• Can students identify words in sentences that signal past actions? • Can students complete sentences using the simple past tense?
Moderate Support	• Can students complete sentences using the simple past tense? • Can students understand the difference between simple past and the past perfect tenses?
Light Support	• Can students generate original sentences in which they use the simple past and past perfect tenses? • Can students explain the order of events using past and past perfect tenses?

Preview or Review Week 1 ELA Mini-Lessons

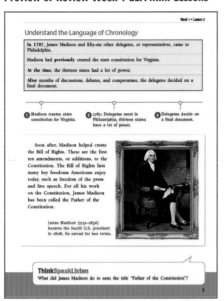

"Understand the Language of Chronology," page 5

Student Objectives

LANGUAGE

Purpose:
- I can create a time line.

Form:
- I can use the language of chronology.

CONTENT
- I can explain the creation of the U.S. Constitution and Bill of Rights.

Additional Materials
- Unit Presentation
- *Texts for Close Reading* booklet
- Think-Speak-Listen Flip Book
- Student journal

Language Transfer Support

Students whose first language is Arabic, Hebrew, Farsi, or Urdu may need additional support in reading and interpreting a horizontal time line that is meant to be read from left to right. Students from right-to-left-reading cultures may associate the earliest event on a time line with the far right entry and the latest event with the far left entry.

2 Understand the Language of Chronology

Engage Thinking

Point to panel 2 and read the first sentence aloud. **Ask**: *What does the word previously tell us?* Elicit answers. Explain that words like previously and after help us understand the order of events.

Turn and Talk: *What did James Madison create before the U.S. Constitution?*

Read and View Closely: Recognize Chronology

Have students look at the chart. **Say:** *Writers of history tell about important events in the order in which they happened. They give us clues about the order things happened, or their chronology, by using time-order words.* Read the chart with the students. Point out the time-order words in bold. **Ask:** *How does 'In 1787' help us understand the order of events?* Help students answer using the sentence frame: *'In 1787' helps us understand the order of events by _____.* Explain that knowing the year and date is one way we know the sequence of events. Explain that we can also use words like *first, after that,* and *finally* to tell the order of events.

Differentiated Instruction
Build Language: Understand the Language of Chronology

Read the time line. **Ask:** *What time-words can we add to the sentences?* Encourage students to use *first, after that,* and *finally* to show the chronology. Use the Differentiated Instruction to practice understanding the language of chronology in a way that best matches the levels of your students.

Think-Speak-Listen: Use the following sentence frame or the Think-Speak-Listen Flip Book to guide discussion: *James Madison earned the title "Father of the Constitution" by _____.*

☑ Use Oral and Written Language: Create a Time Line

Task: *Work with a partner to create a time line for what you have learned about the creation of the United States Constitution. Write complete sentences in your own words that use time-order words to show the order of events. Then share your time line with the group.*

(S) _____, *Madison wrote a constitution for Virginia.* _____, *he went to Philadelphia.*

(M) _____, *Madison created the constitution of Virginia.* _____, *he joined other delegates in Philadelphia.*

(L) _____ *his work on the Virginia state constitution, James Madison* _____. _____, *he joined* _____.

 Wrap Up

Today we learned the importance the language of chronology. Why is it important to use time-order words correctly in a text?

Turn and Talk: *Use time-order words to describe your class schedule.*

👥👥 Differentiated Instruction
Build Language: Understand the Language of Chronology

Ⓢubstantial Support

Model: Read aloud the last sentence in the chart and point out the word *After*. **Say:** *I see the word after and recognize a time-order word. Time-order words help me understand when something happened and in what order. First, the delegates had discussions and debates and made compromises. After that, they decided on a document.* Explain that the words first, and after that also tell us the order of events.

Practice: Write *first*, *after that*, and *finally* on the board. **Say:** *We can use these words to retell events in order.* Distribute BLM 1. Help students number the events in the order in which they occur. Then, add time-order words to the sentences and rewrite each sentence in chronological order using time-order words.

Extend: Have pairs continue the activity on the Extend section of BLM 1.

Challenge: Ask partners to describe their daily routine using *first*, *after that*, and *finally*.

Ⓜoderate Support

Model: Read aloud the first two sentences in the chart and point out the words *in 1787* and *previously*. Remind students that *previously* refers to an event that happened before another event. **Say:** *I notice that some writers tell the specific time that something occurred, such as "In 1787." Other times, they may use time-order words such as first, then, and finally or phrases such as after that and at the time.*

Practice: Distribute BLM 2. Help students number the sentences in the order they occurred.

Extend: Have students work with a partner to rewrite the sentences from the Practice activity in the correct chronological order adding time-order words from the box.

Challenge: If students are ready, have them do the Practice activity in the Light Support section.

Ⓛight Support

Use the text on pp. 4-5 in the *Texts for Close Reading* to complete the following activities.

Practice: Working in pairs, ask students to list the time-order words they find in the text. Ask students to suggest additional time-order words to add to the list.

Extend: Have partners compose new sentences using time-order words to summarize the events after the convention in Philadelphia.

Challenge: If students are ready, compare and contrast the presentation of information in the chart and in the time line. **Ask:** *Why are time-order words such as previously and after not used in the time line?* Elicit answers. Explain that a time line shows the order of events visually, but a text needs time-words to convey the order of events.

☑ Formative Assessment

Substantial Support	• Can students identify time-order words with some help? • Do students choose appropriate time-order words to describe a sequence of events or actions?
Moderate Support	• Can students identify time-order words with little help? • Can students put sentences in order and select appropriate time-order words to complete them?
Light Support	• Do students understand the importance of time-order words in text? • Can students use time-order words to compose a chronology based on historical text?

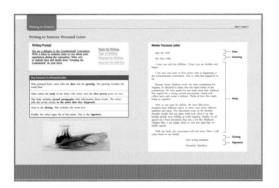

"Writing to Sources," pages 6–7

Student Objectives

LANGUAGE
Purpose:
- I can analyze a personal letter.

Form:
- I can analyze and identify the features of a personal letter.

CONTENT
- I can describe the features of a personal letter.

Additional Materials
- Unit Presentation
- Think-Speak-Listen Flip Book
- Student journal

Language Transfer Support

Students whose first language is Cantonese, Haitian Creole, Hmong, Korean, or Vietnamese may need support in using articles correctly when speaking and writing. There is either no article in their native language, or no difference between **a** and **the**.

3 Writing to Sources: Personal Letter

Engage Thinking

Tell students that they will read and analyze a personal letter so that they can identify its features. Read aloud the prompt.

> You are a delegate to the Constitutional Convention. Write a letter to someone close to you about your experiences during the convention. Make sure to include facts and details from "Creating the Constitution" in your letter.

Say: *Let's ask questions to make sure we understand the prompt.* **Ask:** *What type of writing is it? Who will the writer write as? What will the writer write about? Where will the writer get some of his details?*

Differentiated Instruction
Read and View Closely: Analyze a Personal Letter

Say: *Let's analyze the four features of a personal letter. The first feature is the format of the letter. The format includes the date, the salutation, the body of the letter, and the closing. Turn to a partner. Point out the date.* Check that students can identify the date. Continue with the salutation, body, and closing.

Say: *The second feature of a personal letter is a first person point of view. As I read, look for the point of view.* Read aloud the date, the greeting, and the first paragraph. Check that students can identify **I** as the first person point of view.

Say: *A third feature of a personal letter tells about events clearly in the order they happened. As I read, listen for the order of events.* Read aloud the body of the letter. **Say:** *Turn to a partner. Which words help you identify the order in which events happened?* Check that students can identify word such as **next** and **finally**.

Say: *The writer talks about how the events affected him. Turn to your partner, find an example of how the writer felt about an event.* Check that students can identify how the events affected Hamilton.

Briefly recap the four features of a personal letter. Then continue the lesson using Differentiated Instruction that best fits the needs of your students.

Share Your Understanding

Bring the students back together. **Ask:** *What did we learn about the four features of a personal letter?* Review the features as needed.

✓ Final Writing Assignment

Use the *English Language Development Assessment* to assess students' writing for their ELA writing assignment.

👥 Differentiated Instruction
Read and View Closely: Analyze a Personal Letter

Ⓢubstantial Support

Model: Distribute BLM 1. **Say:** *Let's read and analyze another personal letter that answers the prompt. What parts make up the format of the letter? Where are they?* Model answering the questions by pointing out the date. Then guide the class to identify the salutation, body, and closing.

Practice: Continue reading the letter and ask the same questions that you asked about the Mentor Personal Letter in the book. Invite students to answer.

Extend: Have students in pairs complete the activities on BLM 1. Then check answers with the group.

Challenge: Review the four features of a personal letter by asking questions such as *When was the letter written? How does Hamilton feel about being away from his family?* Encourage students to use academic language as well as their own words to discuss the text.

Ⓛight Support

Practice: Distribute BLM 2. **Say:** *This is the Personal Letter Mentor Text that you read in class on Day 1. We will look more closely at the four features of a personal letter.* Do items 1–3 with students.

Extend: Have students work with partners to number the events in the order they appear in the letter. Then check answers with the whole group.

Challenge: Have students work in pairs to take turns retelling the main events of the story, including how Hamilton felt. Remind students to use transitional words such as **next, then,** and **finally.** Have some pairs share their summaries with the class.

Ⓜoderate Support

Model: Draw students' attention to the Personal Letter Mentor Text in the book. **Say:** *Let's analyze the four features of a personal letter.* Make the chart below. **Say:** *The format includes a date, salutation, body, and closing.* Elicit examples of those parts from the text and write them on the chart.

Personal Letter Feature	Example from Mentor Text
1. Includes a date, a salutation, a body, and a closing.	"July 30, 1787 My Dear Wife," "Your devoted husband, Alexander Hamilton"
2. Uses the first person point of view.	
3. Tells about events clearly and in the order they happened.	
4. Explains how events affected him or her.	

Practice: Work with students to complete the chart with the rest of the parts of the letter.

Extend: Monitor student partners. Tell them to use the chart they created to ask each other questions about the text., such as: *When was the letter written? What is an example of first person? Which event happened last?* Encourage students to use academic language as well as their own words to discuss the text.

Challenge: Have students work in pairs to take turns retelling the main events of the story. Have some pairs share their summaries with the class.

✅ Formative Assessment

Substantial Support	• Do students recognize the criteria for a personal letter in the Mentor Personal Letter?
Moderate Support	• Do students recognize the ways in which the Mentor Personal Letter meets the criteria for a personal letter? • Can students describe the features of a personal letter in their own words?
Light Support	• Do students recognize criteria and analyze how the Mentor Text meets the criteria for a personal letter? • Can students describe in their own words how the writer meets the criteria for a personal letter?

Preview or Review Week 1 ELA Mini-Lessons

"Voting Rights Act Address," pages 8–9

Student Objectives

LANGUAGE
Purpose:
• I can summarize a speech.
Form:
• I can understand modal auxiliaries.
CONTENT
• I can understand a historic speech.

Additional Materials
• Unit Presentation
• *Texts for Close Reading* booklet
• Think-Speak-Listen Flip Book
• Student journal

Language Transfer Support

Although the concept of modality is universal, many languages, including Spanish and Arabic, do not use modal auxiliaries. Students may need extra support to understand and use modal auxiliaries such as must. These helping verbs do not follow conventional English grammar rules—for example, there is no **-s** or **-es** in the third person singular, and two modals cannot be used in the same sentence. Also, modals such as **can** and **must** have multiple meanings and functions.

4 Read "Voting Rights Act Address"

Build Background and Vocabulary

Display the images and explain their importance in the text. If students have already read the text, ask them what they remember. Invite students to share their cultural experiences and knowledge of the meaning of civil rights.

Read Aloud the Text

Read panel 1 and ask *wh-* questions, such as *Who is this? What movement do you think he supported?* Repeat with panels 2 - 8. After reading, **ask:** *What is the main point of the speech?* Invite students to share their ideas using this sentence frame: *I think the main point is _____.* Then refer to the Essential Question. **Say:** *This text refers to a speech that happened a long time ago. It is a historic speech.*

Think-Speak-Listen: Use the following sentence frame or the Think-Speak-Listen Flip Book to guide discussion: *It is important for all citizens to have the right to vote because _____.*

♦♦♦ Differentiated Instruction
Build Language: Understand Modal Auxiliaries

Write and read aloud the last sentence from the speech. Have students repeat. Underline *must* and *act*. **Say:** *The word must is a helping verb that expresses strong feeling. The word must in this sentence lets us know the speaker's strong feeling that action is needed.* Explain that must is a modal along with words like *can, might,* and *should*. Use the Differentiated Instruction to practice understanding modal auxiliaries in a way that best matches the levels of your students.

☑ Use Oral and Written Language: Summarize a Speech

Task: *Imagine that you are writing the script for a film that summarizes the presidency of Lyndon Johnson. Working with a partner, write about Johnson's Voting Act Rights speech. Use modals in your script.*

(S) *President Johnson said all citizens _____ vote. We _____ vote no matter what race we are.*

(M) *President Johnson said everyone _____ and _____ be allowed to vote.*

(L) *In his speech, President Johnson said we _____ and we _____ follow the Constitution.*

Use this opportunity to assess students using the rubric in *English Language Development Assessment.*

↻ Wrap Up

Today we learned the importance of understanding modals. How are they useful in reading and writing?

Turn and Talk: *What problem is stated in the speech? What does the President say we must do?*

👥👥 Differentiated Instruction
Build Language: Understand Modal Auxiliaries

Ⓢubstantial Support

Model: Read panel 3 aloud. **Say:** *I notice the words can, should, and must. I know these words are helping words.* Remind students that *must* is used to express a strong feeling. Explain that *can* is used to express ability as in *I can speak English*, or to ask permission as in *Can I open the window? Should* is used to express obligation as in *Everyone should be allowed to vote*. Explain that modals add meaning to the main verb. Other examples of this type of verb are *could, may, might, will, would,* and *shall.*

Practice: Distribute BLM 1. Help students find the modal auxiliary in each sentence. Then discuss each sentence and how the modal auxiliary is used.

Extend: Have students work with a partner to complete each sentence to show how the modal auxiliary is used.

Challenge: If students are ready, have them find the modal auxiliaries in panels 4 and 6.

Ⓜoderate Support

Model: Read panel 3 aloud. **Say:** *I notice the words can, should, and must. I know these words are helping words called modals.* Remind students that must is used to express a strong feeling, can is used to express ability, and should is used to express obligation. Explain that modals add meaning to the main verb. Other examples of modals are *could, may, might, will, would,* and *shall.*

Practice: Ask students to look for other modal verbs in panels 4, 6, 7, and 8. Discuss their meaning as a group. Explain that *shall* in panel 7 expresses a strong intention. Distribute BLM 2. Help students underline the modal auxiliary in each sentence and draw a line to the main verb.

Extend: Have students work with a partner to write a sentence using each modal auxiliary given.

Challenge: If students are ready, ask them to explain whether a modal they've learned expresses likelihood, ability, permission, or obligation.

Ⓛight Support

Use the text on pp. 6–9 in the *Texts for Close Reading* to complete the following activities.

Practice: Remind students that a modal auxiliary is a type of verb that is used to show likelihood, ability, permission or obligation. They are considered helping verbs and do not follow regular English grammar rules. In pairs, have students list the sentences that include modal verbs in paragraphs 6 and 7.

Extend: In pairs, have students determine whether the modal in each sentence is showing likelihood, ability, permission, or obligation. Ask them to give reasons for their choices.

Challenge: Working with a partner, have students write 2–3 sentences about a civil rights issue they care about using modal auxiliaries.

☑ Formative Assessment

Substantial Support	• Are students able to identify modal auxiliaries in a text with help? • Can students unscramble sentences using modal verbs as a clue?
Moderate Support	• Can students identify modal auxiliaries with little help? • Can students identify modal auxiliaries in a text and explain what purpose they serve?
Light Support	• Can students identify and explain the purpose of modal auxiliaries? • Are students able to write sentences containing modal auxiliaries?

Preview or Review Week 1 ELA Mini-Lessons

"Susan B. Anthony," page 10

5 Read "Susan B. Anthony"

Build Background and Vocabulary

Point out the photograph of Susan B. Anthony and explain that she worked for civil rights in the 1800s. **Say:** *Texts on a similar topic share the same terms and vocabulary.* Invite students to share their cultural experiences and knowledge of the meaning of civil rights.

Read Aloud the Text

Read the text aloud, panel by panel. Remind students that they have been reading about people in history who worked for civil rights. To support comprehension, ask students to find images that match words in the text. Draw students' attention to the last two photographs. **Say:** *These photos show one of the ways that Susan B. Anthony helped change history.*

Think-Speak-Listen: Use the following sentence frame or the Think-Speak-Listen Flip Book to guide discussion: *Both Susan B. Anthony and Lyndon B. Johnson _____.*

👥👥 Differentiated Instruction
Build Language: Use Facts and Examples to Explore Word Meaning

Ask partners to use a T-chart to list words from the paragraph that they know and don't know. Use the words on students' lists to help you clarify meaning. Arrange students in groups according to language acquisition level or select the level of instruction that best matches your students. Use the Differentiated Instruction to practice analyzing word meaning in a way that best matches the levels of your students.

☑ Use Oral and Written Language: Write a Speech About Civil Rights

Task: *Work in groups to explore word meaning to write a speech about civil right issues. Begin with the sentence frames. Use a print or online dictionary for support.*

Ⓢ   *Education is important for all because _____.*

Ⓜ   *Slavery is a stain on a society because _____.*

Ⓛ   *The nation needs suffrage because _____.*

↩ Wrap Up

Today we learned how important it is to explore word meaning. How do we determine word meanings?

Turn and Talk: *Explore with your partner your understanding of "civil rights" from your studies. Take turns giving examples of civil rights.*

Differentiated Instruction
Build Language: Use Facts and Examples to Explore Word Meaning

Substantial Support

Model: Say: *What does the word **vote** mean? Susan B. Anthony is famous for having helped women get the right to vote. In panel 2, I see "equal rights" in the text and a photo of women holding signs. In panel 3, I see "right to vote in national elections. I also see the banner in the last photo. I understand that Anthony fought for women to take part in elections.*

Practice: Explain that voting is the act of officially stating your opinion or choice. Ask students to describe a time when they voted on something, such choosing a game to play, choosing a family activity, voting for something in class. Distribute BLM 1. Help students complete the activity.

Extend: Have students work with a partner to complete the sentences using what they know about the word *vote*.

Challenge: If students are ready, help them write an original sentence using the word *vote*.

Moderate Support

Model: Say: *I see the word labor in second sentence. When I come across a word I do not know, I look for examples in the text to help me find the meaning.* Read aloud the first paragraph and have students repeat. **Ask:** *What words in this sentence help us understand the word labor?*

Practice: Distribute BLM 2. Help students complete the activity.

Extend: Have students work with a partner to use what they know about the meaning of *labor* to complete several sentence frames in BLM 2. Have them share their sentences with the class.

Challenge: If students are ready, help them generate original sentences using the word *labor*.

Light Support

Use the text on p. 20 of the *Texts for Close Reading* to complete the following activities.

Practice: Display a Frayer Model with *suffrage* in the middle oval and ask students to suggest a definition, facts and characteristics, examples, and nonexamples to complete it. **Ask:** *How has exploring suffrage in this way helped your understanding of the word's meaning?*

Extend: Read aloud the last sentence is paragraph 1. **Say:** *Imagine you were just given the right to vote. Describe how you felt when you didn't have suffrage and what you did to change this.*

Challenge: Have partners generate sentences using the word *suffrage*. Ask students to discuss the words elections and lobbied and generate sentences using these words.

☑ Formative Assessment

Substantial Support	• Do students understand the value of going beyond a definition to explore a word's meaning? • Can students demonstrate understanding of a word's meaning by completing a sentence frame?
Moderate Support	• Can students participate in exploring word meaning through examples, characteristics, and other means? • Can students complete a sentence frame to demonstrate understanding of a word's meaning?
Light Support	• Can students explore word meaning by using a Frayer Model? • Can students generate sentences that contain the word *suffrage*?

Preview or Review Week 2 ELA Mini-Lessons

"Understand Pronoun-Antecedent Agreement," page 11

Student Objectives

LANGUAGE
Purpose:
• I can describe famous Americans.
Form:
• I can understand pronoun-antecedent agreement.
CONTENT
• I use domain-specific vocabulary related to nonfiction text.

Additional Materials
• Unit Presentation
• *Texts for Close Reading* booklet
• Think-Speak-Listen Flip Book
• Student journal

Language Transfer Support

Note that speakers of Hmong, Vietnamese, or Haitian Creole may need additional support with pronoun-antecedent agreement. In these languages, the third person pronoun is gender-free, or the personal pronoun is omitted. Speakers of Cantonese or Korean may also need support, because those languages do not require number agreement with antecedents. Provide sentence frames as well as structured opportunities for students to use pronouns in spoken English.

6 Understand Pronoun-Antecedent Agreement

Engage Thinking

Display the chart and read the chart headings. **Say:** *We are going to read about James Madison and Susan B. Anthony.* Encourage a discussion of what students know about the Constitution. **Ask:** *How do you think changes to our Constitution get made? Why are changes necessary to our Constitution?*

Read and View Closely: Recognize Pronouns and Their Antecedents

Ask: *What is a noun?* Elicit from the class that a noun names a person, place, or thing. **Ask:** *What is a pronoun?* Elicit that a pronoun takes the place of a noun in a sentence. Write *he, she, it, they* on the board. Read panel 1 in the chart. **Ask:** *What do you notice about the underlined words?* Elicit that "He" in the second column refers to the proper noun "James Madison" in the first column. Continue in this way with the rest of the chart. **Ask:** *What do you notice about the pronoun "they?"* Elicit that "they" refers to both males and females. The pronoun does not change.

Think-Speak-Listen: Use the following sentence frame or the Think-Speak-Listen Flip Book to guide discussion: *James Madison, Lyndon Johnson, and Susan B. Anthony worked to protect people's rights by _____.*

👥 Differentiated Instruction
Build Language: Understand Pronoun-Antecedent Agreement

Say: *Like the nouns they replace, pronouns are singular or plural. **He** is singular because it stands for one person, James Madison.* Use the Differentiated Instruction to practice understanding pronoun-antecedent agreement in a way that best matches the levels of your students.

☑ Use Oral and Written Language: Describe Famous Americans

Task: *Students work in small groups to complete sentences that describe how James Madison, Susan B. Anthony, and women such as Elizabeth Cady Stanton and Lucretia Mott improved the lives of people. Use pronouns in place of names in your descriptions. Explain your choice of pronouns to the rest of the class.*

(S) *James Madison is a famous American. _____ helped write the Constitution.*

(M) *Susan B. Anthony improved lives. _____ spoke against _____.*

(L) *Elizabeth Cady Stanton and Lucretia Mott are heroes because _____.*

🔄 Wrap Up

Today we learned how important it is to choose the correct pronouns. Why do you think choosing the correct pronoun matters?

Turn and Talk: *Talk about someone you admire in science or another subject area using pronoun-antecedent agreement.*

👥👥 Differentiated Instruction
Build Language: Understand Pronoun-Antecedent Agreement

Ⓢ ubstantial Support

Model: Say: *I know that a noun is a person place or thing. I know a pronoun takes the place of a noun. Feminine means female. Masculine means male. Singular is one. Plural is more than one. She stands for singular feminine; he stands in for singular masculine; it replaces a singular thing; they replaces plural masculine and/or feminine.*

Practice: Distribute BLM 1. Help students read each sentence and fill in the blank with the missing pronoun. Have students draw a line to the antecedent the pronoun repalces. Then, discuss why each pronoun is used.

Extend: Have students work with a partner to find the antecedents to the pronouns in the sentences. Have students discuss with their partner the reason why each pronoun is used.

Challenge: Write the pronouns he, she, it, they. If students are ready, help them choose a pronoun and write an original sentence, drawing a line from the pronoun to the antecendent.

Ⓜ oderate Support

Model: Say: *I know that pronouns take the place of nouns. I see the first underlined word is the noun. The second underlined word is a pronoun. They are linked. The underlined pronoun refers back to the underlined noun.*

Practice: Distribute BLM 2. Help students complete the chart with the correct pronoun to replace the underlined antecedent.

Extend: Have students work with a partner to complete the sentences with the correct pronoun. Then have students draw a circle around the antecedent and draw a line to connect them.

Challenge: If students are ready, hep them explain how they determined which pronoun to use when they completed the BLM. Then, help students write two original sentences using a pronoun and antecedent. Remind students to draw a line connecting the pronoun to the antecedent.

Ⓛ ight Support

Practice: Remind students that singular pronouns such as *I, she, he,* and *it* take the place of singular nouns and that plural pronouns such as *we* and *they* take the place of plural nouns. Model identifying the antecedents for the pronouns in the text and labeling them as *singular* or *plural*.

Extend: Ask students to label each of the rest of the highlighted pronouns in the text as singular or plural. Have partners expand on the information in the following sentences by writing original sentences in which they use pronouns for the antecedents. James Madison wrote a constitution for Virginia. All people are created equal. Susan B. Anthony helped change the Constitution.

Challenge: Ask students to write a paragraph on the famous American of their choice and use appropriate pronouns throughout. Have them read their paragraphs aloud to the class.

☑ Formative Assessment

Substantial Support	• Do students understand the difference between nouns and pronouns? • Can students select pronouns that agree with their antecedents in sentence frames?
Moderate Support	• Can students distinguish between singular and plural pronouns? • Can students substitute appropriate pronouns for nouns in sentences?
Light Support	• Can students generate original sentences in which they use pronouns that agree in number with their antecedents?

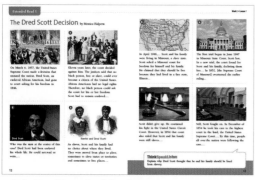

"The Dred Scott Decision," pages 12–13

Student Objectives

LANGUAGE

Purpose:
• I can draw inferences.

Form:
• I understand noun phrases: appositives.

CONTENT
• I can analyze information about a historical figure.
• I use text details to draw inferences about informational social studies.

Additional Materials
• Unit Presentation
• *Texts for Close Reading* booklet
• Think-Speak-Listen Flip Book
• Student journal

Metacognitive Prompt: Selective Attention

Today, we will begin reading about a Supreme Court decision in the 1800s that had far-reaching effects. As you read, pay special attention to what the text and photographs tell you about the man at the center of the court's decision.

7 Read "The Dred Scott Decision"

Build Background and Vocabulary

Display the photos of Dred and Harriet Scott. Ask students to preview the photographs and skim over the text to form a first impression of Dred Scott and clarify any words they may not understand.

Read Aloud the Text

Read the text aloud, panel by panel. **Say:** *Dred and Harriet Scott were enslaved for most of their lives. Dred Scott felt that he and his family deserved to be free.* Have students write down any words or phrases that occur to them about Scott and his struggles. Support this process by thinking aloud and modeling selective attending to key words, phrases, and other types of information. **Ask:** *Who was Dred Scott? What did the court decide? Why? How did people react to the Supreme Court's decision?*

Think-Speak-Listen Use the following sentence frame or the Think-Speak-Listen Flip Book to guide discussion: *Dred Scott and his family thought _____.*

👥 Differentiated Instruction
Build Language: Use Appositives

Display and read aloud the last sentence in panel 1. Circle *an enslaved African American*. Explain that this is called an appositive. An appositive is an explanatory phrase that identifies or renames a noun or pronoun. Use the Differentiated Instruction to practice using appositives in a way that best matches the levels of your students.

✓ Use Oral and Written Language: Draw Inferences

Task: *Imagine that you are part of a team of history detectives looking for clues about Dred Scott that are not directly stated in the text. Work with your team to write two or three smart guesses about Scott from the text and photographs. Present your sentences to the class using the following frames, offering reasons for your guesses.*

(S) *Scott was courageous, because _____.*

(M) *Scott must have been disappointed with _____.*

(L) *He also must have been angry when the court said _____ and frustrated with being forced to _____.*

Use this opportunity to assess students using the rubric in *English Language Development Assessment.*

🔄 Wrap Up

Today we learned about appositives. Why do you think writers use them?

Turn and Talk: *We study the Dred Scott decision in social studies. Why do you think its such an important part of U.S. history?*

👥 Differentiated Instruction
Build Language: Use Appositives

Ⓢubstantial Support

Model: Say: *What is the purpose of an appositive? I know follows its subject, and is between two commas. In panel 1, I read: "Dred Scott, an enslaved African American, had gone to court asking for his freedom in 1846." I see that the appositive explains and renames Dred Scott.*

Practice: Distribute BLM 1. Help students complete the activity.

Extend: Have students work with a partner to complete the activity on the BLM.

Challenge: Write the following sentence on the board and ask students to look at panel 5 and find the appositive to complete the sentence: *Scott and his family were living in Missouri, _____.*

Ⓜoderate Support

Model: Say: *I know an appositive explains or renames the noun or pronoun it follows. An appositive is between two sets of commas.*

Practice: Display and read aloud the last sentence in panel 1. **Ask:** *What is the appositive in the sentence? What does it rename?* Distribute BLM 1. Help students complete the task.

Extend: Have students work with a partner to complete the BLM.

Challenge: If students are ready, help them write an original sentence using an appositive.

Ⓛight Support

Use the text on pp. 12-19 in the *Texts for Close Reading* to complete the following activities.

Practice: Say: *I know an appositive explains or renames the noun or pronoun it follows. An appositive is between two sets of commas.* Display and read aloud this sentence from panel 1: "Dred Scott, an enslaved African American, had gone to court asking for his freedom in 1846." Ask students to identify the appositive and what it renames.

Extend: Underline the appositives in these two sentences: The justices said that no black person, free or slave, could ever become a citizen of the United States. The Blow family, descendants of Dred Scott's original owner, purchased the Scotts and then set them free. Ask volunteers to cross out the subject and commas in each sentence and read them aloud. As a class, discuss the difference and the effect on the sentence.

Challenge: Write three original sentences about Dred Scott, all containing appositives.

☑ Formative Assessment

Substantial Support	• Can students identify and define an appositive in a sentence?
Moderate Support	• Can students identify and define an appositive in a sentence? • Can students add an appositive to an existing sentence?
Light Support	• Can students identify and define an appositive in a sentence? • Can students write original sentences containing appositives?

Preview or Review Week 2 ELA Mini-Lessons

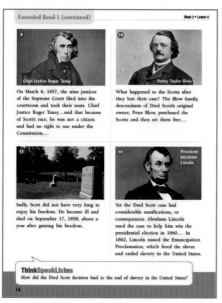

"The Dred Scott Decision," page 14

Student Objectives

LANGUAGE
Purpose:
• I can give a lecture about Dred Scott.
Form:
• I can analyze an author's reasons and evidence.
CONTENT
• I can read a historical account.

Additional Materials

• Unit Presentation
• *Texts for Close Reading* booklet
• Think-Speak-Listen Flip Book
• Student journal

Metacognitive Prompt

As we read today, make a connection between Lyndon Johnson's "Voting Rights Act Address" on pages 8–9 and today's text. Compare ways that reasons and evidence support opposite views about civil rights.

8 Analyze Author's Reasons and Evidence

Engage Thinking

Encourage students to make a personal connection to Dred Scott's fight for freedom. **Say:** *Dred Scott believed that he and his family had a right to freedom from slavery. Freedom was so important to him that he kept on fighting.*

Turn and Talk: Ask: *What freedoms are important to you? Why?*

Read and View Closely: Analyze Author's Reasons and Evidence

Have students look at panel 9. **Ask:** *Who is in the picture?* Elicit answers. Read the text. **Ask:** *What argument did the Chief Justice make in the Dred Scott case?* Elicit answers. **Say:** *The author gives us the reason. He writes that the Chief Justice said Dred Scott was not a citizen so he had no right to sue.* Read panels 10 - 12. While doing a close reading of the text, focus on the reasons and evidence that support important points. Use the Differentiated Instruction to practice analyzing an author's reasons and evidence in a way that best matches the levels of your students.

Think-Speak-Listen: Use the following sentence frame or the Think-Speak-Listen Flip Book to guide discussion: *The Dred Scott decision led to the end of slavery in the United States because _____.*

👤👤👤 Differentiated Instruction
Build Language: Use Irregular Verbs

Point to *took* in panel 9. Remind students that irregular verbs do not add -ed to show past action. Show the Irregular Verbs Chart. **Say:** *We must remember the spelling of irregular verbs to know when the action happens.* Write the irregular past tense forms of the verbs on the chart.

☑ Use Oral and Written Language: Give a Lecture on Dred Scott

Task: *Working with a partner, prepare a lecture about Dred Scott. Look at the sentence frames and find evidence in the text to complete them. Then give your lecture to another pair.*

(S) *Dred Scott was a very determined person. He lost but he decided _____.*

(M) *The Scott family gained their freedom. Peter Blow _____ and gave them _____.*

(L) *The Dred Scott decision eventually helped free the slaves. Abraham Lincoln _____ and in 1862, _____.*

🔄 Wrap Up

Today we learned how to analyze an author's reasons and evidence. Why is this important?

Turn and Talk: *How do you think it felt to be Dred Scott? What reasons can you give for your feelings?*

👥👥 Differentiated Instruction
Build Language: Use Irregular Verbs

Ⓢ ubstantial Support

Model: Reread panel 9 aloud. **Say:** *I remember that the Chief Justice said Dred Scott was not a citizen. Only citizens can sue in the Supreme Court. The author tells us the reason for the Chief Justice's decision.*

Practice: Ask: *What happened to Dred Scott after the court case?* Elicit answers. **Say:** *Let's reread panels 10 and 11.* Distribute BLM 1 and help students fill in the sentence frames using evidence based on a close reading of the text.

Extend: Have students work with a partner to answer the questions on the BLM.

Challenge: If students are ready, **ask:** *How does the author show that Scott's struggle was important?* Elicit answers. Point to panel 12 and model putting evidence in your own words. **Say:** *Abraham Lincoln spoke against the Dred Scott decision. Then, when he became President, he freed the slaves.*

Ⓛ ight Support

Use the text on pp. 12-19 in the *Texts for Close Reading* to complete the following activities.

Practice: Help students fill in the chart.

Page	Question	What the Text Says	In Other Words
19	What did the Supreme Court's decision mean for all African Americans?	"Because of Scott's race, he was not a citizen and had no right to sue."	African Americans were not citizens and had few or no rights.

Extend: Have students work in pairs to fill in the following chart.

Page	Question	What the Text Says	In Other Words
19	How does the author show that Scott's struggle was important?	"The Dred Scott case had considerable consequences... the Emancipation Proclamation... freed the slaves."	Scott's struggle helped lead to the end of slavery.

Challenge: Ask students to summarize how the actions of Dred Scott led to the end of slavery.

Ⓜ oderate Support

Model: Ask students to read panel 9. Focus on the author's reasons and evidence in the text. **Ask:** *What did the Supreme Court's decision mean for all African Americans?* Point to the panel and **say:** *Because of Scott's race, he was not a citizen and had no right to sue.* Ask students to think about that statement and put it in their own words.

Practice: Distribute BLM 2. Help students answer the questions by closely rereading the text and looking for evidence.

Extend: Ask: *How does the author show that Scott's struggle was important?* Point to panel 12 and ask students to put what it says in their own words. Then have students work with a partner to answer the questions in the Extend activity.

Challenge: If students are ready, **ask:** *How did the Dred Scott decision lead to the end of slavery?* Have them give reasons using their own words.

☑️ Formative Assessment

Substantial Support	• Can students reference text to find text-based answers? • Can students recognize important details?
Moderate Support	• Can students analyze an author's reasons and evidence in their own words? • Can students find evidence in a text to support an author's statement?
Light Support	• Are students able to draw conclusions, make inferences, and provide text descriptions? • Can students demonstrate understanding of the author's reasons and evidence by summarizing the key details?

Preview or Review Week 2 ELA Mini-Lessons

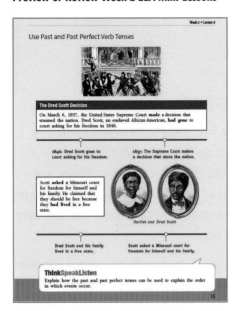

"Use Past and Past Perfect Verb Tenses," page 15

Student Objectives

LANGUAGE
Purpose:
• I can recount events.
Form:
• I can use past and past perfect verb tenses.
CONTENT
• I can analyze a social studies text.

Additional Materials
• Unit Presentation
• *Texts for Close Reading* booklet
• Think-Speak-Listen Flip Book
• Student journal

Language Transfer Support

Note that the past and past perfect verb tenses may be challenging for students whose first language is Chinese, Thai, Hmong, Vietnamese, or Haitian Creole—because these languages do not have tense inflections. These languages indicate time through context, or by adding words that express time. Provide additional writing and speaking opportunities for mini students to master English past and past perfect verb tenses.

9 Use Past and Past Perfect Tenses

Engage Thinking

Read aloud panel 5. **Say:** *Scott asked a Missouri court for freedom. He said they should be free because they had lived in a free state.* **Ask:** *What action happened first?* Elicit answers.

Turn and Talk: *Use the past tense to talk about what you did yesterday.*

Read and View Closely: Recognize a Sequence of Events

Explain that writers of history tell the events of the past in the order they happened. One way to show order is to use words such as *first, next, then,* and *finally*. Authors can also supply years and dates. Read aloud the first time line on page 13. **Ask:** *What helps us to know when these events in Dred Scott's life happened?* Elicit answers. **Say:** *Authors can also tell us the order of events through verb tenses.* Point out the verbs in bold in the first paragraph. **Say:** *There are two actions in the past in this paragraph. Made tells us one past event and had gone tells us another. These verbs together show that one past event happened before another past event.* Explain that the past perfect verb phrase *had gone* tells us that the action happened before the past tense action *made.*

👥 Differentiated Instruction
Build Language: Use Past and Past Perfect Verb Tenses

Read the first paragraph on the chart. Remind students that *made* and *had gone* give us information about which event happened first. Use the Differentiated Instruction to practice using past and past perfect verb tenses in a way that best matches the levels of your students.

Think-Speak-Listen: Use the following sentence frame or the Think-Speak-Listen Flip Book to guide discussion: *The past and past perfect tenses can be used to explain the order in which events occur because _____.*

☑ Use Oral and Written Language: Recount Events

Task: *Create a summary that explains a sequence of events in Dred Scott's struggle for freedom. Write a complete sentence that uses past or past perfect verb tenses to describe the event, then place the sentences in order on the board.*

(S) *Dred Scott _____ a slave. He _____ to be free.*
(M) *Dred Scott _____ the Missoucourt for freedom because he _____ in a free state.*
(L) *The Supreme Court _____ by its decision. They said _____ and therefore _____.*

🔄 Wrap Up

Why do you think it is important for writers of history to explain what happened in the correct order?

Turn and Talk: *Talk about your day today. What happened in the past? What happened before that?*

♦♦♦ Differentiated Instruction
Build Language: Use Past and Past Perfect Verb Tenses

Ⓢubstantial Support

Model: Remind students that verbs can help tell the order in which events in the past happened. Read the first sentence aloud and have students repeat. **Say:** *I see the verb made and I know it's a past tense verb. Stunned is also a past tense verb. It has an -ed ending. I also know the action happened in the past because of the date.*

Practice: Distribute BLM 1. Have students choose the correct verb from the box to complete each sentence. Then, have them write whether the verb is in the present or past tense.

Extend: Have students work with a partner to continue the activity in the Extend section of BLM 1.

Challenge: If students are ready, introduce the past perfect verb tense.

Ⓜoderate Support

Model: Remind students that authors tell the order in which events in the past happened by using sequence words, dates, and verb tenses. Read the first sentence aloud and have students repeat. **Say:** *I see that this sentence includes a date and two past tense verbs, made and stunned. These things help me know that the action happened in the past.*

Practice: Distribute BLM 2. Help students complete the activity.

Extend: Have students work with a partner to continue the activity in the Extend section of BLM 2.

Challenge: If students are ready, model labelling past and past perfect verbs in the *Texts for Close Reading*. Discuss whether they are past or past perfect tense.

Ⓛight Support

Use the text on p. 15 in the *Texts for Close Reading* to complete the following activities.

Practice: Ask students to reread paragraph 1. **Say:** *Verbs in the past tense describe past actions. Verbs in the past perfect tense describe past actions that happened before other past actions.* Have pairs work together to find the past perfect verbs in the paragraph. Then ask them to explain the events in the paragraph in their own words, using the past perfect verbs as a guide to the event that happened first. Help as needed.

Extend: Have pairs continue the activity by finding the past and past perfect verbs in paragraph 2. Then ask them to write about the events in the paragraph in their own words, using the past perfect verbs as a guide to the event that happened first.

Challenge: Say: *When the past tense and the past perfect tense are used together, they show a relationship between two actions.* Ask students to explain what the relationship is in their own words.

☑ Formative Assessment

Substantial Support	• Can students recognize verbs in the past tense? • Can students understand why the past tense is used?
Moderate Support	• Can students use verb tense as a guide to the correct order of events? • Can students identify past and past perfect verb tenses?
Light Support	• Do students understand the relationship between past tense verbs and past perfect tense verbs? • Can students generate original sentences using past and past perfect verb tenses?

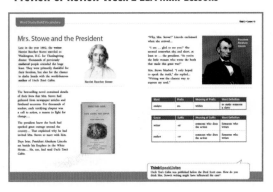

"Mrs. Stowe and the President," pages 16–17

Student Objectives

LANGUAGE
Purpose:
• I can create a chart.
Form:
• I can use prefixes and suffixes.
CONTENT
• I can analyze historical fiction of the Civil War era.

Additional Materials
• Unit Presentation
• *Texts for Close Reading* booklet
• Think-Speak-Listen Flip Book
• Student journal

Language Transfer Support

Students who are learning English may need additional support as they analyze compound words. Some students may not recognize the meaning of one or both words that compose the compound. Also, the meanings of the two words in a compound do not always reveal the meaning of the compound word, as in **brainstorm** and **dragonfly**.

10 Read "Mrs. Stowe and the President"

Build Background and Vocabulary

Display the Harriet Beecher Stowe image from the image bank and explain her importance to the text. If students have read the text, ask what they remember about the author or novel. Invite students to share their cultural experiences and knowledge of the meaning of civil rights.

Read Aloud the Text

Read the first paragraph. To support comprehension, ask *wh-* questions, such as *Where was the author in 1862?* Continue reading the rest of the text. **Ask:** *Why was Mrs. Stowe important to the President of the United States?* Invite students to share their thoughts using the sentence frame: *Mrs. Stowe was important to Abraham Lincoln because _____.* Refer to the Essential Question and invite students to comment on why laws evolve. Explain that the text is historical fiction.

Think-Speak-Listen: Use the following sentence frame or the Think-Speak-Listen Flip Book to guide discussion: *I think Mrs. Stowe's writing might have influenced the case by _____.*

Differentiated Instruction
Build Language: Use Prefixes and Suffixes

Explain that a prefix adds meaning to the beginning of a word and a suffix adds meaning to the end of word. Use the common prefixes and suffixes chart to teach the meanings of common prefixes and suffixes. Use the Differentiated Instruction to practice using prefixes and suffixes in a way that best matches the levels of your students.

☑ Use Oral and Written Language: Create a Chart

Task: *In pairs, have students make a T chart for the prefix en- and the suffix -er. Then, have pairs use the sentence frames to tell the group what they've learned.*

(S) *The word enslaved has the prefix _____. En- means _____. So, enslaved means _____. The word writer has the suffix _____. -Er means _____. So, writer means _____.*

(M) *The word enslaved _____ prefix _____. _____ means _____. So enslaved means _____. The word writer _____ suffix _____. _____ means _____. So, _____ means _____.*

(L) *I know the word enslaved _____ prefix _____ which means _____. So enslaved means _____. The word writer _____ suffix _____ which means _____. So, _____ means _____.*

Wrap Up

Today we learned about the importance of prefixes and suffixes. How does knowing them help you?

Turn and Talk: *What word you've learned with a suffix describes Harriet Beecher Stowe?*

👥 Differentiated Instruction
Build Language: Use Prefixes and Suffixes

Ⓢubstantial Support

Model: Write *thankful* on the board. Underline *-ful* and **say:** *I see that the word thankful has two parts, thank and ful. The suffix -ful at the end means "full of." So, thankful means "full of thanks."* Write the word prefix on the board. Underline pre-. **Say:** *The prefix pre- means "before." The word prefix means "to place in front."*

Practice: Distribute BLM 1. Help students underline the words with the suffix *-ful* and the prefix *pre-*. Then have students write the definition of the new words. Allow them to use a dictionary as needed.

Extend: Have students work with a partner to continue the activity on the BLM.

Challenge: If students are ready, help them use a different word with the prefix *pre-* or the suffix *-ful* in a sentence.

Ⓜoderate Support

Model: Write the words *thankful* and *prefix* on the board. Underline *-ful* and *pre-*. Remind students that suffixes occur at the end of words and prefixes occur at the beginning. Review the prefix *anti-* meaning against. Write this sentence on the board: *In the 1800s, the antislavery movement became stronger.* **Ask:** *Can you guess what antislavery means?* Elicit answers. Review the suffixes -ness (state of being) and -able (capable of being) in the same manner.

Practice: Distribute BLM 2: Help students underline and write a definition for the words with suffixes or prefixes.

Extend: Have students work with a partner to continue the activity in the Extend section of the BLM.

Challenge: If students are ready, help them make a list of words they know with prefixes and suffixes and their meaning.

Ⓛight Support

Use the text on p. 10 in the *Texts for Close Reading* to complete the following activities.

Practice: Review the prefixes and suffixes the students have learned. Have students look for a word with the prefix *-en*, the suffix *-er*, the suffix *-dom* and the suffix *-or* in paragraph 1. Have them list the words they find.

Extend: Working in pairs, have students create a prefix and suffix chart.

Word	Prefix/ Suffix	Meaning of Prefix/Suffix	Word Definition
enslave	en-	within	to make someone a slave
writer	-er	someone who does the action	someone who writes
freedom	-dom	a place	a state of being free
author	-or	someone who does the action	someone who writes

Challenge: Ask students to build their own words using prefixes and suffixes. Have them write two to three of their own sentences about what they learned about Mrs. Stowe, using at least one word containing a prefix or suffix in each sentence. Help them think through the process if needed.

☑ Formative Assessment

Substantial Support	• Can students identify a prefix and a suffix? • Do students understand that adding a prefix or a suffix to a word changes a word's meaning?
Moderate Support	• Can students identify prefixes and suffixes? • Can students analyze words with prefixes and suffixes and explain what they mean?
Light Support	• Can students analyze words with prefixes and suffixes and explain what they mean? • Can students write original sentences using prefixes and suffixes?

Preview or Review Week 3 ELA Mini-Lessons

"Thurgood Marshall's Liberty Medal Acceptance
Speech," pp. 18–19

Student Objectives

LANGUAGE
Purpose:
• I can write a news article.
Form:
• I can use subordinating conjunctions.
CONTENT
• I can analyze the civil rights movement by
reading speeches.

Additional Materials
• Unit Presentation
• *Texts for Close Reading* booklet
• Think-Speak-Listen Flip Book
• Student journal
• Subordinating Conjunctions Chart

Metacognitive Prompt: Summarizing

*As you read the speech, pause after each
panel to summarize what you have read
so far. This will help you understand and
remember the main ideas and key details
in the speech. It will also help you identify
points that are unclear, so that you can
reread the panel and ask and answer
questions to increase your understanding.*

11 Read "Thurgood Marshall's Liberty Medal Acceptance Speech"

Build Background and Vocabulary

Display the images explain their importance to the text. If students have already read
the text, ask them what they remember and invite them to share what they know. Invite
students to share their cultural experiences and knowledge of the meaning of civil rights.

Read Aloud the Text

Point to panel 1. To support comprehension, ask students to find images in the picture
that match words in the text (Thurgood Marshall, justice, Supreme Court, etc.) and ask
wh- questions, such as: *What do you think this person's job is?* Elicit answers. Repeat with
panels 2–8. After reading, **ask:** *What is this speech about?* Invite students to share their
ideas. Refer to the Essential Question. Then tell students that this text is a speech.

Think-Speak-Listen: Use the following sentence frames or the Think-Speak-Listen Flip
Book to guide discussion: *The cases of Heman Sweatt and Dred Scott were the same
because _____. The cases of Heman Sweatt and Dred Scott were different because _____.*

👤👤👤 Differentiated Instruction
Build Language: Use Subordinating Conjunctions

Explain that subordinating conjunctions are used to combine ideas. Words such as
although, because, if, after, unless, and *when* are subordinating conjunctions. Use the
Subordinating Conjunctions Chart to introduce common subordinating conjunctions
and model their use. Use the Differentiated Instruction to practice using subordinating
conjunctions in a way that best matches the levels of your students.

☑ Use Oral and Written Language: Write a News Article

Task: *Write a news article about the experiences of Heman Sweatt. Use the sentence
frames below to help you.*

(S)   *Heman Sweatt was an _____. He wanted to go to _____. He didn't go because
_____.*

(M)   *Heman Sweatt was _____. He wanted to _____ but he couldn't because _____.*

(L)   *Heman Sweatt was _____. His dream was to _____ but he wasn't _____
because of _____.*

🔄 Wrap Up

*Today we learned how to use subordinating conjunctions. How does using subordinating
conjunctions help us summarize Marshall's speech?*

Turn and Talk: *What was the most important thing you learned from Marshall's speech?*

👤👤👤 Differentiated Instruction
Build Language: Use Subordinating Conjunctions

Ⓢubstantial Support

Model: Read sentence 2 in panel 6. **Say:** *I see the word because. I know that we can use because to connect sentences and ideas.* Explain that the first idea is *they denied Heman admission* and the second idea is *his color was not theirs.* **Say:** *I know the word because shows the relationship between the two ideas. Because tells me the reason Heman was not accepted into law school. He was not accepted because his color was not theirs.* Remind students of other subordinating conjunctions they might know such as *although, if, after, unless,* and *when.*

Practice: Distribute BLM 1. Help students underline the subordinating conjunction and write the two ideas in each sentence.

Extend: Have students work with a partner to continue the activity on the Extend section of BLM 1.

Challenge: If students are ready, have them complete the Practice activity on BLM 2.

Ⓜoderate Support

Model: Read sentence 2 in panel 6. Point out that the word *because* connects one idea that has a subject and verb, "they denied Heman admission," to another idea that has a subject and verb, "his color was not theirs." **Say:** *When I see a subordinating conjunction like because, I know that ideas are being connected and what the relationship between the ideas is.* Remind students of other subordinating conjunctions they've learned from the Chart.

Practice: Distribute BLM 2. Help students choose the best subordinating conjunction to combine the two ideas. Then, write the sentence using the correct subordinating conjunction.

Extend: Have students work with a partner to continue the activity on the BLM.

Challenge: If students are ready, ask them to combine the following two ideas with a subordinating conjunction: *we can run from each other* and *we cannot escape each other. Have students choose their own subordinating conjunction.*

Ⓛight Support

Use the text on pp. 22-29 in the *Texts for Close Reading* to complete the following activities.

Practice: Have students work with a partner to link the ideas *We can run from each other* and *we cannot escape each other* by adding a subordinating conjunction to create a new sentence. Then have pairs link the ideas *you were kind enough to invite me here* and *I'm not going to bore you with a speech* by adding a subordinating conjunction.

Extend: Ask students to write 2–3 summary sentences about the speech. Each sentence should contain a subordinating conjunction.

Challenge: If students are ready, ask them to explain the reason it's important to recognize and use subordinating conjunctions.

☑ Formative Assessment

Substantial Support	• Are students able to recognize a subordinating conjunction in a sentence? • Are students able to identify the ideas linked by subordinating conjunctions?
Moderate Support	• Are students able to identify the ideas linked by subordinating conjunctions? • Can students select the correct subordinating conjunction to use in a sentence?
Light Support	• Can students see the relationship between ideas signaled by subordinating conjunctions? • Are students able to summarize a text using subordinating conjunctions?

Preview or Review Week 3 ELA Mini-Lessons

"Thurgood Marshall's Liberty Medal Acceptance Speech," page 20

Student Objectives

LANGUAGE
Purpose:
• I can give a lecture.
Form:
• I can analyze reasons in a speech.
CONTENT
• I can analyze the civil rights movement.

Additional Materials
• Unit Presentation
• *Texts for Close Reading* booklet
• Think-Speak-Listen Flip Book
• Student journal

Metacognitive Prompt: Grouping

Today we will read the rest of Thurgood Marshall's speech. As you read, jot down words and ideas from this and other recent texts about the struggle for equal rights. Draw a web or other type of diagram in which you group together words and ideas and show their connections.

12 Analyze Reasons in a Speech

Engage Thinking

Display the images. **Ask:** *Why do you think the people are protesting in panel 9?* Read the text. **Ask:** *What does the text tell you?*

Turn and Talk: *What events do you know about that relate to racism and civil rights? Share your ideas with a partner.*

Differentiated Instruction
Read and View Closely: Analyze Reasons in a Speech

Read aloud panels 10–12. To get students thinking about Thurgood Marshall's reasons for the beliefs he held, ask questions such as: *What does Thurgood Marshall say about freedom in panel 12?* Model searching the text for answers and putting the information in your own words. **Say:** *Thurgood Marshall said: We will only attain freedom if we learn to appreciate what is different. To me, he is saying that all people will be equal when we celebrate our differences.* Use the Differentiated Instruction to practice analyzing reasons in a speech in a way that best matches the levels of your students.

Think-Speak-Listen: Use the following sentence frame or the Think-Speak-Listen Flip Book to guide discussion: *Marshall and Johnson thought it was important to protect people's rights because _____.*

Build Language: Condense Ideas

Explain that to condense ideas means to shorten or summarize. Read aloud the first sentence in panel 9. Underline *Afro, white or blue* in the sentence. **Say:** *This condensed list is shorter and less repetitive than if Marshall had written "people who are African American, people who are white, or people of any other color."*

☑ Use Oral and Written Language: Give a Lecture

Task: *In pairs, write your own speech about the struggle for civil rights in the U.S. Use evidence from Thurgood Marshall's speech and "The Dred Scott Decision." Then give your speech to another pair.*

Ⓢ   Dred Scott wanted _____ from slavery. Heman Sweatt wanted _____.

Ⓜ   Dred Scott changed history because _____. Heman Sweatt also changed history when he _____.

Ⓛ   Abraham Lincoln and Thurgood Marshall both believed _____. They change the course of US history by _____.

Wrap Up

Today we learned to analyze reasons in a speech. Why did Thurgood Marshall believe that if some people are not free, all people are not free?

Turn and Talk: *What are some effects of racism? What can we do about them?*

👥 Differentiated Instruction
Read and View Closely: Analyze Reasons in a Speech

Ⓢubstantial Support

Model: Say: *What were some of Thurgood Marshall's beliefs? In panel 9 I see that Marshall said, "None of us...will ever rest until we are truly free."* Explain that reading the text closely, we can find reasons and evidence for Marshall's beliefs.

Practice: Distribute BLM 1. Model the activity by asking the first question and explaining the text-based answer given. Work with students to find text-based answers to the rest of the questions in the chart.

Extend: Have students work with a partner to continue the activity on the BLM.

Challenge: If students are ready, ask them to answer questions on the BLM in their own words.

Ⓜoderate Support

Model: Say: *I wonder what beliefs Thurgood Marshall had? I see in panel 9, "None of us...will ever rest until we are truly free." So, one belief is that everyone needs to be free; otherwise no one is.* Explain that to understand the reasons for one person's point of view, it helps to read what they've said and think about the reasons they feel the way they do. Model asking a question, reading the text closely for evidence, then answering the question in your own words.

Practice: Distribute BLM 2. Help students answer the questions on the BLM.

Extend: Have students work with a partner to continue the activity on the BLM.

Challenge: If students are ready, ask them to discuss what they think is the main point of the speech and why.

Ⓛight Support

Use the text on pp. 22-29 in the *Texts for Close Reading* to complete the following activities.

Practice: Ask students to review paragraph 6. **Ask:** *Why does racism fail, sooner or later? Look for reasons in the text in paragraph 6.* Point out *Hatred generates fear; and fear, once given a foothold, binds, consumes and imprisons.* and *No one benefits from racism.* In pairs, have students put these thoughts into their own words.

Extend: Ask students to look closely at the conclusion of the speech. **Ask:** *What conclusion does Marshall reach?* Direct them to paragraph 11. **Ask:** *What does Marshall suggest that we can do to end racism and why?* Then, ask students to analyze the reasons for Marshall's concluding words in pairs.

Challenge: If students are ready, ask them to summarize the text in a few sentences and then tell you why they chose their key points.

☑ **Formative Assessment**	
Substantial Support	• Can students reference text to find text-based answers? • Can students understand the reasons for a point of view?
Moderate Support	• Can students reference text to find text-based answers? • Can students put text-based answers in their own words?
Light Support	• Can students put text-based answers in their own words? • Can students draw conclusions from the text?

Preview or Review Week 3 ELA Mini-Lessons

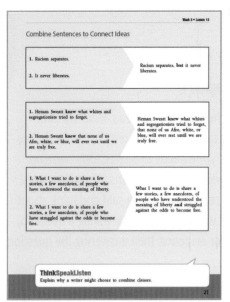

"Combine Sentences to Connect Ideas," page 21

Student Objectives

LANGUAGE
Purpose:
• I can make a movie strip.
Form:
• I can combine sentences to connect ideas.
CONTENT
• I can analyze a historical speech.

Additional Materials
• Unit Presentation
• *Texts for Close Reading* booklet
• Think-Speak-Listen Flip Book
• Student journal

Language Transfer Support

Note that some students may need additional support with the mechanics of sentence-combining to produce compound and complex sentences. Help students locate subjects and verbs as they analyze sentences that combine two or more ideas. Highlight words that express the relationships between ideas. Provide practice with combining two short sentences that have a basic subject-verb structure. Gradually build to more complex sentence structures.

13 Combine Sentences to Connect Ideas

Engage Thinking

Write these sentences on the board and read them aloud: *Thurgood Marshall told some stories. + Thurgood Marshall spoke against racism. = Thurgood Marshall told some stories and spoke against racism.* Explain that you have combined sentences and ideas using *and*.

Read and View Closely: Recognize Opportunities to Combine Sentences

Write these sentences on the board and read them aloud: *I want to share a few stories. The stories are about people who understand freedom.* Ask: How are these sentences related? Elicit answers. Say: Both sentences are about stories. It is possible to combine these sentences into one sentence that shows both ideas. Write and read aloud the new sentence: *I want to share a few stories about people who understand freedom.* Point out the repetition of the subject in boxes 1 and 3 and the repetition of the verb in box 2. Explain that we can combine sentences that use the same subject or verb to connect ideas. This allows us to write with less repetition.

👥 Differentiated Instruction
Build Language: Combine Sentences to Connect Ideas

Point to the text: *Racism separates. It never liberates.* **Say:** *The sentences describe two effects of racism. They can be combined to connect these two ideas.* Read aloud the combined sentence: *Racism separates, but it never liberates.* Use the Differentiated Instruction to practice combining sentences to connect ideas in a way that best matches the levels of your students.

Think-Speak-Listen: Use the following sentence frame or the Think-Speak-Listen Flip Book to guide discussion: *A writer might choose to combine clauses in order to _____.*

☑ Use Oral and Written Language: Make a Movie Strip

Task: *In your group make a movie strip about what you've learned about the Civil Rights Movement. Choose pictures from "Liberty Medal Acceptance Speech" and write captions for your movie strip. Combine sentences and ideas.*

Ⓢ *Thurgood Marshall was an _____ and a _____ on the United States Supreme court.*

Ⓜ *Heman Sweatt was an _____ man who had _____.*

Ⓛ *In his speech, Thurgood Marshall shares _____ as well as _____ about civil rights.*

🔄 Wrap Up

Today we learned how to speak and write by combining sentences to connect ideas. Why do you think speakers like Thurgood Marshall do this?

Turn and Talk: *What parts of Marshall's speech were the most memorable to you? Can you combine the ideas into one sentence?*

👥👥👥 Differentiated Instruction
Build Language: Combine Sentences to Connect Ideas

Ⓢubstantial Support

Model: Say: *I remember that we can combine sentences and ideas. I can use the word and to combine them.* Write the sentences on the board: People took risks for liberty. People showed courage for liberty. **Say:** *I see that people took risks and people showed courage. They did these things for liberty. I can put these ideas together using and.* Write this sentence on the board: People took risks *and* displayed courage for liberty.

Practice: Distribute BLM 1. Help students combine the sentences using *and*.

Extend: Have students work with a partner to continue the activity on the BLM.

Challenge: If students are ready, have them combine the following sentences using *but. We can run from each other. We cannot escape each other.* Guide students to forming the sentence: *We can run from each other but we cannot escape each other.*

Ⓜoderate Support

Model: Write these sentences on the board: Heman Sweatt wanted to go to law school. Heman Sweatt was not admitted to law school because of the color of his skin. **Say:** *The second sentence tells me why Heman Sweatt didn't go to law school right away. At first, he was not admitted.* Write this sentence on the board: Heman Sweatt wanted to go to law school, but he was not admitted because of the color of his skin. **Say:** *By using the connecting word but, I can show the relationship between the sentences.*

Practice: Distribute BLM 2. Help students combine the sentences using *and* or *but*.

Extend: Have students work with a partner to continue combining sentences using *and* or *but/*

Challenge: If they are ready, ask them to complete the Practice activity in the Light Support section.

Ⓛight Support

Use the text on pp. 22-29 in the *Texts for Close Reading* to complete the following activities.

Practice: Say: *Writers often combine sentences to make their writing clearer and stronger. One way to do this is to use connecting words to avoid repeating words.* Encourage partners to combine the following sentences using *but*: 1. *Heman Sweatt tried to get into law school. Heman Sweatt was kept out of law school because of his race.* 2. *We can run from each other. /* "*We cannot escape each other.*

Extend: Have students work with a partner to write 3 sentences summarizing Marshall's speech by combining sentences and ideas.

Challenge: If students are ready, have them articulate in their own words the reasons for combining sentences and ideas to improve their reading and writing skills.

☑ Formative Assessment

Substantial Support	• Do students understand that ideas can be connected by combining sentences? • Can students use connecting words such as *and* to produce compound sentences?
Moderate Support	• Can students identify relationships between two ideas in separate sentences? • Can students combine related ideas in compound sentences using *and* and *but*?
Light Support	• Can students explain relationships between two or more ideas in sentences? • Can students combine ideas to write their own original compound sentences?

Preview or Review Week 3 ELA Mini-Lessons

"The Presidential Medal of Freedom," page 22

Student Objectives

LANGUAGE

Purpose:
• I can perform a role play.

Form:
• I can analyze verbs and verb phrases.

CONTENT
• I can understand domain-specific language about informational social studies texts.

Additional Materials
• Unit Presentation
• *Texts for Close Reading* booklet
• Think-Speak-Listen Flip Book
• Student journal

Language Transfer Support

Note that speakers of Cantonese, Haitian Creole, Hmong, Korean, or Vietnamese may need extra support as they analyze and use verbs that have inflectional endings such as **-ed**. In speaking and writing English, these students might say, "President Kennedy want to pay tribute." Use regular verbs to model expressing the past tense in English.

14 Read "The Presidential Medal of Freedom"

Build Background and Vocabulary

Display "The Presidential Medal of Freedom" images and explain their importance in the text. If students have already read the text, ask what they remember. Invite students to share their knowledge of people who've made a difference. Invite students to share their cultural experiences and knowledge of the meaning of civil rights.

Read Aloud the Text

Read the first panel. To support comprehension, ask students *wh-* questions such as *Who is this? Where was this picture taken?* Repeat for panels 2 and 3. Refer to the Essential Question. **Say:** *One reason laws change and improve over time is due to the hard work of people like those awarded the Presidential Medal of Freedom.* Have students share their ideas using this sentence frame: I think laws change because _____. **Say:** *This text is about real people who did things a long time ago. This is called an informational text.*

Think-Speak-Listen: Use the following sentence frame or the Think-Speak-Listen Flip Book to guide discussion: *I think _____ deserves the Presidential Medal of freedom because _____.*

👥👥 Differentiated Instruction
Build Language: Analyze Verbs and Verb Phrases

Point to the phrase will earn in the last paragraph on page 20. **Say:** *The main verb earn tells the action. The helping verb will tells me when the action happens. Will earn is a verb phrase.* Use the Differentiated Instruction to practice analyzing verbs and verb phrases in a way that best matches the levels of your students.

☑️ Use Oral and Written Language: Perform a Role Play

Task: *With a partner, one of you will be President Kennedy and the other will receive the Presidential Medal of Freedom. Use verbs and verb phrases you've learned in your reading to create your role play.*

(S) *I want to pay _____ to you today.*

I am honored to receive _____.

(M) *You have _____ the constitution. I'd like to give you _____.*

I am _____. I will continue to _____.

(L) *Because of your contribution _____, you have earned _____.*

I will _____ because _____.

🔁 Wrap Up

Today we learned about the Presidential Medal of Freedom. Why do you think President Kennedy felt it was so important to honor citizens?

Turn and Talk: *Would you like to receive a Presidential Medal of Freedom? What would you do to get it?*

👥👥 Differentiated Instruction
Build Language: Analyze Verbs and Verb Phrases

ⓢubstantial Support

Model: Write the word established. Model thinking through the meaning of the word. **Say:** *I know that President Kennedy established the Presidential Medal of Freedom. I think it means he created the medal.* Explain that the -ed at the end of the word shows the action happened in the past. **Say:** *Established is the past tense of the verb establish. I look in my dictionary and see that establish means "to cause to be widely known and accepted."* Write this sentence on the board: *In 1963, President Kennedy established the Presidential Medal of Honor* to show how *established* is used in a sentence.

Practice: Distribute BLM 1. Help students complete the activity on the BLM.

Extend: Have students work with a partner to complete the activity on the BLM.

Challenge: If students are ready, have them create a Word Study Chart for the verb phrase *is receiving.*

ⓜoderate Support

Model: Point out the word *promoted* in the first paragraph. **Say:** *To explore the meaning of promoted, I look at the words around it: "men and women who promoted peace."* Explain that a person who gets an award for something related to peace probably helped create peace in some way. **Say:** *The -ed on the end tells me that the action happened in the past.*

Practice: Working together, further explore the meaning of promote. Ask students to use the dictionary and thesaurus to look up and share its meaning, as well as its synonym and antonym. **Say:** *Let's use the word in a sentence. President Lincoln promoted freedom for enslaved people.* Distribute BLM 2. Help students complete the activity.

Extend: Have students work with a partner to continue the activity on the BLM.

Challenge: If students are ready, have them complete a Word Study Chart for the verb phrase *will earn.*

ⓛight Support

Use the text on p. 30 in the *Texts for Close Reading* to complete the following activities.

Practice: Write the verb phrase *were recognized* from paragraph 4 on the board. Have students discuss the meaning of the verb phrase referencing the text and note the main verb and helping verb. Then, find the dictionary meaning, and look at the synonyms and antonyms. Finally, ask pairs to use the phrase in a sentence.

Extend: In pairs, have students continue the activity by analyzing the verb phrase *have turned* from paragraph 4.

Challenge: Have partners write and share original sentences in which they tell about the Presidential Medal of Freedom. Be sure to include verb phrases.

☑ Formative Assessment

Substantial Support	• Can students identify verbs and verb phrases? • Can students analyze a verb using a Word Study Chart?
Moderate Support	• Can students analyze a verb using a Word Study Chart? • Can students use verbs in original sentences?
Light Support	• Can students independently work with partners to analyze verbs and verb phrases? • Can students generate original sentences using verb phrases?

Preview or Review Week 3 ELA Mini-Lessons

"Use Regular and Irregular Verbs," page 23

Student Objectives

LANGUAGE
Purpose:
• I can write a letter.
Form:
• I can use regular and irregular verbs.
CONTENT
• I can analyze historical events related to civil rights.

Additional Materials
• Unit Presentation
• *Texts for Close Reading* booklet
• Think-Speak-Listen Flip Book
• Student journal

Language Transfer Support

Notes that speakers of Cantonese, Haitian Creole, Hmong, Korean, or Vietnamese may need additional support in recognizing and using regular and irregular verbs that have tense, person, and number inflections. During small-group time, for example, provide sentence frames and other structured opportunities for students to practice using these verbs in spoken and written English.

15 Use Regular and Irregular Verbs

Engage Thinking

Display the images. **Ask:** *Who do you recognize in the pictures? What did they do?* **Say:** *President Johnson, Martin Luther King, Jr. and Susan B. Anthony were all important in the history of our country.*

Read and View Closely: Identify Regular and Irregular Verbs

Display the chart. Read the first box aloud and have students repeat. **Say:** *The verb benefit is a regular verb. We add -ed to the end when the action happened in the past.* Read the second box. **Say:** *The verb speak is an example of an irregular verb. This verb in the past tense is spoke.* Explain that many common English verbs are irregular. This means you cannot just add *-ed* to their endings to show the action took place in the past. Because they do not follow rules, you'll need to memorize their spelling. Read the third box. **Say:** *The verb have is irregular, which means the spelling changes when it is in the past tense.*

👥 Differentiated Instruction
Build Language: Use Regular and Irregular Verbs

Explain that regular verbs are formed using *-ed* and irregular verbs change their spelling and must be memorized. Use the Differentiated Instruction to practice using regular and irregular verbs in a way that best matches the levels of your students.

Think-Speak-Listen: Use the following sentence frame or the Think-Speak-Listen Flip Book to guide discussion: *Regular verbs use _____ to show past tense. Irregular verbs change _____ to show past tense.*

✅ Use Oral and Written Language: Write a Letter

Task: *Working in pairs, write a letter to your parents telling them what you have learned about the struggle for civil rights in the United States. Use regular and irregular verbs.*

Ⓢ   *Susan B. Anthony _____ equality for women and African Americans. She _____ the American Equal Rights Association.*

Ⓜ   *Dred Scott _____ freedom but he _____ in the Supreme Court. Finally, Peter Blow _____ so he _____ his freedom.*

Ⓛ   *President Johnson _____ for equal rights. Thurgood Marshall also _____ and _____ the first _____.*

🔄 Wrap Up

Today we learned about using regular and irregular verbs. Why is it important to understand the difference between the two?

Turn and Talk: *What have you learned about how laws evolve over time? Use new verbs you have used in this unit in your answer.*

👥 Differentiated Instruction
Build Language: Use Regular and Irregular Verbs

Ⓢubstantial Support

Model: Write this sentence: *Dred Scott want his freedom.* Underline *want* and **say:** *I see the word want. To make the past tense, I add -ed.* Add *-ed* to want in the sentence. Point to the second box. **Say:** *I see the word speak. The past tense of speak is spoke. It doesn't have an -ed ending. It is a past tense verb.* Explain that for past tense verbs, we need to memorize the spelling.

Practice: Distribute BLM 1. Help students complete the chart of regular and irregular verbs.

Extend: Have students work with a partner to complete the activity on the BLM. Remind them to use the clues about the verb, whether the verb is regular or irregular, to help them.

Challenge: If students are ready call out the present tense of irregular verbs and ask students to tell you the past tense. Occasionally, call out a regular verb and have students say "Stop!" when they catch you.

Ⓜoderate Support

Model: Read aloud the sentences in the top and bottom chart boxes. **Say:** *I see that I can make the past tense of a regular verb by adding -ed, as in benefit/benefited. For irregular verbs, the spelling of the verbs changes when we use them in the past, like have/had. I need to memorize the spelling of irregular verbs.*

Practice: Distribute BLM 2. Help students change the verb in each sentence to the past tense and underline whether the verb is regular or irregular.

Extend: Have students work with a partner to continue the activity in the Extend section of the BLM.

Challenge: If students are ready, have them complete the Practice activity in the Light Support section.

Ⓛight Support

Use the text on p. 30 in the *Texts for Close Reading* to complete the following activities.

Practice: Write the following verbs related to students' reading: *support, fight, learn, gain.* Help students write the past tense forms of the verbs and label them regular or irregular.

Extend: Have students work with a partner to write two to four original sentences recounting what they learned from their readings on civil rights. The sentences should contain both regular and irregular verbs.

Challenge: If students are ready, ask them to tell you in their own words how regular and irregular verbs are different. Ask them why knowing the difference is important to our reading and writing.

☑ Formative Assessment

Substantial Support	• Do students understand the difference between regular verbs and irregular verbs? • Can students correctly choose regular or irregular past tense verbs to complete sentences?
Moderate Support	• Can students change regular and irregular verbs from the present to the past tense? • Can students correctly choose regular or irregular past tense verbs to complete sentences?
Light Support	• Can students generate original sentences using regular and irregular verbs? • Can students understand and explain how regular and irregular past tense verbs are different?

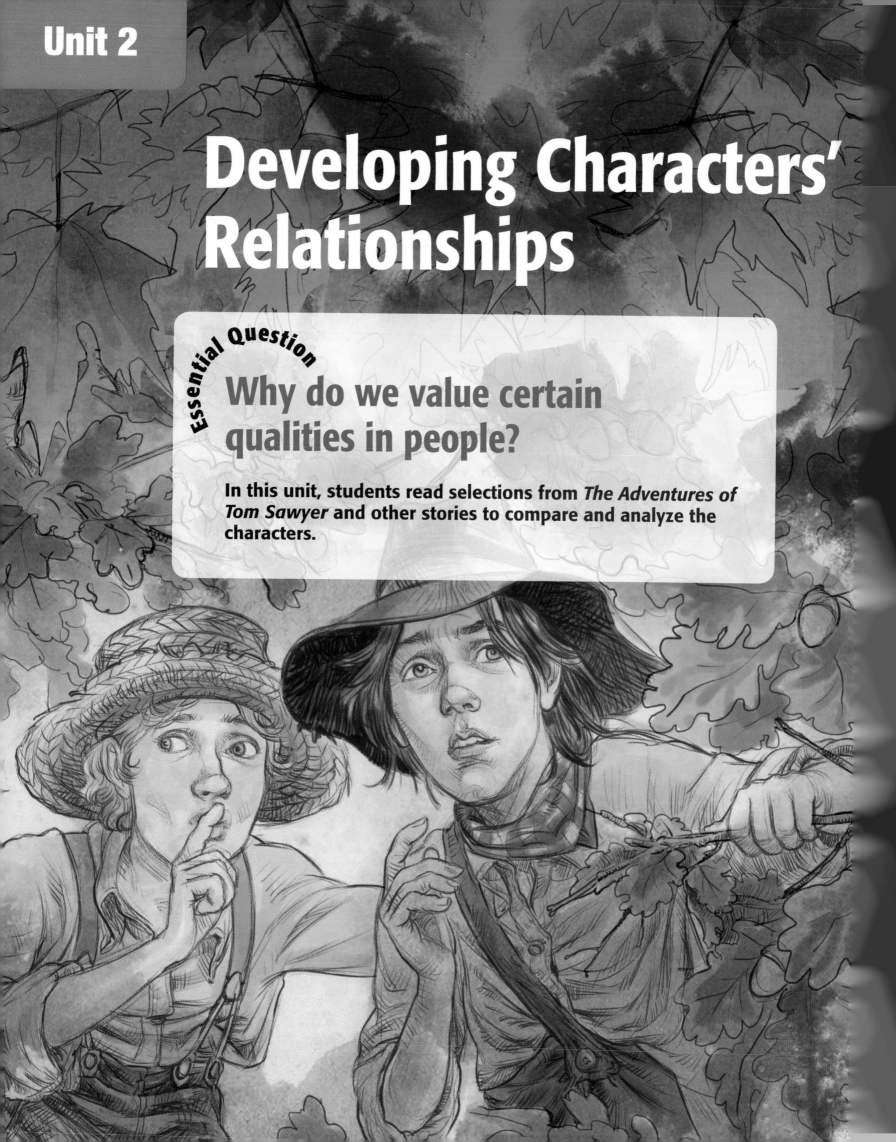

Unit 2

Developing Characters' Relationships

Essential Question

Why do we value certain qualities in people?

In this unit, students read selections from *The Adventures of Tom Sawyer* and other stories to compare and analyze the characters.

Unit 2 Lessons at a Glance

Language Skills

Week 1
- Use Adverbials to Add Detail
- Verb Tenses and Contractions
- Narrative Process Writing
- Understand Literary Language
- Analyze New Words

Week 2
- Understand and Use Interjections
- Condense Clauses
- Understand and Use Verb Tenses
- Use Adverbials to Describe Manner
- Categorize Words

Week 3
- Use Prepositional Phrases
- Use Interjections
- Use Context Clues
- Understand Verb Tenses and Contractions
- Use Compound Words

Lessons

Essential Question

Preview or Review Week 1 ELA Mini-Lessons

"Essential Question," pages 24–25

Student Objectives

LANGUAGE
Purpose:
• I can understand the Essential Question.
CONTENT
• I can understand the topic of the unit.

Additional Materials
• Unit Presentation
• Think-Speak-Listen Flip Book
• Student journal

Introduce Unit 2: Developing Characters' Relationships

Use the short lesson below to introduce the topic of the unit and help students understand the Essential Question.

Build Background and Vocabulary

Draw students' attention to the pictures and questions.

Say: *The topic of this unit is "Developing Characters' Relationships." These pictures and questions introduce the ideas that we will read about.*

Create a 3-column chart. Ask volunteers to read aloud the questions as you label the chart.

Ask: *What does relationship mean? How do we develop relationships with friends and family?*

Encourage a discussion and fill in the chart as below.

Fairness	Loyalty	Kindness
accept differences	trust	give your time and attention
treat everyone equally	cheer each other on	be polite

Ask: *How do these pictures help you understand characters' relationships?*

Help students answer and encourage students to share their cultural knowledge and experiences about the topic.

👤👤👤 Differentiated Instruction
Explain the Essential Question

Read aloud the Essential Question: *Why do we value certain qualities in people?* Review key words by definition and examples: **fairness, loyalty, kindness**. Review the 3-column chart. Encourage students to give examples, for instance of how these qualities are important to building a good team.

Use the Differentiated Instruction to help students at all levels understand the Essential Question.

Then proceed to Lesson 1.

👥 Differentiated Instruction
Explain the Essential Question

Ⓢubstantial Support

Hold up a picture of a sports team. Write: *Team values include fairness, loyalty, and kindness.* Say and have students repeat. Point to each illustration. Explain that **fairness** means accepting differences and being cooperative. Explain that **loyalty** is showing trust and support. Explain that **kindness** means being polite, and giving time and attention to others.

Say: *The very qualities that help build a team are the same values we qualities we value in our own relationships.*

Say: *In this unit we will learn how relationships are built on fairness, kindness, and loyalty.*

Ⓜoderate Support

Say: *We value the qualities of kindness, loyalty, and fairness.*

Point to a picture of a sports team.

Say: *A sports team is a good example of the values of fairness, loyalty, and kindness.*

Write: *The team showed fairness/loyalty/kindness by cheering each other on.* Say the sentence with students. Elicit the correct answer.

Write: *The team's choosing players based only on abilities showed fairness/loyalty/kindness.* Elicit the correct answer.

Say: *Why do we value certain qualities in people? In this unit we will learn how relationships are built on fairness, kindness, and loyalty.*

Ⓛight Support

Say: *Relationships are built on* **kindness, loyalty,** *and* **fairness.**

Elicit examples of **kindness, loyalty,** and **fairness**. Elicit the meaning of the word relationship. Point to a picture of a sports team.

Say: *A sports team is a good example of the values of fairness, loyalty, and kindness.*

Write: *The team showed fairness/loyalty/kindness by cheering each other on.* Elicit the correct answer.

Write: *The team's choosing players based only on abilities showed fairness/loyalty/kindness.* Elicit the correct answer.

Say: *Why do we value certain qualities in people? How do we build relationships? In this unit we will learn how relationships are built on fairness, kindness, and loyalty.*

☑ Formative Assessment

Substantial Support	• Can students, with help, show understanding of key words such as **fairness, loyalty,** and **kindness**?
Moderate Support	• Can students, with help, give examples of key words such as **fairness, loyalty,** and **kindness**?
Light Support	• Can students, give examples of key words such as **fairness, loyalty,** and **kindness**? • Can students show understanding of the word relationship?

"Becky Returns," page 26

Student Objectives

LANGUAGE
Purpose:
- I can re-recreate a dialogue.

Form:
- I can use different kinds of adverbs in text.

CONTENT
- I can identify a novel.
- I can understand different ways people talk.

Additional Materials
- Unit Presentation
- Think-Speak-Listen Flip Book
- *Texts for Close Reading* booklet
- Student journal

Language Transfer Support

Speakers of Chinese or Korean may need additional support in placing adverbs and adverbial phrases after verbs. In these languages, adverbs and adverbial phrases usually come before verbs (e.g., *I will with Susy Harper stay.*).

Students whose first language is Spanish may be familiar with a cognate of the word **adverb** (adverbio).

1 Read "Becky Returns"

Build Background and Vocabulary

If the students have already read the text, ask them what they remember. Invite students to share their cultural experience and knowledge about living in a rural area.

Read Aloud the Text

Point out the image of Mrs. Thatcher next to the first lines of dialogue. To support comprehension, ask students who they think that might be. Ask *wh-* questions, such as Who is that? What is happening? Continue with the remaining dialogue. **Say:** *This reading is an example of a dialogue. A dialogue shows a conversation between two or more characters.* **Say:** *I see the picture of Mrs. Thatcher next to the dialogue. That tells me that she is speaking.* Invite students to share their ideas about the other characters' dialogue. **Ask:** *How does character dialogue help to tell a story?* Then refer to the Essential Question. **Ask:** *Do you think that this story really happened? Could it have?* **Say:** *This is a long story about imaginary characters and events, so it is a novel.*

Think-Speak-Listen: Use the following sentence frame or the Think-Speak-Listen Flip Book to guide discussion: *Tom is _____. Becky is _____.*

Differentiated Instruction
Build Language: Use Adverbials to Add Detail

Read aloud the first paragraph. **Say:** *That first sentence has a lot of information. When we read, we can get information about what happens, and also how, when, and where. Let's look more closely at this sentence.* Point out the two verbs in the sentence, *came* and *gathered*. **Say:** *The verb gathered tells us what people did–they got together. The phrase "at Judge Thatcher's" tells us a detail about where they gathered. Adverbials are important because they add details to the story.* Use the Differentiated Instruction to practice using adverbials in a way that best matches the levels of your students.

☑ Use Oral and Written Language: Re-create a Dialogue

Task: *Using what you learned, write a short dialogue between Becky and Tom about visiting the Widow Douglas. Decide how you will say each line using your own words. Include an adverb or adverbial phrase in at least one line and underline it.*

(S) *Tom: We can run _____ to her house. Becky: _____, she will have ice cream.*

(M) *Tom: We need to hurry. If we run _____, we should get there _____.*

(L) *Becky: If we turn left _____, it will be a much shorter trip _____.*

Wrap Up

Today we learned about adverbials. Why is it important for authors to use adverbials in their stories?

Turn and Talk: *Turn to your neighbor and use adverbs and adverbial phrases to describe something you did over the weekend.*

👥 Differentiated Instruction
Build Language: Use Adverbials to Add Detail

Ⓢ ubstantial Support

Model: Write: *Morning came and people gathered.* Explain the meaning of *gathered,* to get together. **Say:** came *and* gathered *are both verbs. They tell us what happened. Now let's look at when and where. Phrases that give us more information about verbs are called adverbials.* Read the first part of the first sentence and point to the word *eventually.* **Say:** *Sometimes an adverbial is one word—an adverb. The adverb* eventually *tells us how morning came. This tells me the night felt very long.* Point to the phrase *at Judge Thatcher's.* *This adverbial tells us where they gathered.*

Practice: Distribute BLM 1. Help students complete the sentences with the correct adverbials.

Extend: Have students work with partners to choose adverbial phrases. Then have them write the phrases to complete the sentences.

Challenge: If students are ready, have them write their own sentences using adverbials.

Ⓜ oderate Support

Model: Read the first sentence and have students repeat. *Ask: What verbs do you see?* Point out the verbs *came* and *gathered.* Explain the meaning of *gathered* if necessary. **Say:** *The verbs in a sentence tell us the action that happened. Let's look at some of the phrases that tell us when, where, and how it happened.* Discuss what kind of information the phrases *eventually* and at *Judge Thatcher's* tell about the verbs. Then model finding adverbial phrases in Becky's first line. **Say:** *First I look at the verb, stay. I look for words that describe that verb. I see the words "with Susy Harper." The phrase gives details about the verb. It answers the question "where did she stay?"*

Practice: Distribute BLM 2. Help students complete the chart. Help them first find verbs from the text first *(stop, stay, climb, came, get back, gather),* then identify adverbials, and write what the phrase describes.

Extend: Have students work with a partner to write their own sentences, using other adverbials to describe the same verbs.

Challenge: Have students find adverbials in other books of their choice. Ask them to explain what the adverbial tells them.

Ⓛ ight Support

Use the text on pp. 4-5 in the Texts for Close Reading to complete the following activities.

Practice: Remind students that adverbials modify verbs and answer questions such as *how, where,* and *when.* Ask students to read paragraphs 4–6. Help them find the adverbial phrases that answer the following questions: *How was Becky to behave at Susy Harper's? Where did Tom want to stop? How often did the Widow Douglas have ice cream?*

Extend: Have students make a chart of adverbials from the reading, the verbs they modify, and details they describe about the verb.

Challenge: Have students write new sentences with each of the adverbials in the chart.

☑ Formative Assessment

Substantial Support	• Are students able to identify adverbial phrases? • Can students choose appropriate adverbials for sentences?
Moderate Support	• Can students identify adverbial phrases? • Can students write sentences using adverbial phrases?
Light Support	• Can students find and identify adverbial phrases in a longer text? • Can students explain what information adverbial phrases add to a sentence?

Preview or Review Week 1 ELA Mini-Lessons

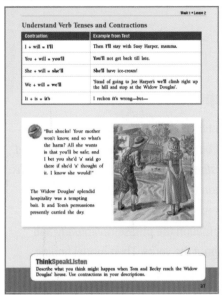

"Understand Verb Tenses and Contractions," page 27

Student Objectives

LANGUAGE
Purpose:
• I can make a persuasive presentation.
Form:
• I can use verb tenses and contractions.
CONTENT
• I can recognize realistic fiction.

Additional Materials

• Unit Presentation
• Think-Speak-Listen Flip Book
• *Texts for Close Reading* booklet
• Student journal

Language Transfer Support

Note that speakers of Spanish, Haitian Creole, or Hmong may use the present tense in place of the future tense. Provide students with extra practice in using **will** or its contraction in statements about the future.

Spanish speakers will be familiar with contractions from Spanish. For example, *del* is a contraction of *de + el* and *al* is a contraction of *a + el*.

2 Understand Verb Tenses and Contractions

Engage Thinking

Remind students that the conversations are written the way people talk. Read aloud Becky's first line. **Say:** *Becky says "you'll." This word is a short form of two words. The author uses "you'll" because this is the way people talk.*

Read and View Closely: Recognize Contractions

Read part of the dialogue from the story. Then have a volunteer find the word *you'll* in the chart on the page and read what it means. Ask other volunteers each to read aloud the other contractions. **Say**: *All of these words in the chart are contractions. They are two words joined to make one word.* Have volunteers read the sentences. For each sentence have them tell you which word is the contraction and what it means.

👥 Differentiated Instruction
Build Language: Verb Tenses and Contractions

Review that contractions are a short way to say two words. Point to the left column. **Say:** *In* I will, *an apostrophe takes the place of the letters wi, to make I'll. The word* will *means that the action is going to happen in the future.* Point out that understanding how to use contractions is important so that we can write the way people really speak. Use the Differentiated Instruction to practice verb tenses and contractions in a way that best matches the level of your students.

Think-Speak-Listen: Use the following sentence frame or the Think-Speak-Listen Flip Book to guide discussion: *When Tom and Becky reach Widow Douglas' house, I think _____ see _____.*

☑️ Use Oral and Written Language: Persuade Becky to Visit the Widow Douglas

Task: *Help Tom convince Becky to visit the Widow Douglas. Write sentences that would persuade Becky to go. Use contractions with will to tell Becky what will happen if she goes. Say your sentences aloud to the group.* Use this opportunity to assess students using the rubric in *English Language Development Assessment.*

S *_____ have fun! _____ love it! _____ be glad.*

M *You know _____ have fun! _____ love it, and _____ be glad to see us. Then _____ give us ice cream!*

L *When we go, _____ have fun. _____ love it, and _____ be glad to see us. When we get there, _____ give us ice cream!*

🔄 Wrap Up

Today we learned that contractions are short forms of two words that people use when they speak. Why is it important to know how to write contractions?

Turn and Talk: *Use contractions to tell your partner about what you did in math class yesterday.*

👥 Differentiated Instruction
Build Language: Verb Tenses and Contractions

Ⓢubstantial Support

Model: Display the chart on page 25. **Say:** *This chart shows some of the words the characters say in the story.* Read aloud the first example sentence. Explain that *I'll* is a short way to say "*I will.*" Remind students that *will* is added to verbs to show that the action will happen in the future. Point to the left column: *I + will = I'll*. Write "I will." Then erase the "wi" and draw in the apostrophe as you explain that it takes the place of those letters. Say a few more sentences with I'll, having students repeat after you: *I'll read the book tomorrow. I'll take the bus in the morning. I'll ride my bike after school. I'll see you later.*

Read aloud the second and third row of the chart, and teach the contractions *you'll* and *she'll* in the same way.

Practice: Distribute BLM 1. Read aloud the directions. **Say:** *As we read, we'll circle the contraction.* Guide students to fill in the equations to show how to form contractions.

Extend: Have pairs match the contraction with the two words. Ask how they figured out the answers.

Challenge: If students seem ready, have them find the contractions on BLM 2 for moderate support.

Ⓜoderate Support

Model: Point out the word *I'll* in the first line of Tom's dialogue. **Say:** *I see the contraction I'll. A contraction is a short form of two words.* Read aloud the first three examples in the Contractions chart. Point out that in these examples, a pronoun and the word *will* are combined. Write "I + will" Cross out the letters wi and draw in the apostrophe, explaining that it takes the place of the missing letters. Review the remaining examples in the chart in the same way. **Say** *"Will" means the action is going to take place in the future. So, "I'll tell" means "I will tell" in the future. The verb is indicates something happening in the present.* Say a few more sentences with contractions, having students repeat after you: *I'll talk to your mother about it. We'll have a great time. You'll love it there!*

Practice: Distribute BLM 2. Read aloud the sentences while students circle the contractions.

Extend: With a partner, have students complete the activity and write sentences.

Challenge: If students are ready, have them read pages 4 and 5 in *Texts for Close Reading* to look for contractions.

Ⓛight Support

Use the text on pages 4–5 in the *Texts for Close Reading* for the following activities.

Practice: Working in pairs, have students choose paragraph 2, 6, or 13. Ask them to make a chart with one column listing the contractions they find and the second column listing the two words used to make the contraction.

Extend: Using their chart, have students pick out the contractions that use the word *will* and describe the action that will take place in the future.

Challenge: Ask the students to write a new dialogue between Becky and Tom in which Becky tries to persuade Tom not to go to visit the Widow Douglas, using at least five different contractions.

☑	Formative Assessment
Substantial Support	• Can students recognize contractions? • Can students understand how contractions are formed?
Moderate Support	• Can students explain what a contraction stands for? • Can students describe why an apostrophe is used?
Light Support	• Can students identify contractions in a text and determine their meanings? • Can students describe action that will take place in the future?

Preview or Review Week 1 ELA Mini-Lessons

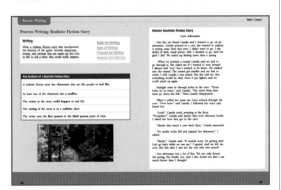

"Process Writing," pages 28–29

Student Objectives

LANGUAGE

Purpose:
• I can analyze a realistic fiction story.

Form:
• I can analyze and identify the features of a realistic fiction story.

CONTENT
• I can describe the features of a realistic fiction story.

Additional Materials
• Unit Presentation

3 Process Writing: Realistic Fiction

Engage Thinking

Tell students that they will read and analyze a realistic fiction story so that they can identify its features. Read aloud the writing topic.

Write a realistic fiction story that incorporates the features of the genre.
Include characters, events, and settings that are made up but true to life.

Say: *Let's ask questions to make sure we understand the writing topic. What type of writing is it? What will the writer write about? What features will the writer include in her story?*

👥 Differentiated Instruction
Read and View Closely: Analyze a Realistic Fiction Story

Say: *Listen and follow along as I read aloud this realistic fiction story. When I finish, we will analyze the five features of realistic fiction.* Read the mentor realistic fiction. **Say:** *Turn to a partner. Who are the main characters?* Check that students can identify the two main characters. Ask students if they seem like people they might meet in real life. Explain that this is the first feature of realistic fiction.

Say: *The second feature in realistic fiction is that at least one character deals with a conflict or has a problem. Turn to a partner. What problem does a character face?* Check that students can identify a conflict.

Say: *The third feature in realistic fiction is that the story events could happen in real life. Could two girls explore a cave in real life?* Check that students understand how this is realistic.

Say: *The fourth feature is that the story's setting is realistic. Turn to your partner. What makes this story seem to happen in a real place?* Find examples in the text. Check that students can find examples of a realistic setting and can identify the real state it takes place in (Utah).

Say: *A realistic fiction story is told from a first person or third person point of view. Which is this? How do you know?* Check that students can identify the point of view using examples from the text. Use the Differentiated Instruction to practice analyzing a fiction story in a way that best matches the level of your students.

Share Your Understanding

Bring the students back together. **Ask:** *What did we learn about the five features of realistic fiction? Review the features as needed.*

✓ Final Writing Assignment

Use the English Language Development Assessment to assess students' writing for their ELA writing assignment.

👤👤👤 Differentiated Instruction
Read and View Closely: Analyze a Realistic Fiction Story

Ⓢubstantial Support

Model: Distribute BLM 1. **Say:** *Let's read and analyze another realistic fiction story that answers the writing topic.* Read the story. **Ask:** *Do the characters talk and act like real people?* Model answering the question using examples from the text.

Practice: Continue asking *yes/no* questions similar to those that you asked about the Mentor Realistic Fiction Story. Invite students to answer and model forming complete sentences for them to repeat as needed.

Extend: Have students work in pairs complete the activity on the BLM.

Challenge: Guide student partners to use the activity on the BLM to make sentences about the text. Examples: *An example of the realistic setting is the "drip, drip, drip" of water in the cave. Maria talks like a real person when she says, "Umm."* Monitor and help the students to answer in complete sentences.

Ⓛight Support

Practice: Distribute BLM 2. **Say:** *This is the mentor realistic fiction story. We will look more closely at how writers include the five features of a realistic fiction story.* Do items 1–5 with students.

Extend: Have students work in pairs. Tell them to take turns using the questions on the BLM to make sentences that define the five features of realistic fiction. Examples: *A setting in a realistic fiction story can be a real place, like Utah. In realistic fiction, people talk like people do in real life.* Invite some pairs to say their sentences to the class.

Challenge: Have student partners join another pair. The pairs take turns asking each other questions about the five features of realistic fiction in the story. Tell them to use examples from the text in their answers. Examples: *Is the setting of Cave Adventure like a real place? Does the dialogue sound like how real people talk?* Remind students to make comments that contribute to the discussion and respond to the remarks of others.

Ⓜoderate Support

Model: Draw students' attention to the Mentor Realistic Fiction Story in their book. **Say:** *Let's analyze how the writer incorporates the five features of a realistic fiction story.* Make the chart below. Have students identify the main characters and give examples of how they act and talk

Features of Realistic Fiction	Examples from the Text
1. Characters are like people in real life.	Camila and Maria are "two friends." They talk realistically. For example, Maria says, "Umm—okay."
2. At least one character deals with a conflict.	
3. Story events could happen in real life.	
4. The story takes place in a realistic setting.	
5. The story is told from first person or third person point of view.	

Practice: Work with students to complete the chart using examples from the text.

Extend: Have students work with partners. Tell them to use the chart they created and to find another example from the text that illustrates each feature in the chart.

Challenge: Have partners use the chart to ask each other questions about the features of realistic fiction. Examples: *Is Camila like a real person? What conflict does Maria have?*

☑ Formative Assessment

Substantial Support	• With support, can students write details about characters in the text and the visual? • With support, can students use details to explain a character's feeling or behavior?
Moderate Support	• With some support, can students describe details about characters in the text and visual? • With some support, can students use details to explain a character's behavior or feelings?
Light Support	• Can students identify details about characters? • Can students use details to explain a character's feelings or behavior?

Preview or Review Week 1 ELA Mini-Lessons

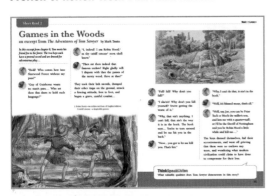

"Games in the Woods," pages 30–31

Student Objectives

LANGUAGE
Purpose:
• I can entertain using literary language.
Form:
• I can understand literary language.
CONTENT
• I can understand realistic fiction.

Additional Materials

• Unit Presentation
• Think-Speak-Listen Flip Book
• *Texts for Close Reading* booklet
• Student journals

Language Transfer Support

Today, English has only one second person pronoun: you. In many other languages, there are formal and informal ways to say "you." In the past, English also had a second word for you, the word thou. The word you was formal—it was formal, similar to the Spanish Usted, French vous, or German Sie. The word thou was informal, similar to Spanish *tú*, French *tu*, or German *du*.

4 Read "Games in the Woods"

Build Background and Vocabulary

Display the panels and explain their importance in the story. Invite students to describe the boys in the pictures. **Ask:** *Where are the boys? What game do you think they are playing? What games do you play outside?* Invite students to share their cultural experience and knowledge about playing games outdoors.

Read Aloud the Text

Read aloud the first page of the text . Help identify unfamiliar words. **Ask:** *Who is speaking in this story? What is happening in the picture?* Repeat with the next page. After reading, **ask:** *How does the dialogue help explain what the boys are doing?* Invite students to share their ideas. Then refer to the Essential Question and the question Why do we value fairness? **Say:** *How does this story show fairness? Why fairness important?* Invite students to respond. **Say:** *This story is not about real people, so it's fiction. But it seems real. We call this type of story realistic fiction.*

Differentiated Instruction
Build Language: Understand Literary Language

Say: *Literary language is a different form, or dialect, of English. In this story, the boys use an old form of English.* Read Joe's first line. **Say:** *The word* thou *is an older form of* you. *The word* art *is an older form of the verb* are. *So* art thou *is* are you. *So Joe is asking "Who are you that dares to talk to me this way?"* Repeat with Joe's first line on p. 31 and the word *sha'n't* (shall not.) **Say:** *Understanding literary language helps us know what the characters are saying.* Use the Differentiated Instruction to practice understanding literary language in a way that best matches the levels of your students.

Think-Speak-Listen: Use the following sentence frame or the Think-Speak-Listen Flip Book to guide discussion: *Tom Sawyer shows the qualities _____, _____, and _____.*

☑ Use Oral and Written Language: Entertain Using Literary Language

Task: *Pretend Tom and Joe have met again for more games in the woods. This time, Joe is Robin Hood. Rewrite the lines to show what Tom and Joe say. Use literary language such as thou, art, thee, thy and sha'n't. Perform your lines for the class.*

(S) **Tom:** *Stop! Who are you?* **Joe:** *I won't stop! I am Robin Hood!* **Tom:** *What! You are an outlaw!*

(M) **Tom:** *Stop there! Drop your sword. I am the Sheriff. Who are you?* **Joe:** *I won't stop for I am Robin Hood!* **Tom:** *What? You are an outlaw!*

(L) **Tom:** *Stop! I am the Sheriff of these woods. Who are you that dares to show your sword?* **Joe:** *I won't stop for I am Robin Hood!* **Tom:** *Then you are a famous outlaw!*

Wrap Up

Today we learned about literary language and how authors can use different dialects in a story. Why is it important to understand literary language in a story?

Turn and Talk: *Use literary language to describe stopping someone from crossing a busy street.*

👥👥 Differentiated Instruction
Build Language: Understand Literary Language

Ⓢ ubstantial Support

Model: Read aloud the second paragraph in panel 2. Point out the words *art* and *thou*. **Say:** *Tom and Joe are pretending to be characters from another time, talking the way people spoke back then.* Make a chart to show old English words and their meaning. In one column list *art, thou, thy, shall, sha'nt*. In a second column, write the meanings: *are, you, your, will, won't*. Ask students to reread the sentence, *"Then art thou indeed that famous outlaw?"* Then have a volunteer look at the chart to find the meanings of *art* and *thou* on the chart. Have another student say the sentence replacing those words. Repeat with other sentences containing the old English words.

Practice: Distribute BLM 1. Help students write the meaning of each Old English word.

Extend: Have students work with a partner to complete the Extend activity on the BLM.

Challenge: Say a sentence with *are you* and ask students to say back with *art thou. (Are you hungry? Are you going to the park?)*

Ⓜ oderate Support

Model: **Say:** *In this story, Tom and Joe use old English words as they play their game. I can understand the game they play when I understand the literary language.* Display the first paragraph of panel 2. **Ask:** *What literary language do the boys use in this part of the story?* Help students identify *thy* and *shall*. **Say:** *If thy means "your" and shall means "will," what does this sentence mean?* Have a volunteer read the sentence, replacing the old English words: *I am Robin Hood, as your caitiff carcase soon will know.* Repeat for other sentences, defining the terms and asking students to replace them. Then make a chart and list the old English words *art, thou, thy, shall, sha'n't* in one column. Have students help you list the modern meanings in a second column.

Practice: Distribute BLM 2. Help students rewrite the sentences using modern English.

Extend: Have students pairs complete the Extend activity on the BLM.

Challenge: Have pairs write new sentences with old English words, exchange them and change them to modern English.

Ⓛ ight Support

Use the text on pages 6–9 in the *Texts for Close Reading* for the following activities.

Practice: **Say:** *In their game, Tom and Joe not only try to dress the part, but speak the way people did during that time.* Ask student pairs to identify the literary language in paragraphs 7-11. For each example, have them write an explanation of the sentence's meaning. Ask partners to create a chart listing all the old English terms they find in one column and giving their modern meanings in a second column. Encourage them to consult a dictionary for words they don't know.

Extend: **Ask:** *How can the reader tell when the Tom and Joe are pretending to be in Sherwood Forest and when they are speaking to each other?*

Challenge: Have students write out a short dialogue describing something they do not like, using literary language terms they learned.

☑ **Formative Assessment**	
Substantial Support	• Are students able to read literary language? • Can students recognize the difference between modern language and literary language?
Moderate Support	• Can students identify literary language? • Can students translate sentences that use literary language to demonstrate their understanding?
Light Support	• Can students identify and explain the meanings of examples of literary language? • Can students write original sentences using literary language?

Preview or Review Week 1 ELA Mini-Lessons

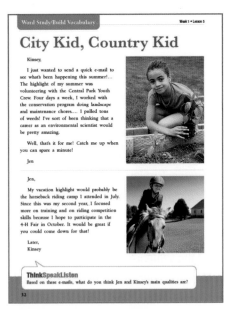

"City Kid, Country Kid," page 32

Student Objectives

LANGUAGE
Purpose:
• I can use science words in an e-mail.
Form:
• I can analyze new words in context.
CONTENT
• I can use science words about the environment.

Additional Materials
• Unit Presentation
• Word Study Chart
• Think-Speak-Listen Flip Book
• *Texts for Close Reading* booklet
• Student journals

Language Transfer Support

Some of the longer words in this text are derived from Latin. Students whose first language is a Latinate language may know cognates of words in this lesson (*conservation, maintenance, scientist, competition, participate.*)

5 Read "City Kid, Country Kid"

Build Background and Vocabulary

Display the panels. If students have already read the text, ask them what they remember. Invite students to share their cultural experience and knowledge of the city or the country. Invite them to describe what the two pictures show. **Say:** *Where is each girl? What activity is each girl doing? What activities do you like to do in the summer?*

Read Aloud the Text

Read panel 1. To support comprehension, ask students *wh-* questions, such as *Who wrote this letter? Who is she writing to? What is the girl doing in the picture?* Repeat with panel 2. After reading, model how to describe the pictures. *This picture shows Jen helping at Central Park. Jen is putting plants in a wooden box.* Invite students to share their ideas. Then refer to the Essential Question. **Ask***: What qualities do you learn about Jen and Kinsey?*

Think-Speak-Listen: Use the following sentence frame or the Think-Speak-Listen Flip Book to guide discussion: *I think Jen and Kinsey's main qualities are _____.*

👥 Differentiated Instruction
Build Language: Analyze New Words

Explain to students how to use context to help analyze the meaning of a new word in a text. **Say***: Analyzing new words is important because it helps us understand everything we read. When I see a word that I don't know, first I look at the word in context—I look at the other words around it, and at the pictures. I look for clues.* Point to the word conservation. **Ask***: What clues help you understand the word conservation? The girl is working outside, so conservation has something to do with the outdoors.* Explain that after looking at the word in context, you will also using a dictionary to look up meanings, and charts to help you organize information about the words. Use the Differentiated Instruction to practice analyzing new words in a way that best matches the levels of your students.

☑ Use Oral and Written Language: Write an E-mail

Task: *Imagine you have a summer job outdoors. Write an e-mail to a friend about what you did. Reread Jen's letter to get ideas. Use science words about the outdoors, words like conservation, landscape, environment. Use these example sentences to help you.*

Ⓢ *I have a new job. I am working in _____. I am_____. The work is good for _____/*

Ⓜ *Hi. Here's a quick e-mail about my new job. I am working _____. I _____ .*

Ⓛ *I just wanted to send a quick e-mail. I'm working _____. The work I do is for _____.*

↩ Wrap Up

Today we learned how to analyze a word's meaning. Why is it important to understand the meaning of new words in a text?

Turn and Talk: *Tell your partner a new word you have recently learned in science or history. Explain how you found out the meaning.*

👥👥 Differentiated Instruction
Build Language: Analyze New Words

Ⓢubstantial Support

Model: Read aloud the first e-mail and point out the word *weeds*. **Say:** *When I get to a word I don't know, I have to find out what it means.* Discuss with students how to analyze a new word using the Word Study Chart. Point to the picture and ask where the girl is working. Read the sentence and pantomime pulling out the weeds. **Ask:** *If I pull out weeds, are those plants I want or plants I don't want?* Explain that we pull them out because they are plants we don't want in the garden.

Practice: Distribute BLM 1. Work with students to fill out the chart for the words on the page. Have them help to find words in the text, and to look up the word in a dictionary. For *conservation*, you can use the cognate *conservar* or *conservación*.

Extend: With a partner, have students look up the definitions to fill in the Word Study Chart on the BLM. Then have them choose one word and fill in the second chart.

Challenge: If students are ready, have them make up sentences with new words.

Ⓜoderate Support

Model: Read aloud the first e-mail. Ask students to identify words that are unfamiliar. **Say:** *Sometimes you may not know the meaning of a word. This is often true with science words you have not seen before.* Discuss what it means to look at a word in context. **Say:** *I'm not sure what landscape means. I look at it in context and see the clue "doing chores." I think landscape has to do with working with the land. Then I'll look up the meaning of landscape in a dictionary.*

Practice: Distribute BLM 2. Help students complete the Word Study Chart for two new words.

Extend: Have students work in pairs to do the activity in the Extend section of the BLM.

Challenge: Have students use p. 10 of the *Texts for Close Reading*, to select one new word and fill out the Word Study Chart.

Ⓛight Support

Use the text on p.10 in the *Texts for Close Reading* to complete the following activities.

Practice: Help students look for new words in paragraphs 2–3. Suggest that they include science words such as *conservation, landscape,* or *environmental*. For each word have them list the definition, part of speech, synonyms, antonyms, and a context sentence.

Extend: Have students work in pairs to identify new words in paragraph 6 and continue their chart.

Challenge: Have students write original sentences using the new science words they have learned.

☑ Formative Assessment

Substantial Support	• Can students use pictures and context clues to determine word meanings? • Can students use a dictionary and thesaurus to identify definitions and synonyms?
Moderate Support	• Can students use context clues and other resources to analyze unfamiliar words in a text? • Can students apply their understanding to support their comprehension of a text?
Light Support	• Can students recognize and analyze unfamiliar words in a text using a Word Study Chart? • Can students explain how to use context clues to help them analyze new words?

Preview or Review Week 2 ELA Mini-Lessons

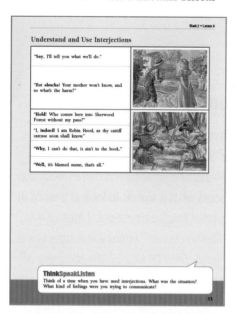

"Understand and Use Interjections," page 33

Student Objectives

LANGUAGE
Purpose:
• I can express emotions in a role-play.
Form:
• I can use interjections in a dialogue.
CONTENT
• I can understand realistic fiction.

Additional Materials
• Unit Presentation
• Think-Speak-Listen Flip Book
• *Texts for Close Reading* booklet
• Student journal

Language Transfer Support

Every language has interjections, which need to be learned just like everything else in a new language. Most languages seem to have the interjection "ah" or "oh," but other sounds are unique and may even mean something completely different in a different language.

6 Understand and Use Interjections

Engage Thinking

Display the panels. Read the first sentence and have students repeat. **Say:** *We could read this sentence without the word "say." I'll tell you what we'll do.* Explain that some words we say and read don't add meaning, but they add expression or emotion to what we say.

Turn and Talk: *What kinds of words do you use to get someone's attention? What about when you are surprised by something?*

Read and View Closely: Recognize Interjections

Say: *This chart helps us see which words in dialogue from the stories show an emotion or call attention to something.* Read the chart. Point out that interjections are more often used in speaking than in writing. As they read, students may see interjections in dialogue. **Say:** *When I read dialogue, recognizing interjections is important because tell us a character is showing an emotion. When I write, I can use interjections in my dialogue to show the characters' emotions and expressions.*

👥👥 Differentiated Instruction
Build Language: Understand and Use Interjections

Read the first two sentences. **Ask:** *What does the interjection "shucks" tell us?* Elicit that *shucks* shows Tom's disappointment. Have a volunteer read the sentence with and without the interjection. Make a list of interjections people use everyday, like *Oh, wow, ooh, Oh no!, Umm, oops.* Use the Differentiated Instruction to practice understanding and using interjections in a way that matches the level of your students.

Think-Speak-Listen: Discuss a time students used interjections or use the Think-Speak-Listen Flip Book to guide discussion.

☑ Use Oral and Written Language: Express Emotions in a Role Play

Task: *Imagine you are thinking of a game to play with a friend. Collaborate with a partner to act out what you would say. Act out your scene for the group. Use some of these sentences. Add interjections.*

Ⓢ *Character 1: _____, let's play a game. Character 2: OK, what should we play? _____, I can't think of anything.*

Ⓜ *Character 1: _____, I know! Let's play _____. Character 2: _____, that's a great idea!*

Ⓛ *Character 1: _____, I forgot. I have to go home soon. Character 2: _____, that's too bad. _____, how about tomorrow?*

🔄 Wrap Up

Today we learned about using interjections. Why is it important to be able to recognize and use interjections when we read and write?

Turn and Talk: *Describe when you might use interjections when playing a sport.*

👥 Differentiated Instruction
Build Language: Understand and Use Interjections

Ⓢubstantial Support

Model: Display the chart. Read aloud the first example and have students repeat. Explain that the word *say* in this sentence does not mean *speak*. It's a word people use when they are excited about a new idea. The word we hear more often now is *hey*. Write: *Hey, let's go buy some snacks! Hey, I have an idea!* Read each sentence aloud and have students repeat. Make a list of other interjections: *Wow, Aww, Hmm.* Explain the emotion for each one. **Say:** *We say wow when we're surprised and excited. We say aww when we're disappointed or sad. We say Hmm when we don't feel sure.* For each one, say a sentence and have students repeat, adding the interjections and saying it with emotion. For example, say *Thanks for the present.* Point to "wow" and have students say excitedly, *Wow, thanks for the present!*

Practice: Distribute BLM 1. Work with students to add interjections to complete each sentence.

Extend: With partners, have students choose an interjection from the box and rewrite each sentence adding that word.

Challenge: If students are ready, have students identify interjections in other sections.

Ⓜoderate Support

Model: Read aloud the first example. Explain that *say* is an old fashioned way to say *hey*. Both words are interjections, words that add emotions or expression. Read each of the other examples, with and without the interjections. Point out that *Why* in the fifth sentence is not a question but a way of emphasizing what he is saying. Ask students to help think of other interjections. **Say:** *What do we say when we are embarrassed about a mistake? When we are surprised? When we are disappointed? When we feel unsure?* Write *oops, wow, aww, hmm.* Say sentences and ask volunteers to add one of the four interjections. For example, they might add *Aww* to *I'm sorry you can't come.*

Practice: Distribute the BLM 2. Work with the students to complete the activity in the Practice section.

Extend: Have students work with a partner to write their own sentence on the BLM, choosing interjections to include. **Ask:** *How do the interjections you added show emotion?*

Challenge: If students are ready, have them read paragraphs 20 and 21 on p. 8 of *Texts for Close Reading*. Ask them to identify and describe an interjection used in each paragraph.

Ⓛight Support

Use the text on pp. 6-9 in the *Texts for Close Reading* to complete the following activities.

Practice: Remind students that interjections are words that are not important to the meaning of a sentence but express an emotion or call attention to something we say. Have students list the interjections in paragraphs 19–22. (*Now, Why, Well, Well*) Ask partners to read the sentences to each other with and without the interjection to see how it changes the expression of the sentence.

Extend: Have students come up with other interjections. Prompt by asking them to list words we say when we express surprise, embarrassment, disappointment, or uncertainty. (*wow, oops, aww, hmm or umm*).

Challenge: Have partners write original sentences for a short dialogue, showing examples of the use of interjections.

☑ Formative Assessment

Substantial Support	• Can students recognize interjections? • Can students add interjections to sentences?
Moderate Support	• Can students identify and describe interjections? • Can students choose interjections to add to original sentences?
Light Support	• Can students list interjections that are used in an authentic text? • Can students write a dialogue with interjections?

Preview or Review Week 2 ELA Mini-Lessons

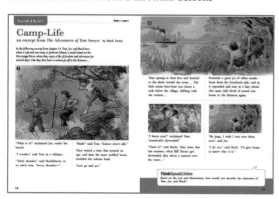

"Camp-Life," pages 34–35

Student Objectives

LANGUAGE

Purpose:
• I can retell a story.

Form:
• I can condense clauses.

CONTENT
• I can understand realistic fiction.

Additional Materials
• Unit Presentation
• Think-Speak-Listen Flip Book
• *Texts for Close Reading* booklet
• Student journals

Metacognitive Prompt: Making Inferences

Today we will practice using information in the text to make inferences about characters.

To make an inference, think about what characters say and how they say it. Then use what you know to decide what you think of the characters.

---

7 Read "Camp Life"

Build Background and Vocabulary

Display the panels. **Ask:** *Where are the boys? What are they doing?* Invite students to share their cultural experience and knowledge of playing or exploring outside.

Read Aloud the Text

Read panel 1. To support comprehension, ask *wh-* questions, such as *Who are the characters? What can you tell about them from how they dress? What problem do they have?* Repeat with panels 2, 3, and 4. **Say:** *Readers make inferences, or guesses, about characters in stories based on the way they dress, talk, and act. What inferences can you make about these characters?* Invite students to share their ideas. Then refer to the Essential Question. **Ask:** *What quality do the boys have?* Invite students to respond. **Say:** *This story is not about real people, so it's fiction. But it seems real. We call this type of story realistic fiction.* Use this opportunity to assess students using the rubric in *English Language Development Assessment.*

Think-Speak-Listen: Use the following sentence frame or the Think-Speak-Listen Flip Book to guide discussion: *I would describe the Joe as _____. I would decribe Tom as _____.*

👥 Differentiated Instruction
Build Language: Condense Clauses

Explain that a clause is a group of words that includes a subject and a verb. Display the fifth paragraph from panel 1. **Say:** *Let's look at this sentence. The clauses are "They waited a time that seemed an age," "then the same muffled boom troubled the solemn hush." The word* and *joins the two clauses. Instead of writing a lot of short choppy sentences to state separate ideas, the writer has put together more than one idea in the same sentence. When writers condense clauses, it helps the writing flow more smoothly.* Use the Differentiates Instruction to practice condescending clauses in a way that best matches the level of your students.

Use Oral and Written Language: Retell a Story

Task: *A summary is a retelling of a story in your own words. Collaborate with your peers to write a summary of "Camp-Life." Include more than one idea in a sentence. Look for ways to condense ideas that are connected. Read your summary to the group.*

Ⓢ *Tom, Joe, and Huck hear _____. They see _____.*

Ⓜ *Tom, Joe, and Huck heard _____ and saw _____, _____.*

Ⓛ *When night came, they _____ and _____, _____.*

🔄 Wrap Up

Today we learned about condensing clauses in writing. Why is it important to know how to condense clauses?

Turn and Talk: *Describe a weekend activity in one to two sentences. Be sure to condense clauses.*

👥👥 Differentiated Instruction
Build Language: Condense Clauses

Ⓢubstantial Support

Model: Write: *They sprang to their feet. They hurried to the shore toward the town.* Read the sentences aloud and have students repeat. **Say:** *These two sentences have the same subject, they. I can join them together, or condense them.* Read aloud the first sentence in panel 2 and have students repeat. Explain that there are many ways to condense sentences. **Say:** *The author condensed the ideas by using the word and.*

Practice: Distribute BLM 1. Help students look at the pictures in each panel and condense the sentences.

Extend: Have students work with a partner to condense the clauses to form one sentence. Encourage students to look at the images in each panel.

Challenge: If students are ready, help them write two clauses about what is happening in the image in panel 1, then condense the clauses.

Ⓜoderate Support

Model: Read aloud the first paragraph in panel 2. Ask students to help you list the different ideas in the sentence, for example, *The boat was a mile from the village. The boat was drifting with the current.* Explain that the writer has condensed two ideas into one sentence. **Ask:** *What did the writer do to condense the two ideas?* Point out that there is a comma between them and that the second one is a *clause*, not a complete sentence, so the writer left out words "The boat was" or "It was." Explain that another way to condense sentences is to use the word *and* between two ideas.

Practice: Distribute BLM 2. Help students look at the pictures and condense the clauses to create one sentence.

Extend: Have students work with a partner to write at least two clauses describing the remaining pictures. Then, have them combine the clauses.

Challenge: If students are ready, challenge pairs to select two sentences on p. 12 in the *Texts for Close Reading* that contain more than one clause. Have students identify the clauses.

Ⓛight Support

Use the text on pp. 12-19 in the *Texts for Close Reading* to complete the following activities.

Practice: Have students read paragraph 1. Help students identify the clause in each sentence.

Extend: Have students work with a partner to find three sentences that contain multiple clauses on p. 13. Ask them to identify the clauses in the sentences and discuss which ideas have been combined. Then ask students to discuss how the story would be different if the clauses were not condensed. **Ask:** *How did the author connect ideas in the sentence?*

Challenge: Have partners write pairs of related sentences and then combine clauses to condense the sentences.

☑ Formative Assessment

Substantial Support	• Can students recognize condensed sentences? • Can students write sentences using clauses?
Moderate Support	• Can students identify clauses in sentences? • Can students combine sentences into one sentence with more than one clause?
Light Support	• Can students identify and explain the use of clauses in a story? • Can students write original condensed sentences?

"Camp-Life," page 36

Student Objectives

LANGUAGE
Purpose:
- I can write and illustrate a scene from a story.

Form:
- I can use verb tenses.

CONTENT
- I can describe a realistic fiction story.

Additional Materials
- Unit Presentation
- Think-Speak-Listen Flip Book
- *Texts for Close Reading* booklet
- Student journal

Metacognitive Prompt: Making Inferences

Today we will continue to practice making inferences. However, we will make inferences from visuals, rather than information in the text. Focus on the illustrations as we read.

8 Analyze Visual Elements

Engage Thinking

Display the text and images for page 32. **Say:** *This part of the story focuses on what the boys are doing. When I look at the pictures, I can see how the boys are dressed and what they doing.* Have students look at the first picture. **Ask:** *What details do you see in the picture?*

Turn and Talk: *Based on the first image, what are the boys doing?*

Differentiated Instruction
Read and View Closely: Analyze Visual Elements

Display panel 5. **Say:** *I see in this picture that the boys look worried. I am making an inference, or a guess, based on the pictures. Then I read the text.* Read panel 5. *Now, I know more. The picture helps me to understand the setting and meaning of the text.* Repeat for panels 6 and 7. **Say:** *Looking for details in the pictures is important because it helps me understand more about the characters, setting, and events.* Use the Differentiated Instruction to practice analyzing visual elements in a way that best matches the levels of your students.

Think-Speak-Listen: Use the following sentence frame or the Think-Speak-Listen Flip Book to guide discussion: *The boys feel "like heroes" because _____ and _____.*

Build Language: Understand and Use Verb Tenses

Say: *Verbs have different tenses that tell when that action takes place. In the sentence "I listen," the verb listen is in the present. The action is happening now.* Read aloud the first sentence in panel 5. **Say:** *In this sentence, listened and watched are in the past* Point out the -ed ending. Read the second sentence in panel 6. Ask students to identify the verbs. **Say:** *The verbs was and were are in the past. They are irregular, so they do not end in -ed.* Create a chart to show verbs in the past and present.

Present	listens, listen	watch, watches	Is, are
Past	listened	watched	was, were

✓ Use Oral and Written Language: Write and Illustrate a Scene from the Story

Task: *The boys realize their families believe they have drowned. As they sit around the fire, they are silent. Write a sentence to explain what the boys are thinking.*

(S) *The boys think _____.*

(M) *The boys are thinking _____ and _____.*

(L) *While sitting around the fire, the boys _____.*

Wrap Up

Today we learned about looking closely at visuals. Why is it important to analyze the illustrations when we read a story?

Turn and Talk: *How do visuals help you understand a topic in social studies or science?*

👥 Differentiated Instruction
Read and View Closely: Analyze Visual Elements

Ⓢubstantial Support

Model: Read aloud panel 5 and point to the picture. **Say:** *In the story, I read that the boys listened and watched. What are they doing in the story? The picture shows them watching. And this one is putting his finger to his lips.* Gesture putting your finger to your lips and ask students to do the same. **Ask:** *What is he telling the others? To be quiet. That detail isn't in the words on the page. We learned that by analyzing the picture.* Point out that sometimes information is in the text but we may need the picture to help understand it. Point to the words *steam ferry-boat.* **Say:** *The text tells us there's a steam ferry-boat, but what is that exactly? We might not know what a ferry-boat is until we see it in the picture.*

Practice: Distribute BLM 1. Work with students to complete the activity in the Practice section.

Extend: Have students work with a partner to complete the Extend section of the BLM.

Challenge: If students are ready, help them analyze the image in panel 2. Ask guiding questions such as: *What do you see in the water? Why is there smoke? How do the boys feel?*

Ⓜoderate Support

Model: Display the images. **Ask:** *What are some reasons we look at the pictures in a story?* List student responses. Elicit that pictures help us to understand words we don't know, give us details not in the text, or just add interest. Read aloud panel 6. Ask students to describe the picture. Have a volunteer read the newspaper headline. **Say:** *When I read the text, I know the boys think their families are heart broken. The image of a newspaper headline helps me understand what they are thinking.* Point out that the visual on that page is an example of something that is not in the text. Ask students to look through the pictures to find an example of something that is described in the text, for example the boys watching, or the ferry-boat.

Practice: Distribute BLM 2. Prompt students to notice details in the pictures. **Ask:** *Which words in the story does the picture go with?*

Extend: Have students work in pairs to complete the Extend section of the BLM.

Challenge: If students are ready, work with them to analyze Tom's facial expression on page 15 of *Texts for Close Reading*.

Ⓛight Support

Practice: Working in pairs, have students reread the story on pages 14–15 of *Texts for Close Reading* and study the illustration. Ask them to analyze Tom's facial expression in the picture and tell the clues it provides to Tom's feelings.

Extend: Have student pairs select one image from pages 16–19 in *Texts for Close Reading*. Ask them to answer the following questions: *Which words in the story does the picture relate to? What details do you learn about the characters, setting, or events from the picture? How else does the picture add to your understanding of the story?*

Challenge: Ask students to answer the following question: *How do visuals help you to make inferences about a story?*

☑ Formative Assessment

Substantial Support	• Can students reference the illustrations to find answers? • Can students describe what the illustrations show?
Moderate Support	• Can students reference specific details in the illustrations? • Can students infer the meaning of those details?
Light Support	• Can students describe facial expressions of characters in the illustrations? • Can students draw inferences from illustrations?

Preview or Review Week 2 ELA Mini-Lessons

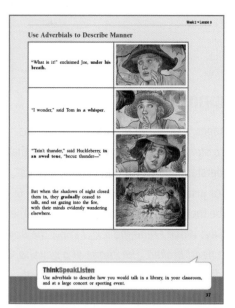

"Use Adverbials to Describe Manner," page 37

Student Objectives

LANGUAGE
Purpose:
• I can describe action in a journal entry.
Form:
• I can use adverbials.
CONTENT
• I can comprehend realistic fiction.

Additional Materials
• Unit Presentation
• Think-Speak-Listen Flip Book
• *Texts for Close Reading* booklet
• Student journal

Language Transfer Support

Note that speakers of Hmong, Chinese or Korean may need additional support in the use of adverbs and adverbial phrases. Adverbs are not used in Hmong; instead, two adjectives or two verbs may be used in place of an adverb. (Example: *I walk fast fast* for *I walk very fast.*) In Chinese and Korean, adverbs and adverbial phrases may precede verbs, while in English they typically follow verbs.

9 Use Adverbials to Describe Manner

Engage Thinking

Walk across the front of the room slowly. **Ask:** *What am I doing? I'm walking. How am I walking?* Write the sentence *I am walking slowly.* Underline the word *slowly*. Tell students that the word *slowly* describes the verb *walking*. It tells how you are walking. Explain that *slowly* is an adverb. Point out that many adverbs end in the letters -ly.

Read and View Closely: Recognize Adverbials

Display the image for panel 1. **Ask:** *Which character is in this visual? What is he doing?* **Say:** *We see in the picture he is whispering. He's talking quietly. Remember what kind of word quietly is? An adverb.* Read the page. Point out the phrase *under his breath* in the first sentence. **Say:** *The author chose another way to say quietly—under his breath.* Explain that sometimes a group of words is used to describe an action. Phrases and words describing verbs are called adverbials. **Say:** *The phrase "under his breath" describes the verb* exclaimed. *It tells how Joe exclaimed. Understanding adverbs and adverbials is important because they give us more details about the actions.*

👥 Differentiated Instruction
Build Language: Use Adverbials to Describe Manner

Look at the chart again. **Say**: *We talked about adverbials—words or phrases that tell us something about the verb in the sentence. One way that we can remember what an adverb or adverbial does is that it adds information to the verb. What information does the adverbial "in a whisper" add?* Invite student responses. Use the Differentiated Instruction to practice understanding and usage of adverbials in a way that matches the level of your students.

Think-Speak-Listen: Discuss how to use adverbials to describe how you would talk in different situations or use the Think-Speak-Listen Flip Book to guide discussion.

☑ Use Oral and Written Language: Describe Action in a Journal Entry

Task: *Describe what you did one day or evening this week. For each verb you used, describe how you did the action, using an adverbial. Examples:*

 I went to the park. I walked there very quickly. I played for a long time. I was tired. I saw my friend across the park. I yelled in a loud voice. She heard me and ran over quickly. We climbed carefully over the rocks.

 My friend and I went to the park. We ran there quickly. We shouted in excited voices. We climbed on the rocks carefully. We went home, tired, walking at a slow speed.

🔄 Wrap Up

Today we learned to use adverbials to describe how something is done. Why is it important to know how to read and write adverbials?

Turn and Talk: *What adverbials would you use to describe getting ready for school?*

ᨔᨔᨔ Differentiated Instruction
Build Language: Use Adverbials to Describe Manner

Ⓢ ubstantial Support

Model: Read aloud the second sentence. **Say:** *The sentence tells us what Tom said. What were his words?* Explain that the sentence also tells us how he said the words. **Say:** *Read the last three words and look at the picture. Did he speak loudly, or was he whispering? Words or phrases that tell us how someone does an action are called adverbials. They describe the verbs. Some adverbials are single words—adverbs, and some are phrases.* Read the first example and explain that the phrase *under his breath* also means quietly. Write these words and phrases: *in a loud voice / loudly / in a quiet voice / quietly.* Then write a sentence, for example *"No, I don't," said Ali.* Ask volunteers to repeat the sentence adding one of the adverbials and speaking in a quiet or loud voice.

Practice: Distribute BLM 1. Read the sentences aloud and work with students to help them identify the verbs and adverbials.

Extend: Have students work with a partner to complete the Extend section on the BLM.

Challenge: If students are ready, work with them to rewrite one of the sentences using a different adverbial. Discuss how the new adverbial affects the sentence's meaning.

Ⓜ oderate Support

Model: Display the chart. Read aloud the second sentence. *Say: When I see an adverbial, I know that it is going to describe the verb in the sentence. First, I ask myself, "What is the verb, or action? In this sentence, the verb is* said. Point to the bold phrase, **in a whisper**. *Say These words tell me more about the action, "in a whisper" describes how Tom spoke.* Discuss each of the pictures on the page, having volunteers read the text and identify the verb and the adverbial. Remind students that an adverbial can be a single word, an adverb like *gradually* in the last sentence, or it can be a phrase, a group of words as in *in a whisper* in the second sentence.

Practice: Distribute BLM 2. Guide students to identify the adverbials and verbs to complete the chart.

Extend: Have students work with a partner to complete the Extend section on the BLM.

Challenge: If students are ready, guide them to practice writing their own sentences about Huck, Tom, and Joe, using one adverbial in each sentence.

Ⓛ ight Support

Practice: Working in pairs, have students read paragraphs 6 through 9 on page 15 of *Texts for Close Reading*. Guide them to identify the adverbials that describe how the boys speak. **Ask:** *Which verb does each adverbial describe or modify? How do adverbials help you know how to read the words the characters say? How do adverbials make the story more interesting?*

Extend: Working in pairs, have students practice using adverbials. Ask them to write a dialogue between Tom, Huck, and Joe as they sit at the campfire. One student writes a sentence. The partner adds to the sentence with an adverbial or adverbial phrase. Have partners take turns doing each task.

Challenge: Have students compose a paragraph based on the images. Be sure that they include at least three adverbials or adverbial phrases.

☑ Formative Assessment

Substantial Support	• Do students understand what adverbials are? • Can students identify the verbs that adverbials describe?
Moderate Support	• Can students identify adverbials and the verbs they modify? • Can students write sentences using different adverbials to describe the action?
Light Support	• Can students identify adverbials and the verbs they modify? • Can students write and expand sentences that include adverbials?

"All Together Now!" page 38

Student Objectives

LANGUAGE

Purpose:
• I can make category word cards for a game.

Form:
• I can categorize words.

CONTENT
• I can understand words related to speech and visual arts.

Additional Materials

• Unit Presentation
• Think-Speak-Listen Flip Book
• *Texts for Close Reading* booklet
• Student journal
• Index cards

Language Transfer Support

A key word in this lesson—*mural*—has an exact cognate in a number of Roman languages, including Spanish, French, and Portuguese. In all these languages, the cognate is *mural*. The word is derived from the Latin word *muralis*.

You might mention that the Mexican artist Diego Rivera is a world-renowned muralist.

10 Read "All Together Now!"

Build Background and Vocabulary

Display the "All Together Now!" images and explain their importance in the story. If students have already read the story, ask them what they remember. **Ask:** *When have you worked in a group to create something?* Invite students to share their cultural experience and knowledge of working in a group.

Read Aloud the Text

Read panel 1. To support comprehension, ask *wh-* questions, such as *Where does this story happen? What does Caleb do?* Repeat with panel 2. Tell students to make note of new words. After reading, discuss how to use context clues to figure out meanings. Model using context clues for the word *sketching*: *When I read a word I don't know, I look for context clues, other words in the sentences or paragraph. I see "in his notebook." So that tells me sketching is something done on paper. I can also use visual clues. The pictures show drawings, so sketching might mean drawing.* Remind students they can look up words to find their exact meaning.

Refer to the Essential Question. **Say:** *What qualities does Caleb show in this story?* Invite students to respond. **Say:** *This story is realistic fiction. It tells us how art is made.*

Think-Speak-Listen: Use the following sentence frame or the Think-Speak-Listen Flip Book to guide discussion: *The character _____ is most like Tom Sawyer because _____.*

👥👥 Differentiated Instruction
Build Language: Categorize Words

Read the first paragraph. **Say:** *We talked about using context clues to figure out word meanings. When we learn new words, a good way to understand and remember them is to categorize—put them into groups, or categories.* Use the Differentiated Instruction to practice categorizing words in a way that best matches the levels of your students.

☑ Use Oral and Written Language: Make Category Word Cards for a Game

Task: *Work in a group to make word cards for a card game. Pick a topic such as sports. Brainstorm a list of activities. Write each word on an index card. Then sort them into groups. Label the categories, for example indoor activities, outdoor activities. Turn the cards over and make a color circle on each card. Use a different color for each category. Use the cards to play card games, for example Go fish!*

🔄 Wrap Up

Today we talked about categorizing words. Why is it important to know how to put words into groups, or categories?

Turn and Talk: *Work with a partner. Each of you chooses a category of words. Take turns naming words in your category for your partner. See how many words you can name in 15 seconds. Then switch categories and try again.*

♟♟♟ Differentiated Instruction
Build Language: Categorize Words

Ⓢubstantial Support

Model: Read the first paragraph. **Say:** *Let's list some words from our story. We are going to use a chart to sort them.* Explain the process of sorting. **Say:** *First, we list some of our words.* Write *swimming, skiing, fishing, ice skating.* Ask a volunteer to read the words. *Then, we put them in groups. We look for things that are the same.* Circle *swimming, fishing,* and underline *skiing, ice skating.* **Say:** *I just made two groups of summer activities. Those are our categories.* Point out that there may be other ways to group.

Practice: Distribute BLM 1. Reread paragraphs 2 and 3. Then point to the following words where they occur in the text: *mural, sketch, photo, painting, printout* and read the sentences again. Ask students to write the five words in the top of the chart and take turns reading them aloud. Ask students to tell you what they know about each word. Guide them to group all the ones you can make with a brush or pencil, and those for which you need technology Have them write the groups. Then ask for ideas for the labels.

Extend: Have partners complete the Extend section, working together to tell what they know about each word.

Challenge: If students are ready have them write sentences using some of the words they sorted.

Ⓜoderate Support

Model: Point out the words mural, sketch, and photo. Discuss the meaning of each word. **Ask:** *When I think about these words, I first think about what they all have in common. They are all words that name types of pictures. We can categorize these words and understand their differences in meaning.* Read the three paragraphs on the page. As you read, list these verbs from each paragraph: *discussed, talked, glanced, shouted, called, looked, said.* Tell students you are going to work together to list some verbs using a Word Sort.

Practice: Distribute BLM 2. Have students list the five words in the chart. **Ask:** *Which words do you think go together?* Invite student responses. Offer information about the meaning of the words if needed. Have students sort the words and list them, suggesting ways to sort. Then ask students to label each group based on the differences between them.

Extend: Have students work in pairs to complete the Extend section of the BLM.

Challenge: Have students find verbs about communicating from p. 20 of *Texts for Close Reading* and sort the words.

Ⓛight Support

Practice: Have student pairs read p. 20 of *Texts for Close Reading* and list the words that name types of pictures: *mural, sketch, photo, painting, printout.* Explain the sorting process. Have students sort the words into two groups based on a common feature and label the two groups. Ask them to explain their choices.

Extend: Ask students to find verbs from the text that have to do with communicating or interacting with others (for example, pointing, glancing, speaking). Have them make a new word sort chart to sort the words.

Challenge: Have students in pairs think of two categories and make two lists of words. Then have them rewrite the list without grouping the words and give it to their partner to sort. Ask if they decided on the same categories.

☑ Formative Assessment

Substantial Support	• Can students sort words into groups based on an identified difference?
Moderate Support	• Can students identify a similarity and a difference between two words?
Light Support	• Can students identify a difference between words and sort them into groups based on this difference? • Can students generate sentences using these words?

Preview or Review Week 3 ELA Mini-Lessons

"Use Prepositional Phrases," page 39

Student Objectives

LANGUAGE

Purpose:
- I can describe places and locations on a map.

Form:
- I can use prepositional phrases.

CONTENT
- I can comprehend realistic fiction.

Additional Materials
- Unit Presentation
- Think-Speak-Listen Flip Book
- *Texts for Close Reading* booklet
- Student journal

Language Transfer Support

Note that students whose first language is Spanish may need support in differentiating between the prepositions *on* and *in*. These prepositions are not differentiated in the Spanish language; the Spanish word *en* is used for both. Point out items that are *on* your desk and other items that are *in* your desk. Explain that when referring to location, *in* means "within" or "inside."

11 Use Prepositional Phrases

Engage Thinking

Display the text and images. **Ask:** *What do you think the arrows might mean?* Invite students to offer their ideas. **Ask:** *How might the arrows help us understand the story?*

Turn and Talk: *What words can you use to tell how to get from one place to another?*

Read and View Closely: Recognize Prepositional Phrases

Read aloud the first sentence. **Say:** *We get a lot of information from sentences. We talked before about what characters do and how they do the actions—they are moving quickly.* Point to the picture and the arrows, and words in bold. **Say:** *"to the shore" is a prepositional phrase. and so is "toward the town." The phrases tell us where and in what direction the boys hurried.* Continue reading the other examples in the chart.

👥👥👥 Differentiated Instruction
Build Language: Use Prepositional Phrases

Display panel 1. **Say:** *We looked at some prepositional phrases on the page. Prepositional phrases all start with prepositions.* Name a few prepositions: *up, down, in* and ask students if they can think of any others. Remind students that it's important to recognize and use many different prepositions so that we can understand specific information when we read about where characters are, the direction things are moving, or when things happen. Use the Differentiated Instruction to practice using prepositional phrases in a way that best matches the level of your students.

Think-Speak-Listen: Use the following sentence frame or the Think-Speak-Listen Flip Book to guide discussion: *First, I go _____ from _____. Then I go _____ to _____. Next, I go _____ at _____.*

☑️ Use Oral and Written Language: Describe Places and Directions on a Map

Task: *In a peer group, use your imaginations to draw a simple map of Jackson Island and the surrounding area where the story of Tom, Huck, and Joe takes place. Label the island, river, campsite, and village. Then use the map to describe directions with prepositional phrases.*

(S) *The island is _____ from the village. The river flows _____ the island. (across / around)*

(M) *The island is _____ the village, and the campsite is _____ the island, _____ the village. (across from / around / past)*

(L) *The island is _____, and the campsite is _____. (across from the village / around the island, past the village)*

🔄 Wrap Up

Today we learned about prepositions and prepositional phrases. Why is it important to be able to understand and use prepositional phrases when you read and write?

Turn and Talk: *Describe how you get home, using prepositional phrases.*

👤👤👤 Differentiated Instruction
Build Language: Use Prepositional Phrases

Ⓢubstantial Support

Model: Read the first sentence of the chart. Remind students that this sentence has a lot of information. **Ask:** *What did the boys do? They sprang to their feet and hurried. That means they jumped up quickly. Now let's look at the other part of the sentence—it tells us more about where they went.* Read the words to and toward and ask students to repeat them. Discuss that *to* and *toward* are both prepositions that tell direction. *To the shore* is a prepositional phrase. It tells where the boys went. *Toward the town* is another one. It tells us the direction they went.

Practice: Distribute BLM 1. Work with students to find the prepositions and phrases.

Extend: Have students work with a partner to complete the Extend section on the BLM.

Challenge: If students are ready, work with them to write new sentences with two of the prepositions.

Ⓜoderate Support

Model: Display the chart on and read the first sentence. **Ask:** *What different kinds of information does this sentence tell us?* Elicit that it tells what the boys did, how they did it, and also where. **Say:** *This sentence has two prepositions–to and toward. The prepositional phrase* to the shore *tells me where they are going. The phrase* toward the town *tells me the direction.* Ask volunteers to read each of the sentences on the page. Discuss each preposition and prepositional phrase, explaining their meanings if necessary.

Practice: Distribute BLM 2. Work with students to identify the prepositions and prepositional phrases.

Extend: Have students work with a partner to use one of the prepositional phrases from the Practice section in an original sentence..

Challenge: Have pairs look at the picture on p. 19 in *Texts for Close Reading*. Ask them to write two sentences about the picture, including prepositional phrases. Remind them to look at surroundings, and the location of objects.

Ⓛight Support

Use the tet on pp. 12-19 in the *Texts for Close Reading* booklet for the following activities.

Practice: Organize students into pairs, and assign one of the following paragraphs to each pair: 2, 6, 12. Have each pair identify the prepositional phrases in their assigned paragraph. Ask them identify which prepositional phrases describe place or direction. **Ask:** *What do prepositional phrases help to describe? Can you think of some other prepositions that are used to describe location or direction?*

Extend: Have students work with a partner to choose one picture from the text. Ask them to write two sentences to describe the direction or location of an object in the picture.

Challenge: Have student pairs exchange the sentences they wrote with another pair. Challenge them to add additional prepositional phrases to the sentences to expand upon the description of the picture.

☑ Formative Assessment

Substantial Support	• Can students recognize prepositional phrases? • Can students choose appropriate prepositions to write in a paragraph?
Moderate Support	• Can students identify the preposition and object in a prepositional phrase? • Can students describe the information given by a prepositional phrase?
Light Support	• Can students identify prepositional phrases and prepositions in sentences? • Can students compose sentences with prepositional phrases that describe the direction or location of an object in a picture?

Preview or Review Week 3 ELA Mini-Lessons

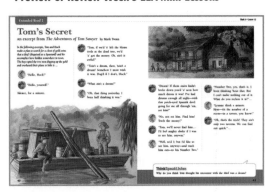

"Tom's Secret," pages 40–41

Student Objectives

LANGUAGE
Purpose:
• I can write a dialogue with interjections.
Form:
• I can form interjections.
CONTENT
• I can comprehend realistic fiction.

Additional Materials
• Unit Presentation
• Interjections Chart
• Think-Speak-Listen Flip Book
• *Texts for Close Reading* booklet
• Student journal

Metacognitive Prompt

Today we will practice hearing what we read in our minds. We want to hear how characters are speaking their words because that will help us to understand what they are saying.

12 Read "Tom's Secret"

Build Background and Vocabulary

Display the image of Tom and Huck. If the students have already read the text, ask them what they remember. Invite them to describe the picture. **Ask:** *What do you think the boys are doing? What do their expressions tell you?*

Read Aloud the Text

Read aloud the first page. Explain slang terms such as ain't, 'tain't, and dog'd. To support comprehension, ask *wh-* questions, such as *Who is speaking? What are they talking about?* Repeat with the next page. After reading, *ask: What do Tom and Huck plan to do next?* Model thinking through the answer: *I think the boys are going to try to find the thief at a tavern. They think that the number two is a room number.* Then refer to the Essential Question. *Ask: What qualities of character do Tom and Huck show in this story?*

Think-Speak-Listen: Use the following sentence frame or the Think-Speak-Listen Flip Book to guide discussion: *I think that Tom thought his encounter with the thief was a dream because _____.*

Differentiated Instruction
Build Language: Use Interjections

Have two volunteers read the dialogue. Then point to the word *Oh* in the last line. Ask students to recall what they learned about interjections (see Lesson 6). Remind them that interjections can emphasize a word, help the speaker pause, or show an emotion. **Say:** *It's important to know how to read and write interjections so that we can understand and show characters' emotions, and write the way we speak.* Use the Differentiated Instruction to practice using interjections in a way that matches the level of your students.

☑ Use Oral and Written Language: Write a Dialogue with Interjections

Task: *Work with a partner to write a dialogue between two characters deciding what to play. Use interjections. Present your dialogue to the class. Use the example as a model.* (S = first two lines M= first four lines L= all six lines)

(S)(M)(L) *Character 1: _____ Let's play a game.*

(S)(M)(L) *Character 2: _____, let's play. _____, what should we play?*

(M)(L) *Character 1: _____, I don't know. How about cards?*

(M)(L) *Character 2: _____, ok. _____, which game?*

(L) *Character 1: _____, I know! I just learned how to play _____.*

(L) *Character 2: _____, ok, I like that game!*

⟳ Wrap Up

Today we learned about interjections in dialogue. Why is it important to know how to read and write interjections?

Turn and Talk: *Tell your classmate about a movie or game you liked. Use interjections.*

👤👤👤 Differentiated Instruction
Build Language: Use Interjections

Ⓢubstantial Support

Model: Reread page 40. Then point to the word *oh* in the last line and reread that sentence. Explain that the word *oh* doesn't add meaning. It's an interjection, an extra word we put in. Ask if anyone remembers some of the interjections they have learned and practiced like: *hey, wow, oops*, and some that are not as common today that they saw in their book: *say, shucks.* Display the Interjections Chart and find some of those interjections they know. **Say:** *Tom and Huck use interjections when they speak. The interjection Hello tells me that the characters are greeting each other. Now let's listen for more interjections.* Read the last four paragraphs. Ask students to raise their hands when they hear the words oh, well, or here. Discuss why we use those interjections.

Practice: Distribute BLM 1. Help students find the interjections. Point out that sometimes a comma is included after an interjection.

Extend: Have students work with a partner to complete the Extend section on their BLM. **Ask:** *How do you decide which interjection from the box fits best in each sentence?*

Challenge: If students are ready, work with them to write new sentences using interjections.

Ⓛight Support

Use the text on pp. 22-29 in the *Texts for Close Reading* booklet for the following activities.

Practice: Ask pairs to generate a list of the interjections Tom and Huck use in their dialogue in paragraphs 20-25. **Ask:** *Which interjections show an emotion? What emotion do they show? How do the interjections help you understand the characters and the words they say?* Then ask pairs to use each interjection in their own original sentence.

Extend: Working in pairs, have students write a brief dialogue between Tom and Huck about how they what they would do if they could keep the treasure. Have students include the interjections they listed in the Practice section.

Challenge: Ask students to look at the Interjections Chart and make up sentences with some of the interjections they find there.

Ⓜoderate Support

Model: Reread the text. Point out the word *Oh* and ask anyone if they remember what a word like that is called. Remind students of some of the interjections they have learned and practiced in earlier lessons: *hey, wow, oops,* and some that are not as common today that they saw in their book: *say, shucks.* Display the Interjections Chart and find some of those interjections. Ask volunteers to read some of the interjections on the chart and the descriptions of when we use them. Then ask them to look again at page 41 and see if they can find the words *Here, oh,* and *well.* Have volunteers read the sentences with those interjections.

Practice: Distribute BLM 2. Help students complete the Practice activities. Ask them to explain how using interjections helps make dialogue sound better.

Extend: Have students work with a partner to complete the Extend section on their BLMs. Ask them to read their sentences out loud to one another and then to the class.

Challenge: If students are ready, have them identify interjections on p. 26 in the *Texts for Close Reading*. Then work with them to use this interjection in an original sentence.

☑ Formative Assessment

Substantial Support	• Can students recognize interjections in sentences? • Are students able to choose interjections to add to simple sentences?
Moderate Support	• Are students able to recognize interjections in more complex sentences? • Can students apply their knowledge about interjections to write sentences?
Light Support	• Can students identify interjections in longer texts? • Can students generate sentences using interjections?

Preview or Review Week 3 ELA Mini-Lessons

"Tom's Secret," page 42

Student Objectives

LANGUAGE
Purpose:
• I can write instructions using imperatives.
Form:
• I can understand imperatives.
CONTENT
• I can use context clues to understand realistic fiction.

Additional Materials
• Unit Presentation
• Think-Speak-Listen Flip Book
• *Texts for Close Reading* booklet
• Student journal

Metacognitive Prompt

Today we will practice using clue words in the text to help us guess the meanings of words we do not know.

13 Use Context Clues

Engage Thinking

Display the panels. If the students have already read the story, ask them what they remember. Invite them to describe the picture of Tom and Huck. **Ask:** *What do you think is happening? Are the boys in a town or are they in the country?*

Turn and Talk: *What clues tell you whether the boys are in the country or in town?*

👥 Differentiated Instruction
Read and View Closely: Use Context Clues

Read aloud the first sentence in the second column. **Say:** *Sometimes you will not understand every word in a text. Here's a word I don't know—nip. One way to figure out new words is to use context clues. We look at the context, the words or sentences around the word we don't know.* **Say:** *Tom is telling Huck to get keys, and then he's saying that he'll "nip" auntie's keys. So the word nip must mean "to take."* Explain using context clues are important because they help us to understand words while we are reading. Use the Differentiated Instruction to practice using context clues in a way that matches the level of your students.

Think-Speak-Listen: Use the following sentence frame or the Think-Speak-Listen Flip Book to guide discussion: *Tom's behavior is _____. His behavior tells me that he _____.*

Build Language: Use Imperatives

Say: *In the dialogue, Tom uses imperatives. An imperative is a sentence that is a command. In the sentence "Find him!," Tom is giving Huck a command. An imperative sentence does not have a subject. The subject is you. So Tom is saying to Huck, "(You) find him!"* Have students find another example of an imperative in the same paragraph *(Track the money!).* Then ask volunteers to use imperatives to give a simple direction to another student, for example *Put the book on the table. Take the book off the table.*

☑ Use Oral and Written Language: Write Instructions Using Imperatives

Task: *With a partner, choose something you both know how to do. Write a list of instructions on how to accomplish it. Write your instructions as imperatives.*

Example: How to Do a Cartwheel

 Spread your feet. Raise your arms. Look to the left. Point your foot.

Ⓜ *Spread your feet a little wide. Raise your arms over your head. Point your left food.*

Ⓛ *Spread your feet a little wider than your hips. Raise your arms over your head. Point your lead foot in the direction of the cartwheel.*

🔄 Wrap Up

Today we learned how to use context clues. How does using context clues help you understand a story?

Turn and Talk: *Describe how context clues can help you read a social studies text.*

👥👥 Differentiated Instruction
Read and View Closely: Use Context Clues

Ⓢubstantial Support

Model: Read aloud paragraph 2 and model identifying the word *reckon* as an unfamiliar word. **Say:** *When Tom says, "I reckon that's the very No. 2 we're after," I'm unsure what reckon means. Let's use a chart to help use identify the clues that we can use to understand this word.* Repeat with *nip* in paragraph 4.

Practice: Distribute BLM 1. Help students complete the activity. Have students refer back to the text to identify the context sentences, information they know, and possible meanings for the other words. Help them to reword the sentence to see if their meaning makes sense.

Extend: Ask students to tell their partners what they think each word means. Then have the pairs work together to make up two new sentences with two of the words.

Challenge: If students seem ready, help them use context clues to find the meaning of another difficult word in the text.

Ⓜoderate Support

Model: Have a volunteer read the first paragraph in the second panel. Ask students what words were unfamiliar. **Ask:** *What are some things we can do when we see an unfamiliar word?* Discuss that before you look up the word or ask someone else the meaning, you can use context clues to try to figure out the meaning. **Say:** *The context is the paragraph or sentence the word is in or near. Sometimes you might find a context clue in the same sentence. Sometimes it might be in that paragraph or in a different paragraph.*

Practice: Distribute BLM 2. Help students complete the chart.

Extend: Have students work with a partner to use each word from they learned in the Practice section in a new sentence.

Challenge: If students are ready, have them read paragraph 6 on p. 23 in *Texts for Close Reading*. Then guide them to use context clues to figure out the meaning of the words *misfortune* and *wakefulness*.

Ⓛight Support

Use the text on pp. 22-29 in the *Texts for Close Reading* booklet for the following activities.

Practice: Have students read paragraphs 29-33. Ask students to identify two to three unfamiliar words and the context clues that help them understand the word and to write what they think the word means.

Extend: Have students work with a partner to list other unfamiliar words and to find their meaning. Then have them work together to write original sentences using the new words.

Challenge: For students who seem comfortable using context clues, have them work with students who need help identifying the context. Ask them to write instructions for a step by step reference chart on how to use context clues, for example *1. I write the word. 2. I read the sentence and the paragraph.*, etc.

☑️ **Formative Assessment**	
Substantial Support	• Do students recognize context clues? • Are students able to use context clues to identify a word's meaning?
Moderate Support	• Can students infer word meanings from context clues? • Are students able to demonstrate their understanding of unfamiliar words by using them in complete sentences?
Light Support	• Can students find and use context clues in a longer text? • Can students write original sentences using context clues?

Preview or Review Week 3 ELA Mini-Lessons

"Understand Verb Tenses and Contractions," page 43

Student Objectives

LANGUAGE

Purpose:
• I can write a letter using contractions.

Form:
• I can understand verb tenses and contractions.

CONTENT
• I can understand personal expression in realistic fiction.

Additional Materials
• Unit Presentation
• Think-Speak-Listen Flip Book
• *Texts for Close Reading* booklet
• Student journal

Language Transfer Support

Some languages, such as Chinese and Hmong, do not have verb tenses as English does. Provide students with extra practice in using verbs in the past and future tenses.

14 Understand Verb Tenses and Contractions

Engage Thinking

Display the panels. Invite students to describe each picture. **Ask:** *In each picture, what are the characters doing? (speaking).* **Say:** *When we read dialogue we are reading how characters speak. A good writer writes dialogue the way people really talk. Sometimes when we speak, we shorten our words with contractions.*

Turn and Talk: *What picture clues tell you that the characters are speaking to each other?*

Read and View Closely: Identify Contractions

Read this sentence: *That's what I've found out, Huck.* **Say:** *The author did not write "That is what I have found" because that's not the way people talk. When we talk and when we write dialogue, we use contractions.* Ask students to look at the chart. Have volunteers read aloud each contraction. **Ask:** *What two words formed each contraction? What letters were replaced by the apostrophe?* Then read the sentence. Point out that some contractions are formed from pronouns and verbs. However, three are formed from a verb and the word not: hadn't, don't, and won't. The pronunciation of do changes when it is contracted with not, and *will not* changes to won't.

👥 Differentiated Instruction
Build Language: Understand Verb Tenses and Contractions

Say: *We identified the contractions in the chart. Each contraction is made up of a verb and another word. Understanding the verb in the contraction will help us recognize the verb's tense, or the time of the action. Let's look more closely at the examples in the chart to help use better understand verb tenses and contractions* Use the Differentiated Instruction to practice understanding of verb tenses and contractions in a way that matches the level of your students.

Think-Speak-Listen: Use the following sentence frame or the Think-Speak-Listen Flip Book to guide discussion: *Last week, I _____. Next week, I'll _____.*

☑ Use Oral and Written Language: Write a letter Using Contractions

Task: *Work together to make a weekend plan. Use present and future contractions.*

ⓢ   *I'll go to the park tomorrow, but I won't play soccer. I don't want to run.*

Ⓜ   *I'll go to the park with my friend. She'll play soccer, but I won't play because my leg hurts. I don't want to play on a bad leg.*

Ⓛ   *We'll go to the park tomorrow, but some of us won't play. My leg hurts, so it's better if I don't play. Cara wants to play so she'll be on the team.*

🔄 Wrap Up

Today we learned that verb tenses work with contractions. How does understanding verb tenses and contractions help us understand a story?

Turn and Talk: *Using contractions, describe your favorite and least favorite chores.*

👥 Differentiated Instruction
Build Language: Understand Verb Tenses and Contractions

ⓈUbstantial Support

Model: First focus on the contractions with present tense verbs in the chart. Read aloud the fourth contraction: that + is = *that's*. **Say:** *The contraction that's means "that is." Ask students which of those words is the verb.* Point out that the verb "*is*" is in the present tense. Read aloud the example from the text. Then discuss the next present tense contraction, *you're* in the same way. Compare the two contractions, *don't* and *won't* in the last example. Point out that *won't* in the last example is in the future. Read the example sentence. Then give another example: *Don't bring your books home. You won't have to read them tonight.*

Practice: Distribute BLM 1. Work with students to complete the chart.

Extend: Have students work with a partner to complete the sentences on the BLM.

Challenge: If students are ready, have them create new sentences based on the ones on the BLM.

Ⓜoderate Support

Model: Ask volunteers to take turns reading the contractions in the chart. Then go back over each one, focusing on whether they are in the past, present, or future. Read aloud the first contraction: had + not = *hadn't*. **Say:** *The contraction hadn't means "had not." The verb had is the past tense. Huck is saying the stairs broke in the past. Understanding the tense helps me understand what has already happened in the story.* For each of the examples, ask students to help you identify the tense.

Practice: Distribute BLM 2. Work with students to complete the chart.

Extend: Have students work with a partner to write two sentences about "Tom's Secret." Have volunteers share their sentences with the group, and ask the rest of the group to identify the contraction.

Challenge: If students are ready, have them use the contraction *I'd* in a sentence about "Tom's Secret."

Ⓛight Support

Practice: Discuss with students contractions with present tense verbs (*I've, that's, you're, don't*), past tense verbs (*hadn't*), and future tense verbs (*won't*). Then discuss the conditional verb would in the contraction *I'd*. Have student pairs read paragraphs 17–20 on pages 25–26 of *Texts for Close Reading*. Ask students to look through the text with a partner and find examples of contractions that are in the present, past, future, or conditional tense.

Extend: Have partners compose sentences that tell about Tom's plan to find the money. Ask them to use contractions with verbs in the past, present, and future as well as the conditional in their sentences.

Challenge: Ask students to include sentences with other pronouns contracted with *have, is,* and *are,* such as *you've, he's,* and *they're.*

☑ Formative Assessment

Substantial Support	• Can students use identify the words that make up a contraction? • Are students able to recognize present tense contractions?
Moderate Support	• Can students explain what a contraction stands for? • Can students generate sentences with contractions in the past and present?
Light Support	• Can students generate original sentences with contractions in the three simple tenses and the conditional?

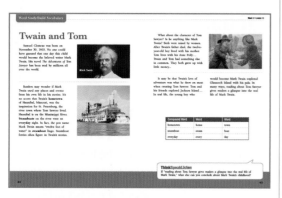

"Twain and Tom," pages 44–45

Student Objectives

LANGUAGE
Purpose:
• I can make compound word game cards.
Form:
• I can form compound words.
CONTENT
• I can comprehend a biography.

Additional Materials

• Unit Presentation
• Compound Words Chart
• Think-Speak-Listen Flip Book
• *Texts for Close Reading* booklet
• Student journal
• Index cards

Language Transfer Support

Point out how compound words work in students' first languages. Spanish compounds include *paraguas* (umbrella–"stops waters"), *rascacielos* (skyscraper), *tragalibros* (bookworm–"swallows books"), and *lavamanos* (bathroom sink–"washes hands").

15 Read "Twain and Tom"

Build Background and Vocabulary

Say: *The book "Tom Sawyer" was written by Mark Twain. He used his experiences growing up in Missouri when he wrote the book.* **Ask:** *What do you think the image of the boat might suggest about Twain's life?* Invite students to share their cultural experience and knowledge of Mark Twain and Tom Sawyer.

Read Aloud the Text

Read panel 1. To support comprehension, discuss unfamiliar vocabulary. Ask *wh-* questions, such as *Who was Mark Twain? Why is he a well-known person?* Repeat with panels 2 and 3. After reading, **ask:** *How did growing up along the Mississippi River affect Mark Twain?* Model thinking though the answer: *He used what he knew to write his books. The text says the place he grew up was the setting for Tom Sawyer, and the adventures Tom had may have been based on Twain's life.* Then refer to the Essential Question. **Ask:** *What qualities did Mark Twain and Tom Sawyer share?* **Say:** *This text describes someone's life. This type of nonfiction is called a biography.*

Think-Speak-Listen: Use the following sentence frame or the Think-Speak-Listen Flip Book to guide discussion: *I can conclude _____ about Mark Twain's childhood.*

👥 Differentiated Instruction
Build Language: Use Compound Words

Read paragraph 2. Write: *hometown, steamboat, everyday.* Ask volunteers to read aloud the words. Then ask students what familiar words they see. **Say:** *Words that are made of two smaller words are called compound words. The meaning is often based on the meanings of the two smaller words.* Ask students to tell you the two words they see in each of the compound words. Use the Differentiated Instruction to practice using compound words in a way that matches the level of your students.

✓ Use Oral and Written Language: Make Compound Word Game Cards

Task: *Work in a group. Choose eight compound words from the Compound Words Chart. Write each word on an index card in large letters. Draw a line between the two parts of each word. Then cut the cards on the lines. Mix the cards and lay them face down. Each player picks two cards to try to make a compound word. If you make a word, say the word, its parts, and its meaning.*

🔄 Wrap Up

Today we learned that compound words are words that are made by joining two words together. How can compound words help in adding details to a story?

Turn and Talk: *List compound words about things found at your school.*

Differentiated Instruction
Build Language: Use Compound Words

Substantial Support

Model: Reread panel 2 and point out the word steamboat in the last line. **Say:** *The word steamboat is a compound word. It's made from the words steam and boat.* Display the Compound Words Chart. Ask volunteers to help you read a few of the words. Have students raise their hands if they recognize a word they hear.

Practice: Distribute BLM 1. Help students complete the chart for each of the compound words.

Extend: Have students work with partners to complete the Expand section of the BLM.

Challenge: If students are ready, work with them to complete a chart for more compound words and then use each word in a sentence that demonstrates its meaning.

Moderate Support

Model: Have volunteers read the panels. Then reread the last sentence in panel 2 and guide students to identify the compound word, *steamboat*. Ask them what words they see within that word. Then ask them to find the words *everyday* and *hometown* in that same paragraph. Ask students to tell you what the two words are that make up each of the compound words. Display the Compound Words Chart. Have volunteers take turns reading the words.

Practice: Distribute BLM 2. Work with students to complete the chart for *steamboat* and use the word in a sentence.

Extend: Working with a partner, have students complete the chart for the words *hometown* and *everyday*. Then have pairs use each word in a sentence.

Challenge: If students are ready, have them identify two additional compound words in paragraph 2 on p. 30 of *Texts for Close Reading*. Guide them to complete a chart for each and use them in sentences.

Light Support

Use the text on p. 30 in the *Texts for Close Reading* booklet for the following activities.

Practice: Help students read paragraph 2 and identify five compound words *(hometown, steamboat, everyday, boyhood, whitewashed)*. Ask them to make a chart to show the five compound words, the two words in each, and their meaning. Have them complete the chart and then use each word in a sentence.

Extend: Have student work with a partner to write a brief summary using at least three compound words.

Challenge: Explain that some compounds are written as two words. They are called open compounds. Ask students to find the open compound in the text that means "a name used by a writer." (pen name)

✓ Formative Assessment

Substantial Support	• Can students complete a graphic organizer to analyze a compound word with the teacher's help?
Moderate Support	• Can students recognize the two small words that make a compound word? • Can students complete a graphic organizer to analyze compound words and use them in a sentence?
Light Support	• Can students identify compound words in a longer text? • Can students analyze those compound words and use them in sentences?

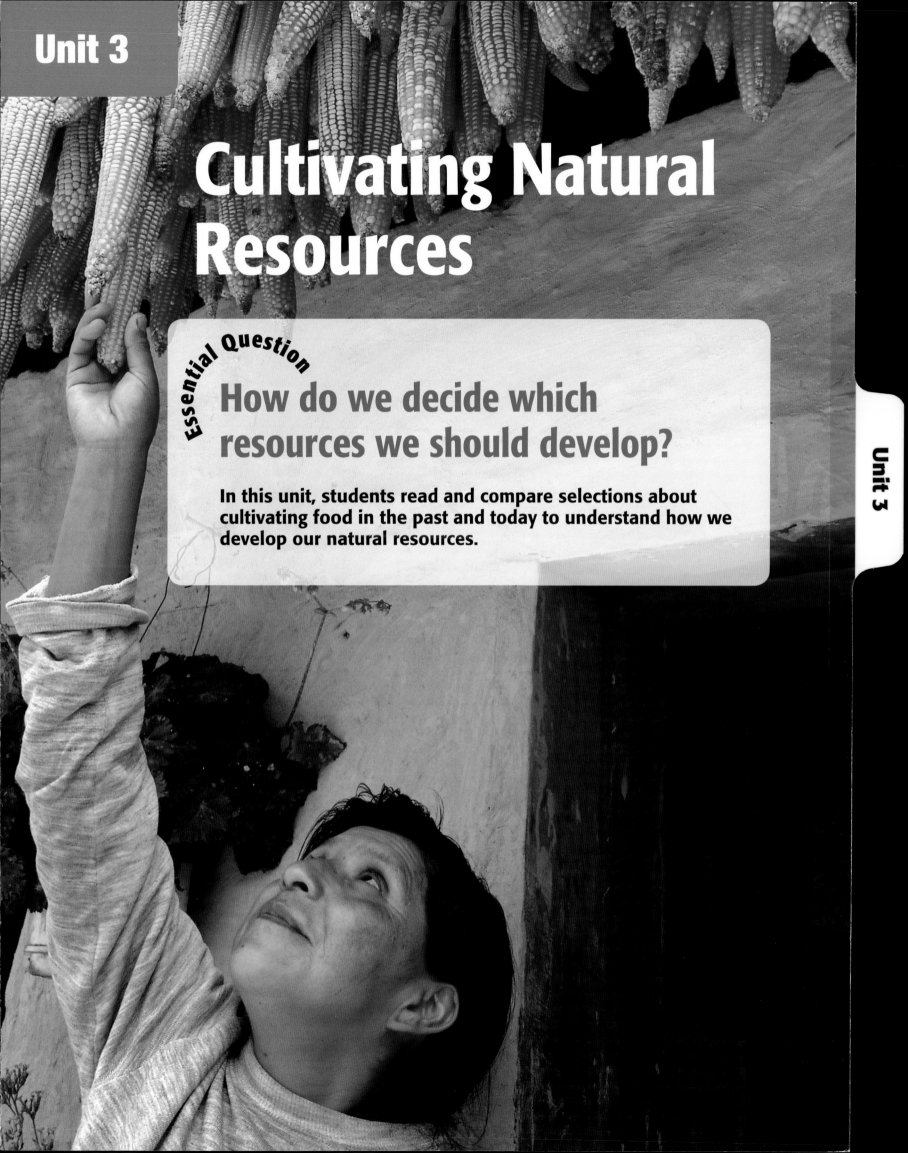

Cultivating Natural Resources

Essential Question

How do we decide which resources we should develop?

In this unit, students read and compare selections about cultivating food in the past and today to understand how we develop our natural resources.

Unit 3 Lessons at a Glance

Language Skills

Week 1
- Use Shifts in Verb Tense to Explain
- Express Cause and Effect
- Informative Writing to Sources
- Use Infinitives as Adverbials
- Analyze Words in Context

Week 2
- Recognize Prepositional Phrases
- Use Prepositional Phrases to Indicate Location
- Understand Temporal Language
- Connect Two Ideas in a Sentence
- Use Multiple-Meaning Words

Week 3
- Understand Shifts in Verb Tense
- Understand Subject-Verb Agreement
- Use the Past and Present Verb Tenses
- Identify Words Related to Art
- Use Adverbs to Describe Verbs and Adjectives

Lessons

Preview or Review Week 1 ELA Mini-Lessons

"Essential Question," pages 46–47

Student Objectives

LANGUAGE

Purpose:
• I can understand the Essential Question.

CONTENT
• I can understand the topic of the unit.

Additional Materials
• Unit Presentation

Introduce Unit 3: Cultivating Natural Resources

Use the short lesson below to introduce the topic of the unit and help students understand the Essential Question.

Build Background and Vocabulary

Draw students' attention to the Essential Question spread on the Unit Presentation.

Say: *The topic of this unit is "Cultivating Natural Resources." These pictures and questions introduce the ideas that we will read about.* **Cultivate** *means to grow crops, or to prepare and use the land for growing.*

Create a 2-column chart. Ask volunteers to read aloud the questions on the spread as you label the chart. Encourage a discussion and fill in the chart as below.

Ask: *How do these pictures help you understand cultivating natural resources?*

Help students answer and encourage students to share their cultural knowledge and experiences about the topic.

Cultivate	Not Cultivate
plants	forest
animals	oil, coal
	wild animals

👥 Differentiated Instruction
Explain the Essential Question

Read aloud the Essential Question: *How do we decide which resources we should develop?* Review key words by definition and examples: **consider, natural resources, cultivate, environment.** Review the 2-column chart. Encourage students to give examples, for instance of how we use the natural resources on the chart.

Use the Differentiated Instruction to help students at all levels understand the Essential Question. Display or invite students to access the unit opener video for Unit 3. After the video **ask:** *How do these pictures and the video help you answer the Essential Question?*

Then proceed to Lesson 1.

ᴬᴬᴬ Differentiated Instruction
Explain the Essential Question

Ⓢubstantial Support

Write: *We consider food choices everyday.* Have students repeat. Point to the first illustration. Explain that we cultivate some of the food we eat. Discuss the meaning of **consider**, to think about or care about. Point to the second illustration. Discuss that some resources, like oil are limited. Point to the third illustration. Explain that trees are a natural resource that need to be protected by planting new trees.

Write the words **cultivate** and **consider**. Review the meanings by saying them in sentences: *We cultivate crops.* Say the sentence with students. *We consider the feelings our friends and family.* Say the sentence with students.

Say: *In this unit, we will learn how we cultivate a plant for food.*

Ⓜoderate Support

Say: *We value our environment.*

Point to the picture of the men working the oil derrick.

Say: *The men are digging for oil.*

Ask: *Can we cultivate oil? Why or why not?*

Write: *We cultivate plants/oil/trucks for food.* Elicit the correct answer.

Write: *We consider/cultivate/use the feelings of our friends and family.* Elicit the correct answer.

Say: *Why must we consider the environment? In this unit we will learn how we cultivate a plant for food.*

Ⓛight Support

Say: *We value our environment.*

Point to the picture of the men working the oil derrick.

Say: *The men are digging for oil. Can we cultivate oil? Why or why not?*

Point to the first photo.

Ask: *Why do we cultivate plants?*

Write the words **consider** and **cultivate.** Ask students to use the words in new sentences. Prompt if necessary by asking questions. *What crops can we cultivate? Do you consider the feelings of your friends?*

Say: *Why must we consider the environment? What other kinds of things do we consider everyday? In this unit we will learn how we cultivate a plant for food.*

☑ Formative Assessment

Substantial Support	• Can students, with help, show understanding of key words such as **cultivate** and **consider**?
Moderate Support	• Can students show understanding of key words such as **cultivate** and **consider**?
Light Support	• Can students use of key words such as **cultivate** and **consider** in sentences?

Preview or Review Week 1 ELA Mini-Lessons

"The Structure of a Corn Plant," page 48

Student Objectives

LANGUAGE
Purpose:
- I can explain the development of corn.

Form:
- I can identify shifts in verb tense.

CONTENT
- I can recognize informational texts.

Additional Materials
- Unit Presentation
- *Texts for Close Reading* booklet
- Think-Speak-Listen Flip Book
- Student journal

Language Transfer Support

Students whose first language is Haitian, Creole, Hmong, Korean, or Vietnamese may need additional modeling to pronounce words from the text that have r-controlled vowels, such as **first, corn, supported, occurs, fertilization,** and **kernels.**

1 Read "The Structure of a Corn Plant"

Build Background and Vocabulary

Display the panels and explain their importance in the text. If students have already read the text, ask them what they remember. Invite students to share their cultural experiences and knowledge on corn, such as how corn is grown, harvested, or cooked.

Read Aloud the Text

Read panel 1. To support comprehension, ask students to find an image in the picture that matches a word in the text (corn) and ask *wh-* questions, such as *What kind of plant do you see?* Repeat with panels 2–4. After reading, model thinking through the Essential Question. **Ask:** *Why do you think corn was corn developed as a natural resource? Corn can grow in hot, dry, wet or cool climates. I think corn was developed as a natural resource because it is adaptable.* Invite students to share their ideas. **Ask:** *How do you know this text is nonfiction?* Invite students to respond. **Say:** *This nonfiction text gives us facts or information about corn. We call this an informational text.*

Think-Speak-Listen: Use the following sentence frame or the Think-Speak-Listen Flip Book to guide discussion: *A cornfield is _____. It has _____. Corn is _____.*

👥 Differentiated Instruction
Build Language: Use Shifts in Verb Tense to Explain

Show the panel 1 image. Write: *People cultivated corn thousands of years ago. Corn grows in different types of climates.* Help students identify the verbs in the sentences. Point to **cultivated** and then to **grows**. **Say:** *The first sentence gives information about the past. The second sentence gives scientific information about the present. We use the past tense to explain history facts and the present tense to explain science facts.* Use the Differentiated Instruction to practice identifying and using shifts in verb tense in a way that best matches the levels of your students.

☑ Use Oral and Written Language: Explain the Development of Corn

Task: *Work with your partner to use verbs in the past tense to describe the history of corn and verbs in the present tense to tell how corn grows. Share your sentences.*

Ⓢ *Corn was first cultivated _____. People migrated. They spread the crop _____.*

Ⓜ *Corn was first cultivated _____. As people migrated, they _____.*

Ⓛ *First cultivated _____, corn was _____ as people _____.*

🗣 Wrap Up

Today we learned how important shifts in verb tense are in describing historic and scientific information. Why is it important to use verb shifts correctly?

Turn and Talk: *Use shifts in verb tense to describe what you know about natural resources.*

👤👤👤 Differentiated Instruction
Build Language: Use Shifts in Verb Tense to Explain

Ⓢubstantial Support

Model: Read the text in panel 1. Model recognizing shifts in verb tense. **Say:** *When I read the word cultivated, I see the -ed ending. This tells me that the verb is in the past tense. So I know that it describes something that happened already in history. Then I see the verb grow. This verb is in the present tense. It tells me about a science fact that happens now.* Continue with Panels 2–4, but invite students to help you recognize shifts in verb tense.

Practice: Distribute BLM 1. Encourage students to help you complete the sentences. Check understanding and reteach as necessary.

Extend: Have pairs complete the activity on the BLM. **Say:** *Think about the information. Does it happen in the past or can it happen now?*

Challenge: If students are ready, help them to form new sentences with some of the words on the BLM.

Ⓜoderate Support

Model: Point out that panels 1 and 2 explain the history of corn and that panels 3 and 4 explain the science of a corn plant. Display the following sentences: *Corn is an adaptable plant that can grow in different climates. As people migrated, they grew corn in other regions.* Model recognizing shifts in verb tense. **Say:** *When I read the present tense verbs is and can grow, I know the information is a fact about corn today. When I read the past tense verbs migrated and grew, I know the information is about the history of corn.* Point out that **grew** is the irregular past tense of the verb **grow**.

Practice: Distribute BLM 2. Work with students to complete the task.

Extend: Have pairs complete the activity in the BLM.

Challenge: If students are ready, have them write new sentences with pairs of verbs in the past and in the present.

Ⓛight Support

Use the texts on pp. 4-5 in the *Texts for Close Reading* booklet for the following activities.

Practice: Have students read paragraph 1. Work together as a class to identify each verb, its tense and whether it is used to explain a history or a science fact.

Extend: Have partners analyze the verbs in paragraphs 2 and 3 to identify scientific and historic information. Have them use some of the verbs in new sentences. Remind students to look for shifts in verb tense to help them.

Challenge: Have one partner assume the role of historian and the other the role of scientist. Ask each student to compose a sentence about corn from his or her professional point of view. Have partners read aloud their sentences. Then have students switch roles and write new sentences about corn.

☑ Formative Assessment

Substantial Support	• With support, can students distinguish between simple present and simple past tense verbs? • With support, are students able to complete sentence frames using cues for shift tenses?
Moderate Support	• Are students able to recognize why verb tenses may shift in a nonfiction informational text? • Can students complete sentences using appropriate verb tenses?
Light Support	• Do students understand that verb tenses shift for different disciplines? • Can students generate new sentences using verbs with appropriate verb tenses for history and science?

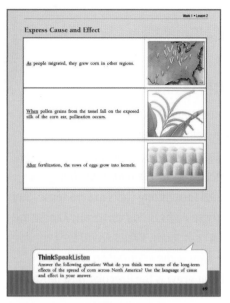

"Express Cause and Effect," page 49

Student Objectives

LANGUAGE

Purpose:
- I can describe cause and effect in an interview.

Form:
- I can recognize the language of cause and effect.

CONTENT
- I can describe cause-and-effect relationships related to the corn plant.

Additional Materials
- Unit Presentation
- *Texts for Close Reading* booklet
- Think-Speak-Listen Flip Book
- Student journal

Language Transfer Support

Note that the words **cause** and **effect** have cognates in several European languages, including Spanish *(la cause/el efecto)* and French *(la cause/l'effet)*. Encourage students to look for other words in the text on page 48 that are similar to words in their first language.

2 Express Cause and Effect

Engage Thinking

Display the chart. **Ask:** *What do the ears of corn show on the map?* **Say:** *The ears of corn show the regions where corn grows.* Read the text. **Ask:** *What did we learn about why corn grows in many different regions?* **Say:** *We learned that corn grows different regions because of the migration of people from what is now Mexico.*

Turn and Talk: *What other things do you think caused corn to be planted across North America?*

Read and View Closely: Recognize the Language of Cause and Effect

Have students look at the chart. **Say:** *This chart helps us to recognize the language of cause and effect.* Read the first row. **Say:** *The word* as *helps me recognize a cause: people migrated, or moved, from place to place. What was the effect? Corn grew in other regions. So, now I know why corn grows in many different regions.* Continue with the remaining sentences. **Ask:** *What are the cause and effect?* Help students answer using this sentence frame: *The cause is _____. The effect is _____.* **Say:** *Words such as* after, when *and* as *are signal words. They signal for a cause and effect.*

👥 Differentiated Instruction
Build Language: Express Cause and Effect

Say: *We identified signal words that help us recognize cause and effect. Now we can use these words to express cause and effect.* Use the Differentiated Instruction to practice expressing cause and effect in a way that best matches the levels of your students.

Think-Speak-Listen: Use the following sentence frame or the Think-Speak-Listen Flip Book to guide discussion: *As corn spread across the continent, _____.*

☑ Use Oral and Written Language: Describe Cause and Effect in an Interview

Task: *With your partner, take turns playing the roles of an expert on corn development and a television interviewer who asks questions.*

(S) *When does pollination occur? When _____.*

(M) *How did corn spread across the continent? As _____.*

(L) *What happens after fertilization? After _____.*

🔄 Wrap Up

Today we learned to recognize and use the language of cause and effect. How does knowing what happened and why help you to better understand a topic?

Turn and Talk: *Explain why pizza became a popular food.*

👥 Differentiated Instruction
Build Language: Express Cause and Effect

Ⓢubstantial Support

Model: Read the text in panel 1 of the chart. Model recognizing a cause and its effect. **Say:** *People grew corn in other regions. That is what happened, or the effect. To find the cause, I ask "Why did it happen?"* Continue with panels 2 and 3.

Practice: Distribute BLM 1. Work with students to complete the Practice activity. Point out that the cause does not have to come first in the sentence.

Extend: Have students work in pairs to complete the Extend activity as a class. Monitor students' work and help as necessary.

Challenge: If students are ready, start a sentence about cause and effect and have them finish it, for example, When it started to rain, _____.

Ⓜoderate Support

Model: Read the text in panel 3. Model identifying a cause and effect, using a signal word as a cue. **Say:** *I read that rows of eggs grow into kernels. That is what happens, or the effect. What is the cause? The first word in the sentence is* after. *It is a signal word that helps me identify the cause. I read the words 'after fertilization'. So I know that fertilization causes the rows of eggs to grow into kernels.*

Practice: Work with students to identify the cause and effect in panel 1. Have them identify the signal word that points them to the cause. Then have them state the effect from the remainder of the sentence.

Extend: Have students work in pairs to identify the cause and effect in panel 2 by completing this sentence frame: **Pollination _____ because _____.** Point out that the word when helps to point them to the text that describes the cause of pollination.

Challenge: If students are ready, guide students in recognizing cause-and-effect sentences in extended text using paragraphs 1 and 6 on pages 4 and 5 in their *Texts for Close Reading.*

Ⓛight Support

Practice: Distribute BLM 2. Complete the Practice activity as a class.

Extend: Have students work in pairs to complete cause-and-effect sentences in the Extend activity on the BLM. Remind students to use signal words when needed. Ask pairs to share their sentences with the class.

Challenge: If students are ready, explain that effects can be stated before causes in cause-and-effect sentences. Model changing the third sentence from the chart. Write: *The rows of eggs grow into kernels after fertilization.* Have students try changing the order with other sentences.

☑ Formative Assessment

Substantial Support	• With support, can students recognize the difference between causes and effects? • With support, can students complete sentence frames that show cause-and-effect relationships?
Moderate Support	• Can students use cues to identify causes, effects, and signal words with little or no assistance? • Can students generate cause-and-effect sentences using sentence frames?
Light Support	• Can students write cause-and-effect statements? • With support, can students reverse cause-and-effect statements to show effects before causes?

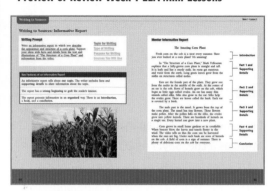

"Writing to Sources," pages 50–51

Student Objectives

LANGUAGE
Purpose:
- I can analyze an informative report.

Form:
- I can identify the parts of an informative report.

CONTENT
- I can recognize an informative report.

Additional Materials
- Unit Presentation

3 Writing to Sources: Informative Report

Engage Thinking

Tell students that they will analyze an informative report so that they can recognize its parts. Read aloud the prompt.

> Write an informative report in which you describe the appearance and structure of a corn plant. Support your ideas with facts and details from the text and illustrations of "The Structure of a Corn Plant" and information from the video "Corn from the CSA."

Say: *Let's ask questions to make sure we understand the prompt. What will the writer write about? What type of writing is it? Where will the writer get some of his facts and details?*

👤👥👥 Differentiated Instruction
Read and View Closely: Analyze an Informative Report

Say: *As I read aloud the report, I will stop so that we can analyze it. In the first paragraph, the writer introduces a single subject. As I read, look for this topic.* Read the paragraph and pause. **Say:** *Turn to a partner. What is this report about?* Check that students can identify the topic.

Say: *Writers use facts and details to share and support information. Listen for facts and details as I read.* Read the second paragraph. **Say:** *Turn to your partner. Tell some facts and details about corn.* Have students share their information with the class. **Ask:** *Where did the writer get his information?* Check that students can identify the source.

Continue in this way with the next three paragraphs.

Say: *An informative report ends with a conclusion.* Check students understand how the conclusion references the introduction. **Say:** *Let's look at the overall structure of the report. Turn to your partner. Is the report organized in a logical way?* Check that students can identify an introduction, body, and conclusion.

Then continue the lesson using Differentiated Instruction that best fits the needs of your students.

Share Your Understanding

Bring the students back together. **Ask:** *What did we learn today about an informative report?* Review the structure as needed.

Final Writing Assignment

Use the *English Language Development Assessment* to assess students' writing for their ELA writing assignment.

👥 Differentiated Instruction
Read and View Closely: Analyze an Informative Report

Ⓢubstantial Support

Model: Distribute BLM 1. **Say:** *Let's read and analyze another informative report that answers the prompt.* Read the first paragraph and pause. **Ask:** *What is the topic of the report?* Model answering the question.

Practice: Continue reading the report and ask the same questions that you asked about the mentor text. Invite students to answer. Help students to understand any unfamiliar words.

Extend: Have students in pairs complete the activity on the BLM.

Challenge: Have students work in pairs to discuss elements of an informative report. They should ask each other *yes/no* and *wh-* questions, such as: *Is the report logically organized? Which detail helps to explain the kernels?*

Ⓛight Support

Practice: Distribute BLM 2. **Say:** *We will look more closely at the Mentor Informative Report to see how writers incorporate the features of an informative report.* Do items 1 and 2 with students.

Extend: Have students work in pairs to complete items 3 and 4.

Challenge: Write on the board: *What is the main idea of each paragraph? What details help you understand this idea?* Have students work in pairs to discuss each paragraph in the report. Tell them to refer to the text to give examples as they answer. Encourage students to affirm their partner's responses, or to ask questions to learn more.

Ⓜoderate Support

Model: Draw students' attention to the Mentor Informative Report in their book. **Say:** *Let's analyze how the writer uses the features of an informative report.* Make the chart below. **Say:** *The writer introduces the topic and uses facts and details to support it. For example, the writer describes the corn plant as "straight and tall and leafy."* Write this on the chart. text.

Features of an Informative Report	Examples from the Text
1. Uses facts and details to support information.	"straight and tall and leafy"
2. Organizes the report in a logical way.	
3. Includes an introduction, a body of text, and a conclusion.	

Practice: Work with students to complete the chart with examples from the text for the other two features.

Extend: Have students work with a partner. Tell them to use the chart to discuss the elements of an informative report, such as: *Which detail helps the reader understand _____?* Provide sentence frames to help students respond or ask questions: *I agree that _____. Can you tell me why you say that _____?*

Challenge: Have pairs of students explain how the body of the report is logically organized. They should summarize each paragraph, determine the main idea of the paragraph, and describe how the facts and detail support it.

☑ Formative Assessment

Substantial Support	• Do students recognize the criteria for an informative report in the Mentor Informative Report?
Moderate Support	• Do students recognize the ways in which the Mentor Informative Report meets the criteria for an informative report? • Can students describe the features of an informative report in their own words?
Light Support	• Do students recognize criteria and analyze how the Mentor Text meets the criteria for an informative report? • Can students describe in their own words how the writer meets the criteria for an informative report?

Extend and Scaffold Academic Language for Writing
Analyze the Mentor Text: Language Purpose and Structure

Introduction
All Levels of Support

Materials List
- **Mentor Text L** BLM X Light Support
- **Writing Frames Teacher Page** BLM Y
- **Writing Frames Student Page** BLM Z

- Have a copy of BLM Y to refer to during the lesson.

- Distribute BLMs X and Z to each student.

- Read aloud the writing prompt on BLM X. Explain that students will read and analyze the language one writer used to respond to this prompt.

- Have students follow along as you read aloud paragraph 1 of "The Amazing Corn Plant."

- Point out the phrase *Ears are the female part of the plant* and the words that indicate the writing frame in bold. **Ask:** *Why did the author use this language? What is its purpose?* Help students understand that the author uses the structure _____ *are* _____ *of the* _____. to explain a particular part of the corn plant. **Ears** is being presented as *the female part of the plant.*

- Have students write this frame into the "Explain" row of their Writing Frames worksheet (BLM Z). Tell students this is one writing frame they can use in their writing to provide an explanation.

- Analyze other bolded phrases in paragraph 1. Explain their purpose and help students add the writing frames to BLM Z.

- Follow these steps as you read additional paragraphs.

- Read aloud the writing prompt on BLM Z. Work with students to generate additional writing frames they could use as they write a response to this prompt. Refer to BLM Y for examples.

Based on students' needs, conduct additional lessons using the differentiated instruction and tools provided.

Light Support
Differentiated Instruction

Materials List
- **Mentor Text L** BLM X Light Support
- **Writing Frames Teacher Page** BLM Y
- **Writing Frames Student Page** BLM Z

Students will need their copies of BLMs X and Z from the initial lesson. Refer to the chart below and your copy of BLM Y during the lesson.

- Explain that students will reread "The Amazing Corn Plant" to analyze more phrases and sentences that the writer used.

- Reread the text with students one paragraph at a time.

- Ask individuals or partners to find and underline each phrase in the chart below, read the sentence it appears in, and try to determine the sentence's purpose in the text.

- Provide explanation as necessary, then have students add the writing frames to the "Other Academic Phrases and Sentences" column of BLM Z.

- Encourage students to generate related writing frames and add them to their chart.

LIGHT SUPPORT		
Purpose	**Phrase/Sentence (paragraph)**	**Frame**
Cite Source	In "The Structure of a Corn Plant," Mark Felkonian explains... (2)	In [source], [name] explains that _____.
Add Details/ Facts	...a mature corn plant is straight and tall and leafy, with a sturdy... (2)	A _____ is _____, with _____.
Add Details/ Facts	Rows of kernels grow on the cob, which begin as little... (3)	__ _____ which begin as _____.
Sequence of Events	After the pollen falls on the silks, the eggs in the ear grow...(3)	After the _____, the _____ _____.
Add Details/ Facts	When warm breezes blow, the leaves and tassels of the tall... (4)	When _____, the _____ _____.

(M)oderate Support

Materials List
- **Mentor Text M** BLM A Moderate Support
- **Writing Frames Teacher Page** BLM Y
- **Writing Frames Student Page** BLM Z

Use the mentor text (BLM A) and the phrases and sentences appropriate for the support level you are targeting.

- Distribute BLM A. Students will also need their copy of BLM Z.

- Read aloud BLM A as students follow along.

- Then reread the text one paragraph at a time, stopping after each paragraph to focus on the bolded and underlined phrases and sentences. Work with students to understand the purpose of each phrase within the text. Have students write the corresponding writing frame in the "Other Academic Phrases and Sentences" column of BLM Z.

- Have partners practice using one or more of these writing frames to expand an idea in the essay they are writing. Have students share their examples with other members of the group.

MODERATE SUPPORT		
Purpose	**Phrase/Sentence (paragraph)**	**Frame**
Location	They grow out from the nodes in the middle of the stalk. (3)	_____ in the middle of _____.
Sequence of Events	After the pollen falls on the silks, the ovules grow... (4)	After the _____, the _____ _____.
Add Details/ Facts	Every kernel can grow into a new plant. (4)	Every _____, can _____ _____.
Number	There are hundreds of kernels on a single ear... (4)	There are hundreds of _____ on _____.
Cite Source	The video tells us that the corn can be harvested... (5)	The [source] tells us that _____ when _____.

(S)ubstantial Support

Materials List
- **Mentor Text S** BLM B Substantial Support
- **Writing Frames Teacher Page** BLM Y
- **Writing Frames Student Page** BLM Z

Students will need their copy of BLM Z from the initial lesson.

- Distribute BLM B.

- Follow the procedure explained in the Moderate Support lesson.

SUBSTANTIAL SUPPORT		
Purpose	**Phrase/Sentence (paragraph)**	**Frame**
Location	They grow out from the middle of the stalk. (3)	_____ from the middle of _____.
Sequence of Events	Then the video tells us... (5)	Then _____, _____.
Add Details/ Facts	Every kernel can start a new plant. (4)	Every _____, can _____ _____.
Number	There is plenty of tasty corn on the cob to eat. (5)	There is plenty of _____ to _____.
Cite Source	Then the video tells us that the corn can be picked... (5)	The [source] tells us that _____ when _____.

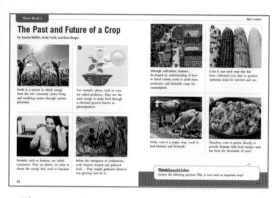

"The Past and Future of a Crop," pages 52–53

Student Objectives

LANGUAGE

Purpose:
- I can use visual information to support a statement.

Form:
- I can identify infinitives used as adverbials.

CONTENT
- I can understand key details about corn cultivation.

Additional Materials
- Unit Presentation
- Using Infinitives as Adverbials Chart
- *Texts for Close Reading* booklet
- Think-Speak-Listen Flip Book
- Student journal

Language Transfer Support

Note that the functions of infinitives in English may be challenging to native speakers of Chinese, Haitian Creole, Hmong, Korean, Spanish, or Vietnamese. In each of these languages, there is no distinction between gerunds and infinitives, and the word *to* in an infinitive can be mistaken for the preposition *to*. In Haitian Creole, infinitives are not used to express purpose.

4 Read "The Past and Future of a Crop"

Build Background and Vocabulary

Display the panels. Explain that photographs, diagrams, and illustrations provide information, just as words do. Invite students to share their cultural experiences and knowledge on corn crops, such as when crops are planted and harvested.

Read Aloud the Text

Read panels 1 and 2. To support comprehension, ask students to consider how the photo and diagram show what the text describes. Ask questions, such as: *How does the photo show living matter and energy? How does the diagram explain how plants use the sun's energy?* Repeat with panels 3–8. After reading, model thinking through the Essential Question. **Ask:** *How did corn become a major crop?* **Say:** *In Panel 7, I see that corn is used to feed cows. It is a good food source for livestock.* Invite students to share their ideas: I think that corn became a major crop because _____. **Ask:** *How do you know this text is nonfiction?* **Say:** *This text explains how corn became an important food crop. We call this type of nonfiction an informational text.*

Think-Speak-Listen Use the following sentence frame or the Think-Speak-Listen Flip Book to guide discussion: *Corn is an important crop because _____.*

👥👥👥 Differentiated Instruction
Build Language: Use Infinitives as Adverbials

Display panel 2. Display the Using Infinitives as Adverbials Chart. Remind students that they learned about adverbials in Unit 3. Help students identify the infinitive phrase and the verb it modifies in the sentence on the chart. **Ask:** *How do plants use the sun's energy?* **Say:** *They use it to make food. The infinitive phrase* to make *tells more about the verb* use *in this sentence. Infinitives used as adverbials act like adverbs by answering questions such as* why? *and* how? Use the Differentiated Instruction to practice using infinitives as adverbials in a way that best matches the levels of your students.

✅ Use Oral and Written Language: Use Visual Information to Support a Statement

Task: *Imagine that you and your partner are preparing for a debate. You support the statement: Corn is an important crop. Select two images from the text in your book and write statements that tell how each shows the importance of corn as a crop.*

(S) *Corn is a major crop. It is used to feed _____.*

(M) *Today, corn is an important crop. It is used to _____.*

(L) *Today, corn is a major crop because it is _____.*

🔄 Wrap Up

Today we learned how infinitives can be used as adverbials to tell more about a verb, such as how, why, when, and where. Why is it important to give more details about verbs?

Turn and Talk: *Use infinitives as adverbs to describe how corn uses the sun's energy.*

👥👥 Differentiated Instruction
Build Language: Use Infinitives as Adverbials

ⓢubstantial Support

Model: Teach infinitives using the Using Infinitives as Adverbials Chart. Then model recognizing infinitives used as adverbials. Point to panel 2. **Say:** *I read the text to help me interpret the diagram. The text says that plants use the sun's energy. How do they use the sun's energy? They use it to make food. To make is an infinitive. It starts with the word to plus the basic verb make. It answers the question of how plants use the sun's energy.*

Practice: Distribute the BLM 1. Complete the activity as a class. Encourage students to help identify the infinitives used as adverbials and to tell whether they answer the question **how** or **why**.

Extend: Have pairs complete the activity in the BLM. Monitor students' work and provide additional support as needed.

Challenge: Have students write sentences using some of the infinitives on the BLM.

ⓛight Support

Practice: Have students use "The Past and Future of a Crop" from *Texts for Close Reading*. Remind students that infinitives consist of the word *to* plus a basic verb. To be used as adverbs, infinitives must tell more about the verb in a sentence. Have partners read paragraph 1 on page 6 and identify two infinitives used as adverbs.

Extend: Put students in pairs. Assign each pair one of the following paragraphs and question:

Paragraph 2: Why did humans breed certain seeds?

Paragraph 3: How is corn used today?

Paragraph 4: How is heat energy from burning corn used?

Tell pairs to write their answer in a complete sentence and to underline the infinitive used as an adverbial.

Challenge: Have students read paragraphs 8, 9, 10 and 11 on pages 8 and 9. **Ask:** *Why do you think we should grow corn?*

ⓜoderate Support

Model: Teach infinitives using the Using Infinitives as Adverbials Chart. Point out that corn is described as an important crop in panels 6–8. Read the text in panel 8. Model identifying the infinitive used as an adverbial. **Say:** *When I see the word to followed by the basic verb produce, I know this is an infinitive. I think the infinitive to produce is used as an adverb because it tells more about the verb cultivated. It tells why corn has been cultivated over time: to produce optimum traits for survival and use.*

Practice: Distribute the BLM 2. Work with students to complete the Practice section.

Extend: Have pairs complete the activity in the BLM. Discuss their answers as a group.

Challenge: If students are ready, model recognizing infinitives used as adverbials in extended text using paragraph 4 in *Texts for Close Reading* on page 7.

☑ Formative Assessment

Substantial Support	• With support, can students identify an infinitive phrase beginning with to? • With support, are students able to complete sentence frames with infinitives used as adverbials?
Moderate Support	• Are students able to recognize the verb that an infinitive modifies as an adverbial? • Can students use infinitives as adverbials in sentence frames?
Light Support	• Can students identify infinitives used as adverbials and the verbs they modify? • Can students compose sentences that include infinitives used as adverbials?

Preview or Review Week 1 ELA Mini-Lessons

"Paul Bunyan and the Great Popcorn Blizzard," page 54

Student Objectives

LANGUAGE
Purpose:
• I can recount events in a tall tale.
Form:
• I can analyze words in context.
CONTENT
• I can understand characteristics of a tall tale.

Additional Materials
• Unit Presentation
• Analyze Words in Context Chart
• *Texts for Close Reading* booklet
• Think-Speak-Listen Flip Book
• Student journal

Language Transfer Support

Students whose first language is Cantonese, Haitian Creole, Hmong, Korean, or Vietnamese may need additional support as they explore past tense verbs since these languages do not use inflectional endings to change verb tense.

5 Read "Paul Bunyan and the Great Popcorn Blizzard"

Build Background and Vocabulary

Display the panels. If students have already read the story, ask them what they remember. Invite students to share their cultural experiences and knowledge on Paul Bunyan or about popcorn.

Read Aloud the Text

Read panel 1. To support comprehension, ask students to find images that match words in the text. Ask questions, such as: *What event does the picture illustrate?* Repeat with panels 2 and 3. After reading, **ask:** *How is all that popcorn like a blizzard?* Model thinking through the answer: *I know that a blizzard is a storm with strong winds and deep snow. In panel 3, the text says that the popcorn covered the entire state, and the picture shows how deep it was. The popcorn was like a terrible snow blizzard that won't melt.* Invite students to share ideas, using: *The popcorn blizzard was _____.* **Ask:** *Could a story like this really happen, or could Paul Bunyan be a real person?* Elicit answers. **Say:** *Tall tales exaggerate real people and events to make a story funny and entertaining.*

Think-Speak-Listen: Use the following sentence frame or the Think-Speak-Listen Flip Book to guide discussion: *People enjoy tall tales because they are _____.*

👤👤👤 Differentiated Instruction
Build Language: Analyze Words in Context

Show panel 1. Write: *Paul Bunyan traveled through the great Midwest with his sidekick, Babe the Blue Ox.* Explain to students that they can look for clues in the sentence to learn the meaning of **sidekick.** Help students identify the words **traveled** and **with** as context clues. **Ask:** *What do these words tell you about Paul Bunyan and Babe?* Elicit answers. **Say:** *They went places together, so a sidekick may be a kind of friend.* Verify the meaning using a dictionary. Use the Differentiated Instruction to practice analyzing words in a way that best matches the levels of your students.

☑ Use Oral and Written Language: Recount Events in a Tall Tale

Task: *Make a list of new words from the Paul Bunyan story. Choose one to three words to research in a dictionary. Then use these words to tell what Paul Bunyan does to get rid of the popcorn after the great blizzard.*

(S) *Paul Bunyan asked his team _____. Babe helped them _____.*

(M) *Paul Bunyan got _____ and they _____. Babe _____.*

(L) *Paul Bunyan gathered his team and Babe so they could _____.*

🔄 Wrap Up

Today we learned how to use context clues to analyze a new word in context. How does analyzing a word in context help us to understand a story or other text?

Turn and Talk: *Use some of the new words you learned in your own tall tale or story to describe what happened.*

♦♦♦ Differentiated Instruction
Build Language: Analyze Words in Context

Ⓢ ubstantial Support

Model: Referring to the Analyze Words in Context Chart, model how to analyze the word **sidekick**. Point to panel 1. **Say:** *In the picture, Paul and his sidekick look like friends. The dictionary meaning of sidekick is "a helpful partner." So a sidekick is like a helper. A word that means the opposite would be enemy. The dictionary also showed me that the word is a noun and that it has two syllables.*

Practice: Distribute BLM 1. Help students complete the activity.

Extend: Have partners complete the BLM activity, supporting the students as needed.

Challenge: If students are ready, help them find context clues for the multiple-meaning word **cleared**.

Ⓜ oderate Support

Model: Use the Analyze Words in Context Chart to review how you analyzed the word sidekick in panel 1. **Say:** *I looked at the other words in the sentence and saw traveled and with as clues that a sidekick might be a friend. Then I checked a dictionary and saw that a sidekick can be a "helpful partner." A word that is similar to sidekick could be helper. A word with the opposite meaning could be enemy. The dictionary also told me that the word is a noun and that it has two syllables.*

Practice: Distribute BLM 2. Point out the word **cleared** in panel 2, and read aloud the sentence. Work with students to complete the task.

Extend: Have pairs complete the activity in the BLM using an online or print dictionary. Point out that **clear** or **cleared** can have more than one meaning.

Challenge: If students are ready, model analyzing the word **scorching** in paragraph 4 in *Texts for Close Reading* on p.10.

Ⓛ ight Support

Use the text on p. 10 in the *Texts for Close Reading* booklet for the following activities.

Practice: Review how word meaning can be analyzed using context clues and how a dictionary can be used as a tool to find more information. Have partners read paragraph 4. Guide pairs in analyzing the word **scorching**, using an Analyze Words in Context Chart.

Extend: Write the following questions for paragraphs 1 and 2. Have partners write their answers in complete sentences and underline the words used in context. Paragraph 1: *What are context clues for the meaning of* **settle**? Paragraph 2: *How does the knowing the kind of work Paul and his team did help you understand the meaning of* **lumberjacks**?

Challenge: If students are ready, **ask:** *How could a dictionary help you use words to exaggerate characters and events in a tall tale?* Guide students in their responses.

☑ Formative Assessment

Substantial Support	• With support, can students recognize context clues? • With support, can students complete a Word Study Chart? • Can students complete sentence frames to demonstrate understanding of new words?
Moderate Support	• Can students use context to determine word meaning? • With moderate support, can students analyze a word using a Word Study Chart?
Light Support	• Can students identify context clues with little or no support? • Can students independently analyze words using a Word Study Chart?

Preview or Review Week 2 ELA Mini-Lessons

Week 2 • Lesson 6	

Recognize Prepositional Phrases

Text	Effects
"The Structure of a Corn Plant"	As people migrated, they grew corn <u>in other regions</u>.
	<u>As a result</u>, the crop soon spread <u>across the continent</u>.
"The Past and Future of a Crop"	<u>Through cultivation</u>, humans ... developed an understanding <u>of how</u> to breed certain seeds to yield more productive and desirable crops <u>for consumption</u>.
	Corn is one such crop that has been cultivated <u>over time</u> to produce optimum traits <u>for survival and use</u>.

ThinkSpeakListen
Explain how a prepositional phrase is formed, and identify some prepositional phrases in "Paul Bunyan and the Great Popcorn Blizzard."

"Recognize Prepositional Phrases," page 55

Student Objectives

LANGUAGE
Purpose:
- I can inform an audience in an interview.

Form:
- I can recognize and use prepositional phrases.

CONTENT
- I can understand key details about informational science content.

Additional Materials
- Unit Presentation
- *Texts for Close Reading* booklet
- Think-Speak-Listen Flip Book
- Student journal

Language Transfer Support

Students whose first language is Cantonese may tend to omit prepositions when speaking and writing English. Speakers of Cantonese do not use prepositions in the same way they are used in English.

Note that students whose first language is Spanish may need additional support to differentiate the prepositions **in** and **on**, which are not differentiated in Spanish.

6 Recognize Prepositional Phrases

Engage Thinking

Display the image for panel 4 from "The Past and Future of a Crop." Read the text. **Ask:** *When did people hunt and gather corn?* **Say:** *People hunted and gathered corn before the emergence of civilizations.* **Ask:** *What word or words in the text tell when people hunted and gathered corn?* Invite students to respond.

Read and View Closely: Recognize Prepositional Phrases

Display the chart. Read the first sentence and point to the underlined phrase. Then reread the sentence without the phrase. **Say:** *The phrase* in other regions *tells me where people grew corn. I know that people grew corn in many different places. The phrase* in other regions *is an example of a prepositional phrase.* Continue with the remaining sentences. **Ask:** *What additional information does the phrase tell us?* Help students answer using this sentence frame: *The phrase _____ tells us _____.* **Say:** *Prepositional phrases give us information by answering questions such as when, where, why, and how.*

👥 Differentiated Instruction
Build Language: Recognize Prepositional Phrases

Say: *Prepositions, such as* in, for, across, to, *and* under, *are connecting words that link nouns or pronouns to the rest of a sentence.* Point to a prepositional phrase. **Say:** *A prepositional phrase is a group of words that begins with a preposition and usually ends with a noun or pronoun.* Point to the third sentence. **Say:** *I see the preposition* for. *Then I see the noun* consumption. *This phrase tells me how people used corn. They used it* for consumption, *or to eat.* Use the Differentiated Instruction to practice recognizing prepositional phrases in a way that best matches the levels of your students.

Think-Speak-Listen: Use the following sentence frame or the Think-Speak-Listen Flip Book to guide discussion: *To make a prepositional phrase, I add _____ to a _____.*

☑ Use Oral and Written Language: Inform an Audience in an Interview

Task: *With a partner, take turns playing the roles of a radio show host and a farmer being interviewed. Ask and answer questions about growing corn. Use prepositional phrases.*

 When do you harvest corn? I harvest corn _____.

Ⓜ *How did people harvest corn in the past? People harvested corn _____.*

Ⓛ *What do you do when you are growing and harvesting corn? First, when I am growing corn, I plant my corn _____.*

 Wrap Up

Today we learned to recognize prepositional phrases in sentences. How do prepositional phrases help us learn about a topic?

Turn and Talk: *Use sentences with prepositional phrases give additional information about how other food crops, such as rice or tomatoes, are grown.*

▲▲▲ Differentiated Instruction
Build Language: Recognize Prepositional Phrases

ⓢubstantial Support

Model: Write the sentence "Paul Bunyan cleared giant oak trees from the forests." **Say:** *I see the preposition* from. *If I look across the sentence, I see the noun* forests. *So I know that* from the forests *is the prepositional phrase. It tells me where the oak trees were.* Write the sentence: *Paul Bunyan traveled through the Midwest.* **Say:** *I see the preposition* through. *If I look across the sentence, I see the noun* Midwest. *So I know that* through the Midwest *is the prepositional phrase. It tells me where Paul Bunyan traveled.*

Practice: Distribute BLM 1. Complete the Practice activity as a class.

Extend: Have students work in pairs to complete the Extend activity in the BLM.

Challenge: If students are ready, work together as a class to answer the Challenge question. Read the sentence without the prepositional phrase. **Ask:** *What do we learn from this sentence?* Read the sentence with the prepositional phrase. **Ask:** *What information does the prepositional phrase add?*

ⓜoderate Support

Model: Read the last sentence. **Say:** *I see two prepositional phrases here:* over time *and for* survival and use. Over time *tells me when corn was grown and* for survival and use *tells me why it was useful.*

Practice: Distribute BLM 2. Work with students to complete the activity in the Practice section.

Extend: Have students work in pairs to complete the Extend activity in the BLM.

Challenge: If students are ready, ask them to reread the sentences in the chart. For each one, ask them to explain what the prepositional phrase tells them.

ⓛight Support

Use the text on pp. 4-5 in the *Texts for Close Reading* booklet for the following activities.

Practice: Have students read paragraph 4. Help them write a sentence about how the corn ear grows, using one of the following prepositional phrases: *in the middle, from a leaf node, of the stalk.*

Extend: Lead a brief discussion on the purpose of prepositional phrases. **Ask:** *How can recognizing prepositional phrases help us read texts and stories?* Have students work in pairs to identify prepositional phrases in paragraph 4. Monitor students' work and ask pairs what kind of information these phrases add to the sentence to check understanding.

Challenge: If students are ready, have them write four sentences about the growth of corn. Encourage them to use information in paragraph 4. Remind students to use prepositional phrases in their writing.

☑ Formative Assessment

Substantial Support	• With support, are students able to recognize prepositional phrases? • Can students use sentence frames to complete prepositional phrases?
Moderate Support	• With support, can students identify the type of information provides a prepositional phrase provides? • With support, can students use specific prepositional phrases to generate sentences?
Light Support	• Can students identify the type of information a prepositional phrase provides? • Can students write original sentences using prepositional phrases?

Preview of Review Week 2 ELA Mini-Lessons

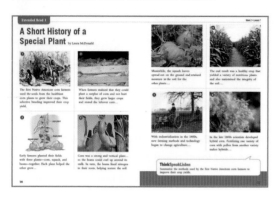

"A Short History of a Special Plant," pages 56–57

Student Objectives

LANGUAGE
Purpose:
• I can explain information with a diagram.
Form:
• I can identify prepositional phrases that indicate location.
CONTENT
• I can read an informational text about the history of corn farming.

Additional Materials

• Unit Presentation
• *Texts for Close Reading* booklet
• Think-Speak-Listen Flip Book
• Student journal

Metacognitive Prompt: Making Inferences

As we read, focus on what you are hearing. Think about what the text says and ask yourself if you understand, or comprehend what it says. If you do not or if you have a question, ask your teacher.

7 Read "A Short History of a Special Plant"

Build Background and Vocabulary

Display the panels. If students have already read the story, ask them what they remember. Invite students to share what they know about corn; its history and how it is grown.

Read Aloud the Text

Display Panel 1. To support comprehension, ask students to find images in the picture that match words in the text (Native American, corn plants, crops, etc.) and ask questions, such as *How did the Native American corn farmers produce so much corn?* Repeat with panels 2– 8. After reading, model thinking through the Essential Question. **Ask:** *How did Native American farmers choose which crops to grow together?* **Ask:** *How can we tell this is a nonfiction text?* Elicit responses.

Think-Speak-Listen: Use the following sentence frame or the Think-Speak-Listen Flip Book to guide discussion: *Early Native American corn farmers used _____.*

👥 Differentiated Instruction
Build Language: Use Prepositional Phrases to Indicate Location

Display Panel 5. Write: *The squash leaves spread out on the ground.* Circle **spread** and underline **on the ground.** Remind students that a prepositional phrase includes a preposition such as **above, in, on, over, around** or **under** and a noun or a pronoun. Help students identify the prepositional phrase in the sentence. **Ask:** *What does the prepositional phrase on the ground tell us?* Elicit answers. **Say:** *It tells us where the leaves spread. They spread on the ground.* Prepositional phrases can tell us where a person is or where an action takes place. Use the Differentiated Instruction to practice prepositional phrases to indicate location in a way that best matches the levels of your students.

✔️ Use Oral and Written Language: Explain Information with a Diagram

Task: *With your partner, prepare a diagram to explain why corn, beans, and squash grow well together. Use complete sentences with prepositional phrases to give details about where crops and their different parts grow.*

(S) *Bean plants curl _____.*

(M) *The beans restored the soil when they fixed nitrogen _____.*

(L) *As the plants were growing, the squash leaves spread _____ and kept moisture _____.*

🔁 Wrap Up

Today we talked about prepositional phrases. What kind of information do they give us?

Turn and Talk: *Explain how Native American methods improved corn crops. Use prepositional phrases that describe where the plants and their parts grew in your answer.*

👥 Differentiated Instruction
Build Language: Use Prepositional Phrases to Indicate Location

Ⓢubstantial Support

Model: Write the prepositions **in, on, over, around, from, through,** and **under**. Say: *Prepositions like these answer the question* where? Point to the sentence "Meanwhile, the squash leaves spread out on the ground and retained moisture in the soil for other plants" on panel 5. Point out the phrase "in the soil." **Say:** *I see the preposition in. The preposition is followed by the noun soil. The phrase in the soil tells me where the squash leaves kept the moisture.*

Practice: Read panel 4. Instruct students to identify two prepositional phrases that answer the question **where**? in the text. **Ask:** *What do these prepositional phrases tell us about how corn and beans grew?*

Extend: Ask students to form pairs and explain to each other how planting corn and beans together helped plants grow. Remind students to use the prepositional phrases they identified in panel 4 during the Practice activity

Challenge: Work with students to write sentences with prepositional phrases about planting corn and beans.

Ⓜoderate Support

Model: Read the text from panel 4. Say: *I see two prepositional phrases here: around its stalk and in their roots. Around its stalk tells me where the bean plants curled up when planted next to the corn, and in their roots tells me where the beans kept the gas nitrogen to help the soil.*

Practice: Distribute BLM 1. Work with students to complete the activity in the Practice section.

Extend: Ask students to work in pairs to complete the Extend activity on the BLM.

Challenge: If students are ready, ask them to read paragraph 2 on p. 12 from the *Texts for Close Reading.* Have them look for prepositional phrases.

Ⓛight Support

Have students use pp. 12–15 in the *Texts for Close Reading* booklet to complete the following activities.

Practice: Distribute BLM 2. Ask students to read paragraph 2. Help students complete the Practice activity on the BLM.

Extend: Have students work in pairs to complete the Extend activity on the BLM.

Challenge: If students are ready, have them find and list prepositional phrases from more paragraphs in the text.

☑️ Formative Assessment

Substantial Support	• With support, are students able to identify prepositional phrases that indicate location? • Can students complete sentence frames using prepositional phrases that tell where?
Moderate Support	• Can students use a prepositional phrase in a sentence to add details about location? • With support, can students write and original sentence using prepositional phrases to indicate location?
Light Support	• Can students identify the information a prepositional phrase provides about location? • Can students write original sentences using prepositional phrases to indicate location?

"A Short History of a Special Plant," page 58

Student Objectives

LANGUAGE
Purpose:
- I can integrate information to explain a topic.

Form:
- I can understand temporal language.

CONTENT
- I can integrate information to understand nonfiction text.

Additional Materials
- Unit Presentation
- *Texts for Close Reading* booklet
- Think-Speak-Listen Flip Book
- Student journal

Metacognitive Prompt: Making Inferences

As we read, think about what you have already learned about corn and connect your knowledge with the new information in the text.

8 Integrate Information

Engage Thinking

Display Panel 9. **Ask:** *What do you remember about the first part of this article? How did early corn farmers grow their crops?*

👥 Differentiated Instruction
Read and View Closely: Integrate Information

Read aloud panel 8. **Say:** *Panel 8 tells me that scientists put pollen from one variety of corn onto another in the 1800s to develop hybrid corn.* Read Panel 9. **Say:** *Panel 9 tells me that hybrid corn was better and more plentiful. This information explains why the development of hybrid corn described in panel 8 was important.* Direct students to read panels 10–12. **Ask:** *How does the information help you to understand the importance of hybrid corn?* Help students to integrate the information. Use these sentence frames: *I learned _____ in panel _____. This tells me more about why hybrid corn is important because _____.* Use the Differentiated Instruction to practice integrating information in a way that best matches the levels of your students.

Build Language: Understand Temporal Language

Point to the first sentence in panel 8. **Say:** *I see the phrase "In the late 1800s." This phrase tells me when scientists developed hybrid corn.* Then point to the first sentence in panel 10. **Say:** *I see the word* Today. *This tells me that the sentence is describing the present.* Explain to students that writers use certain words and phrases to let readers know the order of events in an article and to tell when something happened.

Think-Speak-Listen: Use the following sentence frame or the Think-Speak-Listen Flip Book to guide discussion: *Native American Farmers planted _____. Today's farmers use _____.*

☑ Use Oral and Written Language: Integrate Information to Explain a Topic

Task: Work with a partner. Imagine that you are scientists who have interviewed farmers about why they grow hybrid corn. Using the information provided in panels 9–12, write sentences explaining why hybrid corn is a popular crop.

Ⓢ   *Farmers like hybrid corn because _____.*

Ⓜ   *Farmers found that hybrid corn _____.*

Ⓛ   *Hybrid corn has continued to improve, as scientists _____.*

Wrap Up

Today we learned to add new information to what we already know about a topic. Ask: *How does putting new and old information together help us understand a topic?*

Turn and Talk: *Why did methods used to farm corn begin to change in the 1800s?*

👥 Differentiated Instruction
Read and View Closely: Integrate Information

Substantial Support

Model: Read the text in panel 9 aloud. **Say:** *Panel 9 tells me that hybrid corn produced healthier crops so that more corn could be grown more quickly.* Read the text in panel 10 aloud. **Say:** *This text starts with Today. This tells me that the text is now talking about the present. The text also tells me that corn is a very important crop today, and that most corn is hybrid corn. The information in panel 10 then tells me how the events in panel 9 are important for corn farming today.*

Practice: Distribute BLM 1. Complete the Practice activity as a class.

Extend: Have students work in pairs to complete the Extend activity in the BLM.

Challenge: Ask students to explain how they selected the sentences on the BLM.

Moderate Support

Model: Read the text in panel 11 aloud. **Say:** *Panel 11 tells me that scientists today create better hybrid corn by mixing DNA from different varieties of corn.* Read the text in panel 12 aloud. **Say:** *In panel 12, the text tells me that changes to the DNA of corn crops make them stronger so that dry weather and insects do less damage to them. Reading panel 12 gives me more details about how the changes to corn in panel 11 make corn better.*

Practice: Distribute BLM 2. Instruct students to complete the Practice activity.

Extend: Ask students to work in pairs to complete the Extend activity on the BLM.

Challenge: If students are ready, have one student write a sentence based on the text and another student add a related detail.

Light Support

Use the text on pp. 12–19 in *Texts for Close Reading* for the following activities.

Practice: Direct students to read paragraphs 11 and 12. Instruct students to write three sentences, explaining the development of hybrid corn, the importance of hybrid crops today, and how the development of hybrid corn has affected corn farming today.

Extend: Have students work in pairs to read paragraphs 14 and 15. Ask students to write a sentence explaining the risks of modern farming methods. Instruct students to read paragraph 4 on page 14 and paragraph 7 and write a one- or two-sentence explanation of how the information in these paragraphs helps us to understand the dangers associated with modern farming practices.

Challenge: If students are ready, instruct them to work in pairs to review the text. Ask students to write a short paragraph explaining the development of modern methods used to grow corn and the advantages and disadvantages of these methods.

☑ Formative Assessment

Substantial Support	• With support, can students use knowledge from previous readings to understand new information on a topic? • With support, can students understand temporal language as a way to discuss time and the order of events?
Moderate Support	• With support, can students synthesize knowledge from different parts of a text to build knowledge about a topic? • Can students use temporal language as a way to discuss time and the order of events?
Light Support	• Can students use prior knowledge to integrate new information about a topic? • Can students use temporal language to put time and events in order?

Preview or Review Week 2 ELA Mini-Lessons

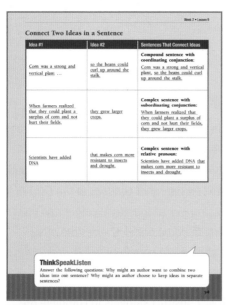

"Connect Two Ideas in a Sentence," page 59

Student Objectives

LANGUAGE
Purpose:
- I can persuade an audience with an advertisement.

Form:
- I can use conjunctions and relative pronouns to connect ideas in compound and complex sentences.

CONTENT
- I can connect ideas in a scientific, nonfiction text.

Additional Materials
- Unit Presentation
- *Texts for Close Reading* booklet
- Think-Speak-Listen Flip Book
- Student journal

Language Transfer Support

In Chinese and Vietnamese, conjunctions are used in pairs (e.g., *Although it was raining, but the sun was shining*). Students whose first language is Chinese or Vietnamese may add extra conjunctions when connecting two ideas in a sentence. They may also need more support in distinguishing between subordinate and independent clauses. Explain to English Learners that every sentence needs at least one independent clause.

9 Connect Two Ideas in a Sentence

Engage Thinking

Display panel 7. Read the text with students. Then write: *Industrialization in the 1800s brought new farming methods and technology, so agriculture changed.* **Say:** *This sentence contains two ideas: industrialization brought new farming methods and agriculture changed.* **Ask:** *What word tells us that these two ideas are connected?*

Turn and Talk: *When reading a text, what are some examples of words that tell you two ideas are connected?*

Read and View Closely: Connect Ideas

Have students look at the chart. Point to the first row of the chart. **Ask:** *What word connects Idea #1 and Idea #2?* Model thinking through the answer. **Say:** *Corn was a strong and vertical plant, so the beans could curl up around the stalk. The connecting word so helps us understand how the ideas are connected.* Continue with the remaining sentences.

Differentiated Instruction
Build Language: Connect Two Ideas in a Sentence

Review the words **so, when,** and **that** from the chart. Read the sentence in the first row. **Say:** *I see the coordinating conjunction so. Coordinating conjunctions connect two clauses that can each stand alone as a sentence.* Read the second sentence. Point out that the two parts of the sentence could each be a whole sentence. Demonstrate by having two volunteers read the two parts, without the word so. Then read the last row and point out that this is not the case when you use the word that. Discuss that sometimes the two ideas that are connected are whole sentences, and sometimes they are not. Use the Differentiated Instruction to guide students in connecting two ideas in a sentence in a way that best matches the levels of your students.

Think-Speak-Listen: Use the following sentence frame or the Think-Speak-Listen Flip Book to guide discussion: *An author may combine two ideas in a sentence because _____.*

☑ Use Oral and Written Language: Persuade an Audience with an Advertisement

Task: *With your partner, imagine that you are selling hybrid corn seeds to farmers. Write an advertisement to persuade farmers that hybrid corn seeds are better. Use conjunctions and relative pronouns to make connections between your ideas.*

(S) *Hybrid corn seeds make healthy crops, _____.*

(M) *Hybrid corn became popular _____.*

(L) *Scientists have continued to develop new forms of hybrid _____.*

Wrap Up

Today we learned to connect related ideas in a sentence. How can using conjunctions and relative pronouns to connect ideas in a sentence help us when speaking and writing?

Turn and Talk: *Use conjunctions to tell your partner about the vegetables you see at the grocery store.*

👥 Differentiated Instruction
Build Language: Connect Two Ideas in a Sentence

Ⓢubstantial Support

Model: Write the sentence: *Most farmers use hybrid crops because they make better corn.* **Say:** *I see two ideas in this sentence: Most farmers use hybrid crops and hybrid crops make better corn. The word because tells me how the two ideas are connected. The fact that hybrid crops make better corn is the reason why most farmers use them.*

Practice: Distribute BLM 1. Complete the activity as a class.

Extend: Have students work in pairs and have them complete the activity in the BLM. Monitor students' work and help as needed.

Challenge: If students are ready, give them two ideas and ask them to connect them in one sentence.

Ⓜoderate Support

Model: Write the sentence: *Modern scientists mix the DNA of different corn plants, so the crops become healthier.* **Say:** *I see two ideas in this sentence:* Ask students to identify the two ideas. (*Modern scientists mix the DNA of different corn plants* and *the crops become healthier*). What word tells me how the two ideas are connected? (*Mixing the DNA of different corn plants makes the crops healthier*).

Practice: Distribute BLM 2. Complete the Practice activity as a class. Monitor students' work and help as needed.

Extend: Have students work in pairs to complete the Extend activity in the BLM.

Challenge: If students are ready, give them pairs of ideas and have them write sentences connecting them.

Ⓛight Support

Use the text on pp. 12-19 of *Texts for Close Reading* for the following activities.

Practice: Have students work in pairs and discuss the history of corn farming. **Ask:** *How have farmers and scientists improved corn plants over time?* Remind students to use conjunctions and relative pronouns to connect ideas.

Extend: Ask students to write 1–3 sentences about the advantages and risks of modern farming methods, using conjunctions and relative pronouns to connect their ideas. Have students share their sentences with the class.

Challenge: Have students form pairs. **Ask:** *Is it a good idea for farmers and scientists to develop more varieties of hybrid corn?* Direct one member of each student pair to argue that it is a good idea to develop more varieties of hybrid corn, and the other to argue that it is a bad idea to do so. Have pairs share their ideas with the class.

☑ Formative Assessment

Substantial Support	• With support, can students identify a connecting word and two ideas in a compound or complex sentence? • With support, can students use a conjunction to connect two related ideas?
Moderate Support	• With support, can students combine related ideas in compound and complex sentences? • With support, can students correctly use conjunctions or relative pronouns to connect ideas in a sentence?
Light Support	• Can students identify and explain relationships between ideas in sentences? • Can students select appropriate conjunctions or relative pronouns to combine ideas in a sentence? • Can students form compound and complex sentences to connect ideas?

Preview of Review Week 2 ELA Mini-Lessons

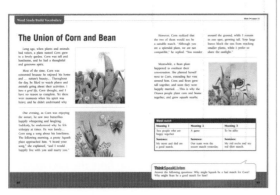

"The Union of Corn and Bean," pages 60–61

Student Objectives

LANGUAGE
Purpose:
- I can analyze a list of multiple meanings of a word.

Form:
- I can identify nouns, verbs, and adjectives.

CONTENT
- I can recognize the characteristics of a myth.

Additional Materials
- Unit Presentation
- *Texts for Close Reading* booklet
- Think-Speak-Listen Flip Book
- Student journal

Language Transfer Support

Note that Spanish does have any words that begin with an initial **s**-blend. Words that begin with an initial **s**-blend in English begin with an **e** in Spanish. Students whose first language is Spanish may therefore have trouble pronouncing words with initial **s**-blends, such as **spirit**.

10 Read "The Union of Corn and Bean"

Build Background and Vocabulary

Display the panels. If students have already read the story, ask them what they remember. Invite students to share their cultural experiences and knowledge on myths, especially any mythological stories they've read or characters they know.

Read Aloud the Text

Read aloud the text. To support comprehension, ask students to find images that match words in the text (plants, corn, garden) and ask questions, such as *How does corn feel?* Repeat with panels 2 and 3. After reading, model thinking through the Essential Question. **Ask:** *Why did Corn decide to marry Bean and not Squash?* Invite students to share their ideas using: *Corn decided to marry bean because _____.* **Ask:** *Did this story really happen?* Invite students to respond. **Say:** *Corn and Bean have human faces and they can talk. These details tell me that the text is fiction. We call this type of fiction a myth. Myths are often told to explain something that happens in nature.*

Think-Speak-Listen: Use the following sentence frame or the Think-Speak-Listen Flip Book to guide discussion: *Squash is a bad match because _____. Bean is a good match because _____.*

👥 Differentiated Instruction
Build Language: Use Multiple-Meaning Words

Display panel 3. Point out the word match. **Ask:** *What does* match *mean?* Elicit answers. **Say:** *Since Squash wants to marry Corn and live with him, I know that match must mean a couple. But match can mean to be alike. The word match is an example of a multiple-meaning word.* Use the Differentiated Instruction to practice using multiple-meaning words in a way that best matches the levels of your students.

✓ Use Oral and Written Language: Analyze a List of Multiple-Meanings of a Word

Task: *Work with a partner to make a list of different meanings for the word squash as a noun and a verb. Use a dictionary to help you. Then choose one meaning and write a sentence using the word squash with that meaning. Read the sentence aloud for your partner. Use context clues to guess the meaning of squash in each other's sentences.*

(S) *My mother always _____ the _____ in the oven.*

(M) *In Roman times, people _____ on grapes and _____ them to make wine.*

(L) *We are tired because we _____ two games of _____ today.*

🌀 Wrap Up

Today we learned to choose between multiple meanings of the same word. This knowledge helps us to understand what we read and to write more interesting texts.

Turn and Talk: *With a partner, discuss how would you use context clues in a sentence with the word match to figure out which meaning is being used.*

👤👤👤 Differentiated Instruction
Build Language: Use Multiple-Meaning Words

Ⓢubstantial Support

Model: Write the sentence: *Bean plant planted herself next to corn.* Underline **plant** and circle **planted**. **Ask:** Do *plant* and *planted* mean the same thing? Elicit answers. **Say:** *No, it's a multiple-meaning word. The word **plant** is a noun that refers to things that grow. The word **planted** is the past tense of the verb **to plant** which means to put in the ground to grow. The word **plant** can also mean a factory or a workshop.*

Practice: Distribute BLM 1. Read the Multiple-Meaning Word Chart and work with students to identify the correct meaning of the word **spot** in each sentence.

Extend: Have students work in pairs to complete the Extend activity on the BLM.

Challenge: If students are ready, help them to make new sentences with two different meanings of a multiple-meaning word.

Ⓜoderate Support

Model: Write the sentence: *Corn had a heavy spirit.* Underline **spirit** and **say:** *The word **spirit** is an example of a multiple-meaning word. In this sentence it means "mood" or "feelings." We know that Corn was sad. But spirit can also mean a part of a person that is not the body, a soul, or it can mean enthusiasm, such as team spirit.*

Practice: Distribute BLM 2. Work with students to identify the correct meaning of multiple-meaning words in context.

Extend: Have partners complete the Multiple-Meaning Word Chart on the BLM for the word **spot**.

Challenge: If students are ready, have them work in pairs to write sentences using more multiple-meaning words and showing their understanding of the different meanings.

Ⓛight Support

Use the text on p. 20 in the *Texts for Close Reading* booklet for the following activities.

Practice: Have students read paragraph 6. Ask students to identify two different meanings of the word **plant**.

Extend: Direct student pairs to use an online or print dictionary to find two additional meanings of the word **plant**. Have them write sentences showing the two meanings.

Challenge: If students are ready, write the words **spirit**, **heavy** and **squash** on the board. Put students in pairs and ask them to choose one word and create a Multiple-Meaning Word Chart. Demonstrate how to create a chart.

Word: spot		
Meaning 1: a small mark or bump (noun)	Meaning 2: a particular place (noun)	Meaning 3: to see or notice (verb)
Sentence: He had a red spot on his nose.	Sentence: This looks like a nice spot for a picnic.	Sentence: Did you spot her in the crowd? She was wearing a red hat.

☑ Formative Assessment

Substantial Support	• Can students understand the difference in the meanings of multiple-meaning words? • With support, can students use context clues to determine the meaning of multiple-meaning words?
Moderate Support	• Can students use context clues to determine the meaning of multiple-meaning words? • Can students use selected meanings of multiple-meaning words in the correct context?
Light Support	• Are students able to select a meaning of a multiple-meaning word in a dictionary that fits the context in which the word is used? • Can students generate sentences with different meanings of multiple-meaning words?

Preview or Review Week 3 ELA Mini-Lessons

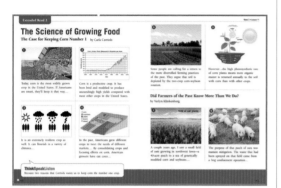

"The Science of Growing Food," pages 62–63

Student Objectives

LANGUAGE
Purpose:
- I can state and support an opinion with logical reasons.

Form:
- I can understand shifts in verb tense.

CONTENT
- I can analyze and choose a point of view.

Additional Materials
- Unit Presentation
- *Texts for Close Reading* booklet
- Think-Speak-Listen Flip Book
- Student journal

Metacognitive Prompt: Advance Organization

Before students begin reading, say: Today, we will use the strategy of advance organization. Before we read, we can preview the article to get an idea of the content and get a sense of how the article is organized. The author states an opinion in panel 1. This is the main idea of the article. The author then gives key details to support the opinion in panels 2, 3, and 4.

11 Read "The Science of Growing Food"

Build Background and Vocabulary

Display the panels. If students have already read the story, ask them what they remember. Invite students to share their cultural experiences and knowledge about growing corn.

Read Aloud the Text

Read the text in panel 1. To support comprehension, ask students to find images that match words in the text and ask **wh**- questions, such as *What is the author's opinion of corn grown in the United States? What does she want Americans to do?* Repeat with panels 2–4. After reading, model thinking through the Essential Question. **Ask:** *What is one reason that corn is the number one crop?* **Say:** *In panel 2, the text says people have changed corn so that the plants produce a lot.* Invite students to share their own ideas using: *I think corn is the number one crop because _____.* **Ask:** *How do you know this article is nonfiction?* Elicit responses. **Say:** *The text and images give facts about corn.*

Think-Speak-Listen: Use the following sentence frame or the Think-Speak-Listen Flip Book to guide discussion: *Corn grows _____. Corn has helped farmers _____.*

👥 Differentiated Instruction
Build Language: Understand Shifts in Verb Tense

Display panel 2. Have students identify the verbs in the first two sentences. **Ask:** *Which verbs are in the present? Which verbs are in the past?* Elicit answers. **Say:** *The author talks about growing corn in the past and present to give reasons why corn is important. The author uses shifts in verb tense to help readers know what time period she is talking about.* Use the Differentiated Instruction to practice shifts in verb tense in a way that best matches the levels of your students.

✓ Use Oral and Written Language: State and Support an Opinion with Logical Reasons

Task: *The author believes corn should stay as the number one crop in America. Do you agree or disagree? Write a sentence that states your opinion. Then write at least two logical reasons to support your opinion. Share your opinion and listen to others.*

(S) *I think that _____ because _____. I don't think that _____ because _____.*

(M) *I agree/disagree that _____. One reason is because _____.*

(L) *I believe that _____ as _____ because _____ and _____.*

↩ Wrap Up

Today we learned that an author shifts in verb tense can signal a shift in time. Why is it important to understand shifts in verb tense?

Turn and Talk: *Tell about what you do to get ready for school. Use shifts in verb tense to tell about things you do every day as well as things you have done in the past.*

👤👤👤 Differentiated Instruction
Build Language: Understand Shifts in Verb Tense

Ⓢubstantial Support

Model: Distribute BLM 1. Read the first sentence. Then model identifying verb tenses. **Say:** *In the first sentence, I see the word* Today, *so I know the sentence is about the present.*

Practice: Work with students to complete the Practice activity on BLM 1. Guide them to find the past tense verb. **Say:** *A verb with an* **-ed** *ending is past tense.* Point out that some verbs do not end in **-ed**, like **was** and **grew**. **Say:** *The first sentence is about the present. The second sentence is about something that happened in the past.*

Extend: Have partners complete the Extend activity on the BLM.

Challenge: If students are ready, have them form sentences with some of the verbs they identified. **Say:** *In panel 4, the verb in the first sentence is grew. This is the past tense of grow. The spelling is different in the past tense.*

Ⓜoderate Support

Model: Write these sentences based on the line graph in panel 2: *Corn is a productive crop. It has been modified to produce high yields.* Model identifying verb tenses. **Say:** *I see the present tense verb* is *in the first sentence. This tells me that corn is a productive crop now. In the second sentence, I see the verb* modified. *The ending* -ed *tells me that this verb is past tense.* **Ask:** *What do you notice about the verbs? They shift tenses.*

Practice: Work with students to identify verbs and verb phrases in panels 3 and 4. **Ask:** *Which verbs are in the present? Which verbs are in the past? Where do you see the verbs shift tense?*

Extend: Have partners use the text in panel 4 to answer the following question: *In addition to past tense verbs, how does the author let you know she is talking about the past?*

Challenge: If students are ready, have them analyze paragraph 5 on p. 24 in *Texts for Close Reading.* Have them determine the verbs' tenses and identify where the tenses shift.

Ⓛight Support

Use the text on pp. 22-29 in the *Texts for Close Reading* booklet for the following activities.

Practice: Have students read paragraph 5. Distribute BLM 2. Have students complete the chart by identifying the verbs and their tenses. **Ask:** *Why do the verbs shift from one tense to another in this paragraph?* Guide students in their responses.

Extend: Have partners complete the Extend activity on the BLM.

Challenge: Have students explain how they know when to use a present tense verb or a past tense verb.

☑ Formative Assessment

Substantial Support	• With support, can students identify present- and past tense verbs? • With support, can students identify shifts in verb tense in an informational text?
Moderate Support	• Can students recognize verbs and identify their tenses? • Can students understand when and why an author shifts verb tense?
Light Support	• Are students able to analyze the verbs in an informational text? • Can students understand how and why an author uses shifts in verb tense?

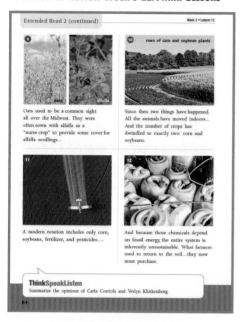

"The Science of Growing Food," page 64

Student Objectives

LANGUAGE
Purpose:
- I can express an opinion with reasons to persuade others.

Form:
- I can understand subject-verb agreement.

CONTENT
- I can compare opinions and understand both sides of a scientific argument.

Additional Materials
- Unit Presentation
- Subject-Verb Agreement Chart
- *Texts for Close Reading* booklet
- Think-Speak-Listen Flip Book
- Student journal

Metacognitive Prompt: Make Connections

Before you read the captions for the illustrations and images, say: Today we will use the strategy of making connections between two texts on the same subject. We will read more about one author's opinion about farmers planting mostly corn crops. Then we'll read a different opinion about the same subject. As you read, you can make connections between the texts to understand both texts better.

12 Compare Opinions

Engage Thinking

Display panel 5. **Say:** *Today, we will read more of "The Case for Keeping Corn Number 1." Ask: What do you remember about the first part of this article? What was the author's opinion?*

👥👥👥 Differentiated Instruction
Read and View Closely: Compare Opinions

Begin by reading panels 5 and 6 to finish the first article. **Ask:** *What does the author say in response to the argument that a corn-soybean rotation depletes the soil?* Then ask students to read the title of the second article. **Ask:** *How might the author's opinion differ from what the first author said about corn? Why do you think so?* Then read the second article panel by panel with students. **Ask:** *What is this author's opinion of the modern rotation of crops?* Help students compare the two articles. Use these sentence frames: *The first author believes that _____. The second author believes that _____.* Use the Differentiated Instruction to practice comparing opinions in a way that best matches the levels of your students.

Think-Speak-Listen: Use the following sentence frame or the Think-Speak-Listen Flip Book to guide discussion: *The opinion of Carla Carriola is _____ because _____. The opinion of Verlyn Klinkenberg is _____ because _____.*

Build Language: Understand Subject-Verb Agreement

Distribute and review the Subject-Verb Agreement Chart. **Say:** *In every sentence, the noun and verb must agree in number. A singular noun has a singular verb, and a plural noun has a plural verb.* Invite students to help you correct the following sentences: *Corn are the most widely grown crop in the United States. People argues that soil is depleted by the two-crop corn-soybean rotation. Oats was a common sight all over the Midwest.*

☑️ Use Oral and Written Language: Express an Opinion to Persuade Others

Task: *Now you have more information about corn as the major crop in the United States. Has your opinion changed? Write whether you think farmers should grow one crop, like corn or soybeans, or many different crops. Provide convincing reasons. Check your sentences for subject-verb agreement. Then try to persuade others in your group.*

(S) *Farmers _____ because _____.*

(M) *In the past, _____, but now _____.*

(L) *Corn _____ because _____ and _____.*

🔄 Wrap Up

Today we learned how to compare two texts on the same subject. How does comparing more than one opinion help us think more deeply about a topic?

Turn and Talk: *Suppose one student wants to have a new vending machine added to your school cafeteria. Another student does not think it's a good idea. Talk about how the two opinions compare and possible reasons the students might use to support their opinions.*

👤👤👤 Differentiated Instruction
Read and View Closely: Compare Opinions

Ⓢubstantial Support

Model: Distribute BLM 1. Then model identifying first author's opinion, using the text in panel 1. **Say:** *In panel 1, I see the author states a fact about corn in the first sentence. I'll write this information in the chart as the topic. The second sentence states a strong opinion, which I'll write next to the word opinion.*

Practice: Guide students to identify the topic and the author's opinion in the second article. **Say:** *The author tells a story about a small patch of oats she saw in a sea of corn and soybeans. I think her opinion is that corn and soybeans have pushed out crops like oats.* **Ask:** *Do you think a personal story is a strong way to state an opinion?*

Extend: Have partners complete the Extend activity on the BLM. **Ask:** *What information do both authors give to support their opinions about corn as the major crop?*

Challenge: If students are ready, ask them to look at the second sentence in panel 1. *Ask: Why is this sentence convincing?* Discuss that the phrase "if Americans are smart" is convincing because everyone wants to be smart.

Ⓜoderate Support

Model: Read the text in panels 1 and 7. Model how to compare opinions. **Say:** *In panel 1, I read the first author's opinion in the second sentence. I don't see a clearly stated opinion by the second author in panel 7, but I think that she doesn't approve of so much land used for genetically modified corn and soybeans. I think "small" and "sea" are clues.*

Practice: Distribute BLM 2. Work with students to fill in each author's opinion. **Ask:** *Do you think starting with a personal story is a convincing way to begin an opinion article? Why or why not?*

Extend: Have partners complete the chart with two reasons each author gives to support her opinion.

Challenge: Guide students to find additional support for the authors' opinions in their *Texts for Close Reading,* paragraph 5 on p. 24 and paragraph 19 on p. 29.

Ⓛight Support

Practice: Have pairs read the first page of each article of "The Science of Growing Food" in *Texts for Close Reading.* Direct them to focus on paragraph 1 and paragraph 13, and compare the opinions of the authors. **Ask:** *What are the authors' opinions about corn as the major crop? What words and phrases do they use to show how they feel?* Assist students in analyzing the text.

Extend: Have partners read pp. 24 and 29 and compare the authors' opinions on new versus old farming practices. Encourage them to write two to three reasons each author gives to support her opinion.

Challenge: Have partners discuss their own opinions about which article was the most convincing and why.

☑ Formative Assessment

Substantial Support	• With support, can students identify an author's opinion? • With support, can students understand how an author supports an opinion?
Moderate Support	• Can students summarize an author's opinion and supporting reasons? • Can students compare two different opinions on the same topic?
Light Support	• Can students identify the opinion of two authors on the same topic? • Can students understand how an author supports an opinion with logical reasons?

Preview or Review Week 3 ELA Mini-Lessons

Use Past and Present Verb Tenses		Week 3 • Lesson 13
Text	**Simple Past**	**Simple Present**
"The Past and Future of a Crop"	Before the emergence of civilizations, early humans hunted and gathered food.	Earth is a system in which energy from the sun constantly cycles living and nonliving matter through various processes.
"A Short History of a Special Plant"	In the late 1800s scientists developed hybrid corn. This corn mixed favorable genetic traits and led to healthier varieties of corn and higher, faster yields...	Fertilizing one variety of corn with pollen from another variety makes hybrids. Almost all corn in the United States grows from hybrid seeds.
"The Science of Growing Food"	A couple years ago, I saw a small field of oats growing in northwest Iowa—a 40-acre patch in a sea of genetically modified corn and soybeans. The purpose of that patch of oats was manure mitigation.	The entire system is inherently unsustainable.

ThinkSpeakListen
Summarize some things about corn that you have learned this week. Use simple present verbs and simple past verbs in your summary.

"Use Past and Present Verb Tenses," page 65

Student Objectives

LANGUAGE
Purpose:
• I can inform an audience in a speech.
Form:
• I can use past and present verb tenses.
CONTENT
• I can use verb tenses to describe past and present farming methods.

Additional Materials
• Unit Presentation
• *Texts for Close Reading* booklet
• Think-Speak-Listen Flip Book
• Student journal

Language Transfer Support

Note that speakers of Chinese, French, or Haitian Creole may need support to form the past tense correctly. These languages have different tense boundaries from English. (e.g., *He has left last week* instead of *He left last week.*)

13 Use Past and Present Verb Tenses

Engage Thinking

Display the panel 1. **Ask:** *When did these events take place?* Read the text with students. **Ask:** *What words tell you that the text describes actions in the past?* (used, improved) Repeat with panel 11 for events that take place in the present.

Read and View Closely: Use Verb Tenses

Have students look at the chart. Point to the first simple past sentence. **Ask:** *What are the verbs in this sentence? What do they tell us about time?* Model thinking through the answer. **Say:** *The verbs are* hunted *and* gathered. *The* -ed *ending tells me they are past tense. They happened in the past.* Then point to the first simple present sentence. **Ask:** *What do the verbs in this sentence tell us about time?* Help students answer using this sentence frame: *The verbs _____ and _____ are in the _____ tense.*

👥 Differentiated Instruction
Build Language: Use the Past and Present Verb Tenses

Point to the sentences in the second row. **Say:** *When you write, decide if an action takes place in the past or present. Add* -ed *to the end of most verbs to make them past tense like* developed *and* mixed. *Present tense verbs like* makes *and* grows *may have an* -s *added to agree with singular subjects.* **Ask:** *Which verbs in the sample sentences are irregular?* Elicit answers. **Say:** *The present tense form of* led *is* lead. Use the Differentiated Instruction to practice using past and present verb tenses in a way that best matches the levels of your students.

Think-Speak-Listen Use the following sentence frame or the Think-Speak-Listen Flip Book to guide discussion: *In the past, corn farmers _____. Today, corn _____.*

✅ Use Oral and Written Language: Inform an Audience in a Speech

Task: *This week you have learned information about corn. Imagine that you are presenting a speech to an audience. With a partner, write three sentences about the history of corn and three sentences about corn today. Be sure to use the correct verb tenses. Share your speech with the group.*

Ⓢ *Today, corn is a _____.*

Ⓜ *Almost all corn in the United States, _____.*

Ⓛ *In the past, Americans _____ to _____.*

🔄 Wrap Up

Today we learned that past and present verb tenses reveal a time period. Why is it important to use tenses correctly in our own writing?

Turn and Talk: *Use past and present verbs to tell a partner about your favorite science topic.*

👥👥👥 Differentiated Instruction
Build Language: Use the Past and Present Verb Tenses

Ⓢubstantial Support

Model: Display the chart and model identifying verb tenses. **Say:** *In the second row, I read the verbs developed and mixed. They both have an -ed ending, so I know they are in the past tense. I think the verb led is an irregular past tense verb. The present tense is lead.* Then read aloud the present tense sentences. Point out the verbs *makes* and *grows*. **Say:** *I know these verbs are in the present tense. They tell me about something that happens now.*

Practice: Distribute BLM 1. Work with students to complete the activity in the Practice section.

Extend: Have partners do the second activity. **Say:** *Look for clues in the sentence that help you decide if you need a past or present tense form of the verb to complete the sentence.*

Challenge: Read the question on the BLM, and model thinking through the answer: **Say:** *When I read the phrase "the first Native American farmers," I think it is a clue that the action happened in the past.*

Ⓜoderate Support

Model: Read aloud the past tense sentences in the second and third rows of the chart. **Say:** *The first verbs I see are developed and mixed. I know the ending -ed added to develop and mix make the past tense. I also see the verbs led, saw, and was. They are all irregular. I know the present tenses are lead, see, and is.* Continue with the present tense verbs. **Say:** *I know the verbs makes, grows, and is are present tense. I see that the verbs make and grow have an s added so they agree with the singular subject.*

Practice: Distribute BLM 2. Work with students to complete the Practice section. Check understanding and reteach as necessary.

Extend: Have pairs complete the Extend section of the BLM.

Challenge: Model thinking through the task on the BLM. **Say:** *The word now is a clue that the sentence talks about the present. The verb led is past tense. I think the verb should be present tense.*

Ⓛight Support

Use the text on pp. 22–29 in the *Texts for Close Reading* booklet to complete the following activities.

Practice: Review past and present tenses of regular and irregular verbs. Then have students read paragraph 19.. Have them identify and list the verbs in the first two sentences. Ask them to write the past tense forms. Then have them rewrite one of the sentences in past tense.

Extend: Assign partners paragraphs 7, 8, and 9. Have them use paragraph 7 to answer the question: *What happened in the past?* Have them use paragraphs 8 and 9 to answer the question: *What is happening now?*

Challenge: If students are ready, have them answer the question: *How does knowing how to use past and present verb tenses help you to understand the information authors use to support their opinions?* Guide students in their responses.

☑ Formative Assessment

Substantial Support	• With support, can students identify the past and present tense forms of regular and irregular verbs? • With support, can students choose the correct verb tense to complete a sentence in the past or present?
Moderate Support	• Can students identify the past and present tense forms of regular and irregular verbs? • Can students provide the correct tense of a verb to talk about the past or the present?
Light Support	• Can students generate the simple past tense form of common regular and irregular verbs? • Can students generate original sentences using the appropriate past or present form of verbs?

Preview or Review Week 3 ELA Mini-Lessons

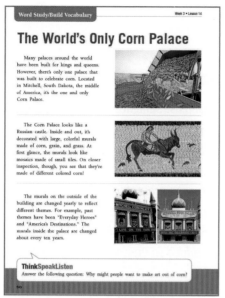

"The World's Only Corn Palace," page 66

Student Objectives

LANGUAGE
Purpose:
- I can use words related to art in an advertisement.

Form:
- I can use a variety of nouns to describe.

CONTENT
- I can analyze an informational science text related to buildings and art.

Additional Materials
- Unit Presentation
- *Texts for Close Reading* booklet
- Think-Speak-Listen Flip Book
- Student journal

Language Transfer Support

Note that speakers of Chinese, French, or Haitian Creole may need support to form the past tense correctly. These languages have different tense boundaries from English. (e.g., *He has left last week* instead of *He left last week.*)

14 Read "The World's Only Corn Palace"

Build Background and Vocabulary

Display the panels. Explain that they show place in North Dakota. Invite students to share their cultural experiences and knowledge on what they know about palaces and castles

Read Aloud the Text

Read panels 1–3. To support comprehension, ask students to find images that match words in the text (corn, Russian Castle, mural) and ask questions, such as *How much corn do you think would be needed to build a palace?* After reading, model thinking through the Essential Question. **Ask:** *Why has corn become a widely grown crop? Why do you think the Corn Palace was built?* **Say:** *I think the Corn Palace celebrates farming and a crop that supports the economy.* Invite students to share their ideas using: *Corn is _____, and South Dakota is _____.* Then refer to the Essential Question. **Ask:** *How do you know this text is nonfiction?* Elicit responses.

Think-Speak-Listen: Use the following sentence frame or the Think-Speak-Listen Flip Book to guide discussion: *Corn comes in _____. South Dakota has _____. Artists can use _____ to _____.*

👥 Differentiated Instruction
Build Language: Identify Words Related to Art

Display the panels. Point out the word ***murals***. **Ask:** *If you don't know what the word* mural *is, how can you determine its meaning?* Elicit answers. Help students identify the words related to *mural* in the sentence, such as large and colorful. **Say:** *A mural is a very large picture on a wall. A text may define topic-related words or give context clues, and you can use illustrations, photographs too. You can also use a dictionary.* Use the Differentiated Instruction to practice identifying words related to art in a way that best matches the levels of your students.

☑ Use Oral and Written Language: Use Words Related to Art in an Advertisement

Task: *With your group, list words related to art and buildings. Look up unfamiliar words. Then create an advertisement to encourage people interested in art to visit the Corn Palace. Use the photos in the text as inspiration. Write a headline and two to three sentences about the Corn Palace. Share your advertisement with the class.*

Ⓢ　*Murals are made of _____.*

Ⓜ　*You will be amazed that mosaics can be _____.*

Ⓛ　*Outside murals are _____, so there is always _____.*

🔄 Wrap Up

Today we learned that nonfiction texts often include specific words related to the topic. Why is identifying and learning these words important to for understanding a topic.

Turn and Talk: *Share specific words you learned in a nonfiction text you recently read.*

👥👥 Differentiated Instruction
Build Language: Identify Words Related to Art

Ⓢubstantial Support

Model: Display panel 2 and read aloud the text. **Say:** *We discussed that murals are large pictures on walls. Usually people use paint to make a mural, but this mural is made of corn, grain, and grass.* Discuss the line that says the murals look like mosaics. Point out the phrase that tells them what a mosaic is (made of small tiles). Explain that to make a mosaic, an artist glues the tiles to a wall.

Practice: Have students help you list some nouns that are things artists make, verbs describing what artists do, and adjectives describing art. Then distribute BLM 1. Work with students to complete the activity in the Practice section.

Extend: Have partners complete the activity in the Extend section of the BLM. **Say:** *Look for a verb that is related to art. Then find an adjective that could be used to describe art.*

Challenge: If students are ready, have them compare the murals in the corn palace to mosaics, using these sentence frames:

(The murals in the corn palace) are made of _____.

(Mosaics) are made of _____.

Ⓜoderate Support

Model: Display the panels. Say: In panel 2, I see the word *murals.* I know this is a word related to art. Ask students to recall what you discussed about murals. **Ask:** *What decorates the walls of the Corn Palace? (murals).* Discuss that murals are usually made by painting. Ask students to find the phrase in the text that tells what these murals are made of. Then discuss mosaics. **Ask:** *What phrase tell you what a mosaic is? (made of small tiles.)*

Practice: Distribute BLM 2. Work with students to complete the Practice section. Ask questions to help students identify words related to art: *What decorates the Corn Palace? What do the murals look like?*

Extend: Have partners complete the Extend section in the BLM.

Challenge: If students are ready, model finding another word related to art in paragraph 5 on page 30 of *Texts for Close Reading*, such as **sketches**. Ask them to describe what they learned from the paragraph.

Ⓛight Support

Have students use the text on p. 30 of the *Texts for Close Reading* for the following activities.

Practice: Demonstrate how to draw a word web. Tell students they will use it to collect words related to art. Write **Art** in the center oval and draw five ovals with lines connecting them to the **Art** oval. Assign each pair paragraphs 1, 2, or 3. Have pairs find art-related words in their paragraph to add them to their word webs for example, *mural, mosaic, sketch*. Ask pairs to share their answers with the class.

Extend: Ask pairs add to their word webs by adding other forms of art they know, and branches to each oval for nouns, verbs, and adjectives related to the art forms.

Challenge: Have students write paragraphs comparing two of the art forms described in the web.

✓ Formative Assessment

Substantial Support	• With support, can students identify words related to art from the text? • With support, can students use words related to art?
Moderate Support	• Can students identify words related to art from the text? • Can students use context and photographs to understand words related to art?
Light Support	• Can students identify words related to art from the text and determine meaning from context and photographs? • Can students independently to analyze words related to art?

Preview or Review Week 3 ELA Mini-Lessons

"Use Adverbs to Describe Verbs and Adjectives," page 67

Student Objectives

LANGUAGE
Purpose:
• I can ask and answer questions about corn.
Form:
• I can identify and use adverbs to describe verbs and adjectives.
CONTENT
• I can use adverbs in sentences about corn.

Additional Materials
• Unit Presentation
• *Texts for Close Reading* booklet
• Think-Speak-Listen Flip Book
• Student journal

Language Transfer Support

Note that speakers of Chinese, French, or Haitian Creole may need support to form the past tense correctly. These languages have different tense boundaries from English. (e.g., *He has left last week* instead of *He left last week*.)

15 Use Adverbs to Describe Verbs and Adjectives

Engage Thinking

Display the panels from "The Past and Future of a Crop" and "The Science of Growing Food." Ask students to tell you what they found most interesting in the selections. Have students share their cultural knowledge and experience about corn.

Read and View Closely: Identify Adverbs

Display the charts. Read aloud the first sentence and point out the word *constantly*. **Say:** *The verb in this sentence is* cycles. *It tells us that the energy of the sun cycles matter through different processes. The word constantly is an adverb that describes the verb cycles. The sun cycles matter constantly, or all the time. Many adverbs answer the question* How? *and end in* -ly. **Say:** *Adverbs can also describe, or give more information about, adjectives.* Continue with the remaining example sentences on the chart.

👥 Differentiated Instruction

Build Language: Use Adverbs to Describe Verbs and Adjectives

Review with students the adverbs they identified in the charts. **Say:** *When you write, you can use adverbs to give precise details about an action or something you describe.* Have students reread the sentences in the charts without the adverbs. **Ask:** *What information is missing?* Elicit answers. **Say:** *Now let's substitute a different adverb in each sentence. Let's use* occasionally *to modify the verb cycles and* moderately *to modify the adjective high. How is the meaning of each sentence changed?* Use the Differentiated Instruction to practice using adverbs in a way that best matches the levels of your students.

Think-Speak-Listen Use the following sentence frame or the Think-Speak-Listen Flip Book to guide discussion: *The adverb _____ modifies _____. The adverb tells _____.*

☑ Use Oral and Written Language: Ask and Answer Questions About Corn

Task: *With a partner, write questions based on what you've learned about corn as a natural resource in Unit 3. Take turns asking and answering questions with another pair. Record their answers in complete sentences and circle the adverbs they use.*

Ⓢ *How important is corn? Corn is _____ important.*

Ⓜ *How important is corn as a crop in the United States? Corn is the most _____.*

Ⓛ *How high are corn yields compared to other crops grown today? Corn yields are _____ and _____.*

↩ Wrap Up

Today we learned that adverbs can be used to describe verbs and adjectives. How do adverbs give more information and exact details about an action or a description?

Turn and Talk: *Use adverbs to describe all the different ways you can think of to walk through a cornfield. Then use adverbs to help describe what you see as you walk.*

👥 Differentiated Instruction
Build Language: Use Adverbs to Describe Verbs and Adjectives

Ⓢ ubstantial Support

Model: Briefly review nouns, verbs, and adjectives. **Say:** *Adverbs can tell more about adjectives and verbs.* Display the charts and model identifying adverbs. **Say:** *In the second sentence, I see the verb gathered. This verb tells me that people gathered or got whatever plants were growing and used them for food. I see the adverb simply in front of the verb. It tells me they only gathered food.* Use the last sentence in the second box to model identifying an adverb that modifies an adjective.

Practice: Distribute BLM 1. Guide students to help you identify the adverbs and the words they modify.

Extend: Have partners do the Extend activity. **Say:** *Read each sentence aloud with your choice. Check that it makes sense in the sentence.*

Challenge: Work with students to replace an adverb in one of the sentences with a different adverb. Explain how the new adverb changes the sentence.

Ⓜ oderate Support

Model: Read aloud the second sentence in the top box and the first sentence in the bottom box. Point out the adverbs. Model identifying how they are used. **Say:** *The adverb simply modifies the verb gathered. It tells me that people only found plants they could eat. The adverb astoundingly modifies the adjective high. It emphasizes how large the corn crops are. Without the adverb, I wouldn't understand how big the corn crop is compared with other crops.*

Practice: Distribute BLM 2. Work with students to complete the Practice activity. Check understanding and reteach as necessary.

Extend: Have partners complete the Extend activity. Encourage them to read their sentences to check that their choice makes sense.

Challenge: Have student replace different adverbs in some of the sentences on the BLM and describe how the change affects the sentences.

Ⓛ ight Support

Practice: Review how adverbs are used to describe verbs and adjectives. Ask partners to read paragraphs 19 and 20 on p. 29 in *Texts for Close Reading*. Have them identify and list adverbs and discuss how they are used. Provide support where needed.

Extend: Have partners read aloud paragraphs 19 and 20 on p. 29, eliminating the adverbs. **Ask:** *How does the meaning change? Is the author's point of view as strongly stated? Why or why not? How does using adverbs affect a persuasive text?*

Challenge: Have partners select two or three sentences from paragraph 20 on page 29 and add adverbs of their own to modify verbs or adjectives to strengthen the author's viewpoint. **Ask:** *How does the addition of strong adverbs make the author's opinion more convincing?*

☑️ Formative Assessment

Substantial Support	• With support, can students identify adverbs and the words they modify? • Can students understand the purpose of adverbs?
Moderate Support	• Can students identify adverbs and the verbs or adjectives they modify? • Can students add or substitute adverbs and explain changes in meaning?
Light Support	• Can students use adverb to modify verbs and adjectives? • Do students understand how the use of adverbs can add details to and elaborate on an author's viewpoint?

Recognizing Author's Point of View

Essential Question

How can other perspectives help us evaluate the world?

In this unit, students read and compare the different perspectives in selections to analyze point of view.

Unit 4

👥 Differentiated Instruction
Build Language: Identify Words Related to Art

Ⓢubstantial Support

Model: Display panel 2 and read aloud the text. **Say:** *We discussed that murals are large pictures on walls. Usually people use paint to make a mural, but this mural is made of corn, grain, and grass.* Discuss the line that says the murals look like mosaics. Point out the phrase that tells them what a mosaic is (made of small tiles). Explain that to make a mosaic, an artist glues the tiles to a wall.

Practice: Have students help you list some nouns that are things artists make, verbs describing what artists do, and adjectives describing art. Then distribute BLM 1. Work with students to complete the activity in the Practice section.

Extend: Have partners complete the activity in the Extend section of the BLM. **Say:** *Look for a verb that is related to art. Then find an adjective that could be used to describe art.*

Challenge: If students are ready, have them compare the murals in the corn palace to mosaics, using these sentence frames:

(The murals in the corn palace) are made of _____.

(Mosaics) are made of _____.

Ⓜoderate Support

Model: Display the panels. Say: In panel 2, I see the word *murals.* I know this is a word related to art. Ask students to recall what you discussed about murals. **Ask:** *What decorates the walls of the Corn Palace? (murals).* Discuss that murals are usually made by painting. Ask students to find the phrase in the text that tells what these murals are made of. Then discuss mosaics. **Ask:** *What phrase tell you what a mosaic is? (made of small tiles.)*

Practice: Distribute BLM 2. Work with students to complete the Practice section. Ask questions to help students identify words related to art: *What decorates the Corn Palace? What do the murals look like?*

Extend: Have partners complete the Extend section in the BLM.

Challenge: If students are ready, model finding another word related to art in paragraph 5 on page 30 of *Texts for Close Reading,* such as **sketches**. Ask them to describe what they learned from the paragraph.

Ⓛight Support

Have students use the text on p. 30 of the *Texts for Close Reading* for the following activities.

Practice: Demonstrate how to draw a word web. Tell students they will use it to collect words related to art. Write *Art* in the center oval and draw five ovals with lines connecting them to the *Art* oval. Assign each pair paragraphs 1, 2, or 3. Have pairs find art-related words in their paragraph to add them to their word webs for example, *mural, mosaic, sketch.* Ask pairs to share their answers with the class.

Extend: Ask pairs add to their word webs by adding other forms of art they know, and branches to each oval for nouns, verbs, and adjectives related to the art forms.

Challenge: Have students write paragraphs comparing two of the art forms described in the web.

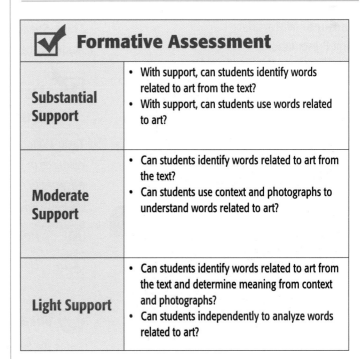

✓ Formative Assessment	
Substantial Support	• With support, can students identify words related to art from the text? • With support, can students use words related to art?
Moderate Support	• Can students identify words related to art from the text? • Can students use context and photographs to understand words related to art?
Light Support	• Can students identify words related to art from the text and determine meaning from context and photographs? • Can students independently to analyze words related to art?

Preview or Review Week 3 ELA Mini-Lessons

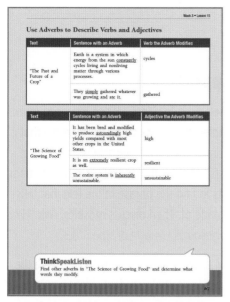

"Use Adverbs to Describe Verbs and Adjectives," page 67

Student Objectives

LANGUAGE

Purpose:
- I can ask and answer questions about corn.

Form:
- I can identify and use adverbs to describe verbs and adjectives.

CONTENT
- I can use adverbs in sentences about corn.

Additional Materials
- Unit Presentation
- *Texts for Close Reading* booklet
- Think-Speak-Listen Flip Book
- Student journal

Language Transfer Support

Note that speakers of Chinese, French, or Haitian Creole may need support to form the past tense correctly. These languages have different tense boundaries from English. (e.g., *He has left last week* instead of *He left last week*.)

15 Use Adverbs to Describe Verbs and Adjectives

Engage Thinking

Display the panels from "The Past and Future of a Crop" and "The Science of Growing Food." Ask students to tell you what they found most interesting in the selections. Have students share their cultural knowledge and experience about corn.

Read and View Closely: Identify Adverbs

Display the charts. Read aloud the first sentence and point out the word *constantly*. **Say:** *The verb in this sentence is* cycles. *It tells us that the energy of the sun cycles matter through different processes. The word constantly is an adverb that describes the verb cycles. The sun cycles matter constantly, or all the time. Many adverbs answer the question* How? *and end in* -ly. **Say:** *Adverbs can also describe, or give more information about, adjectives.* Continue with the remaining example sentences on the chart.

👥 Differentiated Instruction
Build Language: Use Adverbs to Describe Verbs and Adjectives

Review with students the adverbs they identified in the charts. **Say:** *When you write, you can use adverbs to give precise details about an action or something you describe.* Have students reread the sentences in the charts without the adverbs. **Ask:** *What information is missing?* Elicit answers. **Say:** *Now let's substitute a different adverb in each sentence. Let's use* occasionally *to modify the verb cycles and* moderately *to modify the adjective high. How is the meaning of each sentence changed?* Use the Differentiated Instruction to practice using adverbs in a way that best matches the levels of your students.

Think-Speak-Listen Use the following sentence frame or the Think-Speak-Listen Flip Book to guide discussion: *The adverb _____ modifies _____. The adverb tells _____.*

☑ Use Oral and Written Language: Ask and Answer Questions About Corn

Task: *With a partner, write questions based on what you've learned about corn as a natural resource in Unit 3. Take turns asking and answering questions with another pair. Record their answers in complete sentences and circle the adverbs they use.*

(S) *How important is corn? Corn is _____ important.*

(M) *How important is corn as a crop in the United States? Corn is the most _____.*

(L) *How high are corn yields compared to other crops grown today? Corn yields are _____ and _____.*

Wrap Up

Today we learned that adverbs can be used to describe verbs and adjectives. How do adverbs give more information and exact details about an action or a description?

Turn and Talk: *Use adverbs to describe all the different ways you can think of to walk through a cornfield. Then use adverbs to help describe what you see as you walk.*

Unit 4 Lessons at a Glance

Language Skills

Week 1
- Use Present Participles
- Use Adverbials to Describe Time
- Opinion Writing to Sources
- Use Prepositions to Describe Location
- Identify Multiple-Meaning Words

Week 2
- Understand the Language of Comparison
- Use Question Words
- Recognize Differences in Verb Tenses
- Use Conjunctions to Connect Ideas
- Analyze Homographs

Week 3
- Form and Use Irregular Verbs
- Understand Phrasal Verbs
- Understand Pronoun-Antecedent Agreement
- Use Modal Auxiliaries
- Explore Multiple-Meaning Words

Lessons

Essential Question

Preview or Review Week 1 ELA Mini-Lessons

"Essential Question," pages 68–69

Student Objectives

LANGUAGE
Purpose:
• I can understand the Essential Question.
CONTENT
• I can understand the topic of the unit.

Additional Materials
• Unit Presentation

Introduce Unit 4: Recognizing Author's Point of View

Use the short lesson below to introduce the topic of the unit and help students understand the Essential Question.

Build Background and Vocabulary

Say: *The topic of this unit is "Recognizing Author's Point of View." Point of view is who is telling the story.*

Create a 2-column chart.

Say: *First person accounts are eye witness accounts. The narrator is part of the story. A diary is an example of a first person account.*

Elicit other examples.

Say: *Third person accounts are written by a narrator outside the story. A newspaper story is an example of a third person account.*

Elicit responses of other examples.

Say: *A fiction story may be written in either 1st person or 3rd person. This is up to the author.*

First Person Accounts	Third Person Accounts
pronouns: I, me, we	pronouns: they, he, she
diaries	newspapers
speeches	magazines
autobiographies	narrator outside text
narrator inside text	

👥👥👥 Differentiated Instruction
Explain the Essential Question

Display the panels.

Say: *These pictures and ideas introduce what we will read about.*

Read aloud the Essential Question: *How can other perspectives help us evaluate the world?* Review key words by definition and examples: **point of view, perspectives, evaluate**. Review the 2-column chart. Encourage students to use examples, for instance diaries, newspapers, novels, and how reading a wide variety of literature adds to our perspectives and helps us evaluate the world.

Use the Differentiated Instruction to help students at all levels understand the Essential Question.

Then proceed to Lesson 1.

👤👤👤 Differentiated Instruction
Explain the Essential Question

Substantial Support

Write: *She/he teaches school.* Say each sentence and have student repeat. Explain that a narrator is in the story (I), or outside the story (**they, he, she**).

Point to the first picture, and explain that they are searching for gold.

Ask: *If the man wrote a diary about searching for gold, what would he write?*

Help students respond.

Ask: *If a reporter wrote about the man searching for gold, how would he write this?*

Help students respond.

Say: *In this unit, we will learn about different points of view of the same topic.*

Moderate Support

Write: *I teach school. [Teacher name] teaches school. She/he teaches school.* Say each sentence and have student repeat.

Say: In the first sentence, who is speaking?

Point out that **I** is used when a character in a story is telling the story, and **he, she, they** are used if a narrator outside the story is telling it. Point to the picture, and explain that they are searching for gold.

Ask: *If the man wrote a diary about searching for gold, what would he write?* Help students respond using this frame:

Today, at the river _____ searched for gold.

Ask: *If a reporter wrote about the man searching for gold, how would he write this?* Help students respond, using the frame:

Today at the river, _____ searched for gold.

Say: *In this unit, we will learn how different points of view of the same story alters the reader's perspective.*

Light Support

Write **I, we , he, she, they**. Remind students that when we see **I** or **we**, one of the characters is telling the story. If we see **he, she, they**, it means a narrator outside the story is telling the story. Point to the picture, and explain that they are searching for gold.

Ask: *If the man wrote a diary about searching for gold, what would he write?* Have students respond using this answer frame:

Today, at the river _____ searched for gold.

Ask: *If a reporter wrote about the man searching for gold, how would he write this?* Have students respond, using the frame:

Today at the river, _____ searched for gold.

Point to the photos on, and have students create sentences about the photos. **Say:** *In this unit, we learn how different points of view of the same topic alter the reader's perspective. Why is this important to the reader?*

☑️ Formative Assessment

Substantial Support	• Can students, with help, show understanding of point of view?
Moderate Support	• Can students show understanding of point of view? • Can students, with support, give examples of points of view?
Light Support	• Do students clearly show understanding of different points of view? • Can students use pronouns to change the point of view of a sentence?

Preview or Review Week 1 ELA Mini-Lessons

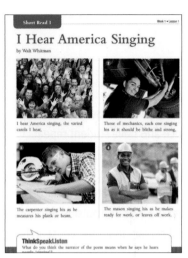

"I Hear America Singing," page 70

Student Objectives

LANGUAGE
Purpose:
• I can explain present participles.
Form:
• I can describe present participles.
CONTENT
• I can use present participles in my writing.

Additional Materials
• Unit Presentation
• *Texts for Close Reading* booklet
• Think-Speak-Listen Flip Book
• Student journal

Language Transfer Support

In some other languages, including Spanish, an infinitive is used in place of a present participle as the complement of a sensory perception verb. For this reason, some Spanish speakers may default to the infinitive form in English and may need additional support to use the present participle in this construction.

1 Read "I Hear America Singing"

Building Background and Vocabulary

Display the panels and explain the importance of the poem. If students have already read the poem, ask them to share what they remember. Ask students to briefly share their experiences with singing individually or in groups with other people.

Read Aloud the Text

Have students read the text. Explain to students that the word *singing* is an example of a present participle. **Say:** Singing *tell us what the people are doing. When you see a word in a sentence that ends in* ing *and it is used to describe what someone is doing, it is a present participle.* America singing, *each one* singing, *carpenter* singing *are examples of* singing *being used as a present participle.* **Ask:** *What are some additional present participles in the poem?*

Think-Speak-Listen: Use the following sentence frame or the Think-Speak-Listen Flip Book to guide discussion: *I think the narrator of the poem means _____ when he says he hears people "singing. .*

Differentiated Instruction
Build Language: Use Present Participles

Say: *Present participles are often used as either adjectives or verbs. They help to express what we see, hear and feel. The verb* sing *becomes a present participle when* ing *is added to make* singing.

Use the Differentiated Instruction to practice using present participles in a way that best matches the level of your students.

☑ Use Oral and Written Language Expression: Describe

Task: *Take turns with a partner. Imagine that you are continuing the text. Create sentences that use* singing *as a present participle.*

ⓢ   *The students love _____.*

Ⓜ   *While getting ready for work, the doctor's _____ awakens her dog.*

Ⓛ   *The _____ bus driver loves his job. His passengers rarely join him in _____ even though he encourages them to participate.*

↺ Wrap Up

We use present participles in our everyday language. How do we form present participles?

Turn and Talk: *Think of a song that represents you. Your song can be a traditional song or a popular song. It could be a song in English or a song in your home language. Share a few of the lyrics with your partner.*

👥 Differentiated Instruction
Build Language: Use Present Participles

Ⓢubstantial Support

Model: Explain that present participles are often used as either adjectives or verbs to describe what people are doing. Work with students to identify present participles that they use when talking to others. Discuss examples of present participles in "I Hear America Singing." Then model how present participles are used. **Say**: *He was playing. We were singing.*

Practice: Distribute BLM 1. Work with students to complete the practice activity on the BLM.

Extend: Have students work in pairs to complete the Extend section of the BLM.

Challenge: If students are ready, ask them to help you list some common actions, such as *singing, dancing, writing,* etc.

Ⓜoderate Support

Model: Explain that present participles are often used as either adjectives or verbs to describe what people are doing. Work with students to identify present participles that they use when talking to others. Have them help you generate a list of some common words: *dancing, running,* etc. Then model how present participles are used in standard English. **Say:** *They were wandering about the store. Running water helped the villagers build the new structure.*

Practice: Distribute BLM 2. Work with students to complete the Practice section.

Extend: Have students work with partners to complete the Extend section of the BLM.

Challenge: If students are ready, have them write sentences using the present participles with the frame *I see/hear someone _____.*

Ⓛight Support

Model: Explain that present participles are a part of our everyday language. Review additional lines in the poem that use present participles besides the ones in the panel.

Practice: Have students create charts. In one column, they list present participles of other verbs they know (*dancing, running,* etc). In a second column, they write the present tense of each verb.

Extend: Have students create a third column that has the past tense of the verb to see how simply changing the ending of a word changes its meaning in a sentence.

Challenge: Have students write sentences using some of the words they listed.

☑ Formative Assessment

Substantial Support	• Can students recognize present participles?
Moderate Support	• Can students complete sentence starters using present participles? Can students identify sensory verbs that require present participles?
Light Support	• Can students generate original sentences in which they use present participles?

Preview or Review Week 1 ELA Mini-Lessons

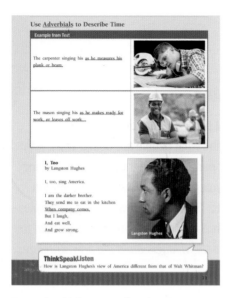

"Use Adverbials to Describe Time," page 71

Student Objectives

LANGUAGE
Purpose:
• I can define adverbs.
Form:
• I can use adverbials to describe time.
CONTENT
• I can use adverbs in my writing.

Additional Materials
• Unit Presentation
• *Texts for Close Reading* booklet
• Think-Speak-Listen Flip Book
• Student journal

Language Transfer Support

Note that speakers of Hmong, Chinese, or Korean may need additional support in the use of adverbs and adverbial phrases. Adverbs are not used in Hmong; instead, two adjectives or two verbs may be used in place of an adverb. (Example: *I walk fast fast* for *I walk very fast.*) In Chinese and Korean, adverbs and adverbial phrases may precede verbs, while in English they typically follow verbs.

---

2 Use Adverbials to Describe Time

Engage Thinking

Say: *Look at the underlined words in the first panel. What do these words tell the audience? What do those words help the reader or listener of the poem to understand about the speaker in the poem?*

Read and View Closely: Recognize Adverbials

Read aloud all of the lines in the third panel. Then read just the underlined words "When company comes." **Say:** *This group of words work together to create an adverbial that describes time. They tell the reader or listener more information about the speaker in the poem. He leaves when others enter the kitchen.*

Think-Speak-Listen: Use the following sentence frame or the Think-Speak-Listen Flip Book to guide discussion: *Langston Hughes's view of America was different from that of Walt Witman because _____.*

👥 Differentiated Instruction
Build Language: Use Adverbials to Describe Time

Read panels 1 through 3. Explain that in each of these panels the subject (person) is doing something (verb). It is important to note not only who is doing something, but when. **Ask:** *Without the adverbial, what would be unknown to the reader/listener?* Elicit answers. **Say:** *The adverbial describes the time when something is happening.* **Say:** *Let's read panel 3 without the adverbial. If we take out "When company comes" what information is missing?* **Say:** *We would have no idea why the speaker is leaving. This line in the poem describes time and helps us to understand the speaker's actions.*

Use the Differentiated Instruction to practice using adverbials to describe time in a way that best matches the level of your students.

☑ Oral and Written Language Expression: Use Adverbials to Describe Time

Task: *Many people sing when they are doing things. Write a 4 line stanza where you describe when you sing. Be sure to use at least 2 adverbials in the stanza.*

S *I love singing when _____.*

M *I love singing when _____ and as I _____.*

L *I'm always singing when _____, and I'm _____ as I _____.*

Wrap Up

Today we learned that adverbials help to describe time. Why is it important for writers to use adverbials?

Turn and Talk: *Use adverbials to describe how you get ready to go to school each morning.*

👤👤👤 Differentiated Instruction
Build Language: Use Adverbials to Describe Time

Ⓢubstantial Support

Model: Read aloud the example sentence in the second box in the chart, **Say:** *The words "as he makes ready for work, or leaves off work" help us understand when the mason sings. He sings his song on two different occasions. He sings when he gets read for work and when he leaves.* Discuss that *makes ready* is another way of saying *gets ready*, "which is the phrase we would usually use. Point out that the words *as* and *when* mean at the same time.

Practice: Distribute BLM 1. Work with students to complete the activity in the Practice section.

Extend: Have students work in pairs to complete the activity in the Extend section of the BLM.

Challenge: If the students are ready, model finding additional adverbials that describe time in "I, Too." Use the line "I'll be at the table."

Ⓜoderate Support

Model: Read aloud the first two sentences and point out the underlined words. **Say:** *In both of these sentences, the word as introduces an adverbial that tells when the subject sings. When does the carpenter sing? (as he measures his plank or beam) When does the mason sing? (as he gets ready to go to work or to go home from work)*

Practice: Then read the lines from the Langston Hughes poem and point out the underlined words. **Say:** *This is also an adverbial that tells when something happens. When do they send the speaker to eat in the kitchen? (when company comes.)* Point out that the words as and when both start adverbials that tell us when something happens. Distribute BLM 2 and work with students to complete the Practice activity.

Extend: Have students work in pairs to complete the activity in the Extend section of the BLM.

Challenge: Ask students to answer each question using an adverbial with as or when. Provide the sentences frames in parentheses if necessary.
When do you like to sing? (I like to sing when _____.)
What do you do when you watch TV? (I _____ when I watch TV.)

Ⓛight Support

Practice: Ask students to read the first two sentences and figure out what they have in common. **Ask:** *What word do both sentences use to introduce an adverbial that tells when something happens?* (as) *When does the carpenter sing?* (as he measures his plank or beam) *When does the mason sing?* (as he makes ready for work, or leaves off work) Then have students read the lines from the Langston Hughes poem in Box 3. Point out the highlighted words and ask what word introduces the adverbial (when).

Extend: Ask: *When does the speaker get sent to eat in the kitchen?* (when company comes)

Challenge: Have partners ask and answer questions about when they do certain things. They should answer each question using an adverbial with *as* or *when*.

☑ Formative Assessment

Substantial Support	• Are students able to recognize adverbials that describe time?
Moderate Support	• Can students answer questions using an adverbial?
Light Support	• Can students ask questions and answer them with original sentences in which they use adverbials to describe time?

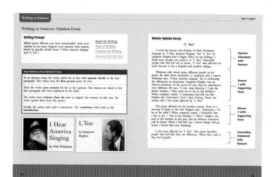

"Writing to Sources," pages 72–73

Student Objectives

LANGUAGE
Purpose:
• I can analyze an opinion essay.
Form:
• I can identify the important parts of an opinion essay.
CONTENT
• I can recognize an opinion essay.

Additional Materials
• Unit Presentation
• *Texts for Close Reading* booklet
• Think-Speak-Listen Flip Book
• Student journal

3 Writing to Sources: Opinion Essay

Engage Thinking

Tell students that they will analyze an opinion essay so that they can identify the important parts. Read aloud the prompt.

> Which poem affected you more emotionally? State your opinion in an essay.
> Support your opinion with reasons based on specific details from "I Hear America Singing" and "I, Too."

Say: *Let's ask questions to make sure we understand the prompt. What will the writer write about? What type of writing is it? Where will the writer get some of his evidence?*

Differentiated Instruction
Read and View Closely: Analyze an Opinion Essay

Say: *As I read aloud the essay, I will stop so that we can analyze it. In the first paragraph, the writer states his opinion about the two poems. As I read, look for the opinions.* Read the paragraph and pause. **Say:** *Turn to a partner. What is the writer's opinion of each poem? Which does the write like best?* Check that students can identify the opinion.

Say: *In the first paragraph, the writer gives two reasons to support the opinion. Turn to a partner. Tell which are the reasons.* Check that students can identify the two reasons. For example, *more inclusive* and *more hopeful and uplifting ending.*

Say: *The writer uses evidence from the text to support his opinions. In this case, it's a quote from the poem. As I read the second paragraph, listen for the evidence.* Read the second paragraph. **Say:** *Turn to your partner. What evidence does the writer include?* Check that students can identify the supporting quote. **Say:** *Turn to your partner. How does the writer explain this quote supports his opinion?* Have pairs discuss and then check that they can identify the reason that the evidence supports.

Continue in this way with all the other paragraphs to identify the opinions and supporting evidence. **Ask:** *How does the writer's conclusion relate to the introduction?* Check that students can identify the two restated reasons the writer gives.

Then continue the lesson using Differentiated Instruction that best fits the needs of your students.

Share Your Understanding

Bring the students back together. **Ask:** *What did we learn today about opinion texts?* Review the structure as needed.

☑ Final Writing Assignment

Use the English Language Development Assessment to assess students' writing for their ELA writing assignment.

👥👥 Differentiated Instruction
Read and View Closely: Analyze an Opinion Essay

Ⓢubstantial Support

Model: Distribute BLM 1. **Say:** *Let's read and analyze another opinion essay that answers the prompt.* Read the first paragraph and pause. **Ask:** *Which poem does the writer like better?* Model answering the question.

Practice: Continue reading the essay and ask the same questions that you asked about the mentor text. Invite students to answer.

Extend: Have students in pairs complete the activity on the BLM.

Challenge: Write on the board: *Inclusive means something that includes, or takes in, all people. Which poem does the writer think is inclusive? Which words show that it is a reason?* In pairs, students discuss the questions and answer in complete sentences.

Ⓛight Support

Practice: Distribute BLM 2. **Say:** *This is the Opinion Mentor Text that you read in class on Day 2. We will look more closely at how writers express their opinions.* Do item 1 with students.

Extend: Have students in pairs complete items 2–4.

Challenge: Write on the board the phrases and related sentence frames:

Because I think = He thinks _____ because _____.
I could relate to = He could relate to _____.
What that says to me = To him _____ says _____.

Tell partners to skim the essay for the phrases. Then they use the sentence frames to restate and explain the writer's reasoning. For example, *Because I think = He thinks "I, Too" had a greater effect on his emotions because it's more inclusive.* Have partners help each other to modify the phrases and make the explanations. Invite some pairs to share their sentences with the class.

Ⓜoderate Support

Model: Draw students' attention to the Opinion Mentor Text in their book. **Say:** *Let's identify the features of an opinion essay.* Guide students to identify the opinion statement the writer gives in the opening statement. Begin a list on the board and write *1. Opinion Statement.*

Practice: Ask, *What two reasons does the writer give to support his opinion?* Have students identify the two reasons. Write *2. Reasons for the Opinion.* Continue in this way as you discuss and write *3. Evidence to Support the Reason* and *4. Conclusion.*

Extend: Using the list on the board, have students work in pairs to talk about the second and third paragraphs. Remind them to ask each other questions and add information. Invite some pairs to share their ideas with the class.

Challenge: Have pairs take turns summarizing the report and telling it to each other. As they do, each partner can ask questions and elaborate on the other's remarks.

☑ Formative Assessment

Substantial Support	• Do students recognize the criteria for an opinion essay in the Mentor Opinion Essay?
Moderate Support	• Do students recognize the ways in which the Mentor Opinion Essay meets the criteria for an opinion essay? • Can students describe the features of an opinion essay in their own words?
Light Support	• Do students recognize criteria and analyze how the Mentor Text meets the criteria for an opinion essay? • Can students describe in their own words how the writer meets the criteria for an opinion essay?

Extend and Scaffold Academic Language for Writing

Analyze the Mentor Text: Language Purpose and Structure

Introduction
All Levels of Support

Materials List
- **Mentor Text L** BLM X Light Support
- **Writing Frames Teacher Page** BLM Y
- **Writing Frames Student Page** BLM Z

- Have a copy of BLM Y to refer to during the lesson.

- Distribute BLMs X and Z to each student.

- Read aloud the writing prompt on BLM X. Explain that students will read and analyze the language one writer used to respond to this prompt.

- Have students follow along as you read aloud paragraph 1 of "I, Too."

- Point out the phrase *I loved the beauty and rhythm of Walt Whitman's language in "I Hear America Singing"* and the words that indicate the frame in bold. **Ask:** *Why did the author use this language? What is its purpose?* Help students understand that the author uses the structure *I loved _____.* to express an opinion. *I loved* is an opinion the author has of *the beauty and rhythm of Walt Whitman's language.*

- Have students write this frame into the "State Your Opinion" row of their Writing Frames worksheet (BLM Z). Tell students this is one writing frame they can use in their writing to give their opinion.

- Analyze other bolded phrases in paragraph 1. Explain their purpose and help students add the writing frames to BLM Z.

- Follow these steps as you read additional paragraphs.

- Read aloud the writing prompt on BLM Z. Work with students to generate additional writing frames they could use as they write a response to this prompt. Refer to BLM Y for examples.

Based on students' needs, conduct additional lessons using the differentiated instruction and tools provided.

Light Support
Differentiated Instruction

Materials List
- **Mentor Text L** BLM X Light Support
- **Writing Frames Teacher Page** BLM Y
- **Writing Frames Student Page** BLM Z

Students will need their copies of BLMs X and Z from the initial lesson. Refer to the chart below and your copy of BLM Y during the lesson.

- Explain that students will reread "I, Too" to analyze more phrases and sentences that the writer used.

- Reread the text with students one paragraph at a time.

- Ask individuals or partners to find and underline each phrase in the chart below, read the sentence it appears in, and try to determine the sentence's purpose in the text.

- Provide explanation as necessary, then have students add the writing frames to the "Other Academic Phrases and Sentences" column of BLM Z.

- Encourage students to generate related writing frames and add them to their chart.

LIGHT SUPPORT		
Purpose	**Phrase/Sentence (paragraph)**	**Frame**
Compare/ Contrast	Like Hughes, I have sometimes felt that I was... (2)	Like [Author], I have sometimes felt _____.
Give Reasons/ Explain	That's one reason why I was more affected by it. (2)	That's one reason why _____ by _____.
Cite Source	Hughes says, "Tomorrow, / I'll be at..." (3)	[Author] says, "_____."
Add Details/ Facts	What that says to me is that, even if I'm feeling left out... (3)	What that says to me is that, _____, _____.
State Your Opinion	I found that very inspiring. (3)	I found that _____.

oderate Support

Materials List
- **Mentor Text M** BLM A Moderate Support
- **Writing Frames Teacher Page** BLM Y
- **Writing Frames Student Page** BLM Z

Use the mentor text (BLM A) and the phrases and sentences appropriate for the support level you are targeting.

- Distribute BLM A. Students will also need their copy of BLM Z.

- Read aloud BLM A as students follow along.

- Then reread the text one paragraph at a time, stopping after each paragraph to focus on the bolded and underlined phrases and sentences. Work with students to understand the purpose of each phrase within the text. Have students write the corresponding writing frame in the "Other Academic Phrases and Sentences" column of BLM Z.

- Have partners practice using one or more of these writing frames to expand an idea in the essay they are writing. Have students share their examples with other members of the group.

MODERATE SUPPORT		
Purpose	**Phrase/Sentence (paragraph)**	**Frame**
Cite Source	But "I, Too" by Langston Hughes had a bigger effect... (1)	"[Source]" by [Author] _____.
Compare/ Contrast	But "I, Too" by Langston Hughes had a bigger effect... (1)	_____ had a [adjective]-er effect on _____.
State Your Opinion	I think more people can connect to "I, Too." (1)	I think _____ can _____ to _____.
Give Reasons/ Explain	The poem affected me for another reason. (3)	The _____ _____ for another reason.
Add Details/ Facts	But he believes tomorrow will be better. (3)	But he believes _____ will be _____.

ubstantial Support

Materials List
- **Mentor Text S** BLM B Substantial Support
- **Writing Frames Teacher Page** BLM Y
- **Writing Frames Student Page** BLM Z

Students will need their copy of BLM Z from the initial lesson.

- Distribute BLM B.

- Follow the procedure explained in the Moderate Support lesson.

SUBSTANTIAL SUPPORT		
Purpose	**Phrase/Sentence (paragraph)**	**Frame**
State Your Opinion	I loved Walt Whitman's language...(1)	I loved _____.
Cite Source	Whitman's language is beautiful. (1)	[Author]'s language in [Source] is _____.
Give Reasons/ Explain	"I, Too" affected me more because it has a... (1)	[Source] _____ by / because _____.
Add Details/ Facts	"I, Too"...has a hopeful ending. (1)	___ has a _____.
Give Reasons/ Explain	But "I, Too" shows that Hughes feels left out. (2)	_____ shows that _____ feels _____.

Preview or Review Week 1 ELA Mini-Lessons

"Gold Country," pages 74–75

Student Objectives

LANGUAGE
Purpose:
• I can retell a story using prepositions.
Form:
• I can identify prepositions.
CONTENT
• I can use prepositions in my writing.

Additional Materials
• Unit Presentation
• *Texts for Close Reading* booklet
• Think-Speak-Listen Flip Book
• Student journal

Language Transfer Support

Students whose first language is Spanish may need support in differentiating between the prepositions on and in. These prepositions are not differentiated in the Spanish language; the Spanish word en is used for both. You might demonstrate the difference by pointing out items that are on your desk and other items that are in your desk. Explain that when referring to location, in means "within" or "inside."

4 Read "Gold Country"

Build Background and Vocabulary

Display the panels. If students have already read the journal, ask them to share what they remember. Also explain that even though this is written as a journal, it is actually fiction. Ask students to share their experiences with traveling within and migrating to the United States.

Read Aloud the Text

Read panels 1 and 2. To support comprehension, ask students to find images in the picture that match words in the text. **Ask:** *What place is this? What is happening? Who is telling the story?* Model thinking through the answers. **Say:** *I don't see a mountain, but I do see an ocean and lots of tall poles. The person telling the story must be near a boat.* Repeat with remaining panels. Invite students to share ideas about the story. Then refer to the Essential Question. **Ask:** *How can other perspectives help us see the world?* **Say:** *Other people's views help us understand the world around us better.* **Say:** *This story is historical fiction. It tells us about events in history though stories.*

Think-Speak-Listen: Use the following sentence frame or the Think-Speak-Listen Flip Book to guide discussion: *Based on his description, "First City" is different from Wong Ming-Chung's home in China because _____.*

👥 Differentiated Instruction
Build Language: Use Prepositions to Describe Location

Ask: *Why are prepositions important?* Elicit answers. **Say:** *Prepositions tell us the time and location something happens.* Display panel 2. **Say: Off** *is a preposition. The prepositional phrase is* off the ship. **Ask:** *What does it tell us?* Elicit answers. **Say:** *It describes the location. It tells us where they were.* Ask students to create a list of all of the other prepositions that they find in the second paragraph. Use the Differentiated Instruction to practice using question words in a way that best matches the levels of your students.

☑ Use Oral and Written Language: Retelling a Story Using Prepositions

Task: *Take turns with a partner. Pretend that you are interviewing Wong Ming-Chung about his experiences. Create questions that use prepositions that describe location.*

(S) *How long have you lived _____?*

(M) *While in San Francisco, how did you become friends with the American boy _____?*

(L) *After you discovered the boy was not American, but he was _____, did that change your friendship?*

🔄 Wrap Up

Today we learned about how important prepositions are in a story or text. What do they tell us about the characters or events in a story or text?

Turn and Talk: *Ask students to turn to a classmate and use prepositions to describe something that they did this morning.*

👥👥 Differentiated Instruction
Build Language: Use Prepositions to Describe Location

Ⓢubstantial Support

Model: **Say:** *Prepositions are often used to explain place and time in a sentence.* **Point to panel 3. Say:** *When I read the word* in*, I stop and look at the words that come after it: my village pond. Then I know where the fish were.* **Model how prepositions are used. Say:** *He was playing in the store. We were skipping through the park. They will be leaving before the day ends.*

Practice: Invite students to help you find additional prepositions in the remaining panels. Then Distribute BLM 1. Work with students to complete the activity in the Practice section.

Extend: Have students work in pairs to complete the Extend section of the BLM.

Challenge: If students are ready, work with them to write new sentences with prepositions based on some of the sentences on the BLM.

Ⓜoderate Support

Model: Explain that prepositions help to describe time and place. This additional information allows the reader to understand the relationship between various items in a sentence. **Say:** *They were playing across the street from the park.* Across the street *and* from the park *both describe location.*

Practice: Distribute BLM 2. Work with students to complete the activity in the Practice section.

Extend: Have students work with partners to complete the Extend activity on the BLM.

Challenge: If students are ready, have them work in pairs to write new sentences with prepositions. They may model their sentences on those on the BLM.

Ⓛight Support

Use the text on pp. 4-5 in the *Texts for Close Reading* booklet for the following activities.

Practice: Create 3 columns. Label column 1: preposition, column 2 phrase: Have students copy the chart. Have them help you generate a list of prepositions from paragraphs 1 and 2, for example, *off, off the ship, in, in the middle of the forest.*

Extend: Put students in pairs. Assign each pair one paragraphs 15, 19, and 20. Ask them to come up with a list of all of the prepositions that describe location and add them to the chart.

Challenge: The excerpt ends with the July 20th entry. Have students use prepositions to describe location to tell what they think might have been included in the next entry made in the journal. Help students think through what prepositions to use.

✓ Formative Assessment

Substantial Support	• Are students able to recognize prepositions? • Are students able to identify prepositions that describe location?
Moderate Support	• Can students recognize prepositional phrases? • Can students express themselves using prepositions?
Light Support	• Are students able to recognize various prepositions that describe time? • Can students generate sentences that use prepositions that describe location?

Preview or Review Week 1 ELA Mini-Lessons

"Annie's New Homeland," page 76

Student Objectives

LANGUAGE

Purpose:
- I can make a guide to a multiple-meaning words.

Form:
- I can identify words that have multiple meanings.

CONTENT
- I can recognize historical fiction.

Additional Materials
- Unit Presentation
- *Texts for Close Reading* booklet
- Think-Speak-Listen Flip Book
- Student journal

Language Transfer Support

Words with more than one meaning can be problematic for students learning English. Emphasize the use of photos and illustrations, as well as textual context clues to determine the correct meaning of unfamiliar words.

5 Read "Annie's New Homeland"

Build Background and Vocabulary

Display the panels. Explain that this story is told from the viewpoint of a young girl who has just come to America in 1892. Ask students to share their cultural experiences and knowledge about what it's like to travel to a new country.

Read Aloud the Text

Read the first paragraph. To support comprehension, ask students to find images in the pictures that match words in the text (steamship, Statue of Liberty, maid, long lines). Ask *wh-* questions, such as *Who are the characters in this story? What is happening? Where is the boat heading?* Repeat with paragraphs 2 and 3. **Ask:** *Where are Annie and her brothers going? Why?* Invite students to answer using the frame: I think Annie and her brothers are _____ because _____. Then refer to the Essential Question. **Say:** *This text is about experiences of people who came to the United States from other countries. It tells about history. It is called historical fiction.*

Think-Speak-Listen: Help students summarize the steps Annie had to take before she was allowed to settle in New York City or use the Think-Speak-Listen Flip Book to guide discussion:

👥 Differentiated Instruction
Build Language: Identify Multiple-Meaning Words

Remind students that context clues can help them figure out what a word means. Ask the students if they see any words that have more than one meaning in the story. Model thinking through the answer. **Say:** *I see the word* deck *in the first panel. I know that a deck can describe a package of playing cards, a structure that extends off of a house, and part of a ship. This must be a multiple-meaning word.* **Ask:** *Based on the story, which of these is the correct meaning? Why?* Invite students to find other words with multiple meanings. Use the Differentiated Instruction to practice identifying multiple-meaning words in a way that best matches the levels of your students.

☑ Use Oral and Written Language: Make a Multiple-Meaning Guide

Task: *Work with a partner. List four multiple-meaning words. Make a guide with a page for each word. Use the word in sentence to show each meaning.* Use this opportunity to assess students using the rubric in *English Language Development Assessment*.

(S) *Bowl: There are grapes in the bowl. I like to bowl on Saturdays.*

(M) *Store: I am going to the store to get groceries. I will store all the groceries on the shelf in the kitchen*

(L) *Stamp: My brother stamps his foot when he's angry. I am collecting stamps as a hobby.*

Wrap Up

Today, we learned about multiple-meaning words. Why is it important to know that some words have multiple meanings?

Turn and Talk: *Ask students to share at least one multiple-meaning word.*

👥 Differentiated Instruction
Build Language: Identify Multiple-Meaning Words

⑤ubstantial Support

Model: Explain that multiple-meaning words are spelled the same but have different meanings. It can be tricky to figure out what they mean. **Say:** *In order to help you to understand the meaning, it is important to see how the word is used in the sentence and in the story. This is called using context. Context often contains clues that give the reader a hint or clue about the meaning of the word.* Work with students to identify multiple-meaning words that they use when talking to others. Discuss examples such as *stamp, float, fit, roll, bowl,* and *store.*

Practice: Distribute BLM 1. Ask students to work with you to determine the multiple meanings.

Extend: Have students work in pairs to do the Extend activity on the BLM. Students may use a dictionary if necessary.

Challenge: If students are ready, work with them to create a pair of new sentences with one of the multiple-meaning words.

Ⓜoderate Support

Model: Explain that some words have two meanings and some have three or more. **Say:** *A* roll *is something that you can eat. What else can it mean?* Discuss that *roll* can also be a verb. Point out that sometimes the same word can have multiple meanings as different parts of speech. Other times, the word may have two meanings as the same part of speech (for example, the noun *deck*)

Practice: Distribute BLM 2. Work with students to complete the Practice section.

Extend: Have students work in pairs to complete the Extend section of the BLM.

Challenge: If students are ready, model finding and using context have them work in pairs to make new sentences showing the meaning of several of the multiple-meaning words.

Ⓛight Support

Have students use page 10 from *Texts for Close Reading* for the following activities.

Practice: Have students reread paragraph 1. Ask them to tell you the two meanings of the word *deck.* Then have them write a sentence showing each meaning.

Extend: Write the words *passed, order* and *cook.* Have partners find the words in the text and write the meanings of how they are used. Then ask them to write another meaning of each word, using a dictionary if necessary.

Challenge: Tell the students to use each word in an original sentence using context clues. For each of the words, ask them to create one sentence for each meaning. It is important that the sentences contain enough details and information that readers, who may be unfamiliar with the words, can use context clues to help them understand the meaning of the word.

☑ Formative Assessment

Substantial Support	• Are students able to recognize multiple-meaning words? • Are students able to define the meanings of words?
Moderate Support	• Can students use multiple-meaning words in different contexts?
Light Support	• Can students use multiple-meaning words in sentences with context clues to show the meaning?

Preview or Review Week 2 ELA Mini-Lessons

"Understand the Language of Comparison," page 77

Student Objectives

LANGUAGE
Purpose:
- I can make a comparison chart.

Form:
- I can recognize when words are used to compare.

CONTENT
- I can use the language of comparison to describe stories and poems.

Additional Materials
- Unit Presentation
- *Texts for Close Reading* booklet
- Think-Speak-Listen Flip Book
- Student journal

Language Transfer Support

Students who speak Hmong, Korean, or Spanish as a native language may need extra support with comparative and superlative adjectives ending in -er or -est. In these languages, comparisons are expressed with separate words.

6 Understand the Language of Comparison

Engage Thinking

Display panel 1. **Say:** *Panel 1 reads "I am the darker brother." The word darker is an example of a comparison word. The speaker is making a comparison between himself and someone else.* **Say:** *Different words help us to understand how things are connected and how they compare to one another. These words help to signal to the reader that two or more things are being compared.*

Read and View Closely: Reading Comparisons

Display panels 1 and 2. **Say:** *In both panels, the writer uses words that a comparison. Panel 1 is from a poem and panel 2 is from a story. Let's look at Panel 3. They (people) are being compared to fish.* **Say:** *What word tells us that two or more things are being compared?* Elicit answers. **Say:** *The word like tells us the people in the harbor are being compared to fish in the village pond.*

👥👥 Differentiated Instruction
Build Language: Understand the Language of Comparison

Read the second row of the chart. **Say:** *When we add -er to words, we can use them to compare.* Write *strange* and *stranger than*. Explain that *stranger than* means more strange. Point out that for some words in the sentence, like *wonderful*, we don't add -er. We use the word *more* instead. Use the Differentiated Instruction to practice understanding the language of comparison in a way that best matches the levels of your students.

Think-Speak-Listen: Help students use the language of comparison to compare Wong Ming-Chung and Annie's first experiences in America or use the Think-Speak-Listen Flip Book to guide discussion.

☑ Use Oral and Written Language: Make a Comparison Chart

Task: *Work in a small group. Write a list of words to compare. Make a chart showing the words with sentence showing comparisons.* Examples:

     The building is taller than the tree.

Ⓜ   *My neighbor's car is as old as their nine-year old dog.*

Ⓛ   *The story "Annie's Homeland" is longer than the poem "I, Too," , but it is shorter than the story "Gold Country."*

Wrap Up

Today we have learned about how words that compare are used in stories and poems. What do they tell us about the characters or events in these texts?

Turn and Talk: *Compare two subjects, using the phrases more* interesting than, easier than, *or* harder than.

👥 Differentiated Instruction
Build Language: Understand the Language of Comparison

Ⓢubstantial Support

Model Display the first two panels. Write the words *dark*, *strange*, *scary*, *funny*, *sad*. Show how we add -*er*, or just -*r* to some words. Then demonstrate that for words ending in -*y*, we take off the -*y* and add -*ier*. The word *sad* gets an extra d before adding the -er. Then remind students that some words like *wonderful* do not have -er. For those we use "more than." Read the last two panels and discuss that when the two things are the same we use as _____ as or *like*.

Practice: Distribute BLM 1. Work with students to do the activity in the Practice section.

Extend: Have students work in pairs to complete the activity in the Extend section of the BLM.

Challenge: If students are ready, work with them to create new sentences with some of the comparative words.

Ⓜoderate Support

Model: Have volunteers read the first two panels. For each one, discuss how the comparative word was formed, for example adding -*er* to dark. Point out that for words ending in *y* like *funny* and *scary*, we take off the *y* and add -*ier*. Say each of the base words, for example *dark*, *strange* and have the students say the comparative, *darker*, *stranger*. Have volunteers read the last two panels. Discuss that in these examples, one is not more than the other, so we can use as _____ as, or _____.

Practice: Distribute BLM 2. Work with students to do the activity in the Practice section.

Extend: Have students work in pairs to complete the activity in the Extend section of the BLM.

Challenge: If students are ready, have partners write more sentences with some of the comparative words.

Ⓛight Support

Have students use pages 6–9 of *Texts for Close Reading* for the following activities.

Practice: Review the language of comparisons with students and check their understanding. If necessary, review how to form comparatives with -*er*, *ier*, *more* _____ *than*, *less* _____ *than*, *as* _____ *as*, or *like*.

Extend: Put students in pairs and ask them to read paragraphs 16–22. Ask them to provide a list of similarities and differences between Runt and his friend from Australia.

Challenge: Throughout the story, Runt makes many comparisons between America and China. Have students discuss with a partner some things that America and China have in common and some things that are different.

☑ Formative Assessment

Substantial Support	• Are students able to recognize when people/places/events are compared? • Are students able to identify words in a poem or story that indicate that a comparison is being made?
Moderate Support	• Can students explain comparisons that are made in different texts? • Can students form comparatives and use them in sentences?
Light Support	• Can students use the language of comparison when retelling the events in a story or a poem? • Can students form comparatives and create original sentences using comparative language?

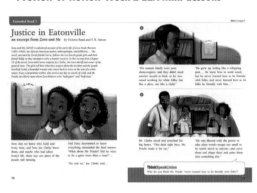

"Justice in Eatonville," pages 78–79

Student Objectives

LANGUAGE

Purpose:
• I can ask questions about a story.

Form:
• I can use question words.

CONTENT
• I can read historical fiction.

Additional Materials
• Unit Presentation
• *Texts for Close Reading* booklet
• Think-Speak-Listen Flip Book
• Student journal

Metacognitive Prompt:

As you read a story, stop and ask questions about what is happening. Asking yourself questions will help you clarify what you read.

7 Read "Justice in Eatonville"

Build Background and Vocabulary

Display the panels. If students have already read the story, ask them to share what they remember. Point out that the author, Zora Neale Hurston, was also an anthropologist, someone who studies different cultures. Invite students to share their experiences and knowledge on different cultures.

Read Aloud the Text

Read panel 1. To support comprehension, ask *wh-* questions such as: *Who are these girls? What are they trying to do?* Model thinking through the answers. Repeat with remaining panels. **Say:** *Questions such as who, what, when, where and why help us understand a text.* Then refer to the Essential Question: How does seeing Mr. Pendir through Joe Clark's perspective help Zora understand him better? **Say:** *Even though this is written as fiction, it is based on the life of a real person, Zora Neale Hurston. This is historical fiction.*

Think-Speak-Listen: Use the following sentence frame or the Think-Speak-Listen Flip Book to guide discussion: *I think Mr. Pendir "never learned how to be friendly with folks" because _____.*

👥👥👥 Differentiated Instruction
Build Language: Use Question Words to Understand a Story

Say: *Sometimes while reading I might be confused about something. Using question words to ask questions as I read gives me more information.* Write: *who, what, where, when, why,* and *how*. Point to the text in panel 1. **Say:** *I see that Zora wants to know more about Mr. Pendir so she asks a question that begins with* **what.** **Ask:** *What new information do we learn about Mr. Pendir from Joe Clark's answer?* Elicit answers. **Say:** *Who is his family?* **Say:** *By asking questions about people and things in the story, we learn more about them.* Use the Differentiated Instruction to practice using question words in a way that best matches the levels of your students.

☑ Use Oral and Written Language: Ask Questions About a Story

Task: *Take turns with a partner. Pretend that you are interviewing the character of Zora about Mr. Pendir. Create questions that will help you to learn more about him.*

Ⓢ *Where did Mr. Pendir _____?*

Ⓜ *What could Mr. Pendir do with _____ _____?*

Ⓛ *How was Mr. Pendir _____ by the _____?*

↩ Wrap Up

Today, we learned about the importance of asking questions when reading a short story. What are some of the questions that we can ask to help us understand a story?

Turn and Talk: *Ask students to turn to a partner and come up with an additional question about Mr. Pendir using the question words discussed in the lesson.*

👥👥 Differentiated Instruction
Language: Use Questions Words to Understand a Story

Ⓢubstantial Support

Model: Say: *Questions that start with who, what, when, where, how and why will help you to learn more about the text.* **Point to Panel 2. Say:** *When I read Mr. Clarke say, "His mama's family were poor sharecroppers" I pause and* **ask:** *What is a sharecropper?* **Say:** *When I read the rest of the sentence "and they didn't want another mouth to feed" I pause and* **ask:** *Why? Asking questions helps me better understand what I have read.*

Practice: Distribute BLM 1. Work with students to complete the activity in the Practice section.

Extend: Have students complete the Extend section of the BLM.

Challenge: Ask: *Why does Zora gasp when she sees the lion mask?*

Ⓜoderate Support

Model: Say: *If stories did not answer who, what, when, where and how, it would be difficult to understand the plot. While reading, you should be thinking about questions that you have about the story.* Explain that sometimes the writer will answer the questions directly, but sometimes we have to ask questions as we read. **Point to Panel 2. Say:** *When I read Mr. Clarke say, "His mama's family were poor sharecroppers" I pause and* **ask:** *What is a sharecropper?* **Say:** *When I read the rest of the sentence "and they didn't want another mouth to feed" I pause and* **ask:** *Why? Asking questions helps me better understand what I have read.*

Practice: Distribute BLM 2. Work with students to complete the activity in the Practice section.

Extend: Have students work with partners to complete the Extend section of the BLM.

Challenge: If students are ready, ask them to create a list of questions that have not been answered so far in the story about Mr. Pendir.

Ⓛight Support

Practice: Have students read paragraphs 26–31 on pages 18–19 in the Texts for Close Reading. Point out that many questions are answered about Mr. Pendir, but there is still much information that we do not know about the young Zora Neale Hurston. Create a word web. In the middle, write young Zora. In the circles, generate questions that you have about this character.

Extend: Have students work in pairs. Have them read paragraph 24 Ask them to come up with a list of questions that this paragraph answers about Mr. Pendir.

Challenge: In addition to who, what, when, where, why and how to generate a list of some of the other ways to start questions about short stories.

✅ Formative Assessment

Substantial Support	• Are students able to ask who, what, when, where, why questions in a story?
Moderate Support	• Can students recognize questions in a story? • Can students generate questions using a variety of question words?
Light Support	• Are students able to recognize how an author answers a question about a character? • Can students generate questions while reading a story?

Preview or Review Week 2 ELA Mini-Lessons

Extended Read 1 (continued) Week 2 • Lesson 8

He reached into a drawer and drew out a lion mask so detailed that Zora and I gasped. "Mr. Pendir breathed life into wood."

"When his fears threatened to swallow him up, he faced them down with the masks he made. His art scared off his fear."...

Zora and I sat with that a moment. Joe Clarke's lips spread across his face in a closed-mouth smile. It was a sad smile, but reassuring.

"I'm going to do justice, girls, but sometimes justice works better in silence.... Don't tell anyone else what you know. Let justice take its course now."

ThinkSpeakListen
What do you think Mr. Clarke meant when he said that Mr. Pendir's "art scared off his fear"?

80

"Justice in Eatonville," page 80

Student Objectives

LANGUAGE
Purpose:
- I can retell a story using different points of view.

Form:
- I can recognize a character's point of view while reading.

CONTENT
- I can explain how point of view is connected to the plot in historical fiction.

Additional Materials
- Unit Presentation
- *Texts for Close Reading* booklet
- Think-Speak-Listen Flip Book
- Student journal

Metacognitive Prompt: Making Inferences

*Today we will read closely to determine the point of view of the story. As we read, pay attention to who is talking. Look for pronouns such as **I, me,** and **we** to help you decide the point of view.*

8 Analyze Point of View

Engage Thinking

Display the panels. Point to panel 4. Remind students that Zora asked a question about Mr. Pendir. **Ask:** *Who is speaking to Zora here?* Elicit answers. **Say:** *While reading, I pay attention to who is speaking. Different words like I, me, you, they, he and she help tell us the point of view.*

Differentiated Instruction
✓ Read and View Closely: Analyze Point of View

Display Panel 5. **Say:** *Learning historical fiction from different characters helps the reader to understand the story. In panel 5, the reader learns even more information about Mr. Pendir.* Point to Panel 5. **Ask:** *Who is telling us more information about Mr. Pendir?* Elicit answers. **Say:** *"Zora and I" tell us that the narrator is speaking from her perspective so this is an example of first person. We also hear from Mr. Clarke when he says " I'm going to do justice girls..." In both of these examples, the speaker uses I. When stories use "I, me, we, us" it is first person.* Use the Differentiated Instruction to practice analyzing point of view in a way that best matches the level of your students. Use this opportunity to assess students using the rubric in *English Language Development Assessment*.

Think-Speak-Listen: Use the following sentence frame or the Think-Speak-Listen Flip Book to guide discussion: *I think Mr. Clarke meant _____ .*

Build Language: Recognize Differences in Verb Tenses

Read aloud panel 4. Draw attention to the verbs ending in *-ed*: *He reached, I gasped, Mr. Pendir breathed.* **Say:** *These three verbs end in -ed. They are regular verbs in the past tense.* Then point out the irregular verbs *drew* and *made*. Discuss that in a story, we often see past tense verbs for telling the story, and present tense verbs in the dialogue. Read aloud the last paragraph in panel 5. Point out that there are several uses of verbs in the dialogue—present tense verbs *works* and *know*, and future *going to do*. The dialogue also has verbs that are used for giving directions—*don't tell*, and *let justice take*. Remind students that being aware of the different forms of verbs will help them understand the meaning of the story.

✓ Use Oral and Written Language: Retell a Story Using Different Points of View

Task: *Work with a partner. Retell the events in the story from the point of view of a narrator (third person), and then as one of the two girls (first person).* Examples:

Zora and Carrie listened to Mr. Clarke. They _____

We listened to Mr. Clarke. We _____ and then _____.

↻ Wrap Up

Today we have learned about point of view in historical fiction. Why is it important to recognize the point of view of a story?

Turn and Talk: *Tell your partner about an argument you had with a friend. Then retell it from the point of view from your friend.*

👥 Differentiated Instruction
Read and View Closely: Analyze Point of View

Ⓢubstantial Support

Model Say: *Understanding the point of view means knowing who is speaking in a story.* Explain that we can tell the point of view by looking for the words *I, you, he, she, we, they.* When we see *I* or *we,* it means that one of the characters is telling the story. Point out the words *Zora and I* in panels 4 and 5. **Say:** *The girl Carrie is telling the story. The story is from her* point of view.

Practice: Distribute BLM 1. Work with students to complete the activity in the Practice section.

Extend: Have students work in pairs to complete the activity in the Extend section of the BLM.

Challenge: If students are ready, provide a sentence in the first person and have them change it to the third person, for example *I went to the park. She went to the park.*

Ⓜoderate Support

Model: Review that *point of view* means who is telling the story. Read aloud the text in Panel 4. **Ask:** *Who is telling the story? How do we know?* Elicit that we can tell the point of view of the story by seeing the words *Zora and I.* Explain that when we see *I* or *we,* we know the *point of view* is *first person,* which means one of the characters is telling the story.

Practice: Distribute BLM 2. Work with students to complete the activity in the Practice section.

Extend: Have students work with partners to complete the Extend section of the BLM.

Challenge: Have partners work together to change additional sentences from first person to third person.

Ⓛight Support

Have students use pages 12–19 in *Texts for Close Reading* for the following activities.

Practice: Discuss that a writer chooses the *point of view* to tell a story. It can be told by a narrator (third person) or it can be told by one of the characters (first person). Remind students that the pronouns *I* and *we* indicate that the story is told from the point of view of a character, or is a personal account of the author. Have students determine the point of view (first person) by looking for the pronouns in the first few paragraphs (I and we).

Extend: Have students work in pairs. Ask them to rewrite one paragraph to change the point of view to third person as though a narrator were telling the story.

Challenge: Have students work in pairs. Have one write a sentence in third person (he, she, they) and the other change it to first person (I, we).

☑ Formative Assessment

Substantial Support	• Are students able to recognize the point of view of a story? • Are students able to identify words in historical fiction that will help them to understand who is telling the story?
Moderate Support	• Can students explain when the point of view changes in historical fiction? • Can students change the point of view of a sentence?
Light Support	• Can students rewrite sentences from different points of view?

Preview or Review Week 2 ELA Mini-Lessons

Use Conjunctions to Connect Ideas

"Use Conjunctions to Connect Ideas," page 81

Student Objectives

LANGUAGE
Purpose:
- I can describe and use conjunctions to connect ideas.

Form:
- I can recognize the use of conjunction words to connect ideas.

CONTENT
- I can explain how conjunctions connect ideas in historical fiction.

Additional Materials
- Unit Presentation
- *Texts for Close Reading* booklet
- Think-Speak-Listen Flip Book
- Student journal

Language Transfer Support

Note that speakers of Chinese, Farsi, or Vietnamese may need additional support when creating sentences with conjunctions. Unlike in English, conjunctions often occur in pairs in those languages. For example, a student may say, *Although, I am hungry, but I do not want to eat.*

9 Use Conjunctions to Connect Ideas

Engage Thinking

Display the chart. Point to the first sentence. **Say:** *This sentence tells us information about Mr. Pendir's family. When we add the conjunction word* and *to the sentence, it adds additional information.* Read the whole sentence in the last column.

Read and View Closely: Recognize Conjunctions

Read aloud the sentence in the last row and column. **Say:** *I notice the word* but. *The word* but *is used to show a contradiction between what has been said about Mr. Pendir.* Point to the part of the sentence: *...but he never learned how to be friendly with folks.* **Say:** *This additional information tells me that Mr. Pendir may have been a hard worker, but he was not friendly. The conjunction* but *shows us how these ideas are connected.*

Think-Speak-Listen: Have students discuss their opinion of "Justice in Eatonville" or use the Think-Speak-Listen Flip Book to guide discussion.

👥 Differentiated Instruction
Build Language: Use Conjunctions to Connect Ideas

Display the chart. **Say:** *Many sentences contain multiple ideas. Conjunctions like* and, so *and* but *help to connect those ideas. Conjunctions also show us the relationship between ideas.* And, so, *and* but *are examples of conjunctions that link ideas.* Point to the last part of the sentence: *...and never learned how to let folks be friendly with him.* **Say:** *The word* and *links the ideas together.* Use the Differentiated Instruction to practice using conjunctions in a way that best matches the levels of your students.

☑ Use Oral and Written Language: Use Conjunctions to Connect Ideas

Task: *Each of the following sentences needs a conjunction. Take turns with a partner to discuss which conjunction word should be used here.*

S *I am brave _____ I am also strong.*

M *I am the brave one, _____ I was the one to jump in to help.*

L *I am brave and strong _____ it was my job to help, _____ my friend was afraid to help me.*

Wrap Up

Today we have learned about conjunctions. What are some of the conjunctions that are used in stories?

Turn and Talk: *Tell your partner two things you want to do. Use a conjunction to connect the ideas.*

☷☷☷ Differentiated Instruction
Build Language: Use Conjunctions to Connect Ideas

Ⓢubstantial Support

Model: Have students read the conjunctions in the chart with you. Explain the difference between *and*, *but*, and *so* by giving simple examples: *I can run and I can jump.* Explain that and is used to join two ideas. *I can dance, but I can't sing.* Explain that *but* is used to contrast two different ideas. *It was raining, so I couldn't go to the park.* Explain that so is used to show a reason.

Practice: Say a sentence with a conjunction and ask students to help you complete it. *I can write and I can _____. I can write, but I can't _____.* Then distribute BLM 1. Work with students to complete the activity in the Practice section.

Extend: Have students work in pairs to complete the Extend activity on the BLM.

Challenge: If students are ready, give them two sentences and ask them to join them using a conjunction.

Ⓜoderate Support

Model: Say: *When I come across these words* and, so, *and* but, *I know that they are linking ideas together. While reading, I am paying attention to the information that comes before and after these words to see how the ideas are related.* Ask students to tell you the difference between how we use *and*, *but* and *so*. Discuss that *and* joins two ideas, that *but* contrasts ideas, and *so* shows cause and effect.

Practice: Distribute BLM 2. Work with students to complete the Extend activity on the BLM.

Extend: Have students work with partners to complete the Extend activity on the BLM.

Challenge: Have partners write two sentences on the same topic and then join them using a conjunction.

Ⓛight Support

Have students use pages 12–19 from *Texts for Close Reading* for the following activities.

Practice: Have students find sentences with *and*, *but*, and *so* in paragraphs 21–27. Ask them to copy the sentences. Then have them explain how the ideas in the sentences are connected. Ask volunteers to explain the difference between linking ideas with *and*, *but*, and *so*. Discuss that *but* contrasts ideas, and *so* shows cause and effect.

Extend: Have students work in pairs. Ask them to replace the conjunctions in the sentences they found with different conjunctions to see how the meaning changes.

Challenge: Ask students to work together to write related ideas using *and*, contrasting ideas using *but*, and ideas showing cause and effect using *so*.

☑ Formative Assessment

Substantial Support	• Are students able to define a conjunction? • Are students able to identify the words that indicate that two ideas are being connected?
Moderate Support	• Can students explain the purpose of using conjunctions in a story?
Light Support	• Can students link multiple ideas together using conjunctions?

Preview or Review Week 2 ELA Mini-Lessons

"Zora Neale Hurston," page 82

Student Objectives

LANGUAGE
Purpose:
- I can use homographs when retelling key details.

Form:
- I can analyze homographs.

CONTENT
- I can explain how words create meaning in a biography.

Additional Materials
- Unit Presentation
- *Texts for Close Reading* booklet
- Think-Speak-Listen Flip Book
- Student journal

Language Transfer Support

Other languages have homographs (Spanish has a few, such as mañana, which means "morning" and "tomorrow"), but English has hundreds, perhaps thousands of them! Homographs are a challenge for English Learners, especially as they read academic texts that use the less common meanings of words English Learners think they already know.

---

10 Read "Zora Neale Hurston"

Build Background and Vocabulary

Display the text. **Ask:** *Who was Zora Neale Hurston?* Elicit answers. **Say:** *Zora Neale Hurston was a writer. She often wrote folklore. Folklore is stories that tell about beliefs and customs that are important to people. Zora stories were based on growing up in the South.* If students have already read the story ask them what they remember.

Read Aloud the Text

Read paragraphs 1-2. Read the sentence in the second paragraph. **Say:** *These details from the biography tell us that she was unique. They also tell us more about her personality.* Read the remaining excerpt and invite students to share their thoughts about Hurston. Use the frame: *Zora Neale Hurston was someone who _____.* **Say:** *"Zora Neale Hurston" is a biography. It is nonfiction. The purpose of a biography is to explain and to provide information about a person.*

👥 Differentiated Instruction
Build Language: Analyze Homographs

Say: *Homographs are words that are spelled the same, but have different meanings.* Read the sentence: "Zora eventually left the South." **Ask:** *What does the word left mean in this sentence?* **Say:** *Left can have different meanings. Does this mean that she turned left or does this mean that she left the area? Based on the context, I realize that she moved from Florida.* Use Differentiated Instruction to practice analyzing homographs in a way that best matches the levels of your students.

Think-Speak-Listen: Use the following sentence frame or the Think-Speak-Listen Flip Book to guide discussion: *Zora is described as _____.*

☑ Use Oral and Written Language: Talk About an Author

Task: *Take turns with a partner. Tell what you know about Zora Neale Hurston, using homographs such as novel, character, work and story. Use a dictionary to help find multiple definitions of these words to help you.*

 Zora Neale Hurston was well liked. She was smart and had a strong _____. The character Zora in Zora and I was based on _____.

M *Zora Neale Hurston believed in hard _____. Much of her published _____ was based on _____.*

L *Zora Neale Hurston offered readers a _____. She is known for publishing _____.*

🔄 Wrap Up

Today, we learned about the importance of finding the correct meaning of a homograph in a story. Why is it important to know the correct meaning?

Turn and Talk: *Share a sentence with a homograph. Explain the meaning of the word.*

👥👤 Differentiated Instruction
Build Language: Analyze Homographs

Ⓢubstantial Support

Model: Say: *Sometimes words are spelled the same way, but they have different meanings. These words are called homographs.* Read the second sentence and discuss the two possible meanings of the word *spent*–passed time, or *spent* money. **Say:** *To figure out the meaning, we look at the context. The sentence says she spent her childhood, so it could not be about spending money.* Give other examples of homographs from the reading: *kind, left, short*. Point out that some homographs have the same spelling but different pronunciations, like *bow*.

Practice: Distribute BLM 1. Work with students to complete the activity in the Practice section.

Extend: Have students work in pairs to complete the Extend activity on the BLM.

Challenge: If students are ready, help them to write two sentences to show the two meanings of the word *spent*.

Ⓜoderate Support

Model: Say: *Homographs are words that have the same spelling, but different meanings. The reader must pay close attention to how the word is being used in a sentence and the details of the sentence.* In the third paragraph read the sentence: *Without her work, many of these traditional stories may have been lost forever.* **Say:** *The word work is an example of a homograph. Work can mean a job or effort, or a collection of materials. Looking at the details of the story, the word work means a body/collection of materials. In this case, her work would be her stories.* List other homographs from the selection: *kind, left, short, spent.* Ask students the meanings they know.

Practice: Distribute BLM 2. Work with students to complete the activity in the Practice section.

Extend: Have students work with partners to complete the Extend activity on the BLM.

Challenge: If students are ready, have them work in pairs to write sentences showing the meanings of several of the homographs you discussed.

Ⓛight Support

Use page 20 from *Texts for Close Reading* for the following activities.

Practice: In paragraph 2, we are told that *Her storytelling cast a spell on the audience.* Point out that spell is a homograph. Write the word and ask students to tell you the meanings they know. Have them decide which definition is appropriate for this sentence.

Extend: Have students work in pairs. Provide a list of homographs: *kind, left, spent, novel, short.* Have them write the meanings, using a dictionary to help if necessary.

Challenge: Ask students to generate at least 3 sentences using one of the homographs from the text. The sentences should use the correct version of the word based on the details that the student provides in the sentence.

☑ Formative Assessment

Substantial Support	• Can students recognize the multiple meanings of homographs?
Moderate Support	• Can students recognize and appropriately use homographs in sentences?
Light Support	• Are students able to differentiate the meaning of a homograph using details from the text? • Are students able to use homographs correctly?

Preview or Review Week 3 ELA Mini-Lessons

Week 3 • Lesson 11

Form and Use Irregular Verbs

Example from "Justice in Eatonville"	Present Tense	Past Tense
Now that we **knew** who Gold and Ivory were, and how Joe Clarke knew them, and maybe who had taken Ivory's life, there was one piece of the puzzle still missing.	know	knew
"He **grew** up feeling like a whipping post."	grow	grew
"At first folks tried to bring him into the circle of town life, but he just couldn't **put** his hurt and mistrust away."	put	put
Mr. Clarke **stood** and stretched his big bones.	stand	stood
"This desk right here, Mr. Pendir **made** it for me."	make	made
He reached into a drawer and **drew** out a lion mask so detailed that Zora and I gasped.	draw	drew

Example from "Zora Neale Hurston"	Present Tense	Past Tense
Zora eventually **left** the South.	leave	left
She **won** many awards for her work.	win	won
She **spent** years collecting and publishing the folklore and stories of southern Americans.	spend	spent

ThinkSpeakListen
Use these irregular verbs to describe the life of Zora Neale Thurston.

"Form and Use Irregular Verbs," page 83

Student Objectives

LANGUAGE
Purpose:
• I can use irregular verbs in a presentation.
Form:
• I can recognize irregular verbs.
CONTENT
• I can explain word meaning in a humor story.

Additional Materials
• Unit Presentation
• *Texts for Close Reading* booklet
• Think-Speak-Listen Flip Book
• Student journal

Metacognitive Prompt

As we read today, remember to pause while listening and reading to check your understanding of the story. You may find it helpful to ask yourself questions such as: Who is speaking or acting? What are they saying or doing? How are they feeling? Why do they feel this way?

11 Form and Use Irregular Verbs

Engage Thinking

Display the charts. Point to the first sentence in the second chart: *Zora eventually left the South.* **Say:** *The writer uses past tense in this sentence. Because a biography is a text that is written about the life of another person, past tense is often used. "Zora Neale Hurston" is written in the past tense to show that the action and events have already taken place.*

Turn and Talk: Tell your partner one interesting thing you remember about the story.

Read and View Closely: Identify Irregular Verbs

Display the chart. *Say: In a text, it is important to know when something took place. The verbs in a sentence help to explain when the action took place.* Read some of the sentences from the chart and point to the present tense verbs. **Say:** *For regular verbs, we add* -ed *for the past, but these verbs are irregular. We don't add* -ed *to these verbs.*

👥 Differentiated Instruction
Build Language: Form and Use Irregular Verbs

Read the fourth sentence of the chart and the verb *stand, stood*. Point out that the verb stretched in the sentence is a regular verb because we add *-ed* in the past. For irregular verbs, we do not add *-ed*. There is no clear pattern for irregular verbs so we need to learn their forms in the past. Point out that it's important to know which verbs are irregular so that you know whether to add *-ed* or whether to use a different form. Read the other irregular verbs in the chart together. Use the Differentiated Instruction to practice forming and using irregular verbs in a way that best matches the level of your students.

Think-Speak-Listen: Help students use irregular verbs to describe the life of Zora Neale Thurston or use the Think-Speak-Listen Flip Book to guide discussion.

☑ Use Oral and Written Language: Explore Multiple-Meaning Words

Task: *Working with a group, create a short presentation about the life of Zora Neale Hurston using past tense irregular verbs. The sentence frames below will get you started.*

Ⓢ *Zora Neale Hurston _____ up in Eatonville. Zora _____ that Mr. Clarke could help her. (grow, know)*

Ⓜ *Zora Neale Hurston _____ to Harlem from Florida. _____ Zora Neale Hurston _____ for a living. (come, write)*

Ⓛ *Zora Neale Hurston _____ others _____. She _____ collecting folklore. (give, spend)*

Wrap Up

Today we have learned about irregular verb forms. Why is it important to know which verbs are irregular? What is different about forming the past of irregular verbs?

Turn and Talk: *Using what we have learned today, explain the difference between a regular verb and an irregular verb.*

👥 Differentiated Instruction
Build Language: Form and Use Irregular Verbs

Ⓢubstantial Support

Model: Point to the portion of the first chart that is labeled "Justice in Eatonville." Highlight the past tense of the verbs. **Say:** *Knew, grew, put, stood, made and drew are all examples of irregular verbs. The present tense of these words is know, grow stand, make, and draw.* **Say:** *We do not add -ed, or -ied to any of these words to form the past tense version of these words. Say each of the present tense verbs and have students repeat the past tense.*

Practice: Distribute BLM 1. Work with students to complete the Practice activity.

Extend: Have students work in pairs to complete the Extend activity on the BLM.

Challenge: If students are ready, work with them to write new sentences using some of the irregular verbs.

Ⓜoderate Support

Model: Have students take turns reading the sentences in the chart, and the present and past tense of each verb. Point out the verb *stretched* in the fourth sentence and remind them that this verb is a regular verb. Ask them to explain how we form regular verbs and what is different about irregular verbs. Read each of the irregular verbs again and have students read the past tense forms.

Practice: Distribute BLM 2. Work with students to complete the activity in the Practice section.

Extend: Have students work with partners to complete the Extend activity on the BLM.

Challenge: Have students work together to write sentences with irregular verbs in the present and past.

Ⓛight Support

Practice: Have students review the first two paragraphs of each story in the Texts for Close Reading, page 12 (Justice) and page 20 (Zora). Create 2 Columns. Label 1 Column Regular Verbs and the Second Column Irregular Verbs. Have students complete the two columns based upon the verbs that they find.

Extend: Put students in pairs. Have students use some of the irregular verbs that they found to create new, original sentences. The students should create two sentences per verb. One sentence should use the present tense of the verb and the other sentence should use the irregular past tense of the verb.

Challenge: Have one student compose a sentence with a verb from the chart in the present and another student change it to past tense.

☑ Formative Assessment

Substantial Support	• Are students able to identify irregular verbs? • Are students able to identify the present and past tense of an irregular verb?
Moderate Support	• Can students recognize irregular verbs? • Can students correctly form the past tense of irregular verbs?
Light Support	• Can students correctly use the past and present tense of irregular verbs in sentences?

Preview or Review Week 3 ELA Mini-Lessons

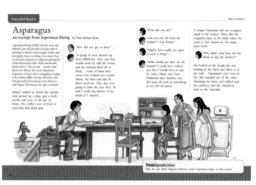

"Asparagus," pages 84–85

Student Objectives

LANGUAGE
Purpose:
• I can to retell details of a story.
Form:
• I can understand phrasal verbs.
CONTENT
• I can explain plot and character details in historical fiction.

Additional Materials
• Unit Presentation
• *Texts for Close Reading* booklet
• Think-Speak-Listen Flip Book
• Student journal

Metacognitive Prompt

As we read today, remember to pause while listening and reading to check your understanding of the story. You may find it helpful to ask yourself questions such as: Who is speaking or acting? What are they saying or doing? How are they feeling? Why do they feel this way?

12 Read "Asparagus"

Build Background and Vocabulary

Display the panels. If students have already read the story, ask them to share what they remember. Explain that it is written as a story, it is actually historical fiction.

Read Aloud the Text

Read the first section. **Say:** *The beginning of the story introduces us to the characters.* On the board, write: *Who are the major characters?* **Say:** *The conversation in the story centers mostly around Miguel and Esperanza. Both characters show emotions. I learn that both characters are upset. Words such as* sharp*,* temper*,* raged*, and* anger *help to describe the emotions of the characters.* Read the remaining excerpt and ask students to share their thoughts using this sentence frame: Miguel and Esperanza's are in conflict because _____. **Say:** *What other words help us to understand their conflict?* Elicit answers. **Say:** *Words like* fire*,* stamped *and* slamming *also help to express how the characters feel.* Refer to the essential question. How does the dialogue between these two characters help us to think about other perspectives?

Think-Speak-Listen: Use the following sentence frame or the Think-Speak-Listen Flip Book to guide discussion: *I think Miguel's behavior made Esperanze angry in this scene because _____.*

👥 Differentiated Instruction
Build Language: Understand Phrasal Verbs

Say: *Phrasal verbs are a group of words that include a verb + a preposition. The combination of these words creates a different meaning than the meaning of each individual word.* Read the first sentence. Write *picked up*. **Say:** *The word* pick *by itself means choose. And the word* up *is the opposite of down. But to* pick up *has a different meaning.* Pick up *is a phrasal verb. It means to lift.* Use the Differentiated Instruction to practice understanding phrasal verbs in a way that best matches the levels of your students.

☑ Use Oral and Written Language: Use Phrasal Verbs to Retell Details

Task: *Work with a partner. Write sentences to retell key details about "Asparagus." Use some of these phrasal verbs:* speak up, pick up, find out, hand in, point out, show up, take off, talk over, throw away, turn down.

(S)   *A group of men _____ from Oklahoma. They said they would _____.*

(M)   *Miguel had to _____ because he didn't want to _____ a day's pay.*

(L)   *Esperanza thought _____. Hearing about Miguel's day made her _____.*

 Wrap Up

Today, we have learned about phrasal verbs and how they are important to the meaning in a story. How can phrasal verbs help us to understand a story?

Turn and Talk: *Use phrasal verbs to share a story with your friend.*

👥 Differentiated Instruction
Build Language: Understand Phrasal Verbs

Ⓢ ubstantial Support

Model: Read aloud the first sentence and review the meaning you discussed of the phrasal verb *pick up*. Confirm understanding by asking students to pick up a pencil or a book. Write the word *pick up* and explain that phrasal verbs are made up of certain verbs plus prepositions like *up, out, off, on*. List other phrasal verbs from the story: *showed up, turned on, speak up*. Discuss the meaning of each one.

Practice: Distribute BLM 1. Work with students to complete the activity in the Practice section.

Extend: Have students complete the Extend activity on the BLM.

Challenge: If students are ready, work with them to write new sentences with phrasal verbs.

Ⓜ oderate Support

Model: Read aloud the first sentence. Ask a volunteer to tell or demonstrate the meaning of *pick up*. Write several phrasal verbs: *pick up, pick out, turn off, turn on, take out*. Explain that phrasal verbs have a verb plus a preposition such as *up, out, off*, or *on*. Point out that sometimes the verb is the same, but which preposition follows it changes the meaning, for example *turn on, turn off*.

Practice: Distribute BLM 2. Work with students to complete the activity in the Practice section.

Extend: Have students work with partners complete the Extend activity on the BLM.

Challenge: If students are ready, have them work in pairs to write more sentences with phrasal verbs.

Ⓛ ight Support

Have students use pages 22–29 of *Texts for Close Reading* for the following activities.

Practice: Review that phrasal verbs are made up of verbs plus a preposition, and that the meaning of the verb is different than the meaning of each of the words. Write some phrasal verbs from the reading: *pick up, catch up, speak up, work out, hold on*. Ask volunteers tell the meanings of the ones they recognize. Discuss the meaning of each one.

Extend: Have students work in pairs. Assign pages 24, 26, 27, 28 to different pairs. Ask them to look for the phrasal verbs you listed and to copy the sentence. (page 24: pick up, page 26: catch up, page 27: speak up, page 28: hold on, work out). Have them read aloud their sentence to the group and tell the meaning of the word in the sentence.

Challenge: Have students pick one of the conversations that take place in the story, "Asparagus." Have them identify who the characters involved are, what they are discussing and how this dialogue helps them to understand the plot.

☑ Formative Assessment

Substantial Support	• Can students understand phrasal verbs in the story?
Moderate Support	• Can students analyze phrasal verbs in the story? • Can students use phrasal verbs in sentences?
Light Support	• Can students analyze words and phrases that the characters and narrator use in order to explain the plot? • Can students use phrasal verbs to gain better understanding of the feeling of the characters?

Preview or Review Week 3 ELA Mini-Lessons

"Asparagus," page 86

Student Objectives

LANGUAGE

Purpose:
• I can compare and contrast characters.

Form:
• I can understand pronoun-antecedent agreement.

CONTENT
• I can explain the similarities and differences between characters in a historical fiction.

Additional Materials
• Unit Presentation
• *Texts for Close Reading* booklet
• Think-Speak-Listen Flip Book
• Student journal

Language Transfer

Today we will practice visualizing, or creating pictures in our mind, as we read. Focus on the illustration on page 87 to make connections with the words and phrases in the text. Create pictures in your mind of the differences between Esperanza's vision and Miguel's vision of how to get ahead in the United States.

13 Compare and Contrast Characters

Engage Thinking

Display the excerpt. **Ask:** *What do you remember about the characters? How are they similar? How are they different?* Elicit answers. **Say:.** *When I read, I look for similarities and differences in the characters to better understand the story.*

👥 Differentiated Instruction
Read and View Closely: Compare and Contrast Characters

Display and read the excerpt. **Say:** *When we compare and contrast characters, we are looking for their similarities and differences. This is important when reading a story because characters do not often agree. When trying to understand a character, we may ask: "What does the character think?" "How does the character feel?" and "What does the character do?" "How are they the same or different from another character?" These questions can also be used when comparing and contrasting characters.* Use the Differentiated Instruction to practice comparing and contrasting characters in a way that best matches the level of your students.

Think-Speak-Listen: Help students compare and contrast Miguel and Esperanze's opinions or use the Think-Speak-Listen Flip Book to guide discussion.

Build Language: Understand Pronoun Antecedent Agreement

Write: *The students read their books.* **Say:** *Students is the antecedent and their is the pronoun. The pronoun their refers to something earlier in the sentence–the students. If the antecedent is plural, the pronoun must be plural. In the sentence "Carl ate his sandwich," **Carl** is a singular antecedent so the pronoun must also be singular–**his**. **His** refers to, or stands in for, **Carl**, which was used earlier in the sentence.*

☑ Use Oral and Written Language: Compare and Contrast Characters

Task: *Imagine that you are telling a friend who has not read "Esperanza Rising" about the story. Work with a partner to say complete sentences that describes Esperanza and Miguel by comparing and contrasting them. Use pronouns such as she, he and they.*

(S) Esperanza moved to California from Mexico. _____ is more _____ than Miguel.

(M) Miguel worked on trains, but now _____. _____ is more _____ than Esperanza.

(L) _____ both _____, but Miguel feels _____.

🔄 Wrap Up

Today we have learned about the similarities and differences between characters. What are some of the details that we can learn by comparing and contrasting characters?

Turn and Talk: *Using what we have learned today, why is comparing and contrasting characters important for the readers to understand characters better?*

♟ Differentiated Instruction
Read and View Closely: Compare and Contrast Characters

ⓢubstantial Support

Model: Display the excerpt and read it aloud. **Say:** *Comparing and contrasting characters can help the reader to understand what a story is about. "Asparagus" is a story with two main characters who have some things in common, but they also have many differences. The similarities and differences between the characters come out when they talk to one another.* Discuss the similarities we can compare: Miguel and Esperanza are both young. They both moved to America. They both live in the same home. Then discuss the differences we can contrast: Esperanza has a temper and wants Miguel to fight. Miguel is hopeful. He is patient and wants to give things more time. **Say:** *Understanding both the similarities and differences of characters helps the reader to understand the plot.*

Practice: Distribute BLM 1. Work with students to complete the activity in the Practice section.

Extend: Have students work in pairs to complete the Extend section of the BLM.

Challenge: If students are ready, have them phrase comparisons using this sentence frame: *Miguel is _____ but Esperanza is _____.*

ⓜoderate Support

Model: Say: *In this part of the story the main characters are Miguel and Esperanza. In order to understand what is happening with the plot, the reader has to focus on the characters. This includes comparing and contrasting them which means looking for similarities and differences. Similarities include their youth and they both migrated to America. Their differences include how they feel about being in America. Esperanza is disappointed and Miguel is hopeful.*

Practice: Distribute BLM 2. Work with students to complete the activity in the Practice section.

Extend: Have students work with partners to complete the Extend section of the BLM.

Challenge: Work with students to understand why character analysis is important to a story.

ⓛight Support

Practice: Students will create two word webs. The first word web should have the name Esperanza in the middle. The connecting webs should include information that you learned about her from the story. The second web should include the name Miguel in the web. The connecting webs should include information that students learned about him from the story.

Extend: Have students work with a partner to take the word webs that they created and compare and contrast Miguel and Esperanza. Have them generate a list of all of the similarities and a second list with all of the differences.

Challenge: Based on the differences and similarities that were generated, identify some of the areas of overlap that students discovered.

☑ Formative Assessment

Substantial Support	• Are students able to explain what it means to compare characters? • Are students able to explain what it means to contrast characters?
Moderate Support	• Can students identify when characters are being compared and contrasted in a story?
Light Support	• Can students analyze characters by comparing and contrasting?

Preview or Review Week 3 ELA Mini-Lessons

"Use Modal Auxiliaries," page 87

Student Objectives

LANGUAGE

Purpose:
• I can use modal auxiliaries in a news report.

Form:
• I can recognize different types of verbs and verb phrases.

CONTENT
• I can understand modal auxiliaries in historical fiction.

Additional Materials

• Unit Presentation
• *Texts for Close Reading* booklet
• Think-Speak-Listen Flip Book
• Student journal

Language Transfer Support

Note that modal auxiliaries do not follow conventional English grammar rules. English Learners may need additional support with using the correct forms of modals and main verbs to express ideas about the present, past, and future. As students explore can and must from the text, help them understand that these modals have multiple meanings and functions.

14 Use Modal Auxiliaries

Engage Thinking

Write and have students repeat: *Miguel can succeed. Miguel might succeed. Miguel must succeed.* Underline can, might, and must. **Say:** *All three statements are about Miguel's succeeding, or doing well. But the modal auxiliaries* can, might, *and* must *change the meaning of succeed.* Can *means Miguel has the ability to succeed.* Might *means it's possible he will succeed.* Must *means it is necessary for Miguel to succeed.*

Read and View Closely: Recognize Modal Auxiliaries

Display the chart. Point to the first picture of Miguel and read the sentence. **Say:** *In this sentence, the word* could *is a modal auxiliary. It tells us what Miguel is able to do. It is paired with the word* dig. *Adding* could *tells me he is able to dig.* Point to the picture of Esperanza and read the sentence. **Ask:** *In this sentence, what verb is it paired with?* Elicit answers. **Say:** *It is paired with the verb* agree. *Both of these examples help the reader to understand what Miguel is capable of doing.*

Think-Speak-Listen: Use the following sentence frame or the Think-Speak-Listen Flip Book to guide discussion: *Miguel and Esperanze's lives would have been different if they had stayed in Mexico because _____.*

👥 Differentiated Instruction
Build Language: Use Modal Auxiliaries

Say: The girl may leave school early. They might go to the store. He must return the library book. *The modals* may/might *and* must *are used to express probability, or the likelihood that something will happen.* Read the last sentence on the page. Point out the modal auxiliary *must* and the verb *work.* **Say:** *When I read* must *before* work, *I know that it is necessary that Miguel works.* Use Differentiated Instruction to practice using modal auxiliaries in a way that best matches the level of your students.

☑️ Use Oral and Written Language: Use Modal Auxiliaries in a News Report

Task: *Collaborate with your group to write a news report based on the dialogue. Use your own words to interpret the problems and solutions that Esperanza and Miguel discuss. Use the following sentence starters and modal auxiliaries to get started.*

Ⓢ   *Miguel told Esperanza he had two choices. He _____ or lay tracks.*

Ⓜ   *Esperanza was _____ to hear what Miguel chose. She asked him, "_____?"*

Ⓛ   *Miguel asked Esperanza what _____. He explained that he _____.*

🔄 Wrap Up

Today we have learned about modal auxiliaries. What do modal auxiliaries express?

Turn and Talk: *Identify three modal auxiliaries that you learned in the text. Then, use these modal auxiliaries to share how you play your favorite sport.*

⚇⚇⚇ Differentiated Instruction
Build Language: Use Modal Auxiliaries

Ⓢubstantial Support

Model: Say: *Words such as* can, could, may, might, must, will, would, shall, should *and* ought *are often used in stories. They are verbs called* modals. *These words help to express the ability of characters. They also express the possibility of what characters can do.* Point to the excerpt and images from the story. **Say:** *Esperanza and Miguel use modals while talking to each other. Throughout this conversation, they use the words* could, can, would, *and* must.

Practice: Distribute BLM 1. Work with students to complete the activity in the Practice section.

Extend: Have students work in pairs to complete the activity in the Extend section of the BLM.

Challenge: If students are ready, work with them to create their own sentences based on the ones on the BLM.

Ⓜoderate Support

Model: Say: Read excerpts from the story. **Say:** *I look for words like could, should and just to know what the characters thinks he or she can or must do. These are verbs called* modals. *They show ability and possibility—what a character can do. In the story, "Asparagus," Esperanza and Miguel use modals to discuss Miguel's ability and the possibility of what's to come. Modal verbs such as* can, could, may, might, must, will, would, shall, should *and* ought *are paired with other verbs.*

Practice: Distribute BLM 2. Work with students to complete the activity in the Practice section.

Extend: Have students work with partners to activity in the Extend section of the BLM.

Challenge: Work with students to understand why modal auxiliaries are very important for character analysis in a story.

Ⓛight Support

Practice: Say: *In our everyday language we use modals just like the characters Miguel and Esperanza did in the story "Asparagus."* Have students locate sentences that contain modal auxiliaries in the Texts for Close Reading on page 28. Ask them to generate a list of the modal auxiliaries that are used in the sentences that in this section of the story.

Extend: Have students work with partners to review the lists. Ask them to take turns explaining what the model auxiliaries express in the sentences.

Challenge: Explain that modal auxiliaries can also be used to show a lack of possibility. Or they can be used to show a character's inability. Have students come up with a list of modal auxiliaries that show what Miguel and Esperanza cannot do or what they think is impossible. For example, *Esperanza can't believe that Miguel dug the ditch.*

☑ Formative Assessment

Substantial Support	• Are students able to identify modal auxiliaries in stories?
Moderate Support	• Can students explain how modal auxiliaries are used in stories?
Light Support	• Can students analyze the meaning and purpose of model auxiliaries?

Preview or Review Week 3 ELA Mini-Lessons

"British English and Me," pages 88–89

Student Objectives

LANGUAGE

Purpose:
- I can explore multiple-meaning words in sentences.

Form:
- I can describe how multiple-meaning words are used in a story.

CONTENT
- I can explain word meaning in a humor story.

Additional Materials
- Unit Presentation
- *Texts for Close Reading* booklet
- Think-Speak-Listen Flip Book
- Student journal

Language Transfer Support

Note that because many English words have multiple meanings, English Learners may need additional support with learning how these words work. Multiple-meaning words can cause confusion for students who translate English words literally. Provide opportunities for students to examine multiple-meaning words in context to determine their meanings and identify their grammatical functions.

15 Read "British English and Me"

Build Background and Vocabulary

Display the panels. If students have already read the story, ask them to share what they remember. **Say:** *Words can take on different meanings depending on where a story is set. As the writer of the story learns, the British meaning of some words is different than the English meaning. Eventually he learns the different words are things he is already familiar with.*

Read Aloud the Text

Read the first section. **Say:** *The beginning of the story introduces the reader to the setting. I know from reading that the narrator is there for a visit. Fletcher asks, "Why don't we get some grub?" What does* grub *mean?* Elicit answers. Read the rest of the excerpt and ask students to share their thoughts. **Say:** *The reader learns that grub can be a worm-like creature or grub can be food. How do we know which one is the correct meaning? It is important to pay attention to details.* Grub *refers to food.*

Differentiated Instruction
Build Language: Explore Multiple-Meaning Words

Point to the third paragraph. **Say:** *At the restaurant Fletcher recommends the "bangers and mash." Banger is a word that has multiple meanings. At first, it is not clear which meaning it has. Using my dictionary, I discover that banger could mean a person who bangs, a sausage, a firecracker or old car. Looking at the details from the story, I notice that they are at a restaurant and that Fletcher is recommending something to eat. Using these details, banger must be a type of food. In this context, banger means sausage.* Point to the fourth paragraph. *The story confirms this meaning when a dish made up of sausage and mash potatoes is served.* Use the Differentiated Instruction to practice exploring multiple-meaning words in a way that best matches the levels of your students.

Think-Speak-Listen: Using this sentence frame, ask student pairs to answer this question: *The character learned that _____ means _____ English.*

☑ Use Oral and Written Language: Explore Multiple-Meaning Words

Task: *Work with your group to explore two or three meanings of words. Use the sentence starters to fill in key details from the story "British English and Me" using multiple-meaning words such as* grub, order, match, meal, *and* expression. *Use a print or online dictionary.*

Ⓢ *When Fletcher suggested getting _____ to eat, the narrator was worried he was talking about a slimy worm.*

Ⓜ *In London, a _____ match is a game. In America the game is called _____.*

Ⓛ *Fletcher knew his cousin was confused when _____. _____ can also mean _____.*

⟳ Wrap Up

Today, we have learned about multiple-meaning words. How can the setting of a story help us to understand which meaning of a word is correct?

Turn and Talk: *Think of another example of a multiple-meaning word and use each meaning in a sentence.*

🏃 Differentiated Instruction
Build Language: Explore Multiple-Meaning Words

Ⓢ ubstantial Support

Model: Read the first sentence in the very last paragraph: *...the streets were full of people going to a football match...* Underline the word *match* and write three meanings, using pictures or gestures to illustrate: 1. a game 2. two things that are alike (draw two socks) 3. something to start a fire (draw a match). Point out that the other words in a sentence, like *football* help you determine which is the right meaning.

Practice: Distribute BLM 1. Work with students to complete the activity in the Practice section.

Extend: Have students work in pairs to complete the activity in the Extend section.

Challenge: If students are ready, help them to compose sentences to show the multiple meanings of a word.

Ⓜ oderate Support

Model: **Say:** *When reading, I may find a word that has more than one meaning. Sometimes, the story will provide enough details that I can determine the meaning just using details from the story.* Read the first sentence in the very last paragraph: *...the streets were full of people going to a football match...* **Say:** *Football is an example of a multiple-meaning word. The word football can be two very different games. In order to determine which type of game of football the author is referring to in "British English and Me," I refer back to the story.* Point to the rest of the sentence. Read: *...which is actually a soccer match in American English.* **Say:** *In this example, the text tells us the meaning here is the British version of the game football.*

Practice: Distribute BLM 2. Work with students to complete the activity in the Practice section.

Extend: Have students work with partners to complete the activity in the Extend section of the BLM.

Challenge: If students are ready, ask them to create more sentences to show the multiple meanings of words.

Ⓛ ight Support

Practice: Have each pair of students fold a paper into four squares. In the middle of the paper, ask them to write the word *banger*. Using a dictionary, have them look up the word *banger*. In each square, they write down one of the definitions and a picture that will help you to recall the meanings of this multiple-meaning word.

Extend: Have students review the pictures that they created. Each partner should take turns presenting the illustrations to the other. The partners should then explore how using the wrong meaning would change the story, "British English and Me."

Challenge: Have students pick one of the other multiple-meaning words used in "British English and Me." Using a dictionary, have them write down the definitions of the word. Then use each of those words in original sentences.

☑️ Formative Assessment

Substantial Support	• Can students identify multiple-meaning words in a story?
Moderate Support	• Can students use details from the text to determine the meanings of multiple-meaning words? • Can students appropriately use multiple-meaning words?
Light Support	• Can students analyze how the setting influences which meaning of a multiple-meaning word is most accurate? • Can students differentiate and explain multiple meanings of words?

Technology's Impact on Society

Essential Question

What value does technology bring to people's lives?

In this unit, students will read and compare literary and nonfiction selections about the role that technology has played in people's lives.

Unit 5 Lessons at a Glance

Language Skills

Week 1
- Understand the Structure of Poetry
- Use Verb Phrases
- Opinion Process Writing
- Use Prepositional Phrases
- Use Noun Suffixes -er, -or

Week 2
- Use Adverbs to Specify Frequency
- Condense Ideas
- Use Prepositional Phrases
- Use Verb Tenses to Convey Times
- Analyze Word Relationships

Week 3
- Connect Ideas
- Link Ideas and Events with Connecting Words
- Use Context Clues to Understand Vocabulary
- Recognize and Distinguish Between Homophones
- Analyze Words with Greek and Latin Roots

Lessons

Preview or Review Week 1 ELA Mini-Lessons

"Essential Question," pages 90–91

Introduce Unit 5: Technology's Impact on Society

Use the short lesson below to introduce the topic of the unit and help students understand the Essential Question.

Build Background and Vocabulary

Draw students' attention to the pictures on pages 82–83.

Say: *The topic of this unit is technology's impact on society. These pictures introduce the ideas that we will read about.*

Create a three-column chart as shown below. Invite students to read the caption for the first picture. Write it in the chart. Explain that a shipyard is a place where you can see technology at work. Cranes that lift boxes are made of steel which was invented in the 1850s. The invention of steel made it possible for trains, skyscrapers, and cars to be built. These technologies changed people's lives. Write the words **crane** and **steel** and explain them. Continue in this way with the other pictures.

A Shipyard	A Textile Factory	A Mobile Phone
shipyard	textile factory	mobile phone
cranes	sewing machine	network
boxes	fabric	satellite
steel	factory workers	Internet

Student Objectives

LANGUAGE
Purpose:
• I can understand the Essential Question.
CONTENT
• I can understand the topic of the unit.

Additional Materials
• Unit Presentation

🏃 Differentiated Instruction
Explain the Essential Question

Display or invite students to access the Unit 1 video and discuss what they have learned. Read aloud the Essential Question: *What value does technology bring to people's lives?* Explain key words by definition and examples: **value, technology,** etc. Encourage students to give examples of things that represent technology (**planes, television,** etc.).

Use the Differentiated Instruction to help students at all levels understand the Essential Question.

Then proceed to Lesson 1.

👥👥 Differentiated Instruction
Explain the Essential Question

Ⓢubstantial Support

Point to the picture of the textile factory.

Write: *Many things are made in factories.* Have students say the sentence with you. Explain that factories are places were many products are made. Point to the picture of the mobile phone.

Gesture and say: *Many thing are made in factories, even mobile phones. In the 1800s, many machines were invented that we use today. Can you think of any inventions from a long time ago?*

Elicit answers.

Say: *In this unit, we will learn about the value that technology brings to our lives.*

Ⓜoderate Support

Point to the picture of the textile factory.

Say: *Many things are made in factories. Clothes are made in factories. The sewing machine was invented in 1846.*

Point to the picture of the mobile phone.

Say: *Even mobile phones are made in factories.*

Write this sentence on the board: *The mobile phone was invented in 1873/1973.* Say the sentence with students. Elicit the correct year.

Ask: *What other inventions can you think of?*

Elicit answers.

Say: *The sewing machine and mobile phone are technologies. When new technologies are invented, our lives change. When new technologies are invented, they change our lives. Depending on our point of view, these technologies add or sometimes don't add value.*

Ⓛight Support

Point to a sewing machine in the picture of the textile factory.

Say: *The sewing machine is an example of an invention that changed people's lives.*

Write: *The sewing machine was invented in 1846/1946.* Say the sentence with students and elicit the correct year.

Say: *The invention of the mobile phone has also changed people's lives.*

Write: *The mobile phone was invented in 1973/1773.* Say the sentence with students and elicit the correct year. Explain that the mobile phone is a new technology and the sewing machine is an old technology. Whenever there is a new technology, our lives change.

Say: *In this unit, we're going to learn what new technologies add, or don't add, to people's lives. Depending on each person's point of view, some technologies add value and some do not.*

☑ Formative Assessment

Substantial Support	• Can students understand key words such as **value** and **technology**? • Can students understand the concept that technology changes people's lives?
Moderate Support	• Can students understand key words such as **value** and **technology**? • Can students brainstorm examples of technologies from the past?
Light Support	• Can students understand the Essential Question? • Can students understand the link between inventions, new technologies, and the societal changes they bring about?

"Technology and the Lowell Mill Girls," page 92

Student Objectives

LANGUAGE

Purpose:
• I can describe the structure of poetry.

Form:
• I can understand the structure of poetry.

CONTENT
• I can read a poem on a social studies topic.

Additional Materials
• Unit Presentation
• *Texts for Close Reading* booklet
• Think-Speak-Listen Flip Book
• Student journal

Language Transfer Support

Note that the short **i** sound in **mill** and **picture** may be unfamiliar to students whose first language is Vietnamese, Hmong, or Khmer. These students may need modeling to produce words with the short **i** sound.

1 Read "Technology and the Lowell Mill Girls"

Build Background and Vocabulary

Display the images and explain any unfamiliar vocabulary. Read the title of the poem and the introduction aloud. If the students have already read the poem, ask them what they remember. Invite students to share what they know about factory work.

Read Aloud the Text

Read the first stanza. Ask students to find images in the picture that match the words in the stanza (women, loom, mill, etc.) and ask *wh-* questions, such as *Where is this? What is the woman in the poem doing?* Continue with stanzas 2 - 3. After reading, **ask:** *Who is the narrator of the poem?* Model thinking through the answer: *The narrator of the poem is the superintendent. He is watching a woman in the mill.* Then, refer to the Essential Question. **Ask:** *How did changes in technology affect this woman's life?* Invite students to respond. Elicit responses. **Say:** *This poem describes a real factory using poetic structure. It is a poem on a social studies topic.*

Think-Speak-Listen: Use the following sentence frame or the Think-Speak-Listen Flip Book to guide discussion: *I think the woman is feeling _____. I think the superintendent is feeling _____.*

Differentiated Instruction
Build Language: Understand the Structure of Poetry

Say: *Poetry looks <u>and</u> sounds different from a story.* Read the first line aloud with students. **Ask:** *How is this different from a story?* Elicit answers. **Say:** *The first line of a story would be a complete sentence; this is not. The first line of a story begins a paragraph. This first line of a poem begins a stanza. A stanza is a group of lines of poetry. Each stanza is separated by a space from other stanzas.* Explain that recognizing how a poem is put together makes it easier to read and to understand the poem. Use the Differentiated Instruction to practice recognizing the structure of poetry in a way that best matches the levels of your students.

☑ Use Oral and Written Language: Describe the Structure of Poetry

Task: *Work in small groups to determine if "A Mill Picture" is, or is not poetry. Share your sentences with the class.*

Ⓢ *"A Mill Picture" is a _____. It has _____ instead of sentences.*

Ⓜ *"A Mill Picture" is _____ because it has _____.*

Ⓛ *"A Mill Picture" is _____ because it _____ and _____.*

 Wrap Up

Today we learned about poetic structure. How does knowing about poetic structure help readers interpret a poem?

Turn and Talk: *Why do you think the person writing about the textile workers chose to write a poem instead of a story?*

👥 Differentiated Instruction
Build Language: Understanding the Structure of Poetry

Ⓢubstantial Support

Model: Say: *When I read the poem, I see that there are groups of lines. Each group of lines is a stanza. There is space between each stanza.* **Ask:** *How many stanzas are there? How many lines are in each stanza? Elicit answers.* **Read the first stanza aloud.** **Say:** *I see the word her and I know the stanza is about a woman. I see the words looms, belts, and gearing. These words tell me that she is in a factory.* Remind students that each stanza gives new information about the topic of the poem.

Practice: Distribute BLM 1. Work with students to choose the words that best complete the sentences about the structure of poetry.

Extend: Working in pairs, have students work out the subject of the poem and the information given in each stanza. Remind them to refer to the poem if necessary.

Challenge: If students are ready, work with them to discuss what the poet is expressing in this poem. Encourage them to use the new vocabulary they've learned to discuss poetry.

Ⓜoderate Support

Model: Reread the first four lines of the poem and model how the punctuation shows they are all one sentence, even though each line begins with a capital letter. Explain that poets are allowed to play with the regular rules of writing prose in order to evoke a feeling. **Say:** *When writing a poem, poets thing carefully about how to organize the text. Sometimes the lines are separated into stanzas. Each stanza relates to the main idea of the poem.*

Practice: Distribute BLM 2. Have students work with you to complete the sentence frames with words they've learned about the structure of poetry.

Extend: Working in pairs, have students work out the subject of the poem and the information given in each stanza. Remind them to refer to the poem if necessary.

Challenge: If students are ready, have them complete the Extend activity in the Light Support section.

Ⓛight Support

Use the text on pp. 4-5 in the *Texts for Close Reading* to complete the following activities.

Practice: Work with students to summarize each stanza. **Say:** *By shifting the description of the setting in stanza one to the possible thoughts of the worker in stanza two, the reader gets a fuller picture of the emotional tone of this place and time.*

Extend: Have students reread the poem. Have students work with a partner and write sentences that tell how the order of the stanzas affects the emotional impact of the poem.

Challenge: Tell students that a quatrain is a four-line poem or stanza that can rhyme in different patterns. Ask students to identify the rhyme pattern in the quatrains in the poem "A Mill Picture" (lines 2 and 4).

☑ Formative Assessment

Substantial Support	• Do students recognize lines and stanzas in a poem? • Can students use sentence frames to explain text structure in poetry?
Moderate Support	• Can students identify elements of the structure of poetry? • Can students use sentence frames to explain the meaning of a poem?
Light Support	• Can students describe how the structure of poetry helps poets evoke emotion? • Can students generate original sentences in which they explain how stanzas in a poem fit together?

Preview or Review Week 1 ELA Mini-Lessons

Use Verb Phrases

"Use Verb Phrases," page 93

Student Objectives

LANGUAGE
Purpose:
• I can perform a monologue.
Form:
• I can use verb phrases.
CONTENT
• I can understand a poem about a social studies topic.

Additional Materials
• Unit Presentation
• *Texts for Close Reading* booklet
• Think-Speak-Listen Flip Book
• Student journal

Language Transfer Support

Students whose native language is Cantonese or Haitian Creole may need extra support recognizing and using verb phrases. In these languages, the verb **be** can be omitted. Students may be accustomed to saying, for example, *the woman working in a factory* instead of *the woman is working in a factory.*

Students whose first language is Spanish may be familiar with the following cognates of words you discuss in this lesson: **verb** *(verbo)* and **phrase** *(frase)*. Encourage students to look and listen for other cognates.

2 Use Verb Phrases
Engage Thinking

Display the photograph from "A Mill Picture." **Ask:** *What is the mill worker doing in the photograph? What else might the mill worker be doing? Is she thinking? About what?* Read the poem. **Ask:** *What does the text tell us about what the woman is doing?*

Turn and Talk: *What action or actions are presented in the poem's text?*

Read and View Closely: Recognize Verb Phrases

Display the chart and read the title. **Say:** *This chart shows that a verb phrase has a helping verb and a main verb.* Read aloud the first row. **Say:** *Look at the boldfaced words. The helping verb is is. The main verb is working. Helping verbs can give the time of the action. The verb tells us the action is in the present.* Repeat with the remaining rows of the chart.

👥 Differentiated Instruction
Build Language: Use Verb Phrases

Say: In the chart, we looked at some of the verb phrases used in the poem "A Mill Picture." Then we learned how verb phrases can be put together to show when actions are happening. Using verb phrases helps readers picture clearly what is happening and when. Use the Differentiated Instruction to practice using verb phrases in a way that best matches the levels of your students.

Think-Speak-Listen: Use the following sentence frame or the Think-Speak-Listen Flip Book to guide discussion: *Verb phrases are formed with _____ and _____. It is necessary to use verb phrases when _____.*

☑ Use Oral and Written Language: Perform a Monologue

Task: *Working with a partner, write sentences from the point of view of a mill worker. Use a verb phrase. Perform your monologue for another pair of students.*

Ⓢ *I have a job in Massachusetts. I am _____ in the town of Lowell. I am _____ at a mill.*

Ⓜ *I moved to Massachusetts and I'm _____ in _____. I'm _____ at _____.*

Ⓛ *I moved _____ and _____. At the mill, I'm _____ as _____.*

🔄 Wrap Up

Today we learned that a verb phrase is made up of a helping verb and a main verb. How do verb phrases help readers imagine and understand actions?

Turn and Talk: *Describe something that you are thinking about using verb phrases. Tell your partner.*

👤👤👤 Differentiated Instruction
Build Language: Use Verb Phrases

Ⓢubstantial Support

Model: Remind students that a verb phrase consists of a main verb and a helping verb. Point to and read aloud the second row of the chart. **Say:** *The verb phrase is gazing is made up of a helping verb is and the main verb gazing. It tells me the action is happening now. Gazing tells me what the action is.* Explain that verb phrases are also used to create questions. Point to the third row on the chart and read the question. **Say:** *In this question, the helping verb is Does and the main verb is thinking.*

Practice: Distribute BLM 1. Help students complete the activity.

Extend: Have pairs work together to complete the activity on the BLM.

Challenge: If students are ready, have them work in pairs and create questions and answers using the following verb phrases: *do you think, I am thinking.*

Ⓛight Support

Use the text on pp. 4–5 in the *Texts for Close Reading* to complete the following activities.

Practice: **Say:** *I know that verb phrases show time and express an action, such as: The Irish woman is working at the mill. The helping verb helps me to understand when something happened. If the action is happening in the past, we need to change the helping verb to the past tense. For example, we need to change the sentence to: The Irish woman was working at the mill yesterday. The helping verb is changes to was.* Direct students to paragraphs 1 and 2 of "A Mill Picture." Have them list the verb phrases they find. Then have them put the verb phrases into the past tense.

Extend: In pairs, have students find verb phrases in paragraphs 3 and 4. After making their list of verb phrases, have them put the verb phrases in the past tense.

Challenge: Working with you, have students choose a verb phrase and write an original past tense sentence.

Ⓜoderate Support

Model: Review the chart with students. Point out each verb phrase and the helping verb and main verb. **Say:** *I notice that in a verb phrase, the helping verb tells me when something happens. If it's happening now, I can use helping verbs like am, is or are. If it's happening in the past, I need to use was or were.* Call attention to the third row of the chart. **Say:** *I see in this example that the helping verb is separated from the main verb.* Point out the helping verb *does* and the main verb *think*. **Say:** *Using does and think this way, I can write a question.*

Practice: Distribute BLM 2. Have students work with you to choose the best verb phrase to complete the sentences. Then have them write the helping verb and main verb. **Ask:** *Are these actions happening in the present or the past?*

Extend: Have pairs work together to complete the activity on the BLM.

Challenge: If students are ready, list other helping verbs on the board, such as: have, has, and can. Help students brainstorm verb phrases.

☑ Formative Assessment

Substantial Support	• Can students recognize main verb, helping verbs, and verb phrases? • Can students identify and write down the helping verb and main verb from a sentence?
Moderate Support	• Can students understand that verb phrases help us know when an action occurred? • Can students complete a sentence with an appropriate verb phrase?
Light Support	• Can students use verb phrases correctly in present and past tense? • Can students generate original sentences using verb phrases?

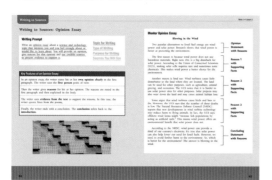

"Process Writing," pages 94–95

Student Objectives

LANGUAGE
Purpose:
- I can analyze an opinion essay.

Form:
- I can write about the features of an opinion essay.

CONTENT
- I can share my ideas in collaborative conversation and in writing.

Additional Materials
- Unit Presentation
- *Texts for Close Reading* booklet
- Think-Speak-Listen Flip Book
- Student journal

3 Process Writing: Opinion Essay

Engage Thinking

Tell students that they will analyze an opinion essay so that they can recognize its parts. Read aloud the writing topic.

> Write an opinion essay about a science and technology topic of your choosing. You will use your own personal experience and/or prior knowledge to help you brainstorm a topic for your essay and develop an opinion statement.

Say: *Let's ask questions to make sure we understand the writing topic. What will the writer write about? What type of writing is it? Where will the writer get some of his details?*

ᴬᴬᴬ Differentiated Instruction
Read and View Closely: Analyze an Opinion Essay

Say: *As I read aloud the essay, we will analyze it to identify how the writer addresses the four features of an opinion essay. Look for the opinion as I read.* Read the first paragraph. **Ask:** *What is the writer's opinion?* Check that students can identify wind power as better than solar power.

Say: *The writer supports her opinion with reasons and supporting facts. Listen for these as I read.* Read the second paragraph aloud. **Say:** *Turn to a partner. Which sentence is a reason? Which presents facts?* Check that students can identify examples of reasons and facts. Help students to understand any unfamiliar vocabulary.

Ask: *Where does the writer get his facts?* Check that students can identify the source. Then continue in this way, asking the class to identify the main reason and supporting facts for the other paragraphs.

Finish reading the essay. **Say:** *The writer ends the essay with a conclusion that restates the introduction. Turn to a partner. How does the introduction relate to the conclusion?* Invite pairs to explain their answers to the class.

Then continue the lesson using Differentiated Instruction that best fits the needs of your students.

Share Your Understanding

Bring the students back together. **Ask:** *What did we learn today about an opinion essay?* Review the structure as needed.

 Final Writing Assignment

Use the *English Language Development Assessment* to assess students' writing for their ELA writing assignment.

👤👤👤 Differentiated Instruction
Read and View Closely: Analyze an Opinion Essay

Ⓢubstantial Support

Model: Distribute BLM 1. **Say:** *Let's read and analyze another opinion essay that answers the writing topic.* Read the first paragraph and pause. **Ask:** *Which sentence is the opinion statement? Model answering the question.*

Practice: Continue reading the essay and ask the same questions that you asked about the mentor text. Invite students to answer.

Extend: Have students in pairs complete the activity on the BLM.

Challenge: Write on the board: *After reading "Wind Is Better," I think _____ power is better. The reason is because _____. A detail to support my reason is _____.* Have students answer the questions with their ideas. Then have pairs compare their answers and help each other to express their ideas.

Ⓛight Support

Practice: Distribute BLM 2. **Say:** *This is the Opinion Mentor Text that you read in class. We will look more closely at how writers use facts and details to support their opinions.* Do item 1 with students.

Extend: Have students in pairs complete items 2–4.

Challenge: Point out that in opinion essays, writers sometimes give an argument against the thing they are for, so they can defeat the reason. **Say:** *In paragraph four, the writer explains a reason not to use wind power. How does the writer argue against this?* Turn to your partner and discuss how the writer turns this argument around. Put students into pairs to discuss the issue. Monitor and help as needed. Then invite pairs to describe to the class how the writer defended wind power against an argument.

Ⓜoderate Support

Model: Draw students' attention to the Opinion Mentor Text in their book. **Say:** *Let's analyze how the features of an opinion essay.* Make the chart below. **Say:** *I write the first feature "Opinion statement" and then I write the example from the text.*

Opinion Essay	Examples
1. Opinion statement	"wind power is better than solar power"
2. Reasons for opinion	
3. Facts and details	
4. Conclusion	

Practice: Work with students to complete the chart with quotes and information from the essay.

Extend: Have students work with a partner. Tell them to discuss examples of how the writer supported the reasons with facts. Remind them to ask each other questions and add relevant information.

Challenge: Have students work with a partner. Tell them to complete these sentence frames: *An opinion the writer gives against wind turbines is that _____. But the writer says _____ to argue against this opinion.*

Have partners discuss the sentences frames and complete them with ideas from the text. Then check that the class understands how the writer turned a negative against wind turbines into a positive.

☑️ Formative Assessment

Substantial Support	• Do students recognize the criteria for an opinion essay in the Mentor Opinion Essay?
Moderate Support	• Do students recognize the ways in which the Mentor Opinion Essay meets the criteria for an opinion essay? • Can students describe the features of an opinion essay in their own words?
Light Support	• Do students recognize criteria and analyze how the Mentor Text meets the criteria for an opinion essay? • Can students describe in their own words how the writer meets the criteria for an opinion essay?

Extend and Scaffold Academic Language for Writing

Analyze the Mentor Text: Language Purpose and Structure

Introduction   All Levels of Support

Materials List
- **Mentor Text L** BLM X Light Support
- **Writing Frames Teacher Page** BLM Y
- **Writing Frames Student Page** BLM Z

- Have a copy of BLM Y to refer to during the lesson.

- Distribute BLMs X and Z to each student.

- Read aloud the writing topic on BLM X. Explain that students will read and analyze the language one writer used to respond to this topic.

- Have students follow along as you read aloud paragraph 1 of "Wind Is Better."

- Point out the phrase *A close look shows that wind power is better than solar power* and the words that indicate the comparison frame in bold. **Ask:** *Why did the author use this language? What is its purpose?* Help students understand that the author uses the structure _____ *is better than* _____ to address the writing topic, which asked the writer to compare and give an opinion.

- Have students write this frame into the "Compare/Contrast" row of their Writing Frames worksheet (BLM Z). Tell students this is one writing frame they can use in their writing to compare something to something else.

- Analyze other bolded phrases in paragraph 1. Explain their purpose and help students add the writing frames to BLM Z.

- Follow these steps as you read additional paragraphs.

- Read aloud the writing topic on BLM Z. Work with students to generate additional writing frames they could use as they write a response to this topic. Refer to BLM Y for examples.

Based on students' needs, conduct additional lessons using the differentiated instruction and tools provided.

Light Support   Differentiated Instruction

Materials List
- **Mentor Text L** BLM X Light Support
- **Writing Frames Teacher Page** BLM Y
- **Writing Frames Student Page** BLM Z

Students will need their copies of BLMs X and Z from the initial lesson. Refer to the chart below and your copy of BLM Y during the lesson.

- Explain that students will reread "Wind Is Better" to analyze more phrases and sentences that the writer used.

- Reread the text with students one paragraph at a time.

- Ask individuals or partners to find and underline each phrase in the chart below, read the sentence it appears in, and try to determine the sentence's purpose in the text.

- Provide explanation as necessary, then have students add the writing frames to the "Other Academic Phrases and Sentences" column of BLM Z.

- Encourage students to generate related writing frames and add them to their chart.

LIGHT SUPPORT

Purpose	Phrase/Sentence (paragraph)	Frame
State an Argument	A close look shows that wind power is better than solar power when it comes to protecting the environment. (1)	_____ shows that _____ is better than _____ when it comes to _____.
Give Reasons	The first reason wind power is better for the environment is because it does not require the use of hazardous materials. (2)	The first reason _____ is better for _____ is because _____.
Add Details/ Facts	In fact, the UCS says offshore wind farms might... (4)	In fact, _____.
Cause and Effect	As a result, wind power offers an environmental plus... (4)	As a result, _____.
Give Opposing Arguments	It's true that solar power can also help lower our dependence on fossil fuels. However, we must... (5)	It's true that _____. However, _____.

Ⓜoderate Support

Differentiated Instruction

Materials List
- **Mentor Text M** BLM A Moderate Support
- **Writing Frames Teacher Page** BLM Y
- **Writing Frames Student Page** BLM Z

Use the mentor text (BLM A) and the phrases and sentences appropriate for the support level you are targeting.

- Distribute BLM A. Students will also need their copy of BLM Z.

- Read aloud BLM A as students follow along.

- Then reread the text one paragraph at a time, stopping after each paragraph to focus on the bolded and underlined content. Work with students to understand the purpose of each phrase within the text. Have students write the corresponding writing frame in the "Other Academic Phrases and Sentences" column of BLM Z.

- Have partners practice using one or more of these writing frames to expand an idea in the essay they are writing. Have students share their examples with other members of the group.

MODERATE SUPPORT

Purpose	Phrase/Sentence (paragraph)	Frame
Compare/Contrast	Wind power and solar power are both popular sources of energy. (1)	_____ and _____ are both _____.
State an Argument	Research shows that wind power is better than solar power because it protects the environment more. (1)	_____ shows that _____ is better than _____ because _____.
Give Reasons	Another reason is because wind power does not use a lot of land. (3)	Another reason is because _____ _____.
Give Examples	...they can use the land for other purposes, such as agriculture and animals. (3)	_____, such as _____ and _____.
Cause and Effect	As a result, wind power is better for the environment. (4)	As a result, _____.

Ⓢubstantial Support

Differentiated Instruction

Materials List
- **Mentor Text S** BLM B Substantial Support
- **Writing Frames Teacher Page** BLM Y
- **Writing Frames Student Page** BLM Z

Students will need their copy of BLM Z from the initial lesson.

- Distribute BLM B.

- Follow the procedure explained in the Moderate Support lesson.

SUBSTANTIAL SUPPORT

Purpose	Phrase/Sentence (paragraph)	Frame
Compare/Contrast	Both wind power and solar power are better than fossil fuel energy. (1)	Both _____ and _____ are better than _____.
Give Reasons	The first reason is because wind power is safer. (2)	The first reason is because _____ is [adjective]-er.
Explain	...solar power is not safe because it uses... (2)	_____ is [not] safe because _____.
Give Reasons	Another reason is because wind power is better for the land. (3)	Another reason is because _____ is _____.
Compare/Contrast	Wind power and solar power are both good. But wind power is better for the environment. (5)	___ and _____ are _____. But _____ is _____.

Preview or Review Week 1 ELA Mini-Lessons

"Eli Whitney's Cotton Gin," pages 96–97

Student Objectives

LANGUAGE
Purpose:
• I can create a movie strip about the cotton gin.
Form:
• I can use prepositional phrases.
CONTENT
• I can recognize an informational social studies text.

Additional Materials
• Unit Presentation
• *Texts for Close Reading* booklet
• Think-Speak-Listen Flip Book
• Student journal

Language Transfer Support

Students whose first language is Spanish, Hmong, or Khmer may need extra support reading and speaking words with the /j/ sound, such as *gin, challenges, engine,* and *changes*. There is no similar sound in their native language. To support these students, you may wish to pre-teach these words and focus on articulating the /j/ sound.

4 Read "Eli Whitney's Cotton Gin"

Build Background and Vocabulary

Display the images and explain any key vocabulary. If students have already read the text, ask them what they remember. Invite students to share what they know about cotton and the cotton gin.

Read Aloud the Text

Read panel 1. Ask students to explain how the drawing and the text work together. **Say:** *I see the drawing of a man, Eli Whitney. The text tells me about his life.* Read panel 2. **Ask:** *What does the picture show? What does the text add?* Model thinking through the answer: *I see in panel 2 the photograph shows a cotton plant. The text helps me realize that cotton must be processed.* Continue with panels 3 - 8. Then refer to the Essential Question. **Ask:** *How did the invention of the cotton gin affect cotton workers' lives?* Invite students to respond. **Say:** *This text is an informational social studies text. It helps readers understand the development of technology to produce cotton.*

Think-Speak-Listen: Use the following sentence frame or the Think-Speak-Listen Flip Book to guide discussion: *Many farmers in the Cotton Belt chose to grow cotton rather than other crops because _____.*

👥 Differentiated Instruction
Build Language: Use Prepositional Phrases

Display panel 4. Write these prepositional phrases *in a box, through small slots,* and *by a hand crank.* **Say:** *I see each phrase begins with a preposition and ends with a noun.* **Ask:** *Which words are prepositions? Which are nouns?* Elicit answers. *Prepositional phrases add important details to a text. They help writers answer questions for readers, such as how, when, and where. They show relationships within a sentence that help readers understand a text.* Use the Differentiated Instruction to practice using prepositional phrases in a way that best matches the levels of your students.

☑ Use Oral and Written Language: Create a Movie Strip About the Cotton Gin

Task: *Working with a group, make a movie strip about Eli Whitney and the cotton gin. Choose pictures from the text to go with your movie strip. Use prepositional phrases to add details. Share your movie strip with another group.* Use this opportunity to to assess students using the rubric in *English Language Development Assessment.*

(S) *A cotton gin pulls cotton _____. The brushes turn _____.*

(M) *A cotton gin works by _____. The brushes _____.*

(L) *First, rotating _____ pulled the cotton fibers. Then, brushes _____.*

🔄 Wrap Up

Today we learned that prepositional phrases help answer questions readers might have. What kind of questions do prepositional phrases answer?

Turn and Talk: *Describe another machine you know about to your partner. use prepositional phrases to discuss how it works.*

👥 Differentiated Instruction
Build Language: Prepositional Phrases

Ⓢ ubstantial Support

Model: Say: *I know that prepositional phrases begin with a preposition like in or to. Let's look for other prepositions.* Display panel 3. Ask students to tell you what prepositions they see in the text. **Say:** *I see the preposition from in the first sentence. I see the preposition for in the second sentence. I know these prepositions begin prepositional phrases.*

Practice: Say: *A prepositional phrase has two parts. It has a preposition like from and a noun or noun phrase. Let's look for the nouns for each of these prepositions.* Read the first sentence in panel 3 aloud. Help students find the noun *fibers*. Read the second sentence. Help them find the noun *engine*.

Extend: In pairs, have students continue the activity in panel 5. After they complete the task, have them share their answers. Write the prepositional phrases *On March 14, 1794, for his cotton gin,* and *by law* on the board. Review the meaning of each prepositional phrase.

Challenge: If students are ready, have them work in pairs to complete the following sentence with a prepositional phrase: The cotton belt produced more cotton that any other place _____.

Ⓛ ight Support

Use the text on pp. 6–9 in the *Texts for Close Reading* to complete the following activities.

Practice: Distribute BLM 2. Work with students to complete the activity. Students will need to use the prepositional phrases they find in the text in their answers.

Extend: Working in pairs, have students continue writing answers in the activity on BLM 2.

Challenge: Have students write answers to the following questions: *What types of words can be part of a prepositional phrase? What information can a prepositional phrase provide?*

Ⓜ oderate Support

Model: Say: *I remember that a prepositional phrase has two parts. There's a preposition like from and a noun or noun phrase.* Point to panel 3. **Say:** *Do you see a preposition in the first sentence?* Elicit answers. **Say:** *From is the preposition and the fibers is the noun. This is a prepositional phrase. Have students find the other prepositional phrase in the panel* (in the engine).

Practice: Distribute BLM 1. Work with students to write the prepositional phrases and underline the noun or noun phrase in each sentence.

Extend: Working with a partner, have students continue writing the prepositional phrases and underlining the noun or noun phrase in each sentence on the BLM.

Challenge: If students are ready, have them read paragraph 9 on page 8 of the *Texts for Close Reading*. With a partner, have them find the prepositional phrase that answers this question: When had slavery spread westward? Have them write a complete sentence to answer the question.

☑️ Formative Assessment

Substantial Support	• Are students able to identify prepositional phrases in the text? • Can students recognize the parts of a prepositional phrase with support?
Moderate Support	• Can students recognize the parts of a prepositional phrase? • Can students distinguish between the prepositions and the object with little support?
Light Support	• Can students explain what information prepositional phrases add? • Can students write original sentences using prepositional phrases?

Word Study/Build Vocabulary   Week 1 • Lesson 5

Lucy Larcom's New England Girlhood

In 1835, when Lucy Larcom was eleven years old, her widowed mother moved her eight children to Lowell, Massachusetts.... Lucy began working at Lowell Mills....

In 1889, she published her autobiography, A New England Girlhood. The work reveals the thoughts and feelings of an observant child about being a mill laborer....

"I never cared much for machinery. The buzzing and hissing and whizzing of pulleys and rollers and spindles and flyers around me often grew tiresome...."

"But in a room below us we were sometimes allowed to peer in through a sort of blind door at the great waterwheel.... It was so huge that we could only watch a few of its spokes at a time...moving with a slow, measured strength through the darkness."

ThinkSpeakListen
Answer the following questions: How did Lucy feel about the machines in the mill? How do you think she felt about the waterwheel? Refer to words in the text to support your opinions.

"Lucy Larcom's New England Girlhood," page 98

Student Objectives

LANGUAGE
Purpose:
• I can create a song or rap.
Form:
• I can use noun suffixes **-er, -or**.
CONTENT
• I can read an autobiographical narrative on a social studies topic.

Additional Materials

• Unit Presentation
• *Texts for Close Reading* booklet
• Think-Speak-Listen Flip Book
• Student journal
• Dictionary

Language Transfer Support

Students whose first language is Spanish may be familiar with the cognate of the word *suffix (sufijo)* studied in this lesson. When reading and speaking, encourage students to look for words that are similar to words in their first language.

5 Read "Lucy Larcom's New England Girlhood"

Build Background and Vocabulary

Display the images and explain key vocabulary. If students have already read the text, ask them what they remember. Invite students to share what they know about factory work.

Read Aloud the Text

Read panel 1. **Ask:** *Who is in the picture?* Elicit answers. Read panel 2. To support comprehension, help students find the pulleys, rollers, spindles, and flyers in the picture. After reading, **ask:** *What is this text about?* Model thinking through the answer: **Say:** *Lucy Larcom talks about her work at a mill.* Then, refer to the Essential Question. **Ask:** *What value does technology bring to people's lives?* Invite students to respond. **Say:** *This text is autobiographical. It gives readers one person's firsthand view of a cloth factory.*

Think-Speak-Listen: Use the following sentence frame or the Think-Speak-Listen Flip Book to guide discussion: *Lucy felt _____ about the machines in the mill. She felt _____ about the waterwheel.*

👥👥👥 Differentiated Instruction
Build Language: Use Noun Suffixes -er, -or

Read the last sentence of the second paragraph. Point out the word *laborer*. **Say:** *Laborer ends in the suffix -er. A suffix is a group of letters added to the end of a base word that changes its meaning.* Explain that *-er* is a suffix added to a word to make a noun. A *laborer* means "a person who performs labor." Invite students to think of other *-er* nouns. **Say:** *Writers use nouns with the suffix -er or -or to say when someone or something does an action. When we see -er or -or after a base word, we have more information about the meaning of the noun.* Use the Differentiated Instruction to practice using the noun suffixes *-er* and *-or* in a way that best matches the levels of your students.

✅ Use Oral and Written Language: Create a Song or Rap

Task: *Work with a partner. Make a song or rap using the suffix -er and/or -or.*

Ⓢ   *Work! Work! Work! I'm a _____. That means I _____. _____! _____! _____! I'm a _____. That means I _____.*

Ⓜ   *Work! Work! Work! I'm a _____ because I work and I'm a _____ because I _____.*

Ⓛ   *Work! work! work! I'm _____ because _____.*

🔄 Wrap Up

Today we learned that by adding suffixes How does this help us understand the text?

Turn and Talk: *Think of a noun that ends in -er or -or to talk about yourself. Tell your partner what it means. Use this sentence frame: A _____ is someone who _____.*

👥👥 Differentiated Instruction
Build Language: Use Words with Noun Suffixes -er, -or

Ⓢubstantial Support

Model: Review the definition of a suffix. **Say:** *I know that -er and -or are suffixes. Suffixes can combine with a base word to make a noun. I also know that a noun is a word that names a person, place, or thing. When I read the word laborer, I know that the word means a person who does labor, or who labors. The suffixes -er and -or mean someone who does something.* Continue reading the next paragraph of the text. **Ask:** *What noun has an -ers ending? Say: The word rollers is a noun made by adding the noun suffix -er to the verb roll. The -s at the end makes the noun plural.*

Practice: Distribute BLM 1. Help students complete the activity.

Extend: Have students work with a partner to complete the activity on BLM 1.

Challenge: Draw the following chart on the board and work with students to add words they know. **Say:** *A Derivations Chart shows how words are formed. Let's create a Derivations Chart for the words we have studied. What are some nouns that end with -er or -or?*

Suffix -er	Suffix -or
laborer	inventor
roller	actor
speaker	visitor

Ⓛight Support

Practice: Direct students to paragraphs 1 and 2 on p. 10 of *Texts for Close Reading*. **Say:** *Let's look for nouns that end in -er or -or and make a Derivation Chart.* Draw a Derivation Chart on the board, with column heads er- and -or. As an example, put laborer under -er and inventor under -or.

Extend: In pairs, have students choose one -er word and one -or word and write original sentences using both the base word and the noun.

Challenge: If students are ready, ask them to explain how learning the meaning of suffixes helps them in their reading. Provide the following sentence frame: *Learning about -er and -or helps me to understand _____.*

Ⓜoderate Support

Model: Write *laborer* and *inventor* on the board. **Say:** *I see the suffix -er in laborer and -or in inventor. I can create a Derivations Chart for the suffixes -er and -or.* Draw the following chart on the board. **Say:** *The suffix -er or -or can change a verb to a noun. Labor is a verb that means "to do hard work." Laborer is a noun. A laborer is "a person who does hard work." Say:* *Explain invent and inventor.*

Suffix -er	Suffix -or
laborer	inventor

Practice: Distribute BLM 2. Work with students to complete the task.

Extend: Working in pairs, have students choose one -er and one -or word and write a definition in their own words. They may use their dictionaries as needed.

Challenge: If students are ready, **ask:** *How does understanding the suffixes -er and -or help us understand new words?* Discuss how understanding a base word and the meaning of a suffix can help us understand new words. Provide the following sentence frame: *Learning about -er and -or helps me to understand _____.*

☑ Formative Assessment

Substantial Support	• Can students understand the meaning of noun suffixes? • Do students understand how noun suffixes are formed?
Moderate Support	• Can students understand the purpose of the suffixes -er and -or. • Can students generate new words using the suffixes -er and -or?
Light Support	• Can students generate original sentences using nouns with the suffixes -er and -or? • Can students explain how learning suffixes helps them with their reading?

Preview or Review Week 2 ELA Mini-Lessons

"Use Adverbs to Specify Frequency," page 99

Student Objectives

LANGUAGE

Purpose:
• I can describe my day.

Form:
• I can use adverbs to specify frequency.

CONTENT
• I can understand an autobiographical narrative on a social studies topic.

Additional Materials

• Unit Presentation
• *Texts for Close Reading* booklet
• Think-Speak-Listen Flip Book
• Student journal

Language Transfer Support

Note that speakers of Haitian Creole or Hmong may need additional support when using adverbs. Students may use an adjective where an adverb is needed, because adjectives and adverbs are used interchangeably in those languages.

6 Use Adverbs to Specify Frequency

Engage Thinking

Display the photograph. **Ask:** *What is the mill worker doing in the photograph? What might she do often in the factory? What might she do sometimes?* Elicit responses.

Turn and Talk: *What information do you get from the photograph? Can you imagine what her day might be like?*

Read and View Closely: Recognize Adverbs

Display the chart and read the title aloud. **Say:** *Let's use the chart to help us recognize adverbs.* Read aloud the first sentence. **Say:** *The word never is an adverb. Never modifies the verb cared. It gives us more information. It answers the question "how often." Lucy never cared for machinery.* Read the second and third sentences aloud. **Say:** *I see in each example, the adverb describes the verb. This gives me more information about Lucy's experience at the mill.*

👤👥👥 Differentiated Instruction
Build Language: Use Adverbs to Specify Frequency

Say: *We know that adverbs modify verbs. Some adverbs modify a verb by describing how often something happens. These are called adverbs of frequency. They answer the questions "how often?" Never is an example of an adverb of frequency. What are some other examples of adverbs of frequency?* Elicit responses and write adverbs on the board. Use the Differentiated Instruction to practice using adverbs to specify frequency in a way that best matches the levels of your students.

Think-Speak-Listen: Use the following sentence frame or the Think-Speak-Listen Flip Book to guide discussion: *My favorite hobby is _____. I often _____. I sometimes _____.*

☑️ Use Oral and Written Language: Describe Your Day

Task: *Work with a partner. Write about your day. Use an adverb of frequency to modify the verbs.*

Ⓢ In the morning, I _____ get to school at 8 am. In the afternoon, I _____ get tired.

Ⓜ In the morning, I _____ at 8 am. In the afternoon, I _____.

Ⓛ _____, I _____ early. Then, I _____ in the afternoon.

🔄 Wrap Up

Today we learned that one way adverbs are used is to specify how often something happens. How does this help readers better understand an autobiographical narrative?

Turn and Talk: *Tell your partner about an activity you like. Be sure to include at least one adverb to show how often you do this activity.*

👥 Differentiated Instruction
Build Language: Use Adverbs to Specify Frequency

Ⓢubstantial Support

Model: Read each sentence in the chart aloud with students. *Say: After reading the second and third sentences, Ask: what is the adverb? What verb does it modify? We see that the verb shows the action. The adverb tells us how frequently the action of the verb happens or happened. Adverbs like often, sometimes, and never answer the question "How often."*

Practice: Distribute BLM 1. Work with students to complete the activity.

Extend: Have students work with a partner to complete the task on the BLM.

Challenge: If students are ready, have them work in pairs to rewrite the following sentence using an adverb of frequency that they have learned: I walk to school.

Ⓜoderate Support

Model: Display the chart. *Say: We know that verbs present the action in a sentence. Adverbs of frequency tells us how often the action happens or happened. Adverbs like often, sometimes, and never answer the question "how often?"*

Practice: Distribute BLM 2. Work with students to complete the task.

Extend: Put students in pairs to complete the activity on the BLM.

Challenge: *Say: Let's look at a sentence from paragraph 6 page 10 of Texts for Close Reading:* "Today, Lucy Larcom's autobiography is often used to study childhood in early America." Draw the following chart on the board and work with students to fill it in.

Verb	Adverb	Who or What?	Frequency
is used	often	autobiography	many times

Ⓛight Support

Use the text on p. 10 in the *Texts for Close Reading* to complete the following activities.

Practice: Ask: *Can you change the meaning of the sentence just by changing the adverb of frequency?* Provide an example. Draw the following chart on the board and work with students to fill it in using paragraphs 5 and 6 on page 10 of *Texts for Close Reading*.

Verb	Adverb	Who or What?	Frequency

Extend: Have partners brainstorm other adverbs that specify frequency: for example, *always, frequently, usually, occasionally, rarely, regularly, seldom.* Have students generate original sentences about things Lucy Larcom may have done during her life using adverbs of frequency.

Challenge: Encourage students to explain in their own words how adverbs of frequency add to the meaning of an autobiographical narrative. Have them demonstrate their idea with one example from the text.

✓ Formative Assessment

Substantial Support	• Can students recognize adverbs of frequency? • Do students add adverbs of frequency to a sentence correctly?
Moderate Support	• Can students understand the adverbs of frequency and the verbs they modify? • Can students write sentences adding an adverb of frequency of their choosing?
Light Support	• Can students explain how adverbs of frequency function in a sentence? • Can students generate original sentences using adverbs of frequency?

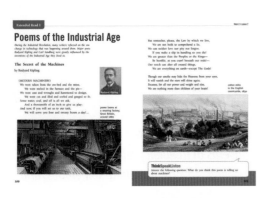

"Poems of the Industrial Age," pages 100–101

Student Objectives

LANGUAGE
Purpose:
• I can create a comic strip about machines.
Form:
• I can condense ideas.
CONTENT
• I can understand condensed ideas is in a poem.

Additional Materials
• Unit Presentation
• *Texts for Close Reading* booklet
• Think-Speak-Listen Flip Book
• Student journal

Metacognitive Prompt: Fix-Up Monitoring

As you read today, remember to stop and think about what you read; then reread to clarify anything you don't understand. Ask questions if you need help understanding something.

7 Read "Poems of the Industrial Age"

Build Background and Vocabulary

Display the images and explain key vocabulary. If students have already read the poems, ask them what the poems are about. Invite students to share what they think it might be like to be a machine.

Read Aloud the Text

Read the introduction to the poem. To support understanding, ask students to find images in the picture that match words in the text (Rudyard Kipling, weaving factory, etc.) and then ask *wh-* questions such as *What do you think the poem will be about?* Read the poem aloud. After reading, **ask:** *Who is "we" in the poem?* Model thinking through the answer: *I can find many clues about who the "we" refers to. The words are spoken from the point of view of a machine.* Invite students to share their ideas using: *I think _____ is speaking in the poem because _____.* Then refer to the Essential Question. **Ask:** *What does presenting machines as living things say about how people value them?* Invite students to respond. **Say:** *This is a poem, but it reveals ideas about people's relationships to technology.*

Think-Speak-Listen: Use the following sentence frame or the Think-Speak-Listen Flip Book to guide discussion: *I think this poem is telling us _____ about machines.*

Differentiated Instruction
Build Language: Condense Ideas

Say: *Let's look at the first line of the poem.* **Ask:** *What words are repeated?* Elicit answers. **Say:** *The author has combined two ideas. One idea is "We were taken from the ore-bed. The other idea is "We were taken from the mine." What words can we leave out to condense these ideas?* Elicit answers. **Say:** *"We were" is used in both sentences. We can combine both of these ideas by using "and." When we combine ideas in this way, our writing becomes less repetitive.* Use the Differentiated Instruction to practice condensing ideas in a way that best matches the levels of your students.

☑ Use Oral and Written Language: Create a Comic Strip About Machines

Task: *Take turns with a partner to create a comic strip about machines. Draw pictures with captions telling their story. Use what you know about condensing ideas.*

Ⓢ   *We are taken _____ and melted _____.*

Ⓜ   *We were _____ and _____. Then, we were _____.*

Ⓛ   *I was _____ and _____ and _____. Then I was _____ and _____.*

⟳ Wrap Up

Today we learned about condensing our ideas. How does this make our writing more effective?

Turn and Talk: *With a partner, think about another poem you have read. Take turns condensing some of the ideas.*

👥👥👥 Differentiated Instruction
Build Language: Condense Ideas

Ⓢubstantial Support

Model: Read line 4 aloud with students. Say: I notice there are many verbs in this sentence. The author uses "and" to combine many ideas. **Ask:** *What ideas is the author condensing?* Elicit responses. **Say:** *The machines were made through many actions. They were cut, filed, tooled, and gauged. The author puts all of these ideas into one line.* Point out that when condensing ideas, words may be omitted or changed as long as the idea remains clear.

Practice: Distribute BLM 1. Help students complete the activity.

Extend: Have students work with a partner to complete the activity.

Challenge: If students are ready, have them work in pairs to answer the following question about the poem. Have them combine two or more ideas from the poem in their answer.

Ⓛight Support

Use the text on pp. 12–19 in the *Texts for Close Reading* to complete the following activities.

Practice: Remind students that condensing ideas means taking multiple ideas and stating them using fewer words. Have students work in pairs to condense the first stanza. **Say:** *First, you will need to understand what the text says. Use the chart to help you.* **Then, say:** *Now combine your two sentences to make one clear, concise summarizing sentence.*

Extend: Say: *We can condense ideas within sentences or within whole texts. Let's reread the poem "The Secret of the Machines." How can we condense the ideas in a few sentences?* Elicit answers. **Say:** *The poem talks about how machines help us in many ways but they don't have human emotions or a human brain.*

Challenge: Encourage students to explain how condensing and combining sentences helps them to write concisely.

Ⓜoderate Support

Model: Read line 4 aloud with students. **Say:** *I notice the author uses "and" to combine many ideas.* **Ask:** *What ideas is the poet condensing?* Elicit responses. **Say:** *The machines were cut. They were filed. They were tooled. They were gauged. The poet uses and to combine these separate ideas into one line. This allows the poet to give a lot of information in one line.* Point out that in condensing ideas, words may be omitted or changed as long as the idea remains clear.

Practice: Distribute BLM 2. Have students read the lines from the poem and find the answers to the questions. Then, have them write answers that condense ideas.

Extend: Put students into pairs. Have students complete the activity in the BLM by reading different lines from the poem and answering the questions. Then, have them condense the ideas using the sentence frames provided.

Challenge: Have students read lines 13–20 of the poem on p. 14 of the *Texts for Close Reading*. Tell them that the stanza references the telegraph and the ocean liner. Help them complete this frame: *Machines allow people to _____ and to _____.*

☑ Formative Assessment

Substantial Support	• Can students interpret relationships among ideas in poetry in order to condense ideas? • Can students complete sentence frames to combine sentences and condense ideas?
Moderate Support	• Can students deconstruct texts to determine related ideas? • Can students combine and condense sentences with conjunctions?
Light Support	• Can students deconstruct text and discern related concepts? • Can students write original sentences that condense the main ideas of a poem?

Preview or Review Week 2 ELA Mini-Lessons

"Poems of the Industrial Age," page 102

Student Objectives

LANGUAGE

Purpose:
- I can create a web diagram of a poem.

Form:
- I can determine the theme of a poem.

CONTENT
- I can understand poetry on a social studies topic.

Additional Materials
- Unit Presentation
- *Texts for Close Reading* booklet
- Think-Speak-Listen Flip Book
- Student journals

Metacognitive Prompt: Imagery

As you read today, practice visualizing, or creating a picture in your mind of what the poet is describing. Use the photographs to make connections with the words and phrases in the text.

8 Determine the Theme of a Poem

Engage Thinking

Display the image. **Ask:** *What do you see in the photograph? How would you describe the building in the photograph?* Read the text title. **Ask:** *What do you think we will learn about the skyscraper from the text?*

Turn and Talk: *What ideas about the skyscraper does the photograph support?*

Differentiated Instruction
Read and View Closely: Determine the Theme of a Poem

Read the poem aloud. **Say:** *The poet presents ideas in the poem that you cannot learn from the photograph.* Ask the students for examples of details from the poem. **Say:** *I can use these ideas to help me understand the meaning of the poem and the underlying idea the poet is making about life.* Use the Differentiated Instruction to practice determining a theme of a poem in a way that best matches the levels of your students.

Think-Speak-Listen: Use the following sentence frame or the Think-Speak-Listen Flip Book to guide discussion: *When Sandburg says the skyscraper has a soul, he means _____?*

Build Language: Use Prepositional Phrases

Read the first sentence of the poem aloud. **Say:** *There are two prepositional phrases in this line. Can you find them?* Elicit answers. **Say:** *I remember that prepositional phrases have two parts. The first part is the preposition. The second part is a noun or noun phrase.* Point out the prepositions and the nouns in each prepositional phrase. **Say:** *Prepositional phrases add important details to a text. They help writers answer questions for readers, such as how, when, and where.*

☑ Use Oral and Written Language: Create a Web Diagram of a Poem

Task: *With your partner, create a web diagram that displays how details from the poem contribute to the theme. On the spokes of the web, write key details of the poem. In the center, write your idea about the theme.*

↻ Wrap Up

Today we learned that we can use details and language to help us analyze the poet's underlying idea, or theme. How does understanding theme help a reader?

Turn and Talk: *State an idea about life that you could use as a theme for a poem. Explain what kinds of details you might use to express your idea.*

🧑‍🤝‍🧑 Differentiated Instruction
Read and View Closely: Determine the Theme of a Poem

Ⓢubstantial Support

Model: Read the poem aloud with students. Distribute BLM 1. **Say:** *I can use a chart to write down important details in the poem. This will help me know what the poet is saying. The theme of the poem is what the poem is about.*

Practice: Work with students to complete the chart on BLM 1. Explain vocabulary and clarify phrases students have difficulty understanding.

Extend: Have students work in pairs to complete the activity on the BLM. **Say:** *How do the details in the chart help you understand the poem. What is the poet saying?*

Challenge: If students are ready, work with them to summarize the theme of the poem.

Ⓛight Support

Use the text on pp. 17–18 in the *Texts for Close Reading* to complete the following activities.

Practice: Remind students that a theme is a universal idea about life in a piece of literature. **Say:** *Since a theme is an idea, we know a theme is abstract, not concrete. Yet it is based on concrete details the poet provides.* **Say:** *Work with a partner and give examples from the text to answer each question.*

Lines	Questions	Text Evidence
1-2	What is the topic of the poem?	
3-9, 23-25	What kinds of activities occur in the skyscraper?	
7-10, 16-18	How do people utilize the technologies in the skyscraper?	
7-13	Why are people important to the skyscraper?	

Extend: Working with a partner, write sentences about the theme of the poem. Use the information in the chart. It should explain why the poet wrote the poem. Begin with this frame: *The poet describes _____ to suggest that _____.*

Challenge: If students are ready, have them answer the following: *How does a reader determine the theme of a poem? Why is it important to understand the theme of a poem?*

Ⓜoderate Support

Model: Read the poem aloud with students. Distribute BLM 2. Review the explanation of what a theme is. **Say:** *I can use a chart to analyze important details in the poem. This will help me determine the theme.*

Practice: Work with students to complete chart on BLM 2. Explain vocabulary and clarify phrases students have difficulty understanding. **Say:** *As we look at details from the text, we notice the poet's choice of words. For example, the verb looms suggests great height. What does the verb pour suggest?*

Extend: Have partners work on the activity on the BLM. They will identify the key elements that make up the theme.

Challenge: If students are ready, have pairs of students summarize the theme of the poem.

☑ Formative Assessment

Substantial Support	• Can students reference text to find text-based answers? • Can students recognize the details of a poem that make up the theme?
Moderate Support	• Can students reference text and respond to text-based questions? • Can students analyze a poem to determine the theme?
Light Support	• Can students cite and interpret text-based evidence? • Can students analyze, interpret, and make inferences to write a statement of theme?

Use Verb Tenses to Convey Time	
Text	**Tense**
We <u>were</u> taken from the ore-bed and the mine, We <u>were</u> melted in the furnace and the pit— We <u>were</u> cast and wrought and hammered to design, We <u>were</u> cut and filed and tooled and gauged to fit.	Past
Some water, coal, and oil is all we ask, And a thousandth of an inch to <u>give</u> us play:...	Present
And now, if you <u>will set</u> us to our task, We <u>will</u> serve you four and twenty hours a day!	Future

ThinkSpeakListen
Describe the things that you have done today, are doing now, and will do later today. Use past, present, and future verb tenses.

"Use Verb Tenses to Convey Times," page 103

Student Objectives

LANGUAGE
Purpose:
• I can write a magazine article on computers.
Form:
• I can use verb tenses to convey times.
CONTENT
• I can determine tense in poetry.

Additional Materials
• Unit Presentation
• *Texts for Close Reading* booklet
• Think-Speak-Listen Flip Book
• Student journal

Language Transfer Support

Students whose first language is Spanish may be familiar with the cognate of the word future: futuro. Encourage students to look for other words that are similar to words in their first language.

9 Use Verb Tenses to Convey Times

Engage Thinking

Display the image. **Ask:** *When was this picture drawn? How can you tell?* **Say:** *You can tell by the machinery and the people's clothing that this is in the past.* Read the first line of the chart. **Ask:** *How can you tell this line is about the past?*

Read and View Closely: Recognize Verb Tenses

Display and read the title of the chart aloud. **Say:** *This chart helps us recognize verb tenses.* Read the chart aloud. **Say:** *I remember that verbs are words that describe actions or states of being. They change tense to show time. Verbs can be used in past, present, or future tense.* Read aloud the second sentence of the chart. **Say:** *The main verb melted is the past tense of the verb melt. The helping verb were is the past tense of the verb be.* **Ask:** *What is the main verb in the third sentence? What is the helping verb?* Help students answer using this sentence frame: *The main verb is _____ and the helping verb is _____.*

👥 Differentiated Instruction
Build Language: Use Verb Tenses to Convey Times

Say: *In the chart, we learned three tenses of verb: past, present, and future. Present tense verbs tell that something is happening now. Past tense verbs tell that something already happened. Future tense verbs tell something that will happening the future.* Use the Differentiated Instruction to practice using verb tenses to convey times in a way that best matches the levels of your students.

Think-Speak-Listen: Use the following sentence frame or the Think-Speak-Listen Flip Book to guide discussion: *Today, I have _____. Now, I'm _____. Later today, I will _____.*

☑ Use Oral and Written Language: Write a Magazine Article on Computers

Task: *Work with a peer group to write a magazine article about computers in the past, computers now, and how computers might be in the future. Use the correct verb tense to express time.*

(S) *Twenty years ago, computers _____ very big. Today computers are _____. In twenty years, computers will _____.*

(M) *Computers were _____ a long time ago. Now they're _____. In the future, I think they will _____.*

(L) *Many years ago, most computers _____ and _____. These days, _____. In the future, I expect _____.*

🔄 Wrap Up

Today we learned how to use different verb tenses to express actions in the past, present, and future. How does using these tenses make writing clearer?

Turn and Talk: *Describe some activity or hobby you enjoy.* **Say:** *what kinds of things you do now, and what you will do in the future.*

👥 Differentiated Instruction
Build Language: Use Verb Tenses to Convey Times

Ⓢ ubstantial Support

Model: Read aloud the first sentence in row 2 of the chart. **Say:** *The verb in this sentence is the present tense is.* Read the first sentence in row 3. **Say:** *I see the word will. Will tells me the action is in the future. Is and will are tense forms of the verb to be.* **Write** *is, are. am* and *will be* on the board. **Ask:** *Do you remember the past tense forms?* Elicit responses. Write *was* and *were.*

Practice: Distribute BLM 1. Work with students to complete the activity.

Extend: Have students work with a partner to complete the activity on the BLM.

Challenge: If students are ready, have them work in pairs to write a sentence about skyscrapers using *are.* Then have then rewrite the sentence using the past tense and the future tense.

Ⓛ ight Support

Use the text on pp. 12–19 in the *Texts for Close Reading* to complete the following activities.

Practice: Draw the columns for the following chart on the board. Work with students to complete the chart.

Text	Verb	Tense
"I am in Lowell..." page 4		
"Cotton was picked...by hand." page 6		
"Whitney received a patent... page 7		
"Kipling's poem...is about technology..." page 12		
"You will find the Mauretania..." page 14		
"the skyscraper looms in the smoke" page 17		

Extend: Tell students to work in pairs to write three sentences about the image on p. 15. Have them choose one of the sentences and rewrite it using the other two tenses.

Challenge: Guide students in answering the following question: What would happen if there were no verb tenses?

Ⓜ oderate Support

Model: Read aloud the first sentence in row 2 of the chart. **Say:** *I see that the verb in this sentence is the present tense verb is. This lets me know that the action is happening in the present.* Read the first sentence in row 3. **Say:** *I see the word will. Will is a helping verb for the main verb set. This tells me that the sentence is in the future tense. Is and will be are present and future tense forms of the verb to be.* Write *is, are. am* and *will be* on the board. **Ask:** *What are the past tense forms?* Elicit responses. Write *was* and *were* on the board.

Practice: Distribute BLM 2. Work with students to complete the activity.

Extend: Have students work with a partner to complete the task on the BLM.

Challenge: Help students write a sentence in the past, present, and future about the image on page 15 of the *Texts for Close Reading*.

☑ Formative Assessment

Substantial Support	• Can students recognize verb tenses and the times they convey? • Can students complete sentences with correct verb tenses of the verb *to be*?
Moderate Support	• Can students complete a chart of the verb forms for the verb *to be* with some assistance? • Can students form the past, present, and future to complete sentences using the verb *to be* correctly?
Light Support	• Can students identify verb tenses in text and change tenses appropriately? • Can students generate original sentences in which they use verb tenses to convey various times?

Preview or Review Week 2 ELA Mini-Lessons

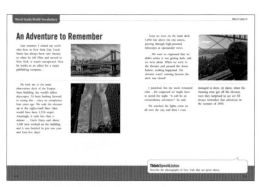

"An Adventure to Remember," pages 104–105

10 Read "An Adventure to Remember"

Build Background and Vocabulary

Display the images and explain key vocabulary. If students have already read the text, ask them what they remember. Invite them to share their cultural experiences they have had visiting cities or historic buildings.

Read Aloud the Text

Read the first panel. Ask students to find images in the picture that match words in the text (New York City, summer, etc.) and ask *wh-* questions, such as: *How do the photograph and the words in the text relate? What information do you gain from the words that you cannot tell from the photograph? How does the photograph add to your understanding?* Repeat with the rest of the text. Have students fill in this sentence frame for each of the panels: *I know the photograph shows _____ because the text also tells me _____.* Then refer to the Essential Question. **Ask:** *What value did the narrator derive from technology?* Invite students to respond and share their own experiences. **Say:** *This text is a personal narrative of historical fiction. It shares with readers one person's experience.*

Think-Speak-Listen: Use the following sentence frame or the Think-Speak-Listen Flip Book to guide discussion: *The first photograph of New York shows _____.*

👥👥 Differentiated Instruction
Build Language: Analyze Word Relationships

Explain that many English words are based on a root. The root is the central part of the word that expresses its meaning. **Say:** *This text is told to us by a narrator.* **Ask:** *What is the root in the word narrator?* Explain that *narrate* is the root. The **-or** suffix means "the person who does something." A narrator is a person who narrates. **Say:** *Many words are based on Latin roots. When you know the root, you can often figure out the meaning of a word. The word may have prefixes, such as un-, and suffixes, such as -or, that affect its meaning. But knowing the root will help you know the word.* Use the Differentiated Instruction to practice analyzing word relationships in a way that best matches the levels of your students.

☑ Use Oral and Written Language: Create a Word Chart

Task: *Work in pairs to create a root chart for the root vent. Use a print or online dictionary to help you. Share your definitions with a group.*

(S) *The noun invention means "something that is _____."*

(M) *The verb prevent means "_____."*

(L) *The adjective adventurous means "_____."*

🔄 Wrap Up

Today we learned that many English words are based on common roots. How does knowing a root help readers unlock the meaning of an unfamiliar word?

Turn and Talk: *Think of a word that uses one of the roots you learned or another Latin or Greek root. Use your word in a sentence. Challenge your partner to define the word.*

♦♦♦ Differentiated Instruction
Build Language: Analyze Word Relationships

Ⓢubstantial Support

Model: Point out the word *editor* in the first paragraph. Write the word *editor* on the board. Circle the word *edit*. **Say:** *I see that the word editor includes the word edit. Edit is the root word. It comes from a Latin word that means "to publish." An editor is someone who fixes or publishes someone's words.* Explain that *publish* means to "prepare something for sale, or for the public."

Practice: Distribute BLM 1. Work with students to complete the chart for the word *editor*. Allow students to use their dictionaries if needed to find multiple words related to *editor*.

Extend: Have students work in pairs to complete the activity on the BLM. Then discuss the answers as a group.

Challenge: If students are ready, have them complete the Practice activity on BLM 2.

Ⓛight Support

Use the text on p. 20 in the *Texts for Close Reading* to complete the following activities.

Practice: Point out the word *literary* in paragraph 1. Draw the following chart on the board, explaining that the root *liter* means "letters."

Latin root and root word: liter, literary

Definition: related to writers or writing; relating to literature

Sentence: The writer hired a literary agent.

Noun	Verb	Adjective	Adverb
literariness	literate	literary	literarily

Have students work in pairs to add three or more related words to the list. Encourage them to use dictionaries to help find words and understand their meanings.

Extend: Have pairs of students use paragraph 2 to find words with the roots listed below. Encourage them to find related words. Then, have them write sentences using a word with the roots *cred-* and *struct-*.

Challenge: How does knowing the meaning of a root help you understand the meaning of an unfamiliar word? In what way does this make your reading more meaningful and enjoyable?

Ⓜoderate Support

Model: Point out the word *spectacular* in the third paragraph. Write it on the board and circle *spec*. **Say:** *I see in this word the common root spec. The root spec means "to see" or "to look." Knowing the meaning of spec can help me figure out the meaning of spectacular.*

Practice: Distribute BLM 2. Help students to complete the word chart for *spec*. Allow students to use their dictionaries if needed to find multiple words related to *spectacular*.

Extend: Have students work in pairs to complete the activity on BLM 2 by completing the sentences with words with the root *spec*. Then discuss the answers as a group.

Challenge: Work with students to look up the meaning of the word root *liter* in and write one or more sentences with the related words.

☑ Formative Assessment

Substantial Support	• Can students understand the significance of a root word? • Can students complete a chart with related words with help? • Can students complete sentences using related words?
Moderate Support	• Can students complete a chart with related words with little help? • Can students complete sentences using related words?
Light Support	• Can students understand and write original sentences using root words? • Can students explain the importance of understanding root words for reading and writing?

"The Making of the Industrial Age," pages 106–107

Student Objectives

LANGUAGE
Purpose:
• I can give a lecture on coal.
Form:
• I can connect ideas.
CONTENT
• I can understand an informational text on a social studies topic.

Additional Materials
• Unit Presentation
• Subordinate Clauses Chart
• *Texts for Close Reading* booklet
• Think-Speak-Listen Flip Book
• Student journal

Metacognitive Prompt

Today we will practice previewing the main ideas of a text and clearly connecting these ideas with key details that support them. Before we read closely, we will look at the pictures and skim the text to get a sense of the main focus of the text.

11 Read "The Making of the Industrial Age"

Build Background and Vocabulary

Display the images and explain key vocabulary. If students have read the text, ask them what they remember. Invite students to share what they know about the machines.

Read Aloud the Text

Read panel 1. **Ask:** *What is happening in this picture? What time period does the picture show? What idea about the industrial era is presented by the picture and the text together?* Repeat with panels 2–4. After reading, **ask:** *What do these images have in common?* Model thinking through the answer: *The images highlight technology during the Industrial Age.* Then refer to the Essential Question. **Ask:** *What value does technology bring to people's lives?* Invite students to discuss how machines and fuel contributed to modern technologies. **Say:** *This text is informational. It helps us understand technology during the Industrial Age.*

Think-Speak-Listen: Use the following sentence frame or the Think-Speak-Listen Flip Book to guide discussion: *In my opinion, steamboats and locomotives were important to the growth of _____.*

Differentiated Instruction
Build Language: Connect Ideas

Show panel 1. **Say:** *Looking at the picture and then reading the text helps us connect ideas. We can also connect ideas using the text alone.* Write: *New technologies allowed different industries to explode.* **Say:** *How do we clarify what technologies we are talking about?* Display the Subordinate Clauses Chart. Review how clauses connect ideas in a sentence. **Say:** *I can add a subordinate clause to add information about technologies.* Write: *that were developed during the industrial age.* **Ask:** *If we add this clause, how would the new sentence look?* Elicit answers. Write: *New technologies that were developed during the industrial age allowed different industries to explode.* **Say:** *Adding clauses lets us connect ideas in a sentence.* Use the Differentiated Instruction to practice connecting ideas in a way that best matches the levels of your students.

☑ Use Oral and Written Language: Give a Lecture on Coal

Task: *Work with a partner to write what you've learned about coal. Give a lecture to the class. Connect ideas using clauses.*

(S) *Coal was an important fuel _____ yielded more energy than wood.*

(M) *Coal was an _____ more energy than wood.*

(L) *Coal was _____ than wood.*

 Wrap Up

Today we learned that we can connect ideas in a text using subordinate clauses. What do clauses do to our writing?

Turn and Talk: *Create sentences that discuss technologies you use today. Use a subordinate clause to connect your ideas.*

👥 Differentiated Instruction
Build Language: Connect Ideas

Ⓢubstantial Support

Model: Display panel 3 and write: *Steam engines ran anywhere that water and wood or coal were available.* Draw a line after anywhere. **Say:** *We can see a steamboat in the picture. A steamboat used a steam engine.* Read aloud the sentence. **Say:** *This sentence connects two ideas about the steam engine using a clause.* **Ask:** *Can you see the clause?* Point out the word that. **Say:** *The word that let's us know that there's a clause. The clause connects ideas about the steam engine.*

Practice: Distribute BLM 1. Work with students to connect ideas.

Extend: Have pairs of students complete the activity by connecting the sentences using clauses.

Challenge: If students are ready, have them work in pairs to combine the following two sentences: *Many machines first appeared during the Industrial Revolution. / Many machines were powered by steam.*

Ⓛight Support

Use the text on pp. 22–29 in the *Texts for Close Reading* to complete the following activities.

Practice: Have pairs of students work together to join the sentences using the words in parentheses. Remind students to refer to the Subordinate Clauses Chart.

1. Most of the changes during the Industrial age originated with the way goods were manufactured and transported. Ripple effects were felt everywhere. (Although)

2. Many people left their farms in rural areas and moved to cities. In cities, they would work in factories that made goods. (where)

James Hargreaves invented the spinning jenny. This hand-powered machine spun yarn ten times as quickly as a regular spindle. (that)

Extend: Have partners read paragraph 10 and find the main idea of the paragraph. Then complete the sentences with clauses.

Watt, Fitch, and Trevithick _____ that _____.

_____ the steam engine, _____.

Challenge: How do adjective and adverb clauses help you connect ideas clearly?

Ⓜoderate Support

Model: Point to panel 3 and write: *Steam engines for factories, steamboats, and steam locomotives could run anywhere that water and wood or coal was available.* Draw a line after anywhere. **Say:** *This sentence connects two ideas about the steam engine using a subordinate clause. Can you identify the clause?* Point out the word *that.* **Say:** *Using a subordinate clause helps the author connect ideas about the steam engine.*

Practice: Distribute BLM 2. Invite students to help you connect ideas using clauses in the Practice activity.

Extend: Put students into pairs. Have them connect ideas using clauses in the Extend activity.

Challenge: If students are ready, have them work in pairs to combine the following two sentences with where: *Many people left their farms in rural areas and moved to cities./ In cities, they would work in factories that made goods*

☑ Formative Assessment

Substantial Support	• Can students identify clauses in a text? • Can students connect ideas using adjective clauses with support?
Moderate Support	• Can students connect ideas using clauses with little support? • Can students use adjective and adverb clauses ?
Light Support	• Can students connect ideas to form sentences containing adjective and adverb clauses? • Can students write an original sentence relating important text-related ideas using adjective and adverb clauses?

"The Making of the Industrial Age," page 108

Student Objectives

LANGUAGE
Purpose:
- I can create a flowchart for coal processing.

Form:
- I can explain key ideas and processes.

CONTENT
- I can understand an informational text on a social studies topic.

Additional Materials
- Unit Presentation
- *Texts for Close Reading* booklet
- Think-Speak-Listen Flip Book
- Student journal

Metacognitive Prompt: Monitoring Comprehension

Today we will focus on checking our comprehension while reading a text. We will stop frequently while reading to restate important ideas in our own words.

12 Explain Key Ideas and Processes

Engage Thinking

Display panel 5. **Ask:** *Who is the person in the picture? What is he doing?* **Say:** *The photograph shows us information about a process. The text explains what the process is.* Read the text. **Ask:** *What do we learn about coal mining?*

👥👥👥 Differentiated Instruction
Read and View Closely: Explain Key Ideas and Processes

Read the text together. **Say:** *To understand the process of mining coal, I look at both images and the text. I get more detailed information in the text.* Show panel 6. **Ask:** *What does the image in panel 6 tell you about the process of mining?* Help students complete the sentence frame: *In panel 6 _____, I see the _____.* **Say:** *Using information from the images and text, I can explain key ideas and processes that led to changes in technology.* Use the Differentiated Instruction to practice explaining key ideas and processes in a way that best matches the levels of your students.

Think-Speak-Listen: Use the following sentence frame or the Think-Speak-Listen Flip Book to guide discussion: *The invention of the steam engine affected the coal industry by _____. The mass production of steel affected other industries by _____.*

Build Language: Link Ideas and Events with Connecting Words

Display and read aloud panel 10. Write the word *then*. Explain that then means next in order. **Say:** *I see the word then. I know then is a connecting word that shows how events are related. I know it connects this sentence to the idea in panel 9, that steel was strong but expensive.* Explain that connecting words such as *first, next, then,* and *finally* show the sequence of events. Write the words on the board. Knowing connecting words can help us explain key ideas and processes.

✓ Use Oral and Written Language: Create a Flowchart for Coal Processing

Task: *With your partner, make a simple flowchart for the sequence of steps in coal mining. Write a sentence for each step in the chart. Use connecting words to show time. Share your sentences with another pair.* Use this opportunity to assess students using the rubric in *English Language Development Assessment.*

(S) *First, miners dug _____. Then, they used _____ to get the coal.*

(M) *First, miners _____. _____, they _____ to get the coal.*

(L) *_____ underground tunnels. _____, they _____.*

🔄 Wrap Up

Today we learned how to explain key ideas and processes from an informational text. How does putting explanations in your own words help assure you understand the text?

Turn and Talk: *Think of a product you use that is made of a metal such as steel. Using connecting words, explain to your partner the steps you take when you use this product.*

👥 Differentiated Instruction
Build Language: Explain Key Ideas and Processes

Ⓢubstantial Support

Model: Read panels 5 - 7 aloud with students. **Say:** *To explain key ideas and processes, I look for several ideas about coal mining. First, workers dug tunnels.* Write this sentence on the board: "After that, they used pickaxes to get coal." **Say:** *For the next idea about coal mining, I can use the word then to express a time sequence. I can use these words to help me explain the next part of a process.*

Practice: Distribute BLM 1. Help students complete the activity.

Extend: Have pairs complete the activity by on the BLM.

Challenge: If students are ready, have them work in pairs to describe the process of how they get to school using connecting words.

Ⓜoderate Support

Model: Display panels 5 - 7. **Say:** *To explain the key ideas and processes of coal mining, I look for key ideas in the text. Underground tunnels were dug. Miners used pickaxes to get coal. If I add sequence words, it's easier to explain the processes. I can say: "First, underground tunnels were dug. Then, miners used pickaxes to get coal." These words express a time sequence. I can use them to help me express when each process happens.*

Practice: Distribute BLM 2. Work with students to add sequence words to explain the processes involved in coal mining.

Extend: Have pairs complete the activity on the BLM.

Challenge: If students are ready, have them work in pairs to describe the process of how they do homework using connecting words.

Ⓛight Support

Use the text on pp. 22-29 in the *Texts for Close Reading* for the following activities.

Practice: Have students read paragraph 4 aloud. **Say:** *Key ideas and processes are supported by the details writers provide. To find the details, I ask questions such as: Why did the process need to change? How was it done before? What were the first, second, and third steps?* Have students use their answers to these questions to explain the process of how producing cotton changed. Remind them to use connecting words.

Extend: Have partners read paragraph 19. Ask students to explain the assembly line process in their own words. Model how to begin. **Say:** *Step 1: Workers placed a car frame on a belt.* Support them with questions such as *What did the belt do? What happened as the car moved?*

Challenge: If students are ready, ask them to describe the process of how they start their days?

✓ Formative Assessment

Substantial Support	• Can students understand key ideas and processes in a text with support? • Can students put the processes of an event in the correct order?
Moderate Support	• Can students understand key ideas and processes in a text with little support? • Can students put the processes of an event in the correct order choosing the correct sequence words?
Light Support	• Can students explain key ideas and processes using sequence words? • Can students explain key details and processes • in their own words?

Preview or Review Week 3 ELA Mini-Lessons

"Use Context Clues to Understand Vocabulary," page 109

Student Objectives

LANGUAGE
Purpose:
- I can write a news report about modern technology.

Form:
- I can use context clues to understand vocabulary.

CONTENT
- I can understand an informational text on a social studies topic.

Additional Materials
- Unit Presentation
- *Texts for Close Reading* booklet
- Think-Speak-Listen Flip Book
- Student journal

Language Transfer Support

Three of the vocabulary words highlighted on page 109 have the past tense inflectional ending -*ed*. Note that speakers of Cantonese, Haitian Creole, Hmong, Korean or Vietnamese may need additional instruction on inflectional endings, because their native language does not use inflectional endings to change verb tense.

13 Use Context Clues to Understand Vocabulary

Engage Thinking

Display the image. **Ask:** *What clues in the picture help you understand more about the train?* Elicit responses. *Things like the steam coming from the train tell me the train has a steam engine.* Read the title of the chart. **Say:** *Words in sentences give you clues to the meaning of words you don't yet know. These are called context clues.*

Read and View Closely: Identify New Vocabulary

Read the chart aloud. **Say:** *In the first column, I see sentences from the text we read, "The Making of the Industrial Age."* **Ask:** *What is the title of the first column of the chart? What words are underlined in these sentences?* Elicit answers. **Say:** *When we read, we often encounter new words. This is often true when we read informational texts.* Read the sentence in the first row. **Say:** *Look for other unfamiliar words in these sentences that are not underlined.* Help students complete this sentence frame for each row: *In row _____, the words I do not know are _____.* **Say:** *Before we can understand a text, we need to identify words that are new to us.*

👥 Differentiated Instruction
Build Language: Use Context Clues to Understand Vocabulary

Say: *Context clues are words that suggest the meaning of nearby words in a text. When I come across words I don't know, I use context clues to help understand what the text says.* In row two, point to *affordability*. **Say:** *I see the words around it like less expensive. Then I have an idea of what affordability means. Using the clues helps me understand the text.* Use the Differentiated Instruction to practice using context clues to understand vocabulary in a way that best matches the levels of your students.

Think-Speak-Listen: Use the following sentence frame or the Think-Speak-Listen Flip Book to guide discussion: *Context clues can be found _____.*

☑ Use Oral and Written Language: Write a News Report About Modern Technology

Task: *Work with a partner to write a short news report about a modern technology. Use context clues to help explain technical or other unfamiliar words in your writing. Use the sentence frames to begin your report. Then read your report to the class.*

Ⓢ *Modern inventors develop new technology.*

Ⓜ *Modern inventors, or people who _____, have developed a new technology. This is _____.*

Ⓛ *Modern inventors who _____ have developed a new technology. It is _____.*

🔄 Wrap Up

Today we learned that we can use context clues to help us understand unfamiliar words. How does this improve our understanding of an informational text?

Turn and Talk: *Describe an invention from history and use context clues to make the meaning of unfamiliar words clear.*

👥 Differentiated Instruction
Build Language: Use Context Clues to Understand Vocabulary

Ⓢubstantial Support

Model: Display the chart. **Say:** *When I read, I see new words. To understand what I read, I need to know what the words mean. Sometimes, there are other words that help me understand a new word. These are context clues.*

Practice: Distribute BLM 1. Work with students to complete the activity.

Extend: Have students work with a partner to complete the activity on the BLM.

Challenge: If students are ready, write this sentence on the board: Nonrenewable resources, such as coal and oil, cannot be replaced if they are used up. **Ask:** *What context clues help us understand the word nonrenewable? What does nonrenewable mean?*

Ⓛight Support

Use the text on pp. 22–27 in the *Texts for Close Reading* to complete the following activities.

Practice: Have students complete this chart about words from the text.

Unfamiliar Word	Clues in Nearby Words	Definition
urban		
dynamite		
methods		

Extend: Say: *A text may define a word, provide a synonym or antonym, give an example or explanation, or provide a tip you can use to infer the meaning.* Have students work with a partner to label the type of content clue for each example in the Practice chart. Then have them choose two of the words from the chart. Tell them to write their own sentences that provide a different kind of context clue for each word.

Challenge: Have students answer this question: How do context clues make understanding informational text easier?

Ⓜoderate Support

Model: Read and explain how to use context clues to determine the meaning of unfamiliar words. Point out the highlighted unfamiliar word in the top row, the highlighted context clue, and the definition in the box on the right. **Say:** *I can look at the unfamiliar words, the context clues, and the definition of the word to clarify its meaning.*

Practice: Distribute BLM 2. Work with students to complete the sentence frames explaining the context clues and definitions of the new words.

Extend: Put students in pairs. Have them complete the activity on the BLM.

Challenge: If students are ready, read this sentence from paragraph 15 on p. 27 of *Texts for Close Reading*. Working with a partner, have them explain the context clue that helps them understand *innovative* and define the word.

Other technology came from new ways of doing things. Steel is an example of how innovative new methods changed an industry.

✔️ Formative Assessment

Substantial Support	• Can students identify context clues? • Can students define and understand words using context clues?
Moderate Support	• Can students identify and explain context clues? • Can students use context clues to understand the meaning of a word?
Light Support	• Can students identify, explain, and label types of context clues and define words using context clues? • Can students write original sentences providing different types of context clues?

Preview or Review Week 3 ELA Mini-Lessons

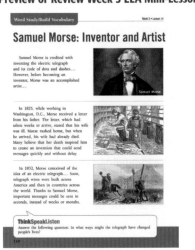

Samuel Morse: Inventor and Artist

"Samuel Morse: Inventor and Artist," page 110

Student Objectives

LANGUAGE
Purpose:
- I can create a chart of homophones.

Form:
- I can recognize and distinguish between homophones.

CONTENT
- I can understand informational text on a social studies topic.

Additional Materials
- Unit Presentation
- *Texts for Close Reading* booklet
- Think-Speak-Listen Flip Book
- Student journal
- Dictionary

Language Transfer Support

The large number of homophones in English present a challenge to English Learners. Homophones even vary within American English dialects. Homophones are common in other languages as well, including Japanese, Cantonese, and Russian. Spanish has far fewer homophones than English, but they do exist. The word *homophone* has a cognate in Spanish, *homófono*.

---

14 Read "Samuel Morse: Inventor and Artist"

Build Background and Vocabulary

Display the images and explain key vocabulary. If students have already read the text, ask them what they remember. Ask students to share what they know about the telegraph and morse code.

Read Aloud the Text

Read the first section. To aid understanding, ask students to describe the portrait. **Say:** *I see a portrait of Samuel Morse, dressed in old-fashioned clothes. The text tells me about his work as an inventor and artist.* Read the next paragraph. **Ask:** *What does the picture show?* Model thinking through the answer: *I see two workers. I think they are in a postal office because I see sorting boxes, letters, packages, and big bags.* **Ask:** *What does the text add?* Elicit answers. Read the third paragraph. Help students share their ideas using: *The picture shows _____. The text says _____.* Then refer to the Essential Question. **Ask:** *What value did the telegraph bring to people's lives?* Invite students to respond. **Say:** *This informational text helps me understand one inventor's idea of the value of technology.*

Think-Speak-Listen: Use the following sentence frame or the Think-Speak-Listen Flip Book to guide discussion: *The telegraph changed people's lives by _____.*

▲▲▲ Differentiated Instruction
Build Language: Recognize and Distinguish Between Homophones

Write: *weak, week.* **Ask:** *How are these words alike? How are they different?* **Say:** *A word that sounds like another word but has a different spelling and meaning is a homophone. Knowing the difference between words that sound alike but have different meanings helps me understand the text I'm reading.* Use the Differentiated Instruction to practice recognizing and distinguishing between homophones in a way that best matches the levels of your students.

☑ Use Oral and Written Language: Create a Chart of Homophones

Task: *Work with a partner to create a chart that lists pairs of homophones and their definitions. Then write a short sentence using each homophone.*

Pairs of Homophones	Definition	Sentence
too two	also one more than one	Morse was an artist, _____. I have _____ ideas for my telegraph.

 Wrap Up

Today we learned that we must choose the right homophone for the meaning intended. Why is it important to spell words that sound alike correctly?

Turn and Talk: *Think of a pair of homophones and use them in one or two sentences about modern communication. Have your partner define and spell each homophone.*

👤👤👤 Differentiated Instruction
Build Language: Recognize and Distinguish Between Homophones

Ⓢubstantial Support

Model: Review that homophones are words that sound alike but have different spellings and meanings. Write the word parts *homo* and *phone*. **Say:** *Homo means "same" and phone means "sound."* Point to the first sentence of paragraph 2. **Say:** *The word* in *sounds like another word I know:* inn. In *means during.* Inn *means a hotel. I can tell from the other words that the author means during.*

Practice: Distribute BLM 1. Help students complete the activity.

Extend: Have students work with a partner to complete the activity on the BLM.

Challenge: If students are ready, have them work in pairs to define *sent* and *cent*.

Ⓜoderate Support

Model: Review homophones. Point out that *homo* means "same" and *phone* means "sound." Model finding the homophone in the first line of paragraph 2. **Say:** *I know another word that sounds like* in. *That word is the homophone:* inn. *I know that* in *means during, and an* inn *is a hotel. Here the author means during.*

Practice: Distribute BLM 2. Work with students to find homophones in the passage and write their definitions.

Extend: Put students in pairs. Have them complete the activity by finding and completing sentences using homophones for *sent*.

Challenge: If students are ready, have them work to find a homophone in the following sentence: It was an amazing feat. Have students list the homophones and write definitions for each.

Ⓛight Support

Use the text on p. 30 in the *Texts for Close Reading* to complete the following activities.

Practice: Review the definition of *homophone* and point out that *homo* means "same" and *phone* means "sound." Have students to find the words that have homophones, list the homophone(s), and to supply definitions of the words.

Paragraph 1: That alone is an amazing feat!

Paragraph 2: After graduation, he went to Europe...

Paragraph 3: Of course, Morse continued traveling for his work
Paragraph 3: ...and, as a result, missed his family dearly.

Extend: Have students work in pairs to write sentences about Samuel Morse and his life using the text and their imaginations. Tell them to use each of the following pairs of homophones correctly in one or two sentences.

feet, feat; to, two; course, coarse; missed, mist

Challenge: Have students write sentences to answer the following questions. How can you recognize homophones? Why is it important to know the spelling and meaning of each homophone?

☑ Formative Assessment

Substantial Support	• Can students determine a homophone for a given word and define each word with some help? • Can students use the correct homophone to complete a sentence frame?
Moderate Support	• Can students determine a homophone for a given word and use the correct homophone to complete a sentence frame? • Can students identify words that have homophones and define both words?
Light Support	• Can students identify words that have homophones and define both words? • Can students write original sentences that use • the correct homophone for the meaning intended?

Preview or Review Week 3 ELA Mini-Lessons

"Analyze Words with Greek and Latin Roots," page 111

Student Objectives

LANGUAGE
Purpose:
• I can give a speech explaining word roots.
Form:
• I can analyze words with Greek and Latin roots.
CONTENT
• I can understand an informational text.

Additional Materials
• Unit Presentation
• *Texts for Close Reading* booklet
• Think-Speak-Listen Flip Book
• Student journal
• Dictionary

Language Transfer Support

Students whose first language is Spanish may know the cognates of the words *telegraph* and *automatically*: *telégrafo* and *automáticamente*.

Verb tense inflections, such as the -ed at the end of *credited*, do not exist in Chinese, Hmong, and Vietnamese. Native speakers of these languages may need support in understanding the purpose and use of such endings.

15 Analyze Words with Greek and Latin Roots

Engage Thinking

Display the chart. **Ask:** *What does each picture show?* Encourage students to connect the pictures to text from previous readings. Read the title of the chart. Read the roots column. **Say:** *The pictures help you understand the highlighted words by showing objects and people.*

Read and View Closely: Recognize Words with Greek and Latin Roots

Read the column titles aloud. **Ask:** *What is underlined in the text? How does this relate to the information in the column labeled "Roots"?* Elicit answers. Read the first row aloud. **Say:** *Compare the underlined parts in the text with the roots.* **Ask:** *What do you notice?* **Say:** *I see that autos was shortened to auto when it helped form a new word.* Read the second and third rows. Ask students to talk about the root words using this sentence frame: *The root _____ is shortened in the word _____.* Explain that recognizing the basic part, such as the letters *a-u-t-o* in *automatically* and the letters *c-r-e-d* in *credited*, will help them recognize other words containing the same root.

👤👥 Differentiated Instruction
Build Language: Analyze Words with Greek and Latin Roots

Say: *Many words in English get their meanings from parts of words from Greek and Latin. We call these basic parts roots. When we learn to recognize these roots, we can use them to help us analyze the meaning of words we don't know.* Read the text in row one. **Ask:** *What is the meaning of the first root, rota?* **Say:** *We see rota in the word rotating. How does an image of a wheel relate to the adjective rotating?* Encourage students to recognize that a wheel moves in a circle. Use the Differentiated Instruction to practice analyzing words with Greek and Latin roots in a way that best matches the level of you students.

Think-Speak-Listen: Use the following sentence frame or the Think-Speak-Listen Flip Book to guide discussion: *Readers can analyze words to discover roots by _____. Discovering roots helps a reader by _____.*

☑ Use Oral and Written Language: Give a Speech

Task: *Work with a partner to write a speech explaining root words. Give your speech to the class.*

Ⓢ *I can tell that the word _____ means _____ because it has the root _____.*

Ⓜ *I can tell that the word _____ means _____ because _____.*

Ⓛ *The word _____ includes the root _____ which means _____. The word means _____.*

🔄 Wrap Up

Today we learned we can analyze Greek and Latin roots in words to help understand unfamiliar words. How is this helpful?

Turn and Talk: *Name an object or invention you use that includes a common root, such as tele or graph, in its name. Challenge your partner to use the root to define the word.*

👥👥 Differentiated Instruction
Build Language: Analyze Words with Greek and Latin Roots

Ⓢubstantial Support

Model: Display the chart. **Say:** *I can use the chart to help me define words using roots. Learning the meaning of roots helps me define the words.*

Practice: Work together to analyze how the root reveals word meaning. **Say:** *We know rota means "wheel" and rotating means "spinning like a wheel." Here, rotating is used as an adjective to describe picks.* Invite students to help you finish the sentence frames:

I watched the rotation of the picks. *Rotation* means "the _____."

The machine rotates. *Rotates* means "to _____."

Extend: Have students work with a partner to complete the definitions.

Word	Definition
automatically	"as if running by _____"
credited	"believed to _____"
telegraph	"machine that sends _____ along _____"

Challenge: If students are ready, have them work in pairs to think of another word that uses the root word auto, and write what it means.

Ⓜoderate Support

Model: Read the chart on and explain how knowing roots can reveal the meanings of multiple words. **Say:** *We know that rota means "wheel" and rotating means "spinning like a wheel." Rotating is used as an adjective to describe picks.* **Ask:** *What if I want to describe the machine's action. What verb with the root rota could I use?* Help students identify *rotates.*

Practice: Distribute BLM 1. Work with students to complete the activity.

Extend: Have students work in pairs to complete the activity on the BLM.

Challenge: If students are ready, ask them to work with a partner to analyze and define the underlined word in the following sentence: Today, Lucy Larcom's autobiography is often used to study childhood in early America.

Ⓛight Support

Use the text on p. 30 in the *Texts for Close Reading* to complete the following activities.

Practice: Distribute BLM 2. Review parts of speech. Remind students that they have studied noun, adjective, and adverb suffixes as well as verb endings, such as *-ing* and *-ed.* Have students complete the Practice activity.

Extend: As students complete the Extend activity on the BLM.

Challenge: Have students answer the following questions.

How does knowing the meaning of a Greek or Latin word root make analyzing the meaning of unfamiliar words easier?

☑ Formative Assessment

Substantial Support	• Can students complete sentence frames to define given words and new words using the meaning of a Greek or Latin root?
Moderate Support	• Can students complete sentence frames to define given words using the meaning of a Greek or Latin root? • Can students supply different parts of speech based on given roots?
Light Support	• Can students supply different parts of speech based on given roots? • Can students define new words based on known roots?

Up Against the Wild

Essential Question

What compels us to survive?

In this unit, students will read and compare selections about characters who are up against the wild and analyze how different genres approach similar themes.

Unit 6 Lessons at a Glance

Language Skills

Week 1
- Understand Verb Tense
- Use Adjectives to Signal States of Being
- Narrative Writing to Sources
- Understand the Structure of a Play
- Use Words with Suffixes **-ly** and **-ily**

Week 2
- Use Adverbs and Adverb Phrases
- Recognize Pronouns and Antecedents
- Recognize and Use Connecting Words
- Form Adverbs from Adjectives
- Use Synonyms to Understand Meaning

Week 3
- Combine Clauses to Connect Ideas
- Condense Ideas
- Use Prepositional Phrases
- Use Sense Imagery to Describe
- Understand Domain-Specific Words

Lessons

Preview or Review Week 1 ELA Mini-Lessons

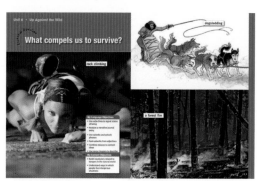

"Essential Question," pages 112–113

Student Objectives

LANGUAGE
Purpose:
• I can understand the Essential Question.
CONTENT
• I can understand the topic of the unit.

Additional Materials
• Unit Presentation

Language Transfer Support

Note that the short /i/ sound in **mill** and *picture* may be unfamiliar to students whose first language is Vietnamese, Hmong, or Khmer. These students may need modeling to produce words with the short /i/ sound.

Introduce Unit 6: Up Against the Wild

Use the short lesson below to introduce the topic of the unit and help students understand the Essential Question.

Build Background and Vocabulary

Draw students' attention to the pictures on pages 112–113.

Say: *The topic of this unit is "Up Against the Wild."*

Create a two-column chart.

Say: *Let's think about what this means.* **Wild** *means untamed. Let's think of examples.*

Write: *Wild/Untamed.* Elicit responses as you fill in the chart. Explain that **up against** means to have a problem with.

Ask: *How can we keep ourselves out of harm's way?*

Continue to fill in the second column of the chart with student responses.

Wild/Untamed	What Do You Do?
animals	avoid them
wilderness	have correct gear
fire	get away
winds	find shelter
tornado	find shelter/get away
hurricane	find shelter/get away
epidemic/illness	get medicine

Ask: *How do these pictures help you understand what it means to be up against the wild?*

Help students answer and encourage students to share their cultural knowledge and experiences about the topic.

👥 Differentiated Instruction
Explain the Essential Question

Draw students' attention to the pictures and questions on pages 112–113.

Say: *These pictures and ideas introduce what we will read about.*

Read aloud the Essential Question: *What compels us to survive?*

Review key words by definition and examples: **compels, wild, dog sledding, forest fire**. Review the two-column chart. Encourage students to give examples using the chart, using the sentence frame:

_____ *compels people to* _____.

Use the Differentiated Instruction to help students at all levels understand the Essential Question.

Display or invite students to access the unit opener video for Unit 6. After the video, *ask: How do these pictures and the video help you answer the Essential Question?*

Then proceed to Lesson 1.

ᴬᴬᴬ Differentiated Instruction
Explain the Essential Question

Ⓢ ubstantial Support

Point to the picture of the rock-climber. Write: *Rock climbing is a sport that is going up against the wild.*

Have students say the sentence with you. Explain that **up against** is an idiom that means *having a problem with*. **Wild** means *untamed*. Give examples of going up against something, like going up against another team in a competition.

Gesture and say: *Danger compels us to survive. Rock climbers use special equipment like ropes. They take special training.*

Point to the second picture. **Say:** *A dog sled is used to travel over snow. It is pulled by dogs.* **Dogsledding** *is the action of using a dog sled. People use dog sleds to hunt, travel, or to race.*

Point to the picture of the forest fire. **Say:** *Forest fires are very dangerous.*

Explain that trees are highly flammable and may catch on fire very quickly making the fire hard to tame.

Say: *A forest fire compels animals to run for safety. In this unit, we will learn what compels us to survive.*

Ⓜ oderate Support

Point to the picture of the rock-climber.

Say: *Danger compels the rock climber to survive. They use special equipment like ropes and take special training.*

Explain that **up against** is an idiom that means *having a problem with*. Give examples of going up against something, like going up against another team in a competition.

Point to the dogsledding picture.

Say: *A dog sled is used to travel over snow and is pulled by dogs.* **Dogsledding** *is a verb that mens using a sled pulled by dogs. People use dog sleds to hunt, travel, or to race.*

Point to the picture of the forest fire.

Say: *A forest fire compels animals to run for safety. When a fire happens in a forest, it is very dangerous.*

Explain that trees are highly flammable and may catch on fire very quickly making the fire hard to tame.

Say: *In this unit, we will learn about what compels living things to survive.*

Ⓛ ight Support

Say: *In the wild, humans and animals will come up against situations that are threatening. In these cases, they are compelled to take actions to survive.*

Elicit examples of different types of threats humans and animals might face in the wild the students know about ,and help as necessary.

Say: *Danger compels a rock climber to use ropes. What kind of danger does a rock climber face?*

Point to the picture of the forest fire.

Ask: *What would compel animals to find safety in a forest fire?*

Say: *In this unit, we will learn what compels living things to survive. We will read how they went up against the wild to survive.*

☑ Formative Assessment

Substantial Support	• Can students, with help, explain what **up against the wild** means? • Can students, with support, show understanding of the key vocabulary word **compel**?
Moderate Support	• Can students, with support, explain what **up against the wild** means? • Can students, with help, show understanding of the key vocabulary word **compel**?
Light Support	• Can students explain what **up against the wild** means? • Can students show understanding of the key vocabulary word **compel**?

Preview or Review Week 1 ELA Mini-Lessons

"Androcles and the Lion," page 114

Student Objectives

LANGUAGE

Purpose:
• I can use explain characters' actions.

Form:
• I can understand shifts in verb tenses.

CONTENT
• I can analyze fables.

Additional Materials
• Unit Presentation
• Think-Speak-Listen Flip Book
• *Texts for Close Reading* booklet
• Student journal

Language Transfer Support

Note that in some languages, including Hmong and Haitian Creole, all verbs in one sentence are in the same tense (e.g., *I remember what happens last year*). Your English Learners may need extra support to understand shifts in verb tense in "Androcles and the Lion."

1 Read "Androcles and the Lion"

Build Background and Vocabulary

Show the text panel images from "Androcles and the Lion" and explain key words and ideas from the text. If students have already read the story, ask them what they remember. Invite students to share their cultural experience and knowledge about lions.

Read Aloud the Text

Read aloud panel 1. Ask students to find details in the images that match words in the text, and ask questions such as, *Where are the characters? What happened?* Repeat with panels 2–3. After reading, **ask:** *What do you think readers learn from this story?* Model thinking through an answer. **Say:** *Androcles was kind and helpful to the lion, so the lion was grateful. What does that tell us about being kind and helping others?* Then, refer to the Essential Question. Discuss how our own need to survive can make us understand and help others in need.

Think-Speak-Listen: Use the following sentence frame or the Think-Speak-Listen Flip Book to guide discussion: *Androcles chooses to help the lion because _____.*

⠀ Differentiated Instruction
Build Language: Understand Verb Tense

Write: *Androcles escaped. While he was wandering in the woods, he came upon a lion.* Point out the verbs *escaped* and *wandering*. **Say:** *The verbs tell us about actions. Some of are about actions that are finished–he escaped, he fled. Fled the simple past tense of the verb to flee. Some of verbs tell us about actions that were ongoing–he was wandering. The verb wandering is in the past progressive tense. In this story, Androcles kept on wandering. It's important to understand verb tenses so that we can tell more about when and how actions happened.* Tell students they will be looking at the endings of verbs to tell the difference between verb tenses. Ask students to name the tense for the verb *came upon* in the last sentence. Use the Differentiated Instruction to practice understanding verb tense in a way that best matches the levels of your students.

☑ Use Oral and Written Language: Explain Characters' Actions

Task: *In the fable, the lion licks Androcles' hand. Why does the lion do this? Discuss this question with your group. Share your sentences with the other groups.*

(S) *The lion _____ because _____.*

(M) *The lion _____ because _____. The lion felt _____.*

(L) *The lion _____ because _____ and _____. The lion wanted _____.*

 Wrap Up

Why is it important to understand verb tenses when you are reading a story?

Turn and Talk: *Tell your partner about a time when you helped someone else. Use appropriate verb tenses.*

👥 Differentiated Instruction
Build Language: Understand Verb Tense

Ⓢubstantial Support

Model: Read aloud panel 1. Then call attention to the verb *escaped*. Explain that the verb *escaped* is in the simple past—it is about an action that already happened. Point out the *-ed* at the end of *escaped*. **Say:** *Most verbs in the simple past end in -ed.* Then read panel 2. Explain that some verbs in the simple past, like *found*, don't have the *-ed* ending. They are irregular. Point to the words *was causing*. Ask students to notice the ending *-ing* on the word. Then have them find that same ending on the words *moaning* and *groaning* in panel 1. **Say:** *The lion was moaning when Androcles found him. The -ing ending tells us the action continued to happen. The thorn kept causing the pain and he kept moaning.* Ask students to look for other verbs ending in *-ing* and *-ed* in panels 2 and 3.

Practice: Distribute Substantial Support BLM 1. Work with students to complete the Practice activity.

Extend: Ask student pairs to complete the Extend activity. Discuss how the shift in verb tense affects the meaning of each sentence on the page.

Challenge: If students are ready, model for them how to identify the past perfect tense in the Practice activity on Moderate Support BLM 2.

Ⓜoderate Support

Model: Read aloud panel 2 and display the text. **Say:** *In the first sentence, I see the verb* came*. I know this is the simple past tense. Then I read the verb phrase* was bleeding*. This tense is the past progressive. This shift in verb tense tells me that the paw kept on bleeding when Androcles came.* Then direct attention to the phrase *had got* in the second sentence. **Say:** *The helping verb* had *lets me know that the tense shifts again. The phrase* had got *is the past perfect tense. This tense means that event of the thorn getting stuck in the lion's paw happened in the past before the event of Androcles finding the thorn.*

Practice: Distribute Moderate Support BLM 2. Work with students to complete the Practice activity.

Extend: Ask student pairs to complete the Extend activity. **Ask:** *What clues help you identify a shift in verb tense?*

Challenge: If students are ready, model finding simple past, past progressive, and past perfect verbs in paragraph 1 on page 4 in *Texts for Close Reading*.

Ⓛight Support

Use the text on pp. 4-5 in the *Texts for Close Reading* to complete the following activities.

Practice: Remind students that there are several different verb tenses used in the story. Ask students to find and list the verbs in simple past. Then have them find and list the verbs paired with the word *was* and the ending *-ing*, the past progressive verbs. Point out an example of the past perfect tense, *A huge thorn had got stuck.* **Say:** *We use the past perfect tense to describe an action that happened before another event in the past.*

Extend: Have students use the simple past and past perfect verb tenses to identify the order of events in the story. (*First a thorn got into the lion's paw, then Androcles found the thorn.*)

Challenge: Have students generate two original sentences about Androcles and the Lion using simple past, past perfect, and past progressive verb tenses.

☑ Formative Assessment

Substantial Support	• Can students find examples of simple past and past progressive verbs? • With support, can students understand shifts in verb tenses?
Moderate Support	• Are students able to identify simple past, past progressive, and past perfect verbs? • Can students understand shifts in verb tenses?
Light Support	• Can students distinguish between the simple past, past progressive, and past perfect verbs? • Can students generate sentences using the simple past, past perfect, and past progressive verb tenses?

Preview or Review Week 1 ELA Mini-Lessons

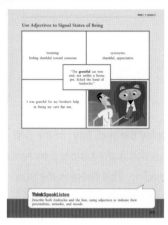

"Use Adjectives to Signal States of Being," page 115

Student Objectives

LANGUAGE
Purpose:
- I can write descriptive titles.

Form:
- I can explain how descriptive words are used to create meaning in a fable.

CONTENT
- I can understand characters' actions in a fable.

Additional Materials
- Unit Presentation
- Think-Speak-Listen Flip Book
- *Texts for Close Reading* booklet
- Student journal

Language Transfer Support

Note that students whose first language is Spanish or Haitian Creole may place adjectives after nouns (e.g., *the cat grateful*). You may wish to review the placement of adjectives in noun phrases.

---

2 Use Adjectives to Signal States of Being

Engage Thinking

Display the chart. **Say:** *We are going to talk about how adjectives help us to understand how a character feels.* Read aloud the middle box. **Say:** *"The grateful cat rose..."* What does the word *grateful* tell us about the cat? Elicit answers. **Say:** *The word **grateful** shows us the lion's feeling. Describing words help us to understand characters in a story.*

Turn and Talk: *Use an adjective to tell your partner how you are feeling today.*

Read and View Closely: Recognize Word Relationships

Read the sentence in the middle of the chart. **Say:** *The chart shows words and ideas that are related to the word* grateful. Write the word **synonym** on the board. **Say:** *A* **synonym** *is a word that has a similar meaning.* **Thankful** *and* **appreciative** *have the same meaning as* **grateful**. *Knowing that the adjective* **grateful** *means the same thing as* **thankful** *or* **appreciative** *helps us understand how the lion feels.*

👥👥 Differentiated Instruction
Build Language: Use Adjectives to Signal States of Being

Ask students if they remember what kind of word describes a noun. **Say:** *Some adjectives give us details about how a character feels.* Read the sentence: *The grateful cat rose and, not unlike a house pet, licked the hand of Androcles.* **Say:** *The adjective **grateful** gives us more information about the lion. It tells us that he is thankful to Androcles. Without the use of **grateful** to tell us about the lion's state of being or how he feels, it may have been unclear why he licked Androcles.* Use the Differentiated Instruction to practice using adjectives to signal states of being in a way that best matches the level of your students.

Think-Speak-Listen: Use the following sentence frame or the Think-Speak-Listen Flip Book to guide discussion: *Androcles is _____. The lion is a _____ lion.*

☑️ Use Oral and Written Language: Write Descriptive Titles

Task: *Work with a partner. Write a new title for the story "Androcles and the Lion." Use an adjective in your new title.*

- **S** *The _____ Man and the _____ Lion*
- **M** *_____ and the _____*
- **L** *The _____ from the _____ Lion*

 Wrap Up

Today we have learned about adjectives that describe a noun by showing a state of being. Why are adjectives important when we analyze characters?

Turn and Talk: *Use one or two adjectives to describe to your partner something you like in school.*

👥 Differentiated Instruction
Build Language: Use Adjectives to Signal States of Being

Ⓢubstantial Support

Model Read aloud the sentence in the middle of the chart. **Say:** *This adjective describes the lion's feelings. The lion is grateful because Androcles removed the thorn.* Point to the two synonyms in the top right square of the chart. Explain that these words are also adjectives that describe feelings. **Say:** *I can use other adjectives to describe feelings: The sad lion moaned. The happy lion licked the hand of Androcles.*

Explain that adjectives can also describe characters' personalities, or what the characters are like. Write these examples: brave, kind, helpful. Point to each adjective. Ask students if each adjective describes the lion or Androcles. Give examples to support the meaning of each word as needed.

Practice: Distribute BLM 1. Guide students to choose the best adjective to complete each sentence.

Extend: Have students work in pairs to write two new sentences using the adjectives they chose in Practice.

Challenge: If students are ready, have them make work together to do the practice on BLM 2.

Ⓜoderate Support

Model: Read aloud the sentence in the middle of the chart. Point out the adjective *grateful* and explain that it describes the noun *cat*. Point out that adjectives often describe the feelings or personalities of characters in stories. Point to the synonyms *thankful* and *appreciative*, and explain that these words are also adjectives. Explain that in some sentences, the adjective is before a noun. In other sentences, the adjective is after a linking verb such as, *is*, *are*, *was*, and *were*. **Say:** *We can use the adjective in two ways. For example: "the grateful lion" or "The lion was grateful." The first example is not a complete sentence, so a verb phrase will need to be added to it: "The grateful lion licked his hand."*

Practice: Distribute BLM 2. Work with students to identify the adjectives.

Extend: Have students work in pairs to create sentences using some of the adjectives from the BLM.

Challenge: Ask students to make a Use Adjectives to Signal States of Being chart using one of the adjectives from the BLM.

Ⓛight Support

Use the text on pp. 4-5 in the *Texts for Close Reading* to complete the following activities.

Practice: Tell students that one way the reader knows that the relationship between the human and the animal is because of how both characters are described. Divide a paper into 2 columns. Label one column "Androcles" and the other column "The Lion." Generate a list of all the adjectives that are used to describe each character.

Extend: Have students work with a partner to review the lists of adjectives. Ask them to discuss which characteristics both the lion and Androcles share and to discuss the differences the two characters have.

Challenge: Ask students to make a Use Adjectives to Signal States of Being chart showing the synonyms, definition and sentences for several different adjectives.

✔️ Formative Assessment

Substantial Support	• Are students able to identify adjectives in a story? • Are students able to use definitions, sentences, synonyms and illustrations to understand adjectives?
Moderate Support	• Can students explain how an adjective can show state of being in a story?
Light Support	• Can students analyze the meaning and purpose of adjectives that show state of being?

Preview or Review Week 1 ELA Mini-Lessons

"Writing to Sources," pages 116–117

Student Objectives

LANGUAGE

Purpose:
- I can analyze a narrative journal entry.

Form:
- I can identify the parts of a narrative journal entry.

CONTENT
- I can recognize a narrative journal entry.

Additional Materials
- Unit Presentation
- Think-Speak-Listen Flip Book
- *Texts for Close Reading* booklet
- Student journal

3 Writing to Sources: Narrative Journal Entry

Engage Thinking

Tell students that they will analyze a narrative journal entry so that they can recognize its parts. Read aloud the writing prompt.

> You are the character of the lion in "Androcles and the Lion." Plan and write a journal entry describing your thoughts and feelings during the events described in the story. Make sure to incorporate specific story events and details from "Androcles and the Lion" in your writing.

Say: *Let's ask questions to make sure we understand the prompt. For example, what type of writing is it?* Model or elicit the following questions from students: *What character will the writer write as? What will the writer write about? Where will the writer get some of the details?*

Differentiated Instruction
Read and View Closely: Analyze a Narrative Journal Entry

Say: *A narrative journal is written using a first person point of view. As I read, look for this.* Read the first two sentences. **Ask:** *Which words show the first person point of view?* Have some students give examples. **Ask:** *Which characters is the I in this story? How do you know?* Elicit words and phrases such as *chased my dinner* and *paw* that show the character is a lion.

Say: *The writer includes the character's thoughts and feelings.* Read the rest of the first paragraph and the second paragraph. **Ask:** *What are some examples of thoughts and feelings the character had?* Have some students give examples.

Say: *A narrative journal uses description to retell what happened. As I read, listen for description.* Read aloud the rest of the Mentor Narrative Journal. **Ask:** *What are some examples of description?* Check that students can offer examples of description.

Say: *A narrative journal entry can include dialogue. What is dialogue?* Elicit from the class that dialogue is what people say. Invite some students to say the dialogue in the lion character's voice.

Continue the lesson using Differentiated Instruction that best fits the needs of your students.

Share Your Understanding

Bring the students back together. **Ask:** *What did we learn today about a narrative journal entry?* Review the structure as needed.

Final Writing Assignment

Use the English Language Development Assessment to assess students' writing for their ELA writing assignment.

👤👤👤 Differentiated Instruction
Read and View Closely: Analyze a Narrative Journal Entry

Ⓢubstantial Support

Model: Distribute BLM 1. **Say:** *Let's read and analyze another narrative journal entry that answers the prompt.* Read the first paragraph and pause. **Ask:** *Which word shows the point of view?* Model answering the question.

Practice: Continue reading the journal entry and ask the same questions that you asked about the Mentor Narrative Journal Entry in their book. Invite students to answer.

Extend: Have students in pairs complete the activity on BLM 1.

Challenge: Guide students to identify the character's thoughts and feelings by asking *yes/no* questions. Examples: *Does the lion feel brave or afraid when he gets a thorn in his paw? How does the man look when he first sees the lion?*

Guide students to answer in complete sentences. Model a response and have the class repeat.

Ⓜoderate Support

Model: Create the chart below with only the headings and text examples. Think aloud as you identify which of the four features the first text example represents.

Examples from the Text	Narrative Journal
I thought "I am going to die…"	Includes the character's thoughts and feelings.
I; My paw	Uses first person point of view.
He looked ready to run away from me when he noticed me.	Uses description to retell what happened.
"Thank you, sir!"	Includes dialogue.

Practice: Have pairs work together to complete the chart with the remaining features.

Extend: Have pairs use the chart to discuss the text. Encourage them to make statements using the examples listed and then to elaborate on their partner's answers, sharing relevant information. For example, *"Thank you, sir!" is an example of dialogue. How do you know it's dialogue? The lion thought it and it's in quotation marks.*

Challenge: Have partners take turns reading a sentence from the story. Their partner identifies which of the features of a narrative journal entry the sentence fulfills. Encourage partners to build on their responses and elaborate on their answers.

Ⓛight Support

Practice: Distribute BLM 2. **Say:** *This is the Narrative Journal Entry Mentor Text that you read in class on Day 1. We will look more closely at how writers answer the prompt and use the features of a narrative journal entry.* Read the entry with students.

Extend: Have student pairs complete the activity in BLM 2.

Challenge: Have pairs of students take turns retelling the second paragraph of the journal entry as if they were the character of the man. Remind them to speak in the first person and include thoughts and feelings, description, and dialogue. Invite some students to share their retelling with the class. For example, *I ran out of the forest. I saw a lion! I was so scared I almost ran away.* Afterwards, have them discuss how the story changes.

✅ Formative Assessment

Substantial Support	• Do students recognize the criteria for a narrative journal entry in the Mentor Narrative Journal Entry?
Moderate Support	• Do students recognize the ways in which the Mentor Narrative Journal Entry meets the criteria for a narrative journal entry? • Can students describe the features of a narrative journal entry in their own words?
Light Support	• Do students recognize criteria and analyze how the Mentor Text meets the criteria for a narrative journal entry? • Can students describe in their own words how the writer meets the criteria for a narrative journal entry?

Preview or Review Week 1 ELA Mini-Lessons

"Brushfire!," pages 118–119

Student Objectives

LANGUAGE
Purpose:
• I can write a dialogue.
Form:
• I can read and understand dialogue.
CONTENT
• I can analyze a play.

Additional Materials

• Unit Presentation
• Understand the Structure of a Play Chart
• Think-Speak-Listen Flip Book
• *Texts for Close Reading* booklet
• Student journal

Language Transfer Support

Note that many English Learners need extra support to understand some conventions of play dialogue. "Brushfire!" contains examples of people speaking incomplete sentences (e.g., *Your suitcase!* and *Out looking for Augie*). As you read with students, explain that the dialogue shows how these characters speak.

4 Read "Brushfire!"

Build Background and Vocabulary

Show the text panel images for "Brushfire!" and explain key words and ideas from the text. If students have already read the play, ask them what they remember. Invite students to share their experiences with reading plays or watching them be performed.

Read Aloud the Text

Read aloud the first page. Ask students to find details in the image that match works in the text. **Ask:** *Where are the characters? What is happening?* Repeat with the next page. **Ask:** *Why do you think Meg looks angry with Ed in the picture?* Model thinking through an answer. **Say:** *Ed and Meg's house is very close to a dangerous brush fire in the canyon. Meg is frustrated with her husband because he isn't taking it seriously.* Invite students to discuss how they would feel if a family member wasn't taking an approaching danger seriously. Then, refer to the Essential Question. Discuss how our need to survive can make us leave a dangerous situation.

Think-Speak-Listen: Use the following sentence frame or the Think-Speak-Listen Flip Book to guide discussion: *Ed is not _____ Meg because _____.*

🏃 Differentiated Instruction
Build Language:
Understand the Structure of a Play

Say: *In a play, actors act out a story on a stage. The people who watch a play are called the audience. The parts of a play are called scenes.* Display the Understand the Structure of a Play Chart and use it to describe the features of a play and the purpose they fulfill. Ask students how each feature helps explain how to perform the play. Use the Differentiated Instruction to practice understanding the structure of a play in a way that best matches the levels of your students.

☑ Use Oral and Written Language: Write a Dialogue

Task: *Work with a partner to write the next few lines of the play. Include dialogue between the main characters and stage directions. Then, perform your lines for the other groups.*

(S) *Ed: Wait for me! I'm going to _____.*
Meg: I'm sorry you had to _____. I'm so glad you are _____.

(M) *Ed: Wait! _____. My life and my family are more important than _____.*
Meg: I'm sorry you had to _____.

(L) *Ed: Wait! _____.*
Meg: I'm sorry _____.

🔄 Wrap Up

Why is it important to understand the structure of a play?

Turn and Talk: *How would you use a play structure to tell a about a conversation you had with a family member?*

👥 Differentiated Instruction
Build Language: Understand the Structure of a Play

Ⓢubstantial Support

Model: Read aloud the text. Then display the Understand the Structure of a Play Chart and discuss each row. **Say:** *These are all parts of the structure of a play. When authors write plays, they include a list of characters. Then they describe the setting.* Point out an example of each play feature in the text. **Say:** *Understanding the structure helps us understand the characters, setting, and events.*

Practice: Distribute BLM 1. Guide student use the cast list and setting to fill out *who, what* and *when*. Then have them look at the stage directions and dialogue to fill out *what* and *why*. Ask volunteers to read aloud what they have written.

Extend: Have partners complete sentences to show they understand the structure of the play. Provide these frames:

The _____ tells us _____.

Challenge: If students are ready, model how to complete the Moderate Support BLM 2.

Ⓜoderate Support

Model: Draw attention to Ed's and Meg's dialogue **Say:** *The author uses bold names and colons to show which character is speaking.* Display the Understand the Structure of a Play Chart. Discuss each line of the chart and explain the purpose of each item in the structure of a play. Then have students find that element. Using the elements of the play structure, including cast list, dialogue and stage directions, summarize page 106 as a group: *In the Acostas' home, Ed plays a tune. He is a film composer. As he plays, a fire comes closer.*

Practice: Distribute Moderate Support BLM 2 and work with students to complete the questions. Then have them fill out the chart.

Extend: Have partners work together to use the elements they filled out in the chart to write sentences about the play.

Challenge: Have students in pairs act out some or all of the play. Have them first practice reading the parts, then do a dramatic reading for a group.

Ⓛight Support

Use the text on pp. 6-9 in the *Texts for Close Reading* to complete the following activities.

Practice: Remind students that all plays follow a similar structure. **Ask:** *How does dialogue appear differently on the page than it does in a story? How do we know where and when a play takes place? How do we know what characters we will see? How do we know what the actors do?*

Extend: Have partner create a five-column chart to show information from the play. They should tell *who* the characters are, *when* and *where* the play takes place, *what* the characters do, and *why* they behave the way they do. Then have students compare Meg's and Ed's reactions to the fire by writing two original sentences about how they behave.

Challenge: Have students in pairs do a dramatic reading of the play, practicing first with each other and then in front of a group.

☑ Formative Assessment

Substantial Support	• Can students identify the elements of play? • Can students use sentence frames to explain the purpose of play elements?
Moderate Support	• Can students understand the structure of a play? • Can students identify purposes about different elements of the play structure?
Light Support	• Can students identify key details about different elements of the play structure? • Can students generate original sentences to analyze play characters?

Preview or Review Week 1 ELA Mini-Lessons

"Sinbad and the Valley of Diamonds," page 120

Student Objectives

LANGUAGE

Purpose:
• I can describe a character.

Form:
• I can use adverbs.

CONTENT
• I can analyze folktales.

Additional Materials
• Unit Presentation
• Think-Speak-Listen Flip Book
• *Texts for Close Reading* booklet
• Student journal

Language Transfer Support

In English, many adverbs are formed by adding *-ly* or *-ily* to adjectives (e.g., *slow/slowly, quiet/quietly*). Note that in some languages, such as Hmong and Haitian Creole, adverbs and adjectives are interchangeable. Some students may need extra practice to recognize the difference between words such as *slow* and *slowly*.

---

5 Read "Sinbad and the Valley of Diamonds"

Build Background and Vocabulary

Display the panels from "Sinbad and the Valley of Diamonds." Explain key words that are important to understanding the text. If students have already read the story, ask them what they remember. Invite students to share their cultural experiences and knowledge about diamonds.

Read Aloud the Text

Read panel 1. Ask students to find images in the picture that match words in the story (diamonds, serpents) and ask questions, such as *What place is this?* Repeat with panel 2. After reading, **ask:** *What do we know about Sinbad?* Model thinking through the answer. **Say:** *I see that Sinbad comes up with a plan to escape danger. He straps a lump of meat to his back so an eagle will grab him. He seems clever.* Then refer to the Essential Question. Discuss the way Sinbad escapes. Point out that in a folktale, there may be ways to escape danger that would not be possible in real life.

Think-Speak-Listen: Use the following sentence frame or the Think-Speak-Listen Flip Book to guide discussion: *First, Sinbad _____. Then Sinbad _____. Finally, Sinbad _____.*

👥👥 Differentiated Instruction
Build Language: Use Words with Suffixes -ly and -ily

Read the last sentence in panel 2. Write the word *speedily* on the board. Underline the suffix *-ily*. **Say:** *Speedily ends in the suffix -ily. Often, words with -ly or -ily describe how something happens. If something happens speedily, it happens quickly.* Explain that knowing how to use suffixes is important because it help writers describe more detail in their stories. Use the Differentiated Instruction to practice using words with suffixes *-ly* and *-ily* in a way that best matches the levels of your students.

☑ Use Oral and Written Language: Describe a Character

Task: *Use words that end in -ly or -ily to describe the Sinbad to your partner.*

Ⓢ   *Sinbad _____ got my attention with some meat on his back.*

Ⓜ   *Sinbad _____ formed a plan and _____.*

Ⓛ   *Sinbad _____.*

🔄 Wrap Up

Today we talked about using words ending in -ly and -ily. Why is it important to know how to use -ly and -ily in a story?

Turn and Talk: *Use words ending in -ly or -ily to describe how a person or animal acted in another story that you read.*

👥 Differentiated Instruction
Build Language: Use Words with Suffixes -ly and -ily

Ⓢubstantial Support

Model: Reread panel 3 and point out the word immediately. **Say:** *If I say " come here immediately," what does that mean? It means come here right now!* Demonstrate by asking two students to stand. To one **say:** *Please come here.* To the other **say:** *come here immediately!* Explain that adding the word immediately gave more information, that the student had to hurry. **Say:** *In the story, Sinbad saw an opportunity–a chance to get out–the word immediately tells us he saw it right away and he was thinking fast.* Point out that words with the suffix -ly add detail.

Practice: Distribute BLM 1. Explain that we can use a vocabulary log to show what we know about a word. Work with students to fill out the log.

Extend: With a partner, have students complete the Extend activity to use the word *immediately* in a new sentence.

Challenge: If students are ready, work with them to complete the Practice activity on Moderate Support BLM 2. Skip the row in the Vocabulary Log for the word *immediately*.

Ⓜoderate Support

Model: Reread panel 1 and guide students to identify the word with the suffix -ly, *accidentally*. Ask a volunteer to tell you what it means to have an *accident* or to do something by *accident*. Have a volunteer pretend to a spill a drink and **say** *Oops, sorry that was an accident!* **Say:** *If I describe what she did I can say she had an accident. Or we can say she spilled the drink accidentally.* Point out that words with the suffix -ly describe actions and add detail to a story.

Practice: Distribute Moderate Support BLM 2. Explain that the vocabulary log can help us understand a word. Work with students to complete the log for the words accidentally and *immediately*. Have students complete the sentences. **Ask:** *How would the meanings of the sentences you wrote be different without the word accidentally?*

Extend: Working with a partner, have students write two original sentences with the words.

Challenge: If students are ready, have them look for words with the suffix -ly or ily in paragraphs 1 and 2 on page 10 of *Texts for Close Reading*. Guide them to complete a Vocabulary Log for each.

Ⓛight Support

Use the text on p. 10 in the *Texts for Close Reading* to complete the following activities.

Practice: Have student pairs reread paragraphs 1–3 and identify a word with the suffix -ly or -ily in each paragraph. Ask them to complete a Vocabulary Log for each word, and use the word in a sentence. **Ask:** *How does the meaning of the word with the suffix differ from the base word?*

Extend: Have students write their own original sentences using the words they found.

Challenge: Have student find the sentence with the word *furious* in the last paragraph. Ask them to add -ly to form the word furiously and use it to describe what the merchants did.

☑ Formative Assessment

Substantial Support	• With support, can students show their understanding of a word with the suffix -ly in a vocabulary log? • Are students able to form a sentence with *immediately*?
Moderate Support	• Are students able to complete vocabulary logs with some support? • Can students generate sentences using words with the suffixes -ly and -ily?
Light Support	• Are students able to recognize and analyze words with the suffixes -ly and -ily? • Can students use words with the suffixes -ly and -ily to generate their own sentences?

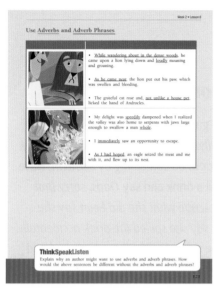

"Use Adverbs and Adverb Phrases," page 121

Student Objectives

LANGUAGE

Purpose:
- I can retell a story.

Form:
- I can recognize adverbs and adverb phrases.

CONTENT
- I can identify how adverbs and adverb phrases are used in fiction.

Additional Materials
- Unit Presentation
- Think-Speak-Listen Flip Book
- *Texts for Close Reading* booklet
- Student journal

Language Transfer Support

In English, adverbs often come after the verbs they modify (e.g., *he walked slowly*). Students whose first language is Cantonese or Korean may typically place adverbs before verbs. As you review sentences with students, point out where authors place adverbs and adverb phrases.

6 Use Adverbs and Adverb Phrases

Engage Thinking

Write: *Sinbad realized his ship had left him behind.* Read the text with students. Then add words to change the sentence: *When he saw the empty beach, Sinbad realized that his ship had accidentally left him behind.* **Ask:** *When did Sinbad know he was left behind? How was he left behind?*

Read and View Closely: Recognize Adverbs and Adverb Phrases

Display the chart and ask students to recall the story about Androcles. Read the first sentence aloud without the underlined words. Then read the underlined words. **Say:** *These words gave us more information. What did they tell us?* Discuss that the word *loudly* gives information about how the lion was moaning and groaning. Remind students that *loudly* is an adverb.

👥 Differentiated Instruction
Build Language: Use Adverbs and Adverb Phrases

Say: *Adverbs describe verbs, adjectives, or other adverbs. Adverbs and adverb phrases add details about how, when, why, or where something happens.* Read aloud the remaining sentences in the chart and have students point out the adverbs and adverb phrases. **Ask:** *What words do they describe?* **Say:** *When you use adverbs and adverbs phrases in your writing, you can add details to tell more about your ideas in a story or text.* Use the Differentiated Instruction to practice using adverbs and adverb phrases to expand sentences in a way that best matches the levels of your students.

Think-Speak-Listen: Use the following sentence frame or the Think-Speak-Listen Flip Book to guide discussion: *Without the adverbs and adverb phrases, this sentences would only tell us _____.*

✔ Use Oral and Written Language: Retell a Story

Task: *Work with your group to list and summarize the main events of "Brushfire!" Then use adverbs and adverb phrases to add details that explain when, where, and how the events happened. Use complete sentences.*

(S) *A fire _____ gets closer. Ed _____ plays the piano. Meg _____ gathers boxes.*

(M) *_____, Ed _____. Meg _____ gathers boxes. As Meg packs, she _____.*

(L) *As a fire gets closer, _____. Meg _____ packs _____. As _____, Meg _____.*

Use this opportunity to assess students using the rubric in *English Language Development Assessment.*

↺ Wrap Up

How can adverbs and adverb phrases clarify a story and make it more exciting?

Turn and Talk: *Summarize an exciting story that you have recently read. Use adverbs and adverb phrases to include important details.*

👥👤 Differentiated Instruction
Build Language: Use Adverbs and Adverb Phrases

ⓈubstantiaI Support

Model: Distribute Substantial Support BLM 1. Review that adverbs and adverbs phrases can be used to add details about how, when, why, or where something happens. **Say:** *In the first sentence, I see the adverb deeply. It tells more about how the thorn cut into the lion's paw so that I know that the wound is serious. So I will circle the word how.*

Practice: Invite students to identify the adverb phrase in the second sentence. **Ask:** *What does the adverb phrase tell you about the thorn?* Continue with the remaining sentences in the Practice activity.

Extend: Have partners do the Extend activity. Monitor their work and provide support as needed. **Say:** *Before you write an adverb or adverb phrase, check that it makes sense in the sentence.*

Challenge: If students are ready, work with them to complete the Practice activity on the Moderate Support BLM 2.

Ⓜoderate Support

Model: Explain that an adverb or adverb phrase can be used to add details to a sentence to tell where, when, why, and how something happened. Read the first sentence in the Use Adverbs and Adverb Phrases chart from the book. **Say:** *I see an adverb phrase at the beginning of the sentence. What information does it give us? I see the adverb while. Does that word tell us when, where, or why? (when).* Then ask them to look at the word loudly and discuss that this adverb tells us how he was moaning.

Practice: Distribute Moderate Support BLM 2. Work with students to complete the Practice activity.

Extend: Have students work with a partner to complete the Extend activity.

Challenge: If students are ready, have them read paragraph 3 in "Sinbad and the Valley of Diamonds" on page 10 in the *Texts for Close Reading.* Work with them to identify adverbs and adverb phrases in the paragraph and explain how they are used.

Ⓛight Support

Use the text on p. 10 in the *Texts for Close Reading* to complete the following activities.

Practice: Ask partners to read paragraph 3. Have them identify and list adverbs and adverb phrases and discuss the details that they add to the story.

Extend: Have partners read aloud paragraphs 1 and 2, and use the adverbs and adverb phrases they find to answer these questions: *Why did the serpents come out at night? When did Sinbad see a chance to escape? Why were the merchants furious?*

Challenge: Have partners select two or three sentences from paragraph 3 and use adverbs and adverb phrases to add details to the story. Invite students to share their sentences.

☑ Formative Assessment

Substantial Support	• With support, can students recognize adverbs and adverb phrases in sentences? • With support, can students understand how adverbs and adverb phrases add details? • With support, can students use adverbs and adverb phrases to expand sentences?
Moderate Support	• Can students identify adverbs and adverb phrases in sentences? • Can students explain how adverbs and adverb phrases are used? • Can students expand and add details to sentences with adverbs and adverb phrases?
Light Support	• Can students understand the purpose of adverbs and adverb phrases added to sentences? • Can students use adverbs and adverb phrases to add details to sentences?

Preview or Review Week 2 ELA Mini-Lessons

"The Law of Club and Fang," pages 122–123

Student Objectives

LANGUAGE
Purpose:
• I can retell a story.
Form:
• I can identify nouns and pronouns.
CONTENT
• I can analyze a character in realistic fiction.

Additional Materials
• Unit Presentation
• Think-Speak-Listen Flip Book
• *Texts for Close Reading* booklet
• Student journal

Metacognitive Prompt: Monitoring Production

Today, we will write and answer questions about a text. When you speak, think about what you are saying. When you write, think about what you are writing use reasons and examples in your responses.

7 Read "The Law of Club and Fang"

Build Background and Vocabulary

Display the panels from "The Law of Club and Fang." Explain that this fictional story is taken from a larger book about sled dogs in Alaska. If students have read the story, invite them to share what they remember and what they know about sled dogs.

Read Aloud the Text

Read panels 1 and 2. Ask students to find images in the picture that match words in the text (straps, harness). Review the names of the characters and ask students to identify Buck in the illustration in panel 2. Ask questions, such as: *Who is in the picture? What happened?* Repeat with panels 3 and 4. Then refer to the Essential Question. Point out that the story is realistic fiction–it shows real aspects of survival during the Alaskan gold rush.

Think-Speak-Listen: Use the following sentence frame or the Think-Speak-Listen Flip Book to guide discussion: *Buck is _____ because in the story _____.*

👤👤👤 Differentiated Instruction
Build Language: Recognize Pronouns and Antecedents

Display panels 1 and 2. Ask volunteers to read the last sentence in panel 1, then the first two sentences in panel 2. Point out the three pronouns used in those sentences: *he, his,* and *him,* all referring to the dog Buck. Write example sentence *"The dog was strong. He was able to pull the heavy sled."* on the board and ask volunteers to read aloud the example sentence. **Ask:** *Which word is replaced by the pronoun* he? Point out that writers use pronouns to replace nouns so they do not have to say the same noun over and over. Use the Differentiated Instruction to practice recognizing pronouns and antecedents in a way that best matches the levels of your students.

☑ Use Oral and Written Language: Retell a Story

Task: *With your partner, write sentences to retell the part of the story. In your sentences, use pronouns correctly to refer to him and other characters.*

(S) *Buck pulled _____. It was _____ first time pulling a sled. _____ wore a harness.*

(M) *Buck pulled the _____. Francois _____ to _____. _____ was shocked and _____ dignity was hurt.*

(L) *Buck was _____. Francois _____ and _____. His _____ was _____, but _____.*

🔄 Wrap Up

Today we learned that pronouns can take the place of nouns in a text or story. Why do writers replace nouns with pronouns?

Turn and Talk: *Use pronouns to describe an animal or person that is a character in a story you have recently read.*

👥👥 Differentiated Instruction
Build Language: Recognize Pronouns and Antecedents

Ⓢubstantial Support

Model: Write two sentence pairs on the board: *"The dog was strong. The dog was able to pull the heavy sled."; "The dog was strong. He was able to pull the heavy sled."* Point out the pronoun **he** in the second sentence pair. **Say:** *To find out what noun the pronoun replaces, I look back at the first sentence. I see the noun **dog**. **He** replaces the noun **dog**.*

Practice: Work with students to look for examples of the pronouns *he, him* and *his* in panels 2 and 3. Have volunteers read aloud the sentences. Then ask students what noun each pronouns replaces, helping them locate the pronouns if necessary. **Say:** *The story is still talking about Buck, so the pronouns replace Buck.*

Extend: Have partners identify pronouns and their antecedents in panel 4.

Challenge: If students are ready, work with them to complete the Practice activity on Moderate Support BLM 1.

Ⓜoderate Support

Model: Display panel 2 from "The Law of Club and Fang" and ask volunteers to read aloud the first few sentences. Point out the pronouns **he** and **him** and ask students who they refer to. If necessary, clarify that they refer to the dog in the picture, Buck. Then have volunteers read sentences from panel 3. After each sentence, ask students to name who or what the pronouns **he**, **him**, or **his** refer to. Point out that they can tell which dog they refer to by looking at the names they follow. For example, the last **he** refers to Buck, rather than Dave. The last **his** refers to Francois, the name that appears earlier in the sentence.

Practice: Distribute Moderate Support BLM 1. Work with students to complete the Practice activity.

Extend: Have partners complete the Extend activity. Ask them to read aloud sentences and have their partners check them.

Challenge: If students are ready, have them read paragraph 3 on page 14 of *Texts for Close Reading*. Ask them to complete the Practice activity on Light Support BLM 2. Support students as needed.

Ⓛight Support

Use the text on pp. 12-19 in the *Texts for Close Reading* to complete the following activities.

Practice: Distribute BLM 2. Work with students to complete the Practice activity using paragraph 3.

Extend: Have partners use paragraph 5 in their *Texts for Close Reading* to complete the Extend activity. Monitor students as they work.

Challenge: If students are ready, have them complete the

✓ Formative Assessment

Substantial Support	• With support, can students identify nouns and pronouns? • With support, can students determine which noun is replaced by a pronoun?
Moderate Support	• Can students recognize pronouns in a story? • Can students identify the previous nouns in a story that pronouns replace?
Light Support	• Can students recognize pronouns in a story and determine which nouns the pronouns refer back to? • Can students use pronouns to understand which characters in a story are referred to?

Preview or Review Week 2 ELA Mini-Lessons

"The Law of Club and Fang," page 124

Student Objectives

LANGUAGE

Purpose:
• I can explain a problem and solution in a journal.

Form:
• I can recognize and use connecting words.

CONTENT
• I can analyze a problem and the solution in realistic fiction.

Additional Materials

• Unit Presentation
• Think-Speak-Listen Flip Book
• *Texts for Close Reading* booklet
• Student journal

Metacognitive Prompt: Grouping

Today we will talk and read about problems and solutions. As you read, look for words the author uses to describe Buck's problems. Look also for words the author uses to describe solutions to the problems. Putting similar ideas into groups can help you understand the story.

8 Analyze Problem and Solution Structure

Engage Thinking

Display panel 5. **Say:** *Today, we will read more of "The Law of Club and Fang."* **Ask:** *What do you remember about Buck in the first part of the story? What challenges did he face?*

👥👥👥 Differentiated Instruction
☑ Read and View Closely: Analyze Problem and Solution Structure

Point to the first sentence in panel 5. **Ask:** *What problem does Buck have?* Read aloud panel 5. **Ask:** *How did Buck try to solve his problem? What happened each time?* Read aloud panel 6. **Ask:** *How did Buck find a solution? Was this solution successful? Why?* Explain that in most stories, the main character faces one or more problems and tries to solve them. **Say:** *Knowing this structure helps me understand the story.* Use the Differentiated Instruction to practice analyzing a problem and solution structure in a way that best matches the levels of your students. Use this opportunity to assess students using the rubric in *English Language Development Assessment*.

Think-Speak-Listen: Use the following sentence frame or the Think-Speak-Listen Flip Book to guide discussion: *Buck learned _____ by _____.*

Build Language: Recognize and Use Connecting Words

Write the words *and, but,* and *so.* **Say:** *These words show the connections between different ideas or events.* Ask students to find these words in the text. **Ask:** *What ideas or events do the words and and so connect?* Elicit answers. Encourage students to review the second sentence on panel 5 and respond to these questions: *What two events or actions are connected by* and? *What connecting word tells you that Buck did not sleep?*

☑ Use Oral and Written Language: Explain a Problem and Solution

Task: *Imagine that you live in Alaska during gold rush in the 1890s. Write a journal entry together to explain one problem you face problem, your attempts to solve it, and your final solution. Use connecting words to relate ideas or events.*

(S) *Our problem was _____. We tried _____. The solution was _____.*

(M) *We had a problem _____. After trying _____, we _____.*

(L) *In the winter, we _____. First, we _____ then _____.*

🔄 Wrap Up

Today we learned how to analyze a problem and solution in a story. How do connecting words help us relate ideas and events to see how the problem is solved?

Turn and Talk: *Recall a problem that a character has in a story you have recently read. How did the character try to solve the problem? What was the final solution?*

👥 Differentiated Instruction
Read and View Closely: Analyze Problem and Solution Structure

Ⓢ ubstantial Support

Model: Read panel 5. Guide students to understand that *miserable* and *disconsolate* mean Buck was unhappy. Distribute BLM 1. Point to the chart. **Say:** *The first sentence says Buck's great problem is sleeping. So, I'll write "sleeping" in the top box. Next, I read what Buck does first to try to sleep. He lays on the snow. I'll write this in the first event box. Then I see a connecting word. The word but tells me that laying on the snow won't work. Buck gets up shivering. I shiver when I'm cold, so I'll write "too cold" in the chart.*

Practice: Invite students to help you identify the next event. **Say:** *Next, we read that Buck wanders from tent to tent. Why doesn't this work?* Have students write what Buck does and why it doesn't work in the second event box.

Extend: Read aloud panel 6. Have partners write the third event and how it leads to a solution. **Ask:** *What does the connecting word so tell you?*

Challenge: If students are ready, work with them to complete the Practice activity on Moderate Support BLM 2.

Ⓜ oderate Support

Model: Distribute Moderate Support BLM 2. Have a volunteers take turns reading aloud sentences in panel 5 and write in their own words what the problem is in the chart in BLM 2.

Practice: Work with students to identify the first three attempts Buck makes to try to solve his problem. Have them write these attempts in the chart, along with the result of each attempt.

Say: *Under* attempt *write what he tried to do—how he tried to solve the problem. Under* result *write what happened when he tried.*

Extend: Ask partners to complete the chart with the event that leads to a solution to the problem.

Challenge: If students are ready, have them read paragraph 10 of "The Law of Club and Fang" on page 17 in their *Texts for Close Reading*. Guide them to identify another attempt by Buck to solve his problem and describe what happened.

Ⓛ ight Support

Use the text on pp. 12-19 in the *Texts for Close Reading* to complete the following activities.

Practice: Have pairs read paragraph 10. **Ask:** *What is the problem that Buck faces? What are the attempts he makes to try to solve this problem? What happens?* Assist students in analyzing the story.

Extend: Monitor partners as they read paragraph 12. Ask them to describe the event that led Buck to realize how he could solve his problem. Have partners create a simple flowchart to show the connection of events and ideas that led to a solution.

Challenge: Ask students to make a list of words from paragraphs 10 and 11 that describe how Buck felt. (For example: *miserable, desolate, forlorn, shivering*) Ask them to describe what they think each word means and to look up meanings of

✓ Formative Assessment

Substantial Support	• With support, can students identify a problem in a story? • With support, can students follow the sequence of events to solve the problem, and recognize how they lead to the solution?
Moderate Support	• With support, can students identify a story problem and connect events that lead to a solution? • With support, can write events that lead to a solution to a problem?
Light Support	• Can students analyze the problem and solution structure of a story? • Can students describe the connection between the events and the solution to the problem?

Preview or Review Week 2 ELA Mini-Lessons

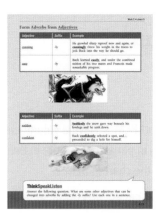

"Form Adverbs from Adjectives, " page 125

Student Objectives

LANGUAGE
Purpose:
• I can tell a descriptive story.
Form:
• I can form adverbs from adjectives.
CONTENT
• I can recognize realistic fiction.

Additional Materials
• Unit Presentation
• Think-Speak-Listen Flip Book
• *Texts for Close Reading* booklet
• Student journal

Language Transfer Support

Note that students whose first language is Hmong or Haitian Creole may need extra support to distinguish between adverbs and adjectives. In those languages, adjectives can be used in place of adverbs (e.g., *the dog barks loud*).

9 Form Adverbs from Adjectives

Engage Thinking

Display the chart. **Ask:** *What character is in the top picture? What character is in the bottom picture? What is each character doing?* Explain that the visuals show us actions of the characters. The sentences from the text describe these actions clearly.

Turn and Talk: *Describe the dogs in each visual, including their appearance and their actions.*

Read and View Closely: Recognize Adjectives and Adverbs

Read the third sentence of the Form Adverbs from Adjectives chart without the underlined word. Then invite a volunteer to read it again with the word. **Ask:** *What did the word add to the sentence? What information did it give us?* Point to the adjective section of the chart. **Say:** *Sudden is an adjective.* Remind students that an adjective describes a noun. **Say:** *The word suddenly is an adverb. Suddenly tells us more about how the snow gave way.* Remind students that an adverb describes a verb and often tells how, when, or where.

👥👥 Differentiated Instruction
Build Language: Form Adverbs from Adjectives

Say: *The chart shows us how we can change adjectives to adverbs.* Read the first row aloud. **Say:** *I see the adjective* cunning. **Ask:** *How do we change the adjective* cunning *to the adverb* cunningly? Remind students that they have seen in a previous lesson how we can use the suffix *-ly* or *-ily* at the end of adjectives to make them into adverbs. Use the Differentiated Instruction to practice forming adverbs from adjectives in a way that best matches the levels of your students.

Think-Speak-Listen: Use the following sentence frame or the Think-Speak-Listen Flip Book to guide discussion: *An example of an adjective that can be changed into an adverb by adding -ly is _____.*

☑ Use Oral and Written Language: Tell a Descriptive Story

Task: *Choose four adjectives from the chart below. Work with your peer group to form adverbs from the adjectives. Work together to write a short story. Use your four adverbs in the story. Read the story aloud.*

calm	perfect	hungry	proud	soft
bold	nervous	necessary	hopeful	lucky

Wrap Up

Today we have learned how to form adverbs from adjectives to help us describe actions. Why is it important to know how to form adverbs?

Turn and Talk: *Describe something you like to do and how you perform this activity or sport. Use adverbs to make your descriptions clear and interesting.*

👥👥 Differentiated Instruction
Build Language: Form Adverbs from Adjectives

Ⓢubstantial Support

Model: Write two example sentences on the board: "Elisa is very careful."and "Elisa carried the drink carefully." Read the example sentences and ask a volunteer to act out the second sentence. Have another student narrate by reading the sentences. **Say:** *We described (Elisa) with the adjective careful. Then we described how she carried the drink. We used the adverb carefully to describe the action. How do we form the adverb carefully? (by adding -ly)* Read a few other familiar adjectives and adverbs from the textbook. Then display the chart. Have students read the adjectives and the adverbs. Discuss the meanings of the ones that are unfamiliar. Read each of the sentences on the page.

Practice: Distribute BLM 1. Work with students to complete the sentences. Some adverbs may work in more than one sentence, so students should choose based on the story.

Extend: Have pairs complete the Extend activity on BLM 1, looking back at the story to help them.

Challenge: Ask students to help you make new sentences using some of the adjectives and adverbs on the chart.

Ⓜoderate Support

Model: Ask volunteers to read each sentence from the Form Adverbs from Adjectives chart. First have students read the sentence without the adverb, and then with it. Discuss the meaning of the adjectives *cunning, easy, sudden,* and *confident.* Help students select the verb that each adverb modifies. Discuss the different spellings shown on the chart, and how the word endings affect how the adverbs are formed.

Practice: Work with students to complete the Practice on BLM 2, forming an adverb to complete each sentence.

Extend: Have pairs of students complete the Extend activity on the BLM, referencing the story as needed.

Challenge: Ask students in pairs to choose five or six adjectives from the chart and form them into adverbs. Have them form sentences using the adjective and then the adverb.

Ⓛight Support

Use the text on pp. 12-19 in the *Texts for Close Reading* to complete the following activities.

Practice: Have pairs find the *-ly* adverbs in the paragraph. Then have them create and complete a chart similar to the one below.

Page	Paragraph	Adverb	Verb Modified	Adjective
13	1	suddenly		sudden
17	10		glowed	
17	10	ignominiously	fled	
17	10			sharp
19	12			aimless

Extend: Have students write two sentence about the characters using an adjective in one sentence and an adverb in another.

Challenge: Have students choose adjectives from the chart, form them into adverbs, and write an original paragraph using the new words.

☑ Formative Assessment

Substantial Support	• Can students add *-ly* to adjectives to form adverbs? • Can students use adverbs to complete sentence frames about the story?
Moderate Support	• Can students add *-ly* to adjectives to form adverbs? • Can students revise a sentence by changing an adjective to an adverb? • Can students use adverbs to complete sentence frames about the story?
Light Support	• Can students add *-ly* to adjectives to form adverbs? • Can students identify related adjectives and adverbs, and identify the verb modified by the adverbs? • Can students write original sentences using adjectives and related adverbs?

Preview or Review Week 2 ELA Mini-Lessons

"Gold Rush!," page 126

10 Read "Gold Rush!"

Build Background and Vocabulary

Display the panels from "Gold Rush!" and explain their importance to the story. If students have already read the story, ask them what they remember. Invite students to share their experiences traveling to new places or going on adventures.

Read Aloud the Text

Read aloud panel 1. **Ask:** *How does the visual relate to the text? Who is in the picture? What are they doing?* Repeat with the other panels, helping students relate the text and visual. **Ask:** *When did the story take place? What event is presented?* Model thinking through the answer. **Say:** *The pictures look old-fashioned. The narrator travels on a steamship. So the story took place in the past. The title tells me there is a gold rush.* Invite students to share their ideas. Then refer to the Essential Question. **Ask:** *Why do Pa and the narrator risk their lives?* Invite students to respond. Explain that a historical fiction story takes place during an event in history. The people are not real, but they could have been.

Think-Speak-Listen: Use the following sentence frame or the Think-Speak-Listen Flip Book to guide discussion: *The narrator means _____ by "our golden future."*

👥 Differentiated Instruction
Build Language: Use Synonyms to Understand Meaning

Review the first paragraph. **Say:** *One way to understand a new word is by using a synonym.* Remind students a synonym is a word that means the same as another word. **Say:** *Look at astonishment in the first sentence.* **Ask:** *What feeling do you think the narrator had when Pa made the announcement?* Guide students to think of words such as surprise. **Say:** *I think of the synonym surprise based on the context. I can substitute it into the sentence to make sure the word works. I can use a dictionary to check the definition or a thesaurus to confirm it is a synonym.* Use the Differentiated Instruction to practice using synonyms in a way that best matches the levels of your students.

☑ Use Oral and Written Language: Write a Historical Article

Task: *Work with a partner to write a historical article informing people about a gold rush. Imagine you are taking part in the event. Write two to three sentences telling people about your experiences. Use three synonyms in your article.*

(S) *I felt _____ and shocked about the decision to _____.*

(M) *I felt _____ about the decision to _____.*

(L) *I felt _____ about _____.*

🔄 Wrap Up

Today we learned how to replace unfamiliar or difficult words with synonyms that we know. How does this help us better understand the meaning of words?

Turn and Talk: *Describe an event in history.*

👥 Differentiated Instruction
Build Language: Use Synonyms to Understand Meaning

Ⓢubstantial Support

Model: Read the first paragraph. Ask students to tell you unfamiliar words, such as *astonishment, announced, prospecting, intended, relented.* Remind them of strategies for figuring out the meanings of words, like looking at visuals or context clues. **Say:** *Look at the phrase "prospecting for gold." What is the man in the picture doing?* (searching, or looking in the water) *Searching may be a synonym—a word that means the same thing. We can look it up to check. Then we can substitute the word "He'd quit his job to go searching for gold."*

Practice: **Say:** *Let's find a synonyms for* announced *and* astonishment *in the same paragraph. So far we know that Pa announced he was quitting his job to go searching for gold. What could announced mean?* (told them, said) *And how would that make the child feel?* (surprised) **Have a volunteer replace the words *astonishment* and *announced* with *surprise* and *said* to see if the sentence makes sense. Have students check a dictionary or thesaurus to verify that the words are synonyms.**

Extend: Have students work in pairs to try to find synonyms for more words in the text, such as *provisions, dogged, chivvied.*

Challenge: Ask students to make up new sentences with words they have analyzed, such as *announced* or *astonishment.*

Ⓜoderate Support

Model: Read the first paragraph. List the words *astonishment, announced, prospecting, intended, relented.* For each word, ask what students know about the word and list any synonyms if students know them. **Say:** *A synonym is a word that has the same meaning as another word. If I don't know the meaning, I can look up a synonym.* Model looking up one of the words students don't know in a thesaurus and list some synonyms. Ask volunteers to reread sentences from the paragraph, substituting any synonyms you have listed.

Practice: Distribute BLM 1. Guide students to complete the Practice. Remind them to use context clues from text and visuals. Encourage them to refer to a print or online dictionary or thesaurus to check the meanings.

Extend: Have pairs complete the Extend activity on the BLM, writing synonyms that they know or look up.

Challenge: Have students write original sentences with words from the story and then rewrite them using synonyms.

Ⓛight Support

Use the text on p. 20 in the *Texts for Close Reading* to complete the following activities.

Practice: Review that a synonym is a word with the same meaning as another word. **Say:** *I can use a synonym to help me understand the meaning of an unfamiliar word.* Distribute BLM 2. Have students work with partners to complete the Practice. Remind them to use context clues as well as a dictionary, and/or a thesaurus to find synonyms and confirm meanings.

Extend: Tell students that finding synonyms can help them relate events in a story. Have pairs work with a partner to complete the Extend activity on BLM 2.

Challenge: Have student pairs write original paragraphs using some of the new words they have learned.

✓ Formative Assessment

Substantial Support	• Can students match pairs of synonyms? • Can students use context clues, a dictionary, and/or a thesaurus to determine synonyms?
Moderate Support	• Can students use context clues, a dictionary, and/or a thesaurus to determine synonyms? • Can students use synonyms to make meanings clear?
Light Support	• Can students use context clues, a dictionary, and/or a thesaurus to determine synonyms? • Can students explain how to determine synonyms? • Can students generate revised sentences using synonyms to make meanings clear?

Preview or Review Week 2 ELA Mini-Lessons

Combine Clauses to Connect Ideas	Week 2 • Lesson 11
Connecting Word	**Type of Relationship Indicated**
Before he had recovered from the shock caused by the tragic passing of Curly, he received another shock.	Sequence
Though his dignity was surely hurt by thus being made a draught animal, he was too wise to rebel.	Contrast
He lay down on the snow and attempted to sleep, **but** the frost soon drove him shivering to his feet.	Contrast
Suddenly the snow gave way beneath his forelegs **and** he sank down.	Result
I begged him to take me along **and** he relented.	Result
But Pa chivvied me along **until** at last we reached the Yukon River .	Duration

Think·Speak·Listen
Describe some of the hardships that you think Klondike gold miners faced. Use some of the connecting words given above.

127

"Combine Clauses to Connect Ideas, " page 127

Student Objectives

LANGUAGE
Purpose:
• I can connect ideas in a journal entry.
Form:
• I can use connecting words to show relationships in sentences.
CONTENT
• I can relate ideas in realistic and historical fiction.

Additional Materials

• Unit Presentation
• Think-Speak-Listen Flip Book
• *Texts for Close Reading* booklet
• Student journal

Language Transfer Support

Students whose first language is Chinese, Vietnamese, or Farsi may use conjunctions in pairs (e.g., *Though Buck tried to sleep, but he was too cold*). Point out that in English, only one conjunction is needed. When you introduce the connecting words, explain or review the structure of sentences with conjunctions.

11 Combine Clauses to Connect Ideas

Engage Thinking

Review the "The Law of Club and Fang" by asking what is happening in each picture. Expand on students' answers with full sentences.

Turn and Talk: *Describe two events from "The Law of Club and Fang."*

Read and View Closely: Recognize Word Relationships

Display chart on the Unit Presentation. Have students review the first row of the chart.
Say: *The first column shows sentences with two ideas joined in one sentence. The second column tells me the relationship–how it connects ideas.* **Ask:** *What relationship does the word* before *show?* Elicit that it shows sequence, or "time order."

👥 Differentiated Instruction
Build Language: Combine Clauses to Connect Ideas

Read aloud the first sentence of the chart. **Say:** *There are two clauses in this sentence. A clause is a sentence part with a subject and a verb.* Clauses *can be combined to connect ideas.* Have students help you identify the two clauses, separated by the comma. **Say:** *The writer connects these ideas using sequence, or time order. The word* before *shows which event happened first.* Explain that combining clauses is important because it helps us understand how events are connected. Use the Differentiated Instruction to practice combining clauses to connect ideas in a way that best matches the levels of your students.

Think-Speak-Listen: Use the following sentence frame or the Think-Speak-Listen Flip Book to guide discussion: *One hardship the gold miners faced was _____. Another hardship was _____.*

✓ Use Oral and Written Language: Connect Ideas in a Journal Entry

Task: *Work with a partner. Imagine that you are one of the characters in "The Law of Club and Fang." Create a journal entry in which you describe events and experiences. Combine clauses with connecting words to show the relationship between ideas. Try to use words that show sequence, result, duration, and contrast.*

(S) On _____, I watched _____ before I _____.

(M) On _____, I watched _____ before _____.

(L) On _____, I _____ before _____.

Wrap Up

Today we have learned how writers combine sentences. Why is it important to know how to combine sentences?

Turn and Talk: *Discuss two events in the past, either in history or in your own life. Combine ideas and descriptions to show clearly how the events related to each other.*

👥 Differentiated Instruction
Build Language: Combine Clauses to Connect Ideas

Ⓢubstantial Support

Model: Point to the word *contrast* in the right column of the chart. **Say:** *We make connections between ideas in different ways.* Contrast *is one kind of connection. We can use words to explain how two things are different.* Point to the word *but* in the third row of the chart. Model using this word to contrast the author's ideas: *Buck wanted to sleep, but the ground was too cold.*

Practice: Distribute BLM 1. **Say:** *We can also show how ideas relate in time order. That is called* sequence. *We use words such as* before *and* after *to show time order. And we can use the word* and *to show a result.* Work with students to complete Practice section of BLM 1.

Extend: Have pairs complete the activity on the BLM. **Say:** *Be sure to complete the clause in a way that shows the relationship.*

Challenge: If students are ready, help them complete this frame to show contrast: *Buck fell through the snow, _____.*

Ⓜoderate Support

Model: Point to the words in the right column of the chart: *sequence, contrast, result, duration.* **Say:** *We make connections between ideas in different ways.* Explain their meaning as necessary. For example, **say** Sequence *means* order. Contrast *means how two things are different.* Result *means what happens because of something else.* Duration *means how long.* Explain the connecting words. For example, ask students to look at rows 3 and 4. **Say:** But *describes a* contrast, *how two ideas are different.* And *describes a* result, Point to row 1. **Say:** *Words about time, like* before *or* after *show sequence.*

Practice: Work with students to complete the Practice section on BLM 2, referring to the story as needed.

Extend: Have pairs work together to complete the Extend activity on the BLM, using information from the story.

Challenge: Have partners write two separate sentences about the story and combine them using words on the chart.

Ⓛight Support

Practice: Ask students to explain the relationships in the chart in their own words. Point out that some connecting words, such as but and and, join sentences in the middle. Others, like before and though, may occur at the beginning. Have pairs use connecting words to combine these sentences about stories they read.

Sequence: Buck was harnessed to the sled. Buck hauled Francois to the forest.

Contrast: A blizzard blew into the pass. We inched along the trail.

Duration: We traveled for a year. We reached the Yukon River.

Extend: Give partners these sentences: *We gathered food and supplies. We set off on the Chilkoot Trail.* **Say:** *Find different ways to combine the sentences using connecting words.* Have partners share their sentences and identify the relationship between ideas.

Challenge: Have students write two short related sentences about Buck and combine them to show how they are related.

☑ Formative Assessment

Substantial Support	• Can students recognize connecting words? • Can students complete sentence to show contrast or sequence?
Moderate Support	• Can students complete a compound or complex sentence and provide the connecting word to show contrast, sequence, or result?
Light Support	• Can students use connecting words to combine sentences to show a given relationship? • Can students combine sentences to show different relationships between ideas and identify the type of relationship? • Can students generate original sentences and combine them using connecting words?

Preview or Review Week 3 ELA Mini-Lessons

"Julie Fights for Survival," pages 128–129

Student Objectives

LANGUAGE
Purpose:
- I can describe characters and events in a news story.

Form:
- I can condense ideas in a story.

CONTENT
- I can understand realistic fiction.

Additional Materials

- Unit Presentation
- Think-Speak-Listen Flip Book
- *Texts for Close Reading* booklet
- Student journal

Metacognitive Prompt

Today we will ask and answer questions as we read a story. Talking about what you read is a good strategy to help you make sure you understand the text.

12 Read "Julie Fights for Survival"

Build Background and Vocabulary

Display the panels from "Julie Fights for Survival" and explain key words and ideas from the story. Invite students to share their cultural experiences and knowledge about what difficulties a person in the wilderness would face.

Read Aloud the Text

Read aloud panel 1. Explain how the image is connected to the text. Discuss and then repeat for panels 2–4. Identify the footnotes and explain the meaning of the unfamiliar words. Ask students to describe Julie and how she feels. After reading, **ask:** *What is Julie afraid of?* Model thinking through the answer, **say:** *Julie is afraid that the lone wolf has taken her bag. The bag contains everything that she needs to survive.* Invite students to share what they know about survival, then ask them to think about the Essential Question: *What compels us to survive?* Explain that this type of story is called realistic fiction.

Think-Speak-Listen: Use the following sentence frame or the Think-Speak-Listen Flip Book to guide discussion: *Jello stole Julie's pack because _____.*

Differentiated Instruction
Build Language: Condense Ideas

Remind students that stories often contain quite a few details and descriptions. Point to panel 3. **Say:** *Writers often condense ideas so that they don't have to list every detail in its own sentence. For example, rather than write, "Her needles and ulo were all in the pack. They were the tools of survival," the author wrote, "Her needles and ulo, the tools of survival, were all in the pack."* Use the Differentiated Instruction to practice condensing ideas in a way that best matches the levels of your students.

☑ Use Oral and Written Language: Describe Characters and Events in a News Story

Task: *The lone wolf has taken Julie's supplies. Write a news story that gives an update on Julie and the wolves. Describe Julie's character as you write about the situation or events in the story. Remember to condense ideas. You may use some of the following words:* independent, brave, lucky, natural, strong-willed, determined, self-reliant.

Examples:

(S) *Julie, a brave girl, is trying to survive in the wilderness.*

(M) *Julie, determined to survive, ran to look for the pack full of tools.*

(L) *The wolf came near Julie, growling with bared teeth, and ran away with the pack.*

Wrap Up

Today we learned about condensing ideas. Why is it helpful to condense ideas when you write?

Turn and Talk: *With a partner, make a prediction about what will happen next with Julie and the wolves.*

••• Differentiated Instruction
Build Language: Condense Ideas

(S)ubstantial Support

Model: Say: *The author gives readers many important details in this story. Instead of listing each detail in its own sentence, the author condenses ideas and creates precise sentences made of many details.* Read Panel 4. **Say:** *"Shivering, she slid into bed and cried."* **Ask:** *What are the different ideas in this sentence?* Help students name the ideas: she is shivering, she got into bed, and she cried.

Practice: Distribute BLM 1 and work with students to complete the activity. For the first chart, students will read the condensed sentence and pull out the ideas.

Extend: Have students work in pairs to complete the Extend activity. For this chart they will read the separate ideas and try to find a sentence in the text that condenses those ideas.

Challenge: If students are ready, ask them to write two separate ideas about what they did this morning. Then have them try to condense them into one sentence.

(M)oderate Support

Model: Display panels 3. Have a volunteer read the first sentence. Ask students to find all of the ideas in the sentence: *She jumped out of bed, she started after Jello, her life was in that pack—food, needles, knives, even her boots.* **Say** *By condensing ideas, the writer doesn't have to list each detail in its own sentence.*

Practice: Distribute BLM 2. Work with students to complete the Practice activity, finding the sentence in the text that condenses the separate ideas.

Extend: In pairs, ask students to complete the Extend activity. For this activity, they will condense the ideas in their own way. Students can also look at the way the ideas were condensed in the text.

Challenge: If students are ready, model for them how to complete the Light Support Practice activity.

(L)ight Support

Use the text on pp. 22-29 in the *Texts for Close Reading* to complete the following activities.

Practice: Ask students to identify at least 3 sentences that condense ideas to complete chart like the following:

Condensed Ideas	Separate Ideas
"The wind chilled her naked body and she stopped to collect her wits."	It was windy, she was naked, she stopped to collect her wits.
"Quickly she pulled them out and clutched them to her chest, but they were of little comfort."	She pulled her clothes out,m clutched them to her chest, she was not comforted by them.

Extend: Ask pairs to decompose the following sentence into the ideas and details that it condenses. Have them write a separate sentence for each idea or detail.

Challenge: If students are ready, ask them to use the ideas they identified in the sentence above and create their own original sentence.

☑ Formative Assessment

Substantial Support	• Do students understand why ideas need to be condensed?
Moderate Support	• Are students able to identify how to condense ideas? • Can students condense ideas in a story?
Light Support	• Are students able to identify ideas that need to be condensed? • Are students able to create original sentences that include condensed ideas from a story?

"Julie Fights for Survival," page 130

Student Objectives

LANGUAGE
Purpose:
- I can ask and answer questions for a news report.

Form:
- I can recognize how prepositional phrases are used to help with details in a text.

CONTENT
- I can understand realistic fiction.

Additional Materials
- Unit Presentation
- Think-Speak-Listen Flip Book
- *Texts for Close Reading* booklet
- Student journal

Metacognitive Prompt

Today we will practice monitoring, or checking, our understanding of the text as we read. As you read, keep asking yourself questions such as: "What just happened?" "What caused that to happen?" "Can I sum up what I've just read?"

13 Evaluate Language Choices

Engage Thinking

Display the panels from "Julie Fights for Survival" and explain key words and ideas from the story. Read aloud panels 5 and 6. Explain how the image is connected to the text. Identify the footnotes and explain the meaning of the unfamiliar words.

Turn and Talk: *Tell a partner how Julie feels.*

👥👥 Differentiated Instruction
Read and View Closely:
Evaluate Language Choices

Say: *Authors have a lot of choices when they decide how to describe what's happening in a story.* Point to panel 5 and read aloud the first sentence. **Say:** *The author uses many descriptive and vivid words to help tell the story. Instead of saying the sun was shining, the author said it's light and loving scent gave her a sense of security. The author chose to give the sun the human characteristic of loving because of how it made Julie feel.* Explain to students that people use language to communicate. The words we choose create imagery and add important plot details. Use the Differentiated Instruction to practice evaluating language choices in a way that best matches the level of your students.

Think-Speak-Listen: Use the following sentence frame or the Think-Speak-Listen Flip Book to guide discussion: *At first Julie felt _____. Then she felt _____. I know this because _____.*

Build Language: Use Prepositional Phrases

Display panels 1 and 2. Point to and read the prepositional phrases. Some of these details are prepositional phrases. List these words on the board: *in, on, beside, next to, below, above.* **Say:** *These are all examples of prepositions. We use them to form prepositional phrases. These phrases tell us about location, where something is happening in the story.*

☑ Use Oral and Written Language:
Ask and Answer Questions for a News Report

Task: *Imagine that you are providing details that will help others to look for Julie for a news interview about Julie. Be sure to use prepositional phrases and language choices that help you describe the character and how she will survive.*

(S) *Where is Julie walking? Julie is walking _____ in.*

(M) *What is in Julie's pack? There are _____ in the pack. She needs _____ in _____.*

(L) *How can Julie survive? What dangers does she face? She _____ in.*

🔄 Wrap Up

Today we talked about the language choices that authors make. How does an author's choice of language change what we read?

Turn and Talk: *Tell your partner something interesting that happened this week. Choose words that make it sound exciting.*

👥 Differentiated Instruction
Read and View Closely: Evaluate Language Choices

ⓢubstantial Support

Model Say: *When we speak and write, we are making choice. The words that we choose depend on our purpose.* Point to panel 3. Have a volunteer read the first sentence. **Ask:** *What are some other ways we could describe what Julie did?* List students' suggestions and add more, for example: *Julie got up. Julie crawled out of bed. Julie got up quickly.* **Ask:** *Why do you think the author chose those words?* Discuss how the use of the word *jumped* paints an image. It tells the reader that there was urgency in what Julie was doing.

Practice: Invite students to help you evaluate more language choices in panels 3 and 4. Select a vivid word or phrase, for example *Shivering, she slid into bed and cried.* Ask for suggestions from students about other ways to give the same information and why they think the author chose these words.

Extend: Have students work in pairs. Ask them to find interesting phrases, copy them, and write another way a writer could say the same thing. Ask partners to evaluate which way gives a more vivid picture.

Challenge: If students seem ready, have them work with a partner on the Practice activity on the Moderate Support BLM 1.

Ⓜoderate Support

Model: Point to panels 3–4. **Say:** *I notice that there are quite a few details in this story. I understand many of these details because of the words and phrases that the author has decided to use.* Ask volunteers to read selected sentences, for example *Shivering, she slid into bed and cried.* Ask other students to suggest different ways the author could say the same thing. As a group evaluate the difference in ways of expressing the same idea. Point out that If writers did not vary their language choices the story might not sound as interesting or exciting.

Practice: Distribute BLM 1. Guide students to complete the chart, finding words in the text. For each phrase students find, evaluate together how the choice of words added to the writing, for example making it sound exciting or suspenseful.

Extend: Ask students to choose two of the rows in the chart and write their ideas about how the language choices paint a picture or add details to the story.

Challenge: If students are ready, have them read paragraphs 4–5 of "Julie Fights for Survival" on page 23 in their *Texts for Close Reading*. Ask them to complete the Practice activity on the Light Support BLM 2.

ⓛight Support

Use the text on pp. 22-29 in the *Texts for Close Reading* to complete the following activities.

Practice: Distribute BLM 2. Have students find phrases to answer the questions. Then for each phrase in the text, ask them to use different words to write what it means in the last column. Discuss the difference in the two ways of saying the same thing, and why the author's choice of words is effective.

Extend: Have students find another phrase or sentence to add to the chart. Then have them add a question about the phrase to ask their partner. Have partners suggest another way of saying the same thing to add to the chart.

Challenge: Ask students to find more interesting phrases or sentences in the text.

✔️ Formative Assessment

Substantial Support	• Can students explain language choice in a story? • Can students suggest alternate language choices?
Moderate Support	• Can students recognize different choices authors make? • Can students explain how language choices affect the meaning of a sentence?
Light Support	• Are students able to describe the affects of different language choices? • Are students able to create original sentences using varied language choices?

Preview or Review Week 3 ELA Mini-Lessons

"Use Sense Imagery to Describe," page 131

Student Objectives

LANGUAGE
Purpose:
- I can describe a picture using sense imagery.

Form:
- I can make sensory words.

CONTENT
- I can understand sensory imagery in realistic fiction.

Additional Materials
- Unit Presentation
- Think-Speak-Listen Flip Book
- *Texts for Close Reading* booklet
- Student journal

Language Transfer Support

When an adjective is used to create sensory images, placement of the adjective may cause problems. In Haitian Creole, Hmong, Spanish, and Vietnamese, adjectives often follow nouns. In Cantonese and Korean, adjectives always follow nouns.

14 Use Sense Imagery to Describe

Engage Thinking

Display the chart and image. Direct attention to the image. **Say:** *The visuals and words in a story help us create images in our minds of the characters, setting, and events. Based on the visual, how would you describe what the girl sees?*

Read and View Closely: Identify Imagery

Have students look at the chart. **Say:** *This chart shows how sense imagery can add details to a story. Imagery is writing that describes something that relates to our senses. This means the imagery describes something that the character sees, feels, smells, or hears.* Read aloud the chart with students. **Say:** *In the first row, the words whistle and whined describe what Julie hears. These words are about the sense of sound. Sense imagery like this helps us to make a picture in our minds of where a story takes place and what happens in the story.*

👥 Differentiated Instruction
Build Language: Use Sense Imagery to Describe

Review the chart. **Say:** *Sensory imagery is used in writing to help create pictures for the reader relating to our five senses.* As needed, mime each sense: seeing, hearing, touching, tasting, smelling and ask students to identify each sense. **Say:** *Sense imagery can make a story seem real.* Work with students to brainstorm different examples of sensory words that might serve as a substitute for the words in the sentences in the chart. Use the Differentiated Instruction to practice using sense imagery to describe in a way that best matches the levels of your students.

Think-Speak-Listen: Use the following sentence frame or the Think-Speak-Listen Flip Book to guide discussion: *I saw _____. I heard _____. I smelled _____. I touched _____.*

☑ Use Oral and Written Language: Describe a Picture Using Sense Imagery

Task: *Working with a partner, discuss the different ways you can use sense imagery to describe the picture at the bottom of the page 119. Make a list of words or ideas. Then write a few sentences, using sense imagery to describe the picture.*

Ⓢ   *Julie's face touched _____. She saw _____. She heard _____.*

Ⓜ   *Julie's face _____. She saw _____ and _____. She heard _____ of the _____. She smelled _____.*

Ⓛ   *Julie _____. She _____ and _____, while she _____.*

🔄 Wrap Up

Today we learned that sense imagery helps a writer describe different sensations for the reader. What does sense imagery add to a story?

Turn and Talk: *Using sense imagery, describe a form of transportation you take to get to school.*

👥 Differentiated Instruction
Build Language: Use Sense Imagery to Describe

(S)ubstantial Support

Model: Remind students that sense imagery is describing with words that relate to sight, sound, touch, and smell. **Say:** *Sense imagery helps us imagine what the characters experience using our senses.* **Read the first row of the chart.** *The sentence has two words that tell the sound of the wind. A whistle is a high, loud noise.* Whistle out loud to support understanding and then invite students to make the sound with you. Then go on to the next row and discuss how it feels to shiver. Have students pantomime shivering from cold.

Practice: Distribute Substantial Support BLM 1. Working with students, help them find sound words in the story. Prompt as needed to find and define words. For example, **say:** *This paragraph tells us a scary sound the dog made.*

Extend: Have students work with partners to choose sound words they wrote to complete the sentences on the page.

Challenge: If students are ready, have them complete the Practice activity for Moderate Support BLM 2.

(M)oderate Support

Model: Remind students that sense imagery is about using words to describe sight, sound, touch, and smell. Use gestures to support understanding of the sensory words in the chart. **Say:** *As I read a story, I look for words that describe things I can see, hear, feel, or smell. Reread row 2.* **Say:** *The word shivering tells me how Julie got into bed. I know when I shiver I am very cold, so this word helps me picture how cold Julie is.*

Practice: Distribute Moderate Support BLM 2. Work with students to complete the chart.

Extend: Have students work with a partner to write original sentences using sense words they have identified.

Challenge: If students are ready, work with them read paragraph 11 on page 26 in the *Texts for Close Reading* and identify sense imagery.

(L)ight Support

Use the text on pp. 22-29 in the *Texts for Close Reading* to complete the following activities.

Practice: Ask students to read paragraphs 11–13 and identify examples of sense imagery. For each example, ask them to classify the sense that the imagery appeals to. Have them make a chart like the one used on BLM 2, listing sentences and words relating to different senses.

Extend: Have partners choose three examples of sense imagery that they identified and use each example in their own sentence.

Challenge: Have pairs to write new examples of sense imagery based on the image on pages 26–27 in *Texts for Close Reading*.

☑️ Formative Assessment

Substantial Support	• With support, can students identify examples of sense imagery? • Can students choose appropriate sense words to complete sentences?
Moderate Support	• Can students identify and classify examples of sense imagery? • Can students appropriately use sense words in new sentences?
Light Support	• Can students recognize and analyze examples of sense imagery in a longer text? • Are students able to generate their own sentences using the examples of sense imagery they identified in the story?

Preview or Review Week 3 ELA Mini-Lessons

"Survival in the Arctic," pages 132–133

15 Read "Survival in the Arctic"

Build Background and Vocabulary

Display and the panels for "Survival in the Arctic." If students have already read the text, ask them what they remember. Invite students to share their experiences with very cold weather.

Read Aloud the Text

Read panel 1. To support comprehension, discuss what the image shows and ask students to identify words in the text that match the pictures. Repeat with panels 2 and 3. After reading, **ask:** *What is the text describing?* Model thinking through the answer, say: *I think the text is about how to survive very cold weather, including what people need to protect themselves.* Then refer to the Essential Question. **Say:** *This text gives information about the steps a person would take to survive very cold weather, so it's nonfiction. We call this type of text an informational article.*

Think-Speak-Listen: Use the following sentence frame or the Think-Speak-Listen Flip Book to guide discussion: *I would want to bring _____ to the North Pole because _____.*

👤👤👤 Differentiated Instruction
Build Language:
Understand Domain-Specific Words

Point to the second image. **Say:** *What words or phrases from the text describe this picture? Can you describe what the word layers means in this situation?* Point out that when we read about a particular subject, we often find words that are specific to that event, job, or activity. **Say:** *Context clues in the text or a dictionary can help us figure out the meanings of these words. Figuring out the meanings helps us understand the text and learn about the topic.* Use the Differentiated Instruction to practice understanding domain-specific words in a way that best matches the levels of your students.

☑ Use Oral and Written Language:
Write Tips for an Arctic Travel Brochure

Task: *With a partner, write a set of tips to be included in a brochure for Arctic Travel. Include domain-specific vocabulary about surviving in severe cold.*

(S) *In extreme cold (temperature), you need (layers). Watch out for (frostbite).*

(M) *You need _____ and _____ to survive in extreme cold weather. You need to watch out for _____.*

(L) *If you are in a place with _____, then you need _____ to survive. You need to watch out for _____ because it can cause _____.*

↩ Wrap Up

Today we learned that domain-specific words are words that relate to a certain subject. Why is it important to figure out the meanings of domain-specific words?

Turn and Talk: *What are some domain-specific words that would you use in math? What are some domain-specific words you use to tell about history?*

👥 Differentiated Instruction
Build Language: Understand Domain-Specific Words

Ⓢubstantial Support

Model: Read the first sentence in panel 2. Model identifying a word in the text about cold weather survival. **Say:** *I read that the first step to survival is layers of clothing. In the photo, I see the person is wearing a lot of clothes.* Name the items of clothing—coat, a hood, warm pants, and gloves. **Say:** *The person is wearing clothes on the outside and more clothes underneath. This helps me understand the meaning of the word layers.*

Practice: Work with students to continue reading panel 2 and listing domain-specific words about cold weather survival. Help students to use context to try to figure out the meaning of *frostbite*. **Ask:** *What does the text say in the next sentence? What happens to the skin? What does the picture show about skin?* Then have them look up frostbite in a dictionary.

Extend: With a partner, have students read panel 3 and add more domain-specific words to their lists. Guide them to use context clues and a dictionary to write a short definition for each word.

Challenge: Ask students to work with partners to write a new sentence with two of the words they discussed.

Ⓜoderate Support

Model: Review using context clues and a dictionary to understand domain-specific words. Then distribute BLM 1. Read panel 2. **Ask:** *What words do you see that tell about cold weather survival?* Model thinking through an answer. **Say:** *In the third sentence, I see the word frostbite. It describes something that can happen in cold weather. In the photo, I see a person's hands. This helps me understand what frostbite is. I'll use a dictionary to help me check this word's meaning.*

Practice: Work with students to fill in the chart. Have them write the sentence from the text in the context box. If the photo shows information about the word, have them write a note about it. Then have them write possible meanings.

Extend: Working with a partner, have pairs use dictionaries to check the meaning of each word. Then have them write sentences using two of the words.

Challenge: If students are ready, have them use BLM 2 for Light Support to analyze the words on page 30 in *Texts for Close Reading*.

Ⓛight Support

Use the text on pp. 22-29 in the *Texts for Close Reading* to complete the following activities.

Practice: Ask students to read paragraphs 1, 2, and 3. Distribute BLM 2. Ask partners to work together to find each word in the text, write the sentence, draw a small "pictograph" to help them think about the word, and write what they think it means. Then have them to use a dictionary to verify and write meanings.

Extend: Have student pairs read paragraphs 4–7 aloud to other partners, explain the meanings of the domain-specific words and show how they figured out the meanings.

Challenge: Have partners create a glossary of domain-specific words to describe what is needed to go on an expedition to the

☑️ Formative Assessment

Substantial Support	• Can students understand domain-specific words? • With support, are students able to identify domain-specific words?
Moderate Support	• Can students identify domain-specific words? • With some support, can students analyze domain-specific words?
Light Support	• Can students recognize and analyze domain-specific words in a text using context clues to aid in determining word meanings? • Can they use a dictionary to verify the meanings of words?

Conflicts That Shaped a Nation

Essential Question

How does conflict shape a society?

In this unit, students will read and compare primary sources, nonfiction texts, and literary texts about the Civil War to understand how conflict shapes a society.

Unit 7 Lessons at a Glance

Language Skills

Week 1
- Understand the Structure of a Diary
- Understand the Language of Sequence
- Informative Writing to Sources
- Connect Ideas
- Analyze Domain-Specific Words

Week 2
- Form and Use Irregular Verbs
- Use Verb Tenses to Convey Time
- Condense Ideas
- Use Adverbials to Add Details about Time
- Use Synonyms and Antonyms

Week 3
- Use Conjunctions to Connect Ideas
- Use Prepositional Phrases
- Use Connecting Words to Link Ideas
- Understand and Use Similes
- Understand Domain-Specific Vocabulary

Lessons

Preview or Review Week 1 ELA Mini-Lessons

"Essential Question," pages 134–135

Student Objectives

LANGUAGE
Purpose:
• I can understand the Essential Question.
CONTENT
• I can understand the topic of the unit.

Additional Materials
• Unit Presentation

Introduce Unit 7: Conflicts That Shaped a Nation

Use the short lesson below to introduce the topic of the unit and help students understand the Essential Question.

Build Background and Vocabulary

Draw students' attention to the pictures on p. 134–135.

Say: *The topic of this unit is "Conflicts that Shaped a Nation."*

Create a two-column chart.

Say: L*et's think about what this means.* **Conflict** *usually means disagreement but this unit is dealing with a specific type of disagreement: war. Let's use the pictures to think of examples of conflicts.*

Write: *Conflict/War.* Elicit responses as you fill in the chart. Explain that **shaped a nation** means that wars had a part in creating America and developing it into what it is today.

Ask: *How do these pictures help you understand how conflict shapes a society?*

Help students answer and encourage students to share their cultural knowledge and experiences about the topic.

Conflict/War	Changes
Revolutionary War	America won it's freedom from the British.
Civil War	The North won, slavery ended.

👥👥👥 Differentiated Instruction
Explain the Essential Question

Read aloud the Essential Question: *How does conflict shape a society?* Review the two-column chart.

Say: *The Revolutionary War caused many changes. The colonists won their freedom from British rule and later created the Constitution forming the United States of America. After the Civil War, northern values prevailed. Slavery ended. The union was preserved. There were many medical advances. Women made some advances, too.*

Display or invite students to access the unit opener video for Unit 7. After the video **ask***: How do these pictures and the video help you answer the Essential Question?*

Use the Differentiated Instruction to help students at all levels understand the Essential Question.

Then proceed to Lesson 1.

👥👥 Differentiated Instruction
Explain the Essential Question

Ⓢubstantial Support

Point to the picture of the Revolutionary War battle. Write: *The Revolutionary War was a conflict between the colonists and the British.*

Point to the picture of the Civil War soldiers. Write: *The Civil War was a conflict between the North and the South.*

Say: *The South had one way of life. The North had another way of life. They could not agree. The Civil War began in 1861 and ended in 1865. The North won. Slavery ended. The union was preserved. Thousands died. Many injuries caused medical knowledge to advance.*

Write: *The Civil War began in 1861.* Say the sentence with students.

Write: *The Civil War ended in 1865.*

Say: *In this unit, we will learn how war changes a society. For example, the Civil War ended of slavery, and the preserved the union. Many injuries caused new advances in medical care.*

Ⓜoderate Support

Point to the picture of the Revolutionary War battle. Write: *The Revolutionary War was a conflict between the colonists and the British.*

Say: *The Revolutionary War was a conflict between the colonists and the British. The colonists in America were fighting for freedom from British rule. This is how the United States of America began.*

Point to the picture of the Civil War Soldiers. **Say:** *The South had one way of life. The North had another way of life. They could not agree. The Civil War began in 1861 and ended in 1865. The North won. Slavery ended. The union was preserved. Thousands died. Many injuries caused medical knowledge to advance.*

Write: *The Civil War began in 1861.* Say the sentence with students.

Write: *The Civil War ended in 1865.*

Say: *In this unit, we will learn how war changes a society. How? For example, the Civil War ended of slavery, and the preserved the union. Many injuries caused new advances in medical care.*

Ⓛight Support

Point to the picture of the Civil War soldiers. **Say:** *The Civil War began in 1861 and ended in 1865. The North won. Slavery ended. The union was preserved. Soldiers fought many battles. Thousands died. Thousands of injuries caused medical knowledge to advance. Point to page 123. World War II ended in 1945. It was a world war. These leaders worked to keep world peace.*

Write: *The Civil War began in 1861/1941.* Say the sentence with students. Elicit the correct answer.

Write: *The Civil War ended in 1865/1945.* Elicit the correct answer. Point to page 123. Discuss the differences between leaders, women soldiers, and soldiers in the painting on page 122.

Say: *In this unit, we will learn how war changes a society. For example, the Civil War ended slavery, preserved the union, and caused medical advances. Today, women serve in the military.*

☑ Formative Assessment

Substantial Support	• Can students say what the Civil War is with help? • Can students show understanding of key words such as **slavery** and **battle** with help?
Moderate Support	• Can students say what the Civil War is? • Can students explain the words **slavery** and **battle** with a little help? • Can students give an example of a change in society as a result of the war?
Light Support	• Can students say what the Civil War is? • Can students explain the words **battle, slavery** and **preserve**? • Can students give an example of a change in society as a result of the war?

Preview or Review Week 1 ELA Mini-Lessons

"Yankee Doodle Boy," page 136

Student Objectives

LANGUAGE
Purpose:
- I can describe an historical event in a diary entry.

Form:
- I can understand the structure of a diary.

CONTENT
- I can recognize a diary as a primary source.

Additional Materials
- Unit Presentation
- *Texts for Close Reading* booklet
- Think-Speak-Listen Flip Book
- Student journal
- Structure of a Diary Chart

Language Transfer Support

Students whose native language is Cantonese, Haitian Creole, Hmong, Korean, or Vietnamese may need additional support with verb tenses when speaking and writing about time and sequence in the past tense. These languages do not use inflectional endings to change verb tense.

1 Read "Yankee Doodle Boy"

Build Background and Vocabulary

Display "Yankee Doodle Boy" panels. If students have read the text, invite them to share what they remember. Invite students to share their cultural experience and knowledge about the American Revolutionary War and keeping a diary.

Read Aloud the Text

Read aloud panel 1. Ask students to find details in the picture that match words in the text (soldiers, marching). Ask questions, such as: *How does the text help you know where the soldiers are?* Repeat with panels 2–4. After reading, **ask:** *What are the soldiers preparing to do?* Refer to the Essential Question: *How does conflict shape a society?* Invite students to discuss how the Battle of Yorktown changed U.S. history. Then **say:** *The text names a place and what real people did. The writer uses I and we. This is a diary of someone's personal experiences.*

Think-Speak-Listen: Use the following sentence frame or the Think-Speak-Listen Flip Book to guide discussion: *The structure of the text helps me understand _____.*

Differentiated Instruction
Build Language:
Understand the Structure of a Diary

Display the Structure of a Diary Chart. Use the chart to discuss the parts of a typical diary entry. **Say:** *A diary entry gives us a personal look into someone's life. If events are historical, we become eyewitnesses to what happened. This makes a diary a primary source of information.* Display and reread aloud panel 3. **Ask:** *What do readers know about what happens?* Elicit answers. **Say:** *As readers, we know only what the writer knows. We are standing with him as he learns information.* Use the Differentiated Instruction to practice understanding the structure of a diary in a way that best matches the levels of your students.

☑ Use Oral and Written Language:
Describe an Event in a Diary Entry

Task: *Imagine that you are a famous person in history. Choose someone you have read about or know of. Write a diary entry to recount an event you experienced. Include what you learned about the text structure of a diary.*

 The day started with _____. Then I _____. I saw _____.

Ⓜ *Today began _____ and then _____ when I _____.*

Ⓛ *When the day began, I _____ before _____ happened and _____.*

Wrap Up

Today we learned about the structure of a diary. How does knowing this structure help us to understand what we read in a diary entry?

Turn and Talk: *Imagine you are a famous person that is alive now. Tell your partner about a day in your life, as though you've written a diary entry.*

👥 Differentiated Instruction
Build Language: Understand the Structure of a Diary

Ⓢubstantial Support

Model: Use the Structure of a Diary Chart to explain diary structure. Display panel 3 and read aloud. **Say:** *When I read, I see the words we and I. These words tell me that the writer experiences the events. I learn new information along with the writer. Words like before dark tell me when events happen.*

Practice: Distribute BLM 1. Encourage students to help you analyze each item and decide if the text comes from a diary or other source. Check understanding and reteach if necessary.

Extend: Have students work in pairs to complete the Extend activity. Provide support as needed, and display the Structure of a Diary Chart for reference.

Challenge: If students are ready, guide them to complete the Practice activity on the Moderate Support BLM 2.

Ⓜoderate Support

Model: Use the Structure of a Diary Chart to explain diary structure. **Say:** *I see the words we and I, which tell me that the writer is describing events that he was a part of. I learn about what happens as he does. He also tells about events in order, using words like before dark.*

Practice: Distribute BLM 2. Work with students to read both sample texts and identify the parts that show one text is a diary entry.

Extend: Distribute BLM 2. Have partners complete the tasks. Monitor students' work and provide support as needed.

Challenge: If students are ready, have them review paragraph 1 on page 4 of their *Texts for Close Reading*. Ask them to underline parts of the paragraph that help them identify the text as part of a diary.

Ⓛight Support

Use the text on pp. 4-5 in the *Texts for Close Reading* to complete the following activities.

Practice: Use the Structure of a Diary Chart to review the parts of a diary entry. Then have students reread paragraphs 1 and 2. Have pairs identify sequential words and personal pronouns. Invite students to help you identify and underline parts in the text that show this is a diary entry.

Extend: Have partners reread paragraph 4. Ask them to write a short paragraph that describes how reading a diary entry versus an account in a social studies book makes readers participants rather than observers of historical events.

Challenge: Have partners work together to compose one or two diary entries that reflect the events of and thoughts about a day at school.

☑ Formative Assessment

Substantial Support	• With support, do students understand the structure of a diary? • With support, can students distinguish a diary entry from other types of text?
Moderate Support	• Do students understand the structure of a diary? • Can students identify a diary entry and distinguish it from other text forms? • Can students compare a diary entry with another text form and note how they differ?
Light Support	• Can students understand and identify the structure of a diary? • Can students use the structure of a diary to write their own diary entry?

Preview or Review Week 1 ELA Mini-Lessons

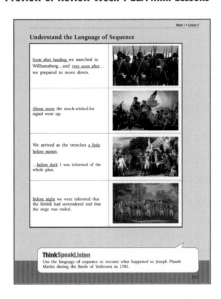

"Understand the Language of Sequence," page 137

Student Objectives

LANGUAGE

Purpose:
- I can describe an event by conducting an interview.

Form:
- I can recognize and understand words that signal sequence.

CONTENT
- I can use sequence to understand a diary entry.

Additional Materials
- Unit Presentation
- *Texts for Close Reading* booklet
- Think-Speak-Listen Flip Book
- Student journal

Language Transfer Support

Students whose first language is Spanish may be familiar with the following cognates of words you discuss in this lesson: **sequence** *(secuencia)* and **order** *(orden)*. Encourage students to look and listen for other words that are similar to words in their first language.

2 Understand the Language of Sequence

Engage Thinking

Display the Understand the Language of Sequence chart. **Say:** *Private Joseph Plumb Martin wrote in his diary about the day the British surrendered at Yorktown. What was the first event that Martin described on that day?* Elicit answers.

Turn and Talk: *How would you write about a series of events that happened in one day? What words would you use to show the order?*

Read and View Closely: Recognize the Language of Sequence

Say: *Martin describes events in the order they happened.* Read aloud the chart. **Ask:** *What words tell about time?* Point out the underlined sequence words on the chart. Tell students that recognizing sequence words will help them follow the order of events.

👥👥 Differentiated Instruction
Build Language: Understand the Language of Sequence

Read aloud row 1. **Say:** *It's important to understand what sequence words are telling you. When did the soldiers march to Williamsburg?* Elicit answers. **Say:** *The key words are soon after. They tell me that first the soldiers landed and then they marched.* Use the Differentiated Instruction to practice understanding the language of sequence in a way that best matches the levels of your students.

Think-Speak-Listen: Use the following sentence frame or the Think-Speak-Listen Flip Book to guide discussion: *First, _____, then _____, later _____, and finally _____.*

☑ Use Oral and Written Language: Describe an Event by Conducting an Interview

Task: *Your partner is a newspaper reporter who has come to interview you, a soldier, about the Battle of Yorktown. Use the language of sequence to answer the reporter's questions and recount your experiences.*

Ⓢ   *When did the signal go up?*
     The much-wished for signal went up _____.

Ⓜ   *When did you hear about the whole plan?*
     We arrived _____, and then _____ we _____.

Ⓛ   *When did you know about the surrender?*
     It was _____ when we heard _____ and knew _____.

 Wrap Up

Today we learned how to recognize and understand the language of sequence. How does this help us when reading about history?

Turn and Talk: *Use the language of sequence to tell about an event you witnessed, saw on television, or read about.*

©2018 Benchmark Education Company, LLC

🧑‍🤝‍🧑 Differentiated Instruction
Build Language: Understand the Language of Sequence

Ⓢubstantial Support

Model: Review sequence words. Display the Understand the Language of Sequence chart. Read aloud row 3.

Say: *I know that this event happened on the same day as the first two events. The signal went up at about noon. Now I see the words a little before sunset that tell me when the soldiers arrived at the trenches. Even though the events are described in order, these words help me keep track and understand the sequence.*

Practice: Distribute BLM 1. Work with students to complete the Practice activity.

Extend: Have partners do the Extend activity. Encourage them to recall the diary excerpts they read and when events happened on the day described.

Challenge: If students are ready, have them work with a partner to complete the Practice activity on the Moderate Support BLM 2.

Ⓜoderate Support

Model: Review sequence words. Display the Understand the Language of Sequence chart. Reread the first two rows.

Say: *These events happened on the same day. I know the order from the sequence or time words and phrases. These help me understand events that happened in quick sequence and the time of day they happened.*

Practice: Distribute BLM 2. Invite students to help you complete the Practice activity.

Extend: Have students work with a partner to complete the Extend activity. Provide support if needed.

Challenge: If students are ready, have them read paragraphs 1–3 on page 4 in their *Texts for Close Reading* and underline the sequence words and phrases. Then have them tell a partner the order of events in their own words.

Ⓛight Support

Use the text on pp. 4-5 in the *Texts for Close Reading* to complete the following activities.

Practice: Have students read paragraphs 1–3 and underline the sequence words and phrases. Then have them write in their own words the order of events, using the sequence language they identified.

Extend: Have partners read paragraphs 5, 7, and 8. Encourage them to ask each other questions about the sequence of events, such as: *Did the soldiers arrive at the trenches before or after sunset?, Did the troops move very soon after the signal, or did they wait?*

Challenge: Have partners create a time line of events in "Yankee Doodle Boy." Have them show one day on the time line with events listed in order under the line. Above the line and over each event, have them write the sequence words that show the order of events.

✅ Formative Assessment

Substantial Support	• With support, can students recognize language used to show sequence? • With support, are students able to understand how the language of sequence helps them to follow events? • With support, can students show the order of events using the language of sequence?
Moderate Support	• Can students recognize and understand language used to show sequence? • Are students able to use sequential language to put events in the correct order?
Light Support	• Can students sequence events using sequential language? • Can students write sentences about events, using sequential language to show the order? • Can students use sequential language to create a time line that shows the order of historic events?

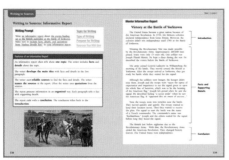

"Writing to Sources," pages 138–139

Student Objectives

LANGUAGE
Purpose:
• I can analyze an informative report.
Form:
• I can identify the parts of an informative report.
CONTENT
• I can recognize an informative report.

Additional Materials

• Unit Presentation
• *Texts for Close Reading* booklet
• Think-Speak-Listen Flip Book
• Student journal

3 Writing to Sources: Informative Report

Engage Thinking

Tell students that they will analyze an informative report so that they can identify its four key features. Read aloud the mentor writing prompt.

> Write an informative report about the events leading up to the British surrender at the Battle of Yorktown. Make sure to include facts, details, and quotations from "Yankee Doodle Boy" in your informative report.

Say: *Let's ask questions to make sure we understand the prompt. What will the writer write about? What type of writing is it? Where will the writer get some of the information?*

👥👥👥 Differentiated Instruction
Read and View Closely:
Analyze an informative Report

Say: *As I read aloud the informative report, we will stop to analyze it. In the first paragraph, the writer uses facts and details to explain the main idea. As I read, look for this.* Read the paragraph and pause. **Ask:** *What is the main idea? What facts and details support it?* Check that students can identify the main idea and some facts and details.

Say: *An informative report uses sources to get information. As I read the second paragraph, listen for the writer's source.* Read the second paragraph. **Ask:** *What source did the writer use?* Check that students understand the writer used Joseph Plumb Martin's diary as a source. Call attention to the fact that the writer uses facts and details in the second paragraph as well. Have students point out a few details.

Say: *The writer also includes quotations from the source. Watch for these as I read.* Read through the fourth paragraph. **Ask:** *Which sentence is quoted from Martin's diary?* Check that students can identify the quotation.

Continue reading the rest of the report. **Say:** *Notice how the report is organized. Turn to a partner and go back and discuss how the ideas are grouped together by paragraph.* Monitor students and help them to see the overall organization. Have partners share their ideas with the class. Point out the conclusion.

Then continue the lesson using Differentiated Instruction that best fits the needs of your students.

Share Your Understanding

Bring the students back together. **Ask:** *What did we learn today about the features of an informative report?* Review the features as needed.

☑ Final Writing Assignment

Use the *English Language Development Assessment* to assess students' writing for their ELA writing assignment.

👥👥 Differentiated Instruction
Read and View Closely: Analyze an informative Report

Ⓢubstantial Support

Model: Distribute BLM 1. **Say:** *Let's read and analyze another informative report that answers the prompt.* Read the first paragraph and pause. **Ask:** *What is this report about? Model answering the question.*

Practice: Continue reading the report and ask *yes/no* questions about the features of an informative report: *Does the report include facts and details? Does the report include quotations? Is the information organized well?*

Extend: Have students in pairs complete the activity on BLM 1.

Challenge: Write these sentence frames on the board:

The writer used _____ as a source.

The main idea of the report is _____.

The writer included details about _____.

The writer used quotations to describe _____.

Have students work together in pairs to complete the sentences with their ideas and information from the text.

Ⓜoderate Support

Model: Draw students' attention to the Mentor Informative Report in their Student Books. **Say:** *Let's analyze how the writer addresses the four features of an informative report.* Make the chart below, with the left column filled out. **Say:** *How did the writer develop and introduce the main idea in the opening?* Elicit from the class the main idea from the first paragraph and write it on the chart.

Informative Report Features	Examples from the Text
1. Develop the main idea	"...the colonies didn't gain full independence until 1781 at the Battle of Yorktown."
2. Include main features	
3. Information from sources	
4. Logical organization	

Practice: Work with students to complete the chart with information from the report.

Extend: Have partners use their charts to make sentences about how the writer addressed the features of an informative report.

Challenge: Have partners take turns asking and answering questions about how the writer included the features of an informative report. For example: *Did the writer have a strong introduction? How did the writer develop the main ideas with facts and details? Did the writer have a strong concluding statement?*

Ⓛight Support

Practice: Distribute BLM 2. **Say:** *This is the Mentor Text that you read in class on Day 1. We will look more closely at how writers include the features of an informative report.* Read the report with students.

Extend: Have student pairs complete the activity on BLM 2.

Challenge: Have students use item 4 on the BLM to discuss how the writer used facts and details to support the main idea of each paragraph. Students should take turns asking and answering questions such as: *What details did the writer include in the paragraph about the army traveling to Yorktown?* Remind students to respond and elaborate on their partner's answers.

☑ Formative Assessment

Substantial Support	• Do students recognize the criteria for an informative report in the Mentor Informative Report?
Moderate Support	• Do students recognize the ways in which the Mentor Informative Report meets the criteria for an informative report? • Can students describe the features of an informative report in their own words?
Light Support	• Do students recognize criteria and analyze how the Mentor Text meets the criteria for an informative report? • Can students describe in their own words how the writer meets the criteria for an informative report?

Extend and Scaffold Academic Language for Writing
Analyze the Mentor Text: Language Purpose and Structure

Introduction
All Levels of Support

Materials List
- **Mentor Text L** BLM X Light Support
- **Writing Frames Teacher Page** BLM Y
- **Writing Frames Student Page** BLM Z

- Have a copy of BLM Y to refer to during the lesson.

- Distribute BLMs X and Z to each student.

- Read aloud the writing prompt on BLM X. Explain that students will read and analyze the language one writer used to respond to this prompt.

- Have students follow along as you read aloud paragraph 1 of "Victory at the Battle of Yorktown."

- Point out the phrase *the powerful nation that exists today is all due to the American Revolution* and the words that indicate the frame in bold. **Ask:** *Why did the author use this language? What is its purpose?* Help students understand that the author uses the structure _____ *due to* _____ to explain why something happened. *The powerful nation that exists* today can be explained by *the American Revolution*.

- Have students write this frame into the "Explain/Give Examples" row of their Writing Frames worksheet (BLM Z). Tell students this is one writing frame they can use in their writing to provide an explanation.

- Analyze other bolded phrases in paragraph 1. Explain their purpose and help students add the writing frames to BLM Z.

- Follow these steps as you read additional paragraphs.

- Read aloud the writing prompt on BLM Z. Work with students to generate additional writing frames they could use as they write a response to this prompt. Refer to BLM Y for examples.

Based on students' needs, conduct additional lessons using the differentiated instruction and tools provided.

(L)ight Support
Differentiated Instruction

Materials List
- **Mentor Text L** BLM X Light Support
- **Writing Frames Teacher Page** BLM Y
- **Writing Frames Student Page** BLM Z

Students will need their copies of BLMs X and Z from the initial lesson. Refer to the chart below and your copy of BLM Y during the lesson.

- Explain that students will reread "Victory at the Battle of Yorktown" to analyze more phrases and sentences that the writer used.

- Reread the text with students one paragraph at a time.

- Ask individuals or partners to find and underline each phrase in the chart below, read the sentence it appears in, and try to determine the sentence's purpose in the text.

- Provide explanation as necessary, then have students add the frames to the "Other Academic Phrases and Sentences" column of BLM Z.

- Encourage students to generate related writing frames and add them to their chart.

LIGHT SUPPORT		
Purpose	**Phrase/Sentence (paragraph)**	**Frame**
Cite Facts	While 1776 was the historic year that... (1)	[Date] was the historic year that _____, _____.
Time/ Duration	...independence from Great Britain, it wasn't until 1781, the final... (1)	It wasn't until [Date] that _____.
Explain/ Give Examples	Soon the Revolutionary Army would be facing the British forces in the battle... (5)	_____ that would change the course of history.
Explain/ Give Examples	The British admitted defeat before nightfall and marked an... (6)	The _____ _____ marked _____ for _____.
Explain/ Give Examples	With that victory, the Revolutionary Army both ended the... (6)	With that _____, the _____ _____.

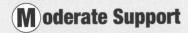 Moderate Support  Differentiated Instruction

Materials List
- **Mentor Text M** BLM A Moderate Support
- **Writing Frames Teacher Page** BLM Y
- **Writing Frames Student Page** BLM Z

Use the mentor text (BLM A) and the phrases and sentences appropriate for the support level you are targeting.

- Distribute BLM A. Students will also need their copy of BLM Z.

- Read aloud BLM A as students follow along.

- Then reread the text one paragraph at a time, stopping after each paragraph to focus on the bolded and underlined content. Work with students to understand the purpose of each phrase within the text. Have students write the corresponding writing frame in the "Other Academic Phrases and Sentences" column of BLM Z.

- Have partners practice using one or more of these writing frames to expand an idea in the essay they are writing. Have students share their examples with other members of the group.

MODERATE SUPPORT

Purpose	Phrase/Sentence (paragraph)	Frame
Give Reasons	The United States became a great nation because of the American Revolution. (1)	_____ became a _____ because of _____.
State Your Opinion/ Contrast	However, the colonies didn't win full independence until 1781... (1)	However, _____ _____.
Explain/ Give Examples	Winning the Revolutionary War was made possible by the Revolutionary Army. (2)	_____ was made possible by _____.
Cite Facts	He described feeling "a secret pride" when he saw the American flag. (4)	He described _____ "_____" when _____.
Explain/ Give Examples	The British lost before nighttime due to... (6)	The _____ _____ due to _____.

 Substantial Support  Differentiated Instruction

Materials List
- **Mentor Text S** BLM B Substantial Support
- **Writing Frames Teacher Page** BLM Y
- **Writing Frames Student Page** BLM Z

Students will need their copy of BLM Z from the initial lesson.

- Distribute BLM B.

- Follow the procedure explained in the Moderate Support lesson.

SUBSTANTIAL SUPPORT

Purpose	Phrase/Sentence (paragraph)	Frame
State Your Opinion/ Contrast	But the United States did not win independence until 1781... (1)	But _____, until _____.
Give Reasons	It was the Revolutionary Army that won the battle. (2)	It was _____ that _____.
Explain/ Give Examples	He describes feeling "a secret pride" because of... (4)	_____ _____ because of _____.
Cite Facts	He describes feeling "a secret pride" because of the American flag. (4)	He describes _____ "_____" when _____.
Explain/ Give Examples	It was a great victory. (6)	It was a _____ _____.

Preview or Review Week 1 ELA Mini-Lessons

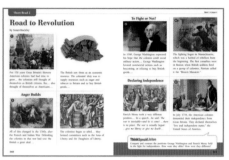

"Road to Revolution," pages 140–141

Student Objectives

LANGUAGE
Purpose:
• I can describe a historical movie.
Form:
• I can connect ideas.
CONTENT
• I can read and understand informational social studies text.

Additional Materials
• Unit Presentation
• *Texts for Close Reading* booklet
• Think-Speak-Listen Flip Book
• Student journal
• Venn Diagram

Language Transfer Support

Students whose first language is Chinese or Vietnamese may need extra support when creating sentences with conjunctions to connect ideas. In these languages, conjunctions often occur in pairs. For example, a student may say, *Although, I am stuck on this problem, but I do not want to ask for help.*

4 Read "Road to Revolution"

Build Background and Vocabulary

Display the panels from "Road to Revolution." If students have already read the text, ask them what they remember. Invite students share their cultural experiences and knowledge of the different ways they've learned about history.

Read Aloud the Text

Read aloud panel 1. Ask students to find details in the picture that match words in the text (colonies, colonists). Ask questions, such as: *Who do you think owns this ship? What is on it?* Repeat with panels 2–8. After reading, refer to the Essential Question. **Ask:** *How does conflict shape a society?* Discuss how these battles led to U.S. independence from Britain. **Say:** *This text is an informational social studies text that explores the history of the United States of America.*

Think-Speak-Listen: Use the following sentence frame or the Think-Speak-Listen Flip Book to guide discussion: *George Washington and Patrick Henry were alike because _____. They were different because _____.*

Differentiated Instruction
Build Language: Connect Ideas

Write: *The colonists' duty was to supply resources such as sugar and tobacco to Britain and to buy British goods.* Point out that the writer has combined three ideas into one sentence. **Say:** *Three ideas are connected because they have the same subject: the colonists' duty. By combining these ideas into one compound sentence, the writer shows how they are connected.* Use the Differentiated Instruction to practice connecting ideas in a way that best matches the levels of your students.

☑ Use Oral and Written Language: Describe a Historical Movie

Task: *Pretend that you have written a movie script based on the text Road to Revolution. Collaborate with your partner to write a short script for a movie trailer that will be used to advertise your movie. The trailer should include the main ideas and key details from the text. Share your trailer with the class.*

(S) *The American colonists did not believe they were being treated fairly by Great Britain _____ they decided to rebel.*

(M) *The American colonists _____ by Great Britain _____ they decided to _____.*

(L) *The American colonists _____ by Great Britain _____ they decided to _____. George Washington wanted to solve the differences peacefully, while Patrick Henry _____.*

Wrap Up

Today we have learned about connecting ideas. How could this help us when we write?

Turn and Talk: *Tell your partner about a speech you have heard. Who gave the speech? What was it about? What do you remember most about the speech or the speaker?*

👥👥 Differentiated Instruction
Build Language: Connect Ideas

Ⓢubstantial Support

Model: Read aloud sentence 2 from panel 2. **Say:** *I see three ideas in the sentence: colonists' duty, supply sugar and tobacco, and buy British goods. Instead of writing several short sentences, the writer combined these ideas into one compound sentence, making the writing more interesting.*

Practice: Read frame 1. **Say:** *One idea is that the Americans thought of themselves as British. Another idea says they thought of themselves as American citizens.* Invite students to help you work through the ideas in the remaining frames.

Extend: In pairs, have students use these sentence frames to identify the connected ideas.

Washington believed _____ but Henry _____.

The start of the war began _____ when _____.

This led to the declaration of the United States of America as _____ on _____.

Challenge: If students are ready, model working through the Extend activity on the Moderate Support BLM 1.

Ⓜoderate Support

Model: Read aloud sentence 2 from panel 2. **Say:** *I see three ideas in the sentence: colonists' duty, supply sugar and tobacco, and buy British goods. Instead of writing several short sentences, the writer combined these ideas into one compound sentence, making the writing more interesting.*

Practice: Provide students with BLM 1. Work through the practice activity with students as they identify the purpose of the conjunctions found in the text.

Extend: Pair students to complete the Extend activity on the BLM. Provide assistance as needed.

Challenge: If students are ready, help them write a short sentence summary of the text. Provide assistance as needed.

Ⓛight Support

Use the text on pp. 6-9 in the *Texts for Close Reading* to complete the following activities.

Practice: Provide students with the BLM 2. Invite students to help you complete the Practice activity. Assist students as needed.

Extend: Have students work in pairs to complete the Extend activity. If needed, provide assistance as the pairs work create original sentences that connect the ideas.

Challenge: If students are ready, have them work on the challenge activity on BLM 2. Provide assistance as needed.

☑ Formative Assessment

Substantial Support	• Can students identify related ideas in the text? • Are students able to use sentence frames to describe the related ideas in the text?
Moderate Support	• Can students identify connected ideas in a text? • Can students generate sentences to show connected • ideas?
Light Support	• Can students identify connected ideas in a text? • Can students generate original sentences that relate connected ideas in a text?

Preview or Review Week 1 ELA Mini-Lessons

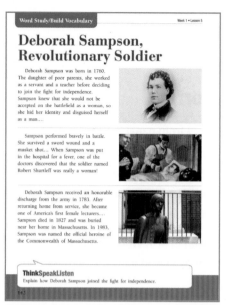

"Deborah Sampson, Revolutionary Soldier," page 142

Student Objectives

LANGUAGE
Purpose:
• I can state opinions and reasons.
Form:
• I can identify domain-specific words.
CONTENT
• I can understand domain-specific words related to informational social studies.

Additional Materials
• Unit Presentation
• *Texts for Close Reading* booklet
• Think-Speak-Listen Flip Book
• Student journal
• Word Web (optional)

Language Transfer Support

Students whose first language is Spanish, Vietnamese, or Hmong may need extra support with adjectives preceding nouns. In these languages, the adjectives follow the nouns they modify (e.g., *She has a shirt yellow*).

5 Read "Deborah Sampson, Revolutionary Soldier"

Build Background and Vocabulary

Display the panels from "Deborah Sampson." Ask students what they remember about the text. Invite students to share their cultural experiences and knowledge about pretending or keeping a secret.

Read Aloud the Text

Read aloud panel 1. Ask students to match the picture and text. Explain vocabulary (servant, independence, battlefield, disguised). Ask *wh-* questions, such as *Who is this? What time period is this?* Repeat with panels 2–3. After reading, **ask:** *Why did Sampson want to be a revolutionary soldier?* Refer to the Essential Question and invite students to discuss how the Revolutionary War changed people's ideas. It allowed women more freedom. Then **say:** *This story is true. We call this type of text an informational text.*

Think-Speak-Listen: Use the following sentence frame or the Think-Speak-Listen Flip Book to guide discussion: *Deborah Sampson joined the fight for independence by _____.*

👥 Differentiated Instruction
Build Language: Analyze Domain-Specific Words

Write: *revolutionary soldier.* **Ask:** *What can help us understand these unfamiliar words?* Invite responses. **Say:** *We can look at related words and phrases in the text, or the context, to figure out the meaning. Then we'll understand the whole text.* Use the Differentiated Instruction to practice analyzing domain-specific words in a way that best matches the levels of your students.

☑ Use Oral and Written Language: State Opinions and Reasons

Task: *Imagine that you and your partner are expressing your opinions in a panel discussion on the topic of Deborah Sampson. Decide if she should have worn a man's disguise and become a revolutionary soldier.*

Ⓢ _____ *think Deborah Sampson should have _____ because _____.*

Ⓜ *I think Deborah Sampson was _____, and she should have _____ because _____.*

Ⓛ *I think Deborah Sampson _____. She _____ because _____ and _____.*

🔄 Wrap Up

Today we learned how to find the meaning of unusual words related to a particular subject. How does this help us to understand unfamiliar words?

Turn and Talk: *Find an unfamiliar phrase or word in a history book. Work with your partner to figure out the meaning using related words in the text.*

👥 Differentiated Instruction
Build Language: Analyze Domain-Specific Words

Ⓢubstantial Support

Model: Say: *I'll find words and phrases in the text that relate to revolutionary soldier.* **Read aloud panel 1. Say:** *I see that Deborah Sampson decided to join the fight for independence. I'll write these words. Now I'll find more related words and write them too. This way, I can figure out the meaning of revolutionary soldier.*

Practice: Distribute BLM 1. Continue through the panels with students. As you read, **ask:** *Which words relate to what a revolutionary soldier is or does?* Invite students to help you complete the Practice section.

Extend: Put students in pairs to complete the Extend section of the BLM. Provide additional support as needed.

Challenge: If students are ready, help them complete the Challenge section of the BLM.

Ⓜoderate Support

Model: Say: *I'll find words and phrases in the text that relate to revolutionary soldier.* **Read aloud panel 1. Say:** *I see that Deborah Sampson decided to join the fight for independence. I'll write these words. Now I'll find more related words and write them too. This way, I can figure out the meaning of revolutionary soldier.*

Practice: Distribute BLM 2. Invite students to help you complete the Practice section. Provide support as needed.

Extend: Put students in pairs to complete the Extend section. Provide support as needed.

Challenge: Model for students how to use paragraph 2 on page 10 of *Texts for Close Reading* to generate a sentence about a revolutionary soldier. Provide support as needed.

Ⓛight Support

Use the text on p. 10 in the *Texts for Close Reading* to complete the following activities.

Practice: Say: *The words* revolutionary soldier *are used for a specific historical subject. To learn their meaning, we can use related words and phrases in the text.* Have students identify and write words and phrases related to a revolutionary soldier. Ask them to generate a sentence to define the phrase.

Extend: Put students in pairs to generate two additional sentences with the words *revolutionary soldier*. Provide minimal support.

Challenge: Ask students to identify words and phrases that relate to the words *honorable discharge* (paragraph 2). Have them list the words or create a Word Web. Then ask them to generate one or two sentences that define an honorable discharge.

☑ Formative Assessment

Substantial Support	• Can students with support identify words and phrases related to *revolutionary soldier*? • Can students complete simple sentence frames to tell about a *revolutionary soldier* with support?
Moderate Support	• Can students identify words and phrases that relate to *revolutionary soldier*? • Can students complete more complex sentence frames to tell about a *revolutionary soldier*?
Light Support	• Can students identify words and phrases that relate to *revolutionary soldier*? • Can students generate sentences from the words *revolutionary soldier*?

Preview or Review Week 2 ELA Mini-Lessons

Week 2 • Lesson 6

Form and Use Irregular Verbs

Example from Texts	Present Tense	Past Tense
Sampson <u>knew</u> that she would not be accepted on the battlefield as a woman...	know	knew
...so she <u>hid</u> her identity and disguised herself as a man.	hide	hid
When Sampson was <u>put</u> in the hospital for a fever...	put	put
...one of the doctors discovered that the soldier named Robert Shurtleff <u>was</u> really a woman!	is	was
After returning home from service, she <u>became</u> one of America's first female lecturers.	become	became

ThinkSpeakListen
Use irregular verbs to describe how Deborah Sampson became a soldier in the fight for independence.

143

"Form and Use Irregular Verbs," page 143

Student Objectives

LANGUAGE
Purpose:
• I can describe a person from history in a speech.
Form:
• I can identify and form irregular verbs.
CONTENT
• I can understand informational social studies text.

Additional Materials
• Unit Presentation
• *Texts for Close Reading* booklet
• Think-Speak-Listen Flip Book
• Student journal

Language Transfer Support

Speakers of Cantonese, Haitian Creole, Hmong, Korean, or Vietnamese may need additional support in using regular and irregular verbs that have tense, person, and number inflections. Provide sentence frames and other structured opportunities for students to practice using these verbs in spoken and written English.

6 Form and Use Irregular Verbs

Engage Thinking

Display the chart. Read the third sentence. Point to the verbs *hid* and *disguised*. **Ask:** *What do you notice about these past tense verbs?* Elicit answers. **Say:** *The past tense takes different forms. Hid is an irregular verb.*

Turn and Talk: *How is a past tense verb usually formed? How can you identify an irregular verb?*

Read and View Closely: Identify Irregular Verbs

Display the chart. Remind students that the past tense of regular verbs is formed by adding the ending *-ed*, but irregular verbs do not follow the rule. Have students identify the underlined irregular verbs in each sentence. **Ask:** *What do you notice about the verb "put"?* Elicit that the present and past tenses have the same spelling. Then **say:** *We can identify irregular past tense verbs by noticing how they are formed.*

Think-Speak-Listen: Use the following sentence frame or the Think-Speak-Listen Flip Book to guide discussion: *Deborah Sampson became a soldier by _____.*

👥👥👥 Differentiated Instruction
Build Language: Form and Use Irregular Verbs

Direct students' attention again to the Past Tense column. **Ask:** *How is the past tense formed for irregular verbs? Do you see any pattern to follow?* Elicit no. Then **say:** *Because there is no pattern, we can use irregular verbs only by memorizing the forms they take. When you use irregular verbs correctly, you demonstrate how well you speak and understand the English language.* Use the Differentiated Instruction to practice forming and using irregular verbs in a way that best matches the levels of your students.

☑️ Use Oral and Written Language: Describe a Person from History in a Speech

Task: *Work with a group to write a speech about Deborah Sampson. Include information about who she was and what she did.* Use this opportunity to assess students using the rubric in *English Language Development Assessment.*

(S) *Deborah Sampson _____. She _____ her identity and disguised herself as a man.*

(M) *Deborah Sampson _____. She _____ her identity and pretended to _____.*

(L) *Deborah Sampson _____. She _____ her identity and _____.*

Wrap Up

Today we learned how to use irregular past tense verbs when we describe the past. Why is it important to form irregular verbs correctly?

Turn and Talk: *Tell your partner about another famous person in history. Be sure to tell who they were and what they did.*

♦♦♦ Differentiated Instruction
Build Language: Form and Use Irregular Verbs

(S)ubstantial Support

Model: Review irregular past tense verbs. **Say:** *Authors use past tense verbs when they write about history. Many are irregular verbs. I need to know how to identify and form irregular verbs so I can understand and use them.* Point to panel 2 of the chart. Read the words *hide* and *hid*. **Say:** *The irregular past tense for hide is hid.*

Practice: Continue to display the chart. Distribute BLM 1. Work together with students to complete the Practice section.

Extend: Put students in pairs to complete the Extend section. Provide support as needed.

Challenge: Remind students that they previously read "Road to Revolution." Model with students how to complete the sentence frames in the Challenge section.

(M)oderate Support

Model: Review irregular past tense verbs. **Say:** *Authors use past tense verbs when they write about history. Many verbs are irregular. I need to be able to identify and use irregular verbs.* Read the words *hide* and *hid* in panel 2 of the chart. **Say:** *The irregular past tense for hide is hid.*

Practice: Continue to display the chart. Distribute BLM 2. **Say:** *Let's identify and use the correct forms of irregular verbs.* Work together with students to complete the Practice section. Provide support as needed.

Extend: Have pairs of students complete the Extend section. Provide support as needed.

Challenge: Model completing the sentence frames in the Challenge section. Use irregular past tense verbs from the chart.

(L)ight Support

Use the text on p. 10 in the *Texts for Close Reading* to complete the following activities.

Practice: Review irregular verbs. Have students generate a new sentence about Deborah Sampson for each verb: *knew, hid,* and *became.*

Extend: Have pairs generate a new sentence drawing from paragraphs 4 and 5. The sentence should use one of these verbs from the chart: *knew, hid, put,* or *became.*

Challenge: Assign alternate groups the irregular past tense verbs *began* (paragraph 9) and *took* (paragraph 10). Have groups generate a new sentence using their verb. Have groups share their sentences. Ask each group to identify the present tense of their verb and explain how the past tense is formed.

☑	Formative Assessment
Substantial Support	• Can students with support identify irregular past tense verbs? • Can students with support generate sentences using frames and irregular past tense verbs?
Moderate Support	• Can students identify and form irregular past tense verbs? • Can students generate original sentences using irregular past tense verbs?
Light Support	• Can students generate original sentences using irregular past tense verbs from the chart? • Can students retell an informational text using new irregular past tense verbs?

Preview or Review Week 2 ELA Mini-Lessons

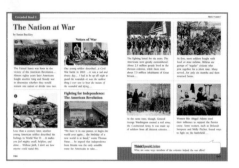

"The Nation at War," pages 144–145

Student Objectives

LANGUAGE
Purpose:
- I can state reasons for the American Revolution in an outline.

Form:
- I can recognize verb tenses that show time.

CONTENT
- I can read and understand informational social studies text.

Additional Materials
- Unit Presentation
- *Texts for Close Reading* booklet
- Think-Speak-Listen Flip Book
- Student journal

Metacognitive Prompt: Elaboration on Prior Knowledge

As you read today, think about what you have already read about the Revolutionary war, and connect that information to the ideas and information in "The Nation at War." How has your knowledge of the Revolutionary War developed and changed?

---

7 Read "The Nation at War"

Build Background and Vocabulary

Display the panels. Invite students to share their cultural experiences and knowledge about the American Revolution.

Read Aloud the Text

Read aloud panel 1. Ask students to find details in the picture that match words in the text (victory, American Revolution). As you read, ask *wh-* questions such as: *What armies do you think are in this picture?* Repeat with panels 2–8. Refer to the Essential Question. Invite students to discuss how the American Revolution changed society. **Say:** *This text gives facts about past wars. It is an informational text.*

Think-Speak-Listen: Use the following sentence frame or the Think-Speak-Listen Flip Book to guide discussion: *The colonists helped with the war effort by _____ and _____.*

👥 Differentiated Instruction
Build Language: Use Verb Tenses to Convey Time

Remind students that verb tenses indicate when an action occurs. **Say:** *Verbs give clues about when events happen. Past tense verbs tell us the action is finished. Present tense verbs tell us the action is happening now, or it happens in general. Future tense verbs tell us an action hasn't happened yet.* Read aloud panel 1 and elicit the verb tense used. **Say:** *These verbs are in the past tense (was, fought, would). They are all irregular verbs.* Use the Differentiated Instruction to practice using verb tenses that convey time in a way that best matches the levels of your students.

☑ Use Oral and Written Language: State Reasons in an Outline

Task: *Imagine you have been asked to write a book on the American Revolution. First you need to outline the reasons for the conflict. With your partner, create an outline of events and information that you think should be included in your book. Share your outline with the group.*

Wrap Up

Today we have learned about verb tenses that convey time. Why is it important to show when something happened?

Turn and Talk: *With your partner, describe what school was like for you last year. Tell about your favorite classes, and if you have the same interests today.*

👥 Differentiated Instruction
Language: Use Verb Tenses to Convey Time

Ⓢubstantial Support

Model: Review verb tenses. Read aloud panel 1. **Say:** *The past tense verbs in this paragraph tell me that events occurred in the past. So, I know that the war happened in the past.*

Practice: Invite students to Read aloud panel 2 and identify the verbs that convey time. Then complete the sentence frames with an appropriate verb:

The United States _____ a united country after the Civil War.

Independence was _____ for long and hard.

Extend: In pairs, have students choose two verbs from panels 3–4 to write sentences about events that happened in the past.

Challenge: If students are ready, provide them with the Moderate Support BLM 1 and model working through the Practice and Extend activities.

Ⓜoderate Support

Model: Review verb tenses. **Say:** *Panel 1 includes verbs that convey time. The verbs was and fought are both in the past tense. So, I know that these actions occurred in the past.*

Practice: Distribute BLM 1. Read aloud panels 2–8 and help students identify and explain the remaining verb tenses. Then help them complete the chart.

Extend: Pair students to complete the Extend activity on BLM 1. Provide assistance as needed.

Challenge: If students are ready, model how to complete the Practice activity on the Light Support BLM 2 using paragraph 4 on page 12 of their *Texts for Close Reading*. Provide assistance as students work through the activity.

Ⓛight Support

Use the text on pp. 12-19 in the *Texts for Close Reading* to complete the following activities.

Practice: Review verb tenses. Distribute BLM 2. Have students read paragraph 4 and complete the activity.

Extend: Have students work in pairs to complete the Extend activity. Provide support as needed.

Challenge: Model for students how to complete the

☑ Formative Assessment

Substantial Support	• Can students identify past tense verbs? • Are students able to identify verb tenses that convey time?
Moderate Support	• Are students able identify verb tenses that convey time in the past? • Can students create four sentences using past tense verbs based on the text?
Light Support	• Can students identify past tense verbs in text? • Are students able to create original sentences using past tense verbs?

Preview or Review Week 2 ELA Mini-Lessons

Extended Read 1 (continued)   Week 2 • Lesson 8

One Nation Indivisible?: The Civil War

In the bloodiest war of our history, the United States fought to keep its unity as a nation.... The two sides... held conflicting beliefs. Issues of slavery and states' rights were at the core of the dispute....

After Abraham Lincoln was elected president of the United States, eleven Southern states left the Union and declared themselves a separate nation. They called it the Confederate States of America, or the Confederacy....

At War in Other Lands

The last war fought... in U.S. territory was the Civil War.... from the twentieth century to the present time... the nation has been involved in wars around the world.

The United States has brought its power to end colonialism... the nation has joined allies defending freedom... fought Communist forces... and... brave American soldiers are fighting for freedom around the world.

ThinkSpeakListen
What are some of the reasons the United States has gone to war?

146

"The Nation at War," page 146

Student Objectives

LANGUAGE
Purpose:
• I can describe a war in a historical skit.
Form:
• I can use primary sources.
CONTENT
• I can understand informational social studies texts.

Additional Materials
• Unit Presentation
• *Texts for Close Reading* booklet
• Think-Speak-Listen Flip Book
• Student journal

Language Transfer Support

Note that some students may need additional support with independent and dependent clauses as groups of related words that have subjects and verbs. For example, native speakers of Cantonese or Vietnamese do not use subjects in subordinate clauses.

8 Analyze Primary Sources

Engage Thinking

Display panels 9–12. **Say:** *What do you think the images are of? During what era or time frame do you think they were taken? Do you think they are valid representations or reliable sources of information? Why or why not?* Elicit responses and discuss.

Turn and Talk: Ask students to compare and contrast the images in panels 9 and 10 with the images in panels 11 and 12.

Differentiated Instruction
✓ Read and View Closely: Analyze Primary Sources

Say: *The people who wrote primary sources were there when the events occurred.* Explain that primary sources include letters, photographs, diary entries, and maps. **Say:** *When reading, it is important to determine a source's truthfulness.* Use the Differentiated Instruction to practice analyzing primary sources in a way that best matches the levels of your students. Use this opportunity to assess students using the rubric in *English Language Development Assessment.*

Build Language: Condense Ideas

Read aloud panel 10. **Say:** *The first sentence contains a lot of information.* Break the information down into separate sentences, and write them on the board for students to see. **Say:** *The author condensed the ideas into one sentence to create more interesting writing.*

Think-Speak-Listen: Use the following sentence frame or the Think-Speak-Listen Flip Book to guide discussion: *Some reasons the United States has gone to war are _____ and _____.*

✓ Use Oral and Written Language: Describe a War in a Historical Skit

Task: *Create a skit that describes what happened in a war. Your skit should tell why the war started, who was involved, and what happened as a result of these wars. Share or perform your skit.*

Ⓢ *The Americans wanted independence from the British. Patrick Henry's speech tells us "give me liberty or give me death."*

Ⓜ *The Americans wanted _____ from _____. Patrick Henry's speech tells us "_____."*

Ⓛ *As we can see from Patrick Henry's speech, _____.*

↺ Wrap Up

Today we learned about how to analyze primary sources. Why is this an important skill to have when reading and writing?

Turn and Talk: *With a partner, talk about a famous speech in history. How does the speech make you believe that the events really happened?*

👥 Differentiated Instruction
Read and View Closely: Analyze Primary Sources

ⓢubstantial Support

Model: Read aloud panel 12. **Say:** *Look at the photograph. It shows us that the claims are valid. This is a primary source. The text says that soldiers are fighting for freedom. The photograph proves that Americans are very proud of that.*

Practice: Read aloud panel 10.

Ask: *What does this illustration show?*

Have students complete the sentence frame: *This image shows us what the _____ looks like.*

Extend: Ask partners to work through Panel 11 as they identify what the image is presenting and possible reasons why.

The image shows us _____.

I believe it shows us that because _____.

Challenge: If students are ready, provide them with the BLM 1 for Moderate Support and help them as they work through the Practice and Extend activities.

ⓜoderate Support

Model: Read aloud panel 12. **Say:** *Look at the photograph. What does it show us? Photographs show us that claims are valid. This is a primary source. The text says that soldiers are fighting for freedom. The photograph proves that Americans are very proud of that.*

Practice: Provide students with BLM 1. Work with them to complete the Practice activity.

Extend: Pair students to complete the Extend activity on BLM 1. Provide assistance as needed.

Challenge: If students are ready, provide students with the Light Support BLM 2 and ask them to read "One Nation Indivisible?: The Civil War" text found on page 16 of *Texts for Close Reading*. Model completing the Practice activity.

ⓛight Support

Use the text on pp. 12-19 in the *Texts for Close Reading* to complete the following activities.

Practice: Review the meaning of primary sources. Distribute BLM 2. Have students read paragraph 14. Work with students complete the Practice activity in the BLM.

Extend: Have students work in pairs to complete the Extend activity on the BLM 2. If needed, provide assistance as the pairs work through the activity.

Challenge: Provide students with the BLM 2 and help them

☑ Formative Assessment

Substantial Support	• Are students able to reference the text to find text-based answers? • Do students understand how primary sources support key details about the topic?
Moderate Support	• Are students able to draw conclusions in response to guided questions about primary sources? • Can students negotiate meaning through text deconstruction?
Light Support	• Are students able to analyze primary sources to better understand historical events? • Can students interpret and draw inferences from the text?

Preview or Review Week 2 ELA Mini-Lessons

"Use Adverbials to add Details About Time," page 147

Student Objectives

LANGUAGE

Purpose:
• I can use adverbs to describe historical events in a news article.

Form:
• I can identify and use adverbials to detail time.

CONTENT
• I can read and understand informational social studies text.

Additional Materials
• Unit Presentation
• *Texts for Close Reading* booklet
• Think-Speak-Listen Flip Book
• Student journal

Language Transfer Support

Note that students whose first language is Chinese, Hmong, or Korean may need support to structure sentences with prepositions and adverbials. In these languages, speakers sometimes omit forms of the verb be before prepositional phrases (e.g., *it on the chair* instead of *it is on the chair*).

9 Use Adverbials to Add Details About Time

Engage Thinking

Display the chart and discuss the first two rows with. **Ask:** *What do you see in the images?* **Say:** *The images give us information about when these events took place.* Read aloud the text. **Ask:** *What do we learn about the events from the text? Which words tell about time?*

Turn and Talk: *Discuss the other two images using words that tell about time.*

Read and View Closely: Recognize Adverbials

Read aloud row 1. Point out the underlined phrase. **Say:** *This phrase is an adverbial. It begins with the adverb* almost. *Adverbs provide more detail in a sentence. Almost eighty years later tells us when Americans fought another war.* Read through the remaining sentences while pointing out the adverbials and discussing what information modify.

Think-Speak-Listen: Use the following sentence frame or the Think-Speak-Listen Flip Book to guide discussion: *The wars have changed society _____.*

👥👥 Differentiated Instruction
Build Language: Use Adverbials to Add Details About Time

Review that adverbials modify a verb and provide more detail in a sentence. Adverbials begin with an adverb. **Say:** *Many adverbials provide information about when, or at what point in time, something happened. In the first sentence, "almost eighty years later" is an adverbial.* **Ask:** *What is the adverb in this phrase?* **Say:** *This adverbial tells us the time frame between wars in the United States. Adverbials that add details about time answer the question* when. Use the Differentiated Instruction to practice using adverbials to add details about time in a way that best matches the levels of your students.

☑ Use Oral and Written Language: Describe Historical Events

Task: *Write a news article with a partner to describe events about conflicts in American history. Include information and details about when the events happened.*

Ⓢ *The American Revolution gave Americans independence from the British. Almost _____, another war was fought.*

Ⓜ *The American Revolution gave Americans _____. _____, another war was fought. This war was called _____.*

Ⓛ *In 1776, the American Revolution _____. _____, another war was fought, _____.*

🔄 Wrap Up

Today we learned about how adverbials are used to add details about time in sentences. How are adverbials helpful to use when you write?

Turn and Talk: *Tell a partner about a science experiment. Use adverbials to add details about when events happen.*

👥👥 Differentiated Instruction
Build Language: Use Adverbials to Add Details About Time

⑤ubstantial Support

Model: Display row 1. **Say:** *The adverb almost introduces the adverbial phrase. Adverbial phrases describe verbs, so I know that the phrase* almost eighty years later *gives details about the verb* fought. *Almost eighty years later answers the question* **when**.

Practice: Read row 2. **Ask:** *When does the soldier describe his feeling?* Elicit responses. **Say:** *The adverbial phrase* less than a century later *provides detail about when the solider described his feelings.* **Ask:** *What question does the adverbial answer?*

Extend: Ask partners to read rows 3 and 4, identifying the adverbials and the question they answer. Provide the following sentence frames:

The adverbial phrase is _____.

It answers the question _____.

Challenge: If students are ready, model for them how to complete the Practice activity of the Moderate Support BLM 1.

Ⓜoderate Support

Model: Display row 1. **Say:** *The adverb* almost *introduces the adverbial phrase. Adverbial phrases describe verbs, so I know that* almost eighty years later *gives details about* fought. *Almost eighty years later answers the question* **when.**

Practice: Distribute BLM 1. Guide students to refer to the text to answer the questions in the Practice section.

Extend: Ask partners to complete the Extend activity on BLM 1. Provide assistance as needed.

Challenge: If students are ready, model for them how to complete the Practice activity on Light Support BLM 2.

Ⓛight Support

Use the text on pp. 12-19 in the *Texts for Close Reading* to complete the following activities.

Practice: Distribute BLM 2. Review adverbials, and have partners complete the Practice activity on the BLM.

Extend: Have partners work together to write their own sentences using adverbials that add details about time in the Extend activity on the BLM. Encourage volunteers to share their sentences with the group.

Challenge: If students are ready, challenge them to write a time line of the events described in "The Nation at War" using adverbials to add details.

☑ Formative Assessment

Substantial Support	• Can students identify an adverb in an adverbial phrase? • With support, can students complete sentence frames to use adverbials that add details about time to a sentence?
Moderate Support	• Can students use adverbial phrases to answer questions about when events happened? • Are students able to write adverbial phrases that add details about time?
Light Support	• Can students analyze a text to identify adverbials that add details about time? • Can students write original sentences using adverbials that add details about time?

"Two Letters from Boston, Massachusetts—1775,"
page 148

Student Objectives

LANGUAGE
Purpose:
• I can describe a soldier in a report.
Form:
• I can use synonyms and antonyms.
CONTENT
• I can analyze letters.

Additional Materials
• Unit Presentation
• *Texts for Close Reading* booklet
• Think-Speak-Listen Flip Book
• Student journal
• Synonym/Antonym Chart
• Dictionary and or thesaurus

Language Transfer Support

The terms for *synonym* and *antonym* are cognates in many languages, including Spanish (*sinomino* and *antonimo*) and French (*synonyme* and *antonyme*).

10 Read "Two Letters from Boston, Massachusetts—1775"

Build Background and Vocabulary

Display the panels. If students have read the letters, ask them what they remember. Invite students to share their cultural experiences and knowledge about the Revolutionary War.

Read Aloud the Text

Read aloud the first letter. Ask students to think about the meaning of unknown words (settled in, faring, threat, camp fever). Ask *wh-* questions such as What is troubling the letter writer? Repeat with the second letter. After reading, model thinking through the Essential Question: *How does conflict shape society?* **Say:** *The life of regular soldiers during the Revolutionary War was hard. People learned to be strong.* Invite students to share their ideas. **Say:** *These letters were written by real people who actually lived. They describe actual events.*

Think-Speak-Listen: Use the following sentence frame or the Think-Speak-Listen Flip Book to guide discussion: *Robert's and John's feelings _____. Robert felt _____, and John felt _____.*

👥 Differentiated Instruction
Build Language: Use Synonyms and Antonyms

Point out the word *clean* in the first letter. Display Synonym/Antonym Chart and draw attention to the word *clean*. **Say:** *A synonym is a word that has the same or a similar meaning. Point to the word* neat *in the synonym column.* Neat *is a synonym for* clean. *Point to the word* dirty *in the antonym column.* **Say:** *An antonym is a word that has the opposite meaning.* Dirty *is an antonym for* clean. Explain that It is important to use synonyms and antonyms because it makes writing interesting and builds vocabulary. Use the Differentiated Instruction to practice using synonyms and antonyms in a way that best matches the levels of your students.

☑ Use Oral and Written Language: Describe a Soldier in a Report

Task: *Pretend that you've interviewed Robert, the first letter writer. Write a news report based on his experiences. Use at least one of the synonyms or antonyms you learned today.*

(S) *Robert settled in at camp and remains _____, but many others are _____. These _____ conditions can cause _____.*

(M) *One of Robert's troubles is _____ brought on by _____. He remains _____.*

(L) *Robert is in _____ spirits despite _____. These _____ conditions can _____.*

🌐 Wrap Up

Today we learned how important synonyms and antonyms are in reading. Why is it important to use synonyms and antonyms correctly in writing?

Turn and Talk: *Use synonyms and/or antonyms to describe an item in the classroom.*

👥 Differentiated Instruction
Build Language: Use Synonyms and Antonyms

Ⓢubstantial Support

Model: Point out the word *happy* in the second letter. **Say:** *A synonym is a word with the same or a similar meaning.* Content *is a synonym for* happy. Remind students that an antonym is a word with the opposite meaning, so sad is an antonym for *happy*. Create a chart for *happy*:

Synonyms	Antonyms
content	sad

Practice: Ask students to help you fill in more synonyms and antonyms for *happy*. Remind students that they can use a dictionary or thesaurus to look up synonyms and antonyms.

Extend: Distribute BLM 1. Ask students to work with a partner to complete the activity.

Challenge: If students are ready, work with them to come up with a synonym and an antonym for *fight* in the second paragraph of John's letter.

Ⓜoderate Support

Model: Point out the word united in the second letter. Display the chart below. **Say:** United *means* together. *Another word that means* together *is* joined. Write *joined* in the synonym column. Guide students to think of an antonym for *united*. Write it in the antonym column. Remind students that they can use a dictionary or thesaurus to look up synonyms and antonyms.

Synonyms	Antonyms
joined	divided

Practice: As a group, work together to come up with synonyms and antonyms for the word *fight* in John's letter. Create a new chart together.

Extend: Distribute BLM 2. Have partners complete sentence frames and form new sentences.

Challenge: If students are ready, read page 20 of *Texts for Close Reading* and model how to use context to find synonyms for the following words t: *disgusted, disease* and *precaution*.

Ⓛight Support

Use the text on p. 20 in the *Texts for Close Reading* to complete the following activities.

Practice: Have students find the word *regular* in paragraph 4 and help them create a Synonyms/Antonyms chart. Have partners use a dictionary or thesaurus to fill in the chart.

Synonyms	Antonyms
ordinary	special

Extend: Have students read paragraph 2. Ask them to work with a partner to find synonyms and antonyms for the following words: *disgusted, disease* and *precaution*. Have partners compose a sentence using the synonyms and antonyms they researched.

Challenge: If students are ready, have partners exchange sentences and rewrite them using different synonyms and antonyms.

☑ Formative Assessment

Substantial Support	• Do students understand what synonyms and antonyms are? • Can students complete sentence frames using synonyms and antonyms?
Moderate Support	• Can students generate simple synonyms and antonyms for common words? • Can students use synonyms and antonyms in sentences?
Light Support	• Can students use reference materials to find synonyms and antonyms? • Can students generate original sentences using synonyms and antonyms?

Preview or Review Week 3 ELA Mini-Lessons

		Week 3 • Lesson 11
Use Conjunctions to Connect Ideas		
Conjunctions		
I have settled in at the army camp. For the most part I am faring well.	**and**	I have settled in at the army camp, and for the most part I am faring well.
The General has instructed We place ornamental ribbons on our hats.	**that**	The General has instructed that we place ornamental ribbons on our hats.
One soldier may wear a heavy coat and a straw hat. Another dresses in moccasins and tattered britches.	**while**	One soldier may wear a heavy coat and a straw hat, while another dresses in moccasins and tattered britches.
Yet despite this, we are united in spirit. We prepare to fight.	**as**	Yet despite this, we are united in spirit as we prepare to fight.

ThinkSpeakListen
Based on your reading and your understanding of conjunctions, write a sentence using the conjunction "while."

"Use Conjunctions to Connect Ideas," page 149

Student Objectives

LANGUAGE
Purpose:
• I can draw conclusions in a letter.
Form:
• I can use conjunctions.
CONTENT
• I can understand conjunctions in letters.

Additional Materials

• Unit Presentation
• *Texts for Close Reading* booklet
• Think-Speak-Listen Flip Book
• Student journal

Language Transfer Support

Note that speakers of Chinese, Farsi, or Vietnamese may need additional support when creating sentences with conjunctions. Unlike in English, conjunctions often occur in pairs in those languages. For example, a student may say, *Although, I am hungry, but I do not want to eat.*

11 Use Conjunctions to Connect Ideas

Engage Thinking

Display the first panel from "Two Letters from Boston, Massachusetts—1775." **Ask:** *What ideas do the men writing the letters express?* **Say:** *The image tells us about what the letter writers see and feel. The text does too.* Read aloud the text. **Ask:** *What do we learn about what happened in the text? How are the ideas connected?*

Turn and Talk: *Why is it important to notice how ideas are connected?*

Read and View Closely: Recognize Conjunctions

Display and read aloud the Use Conjunctions to Connect Ideas chart. **Ask:** *Which words are bolded? What do you notice about these words?* **Say:** *Recognizing conjunctions helps me understand how ideas are related to one another.* Point to the first sentence. **Ask:** *What does the word* and *tell us in this sentence?* Invite students to respond. **Say:** *When I read the word* and*, I know a sentence has two ideas that are similar. I keep reading and I see that Robert has both settled in camp and is faring well.*

👥 Differentiated Instruction
Build Language: Use Conjunctions to Connect Ideas

Say: *Conjunctions are small words that connect ideas.* Tell students that the conjunction and connects ideas that are similar. **Say:** *An independent clause expresses a complete thought. A dependent clause provides additional information but does not express a complete thought.* Use the Differentiated Instruction to practice using conjunctions in a way that best matches the levels of your students.

Think-Speak-Listen: Use the following sentence frame or the Think-Speak-Listen Flip Book to guide discussion: *Robert _____, while John _____.*

☑ Use Oral and Written Language: Draw Conclusions In a Letter

Task: *Working in small groups, write a letter in response to one of the letters. Write from the point of view of Robert's sister or John's wife.*

(S) *Dear Robert, Thank you for your letter. I understand that you _____.*

(M) *Dear Robert, Thank you for _____. I understand _____.*

(L) *Dear John, I am glad to read that _____ and _____. I understand _____. Love, Mary*

Wrap Up

Today we learned to use conjunctions to connect ideas. How does using conjunctions help us understand a text?

Turn and Talk: *Describe an event in history. Use conjunctions to connect ideas.*

👥 Differentiated Instruction
Build Language: Combine Clauses to Connect Ideas

⑤ ubstantial Support

Model: Read aloud the sentence in the right column of the first row. **Say:** *This sentence connects two ideas. The first idea is that Robert has settled in at the army camp. The second idea is that for the most part he is faring well. The conjunction and connects these two ideas.*

Practice: Work with students to complete the following sentence frames with the conjunction *and*. Remind students to refer back to their texts for answers.

Robert and John wrote _____. (letters home)

John thought of his family and _____. (remembered happy times)

Extend: Distribute BLM 1. Ask students to work in pairs to complete the activity.

Challenge: Write the following sentences and have students identify the conjunction.

I think of you and little Sarah each day.

I remain clean, but many others do not.

Ⓜ oderate Support

Model: Have volunteers read aloud the sentence in the right column of the first row. **Say:** *This sentence connects two ideas. Each of these ideas could be expressed in its own sentence. The conjunction and connects them.* **Repeat the process for the other rows.**

Practice: Read the sentences in the chart and identify the conjunctions. Give students the following sentences. As a group, identify the conjunctions and explain how the two ideas in each sentence are connected.

I think of you and little Sarah each day.

I remain clean, but many others do not.

Extend: Distribute BLM 2. Ask partners to complete the activity.

Challenge: If students are ready, ask them to read page 20 of the *Texts for Close Reading*, find three examples of sentences containing conjunctions, and discuss the differences in how the conjunctions are used.

Ⓛ ight Support

Use the text on p. 20 in the *Texts for Close Reading* to complete the following activities.

Practice: Have partners read paragraphs 1–3 and find three examples of sentences containing conjunctions. For each sentence, ask them to identify the two ideas being connected.

Extend: **Say:** *In paragraph 3, it says "I must close now, dear sister, as it is time for military drills." The conjunction as is used here to indicate the timing reason Robert must end his letter.* **Ask** partners to discuss the differences in how the conjunctions they found are used in context.

Challenge: If students are ready, ask them to write three original sentences inspired by Robert and John's letters. All three sentences should contain a conjunction to connect ideas.

☑️ Formative Assessment

Substantial Support	• Can students recognize a conjunction in a sentence? • Can students add the conjunction and to connect ideas in two simple sentences?
Moderate Support	• Can students verbalize how to connect ideas using conjunctions? • Can students join two short sentences by adding a conjunction to connect ideas?
Light Support	• Can students verbalize how ideas are connected, depending on the conjunction used? • Can students generate original sentences that connect ideas by using conjunctions?

Preview or Review Week 3 ELA Mini-Lessons

"The Youth in Battle," pages 150–151

12 Read "The Youth in Battle"

Build Background and Vocabulary

Display the panels. If students have already read the story, ask them to tell what they remember. Invite students to share their cultural experiences and knowledge on how conflict shapes society.

Read Aloud the Text

Read aloud panel 1. Ask students to find the words that indicate that there were many soldiers (brown swarm of running men). Then read aloud panels 2 and 3. **Ask:** *Which words show what life might have been like for the soldiers?* (perspiration, nervous movement). Refer to the Essential Question. **Say:** *From what I've read, I can tell that the war had a huge impact on the way people lived. This is a made-up story, but it seems real and is related to real events. This type of story is called historical fiction.*

👤👥 Differentiated Instruction
Build Language: Use Prepositional Phrases

Remind students that a prepositional phrase is a phrase that describes what is happening. The phrase begins with a preposition that answers questions such as when or where. Read aloud panel 1. **Ask:** *From where did the swarm of running men come?* Invite responses. **Say:** *It came from across the smoke-infested fields. Across is a preposition, and the rest of the phrase is the prepositional phrase.* Display and discuss the Prepositional Phrases Chart with students. Use the Differentiated Instruction to practice using prepositional phrases in a way that best matches the levels of your students.

Think-Speak-Listen: Use the following sentence frame or the Think-Speak-Listen Flip Book to guide discussion: *One time when I was very nervous, _____.*

Student Objectives

LANGUAGE
Purpose:
- I can draw inferences about an imaginary soldier in a letter.

Form:
- I can recognize prepositional phrases.

CONTENT
- I can read a historical fiction story.

Additional Materials
- Unit Presentation
- *Texts for Close Reading* booklet
- Think-Speak-Listen Flip Book
- Student journal
- Prepositional Phrases Chart

☑ Use Oral and Written Language: Draw Inferences About an Imaginary Soldier

Task: *With a partner, write a letter to an imaginary soldier in the Civil War. Ask the solider what it is like on the battlefield, and thank him for his service to the country.*

(S) *Do you battle into _____? What is it like to travel across _____? Thank you for _____.*

(M) *Thanks for your service in _____. Do you go near _____? What is it like in _____?*

(L) *This letter will reach you across _____. You served well in _____. What is it like near _____?*

🔄 Wrap Up

Today we learned about using prepositional phrases. Why is it important to use prepositional phrases in our writing?

Turn and Talk: *Suppose you are giving someone directions to your home. How can prepositional phrases be used?*

Metacognitive Prompt: Making Predictions

Often when we read, we use information in the text to make a special kind of inference called a prediction. A prediction is a guess about what might happen next. After you read today's text, you'll use what you've read to make a guess about what will happen next.

👥 Differentiated Instruction
Build Language: Use Prepositional Phrases

Ⓢubstantial Support

Model: Use the Prepositional Phrases Chart to teach about prepositions and prepositional phrases. **Say:** *When I read a sentence, I look for prepositions first. They tell me where or when something happens. Prepositions often give directions such as in, near, down, or at.*

Point to the first sentence in panel 1. **Ask:** *I see the preposition across. This helps me answer the question "where."*

Practice: Distribute BLM 1. Work with students to complete the Practice activity.

Extend: Distribute BLM 1. Ask partners to complete the Extend activity. Provide support as needed.

Challenge: If students are ready, work with them to complete the Practice activity of the Moderate Support BLM 2.

Ⓜoderate Support

Model: Use the Prepositional Phrases Chart to teach about prepositions and prepositional phrases. **Say:** *A prepositional phrase gives more details about what is happening in a story. Without prepositional phrases, the story would not have as much information about the characters and their actions. For example, I see that the flag tilted forward was near the front. This helps me picture the flag.*

Practice: Distribute BLM 2. Work with students to complete the Practice activity.

Extend: Ask partners to complete the Extend activity on the BLM. They will continue the activity started in the Practice section.

Challenge: If students are ready, have them identify the prepositions and prepositional phrases in paragraph 1 on page 22 of their *Texts for Close Reading*.

Ⓛight Support

Use the text on pp. 22-29 in the *Texts for Close Reading* to complete the following activities.

Practice: Review prepositional phrases. Have students read paragraphs 1, 13, and 14 . On a separate sheet of paper, have pairs make a list of the prepositional phrases they read, and underline each preposition.

Extend: Ask partners to choose three or more of the prepositions they underlined and use them in their own sentences.

Challenge: If students are ready, ask them to add five additional prepositional phrases of their own to the Prepositional Phrases Chart.

✓ Formative Assessment

Substantial Support	• With support, can students identify prepositions and prepositional phrases? • With support, are students able to use prepositions and prepositional phrases?
Moderate Support	• Can students identify prepositions and prepositional phrases with limited help? • Are students able to use prepositions and prepositional phrases with limited help?
Light Support	• Can students identify prepositions and prepositional phrases? • Are students able to use prepositions and prepositional phrases in their own sentences?

Preview or Review Week 3 ELA Mini-Lessons

"The Youth in Battle," page 152

Student Objectives

LANGUAGE
Purpose:
• I can describe a battle in a diary entry.
Form:
• I can use connecting words to link ideas.
CONTENT
• I can read an informational text about a social studies topic.

Additional Materials
• Unit Presentation
• *Texts for Close Reading* booklet
• Think-Speak-Listen Flip Book
• Student journal

Metacognitive Prompt: Making Predictions

Before we read, we can preview the pictures in a story to see if we can make predictions about what will happen. To do this, look at the pictures. Think about what the pictures tell you about what is going to happen.

13 Analyze Author's Language

Engage Thinking

Display panels 4–5. **Say:** *The soldiers in the top picture are in a difficult battle. What do you see in the bottom picture? The soldiers stick together and work together. What words in the text show that the soldiers stick together?*

Turn and Talk: *Tell your partner what you remember so far about the story that we read.*

👥 Differentiated Instruction
Read and View Closely: Analyze Author's Language

Explain to students that authors choose words that will give the reader information about the story and also make the characters and events seem more realistic or dramatic. **Say:** *In panel 4, the author says the regiment was like a firework. What does that make you think of?* (The regiment was loud and energetic.) **Say:** *Each description in the story is a special choice that the author makes.* Use the Differentiated Instruction to practice analyzing author's language in a way that best matches the levels of your students.

Think-Speak-Listen: Use the following sentence frame or the Think-Speak-Listen Flip Book to guide discussion: *I think the narrator of the story feels _____.*

Build Language: Use Connecting Words to Link Ideas

Explain that authors use connecting words and phrases to link events in time. **Say:** *Sometimes these words tell us the order in which events happen, such as first, next, and last. But sometimes words, such as suddenly, and phrases, such as before he knew what happened, can link events in more complicated ways.* Have students read aloud panel 3 to identify the connecting words and phrases that link ideas and events in time. *(instantly, before he was ready to begin)*

☑ Use Oral and Written Language: Describe a Battle in a Diary Entry

Task: *Imagine that you are the youth in this story. Write a diary entry describing the battle. Choose your words carefully to make your descriptions seem realistic or dramatic. Then compare your diary entry with a partner.*

(S) The men in my regiment _____. We finally reached _____. The battle was _____.

(M) My comrades in battle _____. The battle began _____. Then it became _____.

(L) The battle made me feel _____. My comrades _____. Our goal was _____.

 Wrap Up

Today we learned about analyzing an author's language. How might a fiction author's language be different from that of a nonfiction author?

Turn and Talk: *Imagine you are writing the story of your own life. Carefully choose three or four words that describe you. Tell your partner your life story.*

👥👥👥 Differentiated Instruction
Read and View Closely: Analyze Author's Language

Ⓢubstantial Support

Model: Say: *Picking words from the text and analyzing them helps me understand the text in simple terms. In sentence 1 of panel 4, I see the words* proceeds superior. *To me, that means that something is very important. So the regiment gets a lot of important attention until they fade and tire out.*

Practice: Distribute BLM 1. Work with students to complete the Practice activity. Guide students to match phrases from the text with their simplified meanings.

Extend: Ask students to work in pairs to complete the Extend section of the BLM. Help them as needed.

Challenge: If students are ready, work with them to complete the Practice activity of the Moderate Support BLM 2.

Ⓜoderate Support

Model Read paragraph 2 in Panel 4. **Ask:** *Which of these words or phrases means something similar to a loud noise?* **Invite** responses. **Say:** *The sentence "It wheezed and banged with a mighty power" is a more dramatic and literary way to say it made a loud noise.*

Practice: Distribute BLM 2. Work with students to complete the Practice activity.

Extend: Have partners complete the Extend activity. Provide support as needed as pairs complete each sentence frame with a simplified version of the text evidence in the Practice section.

Challenge: If students are ready, read paragraph 20 on page 28 of their *Texts for Close Reading* and model identifying a more simplified meaning of the phrase "rush forward."

Ⓛight Support

Use the text on pp. 22-29 in the *Texts for Close Reading* to complete the following activities.

Practice: In pairs, have students identify a more simplified meaning of the phrases "rush forward," "made his rage into that of a driven beast," and "swirling battle phantoms."

Extend: Have partners continue analyzing paragraph 20. Ask them to rewrite the last sentence of the paragraph in a more simplified version, describing only what the author intended the reader to understand.

Challenge: If students are ready, ask them to complete the following sentence frame to explain why analyzing an author's language choice is so important:

Analyzing an author's language choices is important because _____.

☑ Formative Assessment

Substantial Support	• With help, can students analyze an author's language choices? • Can students understand what an author means when certain language choices are used?
Moderate Support	• Can students analyze an author's language choices with little assistance? • With little support, can students understand what an author means when certain language choices are used?
Light Support	• Can students analyze an author's language choices? • Can students understand what an author means when certain language choices are used?

Preview or Review Week 3 ELA Mini-Lessons

"Understand and Use Figurative Language: Similes" page 153

Student Objectives

LANGUAGE
Purpose:
• I can use similes to describe characters.
Form:
• I can understand and use similes.
CONTENT
• I can read historical fiction.

Additional Materials
• Unit Presentation
• *Texts for Close Reading* booklet
• Think-Speak-Listen Flip Book
• Student journal

Language Transfer Support

Native speakers of Spanish, Cantonese, Korean, Vietnamese, Hmong, or Haitian Creole may need additional support with placing the adjective before the noun it modifies instead of after it, because in these languages the adjective usually or always follows the noun.

14 Understand and Use Figurative Language: Similes

Engage Thinking

Display the chart. Point to the top photo. **Ask:** *What part of the text describes this picture?* **Say:** *The underlined part, or "like that of a weeping urchin." This chart gives us information about the use and understanding of figurative language.*

Turn and Talk: *What word starts all of the underlined sections of text?*

Read and View Closely: Recognize Similes

Read the chart aloud. **Ask:** *How do the pictures help you understand the text?* **Say:** *They help me visualize the underlined part of the sentence.* Point to *like that of a weeping urchin* in the first row. **Say:** *A simile is a comparison using* like *or* as *to describe something. I think, What is being compared? The simile helps me get a clearer picture, or a better understanding, of the youth's face.* Have students read the second and third row. **Ask:** *What are the similes used in these sentences? What do they mean?*

👥 Differentiated Instruction
Build Language: Understand and Use Similes

Say: *Authors use similes to make their writing more interesting to the reader. When I read a simile, I visualize the comparison in my mind. I know that crying creates tears that stream down someone's face. I can picture that when I read the words "weeping urchin."* Have students review the similes in the second and third row and tell why the words are considered a simile. **Say:** *The similes help me better understand the picture the author is trying to create in my mind.* Use the Differentiated Instruction to practice understanding and using similes in a way that best matches the levels of your students.

Think-Speak-Listen: Use the following sentence frame or the Think-Speak-Listen Flip Book to guide discussion: *Being nervous is like _____.*

☑ Use Oral and Written Language: Describe Characters in a Skit

Task: *Describe one of the characters from "The Youth in Battle." Decide which character you will describe. Then use your descriptions to create a skit to perform for the class.*
Ⓢ *The captain is _____. He seems as nervous as a _____.*
Ⓜ *The captain is _____ like a _____. The youth is _____ as a _____.*
Ⓛ *During the battle, the _____ was as _____ as a _____.*

Wrap Up

Today we learned about understanding and using similes. What simile might you use to describe someone who moves very slowly? Very quickly?

Turn and Talk: *Use a simile to describe the battle in the story. Remember to use* like *or* as *in your comparison.*

👤👤👤 Differentiated Instruction
Build Language: Understand and Similes

Ⓢ ubstantial Support

Model: Review similes. Display the chart and **say:** *In the first example, the author is not comparing the crying of a baby to the crying of a soldier. The simile compares the sweaty and dirty perspiration of the soldier running down his face with tears running down the dirty face of a child.*

Practice: Ask a volunteer to read row 2 aloud. **Ask:** *What traits do fireworks have that make them similar to a regiment of soldiers in battle?*

Extend: Have students work together to analyze the simile in row 3. **Ask:** *Are the soldier's eyes really cracking like hot stones? Why is the simile used?*

Challenge: Ask students if they know any similes about animals. Have them complete the following sentences frames or come up with similes of their own:

As busy as a _____.

As sly as a _____.

Ⓜ oderate Support

Model: Review similes. Display the chart and **say:** *In the first example, the author is not comparing the crying of a baby to the crying of a soldier. The simile compares the sweaty and dirty perspiration of the soldier running down his face with tears running down the dirty face of a child.*

Practice: Distribute BLM 1. Work with students to complete the Practice activity.

Extend: Have students work in pairs to complete the Extend activity. Help partners as needed so they can find the simile that correctly restates the sentence.

Challenge: If students are ready, work with them to complete the Practice activity of the Light Support BLM

Ⓛ ight Support

Use the text on pp. 22-29 in the *Texts for Close Reading* to complete the following activities.

Practice: Distribute BLM 2. Ask partners to work together to complete the Practice activity. Have them identify similes from the text.

Extend: Have partners continue with the Extend section and identify more similes from the text. Have partners analyze the similes that they underline.

Challenge: If students are ready, ask them to complete the Challenge section of the BLM with a partner. They may refer back to the text to help them analyze the similes and complete each sentence frame.

☑ Formative Assessment

Substantial Support	• With help, can students recognize similes in a text? • With help, can students understand similes and how they are used?
Moderate Support	• Can student pairs recognize similes in a text? • Can student pairs understand similes and how they are used?
Light Support	• Can students independently recognize similes in a text? • Can students understand similes and what they mean in relation to the text?

Preview or Review Week 3 ELA Mini-Lessons

"Young Patriots," pages 154–155

---

15 Read "Young Patriots"

Build Background and Vocabulary

Display the panels. If students have already read the text, ask them to tell what they remember about the three patriots during the revolution. Invite students to share their cultural experience and knowledge of how conflict shaped our society.

Read Aloud the Text

Read aloud panel 1. Ask students about vocabulary in the text (army, state militia, soldier). Ask students *wh-* questions such as, *How old was Joseph Plumb in 1776? What did he want to do?* Repeat with panels 2–3. Raise the Essential Question. **Ask:** *How does conflict shape a society?* Invite students to discuss how the revolutionary war made America a free nation. **Say:** *This is a true story about real people and real events. This is an informational text.*

👥👥 Differentiated Instruction
Build Language: Understand Domain-Specific Vocabulary

Say: *Texts about social studies or science may have words that we do not know. These words have to do with a specific topic.* Point to the words state militia in panel 1. **Say:** *The text says that Joseph Plumb wanted to join the army. Then it says that he joined a state militia. That lets me know that a militia is similar to an army. I used the context of the sentences to figure out the meaning of the word militia.* Use the Differentiated Instruction to practice building vocabulary related to young patriots in a way that best matches the levels of your students.

Think-Speak-Listen: Use the following sentence frame or the Think-Speak-Listen Flip Book to guide discussion: *A day for a young patriot is _____.*

☑ Use Oral and Written Language: Describe Revolutionary War Jobs

Task: *Work as a group to think of jobs people did during the revolutionary war. Skim the texts from this topic for ideas and vocabulary. Some include soldier, general, or doctor. Make a word web of words and phrases related to that job. Then create a brochure to describe the job.*

(S) *A general does the job of _____. The person must be _____, and _____.*

(M) *A doctor must _____. In the revolutionary war, doctors were _____, _____, and _____.*

(L) *Soldiers are _____. They _____ and _____. They show _____ and _____.*

🔄 Wrap Up

Today we learned vocabulary related to young patriots. How can learning topic specific vocabulary help you when you read or write?

Turn and Talk: *Think about what you learned about Sybil Ludington. Why was she called a young patriot?*

Student Objectives

LANGUAGE
Purpose:
- I can describe a Revolutionary War job in a brochure.

Form:
- I can read and understand domain-specific vocabulary.

CONTENT
- I can read and understand informational social studies text.

Additional Materials
- Unit Presentation
- *Texts for Close Reading* booklet
- Think-Speak-Listen Flip Book
- Student journal
- Dictionary

Language Transfer Support

Cognates are words that share similar meanings and spellings in two languages, such as *soldier* (English) and *soldado* (Spanish). Being aware of cognates can help students understand words that may appear unfamiliar at first but that they already know from their primary language. Encourage students whose primary language is Spanish, French, Italian, or Portuguese to look for cognates as they read.

👥 Differentiated Instruction
Build Language: Understand Domain-Specific Vocabulary

Ⓢ ubstantial Support

Model: Tell students that a dictionary is a good source for looking up difficult words. **Say:** *If I cannot figure out the meaning of a word from the context of the sentence, I will look in a dictionary.* Model how to look up the word "army." **Say:** *When I find the word, I read the different meanings. I find the one that matches what I am reading.*

Practice: Distribute BLM 1. Help students match each word related to the army with its meaning. Guide students through using a dictionary as needed.

Extend: In pairs, have students complete the Extend activity. Provide support as needed.

Challenge: If students are ready, work with them to complete the Practice activity of the Moderate Support BLM 2.

Ⓜ oderate Support

Model: Tell students that making a chart can help them keep track of words they do not know. **Say:** *If I'm reading a text about the revolutionary war, I might start a chart that I can use to list words I come across that I don't know.* Distribute BLM 2 for Moderate Support. *Say: I can use a dictionary to help find the meanings of these words. Militia is defined as "an unofficial army."*

Practice: Work with students to identify all of the words in panel 2 that relate to the army. Work together to find the meaning of each word, either from the dictionary or from the context of the text.

Extend: In pairs have students complete the Extend activity. Support them as needed.

Challenge: If students are ready, model the Practice activity in Light Support.

Ⓛ ight Support

Use the text on pp. 30 in the *Texts for Close Reading* to complete the following activities.

Practice: Ask students to work in pairs to find four words related to Sybil Ludington's bravery. Ask them to list the words on a separate sheet of paper and use both a dictionary and the context of the text to determine the meaning of each word.

Extend: Ask student pairs to repeat the same activity they did in the Practice section for paragraph 4. Ask them to identify three words that have to do with musicians of the revolutionary war. List the words and determine the meaning of each.

Challenge: If students are ready, ask them to complete the following sentence frame:

To find the meanings of words related to _____, I can _____.

✅ Formative Assessment

Substantial Support	• With help, can students learn how to find the meanings of domain-specific vocabulary? • With help, are students able to use a dictionary or context of a text to find the meaning of domain-specific vocabulary?
Moderate Support	• Can students learn how to find the meanings of domain-specific vocabulary? • Are students able to use a dictionary or context of a text to find the meaning of domain-specific vocabulary?
Light Support	• Can students independently find the meanings of domain-specific vocabulary? • Are students able to use a dictionary or context of a text independently to find the meaning of domain-specific vocabulary?

Water: Fact and Fiction

Essential Question

What does water mean to people and the societies they live in?

In this unit, students will read and compare selections about water to understand the importance of water to society.

Unit 8 Lessons at a Glance

Language Skills

Week 1
- Understand the Text Structure of Myths
- Use Similes
- Informative Process Writing
- Use Verb Tenses
- Use Comparative and Superlative Suffixes

Week 2
- Understand Problem and Solution Text Structure
- Link Events with Connecting Words
- Understand Noun and Pronoun Agreement
- Use the Language of Sequence
- Use Suffixes **-ly, -ily, -ize**

Week 3
- Condense Ideas
- Draw Inferences
- Use the Language of Cause and Effect
- Use Words with Suffixes
- Use Simple, Compound, and Complex Sentences

Lessons

Essential Question

Reading

Short Read 1

Language

Writing to Sources

Academic Writing Instruction

Reading

Short Read 2

Word Study & Vocabulary

Language

Reading

Extended Read 1

Language

Word Study & Vocabulary

Reading

Extended Read 2

Language

Word Study & Vocabulary

Language

"Essential Question" pages 156–157

Student Objectives

LANGUAGE
Purpose:
• I can understand the Essential Question.
CONTENT
• I can understand the topic of the unit.

Additional Materials
• Unit Presentation

Introduce Unit 8:
Water: Fact and Fiction

Use the short lesson below to introduce the topic of the unit and help students understand the Essential Question.

Build Background and Vocabulary

Draw students' attention to the pictures.

Say: *The topic of this unit is "Water: Fact and Fiction." These pictures introduce the ideas that we will read about.*

Create a two-column chart as shown below.

Say: *A **fact** is something that is proven to be true. Let's think of texts that give facts.*

Fill in the chart with student responses.

Say: ***Fiction** is a made-up story from the author's imagination. An author may include facts but characters and events are made up. Let's think of texts that are fictional.*

Fill in the chart with student responses.

Fact: Can Be Proved	Fiction: From an Author's Imagination
encyclopedia	stories
reference book	myths
newspapers	tall tales
atlas, maps	fairy tales

👥 Differentiated Instruction
Explain the Essential Question

Read aloud the Essential Question: *What does water mean to people and the societies they live in?*

Explain key words by definition and examples: **community, landscape, fishing, river, lake.** Encourage students to describe the pictures. Explain that there is water in a dry landscape, but living things in that place have adapted by conserving water.

Use the Differentiated Instruction to help students at all levels understand the Essential Question.

Display or invite students to access the Unit 8 video. After the video, **ask:** *How do these pictures and the video help you to answer the Essential Question?*

Then proceed to Lesson 1.

👥👥 Differentiated Instruction
Explain the Essential Question

(S)ubstantial Support

Explain the word **conserve** means "to save and protect." Point to the first two pictures.

Say: *These two places have lots of water. The trees are very green. There are boats on the water. People swim in the water. They fish in the water.*

Explain as needed. Have students repeat the sentences. Contrast these pictures with the dry landscape in last picture. Explain that plants and animals that live in this dry climate conserve water because there isn't much of a water supply.

Ask: *Why is it important to conserve water in all communities? Why?*

Help students answer.

Say: *In this unit we will learn all about the relationship between communities and water.*

(M)oderate Support

Explain the word **conserve** means "to save and protect." Point to the first two pictures.

Say: *These two places have lots of water. The trees are very green. There are boats on the water. People swim in the water. They fish in the water.*

Ask questions as needed. Have students respond. Contrast these pictures with the dry landscape in last picture. Explain that plants and animals that live in this dry climate conserve water because there isn't much of a water supply.

Ask: *Why is it important to conserve water in all communities? Why?*

Help students answer using this frame: *It is important to conserve water because _____.*

Say: *In this unit we will learn all about the relationship between communities and water.*

(L)ight Support

Explain the word **conserve** means "to save and protect." Point to the first two pictures. **Say:** *These two places have lots of water. The trees are very green. There are boats on the water. People swim in the water. They fish in the water.*

Ask questions as needed. Have students respond. Contrast these pictures with the dry landscape in last picture. Explain that plants and animals that live in this dry climate conserve water because there isn't much of a water supply. **Ask:** *In which community would you like to live? Why?*

Provide students with these sentence frames:

I would like to live in the _____ because _____.

Ask: *Why is it important to conserve water in all communities?*

Help students answer using this frame:

It is important to conserve water because _____.

Say: *In this unit we will learn all about the relationship between communities and water.*

☑ Formative Assessment

Substantial Support	• Can students give an example of why water conservation is important with support? • Can students explain the meaning of key words such as **community, river,** and **landscape** with support?
Moderate Support	• Can students give an example of why water conservation is important with a little support? • Can students explain the meaning of key words such as **community, river,** and **landscape** with a little support?
Light Support	• Can students give an example of why water conservation is important in a full sentence? • Can students explain the meaning of key words such as **community, river,** and **landscape**?

Preview or Review Week 1 ELA Mini-Lessons

"The Water Famine," page 158

Student Objectives

LANGUAGE

Purpose:
• I can recount events from a myth.

Form:
• I can understand the language of myths.

CONTENT
• I can comprehend a myth.

Additional Materials
• Unit Presentation
• *Texts for Close Reading* booklet
• Think-Speak-Listen Flip Book
• Student journal

Language Transfer Support

Students whose first language is Spanish may be familiar with the following cognates of words found in the text: *mito* (**myth**), *origen* (**origin**), *beneficios* (**benefits**), and *nectar* (**nectar**). Encourage students to look for other words that are similar to words in their first language.

1 Read "The Water Famine"

Build Background and Vocabulary

Display the image panels and explain key words and ideas from the text. If students have already read the story, ask them what they remember. Invite students to share their cultural experiences and knowledge about myths.

Read Aloud the Text

Read panel 1. To support comprehension, point out images in the pictures that match words in the story. **Say:** *The mean bullfrog forbids, or does not allow, people to get water from the river. He controls its water so people can't use it.* Repeat with panel 2. Then refer to the Essential Question. **Ask:** *What does this story tell you about the importance of water? What happened to the people who didn't have water? (They died of thirst).* Explain that the story is a myth. It is not about real events, but the river it describes is real.

Think-Speak-Listen: Use the following sentence frame or the Think-Speak-Listen Flip Book to guide discussion: *A long time ago, there was a _____. The mean Bullfrog _____. Gluskabe _____ the Monster Bullfrog. Then he _____ a birch tree. The birch tree _____. Finally, the water _____.*

👥 Differentiated Instruction
Build Language: Understand the Text Structure of Myths

Tell students that "The Water Famine" is an "origin myth," a Native American fictional story about the origin of a real river in the state of Maine. If possible, point out the river on a map. Explain that myths follow a specific text structure which often begins with a problem and explain how things came to be or teach lessons or values. Point out that other elements of myths include characters with superhuman powers and a powerful monster. **Ask:** *What is the problem in "The Water Famine?"* Use the Differentiated Instruction to practice understanding the text structure of myths in a way that matches the levels of your students.

✓ Use Oral and Written Language: Recount Events from a Myth

Task: *Pretend that you and your group are a team of news reporters who are reporting on the events from the myth. Work with your group to write complete sentences for a news report that tells what happened. Some group members can play the witnesses who are interviewed. Perform your report for the class.*

Ⓢ   *Reporter: What is the mean bullfrog doing? Witness: The bullfrog is ___ the water.*

Ⓜ   *Reporter: What is happening at the river? Witness: There is a ____ who is ____.*

Ⓛ   *Reporter: What is happening at the river? Witness: There is _____*

🔄 Wrap Up

Today we learned about the elements of myths—problems, monsters, and superhuman characters. Why do people tell myths?

Turn and Talk: *Tell your partner one element of a myth.*

👥 Differentiated Instruction
Build Language: Understand the Text Structure of Myths

Ⓢubstantial Support

Model: Display panel 1 and read the first sentence. **Say:** *Myths begin with a problem.* Write "Problem" on the board. **Say:** *I see the monster bullfrog is controlling the water. So can people get the water? What should I write for the problem?* Under "Problem," write *"People can't get water."* **Say:** *This is a problem because people need water.*

Practice: Distribute BLM 1. **Say:** *In a myth, a character with superhuman powers solves the problem. Many myths also have a powerful monster.* Work with students to match the elements of a myth to examples from the story. Encourage them to look in the story for names or phrases under "Story Details" on the BLM.

Extend: Have partners complete the Extend sentences on the BLM, looking at the matching above for the names or phrases. Then check their work.

Challenge: If students are ready, model reading aloud the sentences in the Extend activity in the BLM. Then have students repeat the sentences.

Ⓜoderate Support

Model: Display the panels. Remind students that this story is a myth. Write four elements of myths on the board: 1) a problem, 2) a character with superhuman powers, 3) a monster, 4) an origin, or an explanation of how a geographical feature was formed. **Say:** *Myths begin with a problem. Usually there is a cruel monster and a hero with powers. This myth tells an origin, or how something was created.* As you read the text aloud, remind students to think about what the problem is, who the monster and hero are, and what geographical feature is created. After reading, ask about each element and write more information next to each one. For example: **ask:** *What is the problem?* Next to *"A problem,"* write *"People can't get water."*

Practice: Distribute BLM 2. Help students complete the Practice chart with the information you discussed.

Extend: Ask partners to complete the Extend sentences using the information in the chart and in the story. Then check their work.

Challenge: If students are ready, have them identify words from the story that state the problem.

Ⓛight Support

Use the text on pages 4–5 in the *Texts for Close Reading* to complete the following activities.

Practice: Say: *Let's review the text structure of a myth by writing a list.* As a group, generate a list that contains these items: 1) a problem, 2) a character with superhuman powers, 3) a monster, 4) an origin or explanation of how a geographical feature was formed.

Extend: Have partners read "The Water Famine" and write the elements of the myth that they find in the story. Ask students to explain how recognizing the text structure of a myth helps them understand its purpose.

Challenge: If students are ready, ask them to write a few sentences to answer the following question: *What is the purpose or function of this myth in Native American culture?*

☑ Formative Assessment

Substantial Support	• Do students understand the structure of myths? • With support, can students match a general description of the structure of a myth to the structure of the myth they read?
Moderate Support	• Can students locate four examples of characteristics of myths in a text? • Can students complete sentences explaining story details that are characteristic of myths?
Light Support	• Do students understand the distinctive functions and structure of myths? • Can students identify and write about details in a story that is characteristic of a myth?

Preview or Review Week 1 ELA Mini-Lessons

"Use Similes," page 159

Student Objectives

LANGUAGE

Purpose:
• I can make comparison game cards.

Form:
• I can recognize and use similes.

CONTENT
• I can analyze similes in a myth.

Additional Materials

• Unit Presentation
• *Texts for Close Reading* booklet
• Think-Speak-Listen Flip Book
• Student journal
• Index cards

Language Transfer Support

English Learners may need additional support with recognizing and using English similes. The use of **like** or **as** can be confusing since it does not always signal a simile, as in *I like red apples* or *the test was not as hard as I thought it would be*. Encourage students to share common similes used in their first languages, such as these in Spanish: *claro como el agua* ("as clear as water") and *hablar como un loro* ("to talk on and on like a parrot").

---

2 Use Similes

Engage Thinking

Display the chart. **Say:** *We will talk about similes, or comparisons, from the myth.* Read aloud both similes, pointing to each image. Explain that these similes from the myth and these images will help us understand ideas more clearly and vividly.

Turn and Talk: *How do vivid descriptions help us picture characters, places, or actions?*

Read and View Closely: Recognize Similes

Say: *The author of the myth uses similes to compare two unlike things. A simile uses the words* as *or* like *to make comparisons.* Explain that the chart lists two similes from the myth. Point out that both similes use the word *as.* Ask students to find *as* in each simile. Explain the key words: *parched* and *brush; nectar.* Point out that the first simile uses *as* to compare dry throats to dry brush, or grass. Read aloud the second row. **Say:** *The phrase "as fast as" tells me this is a simile. A bee takes nectar from a flower quickly, so the author is comparing Gluskabe's speed to a bee.*

👥 Differentiated Instruction
Build Language: Use Similes

Write two new similes on the board, circling *as* and *like*: for example, *His eyes are as blue as the sky. The clouds are fluffy like cotton balls.* **Say:** *Some cultures, such as the Native Americans, use words about things found in nature to describe ideas.* Have students identify the words about things found in nature, and then have them point out what is being compared. **Ask:** *How do these comparisons of things found in nature with something else help you understand what is described?* Invite responses. **Ask:** *Why might some cultures use comparisons with things found in nature to describe characters and actions?* Invite responses. Use the Differentiated Instruction to practice using similes in a way that best matches the levels of your students.

Think-Speak-Listen: Use this sentence frame or the Think-Speak-Listen Flip Book to guide discussion: *Similes in this legend, or myth, use things found in nature because ___.*

☑ Use Oral and Written Language: Make Comparison Game Cards

Task: *With a small group, play a game. Write four adjectives on cards: small, tall, fast, slow. List items under each one: for example, write "snail" below "slow." Pick a card and make a comparison using the word on the card. Use the sentence frames to speak in complete sentences and write your sentence.* Use this opportunity to assess students using the rubric in *English Language Development Assessment.*

Ⓢ The _____ is as slow as a snail _____.

Ⓜ The _____ (is) as _____ as _____.

Ⓛ The _____ is like _____. It is as _____.

🔄 Wrap Up

Today we talked about similes. How does using similes help writers?

Turn and Talk: *Describe something in your school using a simile.*

👥👥👥 Differentiated Instruction
Build Language: Use Similes

Ⓢubstantial Support

Model: Display the chart. Point to the words and image as fast as in the second row. Write: _____ *is as fast as* _____. Model filling in the blanks, for example with *My cat , tiger.* **Say:** *This is a simile. It compares two things. What is it comparing? (my cat, a tiger). We can also write a simile another way.* Write: *My cat is like a tiger.* Explain that *as* and *like* can be used to make similes. Ask students to read the second row in the chart. Discuss that the author is comparing Gluskabe's speed to the speed of a bee taking nectar from a flower. Then read the first row. **Say:** *This smile compares people's dry throats to brush, or grass. Similes often compare things that are not usually alike.*

Practice: Distribute BLM 1. Discuss the words *clear* and *thunder*, explaining the meaning if necessary. Then guide students to use one of those two words to complete each simile and identify what is being compared.

Extend: Ask partners to read aloud the similes on the BLM. Then have them replace the word *glass* with *a window* in the first and last similes. Discuss what they are comparing in each.

Challenge: Have students help you rewrite the sentence "The Monster Bullfrog was big." as a simile.

Ⓛight Support

Use the text on pages 4–5 in the *Texts for Close Reading* to complete the following activities.

Practice: Have volunteers read each row aloud and explain what is being compared in each simile. **Say:** *Comparing the people's throats to parched summer brush and Gluskabe's movement to that of a bee makes the descriptions more vivid. The images would not have been as vivid if the author had written, "The people's throats were dry," and "Gluskabe quickly cut down the tree."* Write *dry* and *fast* on the board. As a group, brainstorm additional similes for these adjectives using *like* or *as*.

Extend: Have partners compose original sentences using the list of similes they brainstormed. Ask them to underline the two things being compared in each new simile.

Challenge: Ask students to list other adjectives and try to write additional similes.

Ⓜoderate Support

Model: Display the chart. Have volunteers read aloud the similes. Discuss what is compared in each. Have students locate the word *as* and point out how the similes are constructed, with *as* on both sides of the adjectives *dry and parched/ fast.* Then write: *The Monster Bullfrog was big.* and *Gluskabe was angry.* Underline the adjectives *big* and *angry.* Model rewriting these sentences using similes to make the underlined adjectives more vivid: *The Monster Bullfrog was as big as* _____. *Gluskabe was as angry as* _____.

Practice: Distribute BLM 2. Guide students to complete the sentences. Discuss the possible answers for each one.

Extend: Write: *The river was fast.* Have students rewrite it to include a simile. Ask them to identify the words that make up the simile and the two things being compared in the new sentence you created together. Then have partners complete the Extend activity on the BLM and read their new sentences aloud.

Challenge: If students are ready, guide them to brainstorm additional similes for the adjectives *dry* and *fast.*

☑	**Formative Assessment**
Substantial Support	• With help, can students recognize similes and the things being compared in them? • Can students select appropriate words to complete sentence frames that contain similes?
Moderate Support	• Can students select appropriate words or phrases to form similes to complete sentence frames? • Can students write their own similes, given adjectives to use?
Light Support	• Can students generate similes from adjectives? • Can students write original sentences using similes they created?

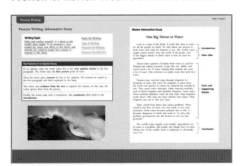

"Process Writing," pages 160–161

Student Objectives

LANGUAGE
Purpose:
- I can analyze an informative essay.

Form:
- I can identify the parts of an informative essay.

CONTENT
- I can recognize an informative essay.

Additional Materials
- Unit Presentation
- *Texts for Close Reading* booklet
- Think-Speak-Listen Flip Book
- Student journal

Language Transfer Support

Note that speakers of Hmong may need extra support with the idea of coordinating conjunctions. Their native language uses two or more main verbs in a sentence without any connection. In other words, they do not connect main verbs with conjunctions or punctuation.

3 Process Writing: Informative Essay

Engage Thinking

Tell students that they will analyze an informative essay so that they can recognize its features. Read aloud the writing topic.

> Select and conduct research on a threat to the world's water supply. In an informative essay, explain the causes and effects of this threat, and describe the solutions people have created to respond to this threat.

Say: *Let's ask questions to make sure we understand the writing topic. What will the writer write about? What type of writing is it? Where will the writer get the information?*

👥👥 Differentiated Instruction

Read and View Closely: Analyze an Informative Essay

Say: *As I read aloud the essay, I will stop to pause so that we can analyze it. In the introduction, does the writer present a main idea and develop it with facts? Listen as I read.* Read the opening paragraph and pause. **Say:** *Turn to a partner and talk about what the main idea is.* Check that students can identify the main idea that agriculture is the biggest threat to water. Check that students can summarize how the writer developed the idea.

Continue to read the second paragraph. **Say:** *An informative essay includes facts. Turn to your partner. How much of Earth's fresh water is used for farming and livestock?* Check that students identify three-quarters of Earth's fresh water. **Say:** *Turn to your partner and discuss what the main idea of this paragraph is. What solution does the writer offer?* After students have discussed the questions, invite volunteers to share their answers with the class.

Continue in the same way with the remaining paragraphs. Help students to understand unfamiliar vocabulary as needed.

Finish reading the report. **Say:** *The writer ends the report with a conclusion. How does the conclusion connect back to the opening statement?* Have partners compare the introduction and conclusion and share their ideas with the class.

Finally, call attention to the overall structure and organization of the report by asking students to identify which paragraphs comprise the introduction, body, and conclusion.

Then continue the lesson using Differentiated Instruction that best fits the needs of your students.

Share Your Understanding

Bring the students back together. **Ask:** *What did we learn today about an informative essay?* Review the features as needed.

✓ Final Writing Assignment

Use the English Language Development Assessment to assess students' writing for their ELA writing assignment.

👥👥 Differentiated Instruction

Read and View Closely: Analyze an Informative Essay

Ⓢubstantial Support

Model: Distribute BLM 1. **Say:** *Let's read and analyze another informative essay that addresses the writing topic.* Read the first paragraph and pause. **Ask:** *What is the main idea in this introduction?* (Agriculture is a big threat to the world's fresh water supply.) Point out that the text detail *It is hard for the world's water supply to meet the needs of all people* supports the main idea in the introduction. **Ask:** *What is the main idea of the essay?* Model reading and analyzing the informative essay features

Practice: Continue reading the essay and ask students to identify the main idea and supporting detail in each paragraph. **Ask:** *What is the main idea of the essay?*

Extend: Have partners complete the Extend activity on BLM 1.

Challenge: Ask *yes/no* questions to guide the students to identify and describe the features of the informative essay. **Ask:** *Does the report have a strong introduction? Does the report include facts and details to support the ideas? Is there a concluding statement? Does it relate to the introduction?* Guide students elaborate on their answers by giving evidence from the text.

Ⓛight Support

Practice: Distribute BLM 2. **Say:** *This is another Mentor Text. We will look more closely at how writers make sure that they address the writing topic and structure a report.* Read the essay aloud, modeling the features of the informative essay.

Extend: Have partners complete the activity on BLM 2. Then check their work.

Challenge: Have students take turns summarizing the essay to their partner. For each paragraph they should mention the cause, the effect, and the solution.

Ⓜoderate Support

Model: Review the Mentor Informative Essay with students. **Say:** *Let's analyze how the writer responds to the writing topic. First, what is the threat to the world's water supply?* Elicit the example of "agriculture."

Practice: Write the chart below on the board. Work with students to identify and describe the three causes of this threat found in the body of the essay. List them on the board:

Agricultural Threats to Water	Effects of Threats	Solutions
1. crops and livestock	use huge amounts of water	Develop crops that use less water.
2. irrigation methods		
3. runoff due to agriculture		

Model how to complete the row. **Say:** *The effect of growing crops and raising livestock is "using huge amounts of water."* Write this on the chart. Then show that the solution is *developing crops that use less water*.

Extend: Have partners complete the rest of the chart. Have them share their charts with the class when they are finished.

Challenge: Have partners discuss how the author organized the information in the essay. For example: *In paragraph two/three/four, _____ causes _____. The effect is _____. The solution is _____.*

☑ Formative Assessment

Substantial Support	• Do students recognize the criteria for an informative essay in the Mentor Informative Essay?
Moderate Support	• Do students recognize the ways in which the Mentor Informative Essay meets the criteria for an informative essay? • Can students describe the features of an informative essay in their own words?
Light Support	• Do students recognize criteria and analyze how the Mentor Text meets the criteria for an informative essay? • Can students describe in their own words how the writer meets the criteria for an informative essay?

Extend and Scaffold Academic Language for Writing
Analyze the Mentor Text: Language Purpose and Structure

Introduction
All Levels of Support

Materials List
- **Mentor Text L** BLM X Light Support
- **Writing Frames Teacher Page** BLM Y
- **Writing Frames Student Page** BLM Z

- Have a copy of BLM Y to refer to during the lesson.

- Distribute BLMs X and Z to each student.

- Read aloud the writing topic on BLM X. Explain that students will read and analyze the language one writer used to respond to this topic.

- Have students follow along as you read aloud paragraph 1 of "One Big Threat to Water."

- Point out the phrase *Yet only about one percent of all that water is fresh and ready for human use* and the words that indicate the writing frame in bold. **Ask:** *Why did the author use this language? What is its purpose?* Help students understand that the author uses the structure _____ *percent of* _____ to add a fact to the text.

- Have students write this frame into the "Add Details/Facts" row of their Writing Frames worksheet (BLM Z). Tell students this is one writing frame they can use in their writing to add a fact to the text.

- Analyze other bolded phrases in paragraph 1. Explain their purpose and help students add the writing frames to BLM Z.

- Follow these steps as you read additional paragraphs.

- Read aloud the writing topic on BLM Z. Work with students to generate additional writing frames they could use as they write a response to this topic. Refer to BLM Y for examples.

> **Based on students' needs, conduct additional lessons using the differentiated instruction and tools provided.**

Light Support
Differentiated Instruction

Materials List
- **Mentor Text L** BLM X Light Support
- **Writing Frames Teacher Page** BLM Y
- **Writing Frames Student Page** BLM Z

Students will need their copies of BLMs X and Z from the initial lesson. Refer to the chart below and your copy of BLM Y during the lesson.

- Explain that students will reread "One Big Threat to Water" to analyze more phrases and sentences that the writer used.

- Reread the text with students one paragraph at a time.

- Ask individuals or partners to find and underline each phrase in the chart below, read the sentence it appears in, and try to determine the sentence's purpose in the text.

- Provide explanation as necessary, then have students add the writing frames to the "Other Academic Phrases and Sentences" column of BLM Z.

- Encourage students to generate related writing frames and add them to their chart.

LIGHT SUPPORT		
Purpose	**Phrase/Sentence (paragraph)**	**Frame**
Cause and Effect	Because of this limited amount of fresh water, there is... (1)	Because of _____, there is _____.
Explain	Most of the water used in farming goes toward watering crops... (3)	Most of _____ _____, or _____.
Add Details/ Facts	In addition, watering methods such as flood irrigation and... (3)	In addition, _____ such as _____ and _____ often _____.
Cause and Effect	Agricultural use of water also causes problems due to runoff. (4)	_____ causes _____ due to _____.
Cause and Effect	As a result of this runoff, fresh water becomes polluted. (4)	As a result of _____, _____ becomes _____.

(M)oderate Support

 **Differentiated Instruction**

Materials List
- **Mentor Text M** BLM A Moderate Support
- **Writing Frames Teacher Page** BLM Y
- **Writing Frames Student Page** BLM Z

Use the mentor text (BLM A) and the phrases and sentences appropriate for the support level you are targeting.

- Distribute BLM A. Students will also need their copy of BLM Z.

- Read aloud BLM A as students follow along.

- Then reread the text one paragraph at a time, stopping after each paragraph to focus on the bolded and underlined content. Work with students to understand the purpose of each phrase within the text. Have students write the corresponding writing frame in the "Other Academic Phrases and Sentences" column of BLM Z.

- Have partners practice using one or more of these writing frames to expand an idea in the essay they are writing. Have students share their examples with other members of the group.

MODERATE SUPPORT

Purpose	Phrase/Sentence (paragraph)	Frame
Problem/ Solution	One of the biggest threats to fresh water... (1)	One of the biggest threats to _____ is _____.
Add Details/ Facts	Almost three quarters of Earth's fresh water is... (2)	Almost _____ quarters of _____ is _____.
Cause and Effect	This causes water shortages. (3)	_____ causes _____.
Cause and Effect	Fresh water becomes polluted due to this. (4)	_____ becomes _____ due to _____.
Problem/ Solution	To solve this problem, governments can ask farmers to not... (4)	To solve this problem _____ can _____ to _____.

(S)ubstantial Support

 **Differentiated Instruction**

Materials List
- **Mentor Text S** BLM B Substantial Support
- **Writing Frames Teacher Page** BLM Y
- **Writing Frames Student Page** BLM Z

Students will need their copy of BLM Z from the initial lesson.

- Distribute BLM B.

- Follow the procedure explained in the Moderate Support lesson.

SUBSTANTIAL SUPPORT

Purpose	Phrase/Sentence (paragraph)	Frame
Problem/ Solution	One of the biggest threats to fresh water... (1)	One of the biggest threats to _____ is _____.
Add Details/ Facts	Also, raising farm animals uses a lot... (2)	Also, _____ uses _____.
Problem/ Solution	One solution is to grow crops that use less water. (2)	One solution is to _____ that _____.
Cause and Effect	Water runoff causes problems, too. (4)	_____ causes _____.
Cause and Effect	Fresh water is polluted because of this. (4)	_____ is _____ because of _____.

Preview or Review Week 1 ELA Mini-Lessons

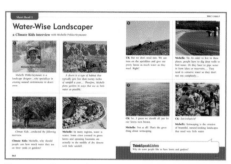

"Water-Wise Landscaper," pages 162–163

Student Objectives

LANGUAGE

Purpose:
- I can summarize information for a news article.

Form:
- I can use verb tenses.

CONTENT
- I can understand information presented in an interview.

Additional Materials
- Unit Presentation
- Verb Tense Chart
- *Texts for Close Reading* booklet
- Think-Speak-Listen Flip Book
- Student journal

Language Transfer Support

Students whose first language is Spanish may be familiar with the following cognates of words found in the text: *natural (natural), desierto (desert), importante (important), posible (possible), clima (climate), region (region), vegetal (vegetable), fruta (fruit), horticultura (horticulture), responsable (responsible),* and *inspiracion (inspiration).* Encourage students to look for other words that are similar to words in their first language.

4 Read "Water-Wise Landscaper"

Build Background and Vocabulary

Display the image panels and explain key words and ideas from the text. If students have already read the text, ask them what they remember. Invite students to share their experiences and knowledge about deserts.

Read Aloud the Text

Read panels 1 and 2. To support comprehension, ask students to find images in the picture that match words in the text. **Say:** *An interview is a text in which one person asks questions and another person answers them.* **Ask:** *What job does Michelle have? What is different about deserts?* Read panels 3 and 4. **Ask:** *Why does Michelle plant gardens that use as little water as possible?* Model thinking through the answer. **Say:** *Michelle works in desert areas that don't get much rainfall. She plans gardens that don't need much water to survive.* Repeat with panels 5–8. Then refer to the Essential Question. Invite students to discuss the role of water in Michelle's work.

Think-Speak-Listen: Use the following sentence frame or the Think-Speak-Listen Flip Book to guide discussion: *People like to have lawns and gardens because _____.*

👤👤👤 Differentiated Instruction
Build Language: Use Verb Tenses

Display the first sentence in panel 4: *In many regions, water is scarce.* Point to the verb *is* and **say**: *This verb is in the present tense. We are talking about something that is happening right now, in the present.* Remind students that verb tenses express time. Explain that most English verbs change their form to show present, past, and future. Display the Verb Tense Chart to review tenses. Use the Differentiated Instruction to practice using verb tenses in a way that best matches the levels of your students.

✔️ Use Oral and Written Language: Summarize Information for a New Article

Task: *In your group, pretend that you are writing a newspaper article about water-wise landscaper Michelle. Write sentences about Michelle and her work. Use verbs in the present, past, or future tenses. Share your sentences with the group.*

(S) *Climate Kids (past) _____ an interview with Michelle. She (present) _____ gardens in ways that use very little water. She hopes people will (future) _____.*

(M) *Climate Kids _____. Michelle _____ landscapes that _____. She hopes _____.*

(L) *Climate Kids _____. Michelle _____. She helps people _____. In the future, Michelle hopes _____.*

🔄 Wrap Up

Today we talked about verb tenses. Why is it important to use verb tenses correctly in a text?

Turn and Talk: *Describe a couple of ways you conserve water now, and what you might do in the future to save water. Use correct verb tenses.*

👥 Differentiated Instruction
Build Language: Use Verb Tenses

Ⓢubstantial Support

Model: Display the Verb Tense Chart. **Say:** *Verbs are words that describe actions or states of being.* Review that verbs have different forms, or tenses, that tell when an action takes place. Read the first sentence on the chart: *I plant beans in my garden.* Then ask a volunteer to read the sentence in the past tense: *I planted beans in my garden.* Remind students of the -*ed* ending for regular verbs in the past. Explain that irregular verbs have different forms in the past and do not have -*ed*.

Have students look at panels 1–4. Point out the present tense verbs: *is, plans, uses.* Then ask them to find a past tense verb with an -*ed* in panel 3 (*conducted*)

Practice: Distribute BLM 1. Work with students to write the past tense form of each verb that follows the sentence.

Extend: Have partners complete the Extend activity. Check their work, and then have them read the sentences aloud.

Challenge: If students are ready, work with them to write new sentences using the verbs in the Verb Tense Chart.

Ⓜoderate Support

Model: Display the panels. Read aloud the first sentence in panel 4. Explain that a writer might use the past, present, or future tense. Discuss when the action in this sentence is happening and how you know. Display the Verb Tense Chart. Ask volunteers to read the sentences in each of the charts. Remind students of the -*ed* ending on regular verbs in the past tense. Have students look at panels 1–4 and find verbs such as *care, use ,*and *plan.* Ask them to tell you what those verbs would be in the past. Point out *is* and *are*, and explain that they are irregular, and do not have -ed for the past tense.

Practice: Distribute BLM 2. Work with students to complete the Practice activity. **Ask:** *What are the verbs in this sentence? How do you know? Does the action take place in the past, present, or future?*

Extend: Have partners complete the Extend activity. **Ask:** *Why is it helpful to use different tenses when you write?*

Challenge: If students are ready, ask partners to write new sentences about the topic, using verbs to convey past, present, and future tense.

Ⓛight Support

Use the text on pages 6–9 in the *Texts for Close Reading* to complete the following activities.

Practice: Have students read paragraphs 1–12 to identify verbs. Work with them to identify if the verbs are in the present, past, or future tense.

Extend: Have partners read paragraphs 13–29. Ask partners to compose new sentences about the topic, using verbs to convey past, present, and future tense. Tell them to use the verbs from the text or other verbs they know. Have them read aloud their sentences with another set of partners.

Challenge: Ask partners to find examples of present and past tense verbs in "Water-Wise Landscaper." Have them write the other tenses of the verbs they find.

☑ Formative Assessment

Substantial Support	• Do students understand the purpose of verb tenses? • Can students form simple sentences with regular past tense verbs?
Moderate Support	• Can students identify verbs and verb tenses? • Can students form sentences with verb tenses using frames?
Light Support	• Can students recognize present, past and future verb tenses? • Can students generate original sentences using present, past, and future verb tenses?

Preview or Review Week 1 Mini-Lessons

"Pecos Bill and the Tornado," page 164

Student Objectives

LANGUAGE

Purpose:
- I can explore words that compare.

Form:
- I can use comparative and superlative suffixes.

CONTENT
- I can analyze tall tales.

Additional Materials
- Unit Presentation
- *Texts for Close Reading* booklet
- Think-Speak-Listen Flip Book
- Student journal

Language Transfer Support

Note that speakers of Hmong, Korean, or Spanish may need additional support as they explore adjectives that have comparative and superlative suffixes. Rather than using word suffixes to show comparative and superlative forms, these languages use separates words that are the equivalents of *more* and *most* in English.

5 Read "Pecos Bill and the Tornado"

Build Background and Vocabulary

Display the image panels and explain key vocabulary and ideas in the text. If students have already read the story, ask them what they remember. Invite students to share their cultural experiences and knowledge with living in dry climates.

Read Aloud the Text

Read panel 1. **Say:** *This story is a tall tale, which is like a myth.* Remind students that in a myth, a problem must be solved and has a character with superhuman powers. Read panels 2 and 3. **Ask:** *Why does Pecos Bill decide to ride the tornado?* Model thinking through the answer. **Say:** *Pecos Bill wants to save the West from drought. So he rides the tornado and squeezes water from it to make it rain.* Then refer to the Essential Question. Invite students to discuss the role that water plays in this tall tale.

Think-Speak-Listen: Use the following sentence frames or the Think-Speak-Listen Flip Book to guide discussion: *The stories are similar because Gluskabe and Pecos Bill _____. The stories are different because Gluskabe _____, but Pecos Bill _____.*

👥 Differentiated Instruction
Build Language: Use Comparative and Superlative Suffixes

Reread the first sentence. Write *roughest* and *toughest* on the board. Underline rough and tough, and circle the suffixes. Write *rougher* and *tougher*, underline the base words, and circle the -er suffixes. **Say:** *The word* tough *in this story means strong. The -est ending shows a comparison that means "most of all." Pecos Bill is the toughest of all the cowboys. We use words with -est when three or more things are being compared. The ending -er also shows a comparison. We use words with -er when two things are being compared.* Work with students to write an example using this sentence frame: *Pecos Bill is _____ than _____.* Use the Differentiated Instruction to practice using comparative and superlative suffixes in a way that best matches the levels of your students.

✓ Use Oral and Written Language: Explore Words That Compare

Task: *Work in small groups to add -er and -est endings to words to describe Pecos Bill. Then use these words and frames to tell how Pecos Bill was different from other cowboys.*

(S) *No one was _____ than Pecos Bill. He was the _____ man in the West.*

(M) *Pecos Bill could ride _____ than other cowboys. He rode the _____.*

(L) *Everyone knew Pecos Bill was _____ than _____. He _____.*

🔄 Wrap Up

Today we learned about using comparative and superlative words. Why is it important to use comparative and superlative words correctly in a story?

Turn and Talk: *Use words that compare to describe a character in a book you read recently.*

👥 Differentiated Instruction
Build Language: Use Comparative and Superlative Suffixes

Ⓢubstantial Support

Model: Read panel 1. **Say:** *The word toughest describes Pecos Bill.* Write the word *toughest* and circle the *-est* suffix. **Say:** *We use comparative and superlative suffixes to compare two or more things. In* toughest*, I see the ending -est. -Est is a superlative. It compares Pecos Bill to many other cowboys.* Ask a volunteer to read the first sentence. Then write the word *tougher* and circle the *-er* suffix. **Say:** *-Er is a comparative. It compares two things. Pecos Bill was tougher than cowboy Joe.*

Practice: Read panel 2. **Say:** *The tornado was ferocious, or very wild. Let's use the comparative and superlative forms of* wild *to compare tornadoes.* As a group, write sentences that use the comparative and superlative forms of *wild*. Provide these sentence frames: *The tornado was _____ than the tornado from the year before. The tornado was the _____ tornado of all time.* Have students add *-er* or *-est* to form the comparative or superlative forms of *wild*.

Extend: Distribute BLM 1. Have partners complete the sentences together.

Challenge: Have students choose one of the words from the BLM and write a new comparison in an original sentence.

Ⓛight Support

Use the text on page 10 in the *Texts for Close Reading* to complete the following activities.

Practice: Review comparatives and superlatives. Point out the superlatives *roughest* and *toughest* in paragraph 1. Then have partners read paragraph 3 and identify three comparatives or superlatives. For each word, ask them to identify what things are being compared and to tell the meaning of the comparative or superlative.

Extend: Have partners create comparatives and superlatives for the words *smart* and *loud*. Then ask them to generate original sentences about the story of Pecos Bill using the *-er* and *-est* forms of the words.

Challenge: If students are ready, explain that the words *more* or *most* usually come before words of two or more syllables: for example, *more powerful* or *most fatal*. Have students generate original sentences about Pecos Bill that use the phrases *more ferocious* and *most terrible*.

Ⓜoderate Support

Model: Read panel 1. **Say:** *The words roughest and toughest compare Pecos Bill to all the other cowboys.* Write the words roughest and toughest and ask a volunteer to circle the suffix -est. **Say:** *Rough and tough are adjectives. Roughest and toughest are superlative forms of those words. They compare three or more things.* Ask a volunteer to read aloud the first sentence again. **Say:** *Pecos Bill is being compared to many other cowboys.* Write rougher and tougher and have volunteers circle the suffixes. **Say:** *These are comparatives. They compare two things. They end with the suffix -er. Using comparatives and superlatives helps us compare things and people.*

Practice: Work with students to use the words rougher and tougher in a sentence that compares Pecos Bill to another cowboy.

Extend: Distribute BLM 2. Have partners complete the activity together.

Challenge: Have students work together to write new sentences using three of the comparatives or superlatives they wrote.

✔️ Formative Assessment

Substantial Support	• Do students understand that *-er* and *-est* suffixes show comparisons? • Can students use sentence frames to explore words with comparative and superlatives suffixes?
Moderate Support	• Can students use the suffixes *-er* and *-est* to form comparatives and superlatives? • Can students generate original sentences using comparatives and superlatives??
Light Support	• Can students distinguish between comparative and superlative forms of words? • Can students generate original sentences using words with comparative and superlative suffixes?

"Understand Problem and Solution
Text Structure," page 165

Student Objectives

LANGUAGE
Purpose:
• I can write a proposal.
Form:
• I can recognize problems and solutions.
CONTENT
• I can understand problem and solution text structure in fictional and nonfiction texts.

Additional Materials
• Unit Presentation
• *Texts for Close Reading* booklet
• Think-Speak-Listen Flip Book
• Student journal

Language Transfer Support

Note that the words *problem* and *solution* have cognates in several languages. These include Filipino (*problema/solusyon*), French (*problème/solution*), German (*Problem*), Haitian Creole (*pwoblém/ solisyon*), Italian (*problema/soluzione*), Russian (*problema*), and Spanish (*problema/solución*). Encourage students to scan the chart to find other words that are similar to words in their first language.

6 Understand Problem and Solution Text Structure

Engage Thinking

Display the image panels from "Pecos Bill and the Tornado." Recount the story about Pecos Bill. **Ask:** *What does the text tell us about the problem in this story? How does the image help you to understand the problem?* **Say:** *The text gives us information about a terrible drought. The image shows dry land and dehydrated livestock from lack of rain.*

Turn and Talk: *What does the text say about who might help solve the problem?*

Read and View Closely: Recognize Problems and Solutions

Display the Understand Problem and Solution chart, and point out the column headings. Explain that every story in this unit has a problem. Have a volunteer read the first problem. **Say:** *What is the problem?* Remind them that *forbade* means "did not let." Have another student read the solution. **Say:** *A solution means how the problem is fixed. The people asked for help.* Recall the story with students. **Say:** *How did asking for help solve their problem?* Words like *help* *can be a clue to recognize problems and solutions. Other clues are the words* problem, figure out, in order to, fix, solve, *and* as a result.

Think-Speak-Listen: Use the following frame or the Think-Speak-Listen Flip Book to guide discussion: *Pecos Bill could have solved the drought by _____ or by _____.*

👥 Differentiated Instruction
Build Language: Understand Problem and Solution Text Structure

Have a volunteer read the second problem on the chart. Review the meaning of the word *scarce*. Ask students to explain the problem. Have another student read the solution. Continue with the third problem and solution. Use the Differentiated Instruction to practice understanding problem and solution text structure in a way that best matches the levels of your students.

☑ Use Oral and Written Language: Write a Proposal

Task: *Work in small groups. Imagine that the people in "The Water Famine" have asked you to solve their problem. Write a proposal that describes three solutions. Present your proposal to another group and have them select one solution.*

(S) *We can _____. Then we will _____. This will _____.*

(M) *First, we will _____. This will _____ because _____.*

(L) *After we _____, we will _____ and _____. The result will be _____.*

🎯 Wrap Up

Today we learned about understanding problem and solution text structure. How can words that signal problem and solution help us understand the events in a text or story?

Turn and Talk: *Describe a problem a character or a real person in a text or story you have read. How was the problem solved? Do you think this was the best solution?*

👥👥 Differentiated Instruction
Build Language: Understand Problem and Solution Text Structure

Ⓢubstantial Support

Model: Display the chart. Read aloud the problem and solution for "Pecos Bill and the Tornado." **Say:** *First, what is the problem?* Review what a drought is. **Say:** *The word* terrible *tells me this problem is bad. What is the solution?* Read aloud the solution. Check that students know the meaning of *tornado*. As you read, gesture squeezing water. Ask students to join you in demonstrating squeezing out water from the tornado. **Say:** *This is a tall tale, not a realistic story. He was able to make it rain by squeezing water from the storm!*

Practice: Invite students to help you label the problem and solution from "The Water Famine." Write: *Monster Frog forbade people from using water. Some people died. The people called Spirit Chief Gluskabe.* **Ask:** *Which sentences describe the problem? Which sentence describes the solution?*

Extend: Have partners show the problems and solution in "The Water Famine" by dividing a paper into two parts and writing "Problem" on one and "Solution" on the other. Have them copy the sentences you wrote in the Practice activity in the appropriate columns. Then have them read the sentences aloud.

Challenge: If students are ready, work with them to identify problem and solution sentences from the "Water-Wise Landscaper" row in the chart. Have them write the sentences in either the "Problem" or the "Solution" column.

Ⓛight Support

Use the text on pages 6–9 in the *Texts for Close Reading* to complete the following activities.

Practice: Distribute BLM 2. Then have students work in partners to read paragraph 4. Have them complete the Practice activity.

Extend: Have partners use paragraphs 16, 17, and 18 to complete the Extend activity and identify problems and solutions. Have them read their sentences aloud.

Challenge: If students are ready, have them complete the Challenge activity on the BLM. Remind them to speak in complete sentences.

Ⓜoderate Support

Model: Remind students of problem and solution text structure. Display the chart. Have a volunteer read the problem for "Water-Wise Landscaper." **Say:** *First, I read that water is scarce because of little rainfall. What does it mean that water is scarce? (there's very little). How are people also causing the problem? (by making green lawns and fountains which use water).* Ask a volunteer to read the solution and explain it in his or her own words.

Practice: Distribute BLM 1. Work with students to complete the Practice activity.

Extend: Have partners complete the Extend activity. Provide support if needed. Check their work. Then have them read aloud their sentences.

Challenge: Have partners read the text and images from "Water-Wise Landscaper" to help them identify more details to answer the Challenge question on the BLM. Encourage them to think about how the solution might solve more than one problem.

☑ Formative Assessment

Substantial Support	• With support, can students recognize a problem and a solution in a story or text? • With support, can students use words and phrases as clues to understand a problem and its solution? • With support, can students ask questions to help them understand the structure of problem and solution in text?
Moderate Support	• Can students recognize a problem and solution in a story or text? • Can students ask questions to understand a problem, including who has the problem, what causes it, and how it can be solved?
Light Support	• Can students recognize a problem and one or more solutions in a story or text? • Can students use questions and answers to understand problem and solution text structure? • Can students understand that a possible solution may lead to another problem and the need for a new solution?

"The Pagoda on the Hill of Imperial Springs," pages 166–167

Student Objectives

LANGUAGE

Purpose:
• I can illustrate a storyboard.

Form:
• I can recognize connecting words that link events.

CONTENT
• I can analyze events in a legend.

Additional Materials
• Unit Presentation
• *Texts for Close Reading* booklet
• Think-Speak-Listen Flip Book
• Student journal

Language Transfer Support

Note that speakers of Chinese, Farsi, or Vietnamese may need additional support when creating sentences with conjunctions. Unlike in English, conjunctions often occur in pairs in those languages. For example, a student may say, *Although, I am hungry, but I do not want to eat.*

7 Read "The Pagoda on the Hill of Imperial Springs"

Build Background and Vocabulary

Display the image panels and explain key words and ideas from the text. If students have read the story, invite them to share what they remember. Invite students to share their experiences or knowledge about dragons in Chinese myths.

Read Aloud the Text

Read panels 1 and 2. To support comprehension, help students identify the characters and the dragons in the text and images. In panels 2–4, clarify that the old man and woman are the dragons, transformed. **Ask:** *What caused the scarcity of water?* Model thinking through the answer: *Panel 2 tells about the scarcity of water.* Scarcity *means there is very little water. I find out that workmen broke into a dragon's cave. This made the dragons angry. So, they made a plan.* Then refer to the Essential Question. **Ask:** *How is the water problem in this story similar to the problem in other stories?* Elicit responses. **Say:** *This story is based on a real person, but it has talking dragons as characters.*

Think-Speak-Listen: Work with students to recount the events in panels 1–4. Use these frames or the Think-Speak-Listen Flip Book to guide discussion: *First, _____. Then, _____. Finally, _____.*

👥 Differentiated Instruction
Build Language: Link Events with Connecting Words

Write connecting words **firstly**, **secondly**, and **finally** on the board. **Say:** *Writers use certain words to show a reader how events in a story are connected.* Point out the second sentence in panel 1. **Say:** *The word* when *connects two events. It shows that both events happened at the same time.* Use the Differentiated Instruction to practice linking events with connecting words in a way that best matches the levels of your students.

☑ Use Oral and Written Language: Illustrate a Storyboard

Task: *With your partner, create and illustrate a storyboard that shows how two events are linked. First, draw one or two pictures to show the events. Then, write a sentence with a connecting word that links the events in sequence and tells what happened. Share your storyboard with your group.*

Ⓢ *The dragons _____. _____ they appeared _____.*

Ⓜ *The dragons _____ they appeared _____.*

Ⓛ *_____ the dragons _____, they _____.*

Wrap Up

Today we learned that connecting words can be used to link story events. How do connecting words help you to understand what happened in a story?

Turn and Talk: *Use connecting words to describe the sequence of events in an action story you have recently read.*

👥👥 Differentiated Instruction
Build Language: Link Events with Connecting Words

Ⓢubstantial Support

Model: Review connecting words with students. **Say:** *Connecting words can be used to link two events in a story.* Write: *There was no water,* and *the people were alarmed.* Ask one group of students to read the first phrase chorally: *There was no water.* Ask a second group to read the second phrase: *the people were alarmed.* Point out the word *and* in the middle. **Say:** *I read that there was no water. That is the first event. Then I read the second event; the people were alarmed. These events are connected with the word* and. *This word tells me that these two events are connected.* Have the entire group read the full sentence.

Practice: Distribute BLM 1. Guide students to complete the Practice activity. **Say:** *As I read the sentence, I look for two different events. Then I look for a word that connects the events.* Help students identify the connecting word *when* in the first sentence. **Ask:** *Which event happened before the other event?*

Extend: Have students work in partners to complete the Extend activity. Provide support as needed. Check their work, and then have students read the sentences aloud.

Challenge: If students are ready, work with them to complete the Practice activity on BLM 1.

Ⓛight Support

Use the text on pages 12–19 in the *Texts for Close Reading* to complete the following activities.

Practice: Support partners as they identify the events in paragraph 1. Have them identify connecting words that link two events in one sentence or in separate sentences.

Extend: Have partners review paragraphs 7 and 8. Have them list the events in order along with any connecting words that link the events. Monitor students as they work.

Challenge: If students are ready, have them insert connecting words in paragraphs 7 and 8 to link two events. For example: **After** *the two dragons then transformed themselves into an old man and a woman, they went to the chamber of the Prince, and appeared to him in a dream.*

Ⓜoderate Support

Model: Review connecting words with students. **Say:** *Connecting words can be used to link two events in a story.* Write: *The dragons left the city after they filled their baskets with water.* Have two volunteers read the first and second underlined events. **Say:** *I see the connecting word* after. *This word connects the event in the first part of the sentence with the event in second part. It also helps us understand the sequence of events. The dragons filled their baskets with water. Then the dragons left the city.*

Practice: Distribute BLM 2. Work with students to complete the Practice activity. Reteach linking events with connecting words as needed. Then have students read the sentences aloud.

Extend: Have partners complete the Extend activity. Encourage them to read aloud their sentences to see if the sequence makes sense. Provide support as necessary.

Challenge: If students are ready, have them choose new connecting words to link the events in the Extend activity. Have them write and then read aloud their sentences.

☑ Formative Assessment

Substantial Support	• With support, can students recognizing connecting words that link two events in a story? • With support, can students add a connecting word to a sentence to link two events?
Moderate Support	• Can students recognizing connecting words that link two events in a story? • Can students link two events in one sentence, using a connecting word?
Light Support	• Can students recognize connecting words in a story and identify the events they connect? • Can students insert connecting words in a story to link events?

Preview or Review Week 2 ELA Mini-Lessons

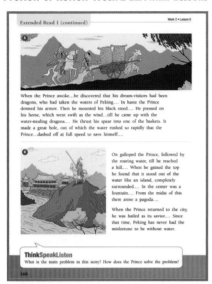

"The Pagoda on the Hill of Imperial Springs," page 168

Student Objectives

LANGUAGE
Purpose:
- I can use provide an eyewitness account in an interview.

Form:
- I can understand noun and pronoun agreement.

CONTENT
- I can comprehend sensory language in a legend.

Additional Materials
- Unit Presentation
- Sensory Language Chart
- *Texts for Close Reading* booklet
- Think-Speak-Listen Flip Book
- Student journal

Metacognitive Prompt: Imagery

Before students read the last two panels of the story, say: Today we will visualize as we read the descriptive language in the legend. We will form a picture in our mind to help us better understand what is happening in the story.

8 Analyze Sensory Language

Engage Thinking

Display panels 1–4. **Ask:** *What event happened at the end of the story?* Have students review panel 4 and describe what they see. Then ask them to imagine the sound of the water rushing into the baskets. **Say:** *Let's talk about how the language in the story helps us imagine what we see and hear in our minds when we read.*

Turn and Talk: *Describe what you see in the image, using words about colors and shapes.*

Differentiated Instruction
Read and View Closely: Analyze Sensory Language

Display panels 5 and 6. Read panel 5. **Ask:** *What does the Prince do? What words help you to picture what happens?* Then read panel 6. **Ask:** *What words help you see him on his horse and hear the water?* Prompt answers: *The prince _____ (galloped) on the horse. The water was _____ (roaring).* **Say:** *Authors use sensory language to describe what we would see, hear, touch, taste, or smell.* Use the Differentiated Instruction to practice analyzing sensory language in a way that best matches the levels of your students.

Think-Speak-Listen: Use these sentence frames or the Think-Speak-Listen Flip Book to guide discussion: *The main problem was _____. The Prince solved the problem by _____.*

Build Language: Understand Noun and Pronoun Agreement

Remind students that a pronoun replaces a noun after the noun is used in a sentence. **Say:** *The noun and pronoun must agree. If the noun is singular, the pronoun is singular. If the noun is masculine, the pronoun must be too.* Write: *The Prince spoke to his ministers. They told him the wells had dried up.* **Say:** *The pronoun* they *refers to the ministers. It is plural because ministers is plural. The pronoun* him *refers to the Prince. It is singular and masculine.* Have students identify the pronouns and the nouns they refer in panel 6.

☑ Use Oral and Written Language: Provide an Eyewitness Account in an Interview

Task: *With your group, imagine that you are watching the Prince catch up to the dragons as they haul away Peking's water. Study panel 5. Then have one member of your group act as a TV reporter who interviews eyewitnesses who saw the action. Have each eyewitness tell what he/she remembers. Review panel 5 again to see how accurate you were.*

(S) *I saw the Prince _____. He _____. Then I heard _____.*

(M) *The Prince _____ and then _____. I heard _____ as _____.*

(L) *After the Prince _____, then he _____. I heard _____ and saw _____.*

↻ Wrap Up

Today we learned how to analyze sensory language. How do vivid words help you to visualize what happens in a story?

Turn and Talk: *Choose a paragraph in the story. Read it aloud to your partner. Then ask your partner what he or she visualized.*

👥👥 Differentiated Instruction
Read and View Closely: Analyze Sensory Language

ⓢubstantial Support

Model: Review a few examples of words that relate to the senses, using the Sensory Language Chart. Read the text in panel 5. Ask a volunteer to read aloud the line: *Then he mounted his black steed.* **Ask:** *What is a steed? What does the author tell us about how the steed looks?* Have another volunteer read the next line. *The author tells us the horse goes as swift as the wind. Those words help us form a picture of how the horse was running. Was it going slowly or quickly?*

Practice: Distribute BLM 1. Guide students through the Practice activity. **Ask:** *Which word in the box would help you visualize what happens?* Check understanding and reteach as necessary.

Extend: Have partners complete the Extend activity on the BLM. Discuss the meaning of the words in the box in advance if necessary. Have students read their sentences aloud.

Challenge: Have students make up new sentences using words from the box in the Extend activity.

ⓜoderate Support

Model: Ask students to close their eyes and listen as you read panel 5. Then ask them to describe the pictures and sounds that the text made them imagine. **Ask:** *What did the horse look like? How was he moving? What was the sound of the water rushing out of the hole?* Display the Sensory Language Chart and have students read some of the words from each column.

Practice: Distribute BLM 2. Read the first question. **Say:** *The Prince was moving fast. The words I read in panel 5 that help me visualize his speed are "haste" and "swift as the wind." I'll write these words as my answer.* Encourage students to help you identify sensory words in panel 5 to answer each question. Check understanding and reteach as necessary.

Extend: Have partners use panel 6 to complete the Extend activity. They may use the illustration to help them visualize.

Challenge: If students are ready, have them work in partners to brainstorm sensory words from the Sensory Language Chart that would match the event in panel 6. Encourage them to write sentences using the words they brainstormed.

ⓛight Support

Practice: Use the text on pages 12–19 in the *Texts for Close Reading* to complete the following activities.

Ask: *What words help you to visualize how the Prince was moving? Which words describe what he saw when he caught up to the dragons?* Have students suggest any additional sensory words they could add to the story to further describe the action.

Extend: Monitor partners as they read paragraph 11. Have them draw one or two pictures that illustrate what they visualize as they read the story. Have them explain how the sensory words help them visualize.

Challenge: Tell students that besides sensory words there are also comparative phrases in the text that help readers visualize, such as *swift as the wind.* Have them analyze paragraph 13 and list phrases that begin with *like* or *as.* Encourage them to write a sentence that states what each phrases helps them imagine.

☑ Formative Assessment

Substantial Support	• With support, can students analyze a story for sensory language? • With support, can students express which senses the sensory words appeal to? • With support, can students understand how authors use sensory language?
Moderate Support	• With support, can students analyze a story for sensory language? • With support, can students express which senses the sensory words appeal to? • With support, can students understand how authors use sensory language?
Light Support	• Can students analyze a story for sensory language? • Can students suggest sensory words to add to a story?

"Use the Language of Sequence, " page 169

Student Objectives

LANGUAGE
Purpose:
• I can use recount the a legend in sequence.
Form:
• I can use the language of sequence to list events in order.
CONTENT
• I can interpret sequence of events in a legend.

Additional Materials
• Unit Presentation
• *Texts for Close Reading* booklet
• Think-Speak-Listen Flip Book
• Student journal

Language Transfer Support

Students whose first language is Spanish may be familiar with the following cognates of words found in the text: *príncipe (prince), nuevo (new), ciudad (city), dragón (dragon), cueva (cave), permiso (permission)* and *tiempo (time)*. Encourage students to look for other words that are similar to words in their first language.

9 Use the Language of Sequence

Engage Thinking

Display the chart. **Say:** *The chart lists events from "The Pagoda on the Hill of Imperial Springs."* Read aloud the boldfaced words, and explain that these words tell us when events happen in the story, or the sequence of events.

Turn and Talk: *Tell your partner the first, second, and third things you did today.*

Read and View Closely: Recognize a Sequence of Events

Read the first row in the chart. **Say:** *The chart lists events in the order they occurred in the myth. First, the digging in the earth disturbed the dragons. The phrase "in digging out the earth" tells me this action caused the breaking of the dragon's cave. I know that action began the series of events. What happened next?* Continue with the remaining events in the chart, paying attention to the order in which they occurred in the myth. **Say:** *I can look for clues to help me follow a sequence of events. When I know the kinds of words to look for, I can follow the order of events in a story more easily.*

👥 Differentiated Instruction
Build Language: Use the Language of Sequence

Say: *The chart shows us words and phrases that help writers express a sequence of events.* Read each row aloud, emphasizing the sequence language. **Say:** *Let's look at what each word or phrase tells us. We know "in digging out the earth" gives us the first event.* **Ask:** *What does "at midnight" tell us?* Review its meaning. Use the Differentiated Instruction to practice using the language of sequence in a way that best matches the levels of your students.

Think-Speak-Listen: Use the following sentence frames or the Think-Speak-Listen Flip Book to guide discussion: *First, _____. Next,_____. Then, _____. Later, _____.*

☑ Use Oral and Written Language: Recount a Legend in Sequence

Task: *Choose a body of water: for example, a river. Work in small groups to create a legend about how the body of water formed or changed, using sequence words. One person tells what happened first, the second person tells what happened next, and so on. Recount the events you created, using these frames. Share your sentences with the class:*

Ⓢ   *First, _____ the land was like a(n) _____. Then, _____.*

Ⓜ   *_____ the land was _____. Then _____. Next _____.*

Ⓛ   *First, _____. Next, _____. Then, _____. Finally, _____.*

Wrap Up

Today we learned how the language of sequence helps writers clarify the order of story events. How does recognizing signal words and phrases help you understand a story?

Turn and Talk: *Recount an event that happened to you. Use sequence language to tell what happened first, next, and last.*

👥 Differentiated Instruction
Build Language: Use the Language of Sequence

ⓢ ubstantial Support

Model: Display the chart. Write the words *First, Next, Then, Finally.* Explain that these words describe a sequence, or the order in which something happens. Read panel 3. Recount the three events using the sequence words: *First, the dragons planned to talk to the prince. Next, they transformed into a man and a woman. Then, they appeared to the prince. Finally, the prince gave his permission for them to leave.* Point out that *next* and *then* can be used in either order, and that we don't always have to use the word *first*. Provide another example: *In haste the Prince donned his armor. Then he mounted his black steed* (panel 5). **Ask:** *What does the Prince do after he hurries to put on his armor? How do you know?*

Practice: Distribute BLM 1 and guide students to complete the Practice activity. Then choral-read the sentences in order.

Extend: Have partners work together to complete the Extend activity on the BLM. After checking their work, have them read the sentences aloud.

Challenge: If students are ready, have them work in partners to recount the events in the Practice activity.

ⓛ ight Support

Use the text on pages 12–19 in the *Texts for Close Reading* to complete the following activities.

Practice: Work with students to identify signal words that describe events in order. List some words such as *First, next, then, last, finally*. Discuss that *next* and *then* are interchangeable, as are *last* and *finally*. Remind them that the word *when* may show events that happen at the same time. Point out that knowing the meanings of signal words help us understand how ideas are connected. Then have students work in partners to reread paragraph 8. Have them discuss the meaning of the sequence words in these sentences.

Extend: Have partners reread paragraph 10 and retell in their own words the events from the start until the Prince finds the dragons. Have them use signal words and phrases to show the sequence.

Challenge: Have students retell the sequence of story events to partners. Remind them to use signal words and speak in complete sentences.

ⓜ oderate Support

Model: Display the chart. Remind students that knowing the meaning of signal words helps them understand the sequence of events in a story. Read row 3. **Say:** *I notice the word* then*. It means the same thing as "next." The next thing the dragons did was to transform, or change, themselves.* Provide another example: *In haste the Prince donned his armor. Then he mounted his black steed* (panel 5). **Ask:** *What does the Prince do after he hurries to put on his armor? How do you know?* Have students read the other examples on the chart. Point out the different uses of the words: When is used to show that something is happening at the same time. *Till* is another way to say *until*, and shows what is happening up to a certain time. Ask students if they know some other words for telling the beginning event and the ones that follow. Suggest that they can use *first, next, then, finally*.

Practice: Distribute BLM 2. Work with students to match each sentence part to the correct event in the sequence.

Extend: Have students work in partners to complete the sentence frames in Extend activity on the BLM. Have them read the sentences aloud.

Challenge: If students are ready, have them work in partners to recount another panel in the story.

☑ Formative Assessment

Substantial Support	• Can students complete a sentence frame using the signal word then? • Can students determine the sequence relationship of ideas and list them using sequence words?
Moderate Support	• Can students match sentence signal words to sentences to create the correct sequence? • Can students complete sentence frames with signal words that show the sequence of events?
Light Support	• Can students explain the relationship of ideas exhibited by signal words? • Can students generate original sentences in which they recount events using signal words?

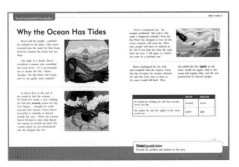

"Why the Ocean Has Tides," pages 170–171

Student Objectives

LANGUAGE

Purpose:
• I can recount an origin story.

Form:
• I can use the suffixes **-ly**, **-ily**, and **-ize**.

CONTENT
• I can understand a pourquoi tale, or origin story.

Additional Materials
• Unit Presentation
• *Texts for Close Reading* booklet
• Think-Speak-Listen Flip Book
• Student journal

Language Transfer Support

Speakers of Hmong may need extra support when forming and using adverbs with the suffixes **-ly** and **-ily.** Adverbs are not used in this language. Two adjectives or two verbs may be used to modify an adjective or a verb.

10 Read "Why the Ocean Has Tides"

Build Background and Vocabulary

Display the image panels and explain key words and ideas from the text. If students have read the myth, ask them what they remember. Invite students to share their experiences and knowledge with other pourquoi tales, or origin stories, they have read.

Read Aloud the Text

Read panel 1. To support comprehension, have students relate the images to the text. **Ask:** *Who is the black bird? Who is the woman? Why is she sitting in the water?* Read panel 2, helping students understand the events. **Ask:** *Why does Raven see the woman?* Suggest the answer: *Raven wants food for his people, but the ocean is too deep.* Invite students to share their ideas using the sentence frames: *Raven wants to _____ the woman so that she will _____.* Then refer to the Essential Question: Ask students to think about why water was important to Raven. **Say:** *This is a pourquoi, or origin, story. It explains why the ocean has tides. Reading a cultural myth helps us realize what is important to people and why.*

Think-Speak-Listen: Use these frames or the Think-Speak-Listen Flip Book to guide discussion: *The problem in the story is _____. The solution to this problem is _____.*

👤👥 Differentiated Instruction
Build Language: Use Suffixes -ly, -ily, -ize

Point to panel 2. Write "He found her inside a cave, holding the tide line securely across her lap." **Say:** *Securely is a word with a suffix.* Review that suffixes are groups of letters, such as *-ly* or *-ize*, added to the end of a base word. **Say:** *A suffix can change the word's use and may alter its exact meaning.* Model thinking through finding the verb that the adverb describes, and what the word securely means. *The base word is the adjective* secure. *Secure means "fastened firmly." The suffix -ly changes* secure *into the adverb* securely. *Writers use words with suffixes to add details. For example, an adverb ending in -ly helps you understand how much or to what extent an action is performed.*

☑ Use Oral and Written Language: Recount an Origin Story

Task: *Work in pairs to explain a myth. First, tell shows the world in the past. Then, tell what event happens. Finally, tell the ending. Write sentences to describe each picture, using words with -ly, -ily, -ize. Use these sentence frames:*

Ⓢ *Long ago, the _____. The _____ changed _____.*

Ⓜ *Long ago, _____. Then the _____ changed _____.*

Ⓛ *In _____, the _____, but _____.*

🔄 Wrap Up

Today we learned how to use words with the suffixes -ly, -ily, and -ize to make actions more specific and detailed. How does this make your writing more descriptive?

Turn and Talk: *Describe what happened to an animal character in a myth or other story you have read. Use adverbs ending in -ly, -ily, or -ize to add to your descriptions of events.*

👥👤 Differentiated Instruction
Build Language: Use the Suffixes -ly, -ily, -ize

Ⓢ ubstantial Support

Model: Say: *This story is a myth.* Review the words *ocean* and *tides.* Explain tides are the regular rising and lowering of ocean water at the shore. Explain that people used this myth long ago to explain how tides began. Read the third line in panel 1 and discuss the word *visualize.* **Ask:** *What word do you see? (visual). A visual is a picture. So to visualize is to imagine, or see a picture in your head.* Then discuss the words *securely* and *momentarily* in the next panel, pointing out the words *secure* and *moment.* **Say:** *Securely is an adverb. It tells me that the woman was holding the tide line in a secure way, or tightly.*

Practice: Distribute BLM 1. Work with students to complete the Practice activity. **Say:** *The suffix -ly means "in a certain way."*

Extend: Have partners complete the Extend activity. Tell them that adjectives that end in *-y* change the *y* to *i* before adding *-ly.* **Say:** *I might say, "Raven flies easily."* Easily *is an adverb formed from the adjective easy.*

Challenge: If students are ready, work with them to create new sentences using *securely* and *visualize.* Have them read aloud the new sentences.

Ⓛ ight Support

Use the text on page 20 in the *Texts for Close Reading* to complete the following activities.

Practice: Discuss how suffixes *-ly* or *-ily* change adjectives. Remind students that the meaning of the adverb is similar to that of the adjective, but the adverb describes a verb. Create this chart and work with students to complete it:

Adjective	Suffix	Adverb	Definition of Adverb
secure			
bare			
momentary			

Extend: Have partners use the words above to discuss and write original sentences about the story.

Challenge: Have students make 4-square charts for each adverb with synonyms, antonyms, sentences, and definitions.

Ⓜ oderate Support

Model: Say: *People told this myth long ago to explain something in nature.* **Ask:** *What is explained?* Review the words *ocean* and *tides.* Explain tides are the regular rising and lowering of ocean water at the shore. **Say:** *I see words with suffixes that make the writing descriptive. The adverb* securely *comes from an adjective. Do you know which adjective?* Cover the *-ly* and ask students to read the word *secure.* **Say:** *The adverb* securely *tells me how the woman was holding the tide line. How was she holding it? In a secure way, tightly.* Then discuss the words *visualize* in panel 1 and *momentarily* in panel 2. Have volunteers tell you what words they see, and discuss what that tells them about the meaning of the words.

Practice: Distribute BLM 2. Work with students to complete the Practice activity.

Extend: Have pairs complete the Extend activity. Remind students that adjectives that end in *-y* change the *y* to *-i* before adding *-ly.* **Say:** *I might say, "Raven hopes to catch food easily."* Easily *is an adverb formed from the adjective* easy.

Challenge: Have students form an adverb from the adjective *uniform* to replace the phrase *in a uniform way (*uniformly). Work with them to create a new sentence using *uniformly*, and choral-read it with them.

☑ Formative Assessment

Substantial Support	• Can students define and analyze adverbs that end in *-ly* or *-ily*? • Can students complete a sentence frame by adding an *-ly* adverb?
Moderate Support	• Cans students define and analyze adverbs that end in *-ly* or *-ily*? • Can students complete sentence frames that include *-ly* adverbs and the verbs they modify?
Light Support	• Can students define, analyze, and form adverbs that end in *-ly* or *-ily* and verbs that end in *-ize*? • Can students generate original sentences using adverbs ending in *-ly* and verbs ending in *-ize*?

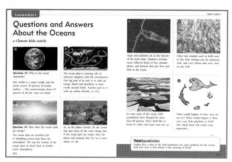

"Questions and Answers About
the Oceans," pages 172–173

Student Objectives

LANGUAGE

Purpose:
• I can write a fact sheet about the ocean.

Form:
• I can combine sentences to condense ideas.

CONTENT
• I can understand a question-and-answer format about an informational text.

Additional Materials
• Unit Presentation
• *Texts for Close Reading* booklet
• Think-Speak-Listen Flip Book
• Student journal

Metacognitive Prompt

Today we will condense text. To condense information, we will combine the main ideas in the text. We will use what we know to help us understand new ideas. Using what we already know can help us understand the meaning of new information and predict upcoming information.

11 Read "Questions and Answers About the Oceans"

Build Background and Vocabulary

Display the image panels and explain key words and ideas from the text. If students have already read the text, ask what they remember. Invite students to share knowledge about oceans from their reading or from their experience.

Read Aloud the Text

Read panel 1. To support comprehension, ask students what the image shows. **Say:** *This photo shows Earth from space.* **Ask:** *What are the blue parts? What can you understand about Earth's oceans by looking at the photograph?* Point out that the photograph of Earth shows much more water than land. **Ask:** *What does the text in panel 1 tell us about how much of the Earth is water?* Have students reread Panel 4. **Ask:** *What does this photograph show? What does the text tell us about a big danger for sea life?* Reread panel 7 and discuss the example of krill needing colder water. Then refer to the Essential Question: **Ask:** *What makes oceans so important to living things, such as krill?*

Think-Speak-Listen: Use the following sentence frames or the Think-Speak-Listen Flip Book to guide discussion: *Fewer krill means _____. Krill need _____.*

👥👥 Differentiated Instruction
Build Language: Condense Ideas

Read aloud panels 1–4. **Say:** *This is an informational text with scientific facts and terms. How can we condense some of these ideas?* Discuss that we combine ideas or group related ideas in sentences. Review combining sentences by compounding subjects, verb, and sentences. Review that descriptive phrases, such as prepositional phrases, can also help condense ideas. **Say:** *It's important to know how to condense ideas so we can connect ideas and make them easier to understand for others.* Use the Differentiated Instruction to practice condensing ideas in a way that best matches the levels of your students.

☑ Use Oral and Written Language: Write a Fact Sheet About the Ocean

Task: *Work with a partner to discuss the importance of the oceans. Use ideas you learned and your own ideas. Condense your ideas by combining ideas.* Use this opportunity to assess students using the *English Language Development Assessment.*

Ⓢ   *The ocean is important because _____ and _____.*

Ⓜ   *The ocean _____ because _____. The ocean has two roles. It _____ and it _____.*

Ⓛ   *The ocean _____ because _____. The ocean has many roles, including _____.*

🔄 Wrap Up

Today we talked about condensing information by combining ideas in clear sentences. Why is it important for writers to be able to condense information?

Turn and Talk: *Describe what you would like to see if you could go under the sea.*

☰☰☰ Differentiated Instruction
Build Language: Condense Ideas

Ⓢubstantial Support

Model: Remind students that to condense ideas means to group related ideas together. Review panel 1. **Say:** *I see two ideas:* The ocean covers 70 percent of Earth's surface. The ocean contains 97 percent of all the water on Earth. *I can condense these ideas into one sentence:* The ocean covers 70 percent of Earth's surface and contains 97 percent of its water.

Practice: Reread panel 2 and discuss the ocean's role in the environment. Help students identify the three parts of this role: (1) soaks up heat, (2) distributes heat evenly, (3) soaks up carbon dioxide. Have students read the second sentence. Ask which two ideas the sentence condenses (soaking up heat, distributing it evenly). Work together to think of other ways to condense those ideas: for example, *The ocean soaks up heat and carbon dioxide.*

Extend: Have partners combine the ideas in panels 3 and 4. Write the following sentence frames and work with students to complete them: *As Earth's atmosphere _____, the ocean _____ from the atmosphere and _____.* After checking their work, have students read aloud their sentences.

Challenge: If students are ready, work with them to condense the ideas in panels 1–4.

Ⓛight Support

Use the text on pages 22–29 in the *Texts for Close Reading* to complete the following activities.

Practice: Remind students that they need to think about what is most important to condense ideas. **Say:** *Let's condense the ideas in paragraph 2. What is the paragraph about? When we condense this information, we want to tell about the importance of the volume and size of the ocean.* Help students complete this sentence frame: *The ocean, which contains _____, covers _____.*

Distribute BLM 2. Have partners complete the Practice activity.

Extend: Have partners complete the Extend activity on the BLM.

Challenge: Have students answer these questions: *How does condensing ideas help you explain information to others? How does condensing ideas help you understand the information yourself?*

Ⓜoderate Support

Model: Remind students that condensing ideas means grouping related ideas. Reread panel 1. Review *ocean, world,* and *surface.* **Say:** *I want to condense the information in panel 1. It is part of the answer to Question #1:* Why is the ocean important? *I see the main idea is the size of the ocean. What two facts tell us about size?*

Help students complete the sentence frames to answer the question, and then have volunteers read the sentences aloud: *The ocean covers _____. The ocean contains _____.*

Say: *Let's combine these ideas:*

The ocean _____ and contains _____.

Practice: Distribute BLM 1. Work with students to complete the Practice activity.

Extend: Have partners complete the Extend activity on the BLM.

Challenge: If students are ready, have them condense ideas about the decrease in krill and its effect, using the following sentence frames: *Krill, which need _____ to breed, are affected by _____. Many animals, such as _____ and _____, depend on krill.*

☑ Formative Assessment

Substantial Support	• Can students recognize related ideas that can be combined in sentences? • Can students complete sentence frames to condense ideas by combining sentences?
Moderate Support	• Can students complete sentence frames with main ideas and related details that can be combined in sentences? • Can students complete sentence frames to condense ideas by combining sentences?
Light Support	• Can students determine main ideas and related details that can be condensed? • Can students generate original sentences that condense main ideas?

"Questions and Answers About the Oceans," page 174

Student Objectives

LANGUAGE
Purpose:
• I can explain how one event affects another event.

Form:
• I can recognize how one action leads to another one.

CONTENT
• I can infer information in a science text.

Additional Materials
• Unit Presentation
• *Texts for Close Reading* booklet
• Think-Speak-Listen Flip Book
• Student journal

Language Transfer Support

Note that the words cause and effect have cognates in several European languages, including Spanish (la cause/el effect) and French (la cause/l'effet). Encourage students to look for other words in the text that are similar to words in their first language.

12 Analyze Cause and Effect

Engage Thinking

Display the image panels and explain how each panel is connected. Point to panel 5. **Say:** *Algae and plankton are at the bottom of the food chain. Some animals like krill eat them.* Point to Panel 7. **Say:** *Krill need cold water to live. What would happen if the water is too warm?* Elicit answers. **Say:** *The krill would die. This is an example of cause and effect.*

Turn and Talk: *Turn to your neighbor and explain what would happen to other animals in the food web if the krill died.*

👤👥 Differentiated Instruction
Read and View Closely: Draw Inferences

Read panels 9–12. Write the word *inference*. **Say:** *In a text, sometimes we are told details, but we also must infer information. In panel 10, we learned that the ocean absorbs carbon dioxide that we create from fossil fuels. In panel 11, we learned that the ocean is becoming more acidic. What can we infer about how fossil fuels affect the ocean?* Explain that when we burn fossil fuels, the air becomes filled with acid, and that when the ocean soaks up carbon dioxide from the air, the ocean becomes too acidic. Use the Differentiated Instruction to practice inferring in a way that best matches the level of your students.

Think-Speak-Listen: Use this sentence frame or the Think-Speak-Listen Flip Book to guide discussion: *Too much carbon dioxide can _____ because _____.*

Build Language: Use Adjectives to Expand Sentences

Read the text in panels 4, 7, and 11. **Say:** *The author used adjectives to describe the ocean water. Can you find the three adjectives?* Give students time to find *warm, cold, acidic.* Point to panel 12. **Say:** *The word* delicate *describes the balance of the ocean.* Explain that *delicate* means "something that can be broken easily." Have students find two other adjectives in panel 12 (protective, strong). **Ask:** *What word do these adjectives describe?* (shells) *What information did we learn by reading those adjectives?* Discuss that some animals need strong shells to survive, and that acidic water causes an effect on the shells. Point out that using adjectives help us understand important ideas and details more clearly.

☑ Use Oral and Written Language: Explain How One Event Effects Another

Task: *Work in small groups to create a pamphlet to explain the effect of the warming of the ocean. Answer this question: How will the warming of the ocean effect its animals? Discuss and write down your answer, using adjectives. Use the sentence frames below.*

(S) *The warming of the ocean will _____ because _____.*

(M) *Krill are the _____ in the food web. If the ocean warms, they _____.*

(L) *The ocean's food web depends upon ___ and if the water is too warm, the ___.*

🔄 Wrap Up

Today we inferred information about causes and effects about the ocean. Why is it important to infer information in a text?

Turn and Talk: *With a partner, discuss a cause and effect in your daily life.*

▲▲▲ Differentiated Instruction
Read and View Closely: Draw Inferences

Ⓢubstantial Support

Model: Display panels 9–12. Reread the text in panel 9 and ask students to help you list information that is stated: for example, *Fish and animals breathe oxygen.* Write the words *infer* and *inference.* **Say:** *To infer, or to make an inference, means we look at information in the text and draw conclusions about information that is not stated in the text.* Refer to the information you listed. **Ask:** *What can we infer about what fish and animals need to live?* Explain that if fish and animals breathe oxygen, they must need it to live. Write: *Fish and animals need oxygen.* **Say:** *This is an inference. It wasn't stated in the text, but we inferred it by reading the text.*

Practice: Invite students to help you draw inferences in panel 8. **Say:** *The questions all begin with "What would happen if..." The text does state the information directly. I have to infer. When I read, "The food web would become unraveled..." I infer that the krill are one of the most important parts of the food web.* Distribute BLM 1, and have partners complete the Practice activity.

Extend: Have students work in pairs to complete the Extend activity on the BLM. After checking their work, have them read their sentences aloud.

Challenge: Challenge partners to complete the Practice activity. Have them read it aloud to each other.

Ⓛight Support

Use the text on pages 22–29 in the *Texts for Close Reading* to complete the following activities.

Practice: Have students create two columns labeled "Stated" and "Inferred." Ask them to write statements that they learned from the text directly, and others that they inferred. Support students to use the language of cause and effect to describe the information. Check their work.

Extend: Have partners compare and contrast their responses in the Practice task. Ask them to read their responses aloud.

Challenge: If students are ready, guide them to write a paragraph that explains the connection between making inference and cause and effect.

Ⓜoderate Support

Model: Explain that sometimes texts state information directly, but other times, not. Display Panels 5–8. **Say:** *As I read, I notice that there are some details that are not stated such as why there isn't as much sea ice.* Write the words *infer* and *inference* and ask if students know the meaning of either word. Explain that to infer or make an inference means to draw conclusions about information that is not in the text. **Say:** *The text tells me that krill like to breed in sea ice. It also tells me the krill population is shrinking. Earlier in the text, it talked about the ocean getting warmer. What can I infer about the reason for the population shrinking?* Discuss that the ocean becoming warmer means less sea ice and less ice for krill to breed in. **Say:** *The text did not tell us the reason directly. We inferred it from the other information.*

Practice: Distribute BLM 2. Work with students to choose the inference in the Practice activity. Read the sentence aloud with students.

Extend: In pairs, ask students to complete the Extend activity. Monitor students' work and provide additional support as needed. Once finished, discuss the answers as a group.

Challenge: If students are ready, have them identify which details and ideas in the Practice activity are "Inferred" or "Stated."

☑ Formative Assessment

Substantial Support	• Can students identify when information is inferred in a text? • Can students complete sentences based on stated and inferred information?
Moderate Support	• Are students able to draw inferences in a text? • Are students able to support their inference from a text?
Light Support	• Are students able to analyze inferences? • Are students able to create original sentences that explain their inferences?

Preview or Review Week 3 ELA Mini-Lessons

Week 3 • Lesson 13

Use the Language of Cause and Effect

Cause	Effect
But if the ocean gets too warm,	then the plants and animals that live in it must adapt—or die.
What would happen if there were very little plankton or krill?	The whole food web could come unraveled.
The ocean is becoming more acidic. What does this mean?...	If the water is too acidic, the animals may not be able to make strong shells.

ThinkSpeakListen
Explain what might happen if the ocean's food web is disturbed.

175

"Use the Language of Cause and Effect," page 175

Student Objectives

LANGUAGE
Purpose:
- I can write an ocean fact sheet.
Form:
- I can use the language of cause and effect.
CONTENT
- I can describe cause and effect in informational texts.

Additional Materials
- Unit Presentation
- *Texts for Close Reading* booklet
- Think-Speak-Listen Flip Book
- Student journal

Language Transfer Support

The words *cause* and *effect* have cognates in a number of Latin-based languages, such as Spanish *(la causa/el efecto)* and French *(la cause/el efecto)*. Students whose first language is Spanish may be familiar with these other cognates of words found in the text: *el océano (ocean), la planta (plant), el animal (animal), adaptar (adapt),* and *ácido (acidic).* Encourage students to look for additional words that are similar to words in their first language.

13 Use the Language of Cause and Effect

Engage Thinking

Display the Cause-and-Effect Chart. Point to the first row. **Say:** *If the ocean gets too warm then the plants and animals that live in the ocean must adapt or die. Why would the plants and animals have to adapt or die?* Elicit answers. **Say:** *They cannot survive in warm water.* One event leads to, or is the result of, the other.

Think-Speak-Listen: Use the following sentence frame or the Think-Speak-Listen Flip Book to guide discussion: *If the ocean's food web is disturbed, then _____.*

Turn and Talk: Turn to your neighbor and explain one effect of warming ocean water.

Read and View Closely: Recognize Cause and Effect

Say: *In informational texts, the order of events is important. One event can cause something to happen. This is called cause and effect. The cause is why something happens and the effect is what happens.* Write this question on the board: "What would happen if there were very little plankton and krill?" **Say:** *This is a question about cause and effect.* Underline *if there were very little plankton.* **Say:** *This is the cause. The answer to the words* What would happen if *is the effect. One way to think about cause and effect is: _____ happens because _____. For example: The food web would become unraveled* **because** *there are very little plankton krill.*

👥 Differentiated Instruction
Build Language: Use the Language of Cause and Effect

Say: *Words such as* **why, if, then, because, when, since** *and* **so** *are used to show cause and effect.* Point to the third row. **Ask:** *What language of cause and effect is used here?* Elicit answers. **Say:** *The word "if" tells us that two events are connected. The animals may not be able to make strong shells* **if** *the water is too acidic.* Use the Differentiated Instruction to practice using the language of cause and effect in a way that best matches the level of your students.

☑ Use Oral and Written Language: Write an Ocean Fact Sheet

Task: *As a small group, write sentences for a fact sheet to state problems about the oceans. Use the sentence frames below. Use the language of cause and effect.*

Ⓢ *Krill are breeding less _____ there is less ice.*

Ⓜ *The oceans are becoming _____ because _____.*

Ⓛ *If _____, then _____. As a result of _____, the _____*

🌀 Wrap Up

Today we talked about cause-and-effect language. Why is it important to use language that expresses cause and effect?

Turn and Talk: *Tell your partner an event that was a result of another event.*

👥👥 Differentiated Instruction
Build Language: Use the Language of Cause and Effect

Ⓢubstantial Support

Model: Display the chart. **Say:** *The chart shows causes and effects, or events that are connected. The first event is the cause. The second one is the event that happens because of the first event.* Read the events in the chart, rewording to make the cause and effect apparent. **Say:** *First, the ocean gets warm. Then the plants and animals must adapt or die. Signal words are clues that tell us that there is a cause and effect.* Write the words *if, then,* and the words *Why, because.* Point to the words in the chart and emphasize the words. **Say:** *If the ocean gets warm, then the plants and animals adapt or die. Why do the plants and animals adapt or die? They adapt or die because the ocean gets too warm. The word* because *tells the cause.*

Practice: Distribute BLM 1. Work with students to complete the Practice activity, re-teaching as necessary.

Extend: Have students work in partners to use cause-and-effect language to write sentences. Have them read aloud their sentences.

Challenge: If students are ready, have them complete the Practice activity on BLM 1.

Ⓜoderate Support

Model: Display the chart. Explain that cause-and-effect language shows how events are connected. **Say:** *Each row lists details about the ocean. When I read the panels in order, I see that each panel is connected to the one before it. One event causes another. One is the cause and one is an effect.* Ask: Which event comes first, a cause or an effect? Point out the words *If/then.* Explain that the word *If* is used to talk about a possible cause, and the word *then* shows the effect.

Practice: Distribute BLM 2. Work with students to complete the Practice activity. Have them read aloud the sentences.

Extend: Have partners work together to complete the Extend activity. Monitor students' work and provide additional support as needed. Once finished, discuss the answers as a group.

Challenge: If students are ready, have them complete the Challenge activity.

Ⓛight Support

Use the text on pages 22–29 in the *Texts for Close Reading* to complete the following activities.

Practice: Write on the board two columns labeled "Cause" and "Effect." Work with students to identify causes and effects from the text and list the information in each column. Have them write sentences using cause-and-effect language to describe the information listed in the columns. Write words for reference such as *if, then, because, as a result, why.* Have them read aloud their sentences.

Extend: Have partners take turns playing an oceans expert and an interviewer to ask and answer questions using cause-and-effect language.

Challenge: If students are ready, encourage them to write a paragraph that cites causes and effects from the text.

☑ Formative Assessment

Substantial Support	• Can students identify cause and effect in an informational science text? • Can students complete sentences describing cause and effect?
Moderate Support	• Are students recognize cause-and-effect words in an informational science text? • Are students able to generate sentences explaining cause and effect?
Light Support	• Are students able to analyze cause and effect? • Are students able to create original sentence using the language of cause and effect to answer questions?

Preview or Review Week 3 ELA Mini-Lessons

"The Great Barrier Reef," page 176

Student Objectives

LANGUAGE

Purpose:
- I can describe the Great Barrier Reef in a guide.

Form:
- I can form words with suffixes ending in **-al, -ity,** and **-ic.**

CONTENT
- I can comprehend an informational science text.

Additional Materials
- Unit Presentation
- *Texts for Close Reading* booklet
- Think-Speak-Listen Flip Book
- Student journal

Language Transfer Support

Students whose first language is Spanish may be familiar with the following cognates of words found in the text: *natural* (natural), *costa* (coast), *diversidad* (diversity) and *clima* (climates). Encourage students to look for other words that are similar to words in their first language.

14 Read "The Great Barrier Reef"

Build Background and Vocabulary

Display the image panels and explain key words and ideas from the text. If students have already read the text, ask them what they remember. Point out Australia on a map or globe and identify the northeastern coast described in the text. Invite students to share their experiences and knowledge about important natural landmarks.

Read Aloud the Text

Point to each image and then read aloud the text. Discuss that the informational text describes the Great Barrier Reef and its struggle to survive. Invite students to share what they know about climate change, and then ask them to think about the Essential Question. **Ask:** *How is the reef affected by changes to the ocean?*

Think-Speak-Listen: Use the following sentence frame or the Think-Speak-Listen Flip Book to guide discussion: *It is/is not important for us to try to save the Great Barrier Reef because _____.*

👥 Differentiated Instruction
Build Language: Use Words with Suffixes

Read the first sentence in panel 1. Write the word *natural*. Point out that *natural* comes from *nature* and circle the suffix *-al*. Remind them that suffixes can change the part of speech of a word. Explain that the noun *nature* becomes the adjective *natural* when the suffix *-al* is added to the end of the word. Discuss the suffix *-ity*, which changes verbs to nouns. Ask students to find a word in panel 1 ending in *-ity* (diversity). Discuss how the adjective *diverse* becomes the noun *diversity*. Point out that the suffix *-ic* can also be used to change nouns to adjectives: for example, the suffix *-ic* changes the noun *optimism* to the adjective *optimistic*. Point out that it is important to understand how to form words with suffixes because it helps us recognize word meanings and expand our vocabulary. Use the Differentiated Instruction to practice understanding words with suffixes in a way that best matches the levels of your students.

☑ Use Oral and Written Language: Describe the Great Barrier Reef in a Guide

Task: *With a partner, describe the visual in panel 3. Use your description to create a visitor guide for the Great Barrier Reef. Include words with the suffixes -al and -ity.*

Ⓢ *The Great Barrier Reef has a ____ beauty. The ____ of life includes many fish.*

Ⓜ *The Great Barrier Reef's ____ is affected by ____. The ____ of marine life ____.*

Ⓛ *The Great Barrier Reef _____. The _____ of marine life _____, while ____*

🔄 Wrap Up

Today we talked about suffixes -al and -ity. Why is it important to know how to form words with suffixes?

Turn and Talk: *Describe something you see in nature. Use the words nature and natural in your description.*

👤👤👤 Differentiated Instruction
Build Language: Use Words with Suffixes

Ⓢ ubstantial Support

Model: Read panel 1. Write the words *nature* and *natural*. Ask students to read them with you. **Say:** Nature *is a noun. To form the adjective* natural, *cross out the -e and add the suffix -*al. Natural *is an adjective. In the text, the word* natural *describes the word* wonders. Then read the last sentence in panel 1. Write the words *diversity* and *diverse* and circle the suffix -*ity*. **Say:** *This suffix changes an adjective to a noun.* Show how to form the noun *diversity* by removing the -e in *diverse* and adding the suffix -*ity*.

Practice: Write the words *diverse, globe, nature*. Discuss the meaning of each word with students, and then work with them to change an adjective to a noun with the suffix -*ity*, or a noun to an adjective with the suffix -*al*. Distribute BLM 1. Guide students to choose the nouns and adjectives for each sentence. Have them read aloud the sentences.

Extend: Have partners work together to write new sentences with their choice of words. Then check their work.

Challenge: If students are ready, have them complete the Practice activity.

Ⓜ oderate Support

Model: Read panel 1. Point out the words *natural* and *diversity*. **Say:** *The word* natural *is an adjective. What noun does it come from?* Write the word *nature* and ask a volunteer to show how to change the noun into the adjective *natural*. Discuss that -*al* is a suffix that forms the adjective. Then discuss the word *diversity*. Write the word and ask a student to circle the suffix -*ity*. Point out that this suffix forms a noun from an adjective. Ask if anyone knows the adjective it comes from, *diverse*, and write the word. Give examples using the words *diverse, diversity, nature, natural* and have students suggest sentences.

Practice: Distribute BLM 2. Work with students to complete the Practice activity. Discuss the parts of speech of each word and the word it comes from (nouns: *nature, globe*; adjective: *diverse*).

Extend: Have partners complete the Extend activity on the BLM. Support students as needed. After checking their work, have them read aloud their sentences.

Challenge: If students are ready, have them work in partners to look up additional words with these suffixes in a print or online dictionary, and identify the suffixes and the parts of speech of each word.

Ⓛ ight Support

Use the text on page 30 in the *Texts for Close Reading* to complete the activities.

Practice: Review the suffixes -*al*, -*ity*, and -*ic*. Ask partners to review the text, and list words that have these suffixes. Guide the students to look up meanings in a print or online dictionary and write the words that they originate from. Have them explain what has to change from the origin words to form the words with suffixes.

Extend: Have partners use the words they identified from the text to write their own sentences using these words. Have them read aloud their sentences.

Challenge: Ask students to brainstorm other words with the suffixes of -*al*, -*ic*, and -*ity* and to write sentences with the words. Have them read aloud their sentences.

☑ Formative Assessment

Substantial Support	• With support, can students identify words with the suffixes -al, -ity, and -ic? • With support, can students complete sentences using words with the suffixes -al, -ity, and -ic?
Moderate Support	• Can students analyze words with suffixes? • Can students use words with the suffixes -al, -ity, and -ic when forming sentences?
Light Support	• Can students identify and analyze words with suffixes in a text? • Can students generate sentences of their own using words with the suffixes -al, -ity, and -ic?

Preview or Review Week 3 ELA Mini-Lessons

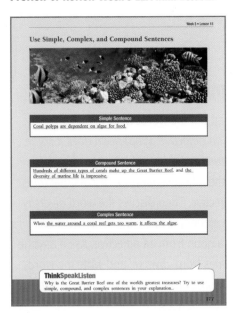

"Use Simple, Complex, and Compound Sentences," page 177

Student Objectives

LANGUAGE
Purpose:
• I can make a poster.
Form:
• I can use simple, compound, and complex sentences.
CONTENT
• I can comprehend an informational science text.

Additional Materials
• Unit Presentation
• *Texts for Close Reading* booklet
• Think-Speak-Listen Flip Book
• Student journal

Language Transfer Support

Note that speakers of Hmong may need extra support with the idea of coordinate conjunctions. Their native language uses two or more main verbs in a sentence without any connection. In other words, they do not connect main verbs with conjunctions or punctuation.

15 Use Simple, Complex, and Compound Sentences

Engage Thinking

Display the chart. Read aloud the simple sentence and the compound sentence. **Say:** *A simple sentence is a complete thought. A compound sentence is made of two simple sentences joined by a conjunction.* **Ask:** *What is the conjunction in this compound sentence?* Review the three conjunctions *and, but,* and *or.*

Turn and Talk: *What is the difference between a simple sentence and a compound sentence?*

Read and View Closely: Recognize Simple, Compound, and Complex Sentences

Have students look at the third sentence. **Say:** *This is a complex sentence. A complex sentence has one independent clause and one dependent clause.* **Ask:** *What makes a clause independent or dependent?* Explain that an independent clause is a sentence that is complete and can stand by itself. A dependent clause is not a complete sentence and cannot stand alone. Point out that dependent clauses can begin with one of these conjunctions: *when, because, if,* or *although.* **Ask:** *In the example, is the dependent clause at the beginning or end of the sentence?* Point out that a dependent clause can either appear at the beginning or at the end of a sentence.

👥 Differentiated Instruction
Build Language: Use Simple, Complex, and Compound Sentences

Say: *Now that we have looked at simple, compound, and complex sentences, we are going to practice using them.* Use the Differentiated Instruction to guide students to use simple, compound, and complex sentences.

Think-Speak-Listen: Use the following sentence frame or the Think-Speak-Listen Flip Book to guide discussion: The Great Barrier Reef is _____. It is _____ and it is _____. As _____, we have to try to save it.

☑ Use Oral and Written Language: Make a Poster

Task: *With a partner, make a poster to persuade people to save the Great Barrier Reef. Include at least one simple sentence, one complete sentence, and one complex sentence on the poster explaining why the Great Barrier Reef is so important.*

Ⓢ   *The Great Barrier Reef is very important because _____.*

Ⓜ   *In the Great Barrier Reef you can see _____ and you can see _____.*

Ⓛ   *When you visit the Great Barrier Reef, you can _____.*

Wrap Up

Today we learned about three different sentence types: simple, compound, and complex. Ask: *Why do good writers use a combination of these sentence types in their writing?*

Turn and Talk: *Tell your partner how you start your homework after school, using this sentence frame for a complex sentence: When I start my homework, I _____.*

👥 Differentiated Instruction
Build Language: Use Simple, Complex, and Compound Sentences

Ⓢ ubstantial Support

Model: Review the simple and compound sentences. **Say:** *I know a simple sentence has one subject and one predicate. And I know a compound sentence has two simple sentences joined together by a conjunction. What are the three conjunctions we learned today?* Review the use of *and, or*, and *but*. Then review the complex sentence. **Say:** *I know a complex sentence has one dependent clause and one independent clause.* Remind students that an independent clause is a complete sentence that can stand alone. Then remind them that a dependent clause is an incomplete sentence, cannot stand alone, and begins with conjunctions such as *when, because, if,* or *although*.

Practice: Distribute BLM 1. Read the aloud the sentences. Work with the students to decide whether each sentence is simple or compound, and circle S or C respectively.

Extend: Have the students work in partners to complete the task. After they read each pair of sentences, have them make a compound sentence by filling in the blank with the correct conjunction. Have them read aloud the sentences.

Challenge: Work with the students to underline the independent clause and circle the dependent clause in each sentence.

Ⓛ ight Support

Use the text on page 30 in the *Texts for Close Reading* to complete the activities.

Practice: Have the students reread paragraph 1. Work with them to underline the simple sentences, circle the compound sentences, and draw boxes around the complex sentences.

Extend: Have students reread paragraph 2. Have them tell a partner what they would like to see and do if they could visit the Great Barrier Reef. Remind them to use simple, compound, and complex sentences in their conversations.

Challenge: Have the students reread paragraph 3 and discuss with a partner why global warming may be harmful to the Great Barrier Reef.

Ⓜ oderate Support

Model: Review the simple and compound sentences. **Say:** *I know the difference between a simple sentence and a compound sentence. A simple sentence is a complete thought. A compound sentence is two simple sentences joined together by a conjunction. What are the three conjunctions we learned today?* Review the use of *and, or*, and *but*. Then review the complex sentence. **Say:** *I know that a complex sentence has an independent clause that can stand alone, and that a dependent clause cannot stand alone.*

Practice: Distribute BLM 2. Read the simple sentences. Work with the students to join each pair together into a compound sentence and fill in the blank with the correct conjunction *and, or,* or *but*.

Extend: Have the students work in partners to complete the task. Work with the students to read each complex sentence, underline the independent clause, and circle the dependent clause.

Challenge: Ask the students to imagine that they could visit the Great Barrier Reef. Have them talk with their partner about what they would like to see and do there. Remind them to use simple, compound, and complex sentences as they discuss.

☑ Formative Assessment

Substantial Support	• Can students identify the parts of simple, compound, and complex sentences with support? • Can students choose the correct conjunction to use in a compound sentence with support?
Moderate Support	• Can students identify the parts of simple, compound, and complex sentences with little support? • Can students choose the correct conjunction to use in a compound sentence with little support?
Light Support	• Can students identify simple, compound, and complex sentences in a text? • Can students use simple, compound, and complex sentences to communicate their thoughts?

The Economic Development of Cities

Essential Question

How do economic changes impact societies?

In this unit, students will read and compare selections about the development of cities to analyze how economic changes impact society.

Unit 9 Lessons at a Glance

Language Skills

Week 1
- Use Past Tense Verbs
- Use Noun Phrases to Add Detail
- Multimedia Writing
- Switch Between Verb Tenses
- Use Context to Explore Word Meaning

Week 2
- Use Irregular Nouns
- Form Complex Sentences
- Use Contractions
- Combine Clauses to Condense Ideas
- Explore Words to Build Vocabulary

Week 3
- Condense Ideas By Listing Nouns
- Use Verb Tense to Convey Time
- Use Introductory Prepositional Phrases to Establish Time
- Analyze Unfamiliar Vocabulary
- Use Commas in a Series

Lessons

Preview or Review Week 1 ELA Mini-Lessons

"Essential Question," pages 178–179

Student Objectives

LANGUAGE
Purpose:
• I can understand the Essential Question.
CONTENT
• I can understand the topic of the unit.

Additional Materials
• Unit Presentation

Introduce Unit 9: The Economic Development of Cities

Use the short lesson below to introduce the topic of the unit and help students understand the Essential Question.

Build Background and Vocabulary

Draw students' attention to the pictures on pages 162–163.

Say: *The topic of this is unit is "The Economic Development of Cities." These pictures introduce the topic and show us things we might see in a busy city.*

Display the two-column chart. Have students think about people and things they might find in a city. Invite students to read the caption for the first picture. Begin to fill in the chart. Elicit other illustrated vocabulary and brainstorm other ideas. Introduce and teach new vocabulary. Continue in this way with the other pictures.

People in a city	Things in a city
crowds	streets
immigrants	factories
community	bridges
workers	businesses
drivers	stores
tourists	theater

Ask: *How do these pictures help you understand the economic development of cities?*

Help students answer and encourage students to share their cultural knowledge and experiences about the topic.

👥👥 Differentiated Instruction
Explain the Essential Question

Point to the Essential Question and read it aloud. Say: **Economy** is about money. **Society** is another way to say "a group of people living together."

Ask: *How do economic changes impact societies? Say: Cities change over time. People move to cities to find work. Sometimes, there are lots of new jobs. The economy is good and people are happy. Other times, there isn't enough money. Then people look for new jobs and move to different cities. Society is impacted, or changed, when people leave.*

Explain that people are connected to the city. When the city changes, people's lives change too. Understanding the question will help students understand the texts and do well in their narrative writing tasks. Use the Differentiated Instruction to help students at all levels understand the Essential Question.

Display or invite students to access the unit opener video for Unit 9. After the video **ask:** *How do these pictures and the video help you answer the Essential Question?*

Then proceed to Lesson 1.

👥 Differentiated Instruction
Explain the Essential Question

Ⓢubstantial Support

Write *My Candy Store* on the board. **Say:** *This is my store. Point to the class and say: You have a good job. And you like candy! Gesture and say: You give me money. I give you candy. You are happy. I am happy, too! Then say: Oh, no. Now you don't have a job. You have no money.*

Write and use students' ideas to complete the second sentence: *The economy used to be good. We all had money. But now, the economy _____.*

Ask: *What happens next?* Elicit ideas. **Say:** *People move to find jobs. When jobs change, cities change too.* **Display the chart. Ask:** *Why do people move to cities? Why do they move away?*

Help students check the correct box. Then help students complete the following sentence frames.

	Jobs	**No Jobs**
People move in	X	
People move out		X

People move to cities for _____.

People move away from cities when _____.

Ⓛight Support

Read the Essential Question again.

Say: *Think about a crowded city with lots of happy people. Now imagine all those people lose their jobs.*

Make a cause-and-effect chart.

Ask: *How would things change?*

Elicit ideas and write them in the chart.

Cause	**Effect**
People move in	They are _____. The city is _____.
People move out	People aren't _____. The city isn't _____.

Say: *People move to cities to find jobs. When there are jobs, more people come. When there are no jobs, people leave. In this unit, you will learn why some cities change over time.*

Ⓜoderate Support

Read the Essential Question. **Say:** *People move to cities for jobs.* Display the chart. **Ask:** *What happens when there are jobs in a city? What happens when there aren't any jobs?*

Point to chart 1 and **say:** *This city has a good economy.* Then point to chart 2 and **say:** *This city has a bad economy.*

Help students fill it chart 2, then ask students to compare the two.

Say: *Cities change over time, and people change too. In this unit, you will learn why some cities change over time. There are reasons why jobs disappear and people move on.*

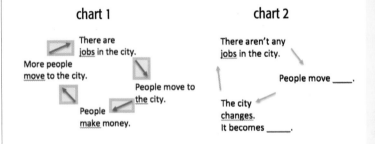

chart 1   chart 2

☑ Formative Assessment

Substantial Support	• Can students give an example of why water conservation is important with support? • Can students explain the meaning of key words such as **community**, **river**, and **landscape** with support?
Moderate Support	• Can students give an example of why water conservation is important with a little support? • Can students explain the meaning of key words such as **community**, **river**, and **landscape** with a little support?
Light Support	• Can students give an example of why water conservation is important in a full sentence? • Can students explain the meaning of key words such as **community**, **river**, and **landscape**?

Preview or Review Week 1 ELA Mini-Lessons

Short Read 1   Week 1 • Lesson 1

The Founding of Chicago
by Vaughn Smith

Native Americans have lived in the Chicago region of Illinois for thousands of years. The area served as home and as a trade center for different tribes...

One tribe...is known as Mound Builders. They built huge mounds of earth, which they used as burial grounds and centers for religious ceremonies...

Jacques Marquette
Louis Jolliet

The first Europeans to discover the Chicago area were Louis Jolliet and Jacques Marquette in 1673. Jolliet was a French Canadian explorer; Marquette was a Jesuit missionary...

Jean Baptiste Point du Sable

The first settler of Chicago was Jean Baptiste Point du Sable...a free black man believed to have been born in Haiti or Santo Domingo. He settled in Chicago around the late 1770s or early 1780s.

ThinkSpeakListen
Summarize the events described in this text.

"The Founding of Chicago," page 180

Student Objectives

LANGUAGE
Purpose:
• I can describe history in a brochure.
Form:
• I can use past tense verbs.
CONTENT
• I can understand key details in a historical account.

Additional Materials
• Unit Presentation
• Think-Speak-Listen Flip Book
• *Texts for Close Reading* booklet
• Student journal

Language Transfer Support

Note that speakers of Chinese, Haitian Creole, Spanish, Hmong, or Vietnamese may need additional support with word order in sentences. In these languages, nouns often precede adjectives.

1 Read "The Founding of Chicago"

Build Background and Vocabulary

Display the panels from the text "The Founding of Chicago" and explain their importance in the text. Explain to students that the events described really happened in the past. Invite students to share their cultural experiences and knowledge of Chicago or other big cities.

Read Aloud the Text

Read aloud panel 1. To support comprehension, ask students to find details in the picture that match words in the text (Native Americans, tribes). **Ask:** *What is the text about?* Repeat with panels 2–4. After reading, **ask:** *How are the four panels connected?* Model rereading panel 4 to find the answer. Refer to the Essential Question: *How do economic changes impact societies?* Model thinking through the answer. **Say:** *I see that Native Americans used the area as a trade center. The visual shows lots of people gathered together.* Invite students to share their ideas. **Say:** *This text is based on facts about the past. We call this type of text an informational text.*

Think-Speak-Listen: Use the following sentence frame or the Think-Speak-Listen Flip Book to guide discussion: *First, _____ lived in _____. Then _____.*

Differentiated Instruction
Build Language: Use Past Tense Verbs

Say: *One way to know that an event happened in the past is by recognizing past tense verbs.* Display the second sentence of panel 1 and point out the verb *served*. **Say:** *Verbs can tell us about time as well as action. I know that "served" is the past tense so I know that this text describes an action in the past. Writers use the past tense to describe events in history.* Use the Differentiated Instruction to practice using past tense verbs in a way that best matches the levels of your students.

☑ Use Oral and Written Language: Describe History in a Brochure

Task: *Imagine that you are writing a museum brochure to describe early history in the Chicago area. Collaborate with your peers to write complete sentences that use past tense verbs.* Use this opportunity to assess students using the rubric in *English Language Development Assessment*.

(S)   *Native Americans _____ in the Chicago area thousands of years ago.*

(M)   *They _____ the areas as their home, and one tribe _____ huge mounds nearby.*

(L)   *The first settler of Chicago _____.*

Wrap Up

Today we learned how important past tense verbs are in reading and writing about history. Why is it important to use past tense verbs correctly in a text?

Turn and Talk: *Describe an event in your city that happened a long time ago.*

👥 Differentiated Instruction
Build Language: Use Past Tense Verbs

Ⓢubstantial Support

Model: Use gestures and act out the meanings of the words *built, burial grounds, missionary, settled* and then check students' understanding of them. Point to served in panel 1.

Say: *Most historical texts are written in the past tense. Past tense verbs indicate that the action already happened.*

Practice: Point to the verb *built* in the second sentence on panel 2. Explain that the present tense of this verb is *build*. Distribute BLM 1. Work with students complete the activity.

Extend: Ask partners to form sentences using these sentence frames:

Native Americans built _____.

Europeans built _____.

Challenge: If students are ready, discuss the verb to be. Reread panel 3 and distribute BLM 2. Explain that *was* and *were* are the past tense verbs of *to be.*

Ⓜoderate Support

Model: Use gestures and act out the meanings of the words *built, burial grounds, missionary, settled* and then check students' understanding of them. **Say:** *Most historical texts are written in the past tense. Past tense verbs indicate that the action took place in the past.* Review the past tense forms of *to be: was* and *were.*

Practice: Distribute BLM 2 and invite students to help you complete the first two sentences. Have them work in pairs to complete the remaining sentences.

Extend: Ask partners to complete the Extend exercise on BLM 2.

Challenge: If students are ready, explain that "have lived" signals the present perfect tense. It uses the helping verb *have* with the past participle *lived* to show something that started in the past and continues now. Have them write two sentences using the present perfect tense.

Ⓛight Support

Practice: Review how to form the past tense in regular and irregular verbs. Have students read "The Founding of Chicago" on page 4 in their *Texts for Close Reading*. Ask them to identify all of the past tense verbs in paragraphs 4 and 5.

Extend: Remind students that verbs such as *be* indicate state of being. Then read aloud the first sentence in paragraph 1 on page 4. **Say:** *The phrase "have lived" signals the present perfect tense. It uses the helping verb have with the past tense form lived to show something that started in the past and continues until now.*

Challenge: Have partners compose new sentences based on what they learned in the text about important events in the history of the United States. Instruct them to use past tense verbs and present perfect verb tenses in their sentences.

☑ Formative Assessment

Substantial Support	• Can students recognize and use regular past tense verbs? • Can students recognize irregular past tense verbs and use them in sentence frames?
Moderate Support	• Can students use the past tense verbs were and was? • Can students complete sentence frames with past tense irregular verbs?
Light Support	• Can students generate original sentences in which they use past tense verbs? • Can students explain what the use of past tense and present perfect tense signify?

Preview or Review Week 1 ELA Mini-Lessons

Use Noun Phrases to Add Detail

Week 1 • Lesson 2

Sentence	Subject	Linking Verb	Noun Phrase
The first Europeans to discover the Chicago area were Louis Jolliet and Jacques Marquette in 1673.	The first Europeans to discover the Chicago area	were	Louis Jolliet and Jacques Marquette
Jolliet was a French Canadian explorer.	Jolliet	was	French Canadian explorer
Marquette was a Jesuit missionary.	Marquette	was	Jesuit missionary
The first settler of Chicago was Jean Baptiste Point du Sable.	The first settler of Chicago	was	Jean Baptiste Point du Sable

ThinkSpeakListen
How do noun phrases give readers information?

181

"Use Noun Phrases to Add Detail," page 181

Student Objectives

LANGUAGE
Purpose:
• I can describe details in a report.
Form:
• I can use predicate nominatives.
CONTENT
• I can recognize informational social studies texts.

Additional Materials
• Unit Presentation
• Think-Speak-Listen Flip Book
• *Texts for Close Reading* booklet
• Student journal

Language Transfer Support

Students who speak Cantonese, Hmong, or Korean as their native language may need extra help with verb forms showing number. In these languages, verb forms do not change to show the number of the subject.

2 Use Noun Phrases to Add Detail

Engage Thinking

Display the chart. **Say:** *We read about the founding of Chicago, a city in Illinois.* Write: *Some tribes. mound builders.* **Say:** *I can link these ideas by using a linking verb.* Write this sentence on the board, and underline the verb were: *Some tribes <u>were</u> mound builders.*

Turn and Talk: *How would you use a noun phrase to add detail to a sentence about Chicago? What word would you use connect the ideas?*

Read and View Closely: Recognize Noun Phrases

Read aloud the first sentence in the chart. **Say:** *We call the verb* were *a linking verb. The noun phrase that comes after the linking verb restates or gives more detail about the subject.* Reread the first sentence and **say:** *The noun phrase "Louis Jolliet and Jacques Marquette" renames the subject "the first Europeans to discover the Chicago area." The subject and the noun phrase are linked by the verb* were.

Think-Speak-Listen: Use the following sentence frame or the Think-Speak-Listen Flip Book to guide discussion: *Noun phrases give readers information because _____.*

👤👤👤 Differentiated Instruction
Build Language: Use Noun Phrases to Add Detail

Read aloud the second sentence. Model identifying the subject, the linking verb, and the noun phrase. **Say:** *In this sentence, the noun phrase "French Canadian explorer" gives us more information about the subject, Jolliet. The subject and the noun phrase are linked by the verb* was. *Writers use noun phrases because they add more detail to the subject.* Use the Differentiated Instruction to practice using noun phrases to add detail in a way that best matches the levels of your students.

☑ Use Oral and Written Language: Describe Details in a Report

Task: *Write a report about the settlers in the Chicago area, using information you learned. Include noun phrases to describe the people in your account.*

Ⓢ *The Chicago area served as _____ for different tribes.*

Ⓜ *One tribe is known _____ because they _____.*

Ⓛ *Jean Baptiste Point du Sable, who _____, was _____.*

🔄 Wrap Up

Today we learned to recognize and to use noun phrases to give more information about a subject. How does recognizing noun phrases help us better understand a text?

Turn and Talk: *Describe a person in history. Use noun phrases to give more information about him or her.*

▲▲▲ Differentiated Instruction
Build Language: Use Noun Phrases to Add Detail

Ⓢubstantial Support

Model: Use gestures and act out the meanings of the words *discover, missionary, settler* and then check students' understanding of them. Read aloud the third sentence. **Say**: *The subject Jolliet is followed by the linking verb was. The noun phrase "French Canadian explorer" renames Jolliet and tells exactly who he was. It adds important detail and meaning to the sentence.*

Practice: With students, read the third sentence. Lead students to identify the subject, the linking verb, and the noun phrase. Discuss how the noun phrase adds meaning to the sentence by renaming and describing the subject.

Extend: Have partners work together to complete the sentence frames in BLM 1.

Challenge: If students are ready, explain that because noun phrases rename the subject in a sentence, their order can be reversed without changing the subject. Model how to reverse the order of the first sentence in the Use Noun Phrases to Add Detail chart. Then ask student pairs to reverse the remaining sentences.

Ⓜoderate Support

Model: Read aloud the sentences in the chart and identify the subjects, linking verbs, and noun phrases (that are not subjects). **Say:** *I know that each noun phrase is related to its subject because it explains or identifies the subject.*

Practice: Work with students to identify the parts of the following sentences:

Chicago was a hub for trading goods.

The area was a good place to found a settlement.

Extend: Ask partners to write original sentences based on the information in the chart. Make sure that they include noun phrases that rename or add detail to the subject. For example: "One of the first Europeans to discover the Chicago area was a Jesuit missionary."

Challenge: Distribute BLM 2. Have students complete the sentences by adding noun phrases to describe the subjects in the sentences.

Ⓛight Support

Practice: Have students read pages 4–5 in their *Texts for Close Reading*. Distribute BLM 2. Have students complete the sentences by adding noun phrases to describe the subjects in the sentences.

Extend: Tell students that recognizing noun phrases in a sentence can help deepen understanding of the subject. Have them work with a partner to answer the following questions:

Where was Jean Baptiste Point du Sable from?

When did Chicago become an incorporated city?

Challenge: Using noun phrases in a sentence can help deepen understanding of the subject. Have students write two original sentences about the early settlers of Chicago based on the informatiion they learned in the *Texts for Close Reading*. Both sentences should include noun phrases.

✓	Formative Assessment
Substantial Support	• Can students identify noun phrases? • With help, can students complete sentence frames that include noun phrases?
Moderate Support	• Can students recognize a sentence pattern that includes a noun phrase? • Can students generate sentences including noun phrases?
Light Support	• Can students identify noun phrases with little or no assistance? • Can students independently write sentences including noun phrases?

Preview or Review Week 1 ELA Mini-Lessons

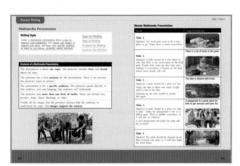

"Process Writing," pages 182–183

Student Objectives

LANGUAGE
Purpose:
• I can analyze a multimedia presentation.
Form:
• I can identify the parts of a multimedia presentation.
CONTENT
• I can recognize a multimedia presentation.

Additional Materials
• Unit Presentation
• Think-Speak-Listen Flip Book
• *Texts for Close Reading* booklet
• Student journal

---

3 Process Writing: Multimedia Presentation

Engage Thinking

Tell students that they will analyze a multimedia presentation so that they can recognize its parts. Read aloud the presentation topic.

> Create a multimedia presentation about a way to improve your community. Use visuals and images to support your ideas, and keep your specific audience in mind as you inform, persuade, and/or entertain.

Say: *Let's ask questions to make sure we understand the presentation topic. What will the writer write about? What type of writing is it? What will the writer include?*

👥👥 Differentiated Instruction
Read and View Closely:
Analyze a Multimedia Presentation

Say: *We're going to look at a multimedia presentation, which is a text combined with visuals, such as photographs or diagrams.*

Say: *As I read aloud the presentation, I will stop so that we can analyze four features of a multimedia presentation. The first feature is having a purpose for the presentation. Let's look at the first slides.* Read the first two slides and then pause. **Ask:** *What is the purpose of this presentation?* Check that students can identify that the presentation is intended to persuade its listeners.

Say: *The second feature is that the presentation will have a specific audience. Who is the audience for this presentation?* Have some pairs share their ideas.

Continue to read through slide 5. **Say:** *The third feature of a presentation is that it includes more than one form of media. Turn to your partner and name the types of media we've seen so far.* Check that students can identify the text and photos.

Say: *The last feature—the images—help you to understand the slide.* Go back to slide 3, of the lake. **Say:** *Turn to your partner and say how the image of the lake helps us to understand the text.* Check that students can relate how the image connects with the description.

Then continue the lesson using Differentiated Instruction that best fits the needs of your students.

Share Your Understanding

Bring the students back together. **Ask:** *What did we learn today about multimedia presentations?* Review the features as needed.

Final Writing Assignment

Use the English Language Development Assessment to assess students' writing for their ELA writing assignment.

👥👥 Differentiated Instruction
Read and View Closely: Analyze a Multimedia Presentation

Ⓢubstantial Support

Model: Distribute BLM 1. **Say:** *Let's read and analyze another multimedia presentation that answers the writing topic.* Read the title and pause. **Ask:** *What is this presentation about?* Model answering the question.

Practice: Continue reading the presentation and ask the same questions that you asked about the Mentor Multimedia Presentation. Invite students to answer. Check that students can connect the images with descriptive words. Help students with any unfamiliar words.

Extend: Have students in pairs complete the activity on BLM 1.

Challenge: Ask *yes/no* and *wh-* questions to help students discuss the features of the presentation. Ask questions such as: *Does the presentation use more than one type of media? Does the presentation have a specific audience in mind? Who? Does the presentation have a purpose? What does it want the audience to do? How do the images support the content?*

Restate students' responses as complete sentences and have them repeat.

Ⓜoderate Support

Model: Draw students' attention to the Mentor Multimedia Presentation in their Student Books. **Say:** *Let's analyze how the writer addressed the presentation topic.* Make the chart below. Read aloud and view the entire presentation. **Ask:** *What is the purpose of this presentation?* Elicit *to clean up the park* and write it on the chart.

Multimedia Presentation Feature	Example from the Text
1. Purpose	to clean up a park
2. Audience	members of the community
3. Forms of media used	photographs
4. Visuals and images support ideas	photographs that match what is being said in the script

Practice: Work with students to complete the rest of the chart for the presentation features. Use one specific slide to fill in the fourth item.

Extend: Have students work with a partner. Tell them to use the chart they made above and to add two more rows. In the rows, they should add notes about what visual images on the other two slides you didn't cover above.

Challenge: Have pairs join another pair to compare charts. They should summarize the information on the slides and describe how the images help support the text. Remind students to elaborate on each other's statements to add to the discussion.

Ⓛight Support

Practice: Distribute BLM 2. **Say:** *These are the slides from the Multimedia Presentation you viewed in class. We will look more closely at how writers use the features of a multimedia presentation.* Read the presentation with students.

Extend: Have student pairs complete the activity on BLM 2.

Challenge: Write: *What are the features of a multimedia presentation? How does this presentation use them to answer the writing topic?* If necessary, review the four features: *purpose, audience, multiple forms of media, and images that relate to text.* Have partners discuss the questions and give examples from the presentation to support their answers. Remind students to elaborate on each other's statements to add to the discussion.

✓ Formative Assessment

Substantial Support	• Do students recognize the criteria for an oral presentation with visuals in the Mentor Multimedia Presentation?
Moderate Support	• Do students recognize the ways in which the Mentor Multimedia Presentation meets the criteria for an oral presentation with visuals? • Can students describe the features of an oral presentation with visuals in their own words?
Light Support	• Do students recognize criteria and analyze how the Mentor Text meets the criteria for an oral presentation with visuals? • Can students describe in their own words how the writer meets the criteria for an oral presentation with visuals?

"Chicago: An American Hub," pages 184–185

Student Objectives

LANGUAGE
Purpose:
• I can express sequence of events in a time line.
Form:
• I can switch between verb tenses.
CONTENT
• I can recognize informational social studies texts.

Additional Materials
• Unit Presentation
• Think-Speak-Listen Flip Book
• *Texts for Close Reading* booklet
• Student journal

Language Transfer Support

Students whose native language is Cantonese, Haitian Creole, Hmong, or Vietnamese may need extra support using and understanding linking verbs. In these languages, *be* is often implied with adjectives. Students are likely to omit the linking verb (e.g., *Chicago big city*).

4 Read "Chicago: An American Hub"

Build Background and Vocabulary

Display the panels from "Chicago: An American Hub." **Say:** *Today you will read about some things that contribute to Chicago's importance as an American city.* Invite students to share their cultural experiences and knowledge of Chicago or other big cities. If students have already read the text, ask them what they remember.

Read Aloud the Text

Read aloud panel 1. Ask students to find images that match words in the text (settlement, river). **Ask:** *How did Chicago begin? How did it change?* Repeat with panels 2–4. After reading, **ask:** *Why did Chicago become one of America's largest cities?* Model rereading Panel 2 to find the answer. Repeat with panels 5–8. Refer to the Essential Question and invite students to discuss how economic changes impact societies. **Say:** *This story is about things that actually happened. We call this an informational social studies text.*

Think-Speak-Listen: Use the following sentence frame or the Think-Speak-Listen Flip Book to guide discussion: *I think that Chicago today might be attractive to new immigrants because _____.*

👥 Differentiated Instruction
Build Language: Switch Between Verb Tenses

Remind students that the verb tense gives clues to when events happen. **Say:** *Switching between tenses helps writers describe both past and present actions in the same text.* Point to the sentence in panel 3. **Say:** *The verb* worked *tells us the action happened in the past.* Next, Read aloud panel 6. **Say:** *The verb* call *is in the present tense, so we know that this is happening now.* Use the Differentiated Instruction to practice switching between verb tenses in a way that best matches the levels of your students.

☑ Use Oral and Written Language: Express Sequence of Events in a Time Line

Task: *In groups, create a time line that shows how Chicago has changed over the years. Use the information in "Chicago, An American Hub."*

(S) *Chicago began as _____.*
Many people _____.

(M) *_____ in factories.*
_____ of nearly 300,000 in 1870.

(L) *Today, Chicago _____.*
_____ a leader in _____.

🔄 Wrap Up

Today we learned about switching verb tenses to show when events occur in a text. How does recognizing and switching between verb tenses help your writing?

Turn and Talk: *Describe what you did this morning and what you are doing now. Switch verb tense as you change from describing the past to describing the present.*

👪 Differentiated Instruction
Build Language: Switch Between Verb Tenses

Ⓢubstantial Support

Model: Use gestures and act out the meanings of the words *settlement, flocked, immigrants* and then check students' understanding of the words. Remind students that verbs can tell us when events happen. Read aloud the second sentence in panel 4. **Say:** *The verb* called *shows that this part of the text happened in the past. It is in the past tense.* Next, read aloud the first sentence in panel 5. **Say:** *The verb* is *shows that this part of the text is happening in the present.*

Practice: Invite students to help you switch the verb tenses in these sentences from the past to the present:

People <u>flocked</u> to this new city.

People <u>worked</u> in factories that produced meat.

Extend: Distribute BLM 1. Ask the students to work in pairs to complete the exercise.

Challenge: If students are ready, have them find irregular verbs in the text. Then have students complete this sentence with the past tense: *Chicago soon _____ one of the largest cities.*

Ⓜoderate Support

Model: Use gestures and act out the meanings of the words *settlement, flocked, immigrants* and then check students' understanding of them. **Say:** *Some past tense verbs are irregular and do not end in -ed.* Point out the verb *became* in panel 4. *Say: The action word* became *is in the past tense, so the events happened in the past.* Point to panel 7. **Say:** *The action word* is *is in the present tense, so the action is happening now.*

Practice: Invite students to help you change the verbs in the following sentences from present tense to past. you may need to explain to students that the verbs are irregular.

Chicago <u>is</u> a vibrant city.

The city <u>draws</u> new immigrants.

Extend: Distribute BLM 2. Ask the students to work with a partner to complete the exercise.

Challenge: Have students complete the following sentences:

In the past, Chicago _____.

Today, Chicago _____.

Ⓛight Support

Practice: Have students read paragraph 3 on page 7 in "Chicago: An American Hub" in *Texts for Close Reading*. Point out two verb tenses: *made* and *knows* and discuss why the past and the present are both used.

Extend: Working with a partner, have students read the heading above paragraph 9 on page 9 and complete the sentence: *The heading tells us to expect the _____ tense because _____.* Then have students find examples in the paragraph to support their answer.

Challenge: Ask students to write two or three original sentences about Chicago using the past, present, and present perfect verb tenses.

☑ Formative Assessment

Substantial Support	• Students recognize two different verb tenses. • Students can switch between two verb tenses with support.
Moderate Support	• Students understand the purpose of switching verb tenses. • Students can switch between verb tenses within sentence frames.
Light Support	• Students recognize more than two different verb tenses and can switch between them. • Students can write original sentences using a variety of verb tenses.

Preview or Review Week 1 ELA Mini-Lessons

"A Tragedy That Brought Change," page 186

Student Objectives

LANGUAGE
Purpose:
• I can analyze word meanings in a chart.
Form:
• I can use context to explore word meaning.
CONTENT
• I can use word meaning in context to understand historical nonfiction.

Additional Materials
• Unit Presentation
• Think-Speak-Listen Flip Book
• *Texts for Close Reading* booklet
• Student journal
• Online or print dictionaries

Language Transfer Support

Students whose first language is Spanish or Cantonese may have difficulty pronouncing the /sh/ sound in words such as *shirtwaist*. Pre-teach this sound and its spelling in small-group settings, focusing on articulation of the sound. Provide additional practice time for students to master the sound and spelling.

5 Read "A Tragedy That Brought Change"

Build Background and Vocabulary

Display the panels from "A Tragedy That Brought Change." Explain that the first image shows women in a clothing factory in the early 1900s. The second and third panels show the fire they will be reading about. Invite students to share their cultural experiences and knowledge of changes initiated by tragic events. If students have read the text, invite them to share what they remember.

Read Aloud the Text

Read aloud panel 1. To support comprehension, ask students to find details in the picture that match words in the text (women working, factory, sewed, fabric). Ask questions, such as: *What place is this? When does this event happen?* Repeat with panels 2–4. After reading, **ask:** *Why were changes needed for factory workers?* Then refer to the Essential Question and invite students to discuss how economic changes impact societies. **Say:** *The text is about a real event that occurred in 1911. This is called historical nonfiction.*

Think-Speak-Listen: Use the following sentence frame or the Think-Speak-Listen Flip Book to guide discussion: *If the factory had _____, then _____.*

👥 Differentiated Instruction
Build Language: Use Context to Explore Word Meaning

Say: *Words can have more than one meaning depending on the way is is used in a text.* Point to the word *regulation* in the last sentence. **Say:** *Regulation can mean "an official rule or law" or "control of a process."* **Ask:** *Would this article about the fire be in a social studies text, or in a science text?* Elicit answers. **Say:** *Since this article is historical, I think it would be in a social studies text, so* regulation *means "an official rule or law."* Use the Differentiated Instruction to practice using context to explore word meaning in a way that best matches the levels of your students.

☑ Use Oral and Written Language: Analyze Word Meanings in a Chart

Task: *Create sa two-column chart. Choose two or three words from the text. Write two sentences, using each word in a different context: science, math, or social studies.*

Ⓢ   *The _____ was five pounds. The weight of their decision was big.*

Ⓜ   *The _____ of the chair was ten pounds. The _____ of their decision was big.*

Ⓛ   *The _____ was _____. The _____ of their _____ was _____.*

🔄 Wrap Up

Today we used context or the type of text to explore word meaning. How does knowing the type of text help you think about what a word might mean in context?

Turn and Talk: *Tell your partner a word "out of context." Ask your partner to think of a context or type of text in which the word could be used.*

👥👥👥 Differentiated Instruction
Build Language: Use Context to Explore Word Meaning

Ⓢubstantial Support

Model: Use gestures and act out the meanings of the words *tragedy, fire, regulations* and then check students' understanding of them. Review with students that the meaning of a word can depend on the type of text or context in which a word is used. Distribute BLM 1. Point to the first chart. **Say:** *I see two different contexts for the word* change*. When I read the first sentence, I think about how the word is used in context. I can also use the words* price, count, amount, *and* money *as clues. I think this is a math sentence. So I'll write* Math.

Practice: Support students in exploring the meanings of the word *weight* in the second chart. Guide them to determine the meaning in each sentence based on its context.

Extend: Have students work in pairs to complete the Extend activity. Provide support as needed.

Challenge: If students are ready, work with them to complete the Practice activity on BLM 2.

Ⓜoderate Support

Model: Use gestures and act out the meanings of the words *tragedy, fire, regulations* and then check students' understanding of them. **Say:** *A word's meaning may be different in a social studies context from its meaning in a science or math context.* Distribute BLM 2. Point to the first chart: **Say:** *When I read the first sentence, I think about* weather. *I know that is a science topic. The second sentence reminds me of what I read about the Triangle Factory fire, so it must have a social studies context.*

Practice: Work with students to complete the second chart. Help students check word meaning in a dictionary.

Extend: Have partners discuss how they would illustrate the word *requirements*, using the example sentences. Have them draw an image for each context on the chart.

Challenge: If students are ready, have them review the phrase *minimum wage*. Ask them to consider how the adjective *minimum* gives a clue about the intended meaning of the word *wage*. **Ask:** *What other meanings are there for the word* wage?

Ⓛight Support

Practice: Have students read "A Tragedy That Brought Change" on page 10 in their *Texts for Close Reading*. Have them find the word *meager* in paragraph 4 and copy the sentence in which it is used. Ask them to determine the context in which the word is used: *social studies, science,* or *math*. Then have them write a second sentence using the word in a different context.

Extend: Have partners review paragraph 4 on page 10. Ask them to choose a word they think could have different meanings in different contexts. Have them check word meaning in a dictionary and then write two sentences showing the word used in two different contexts.

Challenge: If students are ready, have them review the phrase *safety regulations* in paragraph 4. Ask them to consider how this phrase can apply to both social studies and science contexts. Have them write two to three sentences about their ideas.

✔️ Formative Assessment

Substantial Support	• With support, do students understand the value of going beyond a definition and using context to explore a word's meaning? • With support, can students recognize how context can illustrate a word's meaning?
Moderate Support	• Can students go beyond a dictionary definition and use context to explore a word's meaning? • Can students demonstrate an understanding of a word's meaning based on context?
Light Support	• Can students recognize how a word is used in context and apply the context to the word's meaning? • Can students express a word's meaning in different contexts?

Preview or Review Week 2 ELA Mini-Lessons

Week 2 • Lesson 6

Use Irregular Nouns

Sentence	Singular Form	Plural Form
People flocked to this new city, searching for jobs and hoping for a better life.	life	lives
According to the U.S. Census of 1870, nearly 300,000 people called Chicago home.	person	people
The first settler of Chicago was Jean Baptiste Point du Sable...a free black man believed to be born in Haiti or Santo Domingo.	man	men
At the end of the day on March 25, 1911, the women who worked in New York City's Triangle Factory were preparing to go home.	woman	women

ThinkSpeakListen
Create new sentences using the plural nouns listed above.

187

"Use Irregular Nouns," page 187

Student Objectives

LANGUAGE
Purpose:
- I can inform about Chicago's history in a news report.

Form:
- I can understand the use of irregular nouns.

CONTENT
- I can comprehend an informational social studies text.

Additional Materials

- Unit Presentation
- Think-Speak-Listen Flip Book
- *Texts for Close Reading* booklet
- Student journal

Language Transfer Support

Note that speakers of Chinese, Hmong, or Vietnamese may need extra help understanding the concept of irregular nouns. In these languages, there is no plural form for nouns, so the notion of an irregular plural may be particularly hard for these students to grasp.

6 Use Irregular Nouns

Engage Thinking

Display panel 2 of "Chicago: An American Hub." Write: *The new immigrant family had one child. Many children were with the immigrants in Chicago.* **Ask:** *Which sentence best describes the picture?* **Say:** *There are many people in the picture, so the sentence with plural nouns is the best choice.*

Turn and Talk: *What do you notice about the plural and singular nouns in the sentences?*

Read and View Closely: Recognize Irregular Nouns

Display the chart, and point out the underlined nouns in the sentences. Read the first sentence. **Say:** *The plural of most singular nouns is formed by adding -s or -es, such as in the words* jobs *and* clothes. *The plural of the word* life *is different. It is an irregular noun.* Read aloud the singular and plural forms of *life.* **Ask:** *How was the singular* life *changed to make the plural* lives? Elicit answers. Then continue by analyzing the remaining sentences and irregular nouns. **Say:** *The plural of some irregular nouns is formed by changing the f to v before adding -es. Others are formed by changing the vowels, the ending, or respelling the whole word.*

👥 Differentiated Instruction
Build Language: Use Irregular Nouns

Review row 2 of the chart. **Say:** *Using the forms of irregular nouns takes practice. How would you know to use* person *or* people *in this sentence?* Continue with rows 3 and 4. **Say:** *When you write, ask yourself, "Is the noun regular or irregular? Am I writing about one or more than one? Do I need the singular or plural form?"* Ask for ideas from students on how they would make sure they had used the correct form. Use the Differentiated Instruction to practice using irregular nouns in a way that best matches the levels of your students.

Think Speak Listen: Have students create new sentences using the irregular nouns in the chart or use the Think-Speak-Listen Flip Book to guide discussion.

☑ Use Oral and Written Language: Inform About Chicago's History in a News Report

Task: *Imagine you and your partner are editors for a Chicago history magazine. Write a news report, telling about the arrival of immigrants as the city grew.*

Ⓢ *Many immigrant _____ went to school. They had to _____.*

Ⓜ *When they came to the city, many _____ and _____ found work in factories.*

Ⓛ *The work was hard for these _____, but many _____ believed _____.*

Wrap Up

Today we learned that recognizing and correctly using irregular nouns will help us better understand what we read. How can this skill improve our writing?

Turn and Talk: *Describe a visit to a national park and the wildlife that visitors might see there. Use irregular nouns.*

👥👥 Differentiated Instruction
Build Language: Use Irregular Nouns

ⓢubstantial Support

Model: Use gestures and act out the meanings of the words *flocked, searching, settler* and then check students' understanding of them. Refer to the Use Irregular Nouns chart. Read aloud the first row. **Say:** *I see the singular noun* life*. I see it is irregular because the plural* lives *is not formed by adding -s or -es. The plural nouns* people, men, *and* women *are also irregular.*

Practice: Distribute BLM 1. Invite students to help you identify the irregular nouns in each sentence. **Ask:** *Is the irregular noun in the sentence singular or plural?*

Extend: Have partners do the Extend activity. Encourage them to read a sentence with their irregular noun choice to make sure it makes sense before writing the noun.

Challenge: If students are ready, work with them to complete the Practice activity on BLM 2.

ⓜoderate Support

Model: Use gestures and act out the meanings of the words *flocked, searching, settler* and then check students' understanding of them. Explain that the plural forms of some nouns are irregular. Refer to the Use Irregular Nouns chart. Read aloud the singular and plural noun forms. **Say:** *I see that the plural of* life *is not* lifes*. Instead, it is spelled by changing the* f *to* v *before adding* -es. Guide students in reading aloud the sentences and noting the irregular nouns.

Practice: Distribute BLM 2. Work with students to complete the Practice activity. **Say:** *Read the sentence with your choice to see if it makes sense before you write it.*

Extend: Ask partners to complete the Extend activity. Provide support as needed.

Challenge: If students are ready, guide partners to list the plural nouns they find in the text. Then have them write the singular and plural form, and tell which nouns are irregular.

ⓛight Support

Practice: Have students read "A Tragedy That Brought Change" in their *Texts for Close Reading*, paragraph 1. Help students list the nouns, write the plural or singular form, and then identify which nouns are irregular.

Extend: Have partners select a sentence containing the plural form of an irregular noun in paragraph 1 or 4. Encourage them to try rewriting the sentence using the singular form. For example: *At the end of the day on March 25, 1922, each woman who worked in New York City's Triangle Factory was preparing to go home.*

Challenge: If students are ready, have them choose a section of the selection "Chicago: An American Hub," starting on page 6. Have them identify and list irregular nouns and then write their own sentences using the nouns.

☑ Formative Assessment

Substantial Support	• With support, can students recognize irregular nouns in a text and distinguish the singular from the plural form? • With support, can students use irregular nouns correctly in sentences?
Moderate Support	• With some support, can students recognize irregular nouns in a text and correctly identify the singular or plural form used? • With some support, can students determine which form of an irregular noun to use in a sentence?
Light Support	• Do students recognize irregular nouns in a text and understand how to spell both the singular and plural form? • Can students use irregular nouns in their own writing?

Preview or Review Week 2 ELA Mini-Lessons

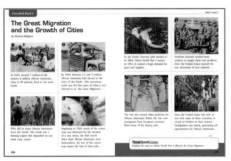

"The Great Migration and the Growth
of Cities," pages 188–189

Student Objectives

LANGUAGE
Purpose:
• I can describe a historical event.
Form:
• I can form complex sentences.
CONTENT
• I can follow a time line of events in an
  informational social studies text.

Additional Materials
• Unit Presentation
• Think-Speak-Listen Flip Book
• *Texts for Close Reading* booklet
• Student journal

Metacognitive Prompt

*Today, we will be reading about the
Great Migration and how it changed the
populations of the South and the North.
As you read, think of ways to keep in mind
when and where events happen. You
may want to look for key words, dates, or
place names that will remind you of what
historical events are described in the text.*

7 Read "The Great Migration and the Growth of Cities"

Build Background and Vocabulary

Display the panels from "The Great Migration and the Growth of Cities." Use this as an opportunity to discuss the similarities between the words *migration* and *immigration*, *migration* refers to moving and *immigration* is a specific type of move (from one's country of origin). Invite students to share their cultural experiences and knowledge about migration and the growth of cities. If students have read the text, ask what they remember and what they know about the Great Migration.

Read Aloud the Text

Read aloud panel 1. To support comprehension, ask questions, such as: *What does rural mean? What kind of work might many people do in a rural area?* Read aloud panels 2–8. After each panel, , **ask:** *How did the lives of African Americans change between 1910 and 1914?* Refer to the Essential Question and invite students to discuss how economic changes impact societies. **Say:** *The text tells about a real event in U.S. history and includes dates and explanations for this event. We call this an informational social studies text.*

Think-Speak-Listen: Use the following sentence frame or the Think-Speak-Listen Flip Book to guide discussion: *World War I affected the Great Migration because _____.*

👥 Differentiated Instruction
Build Language: Form Complex Sentences

Review connecting words and clauses. Then display the second sentence from panel 5. **Say:** *This sentence is a complex sentence with one independent clause that can stand on its own and one subordinate clause that cannot.* Underline each clause. **Ask:** *What word connects the clauses?* **Say:** *Combining two related ideas in one complex sentence makes your writing more interesting.* Use the Differentiated Instruction to practice forming complex sentences in a way that best matches the levels of your students.

☑ Use Oral and Written Language: Describe a Historical Event

Task: *Imagine that you are preparing an online history lesson about events in the Great Migration. Collaborate with your group to prepare a time line. Write complex sentences on the time line to tell what happened in specific years.*

(S) *Before _____, _____ lived in the rural South.*

(M) *After _____, the cotton crop _____ and _____.*

(L) *Because _____, northern factories _____ as a chance for _____.*

🔄 Wrap Up

Today we learned that complex sentences contain an independent and a subordinate clause. How can a complex sentence help you understand how two ideas are connected?

Turn and Talk: *Describe moving to or visiting a new place. Use a variety of simple, compound, and complex sentences.*

👥👥 Differentiated Instruction
Build Language: Form Complex Sentences

Ⓢubstantial Support

Model: Use gestures and act out the meanings of the words *factories, war products, enlisted* and then check students' understanding of them. Write: *Thousands of men enlisted. The Northern factories needed more workers.* **Say:** *If I write all of my sentences like this, they sound choppy. I can form these two sentences into one complex sentence. I'll use the connecting word* after. Write: *After thousands of men enlisted, the Northern factories needed more workers.*

Practice: Distribute BLM 1. Invite students to do the Practice activity with you. **Say:** *As I read the first sentence, I look for two ideas that are expressed in two clauses. I also look for a connecting word.* Help students identify the clauses and the connecting word. **Ask:** *Which clause can stand alone? Which cannot?*

Extend: Have students work in pairs to complete the Extend activity. Provide support as needed.

Challenge: If students are ready, model how to complete the Practice activity on BLM 2.

Ⓜoderate Support

Model: Use gestures and act out the meanings of the words *factories, war products, enlisted* and then check students' understanding of them. Read aloud the last sentence in panel 5. **Say:** *I read two ideas in this sentence. Each idea is expressed in a clause. The word* when *connects them. I know this is a complex sentence because the first clause cannot stand alone. The second clause can.*

Practice: Distribute BLM 2. Work with students to complete the Practice activity. As needed, reteach how to express two ideas in one complex sentence.

Extend: Have partners complete the Extend activity on the BLM.

Challenge: If students are ready, have them read "The Great Migration and the Growth of Cities" Have them select two sentences to use to form a complex sentence by adding a connecting word.

Ⓛight Support

Practice: Have students read paragraph 1 on page 12 of "The Great Migration and the Growth of Cities" in *Texts for Close Reading* and select two ideas that they can use to form a complex sentence. For example: *When they were sent to the South in search of workers, recruiters offered people free train tickets to the North.*

Extend: Have partners read paragraph 3 on page 13. Have them take apart the fourth sentence and write two separate sentences. Then have them choose one of the sentences and use the idea expressed to form a complex sentence with the idea expressed in the last sentence. Monitor students as they work.

Challenge: If students are ready, have them work with a partner to review paragraph 4 on page 13. Have them decide where the text could be improved by forming complex sentences. After they rewrite the paragraph, invite them to read aloud their sentences.

☑ Formative Assessment

Substantial Support	• With support, can students identify the parts of a complex sentence? • With support, can students form a complex sentence, using an independent and a subordinate clause? • With support, can students express the two ideas in a complex sentence?
Moderate Support	• Can students recognize the structure of a complex sentence? • Can students form a complex sentence from two ideas using a connecting word?
Light Support	• Can students recognize an independent and a subordinate clause in a complex sentence? • Can students form a complex sentence from ideas expressed in two separate sentences?

Preview or Review Week 2 ELA Mini-Lessons

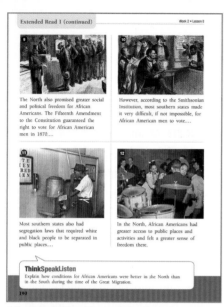

"The Great Migration and the Growth of Cities," page 190

Student Objectives

LANGUAGE

Purpose:
- I can draw conclusions in a historical letter.

Form:
- I can use contractions.

CONTENT
- I can interpret information social studies.

Additional Materials
- Unit Presentation
- Think-Speak-Listen Flip Book
- *Texts for Close Reading* booklet
- Student journal

Metacognitive Prompt

Today we will read the rest of the account of the Great Migration. Reflect on the causes of the Great Migration presented in the text. Then check the text again to confirm your understanding. As we read today's text, pause after reading each panel to reflect on the meaning of the text.

8 Explain Relationships Between Events

Engage Thinking

Display panel 9. **Ask:** *What are people in the picture doing?* Elicit answers. **Say:** *This visual and the visuals in panels 10–12 show a time in the past.* Read the text. **Ask:** *What do we learn from the text that we cannot tell from the pictures?*

Turn and Talk: *How would you compare the images in panels 9–10 to the images in panels 11–12? How are the visual and text in panel 12 different from all the others?*

👥👥👥 Differentiated Instruction
Read and View Closely: Explain Relationships Between Events

Have students review the text. **Say:** *Let's look at relationships that might help us explain events in history.* **Ask:** *How are events related by sequence?* **Say:** *We can also examine how events are alike or different. This is a relationship of comparison or contrast, and a third way to explain events is to show how one event causes or affects another.* Use the Differentiated Instruction to practice explaining relationship between events in a way that best matches the levels of your students.

Think-Speak-Listen: Use the following sentence frame or the Think-Speak-Listen Flip Book to guide discussion: *During the Great Migration, conditions were better in the North because* _____.

Build Language: Use Contractions

Say: *A contraction is a shortened word made by replacing letters with an apostrophe. One common contraction is made from a verb plus not.* Write: *cannot = can't, do not = don't, does not = doesn't,* and *was not = wasn't.* **Say:** *Other common contractions are made by shortening a verb.* Write: *I am = I'm, she will = she'll, they would = they'd,* and *we have = we've.* **Say:** *We can use contractions in the same place that we would use the words the contraction is made from.*

☑️ Use Oral and Written Language: Draw Conclusions in a Historical Letter

Task: *Use the point of view of a young African American during the Great Migration. Compare and contrast events in your life to the way there were before the Great Migration.*

Ⓢ   *Dear Friend, Life in the North isn't _____ life in the South.*

Ⓜ   *Dear Friend, Life in the North _____ life in the South.*

Ⓛ   *Dear Friend, Life in the North _____.*

🔄 Wrap Up

Today we learned how to explain relationships between events, including sequence, comparison and contrast, and cause and effect. How does this help us understand events?

Turn and Talk: *Describe an event in your life. Explain how the event relates to another event you experienced.*

⚇ Differentiated Instruction
Build Language: Explain Relationships Between Events

Ⓢubstantial Support

Model: Use gestures and act out the meanings of the words *social, political, freedom, Constitution* and then check students' understanding of them. **Say:** *To understand this text, I need to know how events are related.*

Practice: Distribute BLM 1. Have students Read aloud panels 1 and 2. **Ask:** *What happens first? What happens later?* Point out the population change over time. **Say:** *In panel 3, I read, "Why did so many African Americans leave the South?" I know I will read about cause-effect relationships.*

Extend: Have partners complete the Extend activity on the BLM.

Challenge: If students are ready, have them complete the sentence frames on Challenge on the BLM.

Ⓜoderate Support

Model: Use gestures and act out the meanings of the words *social, political, freedom, Constitution* and then check students' understanding of them. **Ask:** *What should have been the result of the Fifteenth Amendment?* Point to panel 9. **Say:** *The intended result was freedom to vote.*

Practice: Distribute BLM 2 and help students complete the causes and effects chart.

Extend: Have partners complete Extend activity in BLM 2.

Challenge: Have students use their texts to complete the chart in Light Support.

Ⓛight Support

Practice: Have students read pages 12–19 in their *Texts for Close Reading* and have partners complete this chart.

Paragraph	Cause	Effect
3	The cotton crop was destroyed by boll weevils.	African Americans _____.
3	World War I created _____.	
3	Men joined _____.	African Americans _____.
4	Immigration _____.	

Extend: Have students write the causes that resulted in the Great Migration.

Challenge: Have students complete the sentence frame.

It's important to know how events relate to each other in history because _____.

☑ Formative Assessment

Substantial Support	• Can students complete cause-effect relationship by selecting events from a list? • Can students understand the relationship of sequence and of cause and effect?
Moderate Support	• Can students complete sentence frames to relate multiple causes or effects? • Can students explain relationships of sequence, cause and effect, and compare and contrast?
Light Support	• Can students complete sentences to relate causes and effects? • Can students explain relationships of sequence, cause and effect, and compare and contrast? • Can students explain the importance of relationship of historical events?

Preview or Review Week 2 ELA Mini-Lessons

Combine Clauses to Condense Ideas

Week 2 • Lesson 9

Clauses	Combined into One Sentence
Most African Americans were farmworkers. The loss of the cotton crop meant the loss of their jobs.	**Since** most African Americans were farmworkers, the loss of the cotton crop meant the loss of their jobs.
Immigration was halted. This presented job opportunities for African Americans.	Immigration was halted, **presenting job opportunities for African Americans.**
The North also promised greater social freedom for African Americans. It also promised greater political freedom for African Americans.	The North also promised greater **social and political** freedom for African Americans.
The South was a farming region. It depended on one main crop. That crop was cotton.	The South was a farming region **that** depended on one main crop, **cotton.**

ThinkSpeakListen
Give some reasons why a writer might want to combine clauses into one sentence.

191

"Combine Clauses to Condense Ideas," page 191

Student Objectives

LANGUAGE
Purpose:
• I can recount historical events in a report.
Form:
• I can combine clauses to condense ideas.
CONTENT
• I can interpret informational social studies.

Additional Materials

• Unit Presentation
• Think-Speak-Listen Flip Book
• *Texts for Close Reading* booklet
• Student journal

Language Transfer Support

Note that some students may need additional support with recognizing and understanding independent and dependent clauses as groups of related words that have subjects and verbs. For example, native speakers of Cantonese or Vietnamese do not use subjects in subordinate clauses, and native speakers of Hmong use consecutive verbs, without conjunctions or punctuation, in a single clause.

9 Combine Clauses to Condense Ideas

Engage Thinking

Display the chart. **Ask:** *How is the chart organized?* Point to the first column. **Say:** *A clause has a subject and a verb.* Point to the first sentence in the second column. **Ask:** *What does this sentence do?* Elicit answers.

Turn and Talk: *How is the information in the two clauses and their combined sentence alike? How is it different?*

Read and View Closely: Recognize Clauses

Say: *Let's review how to recognize a clause. A clause has a subject and verb.* **Say:** *Look at the first clause in row 1.* **Ask:** *What is the subject of the clause? What is the verb?* Help students identify the subject *African Americans* and the verb *were*. Repeat with the second clause. **Ask:** *How many clauses are in the combined sentence?* **Say:** *The first clause, beginning with since, is dependent. The second clause is independent. It can stand alone as a sentence.*

👥 Differentiated Instruction
Build Language: Combine Clauses to Condense Ideas

Say: *Let's look at the chart. We see how two clauses can be combined.* Read the first pair of sentences. **Ask:** *In what way do the two clauses relate? What word in the combined sentence helps express this idea?* Point to *since*. Explain that *since* means "because." Then read the combined sentence. Help students see that the combined sentence relates the two ideas clearly. Use the Differentiated Instruction to practice combining clauses to condense ideas in a way that best matches the levels of your students.

Think-Speak-Listen: Use the following sentence frame or the Think-Speak-Listen Flip Book to guide discussion: *A writer combines clauses into one sentence so that _____.*

☑ Use Oral and Written Language: Recount Historical Events in a Report

Task: *Retell the events of the Great Migration in a brief report. Work with a partner to write sentences that tell key events in the order in which they happened.*

Ⓢ *In 1910, many African Americans lived _____ because _____.*

Ⓜ *In 1910, many African Americans _____ because _____.*

Ⓛ *In 1910, _____ because _____.*

Wrap Up

Today we have learned how to combine clauses to condense ideas. How does combining clauses help make writing clear?

Turn and Talk: *Describe an event or type of activity that is important to you. In your description, look for ways to combine clauses to make relationships and ideas clear.*

👪 Differentiated Instruction
Build Language: Combine Clauses to Condense Ideas

Ⓢubstantial Support

Model: Use gestures and act out the meanings of the words *farmworkers, cotton, crop* and then check students' understanding of them. Read the clauses in the first row. **Say:** *I know these are clauses because each has a subject and a verb. When I combine these clauses, I want to keep the important ideas.* Read aloud the combined sentence. **Say:** *In this sentence, the word since means "because." It ties together the idea that the loss of cotton caused a loss of jobs.*

Practice: Distribute BLM 1. Work with students to combine sentences in the Practice activity, reteaching as necessary.

Extend: Have students work with partners to complete Extend on the BLM.

Challenge: If students are ready, model combining the sentences on the BLM Challenge.

Ⓜoderate Support

Model: Use gestures and act out the meanings of the words *farmworkers, cotton, crop* and then check students' understanding of them. Read the clauses in row 3 of the chart. **Ask:** *What is the subject and verb of each clause? What words or ideas repeat in both sentences?* Then have students read the combined sentence.

Practice: Distribute BLM 2 and complete the Practice activity together.

Extend: Have partners complete the Extend activity on the BLM.

Challenge: If students are ready, work with them to complete Challenge the sentence frame on the BLM.

Ⓛight Support

Practice: Have students read the paragraphs listed below in "Migration and the Growth of Cities" in their *Texts for Close Reading*. Have students use connecting words to combine the sentences.

World War I created a need for factory workers.

World War I caused a demand for supplies.

_____, creating _____.

Extend: Have partners combine these sentences:

Many southern states made voting difficult.

Taxes kept black voters from the polls.

Literacy tests were also obstacles.

_____, such as _____ and _____, that _____.

Challenge: Have students combine the sentences above in another way.

☑ Formative Assessment

Substantial Support	• Can students define a clause? • Can students find the subject and verb in a clause? • Can students recognize relationships of ideas that can be linked by *because* and *since*? • Can students use sentence frames to combine sentences using *because* and *since*?
Moderate Support	• Can students define a clause and find subjects and verbs in clauses? • Can students recognize related and repeated ideas in clauses and sentences? • Can students complete sentence frames to combine sentences using subordinate clauses, phrases, and compounds?
Light Support	• Can students identify clauses, subjects, and verbs? • Can students determine relationships between ideas in clauses and sentences? • Can students combine sentences given connecting words that signal relationships? • Can students generate original combined sentences?

Preview or Review Week 2 ELA Mini-Lessons

"The Glassblower's Daughter," page 193

Student Objectives

LANGUAGE

Purpose:
- I can describe a place in a skit.

Form:
- I can determine word meanings using a dictionary, thesaurus, and context clues.

CONTENT
- I can understand realistic fiction.

Additional Materials
- Unit Presentation
- Think-Speak-Listen Flip Book
- *Texts for Close Reading* booklet
- Student journal

Language Transfer Support

Note that students whose first language is Spanish or Hmong may need additional support as they explore adjectives that, in English, appear in front of the nouns they modify. In Hmong and Spanish, adjectives usually follow the nouns they modify.

For students whose first language is Cantonese, Haitian Creole, Hmong, Korean, or Vietnamese, you should provide extra support with the r-controlled vowel sound in enormous, as this sound is not found in these languages.

10 Read "The Glassblower's Daughter"

Build Background and Vocabulary

Display the panels. If students have already read the story, ask them what they remember. Invite students to share their cultural experiences and knowledge of watching artists, making art, and/or visiting museums or displays of art.

Read Aloud the Text

Read aloud the first panel. To support comprehension, ask students to explain what the visual shows. **Ask:** *What does this building look like? What can you see in the rooms?* Repeat with panels 2 and 3, having students relate the text and the photograph. Refer to the Essential Question and invite students to discuss how economic changes impact societies. **Say:** *This story is realistic fiction. It is not about real people. But it seems real, and could be real.*

Think-Speak-Listen Use the following sentence frame or the Think-Speak-Listen Flip Book to guide discussion: *I think the workers who built torpedoes would be _____.*

👥👥 Differentiated Instruction
Build Language: Explore Words to Build Vocabulary

Read aloud the first panel. **Ask:** *What is one descriptive word from the text?* Point out the adjective *fascinating*. **Ask:** *What can we tell from the context?* Explain that the text tells us the *fascinating place* is the art center. **Say:** *Do you know the verb fascinate? It means "to draw attention or interest."* **Say:** *We can use context, related words, as well as a dictionary or thesaurus to explore word meanings.* Use the Differentiated Instruction to practice exploring words to build vocabulary in a way that best matches the levels of your students.

☑ Use Oral and Written Language: Describe a Place in a Skit

Task: *In small groups, create a skit to describe a visit to an art center. Use the information in the story and your imagination. Use a print or online dictionary and thesaurus for support. When you use new words, provide context clues to help others understand.*

(S) *I'm in the art center. I see _____. Two women are _____. My mom is _____.*

(M) *I went to the art center. Inside the building, I saw _____. Then I saw two women _____.*

(L) *I entered the art center, and I saw _____. Then I watched _____. Using _____, she was _____.*

🔄 Wrap Up

Today we learned how to explore words in different ways to develop understanding and to build our vocabulary. How does this help us improve our own writing?

Turn and Talk: *Use some of the new words you have learned in this lesson to describe a skill you would like to learn or a process you would like to see.*

👥 Differentiated Instruction
Build Language: Explore Words to Build Vocabulary

Ⓢubstantial Support

Model: Use gestures and act out the meanings of the words *studio, furnace, melt, orb* and then check students' understanding of them. Remind students there are many ways to learn the meaning of words. Reread the third section.

Ask: *How can I tell a studio is where art is made?* **Say:** *I read that it has a furnace for melting glass. I read that the narrator's mother is making glass in the art center. I can see in the photograph a glass orb, or ball.*

Practice: Ask: *How can we tell what a* furnace *is?* Invite students to explore for context clues, such as "super-hot" and "for melting glass." Remind them that they can look up *furnace* in a dictionary. Work with students to complete the Practice activity from BLM 1.

Extend: Have pairs of students complete the Extend activity from the BLM 1. Once finished, discuss the answers as a group.

Challenge: If students are ready, have them complete the web in the Practice activity from BLM 2.

Ⓜoderate Support

Model: Use gestures and act out the meanings of the words *studio, furnace, melt, orb* and then check students' understanding of them. Remind students there are many ways to learn the meaning of words. Reread the third section. **Ask:** *How can I tell a studio is where art is made?* **Say:** *I read that it has a furnace for melting glass. I read that the narrator's mom is making glass in the art center. I can see in the photograph a glass orb, or ball.*

Practice: Distribute BLM 2. Work with students to complete the Practice activity.

Extend: Have partners complete the Extend activity on the BLM. Monitor students' work and provide additional support as needed. Once finished, discuss the answers as a group.

Challenge: If students are ready, have them use this sentence explore the word *vivid*. Help them to use a dictionary or thesaurus. Then help students write a sentence of their own using the word *vivid*.

Ⓛight Support

Practice: Have students read paragraph 3 in "The Glassblowers' Daughter" in their *Texts for Close Reading*. Create a word web like the example below Have students fill it out for the word *delicate* and then write a sentence using the word.

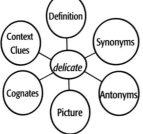

Extend: Have partners define the underlined word in each sentence from paragraph 2. Then have them write their own sentence.

Challenge: Have students complete the sentence frame.

It's important to add new words to my vocabulary because _____.

✔️ Formative Assessment

Substantial Support	• Can students use a dictionary, thesaurus, and/or context clues to complete a word web with the definition, synonyms, antonyms, and a picture? • Can students complete a sentence frame with the word they explored?
Moderate Support	• Can students use a dictionary, thesaurus, and/or context clues to complete a word web with the definition, synonyms, antonyms, and a picture? • Can students use information from a word web to complete sentence frames using the word they explored? • Can students generate an original sentence using an explored word?
Light Support	• Can students use a dictionary, thesaurus, and context clues to help define and understand a word? • Can students generate original sentences with words they have explored?

"Old Cities Revitalize," pages 194–195

Student Objectives

LANGUAGE
Purpose:
• I can create a collage about manufactured items.
Form:
• I can condense ideas to understand meaning.
CONTENT
• I can interpret informational social studies texts.

Additional Materials
• Unit Presentation
• Think-Speak-Listen Flip Book
• *Texts for Close Reading* booklet
• Student journal

Metacognitive Prompt

As you read, recall what you read earlier about America's Great Migration from the rural South to cities in the North. Use what you learned to connect to the new ideas or information in this selection.

11 Read "Old Cities Revitalize"

Build Background and Vocabulary

Display the panels for "Old City Revitalize." If students have already read the text, ask them what they remember. Invite students to share their cultural experiences and knowledge of working around the house or of a parent and family member working.

Read Aloud the Text

Read aloud panel 1. Ask students to find details in the image that match words in the text. **Ask:** *What is the text about?* Repeat with panels 2–8. After reading, **ask:** *Why did the end of War World II lead to an economic boom?* Refer to the Essential Question and invite students to discuss how economic changes impact societies. **Say:** *This type of text gives details about a period in history. It's called an informational text.*

Think-Speak-Listen: Use the following sentence frame or the Think-Speak-Listen Flip Book to guide discussion: *The economic boom affected Americans by creating ___ because ___.*

Differentiated Instruction
Build Language: Condense Ideas by Listing Nouns

Say: *Sometimes a text contains a lot of information that can be shortened, or condensed. One way that we can condense ideas is by listing nouns.* Read the text in panel 1 and point to the nouns listed: *planes, ships, bombs, and other war products.* **Say:** *Rather than writing two sentences: "Many people moved to make planes. Many people moved to make ships." The writer condensed this information by listing the nouns: "Many people moved to make ships, planes, bombs..."* Use the Differentiated Instruction to practice condensing ideas by listing nouns in a way that best matches the levels of your students.

☑ Use Oral and Written Language: Create a Collage About Manufactured Items

Task: *Work with a partner to create a collage with drawings that show items manufactured in cities during and after World War II. Be sure to label your pictures using complete sentences that condense ideas by condensing nouns* Use this opportunity to assess students using the rubric in *English Language Development Assessment*.

 During World War II people made _____, _____, and _____.
After the war people made _____, _____, and _____.

(M) *During World War II people made _____.*
After the war people made _____.

(L) *During the war _____. After the war _____.*

↻ Wrap Up

Today we learned how to condense ideas by listing nouns. How does this help us to better understand the meaning of informational social studies texts?

Turn and Talk: *Describe an event in history or an event in your life. Use sentences that condenses ideas with a list of nouns in your description.*

👥👥 Differentiated Instruction
Build Language: Condense Ideas by Listing Nouns

Ⓢubstantial Support

Model: Use gestures and act out the meanings of the words *economic boom, manufactured, products* and then check students' understanding of them. **Say:** *I can shorten, or condense, a ideas if I want to focus on the key details. The nouns in a text are often key details because they help to identify the people, places, and things that are involved.* **Read aloud panel 3** and **say:** *Listing the nouns* automobiles, furniture, *and* clothing, *is a simple way to explain what was being made at this time.*

Practice: Distribute BLM 1. Work with students to complete the chart, reteaching as necessary.

Extend: In pairs, ask students to complete the Extend activity. Monitor students' work and provide additional support as needed. Once finished, discuss the answers as a group.

Challenge: If students are ready, challenge them to work with a partner to complete the Extend activity on BLM 2.

Ⓜoderate Support

Model: Use gestures and act out the meanings of the words *economic boom, manufactured, products* and then check students' understanding of them. **Say:** *I can shorten, or condense, a text's ideas if I want to focus on the key details. The nouns in a text are often key details because they help to identify the people, places and things that are involved.* **Read the text in Panel 3 and say:** *By listing the nouns* automobiles, furniture, *and* clothing, *it helps to explain what was being made at this time.*

Practice: Distribute BLM 2. Work with students to complete the Practice activity.

Extend: Have pairs complete Extend on the BLM 2. Monitor students' work and provide additional support as needed. Once finished, discuss the answers as a group.

Challenge: If students are ready, ask them to complete the Practice activity from Light Support.

Ⓛight Support

Practice: Have students read paragraphs 2–4 in "Old Cities Revitalize" in their *Texts for Close Reading*. Have pairs find sentences that condense ideas. If needed, help them to look for sentences about how the economy showed growth in the 1940s and 1950s in paragraphs 2 and 3. Look for sentences that show a decline in the economy in the 1960s.

Extend: Point to the picture at the bottom of page 22 in *Texts for Close Reading*. Ask pairs to explain what the picture displays. Then ask students to condense the ideas that are in the text associated with the picture.

Challenge: Have students refer to the text to complete the sentence frame:

_____, _____, _____, and _____ *moved to Lowell after artists turned abandoned factories into studios.*

☑ Formative Assessment

Substantial Support	• Can students list nouns to condense ideas in a text?
Moderate Support	• Can students list nouns and determine how to condense ideas in a text? • Can students explain why ideas need to be condensed in a text?
Light Support	• Can students demonstrate how to condense ideas? • Can students use a list of nouns to explain what information has been condensed?

"Old Cities Revitalize," page 196

Student Objectives

LANGUAGE
Purpose:
• I can analyze a city in a magazine article.
Form:
• I can use verb tense to convey time.
CONTENT
• I can analyze similarities and differences in informational social studies.

Additional Materials
• Unit Presentation
• Think-Speak-Listen Flip Book
• *Texts for Close Reading* booklet
• Student journal

Metacognitive Prompt

As you read, jot down notes about anything you don't understand or want to learn more about. Don't write complete sentences. Instead, write down words or phrases. Circle the ones you think are most important.

12 Compare and Contrast

Engage Thinking

Point to panels 5–8. **Ask:** *What do you see in the pictures? What are the people doing?* Invite ideas. **Say:** *The visuals in the panels show a time in the past.* Ask students to share what they know about cities and suburbs. Read the text for panels 5–12. **Ask:** *What do we learn from the text that we cannot tell from the pictures?*

Turn and Talk: *Turn to your neighbor and explain one similarity and one difference between the cities and the suburbs.*

🏃 Differentiated Instruction
Read and View Closely: Compare and Contrast

Read aloud panels 5–12. **Say:** *If we review the images and the text, we notice that there are two major events taking place: the growth of the suburbs and the decline of the city. In order to understand both events, it is important to compare and contrast them with one another. When comparing, I am looking for similarities. When contrasting, I am looking for differences.* **Say:** *Writers compare and contrast to show how ideas relate to each other.* Use the Differentiated Instruction to practice comparing and contrasting in a way that best matches the level of your students.

Think-Speak-Listen: Use the following sentence frame or the Think-Speak-Listen Flip Book to guide discussion: *Many people left American cities in the decades following WWII because _____.*

Build Language: Use Verb Tense to Convey Time

Say: *When reading informational texts, we should focus on when an event took place. One way we can do that is by paying close attention to the verb tense that is used to describe the event.* Read aloud panel 9. **Say:** Rose, *lost,* and declined *are used to show that these events already happened. They happened in the past so the writer uses past tense verbs.*

☑ Use Oral and Written Language: Analyze a City in a Magazine Article

Task: *Imagine a magazine is studying the recent rebirth of the city of Detroit. They want to put together a magazine article that compares/contrasts large cities and suburbs after War World II. Create a magazine page that uses texts and illustrations.*

S *After War World II, cities like _____ compared to suburbs that _____.*

M *Large cities enjoyed a boom during War World II, but after the war _____; suburbs _____.*

L *The end of World War II led to _____ for many American suburbs; yet, the cities _____ because of _____.*

🔄 Wrap Up

Today we have learned about comparing and contrasting. What do you look for when you compare and contrast things?

Turn and Talk: *With a partner, discuss the similarities and differences between what you do at school and at home.*

👥 Differentiated Instruction
Read and View Closely: Build Language: Compare and Contrast

Ⓢubstantial Support

Model Use gestures and act out the meanings of the words *economic, urban,* and *turn around.* Then check students' understanding. Point to panels 11 and 12. **Say:** *Cities of the 1950s were losing residents. People were moving. Panels 11 and 12 tell us that cities are trying to grow again. I will compare the cities of the 1950s to the time since the 1980s. They are the same in that they are still places struggling with economic downs. They are different because some people are now moving back to cities.*

Practice: Work with students to compare and contrast using the Practice activity on BLM 1. Use information learned from the reading.

Extend: Have students work in pairs to complete the Venn Diagram in the Extend activity. Monitor students' work and provide additional support as needed.

Challenge: If students are ready, challenge them to work with a partner to complete the Extend activity on BLM 2.

Ⓜoderate Support

Model: Use gestures and act out the meanings of the words economic, urban, turn around and then check students' understanding. Point to panels 5–12. **Say:** *I see there are many similarities and differences between cities and suburbs. By comparing and contrasting, I can answer the questions: "How are these things/events alike?" and "How are these things/events different?"*

Practice: Distribute BLM 2. Work with students to complete the first chart in the Practice activity.

Extend: Ask student pairs to complete the Extend activity. Monitor students' work and provide additional support as needed. Once finished, discuss the answers as a group.

Challenge: If students are ready, encourage them to write a few sentences that compares and contrasts the changes that took place in the city of Baltimore.

Ⓛight Support

Practice: Have students read paragraphs 12–15 on pages 27–28 in "Old Cities Revitalize" and help students create a Venn Diagram to compare and contrast Baltimore during different time periods using the headings: "Baltimore in the 1700s and 1800s" and "Baltimore from the 1950s to 1990s."

Extend: Monitor partners as they work in groups to compare and contrast their responses in the Practice task.

Challenge: If students are ready, encourage them to write a paragraph that compares and contrasts the changes that took place in the city of Baltimore.

☑️ Formative Assessment

Substantial Support	• Can students compare and contrast events in an informational social studies text?
Moderate Support	• Are students able to evaluate compare and contrast in an informational social studies text?
Light Support	• Are students able to create original sentences using the language of compare and contrast?

Preview or Review Week 3 ELA Mini-Lessons

Week 3 • Lesson 13

Use Introductory Prepositional Phrases to Establish Time

Sentence	Preposition Indicating Time
During World War II, many people had moved to cities to make planes, ships, bombs, and other war products.	During
Following World War II, the United States experienced an economic boom.	Following
By the late 1960s, many major cities had lost tens of thousands of residents.	By
Between 1960 and 1980, Detroit lost nearly half a million people.	Between
In the decades since the 1980s, the United States has experienced economic ups and downs.	In since

ThinkSpeakListen
Summarize what you have done today, using some of the prepositions listed above.

197

"Use Introductory Prepositional Phrases to Establish Time," page 197

Student Objectives

LANGUAGE
Purpose:
• I can relate observable events in a report.
Form:
• I can make prepositional phrases that establish time.
CONTENT
• I can comprehend an informational social studies text.

Additional Materials
• Unit Presentation
• Think-Speak-Listen Flip Book
• *Texts for Close Reading* booklet
• Student journal

Language Transfer Support

Note that students who speak Cantonese as their native language may need extra support in understanding the use of prepositions. In Cantonese, prepositions are not used the way they are in English. For example, Cantonese speakers might say, "Detroit lost thousands residents," instead of "Detroit lost thousands of residents."

13 Use Introductory Prepositional Phrases to Establish Time

Engage Thinking

Display the chart. Read aloud the sentence in the first row of the chart. **Say:** *The word* during *tells when people moved to cities. Writers use words like* during *to tell when something happened.*

Read and View Closely: Recognize Prepositional Phrases

Say: *This chart shows how prepositional phrases can be used to tell time. Prepositional phrases begin with a preposition such as* during, by, between, in, for, *or to. A noun or a pronoun always follows the preposition. A prepositional phrase helps answer questions "when?" or "where?"* Point to the preposition and noun or pronoun in each prepositional phrase. **Say:** *Each prepositional phrase in the chart tells when something happened.*

👥 Differentiated Instruction
Build Language: Use Introductory Prepositional Phrases to Establish Time

Say: *Prepositional phrases are used to help establish time in writing.* Read the second sentence of the chart. Point out that the prepositional phrase comes at the beginning of the sentence. **Say:** *In the third sentence, I can ask the question, When did the United States experience an economic boom? The word* following *helps me know the boom happened right after World War II.* Use the Differentiated Instruction to practice using introductory prepositional phrases to establish time in a way that best matches the levels of your students.

Think-Speak-Listen: Use the following sentence frame or the Think-Speak-Listen Flip Book to guide discussion: *During the morning, I _____. Following lunch, I _____. Between classes, I _____.*

☑ Use Oral and Written Language: Relate Observable Events in a Report

Task: *You've been asked to write a report about some of the problems cities faced during the 1960s and after. With a partner, write sentences to describe some of the problems. Include prepositional phrases in your sentences.*
(S) *Some cities had problems in _____. Many people moved away since _____.*
(M) *During the 1960s, many people _____. By then, there were _____ and _____.*
(L) *___ the 1960s, many _____. _____ this time, _____, while _____ and _____.*

Wrap Up

Today we learned that prepositional phrases are used to establish time. Why is it important to use prepositional phrases to establish time in your writing?

Turn and Talk: *Use a prepositional phrase to describe an activity you did last summer.*

👥 Differentiated Instruction
Build Language:
Use Introductory Prepositional Phrases to Establish Time

Ⓢubstantial Support

Model: Use gestures and act out the meanings of the words *during, following, by,* and *between.* Then check students' understanding. Remind students that prepositional phrases can be used to establish time. **Say:** *When I read the sentence, "By the late 1960s, many major cities had lost tens of thousands of residents," I see the word* by *followed by the phrase* the late 1960s. *I know that the sentence is stating a time frame.*

Practice: Distribute BLM 1. Work with students to complete the first two rows of the chart.

Extend: Have students work with partners to complete the rest of the chart. Provide help as needed

Challenge: If students are ready, model how to complete the Extend activity on BLM 2.

Ⓜoderate Support

Model: Use gestures and act out the meanings of the words *during, following, by,* and *between.* Then check students' understanding. Remind students that prepositional phrases can be used to establish time. **Say:** *When I read the sentence, "By the late 1960s, many major cities had lost tens of thousands of residents," I see the word* by *followed by the phrase* the late 1960s. *I know that the sentence is establishing, or stating, a time frame.*

Practice: Distribute BLM 2. Have students complete the chart.

Extend: Have partners look at the question for the Extend activity. Provide help as needed.

Challenge: If students are ready, model how to read paragraph 16 on pages 27 in the *Texts for Close Reading.* Demonstrate finding three sentences using prepositional phrases that establish time. Then write out the question that the sentence answers.

Ⓛight Support

Practice: Have students read "Old Cities Revitalize" in *Texts for Close Reading* page 28, paragraphs 16 and 17, with a partner and establish time.

Extend: Have partners write new sentences based on ones from the text, substituting another prepositional phrase that establishes time. For example: *Following World War II, the United States experienced an economic boom. The United States experienced an economic boom after World War II.*

Challenge: If students are ready, have students write new sentences based on one of the visuals on pages 22–29. Have students use at least two prepositional phrases to establish time as they describe the visual.

☑ Formative Assessment

Substantial Support	• Can students identify prepositional phrases? • Can students answer a *when* question using a sentence with a • prepositional phrase?
Moderate Support	• Can students describe prepositional phrases that establish time? • Can students form *when* questions using the information from a prepositional phrase?
Light Support	• Can students analyze prepositional phrases that establish time in a text? • Do students write well-formed answers in complete sentences using prepositional phrases that establish time?

Preview or Review Week 3 ELA Mini-Lessons

"Out of Disaster," page 198

Student Objectives

LANGUAGE
Purpose:
• I can analyze words in a weather report.
Form:
• I can recognize parts of speech of unfamiliar words.
CONTENT
• I can comprehend an informational social studies text.

Additional Materials
• Unit Presentation
• Think-Speak-Listen Flip Book
• *Texts for Close Reading* booklet
• Student journal
• Word Study Chart
• Dictionaries and thesauruses

Language Transfer Support

Note that speakers of Cantonese, Haitian, Creole, Hmong, Spanish, Vietnamese, Korean, or Cantonese may need extra support in understanding the use of adjectives. In Haitian Creole, Hmong, Spanish, and Vietnamese, nouns often precede adjectives. In Cantonese and Korean, adjectives always follow nouns.

14 Read "Out of Disaster"

Build Background and Vocabulary

Display the panels for "Out of Disaster." If students have already read the text, ask them what they remember. Invite students to share their cultural experiences and knowledge of the effects of bad weather on a community.

Read Aloud the Text

Read aloud panel 1. To support comprehension, ask questions such as *What caused life to change in Greensburg?* Repeat with panels 2–3. After reading, ask: *What is the text mostly about?* Refer to the Essential Question and invite students to discuss how economic changes impact societies. Say: *This is an informational text that gives facts about how a community worked together to make itself better.*

👥👥👥 Differentiated Instruction
Build Language: Analyze Unfamiliar Vocabulary

Read aloud panel 1. **Say:** *This nonfiction text is about an historical event. It may have vocabulary words that you haven't seen before.* Help students identify unfamiliar words. **Ask:** *If you don't know what a* tornado *is, how could you determine meaning?* Elicit answers. **Say:** *A text may give clues in the surrounding words, and you can also use pictures and a dictionary.* Use the Differentiated Instruction to practice analyzing unfamiliar vocabulary in a way that best matches the levels of your students.

Think-Speak-Listen: Use the following sentence frame or the Think-Speak-Listen Flip Book to guide discussion: *The tornado _____ Greensburg. The city leaders' response was _____.*

☑ Use Oral and Written Language: Analyze Words in a Weather Report

Task: *Imagine you are a weather forecaster and a hurricane is coming. Give a news flash about the weather. Use a dictionary and thesaurus if possible. Listen to your partner's news flash. What words are unfamiliar?*

Ⓢ *The eye of the _____ is quickly approaching.*

Ⓜ *Be careful and stay inside. The _____ of the hurricane is _____.*

Ⓛ *Alert! Stay inside! The _____ is imminent and the winds are _____.*

🔄 Wrap Up

Today we learned how to analyze unfamiliar vocabulary words by using context clues and other strategies. Why is learning new vocabulary words important?

Turn and Talk: *How would you figure out the meaning of an unfamiliar word in a text?*

👥 Differentiated Instruction
Build Language: Analyze Unfamiliar Vocabulary

Ⓢubstantial Support

Model: Use gestures and act out the meanings of the words *community, destroyed,* and *tornado.* Then check students' understanding. Read aloud the text in panel 1 then distribute BLM 1. Point to the word *familiar* in the text. **Say:** *I see that the word* familiar *comes before a noun,* houses*, so it is probably an adjective that describes* houses*. Then I look at the other words in the sentence for clues. The sentence seems to say that places you call home are* familiar*.*

Practice: Work with students to complete the Practice activity on the BLM. Guide them to tell what they think the word means and then to use a dictionary to check the meaning.

Extend: Have partners complete the Extend activity. Provide assistance as needed.

Challenge: If students are ready, model using a Word Study Chart to analyze the meaning of *embarked* on BLM 2.

Ⓜoderate Support

Model: Use gestures and act out the meanings of the words *community, destroyed,* and *tornado.* Then check students' understanding. Read aloud panel 2, and point out the word *embarked.* Distribute BLM 2. **Say:** *The text says, "Officials embarked on a program." A person who embarks on something is probably starting or setting out in some way.*

Practice: Continue to guide students to complete the Practice activity on BLM 2. Work with students to use dictionaries and thesauruses to check their ideas.

Extend: Have partners complete the Extend activity on BLM 2. Provide assistance as needed.

Challenge: Have students complete the following sentence frame for two challenging words from the text.

I think the word _____ means _____ because _____.

Ⓛight Support

Practice: Ask partners to read paragraph 2 on page 30 in their *Texts for Close Reading.* Ask them to choose a word and analyze it by completing the Word Study Chart.

Word	What I Think It Means	Meaning
Synonym/Antonym:	Picture:	Divided into syllables:
Used in a sentence:	Part of speech:	Morphology or Etymology:

Extend: Ask partners to complete a Word Study Chart for an unfamiliar word in paragraph 3 on page 30.

Challenge: Have students complete the following sentence frame for two challenging words from the text.

I think the word _____ means _____ because _____.

☑ Formative Assessment

Substantial Support	• Do students understand the value of context clues? • With support, can students participate in word analysis using a Word Study Chart?
Moderate Support	• Can students identify context clues that contribute to word meanings? • Can students analyze words using a Word Study Chart?
Light Support	• Can students select unfamiliar vocabulary words from a longer text? • Can students work with partners to analyze word meanings in a Word Study Chart?

Preview or Review Week 3 ELA Mini-Lessons

"Use Commas in a Series," page 199

Student Objectives

LANGUAGE
Purpose:
• I can ask and answer interview questions.
Form:
• I can use commas in a series.
CONTENT
• I can identify informational text.

Additional Materials
• Unit Presentation
• Think-Speak-Listen Flip Book
• *Texts for Close Reading* booklet
• Student journal

Language Transfer Support

Note that speakers of Vietnamese and Hmong use **have** without a subject in place of **there is/are, was/were**. Speakers of Spanish can use **have** with or without a subject, or **there are**.

15 Use Commas in a Series

Engage Thinking

Display the charts. Read aloud the first sentence, pausing between each word in the series. **Say:** *When we write a list of words in a sentence, we need to use commas to separate each word. A comma tells me to take a short pause, or a breath, between reading one word and the next, to keep words in a series separate.* Then read aloud the second sentence, pausing in the same way.

Turn and Talk: *What does a comma tell a reader to do?*

Read and View Closely: Recognize Commas in a Series

Have students look at the second chart. **Say:** *Commas can also help us separate a series of phrases or clauses within a sentence.* Read aloud the first sentence, pausing after each phrase. **Ask***: What makes this series of words different than the examples in the top chart?* **Say:** *We know we use commas to separate words in a list or series. We can also use commas to separate groups of words, like phrases and clauses.* Then read the second sentence aloud, pausing in the same way.

👥👥 Differentiated Instruction
Build Language: Use Commas in a Series

Say: *Now that we have learned about using commas in a series, we are going to practice sentences that include them.* Use the Differentiated Instruction to guide students to use commas in a series according to their language levels.

Think-Speak-Listen: Use the following sentence frame or the Think-Speak-Listen Flip Book to guide discussion: *I plan to _____, _____, and _____.*

☑ Use Oral and Written Language: Ask and Answer Interview Questions

Task: *Write questions to ask someone who survived a bad storm. Remember to ask questions that will require a series or list of items in the answer. Then take turns interviewing your partner.*

Ⓢ *What items do you still have after the storm?*
I still have _____, _____, and _____.

Ⓜ *During the storm, what did you _____?*
I saw _____, _____, and _____ during the storm.

Ⓛ *Can you describe _____? Following the storm, I _____.*

Wrap Up

Today we learned that commas help to separate words and phrases grouped together in a series. Why are commas needed when writing a series of words or phrases?

Turn and Talk *Make a list of the homework you have today. Then tell your partner your list, pausing after each item as if there was a comma there..*

Differentiated Instruction
Build Language: Use Commas in a Series

Substantial Support

Model: Review each box in the charts, and read aloud the sentences. **Say:** *I know that when I make a list of words in a sentence, each word in the list must be separated by a comma.* **Ask:** *Can a series contain phrases instead of single words?* Point to the second set of sentences in the chart and **say:** *Yes, a series can have short phrases such as "homes with yards" or "more open spaces."*

Practice: Distribute BLM 1. Work with the students to read each sentence and decide where to places commas in the series.

Extend: Have the students work in pairs. Ask them to work together to read each sentence and place commas after the phrases as needed.

Challenge: Ask each student to make a list of three students who sit near them in the classroom. Ask them to make a series statement using the sentence frame:

I sit near _____, _____, and _____.

Moderate Support

Model: Review the charts, and read aloud the sentences in the bottom chart. **Say:** *I know that commas are used to separate words in a series or list. I know they are also used with groups of words in a series, like phrases.*

Practice: Distribute BLM 2. Work with the students as they read the sentences containing a series of phrases and place commas where they are needed.

Extend: Have the students work in pairs. Ask them to read the words in each box and create a sentence that uses all three words in a series. Remind them to use commas as needed.

Challenge: Ask each student to make a list of four students who sit near them in the classroom. Ask them to make a series statement using the sentence frame:

I sit near _____, _____, _____, and _____.

Light Support

Practice: Ask the students to reread the last three sentences in paragraph 1 on page 30 of their *Texts for Close Reading*. Work with them to change words and punctuation to turn this into one sentence that contains a series of facts about the tornado.

Extend: Have the students reread paragraph 3 on page 30. Ask them to discuss in pairs how the citizens of Greenburg made their city "stronger, better, greener." Encourage them to use series statements in their comments.

Challenge: Ask the students: *If you could design a town to be safer during a storm, what changes would you make?* Discuss with the group, and encourage the use of series statements.

✓ Formative Assessment

Substantial Support	• Can students use commas between nouns in a series with support? • Can students use commas between phrases in a series with support?
Moderate Support	• Can students use commas between nouns in a series with little support? • Can students use commas between phrases and clauses in a series with little support?
Light Support	• Can students use commas between nouns in a series? • Can students use commas between phrases and clauses in a series?

Transforming Matter

Essential Question

Why do we measure and describe the world?

In this unit, students will read and compare selections about matter to understand how science helps people describe the world.

Unit 10

Unit 10 Lessons at a Glance

Language Skills

Lessons

Preview or Review Week 1 ELA Mini-Lessons

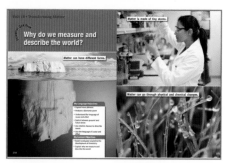

"Essential Question," pages 200–201

Student Objectives

LANGUAGE
Purpose:
• I can understand the Essential Question.
CONTENT
• I can understand the topic of the unit.

Additional Materials
• Unit Presentation

Introduce Unit 10: Transforming Matter

Use the short lesson below to introduce the topic of the unit and help students understand the Essential Question.

Build Background and Vocabulary

Say: *The topic of this unit is "Transforming Matter." Matter is physical substance.*

Draw students' attention to the pictures on pages 200–203.

Say: *These pictures introduce the topic and some of the texts that we will read. Let's make a list of the words that we see in each picture.*

Display the three-column chart. Invite students to read the caption for the first picture. Write it in the chart. Ask students what they notice in the pictures and add vocabulary words to the chart, like the sample below.

Matter Can Have Different Forms	Matter Is Made of Tiny Atoms	Matter Can Go Through Physical and Chemical Changes
iceberg	scientist	grass
water	lab	dew
ice	test tubes	water drops

Ask: *How do these pictures help you understand what it means to transform matter?*

Help students answer and encourage students to share their cultural knowledge and experiences about the topic.

👥 Differentiated Instruction
Explain the Essential Question

Point to the Essential Question and read it aloud: *Why do we measure and describe the world?*

Say: *We measure things around us for many reasons. We measure the temperature so we know if we need a jacket. We measure distance so we know how long a trip will take. Scientists measure things to learn more about the world. They can use the information to develop things which help us, such as new medicine and new technology.*

Explain that solids, liquids, and gases are different forms of matter and can all be measured. Understanding the question will help students understand the stories and do well in their opinion essay writing tasks.

Display or invite students to access the unit opener video for Unit 10.

Ask: *How does the video help you understand why we measure and describe the world?*

Help students answer and encourage them to share their cultural knowledge and experiences about the topic. Continue the lesson using Differentiated Instruction that best fits the needs of your students.

Differentiated Instruction
Explain the Essential Question

Substantial Support

Write: *Chocolate Cake*. Draw a simple measuring cup with labels.

Say: *I am going to bake a cake. Gesture as you say: First, I need one half cup of sugar, 1 cup of flour, and 2 eggs.*

Write and use students' ideas to complete the sentence: *I need to measure the ingredients because _____.*

Ask: *What would happen if I didn't measure the ingredients?* Elicit ideas.

Create the chart below and write in the information. Explain unknown vocabulary. **Ask:** *What can you measure with each tool?* Write ideas on the chart.

	measuring cup?	thermometer?	ruler?
What can you measure with a...	You can measure _____ with a measuring cup.	You can measure _____ with a thermometer.	You can measure _____ with a ruler.

Say: *It's important to measure things to get precise information. Then we can make good decisions about how we interact with our world.*

Moderate Support

Read aloud the Essential Question again.

Say: *There are many ways to measure things around us. For example, we can use a thermometer to measure the temperature of the air outside. Then we know what type of clothes to wear that day.*

Create a chart like the one below and write in the information.

	measuring cup?	thermometer?	ruler?
What can you measure with a...	You can measure _____ with a measuring cup.	You can measure _____ with a thermometer.	You can measure _____ with a ruler.
Why it is important?	It is important because _____.	It is important because _____.	It is important because _____.

Point to picture 1 again.

Say: *Matter can change. How can water become a solid? a liquid? a gas? Help students answer. When we transform water, we measure it in different ways.*

Light Support

Read aloud the Essential Question again.

Say: *Think about different ways to measure things in the world. What do you measure? What tool do you use? Why is it important?*

Make a chart. Elicit ideas and write them in the chart.

What you measure	Tool	Why it's useful
temperature	thermometer	to dress appropriately
length of wall	tape measure	to buy the right-sized bed

Point to picture 1 again. **Say:** *Matter can change. How can water become a solid? a liquid? a gas?*

Help students answer. **Say:** *When we transform water, we measure it in different ways. In this unit, you will learn why we measure things in our world.*

☑ Formative Assessment

Substantial Support	• Can students understand the idea of measuring to describe the world?
Moderate Support	• Can students understand the idea of measuring to describe the world? • Can students give an example of measuring to describe the world?
Light Support	• Can students understand the idea of measuring to describe the world? • Can students give two examples of measuring to describe the world?

Preview or Review Week 1 ELA Mini-Lessons

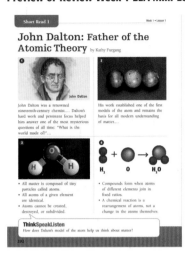

"John Dalton: Father of the Atomic Theory," page 202

Student Objectives

LANGUAGE
Purpose:
• I can describe John Dalton in a speech.
Form:
• I can analyze present and past tense verbs.
CONTENT
• I can understand informational texts.

Additional Materials
• Unit Presentation
• Think-Speak-Listen Flip Book
• *Texts for Close Reading* booklet
• Student journal

Language Transfer Support

Some students may need extra support to understand sentences that include both past tense and present tense verbs. In Hmong and Haitian Creole, verbs within a single sentence do not change tense.

1 Read "John Dalton: Father of the Atomic Theory"

Build Background and Vocabulary

Display the panels from "John Dalton: Father of the Atomic Theory" and explain key words. **Say:** *Today we will read about a chemist named John Dalton who discovered the world is made up of atoms.* Invite students to share their cultural experiences and knowledge about atoms. If students have already read the text, ask them to share what they remember.

Read Aloud the Text

Read aloud panel 1. Ask students to find words in the text that help them describe the man in the image, and ask *wh-* questions, such as: *Who was John Dalton? What did he do?* Repeat with panels 2–4. After reading, **ask:** *Why was John Dalton's work so important?* Refer to the Essential Question: *Why do we measure and describe the world?* Invite students to discuss how John Dalton's work is important to science and measurement. Then **say:** *This text is factual. We call this an informational text.*

Think-Speak-Listen: Have pairs answer the question using this sentence frame: *Dalton's model of the atom helps us think about matter by _____.*

👥👥👥 Differentiated Instruction
Build Language: Switch Between Present and Past Tense

Remind students that verb tense can tell us when events happen. **Say:** *Sometimes writers switch between present and past tense in the same text. They may even switch verb tense in the same sentence.* Read aloud panel 2 and have students find the two verbs. **Say:** *The verb* established *ends in -ed, so we know that John Dalton's work happened in the past. The verb* remains *is in the present tense, so we know Dalton's discoveries are considered to be true today.* Use the Differentiated Instruction to practice switching between present and past tense in a way that best matches the levels of your students.

☑ Use Oral and Written Language: Describe John Dalton in a Speech

Task: *In pairs, write a speech about John Dalton. Include information that shows how we use his work today. Give your speech to the class.* Use this opportunity to assess students using the *English Language Development Assessment.*

(S) John Dalton _____ a famous chemist. His work _____ us understand matter.

(M) John Dalton _____. All atoms of the same element _____ identical.

(L) Dalton's hard work _____. Compounds _____ when _____.

🔄 Wrap Up

Today we learned about switching between present and past tense in a text. Why is it important to switch between present and past tense correctly in a text?

Turn and Talk: *Describe a sports figure or musician who you admire. How does the person's past work affect you today?*

👥👥 Differentiated Instruction
Build Language: Switch Between Present and Past Tense

Ⓢubstantial Support

Model: Use gestures and act out the meanings of the words *renowned, chemist, persistent,* and *mysterious.* Check students' understanding. Read aloud the second sentence in panel 1. Point to helped. **Say:** *The verb helped is in the past tense because the action is complete.* Point to is. **Say:** *The verb is is in the present tense. Even though Dalton finished his work many years ago, the question he asked is still asked today.*

Practice: Write the following sentence frame on the board: Scientists _____ Dalton's model every day, but Dalton _____ many years ago. **Say:** *I see the words every day, so I know that the action of the first verb happens now. I also see the words many years ago, so I know the second verb should be in the past tense.* Invite students to help you plug in two pairs of verbs to complete the sentence.

Extend: Distribute BLM 1. In pairs, have students complete the sentences.

Challenge: Distribute BLM 1. If students are ready, model completing these sentence frames.

Ⓜoderate Support

Model: Use gestures and act out the meanings of the words *renowned, chemist, persistent,* and *mysterious.* Check students' understanding. Point out the second sentence in panel 1. **Say:** *This sentence has verbs in two different tenses.* **Say:** *The verb helped is used because Dalton's work took place in the past. The question "What is the world made of?" is one that people are still asking today, so is is in the present tense.*

Practice: Distribute BLM 2. As a group, write new sentences about John Dalton that switch from present tense to past tense, or from the past tense to the present.

Extend: Distribute BLM 2. Have partners complete the sentences. Support students as necessary.

Challenge: If students are ready, have pairs study paragraphs 4 and 5 on page 5 in their *Texts for Close Reading.* Ask them to find sentences that contain both verbs in the present tense and verbs in the past tense, and discuss the reason for the shift.

Ⓛight Support

Practice: Have students read paragraph 1 on page 4 in their *Texts for Close Reading.* Ask students to circle the verbs *allowed* and *is.* **Ask:** *What do you notice about these two verbs?* Guide students into discussing the tense of each verb. **Say:** *Why do you think the author switched between the past and present tense?*

Extend: Have students work with a partner to study paragraphs 5. Have them point to verbs in the present tense and verbs in the past tense, and discuss the reason for the shift.

Challenge: Have students work with a partner to create a sentence that shifts between the present and past tense. Remind students their sentences must have a change in time frame.

✓ Formative Assessment

Substantial Support	• Do students understand why verb tense changes? • Can students change the verb tense in a sentence?
Moderate Support	• Can students form past tense and present tense verbs? • Can students complete sentence frames with both past and present tense verbs?
Light Support	• Can students discuss the reasons for a shift in verb tense? • Can students write a sentence with both past and present tense verbs?

Preview or Review Week 1 ELA Mini-Lessons

> Week 1 • Lesson 2
>
> **Expand Noun Phrases**
>
> **1. Add academic vocabulary**
> John Dalton was a chemist. | John Dalton was a renowned
> He was renowned. | nineteenth-century chemist.
> He lived in the nineteenth century.
>
> **2. Add comparatives and superlatives**
> Dalton's hard work and persistent focus | Dalton's hard work and persistent
> helped him answer an important question. | focus helped him answer one of the
> The question was one of the most | most mysterious questions of all time.
> mysterious questions of all time.
>
> **3. Add adjectives and reduced clauses**
> All matter is composed of particles. | All matter is composed of tiny
> The particles are tiny. | particles called atoms.
> We call these particles atoms.
>
> **ThinkSpeakListen**
> Explain why a writer might choose to expand noun phrases.
>
> 203

"Expand Noun Phrases," page 203

Student Objectives

LANGUAGE
Purpose:
• I can state an opinion in an editorial.
Form:
• I can recognize noun phrases.
CONTENT
• I can analyze noun phrases in informational texts.

Additional Materials
• Unit Presentation
• Think-Speak-Listen Flip Book
• *Texts for Close Reading* booklet
• Student journal

Language Transfer Support

Using different forms of nouns and adjectives may be difficult for speakers of Hmong, Cantonese, or Mandarin because nouns and adjectives can use the same form (e.g., *They felt **safety** in the home*).

2 Expand Noun Phrases

Engage Thinking

Display the chart. Read aloud the first sentence in each column.

Ask: *Do these sentences mean the same thing? How are they different?*

Turn and Talk: *Discuss what you know about John Dalton.*

Read and View Closely: Recognize Noun Phrases

Say: *A noun phrase is a group of words that functions as a noun. A noun phrase includes words that add detail or description to the noun.* Walk through the chart with students. Explain that each section in the left column lists a way to expand the noun phrase in the original sentence. On the right is a new sentence with an expanded noun phrase. **Say:** *Recognizing noun phrases is important. It lets us see how each sentence is improved by including more detailed information. When we read a text with expanded noun phrases, we learn more about its subjects.*

Think-Speak-Listen: Have pairs complete the task using this sentence frame:
A writer might expand noun phrases because _____.

👥 Differentiated Instruction
Build Language: Expand Noun Phrases

Read the first example in the chart. **Say:** *These three sentences tell us about John Dalton. We can combine details and create one sentence by expanding the noun phrase.* Explain that noun phrases can be expanded in several ways: by adding academic vocabulary, by adding comparatives and superlatives, and by adding adjectives. **Say:** *Expanding noun phrases improves our writing. When we write sentences with expanded noun phrases, we include more detailed information about a subject.* Use the Differentiated Instruction to practice expanding noun phrases in a way that best matches the levels of your students.

☑ Use Oral and Written Language: State an Opinion in an Editorial

Task: *Write an editorial that explains why you believe or don't believe John Dalton was a great scientist. Recall what you learned in the reading. Include an expanded noun phrase in at least one of your sentences.*

(S) *John Dalton was a _____ chemist. He _____ and _____.*

(M) *Dalton's hard work helped him answer _____.*

(L) *Dalton helped figure out that all matter _____.*

Wrap Up

Today we learned how to recognize and expand noun phrases. How does expanding noun phrases help us better understand a subject?

Turn and Talk: *Describe a famous person you admire in a few sentences. Include expanded noun phrases in your sentences.*

![icon] Differentiated Instruction
Build Language: Expand Noun Phrases

(S)ubstantial Support

Model: Use gestures and act out the meanings of the words *academic, vocabulary, chemist,* and *renowned.* Check students' understanding. Read the first example on the chart. **Say:** *These sentences tell us about John Dalton. We can expand the noun phrase to combine clauses and create one sentence.* Read the sentence in the right hand column that contains an expanded noun phrase. **Say:** *This sentence gives the reader more information about John Dalton. Academic vocabulary was added to provide more detail.*

Practice: Say: *Sometimes we can use a noun phrase to combine sentences and create one sentence that is clearer.* Read aloud the third example. Work with students to explain how the noun phrase combined the sentences.

Extend: Distribute BLM 1. Have students work with a partner to complete the Extend activity.

Challenge: If students are ready, have them write a new sentence with an expanded noun phrase.

> *John Dalton was hard-working.*
>
> *He was a chemist.*

(M)oderate Support

Model: Use gestures and act out the meanings of the words *academic vocabulary, chemist,* and *renowned.* Check students' understanding. Point to the second example in the chart. **Say:** *The expanded noun phrase creates a more interesting sentence. It gives more information about the question that Dalton answered.*

Practice: As a group, complete the following sentence frames, then expand the noun phrase to add more detail.

> *John Dalton wanted _____.*
>
> *John Dalton is remembered for _____.*

Extend: Distribute BLM 2. Ask partners to work together to complete the task.

Challenge: If students are ready, discuss the ways of expanding noun phrases and find examples on pages 4 and 5 in their *Texts for Close Reading*: add academic vocabulary; add comparatives and superlatives; and add adjectives and reduced clauses.

(L)ight Support

Practice: Have students read paragraph 1 in their *Texts for Close Reading* to find a noun phrase. Point to "nineteenth-century chemist." **Ask:** *Is this an example of: added academic vocabulary; added comparatives and superlatives; or added adjectives and reduced clauses?*

Extend: Ask partners to point out three more noun phrases. Have them decide if the noun phrase is an example of: added academic vocabulary; added comparatives and superlatives; or added adjectives and reduced clauses.

Challenge: Ask students to generate two original sentences about John Dalton or chemistry. Their sentences should include expanded noun phrases.

☑ Formative Assessment

Substantial Support	• Can students identify noun phrases? • Do students understand why noun phrases are useful?
Moderate Support	• Can students identify noun phrases? • Can students expand noun phrases in sentences?
Light Support	• Can students recognize the various ways noun phrases can be expanded in a text? • Can students generate original sentences with expanded noun phrases?

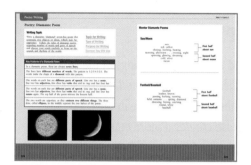

"Process Writing," pages 204–205

Student Objectives

LANGUAGE
Purpose:
• I can analyze a diamanté poem.
Form:
• I can identify the diamanté form.
CONTENT
• I can recognize a diamanté poem.

Additional Materials
• Unit Presentation
• Think-Speak-Listen Flip Book
• *Texts for Close Reading* booklet
• Student journal

3 Diamanté Poetry

Engage Thinking

Tell students that they will analyze a diamanté poem so that they can recognize its features. Read aloud the writing topic.

> Write a diamanté, "diamond," seven-line poem that contrasts two objects or ideas, which may be opposites. Follow the rules of diamanté poetry regarding number of words and parts of speech, and choose your words carefully to focus on the sounds and rhythms of the words.

Say: *Let's ask questions to make sure we understand the writing topic. What will the writer write about? What type of writing is it? How will the writer write the poem?*

Differentiated Instruction
Read and View Closely: Analyze a Diamanté

Say: *We will analyze a diamanté poem to understand its rules.* Display the poem "Football/Baseball." Read it aloud once. Then point to the seven lines. **Say:** *A diamanté poem always has seven lines. What do you notice about how many words there are per line?* Check that the class understands the structure of 1–2–3–4–3–2–1 words per line. Point out that the shape of the poem looks like a diamond, which translates to "diamanté" in Italian.

Say: *Each line has words that are a specific part of speech. Line 1 is a noun. What part of speech are the words in line 2?* Elicit adjectives. **Say:** *Line 3 has words that end in* **-ing.** Elicit the part of speech: verbs. **Ask:** *What kind of words are in line 4?* Elicit the part of speech: nouns. Then point out how the bottom half of the poem has the same number of words as the top, in reverse, and elicit the parts of speech again.

Say: *Look at the first and last words of the poem. What do you notice?* Check that students understand that this is the title of the poem. **Say:** *The words in the top half of the poem describe football, and the words in the bottom half describe baseball. They meet in the center and these ellipses separate them.* Explain that the poem is meant to contrast two different things. Read the poem aloud again telling students to listen for the sound of the words. Finally, read and analyze the other poem by using the same questions as above.

Continue the lesson using Differentiated Instruction that best fits the needs of your students.

Share Your Understanding

Bring the students back together. **Ask:** *What did we learn today about diamanté poetry?* Review the features as needed.

👥 Differentiated Instruction
Read and View Closely: Analyze a Diamanté

Ⓢubstantial Support

Model: Distribute BLM 1. Complete the activity on the BLM for the first poem, "Football/Baseball."

Practice: Say: *Let's read and analyze another diamanté.* Read the "Sun/Moon" diamanté and pause. **Ask:** *How many words does each line have?* Continue asking the same questions you asked about the Mentor Diamanté.

Extend: Help students complete the questions a second time on the BLM for the second poem.

Challenge: Display sentence frames and model how students can use them to talk about the poems. For example:

The season in this poem is _____.

This poem makes me feel _____.

The contrast between _____.

Ⓜoderate Support

Model: Draw students' attention to the Mentor Diamanté Poem "Football/Baseball" in their book. **Say:** *Let's analyze the rules of a diamanté poem.* Count the number of words in each line with students.

Practice: Work with students to determine the parts of speech and purpose of each line in "Football/Baseball." Explain any unfamiliar words.

Extend: Have students pairs determine the parts of speech and purpose of each line in "Sun/Moon." Then have pairs compare their answers. Check the answers with the class.

Challenge: Write: *I like the diamanté titled _____. It's about _____. It makes me feel _____ because _____.*

Have students complete the sentences with their ideas. Encourage students to refer to the words or images in the diamanté. Invite students to share their sentence with the class.

Ⓛight Support

Practice: Distribute BLM 2. **Say:** *This is the Diamanté Mentor Text that you read in class on Day 1. We will look more closely at the rules of diamanté poetry.* Have students complete the activity for the first diamanté "Football/Baseball."

Extend: Have students in pairs complete items 1–4 again for the other diamanté, "Sun/Moon." Invite students to share their answers with the class.

Challenge: Have students choose one of the two diamanté poems. Ask students to complete the following sentence frames:

I like the diamanté titled _____. It's about _____. It makes me feel _____ because _____.

Then have students in pairs discuss their answers, comparing and contrasting their ideas. Remind them to respond to their partner's ideas and contribute to the conversation.

☑️ Formative Assessment

Substantial Support	• Do students recognize the criteria for a diamanté poem in the Mentor Diamanté Poems?
Moderate Support	• Do students recognize the ways in which the Mentor Diamanté Poems meet the criteria for a diamanté poem? • Can students describe the features of a diamanté poem in their own words?
Light Support	• Do students recognize criteria and analyze how the Mentor Text meets the criteria for a diamanté poem? • Can students describe in their own words how the writer meets the criteria for a diamanté poem?

Preview or Review Week 1 ELA Mini-Lessons

"Matter Is Everywhere!," pages 206–207

Student Objectives

LANGUAGE

Purpose:
• I can describe states of matter in a collage.

Form:
• I can analyze prepositional phrases.

CONTENT
• I can understand key facts in informational texts.

Additional Materials
• Unit Presentation
• Think-Speak-Listen Flip Book
• *Texts for Close Reading* booklet
• Student journal

Language Transfer Support

The meaning and usage of prepositions in Spanish do not necessarily correspond to their English meaning and usage. For example, Spanish speakers may use *in* to convey a particular relationship where English speakers would use *on*.

4 Read "Matter Is Everywhere!"

Build Background and Vocabulary

Display the panels from "Matter is Everywhere!" Invite students to share their cultural experiences and knowledge about matter. If students have already read the text, ask them what they remember.

Read Aloud the Text

Read aloud panel 1. Ask students to find words in the text that match images in the picture (matter, mass, volume, object). Ask *wh-* questions such as *What is matter?* Repeat with panels 2–8. Refer to the Essential Question and invite students to discuss how we measure things. Then **say:** *This nonfiction text explains facts about a particular topic. We call this an informational text.*

Think-Speak-Listen: Have pairs complete the activity using this sentence frame: *When liquid water becomes ice, water particles _____.*

Differentiated Instruction
Build Language: Use Prepositional Phrases

Explain that prepositional phrases begin with a preposition, such as *above, at, for, in, on,* and *under,* and end with a noun or pronoun. **Say:** *Prepositional phrases answer the question "Where?" They tell where something is or where it is going.* Point to panel 3 and read the prepositional phrase "in a solid." **Say:** *"in" is a preposition. It tells "where" the particles are.* Use the Differentiated Instruction to practice using prepositional phrases in a way that best matches the levels of your students.

☑ Use Oral and Written Language: Describe States of Matter in a Collage

Task: *With your group, create a collage showing different states of matter: solid, liquid, and gas. Use magazines, construction paper, and other supplies to find and draw pictures to put in your collage. Label the images and write sentences to describe the pictures.*

(S)   *A _____ is a solid. _____ a solid, the particles are close together.*

(M)   *A _____ is a solid because its particles are _____. _____ a solid, _____.*

(L)   *A _____ is a _____ because _____.*

↺ Wrap Up

Today we learned how to use prepositional phrases to help us understand where something is, or where it is going. How do prepositional phrases help us understand a topic?

Turn and Talk: *Tell a partner about an animal you have seen. Use prepositional phrases to explain where it was or where it was going.*

👥 Differentiated Instruction
Build Language: Use Commas in a Series

Ⓢubstantial Support

Model: Review each box in the charts, and read aloud the sentences. **Say:** *I know that when I make a list of words in a sentence, each word in the list must be separated by a comma.* **Ask:** *Can a series contain phrases instead of single words?* Point to the second set of sentences in the chart and **say:** *Yes, a series can have short phrases such as "homes with yards" or "more open spaces."*

Practice: Distribute BLM 1. Work with the students to read each sentence and decide where to places commas in the series.

Extend: Have the students work in pairs. Ask them to work together to read each sentence and place commas after the phrases as needed.

Challenge: Ask each student to make a list of three students who sit near them in the classroom. Ask them to make a series statement using the sentence frame:

I sit near _____, _____, and _____.

Ⓜoderate Support

Model: Review the charts, and read aloud the sentences in the bottom chart. **Say:** *I know that commas are used to separate words in a series or list. I know they are also used with groups of words in a series, like phrases.*

Practice: Distribute BLM 2. Work with the students as they read the sentences containing a series of phrases and place commas where they are needed.

Extend: Have the students work in pairs. Ask them to read the words in each box and create a sentence that uses all three words in a series. Remind them to use commas as needed.

Challenge: Ask each student to make a list of four students who sit near them in the classroom. Ask them to make a series statement using the sentence frame:

I sit near _____, _____, _____, and _____.

Ⓛight Support

Practice: Ask the students to reread the last three sentences in paragraph 1 on page 30 of their *Texts for Close Reading*. Work with them to change words and punctuation to turn this into one sentence that contains a series of facts about the tornado.

Extend: Have the students reread paragraph 3 on page 30. Ask them to discuss in pairs how the citizens of Greenburg made their city "stronger, better, greener." Encourage them to use series statements in their comments.

Challenge: Ask the students: *If you could design a town to be safer during a storm, what changes would you make?* Discuss with the group, and encourage the use of series statements.

☑ Formative Assessment

Substantial Support	• Can students use commas between nouns in a series with support? • Can students use commas between phrases in a series with support?
Moderate Support	• Can students use commas between nouns in a series with little support? • Can students use commas between phrases and clauses in a series with little support?
Light Support	• Can students use commas between nouns in a series? • Can students use commas between phrases and clauses in a series?

👥 Differentiated Instruction
Build Language: Use Prepositional Phrases

Ⓢubstantial Support

Model: Use gestures and act out the meanings of the words *matter, solid, particles,* and *liquid.* Check students' understanding. **Say:** *Prepositional phrases can answer the question "Where?" They tell where something is or where it is going.* Point to panel 4 and **ask:** *Where are the particles?* Write: *The particles are in a liquid.* Underline the prepositional phrase and circle the preposition. **Say:** *The preposition* in *links the word* liquid *to the rest of the sentence.*

Practice: As a group, identify other prepositional phrases in the text that tell location. Use prepositional phrases to complete the following sentence frames together:

Mass is the amount of matter _____.

The particles _____ are packed tightly together.

Extend: Distribute BLM 1. Have students work in pairs to underline the prepositional phrases in the sentences.

Challenge: If students are ready, have them complete the Challenge activity.

Ⓜoderate Support

Model: Use gestures and act out the meanings of the words *particles, gas,* and *liquid.* Check students' understanding. Explain that a prepositional phrase includes a preposition and a noun or pronoun. Point out the prepositional phrase *into a much smaller space* in panel 5. **Say:** *Prepositions are words that give information about where something is. The preposition* into *shows direction.*

Practice: Write: *Particles can barely move _____.* **Ask:** *Where are the particles that can barely move?* Add *in a solid* to complete the sentence. Help students identify the preposition and prepositional phrase.

Extend: Distribute BLM 2. Have pairs complete the sentence frames by adding prepositional phrases.

Challenge: If students are ready, have them complete the Challenge activity.

Ⓛight Support

Practice: Have students read paragraph 3 on page 7 of their *Texts for Close Reading* and identify each of the prepositional phrases.

Extend: Have students complete the sentence frames about paragraph 3.

The particles in a solid _____.

The particles in a liquid _____.

Challenge: Have partners use the prepositions *at, for, in,* and *without* to write sentences about matter.

✔ Formative Assessment

Substantial Support	• Can students locate a prepositional phrase in a sentence with support? • Can students use prepositional phrases to complete a sentence frame with support?
Moderate Support	• Can students identify the elements of a prepositional phrase? • Can students complete a sentence frame with a prepositional phrase?
Light Support	• Can students understand the purpose of prepositional phrases? • Can students generate original sentences containing prepositional phrases?

Preview or Review Week 1 ELA Mini-Lessons

"Balloon Ride," page 208

Student Objectives

LANGUAGE

Purpose:
- I can describe a balloon festival in a magazine.

Form:
- I can analyze precise words.

CONTENT
- I can understand informational texts.

Additional Materials

- Unit Presentation
- Think-Speak-Listen Flip Book
- *Texts for Close Reading* booklet
- Student journal
- Precise Words Chart
- Online or print thesaurus or dictionary

Language Transfer Support

Speakers of non-English languages may need help using and understanding resources such as the dictionary and a thesaurus. You may wish to pair your English Learners with native speakers during activities involving these resources.

5 Read "Balloon Ride"

Build Background and Vocabulary

Display "Balloon Ride" images from the textbook. If students have read the article, invite them to share what they remember. Invite students to share their cultural experiences and knowledge about riding in a hot-air balloon.

Read Aloud the Text

Read aloud panel 1. Ask students to find words in the text that represent the image (dew-dropped grass, damp). Ask wh- questions such as: *What is the time and the setting? What are the people gathering to do?* Elicit responses. Repeat with panels 2–3. Refer to the Essential Question and invite students to say what things need to be measured for a hot-air balloon ride. Then **say:** *This text describes the process of launching a balloon, which is something that could really happen. This is called an informational text.*

Think-Speak-Listen: Have pairs answer the question using this sentence frame: *I think a hot air balloon would be _____.*

👤👤👤 Differentiated Instruction

Build Language: Analyze Precise Words

Say: *Precise word paint a clear picture for readers to picture what a writer describes.* Point to the word *damp* in panel 1. **Say:** *The writer could have used the word* wet. *But* wet *is too general. How is* damp *a more precise or exact word?* Elicit answers. **Say:** *The word* damp *suggests something is only a little wet.* Display Precise Words Chart. **Say:** *You can find more examples of precise words in a thesaurus or dictionary. Using precise words makes writing clearer and more interesting.* Use the Differentiated Instruction to practice analyzing precise words in a way that best matches the levels of your students.

☑ Use Oral and Written Language: Describe a Balloon Festival in a Magazine

Task: *With a partner, pretend you are news reporters assigned to cover a balloon festival where many hot-air balloons are launched. Write three to four sentences describing the event that would help others imagine what you see. Use a thesaurus to find precise words for general words such as fly, fill, rise, and see.*

(S) The balloons _____. The sky _____. The wind _____.

(M) When all of the balloons were _____, they _____.

(L) The balloons _____ as they _____ and _____.

🔄 Wrap Up

Today we analyzed precise words to learn how to choose words that say and describe exactly what we mean. How do precise words make writing more interesting?

Turn and Talk: *Tell your partner about a park or other place you have seen. Describe it a second time, using more precise words. Ask your partner how the descriptions differed.*

👥 Differentiated Instruction
Build Language: Analyze Precise Words

Ⓢubstantial Support

Model: Use the Precise Words Chart to teach students about other examples of precise words. Distribute BLM 1 and explain unknown vocabulary.

Practice: Distribute BLM 1. Encourage students to help you choose a precise word for the bold word in each sentence. Check understanding and reteach if necessary.

Extend: Distribute BLM 1. Have students work in pairs to complete the Extend activity. Provide support as needed, and encourage them to use a dictionary or thesaurus to distinguish word meaning.

Challenge: If students are ready, model finding the verb *land* in a thesaurus. Discuss how different precise words would change the description of a hot-air balloon landing.

Ⓜoderate Support

Model: Use the Precise Words Chart to teach students about other examples of precise words. Focus on general versus precise words and shades of meaning.

Practice: Distribute BLM 2. Work with students to select five precise words to fill in the word web. Guide students to use a dictionary and a thesaurus to check meaning.

Extend: Have partners complete the Extend activity. Monitor students' work and provide support as needed.

Challenge: If students are ready, ask them to find the word *gather* in the first panel of their text. Provide support in using a dictionary or thesaurus to find and list synonyms for *gather*.

Ⓛight Support

Practice: Use Precise Words Chart to review precise and general words. Have students read paragraph 1 in "Balloon Ride" in their *Texts for Close Reading*. Have them find the word *gather* and copy the sentence in which it is used. Provide support using a dictionary or thesaurus to find and list synonyms for *gather*. Ask them to rewrite the sentence with a different precise word. Discuss changes in sentence meaning.

Extend: Have partners read paragraph 2. Ask them to choose a general word in one of the sentences, then find more precise words in a dictionary or thesaurus. Have them rewrite the sentence using the precise word.

Challenge: If students are ready, have them review paragraph 3. Encourage them to write two or three sentences describing the balloon flight on a windy day. Remind them to use precise words.

☑ Formative Assessment

Substantial Support	• With support, can students distinguish general from precise words? • With support, can students analyze a precise word?
Moderate Support	• Can students identify and understand a precise word? • Can students select and use a precise word in a sentence? • Can students use a dictionary or thesaurus to help them select precise words?
Light Support	• Can students analyze the effects of precise words? • Can students use a dictionary or thesaurus to select precise words that reflect intended meaning? • Can students write original sentences using precise words?

Preview or Review Week 2 ELA Mini-Lessons

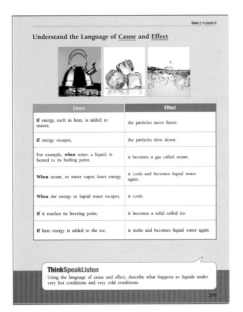

"Understand the Language of Cause and Effect," page 209

Student Objectives

LANGUAGE
Purpose:
• I can express cause and effect in a flowchart.
Form:
• I can recognize and understand words that signal cause and effect.
CONTENT
• I can understand cause and effect in informational texts.

Additional Materials

• Unit Presentation
• Think-Speak-Listen Flip Book
• *Texts for Close Reading* booklet
• Student journal

Language Transfer Support

Students whose first language is Spanish may be familiar with the following cognates of words found in the text: *energía (energy), materia (matter), ejemplo (example), vapor (vapor), líquido (liquid), gas (gas), sólido (solid),* and *partícula (particle).* Encourage students to look for other words that are similar to words in their first language.

6 Understand the Language of Cause and Effect

Engage Thinking

Display the chart and point to the three pictures at the top. **Say:** *Each picture shows water.* **Ask:** *How is the water different in each picture?* Have students share their ideas.

Turn and Talk: *How can you turn water into a solid? a liquid? a gas?*

Read and View Closely: Recognize Cause and Effect

Read aloud the column headings from the chart. **Say:** *Sometimes we can explain by showing causes and effects. A cause is what makes something happen, and an effect is the result.* Read aloud the first sentence. **Say:** *I add heat to energy. What happens? First I add heat, and then the particles move faster. As you read, you can recognize cause and effect by asking: What happened? Why did it happen?* Point to the picture of the ice cube, and **say:** *When the temperate rises, the ice melts.* **Ask:** *What is the cause? What is the effect?*

Think-Speak-Listen: Have pairs answer the question using this sentence frame: *In very (hot/cold) conditions liquids _____.*

👥 Differentiated Instruction
Build Language: Understand the Language of Cause and Effect

Point out the *if* and *when* statements in the cause column on the chart. **Say:** *Certain words signal causes and effects. To find a cause, look for words like* if *and* when. *To find an effect, look for words like* become *and* then. Write: *If heat is added to ice, then it melts.* Elicit which action is the cause, and which is the effect. **Say:** *Understanding the language of cause and effect helps you recognize relationships in text.* Use the Differentiated Instruction to practice understanding the language of cause and effect in a way that matches the level of your students.

☑️ Use Oral and Written Language: Express Cause and Effect in a Flowchart

Task: *Work with a partner. Create a cause-and-effect flowchart that shows how water transforms into its different states. Start with liquid water. Write a cause-and-effect sentence for each step in the flowchart.*

Ⓢ *Water is _____, and then becomes _____.*

Ⓜ *When steam cools, it _____ and _____.*

Ⓛ *If water cools to _____, it _____ and becomes _____, which is _____.*

🔄 Wrap Up

Today we learned signal words that help us identify cause and effect. How does cause and effect help us better understand science?

Turn and Talk: *Describe the effect of a weather event that you observed. Share your ideas on what caused this event.*

👥 Differentiated Instruction
Build Language: Understand the Language of Cause and Effect

Ⓢ ubstantial Support

Model: Use gestures and act out the meanings of the words *energy, boiling point, steam,* and *freezing point.* Check students' understanding. Display the chart. Read aloud the first sentence.

Say: *Heat is added. That's the cause. Then what happens? The effect is that particles move faster.*

Practice: Distribute BLM 1. Invite students to help you identify and label the cause and effect in each sentence. Remind students to look for signal words that help answer these questions.

Extend: Have partners complete the Extend activity. Encourage them to read each sentence aloud with their choice of signal word to make sure it makes sense.

Challenge: If students are ready, have them work with a partner to complete the following sentences frames.

_____ water is heated, _____.

Water turns to _____ when _____.

Ⓜ oderate Support

Model: Use gestures and act out the meanings of the words *energy, boiling point, steam,* and *freezing point.* Check students' understanding. Review cause and effect. Display the Understand the chart. Read the first part of sentence 1. **Say:** *The first part of the sentence is the cause. It tells what happens first: heat is added. The second part tells what happens as a result: the particles move faster.*

Practice: Distribute BLM 2. Invite students to help you complete the Practice activity. Have students read all the sentence parts first.

Extend: Have students work with a partner to complete the Extend activity. Provide support if needed.

Challenge: If students are ready, have partners read the Challenge paragraph and identify the cause and the effect in each sentence.

Ⓛ ight Support

Practice: Have students read paragraph 3 in "Matter Is Everywhere!," in their *Texts for Close Reading.* Ask them to identify the signal word *so* which points to a cause or an effect.

Extend: Have partners rewrite the following sentence in paragraph 3 using if, when, or so: *A set amount of liquid can flow from one container to another and change its shape.*

Challenge: Have partners complete the following sentence to show a cause-and-effect relationship.

Gas particles expand to fill a large space when _____.

☑ Formative Assessment

Substantial Support	• With support, can students recognize causes and effects in text? • With support, can students identify signal words that point to a cause or an effect? • With support, can students complete a sentence frame to complete a cause-and-effect statement?
Moderate Support	• Can students correctly identify a cause and an effect in a sentence? • Do students understand the use of signal words in cause-and-effect statements? • Can students create a cause-and effect sentence using sentence frames as needed?
Light Support	• Can students identify cause and effect within text? • Can students use the language of cause and effect to create sentences?

Preview or Review Week 2 ELA Mini-Lessons

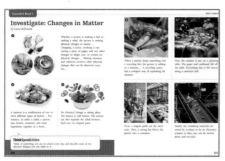

"Investigate: Changes in Matter," pages 210–211

Student Objectives

LANGUAGE

Purpose:
- I can inform by creating a diagram.

Form:
- I can analyze a thesis statement in an informational text.

CONTENT
- I can recognize informational texts.

Additional Materials
- Unit Presentation
- Think-Speak-Listen Flip Book
- *Texts for Close Reading* booklet
- Student journal
- Informational Text Structure Chart

Metacognitive Prompt: Elaboration on Prior Knowledge

Before students begin reading, say: Today we will learn about changes in matter as we read an informational text. Think about the different states of matter we learned in previous articles as you read about mixtures and solutions. Also note how the information is presented.

7 Read "Investigate: Changes in Matter"

Build Background and Vocabulary

Display the panels from "Investigate: Changes in Matter" and explain key words. If students have read the article, invite them to share what they remember. Invite students to share their cultural experiences and knowledge on making mixtures and solutions.

Read Aloud the Text

Read aloud panel 1. Ask students to find details in the picture that match words in the text (chopping a carrot, crushed can). Ask questions, such as: *What physical changes were made?* Repeat with panels 2–11. After reading, **ask:** *Before we read the text, what did you think a mixture was?* Then refer to the Essential Question. Invite students to discuss how matter is measured differently when its form changes. Then **say:** *This text is about making physical changes to matter. This is called an informational text.*

Think-Speak-Listen: Have pairs answer the question using the sentence frame: *In school I use _____ and it changes when I _____.*

Differentiated Instruction
Build Language: Understand the Structure of an Informational Essay

Say: *When writers want to explain something, they can write an informational text.* **Ask:** *How does the writer try to interest readers?* Display and read aloud the Informational Text Structure Chart. **Say:** *Writers start with an introductory paragraph to introduce the topic. The body paragraphs make up details. Then the conclusion summarizes the main idea.* Use the Differentiated Instruction to practice the understanding the structure of an informational text in a way that best matches the levels of your students.

☑ Use Oral and Written Language: Inform by Creating a Diagram

Task: *Choose one of the following mixtures, or come up with your own: a bowl of mixed nuts, a salad, a bottle of oil and vinegar, a container of sand and water. Draw a picture of your mixture. Then draw another picture that shows the mixture separated into its original parts. Write a short informational text to describe it.*

(S) *A mixture is made up of parts. Our mixture is _____.*

(M) *A mixture is made up _____. Our mixture, which is _____, can be separated into _____.*

(L) *A mixture is _____. Our mixture, which is _____, can be _____ and _____.*

🔄 Wrap Up

Today we learned about the structure of an informational text. Why is it important to have a clear beginning, middle, and end?

Turn and Talk: *Tell your partner about a science topic you are interested in. Explain why this topic interests you.*

👥 Differentiated Instruction
Build Language: Understand the Structure of an Informational Essay

Ⓢubstantial Support

Model: Display the Informational Text Structure Chart, and teach the different parts of an essay. Then refer to panel 1. **Say:** *The introductory paragraph helps me decide if I want to continue reading. I'm interested, or hooked, because the writer says in the first sentence that making a bed or a salad is making physical changes to matter. I never thought of these actions this way.*

Practice: Have students help you label the parts of the introductory paragraph in panel 1. **Ask:** *What is the topic, or subject of the text?* Elicit answers. **Say:** *I think the topic is mixtures and solutions.* Help students label the topic and purpose.

Extend: Read aloud panel 2. In pairs, have students answer these questions:

The main idea of the paragraph is _____.

A detail that supports this idea is _____.

Challenge: If students are ready, have them repeat the questions in Extend for panel 3.

Ⓜoderate Support

Model: Display the Informational Text Structure Chart, and discuss the different parts of an essay. Refer to panel 1. **Say:** *When I read the first, or introductory, paragraph of an informational text, I'll decide if I want to continue reading. So, the writer wants to interest me with the first sentence.* **Ask:** *What is interesting about this first sentence?* Elicit answers.

Practice: Distribute BLM 1. Work with students to answer the questions about the structure of the introductory paragraph, using panel 1.

Extend: Have partners analyze the introductory paragraph in panel 1 to identify the topic, purpose, and supporting examples. Provide support as needed.

Challenge: Distribute BLM 1. Have pairs put the sentences in order to show the parts of an informational text.

Ⓛight Support

Practice: Review Informational Essay Structure Chart. Then have students read paragraph 1 in "Investigate: Changes in Matter" in their *Texts for Close Reading*. Distribute BLM 2. Work with them to complete the activity.

Extend: Have students work in pairs to analyze body paragraph 4 on page 14 by completing the Extend activity. Monitor students' work.

Challenge: If students are ready, have them analyze paragraph 5. In pairs, have students say how it relates to the topic sentence in paragraph 1.

☑ Formative Assessment

Substantial Support	• With support, can students understand the purpose of an informational text? • With support, can students identify the parts of an informational text? • With support, can students recognize how the introductory paragraph of an informational text is constructed?
Moderate Support	• Can students understand the purpose and structure of an informational text? • Can students identify and understand the purpose of each part of an introductory paragraph? • Can students identify the main idea and a supporting detail of a body paragraph?
Light Support	• Can students identify the purpose and structure of an informational text? • Can students break down the parts of an introductory paragraph and the purpose of each? • Can students analyze a body paragraph to identify the main idea or point and at least one supporting detail?

Preview or Review Week 2 ELA Mini-Lessons

"Investigate: Changes in Matter," page 212

Student Objectives

LANGUAGE
Purpose:
• I can express a sequence of events in a skit.
Form:
• I can recognize sequencing language.
CONTENT
• I can analyze the sequence of events in an informational text.

Additional Materials

• Unit Presentation
• Think-Speak-Listen Flip Book
• *Texts for Close Reading* booklet
• Student journal

Metacognitive Prompt

*Today, we will practice sequencing. Notice clue words that help the reader understand the order of events, such as **first, then, next,** and **last**. Make sure to use these words when you write and speak to help others understand the steps in a process.*

---

8 Recognize a Sequence of Events

Engage Thinking

Say: *Recycling requires many steps. These steps take place in a specific order.* Explain that one of the first steps is placing the mixture on the spinning table. The other steps follow this one. **Say:** *This is an example of recognizing a sequence, or order, of events.*

Turn and Talk: *Turn to your neighbor and explain one additional event that takes place in the recycling process.*

👥 Differentiated Instruction
Read and View Closely: Recognize a Sequence of Events

Display and read aloud panels 8–11. **Say:** *This part of the text shows the order of events to make a solution. Understanding the sequence helps us understand when and how events happen.* **Say:** *Each picture describes the next step in the process. The text includes details to help me understand what happens.* Use the Differentiated Instruction to practice recognizing a sequence of events in a way that best matches the level of your students.

Think-Speak-Listen: Have pairs answer the question using the sentence frame:
A solution is different from a mixture because _____.

Build Language: Understand Sequencing Language

Say: *There are certain words we should look for to understand the order of events.* Read aloud panel 5. **Say:** *The word* first *tells me that this is the first thing that happens.* Read aloud panel 6. **Say**: *The words next and then tell that one event follows the other one.* Read aloud panel 7. **Ask:** *Which word shows sequence?* Elicit answers. **Say:** *The word finally tells us this is the last step in the sequence.* Additional words include *then, next, after, followed* and *by.*

☑ Use Oral and Written Language: Express a Sequence of Events in a Skit

Task: *The local theater wants to do a show about the recycling process. In a group, create a skit that shows the sequence of events for recycling. Be sure to use the language of sequence to help explain the order of events.*

 First, let's _____

M *The first step in recycling is _____. Next, _____.*

L *The recycling process starts with _____. Then _____ followed by _____ and _____.*

♻ Wrap Up

Today we have learned about recognizing a sequence of events. How does recognizing a sequence of events help you understand an informational social studies text?

Turn and Talk: *Tell your partner how to make a peanut butter and jelly sandwich. Use sequence words to explain the process.*

👥👥 Differentiated Instruction
Build Language: Recognize a Sequence of Events

Ⓢubstantial Support

Model: Use gestures and act out the meanings of the words *recycling center, separate,* and *mixture.* Check students' understanding. Point to panel 5. **Say:** *In these panels, we learn that there are several steps in the recycling process.* The order in which these events happen is important. Point to the word first and **say:** *The word* first *signals the beginning of the process.*

Practice: Distribute BLM 1. Work with students to choose the correct sequence word for each event.

Extend: Have students work in pairs to put events in correct sequence on the Extend activity.

Challenge: If students are ready, have them rewrite the following sentences with sequence words.

The mixture is placed on a spinning table. Cardboard, paper and plastic are taken out. The cans are sorted from other things.

Ⓜoderate Support

Model: Use gestures and act out the meanings of the words *recycling center, separate,* and *mixture.* Check students' understanding. Point to panel 5. **Say:** *In these panels, we learn that there are several steps in the recycling process. The order in which these events happen is important.* Point to the word first and **say:** *The word "first" signals the beginning of the process. Words like next, then and finally also help me recognize the sequence of events.*

Practice: Distribute BLM 2. Work with students to complete the activity, re-teaching as necessary.

Extend: In pairs, ask students to complete the Extend activity. Monitor students' work and provide additional support as needed. Once finished, discuss the answers as a group.

Challenge: If students are ready, ask them to complete the Light Support Practice activity.

Ⓛight Support

Practice: Have students read "Chemical Change vs. Physical Change" on page 13 of "Investigate: Changes in Matter" in their *Texts for Close Reading.* Help them determine the sequence of events that take place during the digestive process. Students should use complete sentences and the language of sequence such as *first, then, next* and *finally.*

Extend: Have pairs create a four-panel illustration that shows the sequence of events in the digestive process. Have students provide captions to show the sequence of events.

Challenge: If students are ready, encourage them to create a visual aid or poster that shows the sequence of events to make a solution, using page 16, paragraphs 5–7.

☑ Formative Assessment	
Substantial Support	• Can students recognize the sequence of events in an informational text?
Moderate Support	• Are students able to evaluate the sequence of events in an informational text?
Light Support	• Are students able to create original sentences and images that show the sequence of events?

Preview or Review Week 2 ELA Mini-Lessons

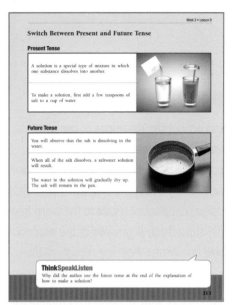

"Switch Between Present and Future Tense," page 213

Student Objectives

LANGUAGE
Purpose:
• I can predict what will happen in a letter.
Form:
• I can explain the difference between present and future.
CONTENT
• I can identify when an informational text switches from present to past tense.

Additional Materials
• Unit Presentation
• Think-Speak-Listen Flip Book
• *Texts for Close Reading* booklet
• Student journal

Language Transfer Support

Spanish, Hmong, and Farsi use the present tense for the future tense; therefore, speakers of these languages may have trouble using the future tense correctly. You may want to pre-teach the future tense in a small group, using sentence frames and ample practice contrasting it with the present tense.

9 Switch Between Present and Future Tense

Engage Thinking

Hold a book in your hand. **Say:** *I have a book. After school, I will go to the library and get another book.* Write the verbs *have* and *will go.* **Say:** *The verb* have *tells about something that is true now. The verb* will go *tells about a prediction in the future.*

Turn and Talk: *Tell your partner about what you're going to do after school.*

Read and View Closely: Recognize Verb Tenses

Display the chart. **Say:** *There are two verbs tenses here: present and future. A verb tense tells when an action or event took place.* Present tense verbs are actions that are happening now or are ongoing. Read aloud the first sentence and point to *dissolves.* Then **say:** *Future tense verbs predict actions in the future. They have the word* will *in front of them.* Read sentence 3 and point to *will observe.*

👥 Differentiated Instruction
Build Language: Switch Between Present and Future Tense

Point to the first sentence under "present tense." **Say:** *The verbs* is *and* dissolves *tell me the actions always happen.* Read sentence 4 under "future tense." **Say:** *The verb* dissolves *is the present tense. But the verb* will result *is the future tense. Writers switch between the present and the future tense to describe actions that can be predicted. The present tense shows action that is constant, and the future tense shows what we can predict.* Use the Differentiated Instruction to practice switching between present and future tense in a way that best matches the level of your students.

Think-Speak-Listen: Have pairs answer the question using the sentence frame: *The author uses the future tense at the end of the explanation because _____.*

☑ Use Oral and Written Language: Predict What Will Happen in a Letter

Task: *In pairs, write a letter about how a recycling program will help your school. In your letter, predict how a new program will change things at school.*

Ⓢ   *We need a new recycling program. A new program will _____ the school clean.*

Ⓜ   *There are many reasons why we need a new recycling program. It _____ and help _____. Students will _____.*

Ⓛ   *A recycling program is _____. It will allow _____ and _____.*

 Wrap Up

Today we have learned about switching from future to present tense. Why is it important to know when something took place while reading an informational text?

Turn and Talk: *Tell your partner what you will do next weekend.*

👤👥 Differentiated Instruction
Build Language: Switch Between Present and Future Tense

Ⓢubstantial Support

Model Use gestures and act out the meanings of the words solution, mixture, and dissolve. Check students' understanding. Read aloud the first sentence. **Say:** *Is and dissolves are present tense verbs.* Read aloud the second sentence. **Say:** *will observe is a future tense verb.* (You may want to point out that "is dissolving" is the present continuous tense, which means the action is happening at the moment.)

Practice: Distribute BLM 1. Work with students to help you switch between present and future tense.

Extend: Distribute BLM 1. Have students work in pairs to complete the activity. **Ask:** *What word should we add to switch from present to future tense?*

Challenge: Write the sentences on the board. Have pairs say how the verbs switch tense.

You will notice that the salt dissolves.

When all of the saltwater dissolves, a solution will result.

Ⓜoderate Support

Model Use gestures and act out the meanings of the words solution, mixture, and dissolve. Check students' understanding. Read aloud the first sentence. **Say:** *Is and dissolves are present tense verbs.* Read aloud the second sentence. **Say:** *will observe is a future tense verb.* (You may want to point out that "is dissolving" is the present continuous tense, which means the action is happening at the moment.)

Practice: Distribute BLM 2. Work with students to complete the Practice activity, re-teaching as necessary.

Extend: In pairs, ask students to complete the Extend activity. Monitor students' work and provide additional support as needed. Explain that students need to add the subject the first two questions.

Challenge: If students are ready, have them find verbs and name the tenses in paragraphs 5–7 on page 16 in their *Texts for Close Reading*.

Ⓛight Support

Practice: Have students read steps 1–6 in the "Investigate Matter: Oobleck" section on pages 18–19 in their *Texts for Close Reading*. Help them write a list of present, past and future tense verbs used in steps 1–6.

Extend: Have pairs rewrite any three steps with a switch in tenses.

Challenge: Have students complete the following sentence frame with the verbs in parentheses.

You _____ a change when you _____ food coloring.

✅ Formative Assessment

Substantial Support	• Can students recognize when a text switches from present to future tense?
Moderate Support	• Are students able to evaluate why a text switches from present to future tense in an informational text? • Can students explain when it is appropriate to use different tenses?
Light Support	• Are students able to create original sentences that switch from present to future tense?

Preview or Review Week 2 ELA Mini-Lessons

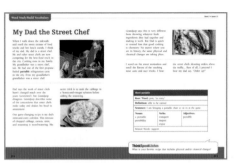

"My Dad the Street Chef," pages 214–215

Student Objectives

LANGUAGE
Purpose:
• I can describe words with the same root in a chart.

Form:
• I can understand root words.

CONTENT
• I can comprehend realistic fiction.

Additional Materials
• Unit Presentation
• Think-Speak-Listen Flip Book
• *Texts for Close Reading* booklet
• Student journal
• Dictionary and thesaurus

Language Transfer Support

Roots often have a Latin origin, and many are used in the Latinate languages. For example, the English word **chemical** is *químicoin* in Spanish and Portuguese, *chimico* in Italian, and *chimique* in French. Ask students if the vocabulary words you discuss look like words in their first language.

10 Read "My Dad the Street Chef"

Build Background and Vocabulary

Display the "My Dad the Street Chef" the panels and explain their importance in the story. If students have already read the story, ask them what they remember. Invite students to share their cultural experiences and knowledge on eating out, particularly if they have visited a street vendor or food truck.

Read Aloud the Text

Read aloud panel 1. Ask students to find words that help them understand the idea and ask questions such as: *What does the narrator describe?* Repeat for panels 2 and 3. After reading, **ask:** *What is the story about?* Model thinking through the answer. **Say:** *The story describes differences in cooking styles between the narrator's father and grandfather.* Refer to the Essential Question. Invite students to discuss what a chef needs to measure. Then **say:** *This story is not about a real person, but it seems real. We call this realistic fiction.*

Think-Speak-Listen: Have pairs answer the question using these sentence frames: *My favorite recipe is _____. There are (physical/chemical) changes when _____.*

👥 Differentiated Instruction
Build Language: Understand and Use Words with Science Roots

Explain that a root word is a basic word with no suffix or prefix added to it. Read the last sentence in panel 1. **Say:** *To understand the meaning of the word portable, I break apart the word. The root word port is from a Latin word that means, "to carry." So, portable means "able to be carried."* Explain to students that they can use a dictionary to help them identify root words and their meanings. Use the Differentiated Instruction to practice understanding and using words with science roots in a way that best matches the levels of your students.

☑️ Use Oral and Written Language: Describe Words in a Chart

Task: *Work with a partner to create a Morphology chart for the word* concoction. *Use a dictionary and thesaurus to help you.*

Root Word:			
Definition:			
Sentence:			
Nouns:	Verbs:	Adjectives:	Adverbs:
Related Words:			

Wrap Up

Today we learned how to understand and use root words. Why is learning about root words important?

Turn and Talk: *Talk with your partner about how you can use root words to help you understand unfamiliar words in math.*

👥 Differentiated Instruction
Build Language: Understand and Use Words with Science Roots

Ⓢubstantial Support

Model: Use gestures and act out the meanings of the words *fresh, ingredients,* and *chemistry.* Check students' understanding. Point out the word *physical* in panel 3. **Say:** *Physi- is from a Latin word that means "from nature." The root gives me a clue about a word's meaning.*

Practice: Distribute BLM 1. Invite students to help you find the root word in *chemical.* As needed, help students use a dictionary to complete the Practice activity.

Extend: Have students work in pairs to complete the Extend activity. **Ask:** *How does the meaning of chem help you understand the word chemistry?*

Challenge: If students are ready, have them write a sentence with the word chemical.

Ⓜoderate Support

Model: Use gestures and act out the meanings of the words *fresh, ingredients,* and *chemistry.* Check students' understanding. Point out the word *physical* in panel 3. **Say:** *Physi- is from a Latin word that means "from nature." The root gives me a clue about a word's meaning.*

Practice: Distribute BLM 2. Work with students to complete the Practice activity. Reteach as necessary.

Extend: Have students work in pairs to complete the Extend activity. **Ask:** *How do root words help you understand a whole word's meaning?*

Challenge: If students are ready, point out the word formula in paragraph 2 on page 20 of their *Texts for Close Reading* and model how to complete a morphology chart for this word.

Ⓛight Support

Practice: Review root words with students. Point out the words *physical* and *chemical* in paragraph 2 on page 20 of their *Texts for Close Reading.* Then assign one of the words to each pair of students. Ask them to complete a morphology chart for their assigned word.

Root Word:
Definition:
Sentence:
Related Words:

Extend: Have students discuss their charts with the group. Then ask them to use their charts to explain how the meanings of *physical* and *chemical* compare.

Challenge: Working in pairs, have students find another example of a word with a root, or have them come up with their own. Ask them to fill out a morphology chart for their chosen word.

☑️ Formative Assessment

Substantial Support	• Can students understand root words? • Can students make connections between root words?
Moderate Support	• Can students use context clues and related concepts to understand the use of root words? • Can students use root words to form sentences?
Light Support	• Can students use root words correctly in sentences? • Can students develop Morphology Chart entries for their assigned word?

Preview or Review Week 3 ELA Mini-Lessons

"Marie M. Daly: Biochemistry Pioneer," pages 216–217

Student Objectives

LANGUAGE
Purpose:
• I can describe Dr. Daly in an interview.
Form:
• I can recognize and use adjectives.
CONTENT
• I can understand informational texts..

Additional Materials
• Unit Presentation
• Think-Speak-Listen Flip Book
• *Texts for Close Reading* booklet
• Student journal

Metacognitive Prompt

As we read today, think about what you already know about the human body. Remember what you have read about the states of matter. Make connections between the text and what you already know.

---

11 Read "Marie M. Daly: Biochemistry Pioneer"

Build Background and Vocabulary

Display panels 1–4 from "Marie M. Daly: Biochemistry Pioneer." If students have already read the text, ask what they remember. Invite students to share their cultural experiences and knowledge of healthy and unhealthy foods.

Read Aloud the Text

Read aloud panel 1. **Ask:** *Who is the woman in the photograph? How do the text and the photograph work together?* Repeat with panels 2–4. Then refer to the Essential Question. Invite students to describe why Dr. Marie Maynard Daly measured and described the effects of cholesterol. Then **say:** *This text is an informational text. Informational texts help us learn more about our world and ourselves.*

Think-Speak-Listen: Have pairs complete the activity using the sentence frame:
It's important for scientists to ask questions about _____ because _____.

👥 Differentiated Instruction
Build Language: Use Adjectives to Provide Detail

Remind students that adjectives describe nouns and give more information about people, places, and things. **Say:** *We use adjectives to add details to sentences.* Use the Differentiated Instruction to practice using adjectives to provide detail in a way that best matches the levels of your students.

☑ Use Oral and Written Language: Describe Dr. Daly in an Interview

Task: *Work with your group. Write interview questions for Dr. Marie M. Daly. Decide how Daly would answer each question. Use details from the text and your imagination. Write her answers in complete sentences. Use adjectives to make your writing descriptive. Then present your interview. Have group members take turns asking and answering questions.*

Ⓢ   *Q: Is your work _____?*
     A: My work is _____ because I help people.

Ⓜ   *Q: Do you think your research is _____?*
     A: I think _____ because I _____ people.

Ⓛ   *Q: Does your research _____ facts about _____?*
     A: I think _____ because I _____.

🔄 Wrap Up

Today we have learned how to use adjectives to add detail to our writing. In what ways do adjectives make writing more descriptive?

Turn and Talk: *Describe a person in history who is important to you. Use adjectives to describe the person's life, work, and/or character.*

👥 Differentiated Instruction
Build Language: Use Adjectives to Provide Detail

Ⓢubstantial Support

Model: Use gestures and act out the meanings of the words *healthful*, *research*, and *profoundly*. Check students' understanding. Read aloud panel 1. **Say:** *In the first sentence, I see the word healthful. I know healthful is an adjective meaning "full of health."* **Ask:** *What noun does healthful describe?* **Say:** *The noun is foods.*

Practice: Distribute BLM 1. Work with students to complete the chart.

Extend: Have student work in pairs to complete the Extend activity. Provide support as needed.

Challenge: If students are ready, model completing the BLM challenge. Add *important* as all or part of the first blank, and *healthful* or *better* in the second blank.

Ⓜoderate Support

Model: Use gestures and act out the meanings of the words *healthful*, *research*, and *profoundly*. Check students' understanding. Read aloud panel 1. **Say:** *In the first sentence, I see the word healthful. I know healthful is an adjective meaning "full of health."* **Ask:** *What noun does healthful describe?* **Say:** *The noun is foods.*

Practice: Distribute BLM 2. Work with students to complete the chart.

Extend: Have student work in pairs to complete the Extend activity. Point out that in some sentence frames, they will use the adjectives or adjective/noun pairs in a new way.

Challenge: If students are ready, model completing the BLM challenge.

Ⓛight Support

Practice: Review adjectives. Have students read paragraphs 1 and 2 on page 22 in their *Texts for Close Reading* and find the adjectives. Have pairs complete a chart with the headings: *adjective* and *noun it modifies.*

Extend: Have students write original sentences about Marie Daly using the following nouns: *research, reactions, questions, understanding.* Encourage students to include at least one adjective to add detail.

Challenge: Have students complete these sentence frames about Marie Daly.

Among her _____ was one about _____.

In her youth, she read _____ about _____.

She attended _____ that had _____.

☑ Formative Assessment

Substantial Support	• Can students recognize adjectives that tell what kind? • Can students select adjectives to complete sentence frames? • Can students supply adjectives to complete sentence frames?
Moderate Support	• Can students recognize adjectives that tell what kind and the nouns they modify? • Can students select different adjectives to complete sentence frames? • Can students supply adjectives to complete sentence frames?
Light Support	• Can students recognize adjectives, the nouns they modify, and the types of detail they provide? • Can students supply adjectives to complete sentence frames? • Can students generate original sentences with adjectives?

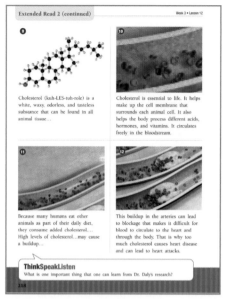

"Marie M. Daly: Biochemistry Pioneer," page 218

Student Objectives

LANGUAGE
Purpose:
• I can express cause and effect in a chart.
Form:
• I can evaluate language choices.
CONTENT
• I can understand informational texts.

Additional Materials

• Unit Presentation
• Think-Speak-Listen Flip Book
• *Texts for Close Reading* booklet
• Student journal

Metacognitive Prompt

Today, we will discuss the enzymes that break down food. When authors share information, they give examples and use vocabulary you may not know. Use context clues to help you understand what you read.

12 Evaluate Language Choices

Engage Thinking

Display panel 5. **Ask:** *What does the diagram show? What do the labels add?* Read the text aloud. **Ask:** *How is the text related to the visual?* **Say:** *The visual show us parts of the digestive system. The text describes processes that occur in this system.*

Turn and Talk: *Tell your partner what you know about the digestive system.*

👤👤👤 Differentiated Instruction
Read and View Closely:
Evaluate Language Choices

Say: *I notice many words that I do not understand.* **Ask:** *Can you list some unfamiliar words?* Students may suggest *metabolism, molecules,* and *enzymes.* **Ask:** *Is a text harder to read when there are words you do not understand? Why would a writer include such words?* Explain that in science writing, a writer uses the language of science. Use the Differentiated Instruction to practice evaluating language choices in a way that best matches the levels of your students.

Build Language: Understand New Vocabulary

Read aloud panels 9–12. **Say:** *Let's make a two-column chart. In the first column, list words we need to know to understand the body processes. Then let's use our word skills to define words in the second column.* Help students select unfamiliar words and write them in the first column. **Say:** *In the first sentence, I need to understand metabolism. I can use the definition of cholesterol in the text: "a white, waxy, odorless, and tasteless substance that can be found in all animal tissue." I can check this definition in a dictionary.*

Think-Speak-Listen: Have pairs answer the question 198 using the sentence frame: *One important thing Dr. Daly's research teaches is _____.*

☑ Use Oral and Written Language:
Express Cause and Effect in a Chart

Task: *Work with a group to create a chart that expresses causes and effects related to cholesterol. Use words or simple pictures to show what cholesterol does, how people may get too much cholesterol, and what too much cholesterol may do to the body. Provide a caption that includes science terms for each item in the chart.*

 Cholesterol makes up _____. The cell membrane is a _____.

Ⓜ *Cholesterol makes up _____ that _____. The cell membrane is _____.*

Ⓛ *Cholesterol _____ that _____. The cell membrane _____.*

Wrap Up

Today we have evaluated language choices made in science writing. Why is it helpful to understand the importance of using science language to explain science facts?

Turn and Talk: *Describe a scientific process. Be sure to use the correct language to refer to events, steps in a process, or characteristics.*

♣♣♣ Differentiated Instruction
Read and View Closely: Evaluate Language Choices

Ⓢubstantial Support

Model: Say: *Panel 5 describes metabolism as a reaction which produces energy. I know* reaction *can mean "an action of a person." But I look at how the term is used in science. I see it is a process that breaks down "complex molecules." I can look up* molecule *in the dictionary: a molecule is the smallest particle of a compound.* Complex *can mean "complicated." Molecules that are complicated have many parts.*

Practice: Distribute BLM 1. Work with students to answer the questions.

Extend: Distribute BLM 1. Have partners use what they have learned from Practice to complete Extend activity. Provide support as needed.

Challenge: If students are ready, help them answer the question in Challenge.

Ⓜoderate Support

Model: Say: *Panel 5 describes metabolism as a reaction which produces energy. I know* reaction *can mean "an action of a person." But I look at how the term is used in science. I see it is a process that breaks down "complex molecules." When I look up* molecule *in the dictionary, I find "a molecule is the smallest particle of a compound." I know* complex *can mean "complicated." So, molecules that are complex or complicated must have many parts.*

Practice: Distribute BLM 2. Work with students to fill in context clues and definitions.

Extend: Distribute BLM 2. Have pairs of students complete the task. Provide support as needed.

Challenge: If students are ready, work with them to answer these questions, referring back to the text for examples.

What does the word pioneering *mean?*

What specific idea does this word suggest?

Ⓛight Support

Practice: Have students read paragraph 7 in "Marie M. Daly: Biochemistry Pioneer" in their *Texts for Close Reading*. Have students list any unknown science words.

Extend: Have pairs answer the following questions. Remind students to use context clues from paragraph 7.

What does the word pioneering *mean? Why does the author call Caldwell a chemist and nutritionist instead of a scientist?*

Challenge: Have students answer the following question.

How do the diagrams on page 27 help your understanding of the word cholesterol?

☑ Formative Assessment

Substantial Support	• Can students understand vocabulary in informational text? • Can students explain why scientific language is important in informational texts?
Moderate Support	• Can students use context clues and the dictionary to define vocabulary in science text? • Can students explain why sentences with scientific language are more appropriate for science writing?
Light Support	• Can students use a variety of methods to define vocabulary in science text? • Can students explain why certain word choices and particular meanings are appropriate to texts? • Can students explain how language choice may vary in biographical versus scientific information?

Preview or Review Week 3 ELA Mini-Lessons

Week 3 • Lesson 13

Use Relative Clauses to Describe Nouns

Sentence	Noun	Relative Clause
Amylase is the enzyme that helps the body process sugars and starches (carbohydrates) like pasta and potatoes.	enzyme	that helps the body process sugars and starches (carbohydrates) like pasta and potatoes.
Cholesterol is essential to life. It helps make up the cell membrane that surrounds each animal cell.	cell membrane	that surrounds each animal cell.
This buildup in the arteries can lead to blockage that makes it difficult for blood to circulate to the heart and through the body.	blockage	that makes it difficult for blood to circulate to the heart and through the body.

ThinkSpeakListen
What types of details can we add to sentences by using relative clauses?

219

"Use Relative Clauses to Describe Nouns," page 219

Student Objectives

LANGUAGE
Purpose:
• I can persuade in a speech.
Form:
• I can use relative clauses to describe nouns.
CONTENT
• I can interpret informational texts.

Additional Materials

• Unit Presentation
• Think-Speak-Listen Flip Book
• *Texts for Close Reading* booklet
• Student journal

Language Transfer Support

In English, speakers use different relative pronouns for people and things (*who*, and *that* or *which*). Note that there is no such distinction in many other languages, including Spanish and Arabic. Students may need extra practice to determine when to use *who* and when to use *that* or *which*.

13 Use Relative Clauses to Describe Nouns

Engage Thinking

Display and review the chart. **Say:** *This chart tells us how to use relative clauses to describe nouns. A relative clause starts with a relative pronoun*: who, whom, which, or that. *A relative clause acts as an adjective. It describes a noun.*

Read and View Closely: Recognize Relative Clauses

Read aloud the first sentence. **Ask:** *What noun does the relative clause beginning with* that *describe?* Elicit ideas. Repeat with the remaining sentences in the chart.

Differentiated Instruction
Build Language: Use Relative Clauses to Describe Nouns

Read aloud the second sentence. Point out the noun *cell membrane*. **Say:** *The relative clause connects the noun,* cell membrane, *to the idea that comes before it. Writers use relative clauses to make stronger sentences without repeating words.* Use the Differentiated Instruction to practice using relative clauses to describe nouns in a way that best matches the levels of your students.

Think-Speak-Listen: Have pairs answer the question using the sentence frame: *We can add details such as _____ by using relative clauses.*

✓ Use Oral and Written Language: Persuade in a Speech

Task: *Work with your group to prepare a speech. Persuade your audience that Dr. Marie M. Daly was one of the most important scientists in history. Include information from the text to support your opinions.* Use this opportunity to formally assess students using the rubric in *English Language Development Assessment.*

(S) *Marie M. Daly is _____. She was a scientist who _____. She studied enzymes that _____.*

(M) *Marie M. Daly is _____. She was _____ who _____. She studied _____ that _____.*

(L) *Marie M. Daly, who _____, is _____. She _____ who _____. She researched _____ that _____.*

Wrap Up

Today we learned how to use relative clauses to add important details about nouns to our writing. How does this make our writing more descriptive?

Turn and Talk: *Describe a person or pet, providing information about your subject's character and/or actions. Use relative clauses to add details to your descriptions.*

👥👥 Differentiated Instruction
Build Language: Use Relative Clauses to Describe Nouns

Ⓢubstantial Support

Model: Use gestures and act out the meanings of the words *enzyme, process,* and *carbohydrates.* Check students' understanding. Read aloud the first sentence. **Say:** *I learn amylase is an enzyme, or substance that aids digestion. The relative clause tells me what the enzyme does. It helps break down sugars and starches (carbohydrates).*

Practice: Review the relative clauses in rows two and three. Help students with difficult vocabulary. Distribute BLM 1. Work with students to complete the task.

Extend: Have pairs complete Extend on the BLM. Provide support as needed.

Challenge: Help students complete these sentence frames with a relative pronoun:

Daly was a scientist _____ answered questions.

She learned facts _____ help people.

Ⓜoderate Support

Model: Use gestures and act out the meanings of the words *enzyme, process,* and *carbohydrates.* Check students' understanding. Read aloud the first sentence. **Say:** *I learn amylase is an enzyme, or substance that aids digestion. The relative clause tells me what the enzyme does. It helps break down sugars and starches (carbohydrates).*

Practice: Distribute BLM 2. Work with students to complete the task. Explain that students need to add who or that at the beginning of the relative clause.

Extend: Have pairs complete the Extend activity. Provide support as needed.

Challenge: If students are ready, help them identify the relative clause and noun modified in the following sentence:

Caldwell was a pioneering nutritionist who specialized in studying enzymes.

Ⓛight Support

Practice: Review relative clauses. Have students read paragraph 2 on page 22 in *their Texts for Close Reading* and find the relative pronoun *that*. In pairs, have them say the relative clause and the noun it modifies.

Extend: Have pairs complete the following sentence frames about Daly and her work, using relative clauses to describe nouns.

Dr. Daly was _____ who _____.

One fact _____ that _____.

Scientists _____ who _____.

An important idea _____ that _____.

Challenge: Have students complete the sentences below and include a relative clause.

Caldwell was _____.

Cholesterol is _____.

☑ Formative Assessment

Substantial Support	• Can students recognize a relative clause and identify the noun it modifies? • Can students match a relative clause with the noun it modifies to complete sentence frames?
Moderate Support	• Can students recognize a relative clause and identify the noun it modifies? • Can students match a relative clause with the noun it modifies to complete sentence frames? • Can students complete sentences by adding original relative clauses?
Light Support	• Can students identify relative clauses and the nouns they modify? • Can students complete sentences using original relative clauses? • Can students generate original sentences with relative clauses?

Preview or Review Week 3 ELA Mini-Lessons

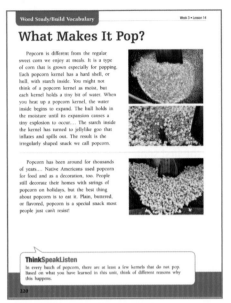

Word Study/Build Vocabulary — Week 3 • Lesson 14

What Makes It Pop?

Popcorn is different from the regular sweet corn we enjoy at meals. It is a type of corn that is grown especially for popping. Each popcorn kernel has a hard shell, or hull, with starch inside. You might not think of a popcorn kernel as moist, but each kernel holds a tiny bit of water. When you heat up a popcorn kernel, the water inside begins to expand. The hull holds in the moisture until its expansion causes a tiny explosion to occur.... The starch inside the kernel has turned to jellylike goo that inflates and spills out. The result is the irregularly shaped snack we call popcorn.

Popcorn has been around for thousands of years.... Native Americans used popcorn for food and as a decoration, too. People still decorate their homes with strings of popcorn on holidays, but the best thing about popcorn is to eat it. Plain, buttered, or flavored, popcorn is a special snack most people just can't resist!

ThinkSpeakListen
In every bunch of popcorn, there are at least a few kernels that do not pop. Based on what you have learned in this unit, think of different reasons why this happens.

220

"What Makes It Pop?," page 220

Student Objectives

LANGUAGE
Purpose:
• I can analyze related words in a chart.
Form:
• I can understand nouns and verbs.
CONTENT
• I can comprehend an informational text.

Additional Materials

• Unit Presentation
• Think-Speak-Listen Flip Book
• *Texts for Close Reading* booklet
• Student journal
• Dictionaries

Language Transfer Support

Several of the related words from "What Makes It Pop?" have Spanish cognates. These include expander (expand), expansión (expansion) and decoración (decoration). Ask students if the words from the text remind them of words in their first language.

14 Read "What Makes It Pop?"

Build Background and Vocabulary

Display the panels from "What Makes It Pop?" If students have already read the text, ask them what they remember. Invite students to share their cultural experiences and knowledge of making popcorn.

Read Aloud the Text

Read aloud panel 1. Ask students to find details in the photos that match the words in the text (kernel, popcorn). Ask questions, such as *What's happening in the photos?* Repeat with panel 2. After reading, **ask:** *What causes popcorn to pop?* Refer to the Essential Question: *Why do we measure and describe the world?* Invite students to discuss why it's important to measure the kernels. Then **say:** *This text gives facts about how cooking popcorn relies on science. Texts that give facts about a science topic or social studies are called informational texts.*

Think-Speak-Listen: Have pairs complete the activity using this sentence frame: *I think some kernels do not pop because _____.*

👥 Differentiated Instruction
Build Language: Analyze Related Words

Say: *Words that have the same root are related.* Point out the word *flavored* in panel 2. **Ask:** *What base word do you see?* Elicit answers. **Say:** *I see the word* flavor *and the suffix -ed. Flavor is a noun and* flavored *is an adjective. Based on this and the clues in the sentence, I think* flavored *means, "having a certain taste."* **Say:** *Looking at related words can help us figure out a word's meaning in a sentence.* Use the Differentiated Instruction to practice analyzing words relationships in a way that best matches the levels of your students.

☑ Use Oral and Written Language: Analyze Related Words in a Chart

Task: *With a partner, think about the word* resist *as it is used in the last sentence of the text. First, look it up in a dictionary. Then find words that are related. Record the words in a Derivations Chart. Write sentences for your words.*

Ⓢ   *Popcorn is _____.*

Ⓜ   *It is hard to _____.*

Ⓛ   *To _____ is _____.*

 Wrap Up

Today we learned how to analyze related words. How does knowing about related words help you when you read?

Turn and Talk: *Describe a type of food that you find irresistible.*

👥 Differentiated Instruction
Build Language: Analyze Related Words

Ⓢubstantial Support

Model: Explain that words are related when they have the same base word. Point out the words *decoration* and *decorate* in panel 2. **Say:** *These two words have related meanings. I can use the other words in the text to help me figure out their meanings. I can also use a dictionary to help me understand these words and other words related to them.*

Practice: Distribute BLM 1. Discuss that a Derivations Chart can help students think about related words. Then work with students to complete the Practice activity from the BLM.

Extend: Ask partners to complete the Extend activity. Provide support as needed.

Challenge: If students are ready, have them list words that are related to the word *expand*.

Ⓜoderate Support

Model: Point out the words *expand* and *expansion* in panel 1. **Say:** *These words are related words because the base word in expansion is expand. Because these words are related, they have related meanings. We can also look at the context clues to help us figure out the meanings of related words.*

Practice: Distribute BLM 2 and work with students to complete the Derivations Chart for the word *expand*. Reteach as necessary. Then have students answer the question.

Extend: Have students work in pairs to complete the Extend activity. **Ask:** *How does finding related words help you understand the text?*

Challenge: If students are ready, model analyzing the related words *moist* and *moisture* in a Derivations Chart.

Ⓛight Support

Practice: Have partners read paragraph 2 on page 30 in their *Texts for Close Reading* and ask them to complete a Derivations Chart for the words *moist* and *moisture*. Ask them to use context clues and a dictionary to explain the meaning and part of speech of each word.

Extend: Have partners find another pair of related words in paragraph 2, make a Derivations Chart for them, and identify the meaning and part of speech for each word.

Challenge: If students are ready, have them write a sentence using two or more of the related words they identified in one of their Derivations Chart.

☑ Formative Assessment

Substantial Support	• Do students understand the concept of related words? • With support, can students analyze related words using a Derivations Chart?
Moderate Support	• Can students use a Derivations Chart and context clues to define related words? • Are students able to generate sentences using related words?
Light Support	• Are students able to use analyze related words using a Derivations Chart and define each word? • Can students identify related words in a text and use the relationship to understand the words' meanings?

Preview or Review Week 3 ELA Mini-Lessons

Use the Language of Cause and Effect

Cause	Effect
When you heat up a popcorn kernel,	the water inside begins to expand.
When the starch inside has turned to goo,	it inflates and spills out.
When the hull explodes,	we hear a popping sound.

ThinkSpeakListen
What else can change from one state to another? What causes the change? What is the effect? Explain using the language of cause and effect.

221

"Use the Language of Cause and Effect," page 221

Student Objectives

LANGUAGE
Purpose:
• I can create a recipe.
Form:
• I can use cause-and-effect language.
CONTENT
• I can read an informational text.

Additional Materials
• Unit Presentation
• Think-Speak-Listen Flip Book
• *Texts for Close Reading* booklet
• Student journal

Language Transfer Support

Note that speakers of Chinese and Vietnamese may need additional support to use complex sentences with subordinate conjunctions. In these languages, conjunctions occur in pairs.

15 Use the Language of Cause and Effect

Engage Thinking

Say: *In the text about popcorn, we read about cause and effect as popcorn changed from kernels to popcorn.* Display the Use the chart and point to the images. Read aloud the first row, pointing out the cause and effect. **Say:** *This is an example of cause and effect. The cause is the reason why something happened. The effect is what happened.*

Turn and Talk: *Tell your partner one effect of hot weather.*

Read and View Closely: Use the Language of Cause And Effect

Remind students that there can be two types of clauses in a sentence. Explain that a cause-and-effect sentence usually contains a dependent clause and an independent clause. Read aloud the first row. **Ask:** *Which clause is dependent and which one is independent?* **Say:** *"When you heat up a popcorn kernel" is the dependent clause and "the water inside beings to expand" is the independent clause.* Repeat with the remaining rows.

👥 Differentiated Instruction
Build Language: Use the Language of Cause and Effect

Say: *Now that we know the two types of clauses within a cause-and-effect sentence, we will practice writing our own.* Use the Differentiated Instruction to guide students to use cause-and-effect language.

Think-Speak-Listen: Have pairs complete the activity using these sentence frames: _____ can change from _____ to _____. The change is caused by _____.

✔️ Use Oral and Written Language: Create a Recipe

Task: *Create a recipe. Include the ingredients you need and explain the process using cause-and-effect language in your sentences.*

Ⓢ *When you mix _____ and _____, the mixture _____.*

Ⓜ *When you mix _____ and _____, the _____ can _____.*

Ⓛ *When you mix _____.*

🔄 Wrap Up

Today we learned about cause-and-effect sentences. Now we can use these types of complex sentences in our own writing.

Turn and Talk: *Tell a partner what might happen in this short story: Inside a popcorn factory, a worker accidentally adds food coloring to the popcorn containers. What are the effects? How is the popcorn different? How does this effect people who buy the popcorn?*

👥 Differentiated Instruction
Build Language: Use the Language of Cause And Effect

Ⓢubstantial Support

Model: Review the chart. Read the example sentences. **Say:** *When you write a cause-and-effect sentence, you must include one dependent clause and one independent clause.* **Ask:** *What is the difference?* **Say:** *A dependent clause is a sentence that cannot stand alone. An independent clause is a sentence that can stand by itself.*

Practice: Distribute BLM 1. Encourage students to help you match the causes with their effects. Check understanding and reteach as necessary.

Extend: Have pairs complete the activity on BLM 1. **Say:** *Read each sentence. Underline the cause and circle the effect.* Provide support as needed.

Challenge: Read the question on the BLM and model thinking through the answer. Then have students complete the challenge on their own. **Say:** *Think about what happens in each sentence. The cause makes something happen. The effect is the thing that happens because of the first thing.*

Ⓜoderate Support

Model: Review the chart. Read the example sentences. **Say:** *When you write a cause-and-effect sentence, you must include one dependent clause and one independent clause.* **Ask:** *What is the difference?* **Say:** *A dependent clause is a sentence that cannot stand-alone. An independent clause is a sentence that can stand by itself.*

Practice: Distribute BLM 2. Work with the students to underline the causes and circle the effects. Check understanding and reteach as necessary.

Extend: Have pairs complete the sentences on BLM 2. Provide support as needed.

Challenge: Have student pairs list the process of how popcorn pops, using cause-and-effect language.

Ⓛight Support

Practice: Have students read paragraph 2 on page 38 of their *Texts for Close Reading.* Work with students to identify the three actions that happen in the paragraph, and their causes. Help as needed.

Extend: Read the first sentence in paragraph 2. Ask students what they think might happen if you tried to make popcorn out of sweet corn. Think of a cause-and-effect sentence starting with: *If you tried to pop sweet corn in the microwave, _____.* Have them work with a partner to answer the question.

Challenge: **Say:** *What if we used popcorn instead of other types of decorations? For example, "If you used popcorn to decorate your clothes, _____. If you use popcorn to fill your pillows, _____." Share your silly effects with a partner. Now create your own cause-and-effect sentences.* Guide students in creating sentences.

☑ Formative Assessment

Substantial Support	• Can students identify cause-and-effect language with support? • Can students use cause-and-effect language with support?
Moderate Support	• Can students identify cause-and-effect language with little support? • Can students use cause-and-effect language with little support?
Light Support	• Can students identify cause-and-effect language? • Can students use cause-and-effect language?

Additional Resources

Additional Resources

Close Reading Protocol

A Close Reading Protocol with Scaffolding Support for English Learners

	FIRST READING	SECOND READING	THIRD READING
	General Understanding of Topic	*Key Ideas, Vocabulary Use, and Text Structure*	*Author's Purpose, Inferences, Opinions, Intertextual Connections, Critical Thinking*
Before Reading	Point out and discuss text features Introduce pre-selected essential vocabulary Set a purpose for reading/listening Ask a leading question (focus/topic) Elicit a specific strategy (prediction)	Set a purpose for reading Promote personal connection to content Provide instructions for specific annotation Ask leading question (key idea) (text structure) Review/reinforce key vocabulary	Set purpose for reading, framing with meaningful and more complex text-dependent questions to discern author's purpose/point of view/bias/intentions/omissions; or questions that frame integration of knowledge and ideas presented in text.
During Reading	Teacher Read-Aloud modeling prosody Think aloud to model interaction Model annotation of essential vocabulary Model interaction with unknown words	Teacher-led Shared Reading and Think-Aloud Read to determine main ideas Read to identify logical connections between ideas Point to signal words—text structures and the organization of ideas presented	Students reread independently targeted sections of text and take notes or make annotations that relate to the purpose for reading.
After Reading	Ask general understanding text-dependent questions Promote academic discussion (pairs) Promote use of essential vocabulary Create vocabulary/concept logs, banks Engage in shared writing	Ask text-dependent questions to identify key ideas, facts, details, examples, etc. Determine relationships between concepts/ideas Identify text structure—sentence/paragraph level Construct graphic organizers/charts/concept maps Engage in writing, collaborative discussion/tasks using textual evidence	Write-Pair-Share summaries/responses Students reflect on learning-implications, cross-content or cross-cultural connections, innovations Work on collaborative tasks including writing assignments and cross-referencing texts on the same topic/author or content.
What All Students Do	Interactive/Shared reading Active listening Annotation—circle unfamiliar words/phrases Ask and answer questions Reference text features Contribute to pair or group conversations Engage in shared writing	Read and reread text Identify what is confusing or difficult to understand Recount the main ideas and details Annotate key ideas and details Make intertextual connections Ask and answer text-dependent questions Contribute to collaborative conversations	Read and reread text Identify what is confusing or difficult to understand Identify author's purpose Articulate inferences, opinions, and problem pose/solve Support/disagree/build on others' ideas Engage in collaborative tasks, extension activities
Metacognition	Preview, skim, gist Use prior knowledge Confirm understanding	Monitoring listening and reading comprehension Selective attention Determine text importance	Make inferences Integrate knowledge Organization and planning
Substantial	Who/What/When/Where/How/Why questions and answer frames Illustrated vocabulary banks/bilingual logs Oral practice/draw/label/dictate Primary language support	Use of graphic organizers/maps/charts/visuals Annotation markers/posters Sentence frames Noting connecting words/phrases Primary language support	Primary language texts on topic/author/content Sentence frames that align with speech/thinking function assigned
Moderate	Conversation mats Question cards Deconstructing and reconstructing key idea	Sentence frames that align with speech/thinking function assigned to support collaborative conversations	Modeled and Think-aloud making inferences Examples and non-examples
Light	Making analogies Using context clues	Understanding cohesion—how ideas are linked Deconstructing compound and complex sentences	Relate text to prior knowledge/experience Question the author/text

Close Reading Strategies

	SUBSTANTIAL	MODERATE	LIGHT
Key Ideas and Details	Story structure GOs Focus on character + setting Story illustrations *Wh* questions and response frames	Story retell Attention to pronouns and antecedents Descriptive language Dialogue (who says what, how, and why)	Summarize part of story Make predictions Make inferences Cite text evidence
Craft and Structure	Story structure GO Focus on sequence of events + plot climax Illustrated vocabulary Word banks	Recognize and identify Text structure Signal/Transition words Word functions in context	Diagram text structures Discuss word nuances
Integration of Knowledge	Story structure GO Focus on plot solution and conclusion Summary frames Reflection/Opinion frames	Inference charts Cross-text or cross-curricular integration using Compare/Contrast charts and matrixes	Making meaning using more complex language structures (reading/speaking/writing)

Corrective feedback is an essential feature of English Language Development instruction.
It is information given to learners regarding a linguistic error they have made.

Corrective Feedback Strategies		
	IMPLICIT	**EXPLICIT**
	Attracts learner's attention without overtly informing the learner that he/she has made an error or interrupting the flow of interaction	Tries to overtly draw the learner's attention to the error made
INPUT PROVIDING: **Correct form is given to students.**	**Recast** The corrector incorporates the content words of the immediately preceding incorrect utterance and changes and corrects the utterance in some way (e.g., phonological, syntactic, morphological, or lexical). L: I went school. T: You went to school?	**Explicit Correction** The corrector indicates an error has been committed, identifies the error, and provides the correction. L: We will go on May. T: Not on May, in May. L: We will go in May.
OUTPUT PROMPTING: **The student is prompted to self-correct.**	**Repetition** The corrector repeats the learner utterance highlighting the error by means of emphatic stress. L: I will showed you. T: I will show you. L: I will show you.	**Metalinguistic Explanation** Corrector provides explanation for the errors that have been made. L: two duck T: Do you remember how to show more than one duck? L: ducks T: Yes, you remember that we need to add "s" at the end of a noun to show the plural form.
	Clarification Request The corrector indicates that he/she has not understood what the learner has said. L: on the it go T: Can you please tell me again? T: Do you mean "it goes in your desk"?	**Elicitation** The corrector repeats part of the learner utterance but not the erroneous part and uses rising intonation to signal the learner should complete it. L: I don't think won't rain. T: I don't think it . . . (*will*) rain.
		Paralinguistic Signal The corrector uses a gesture or facial expression to indicate that the learner has made an error. L: Yesterday I go to the movies. T: (gestures with right forefinger over left shoulder to indicate past)

Benchmark Advance Contrastive Analysis Charts

The Sound-Spelling Contrastive Analysis Charts compare the phonemes (sounds) and graphemes (letters) of English to nine world languages and enable teachers to compare various features at a glance, including:

- Categories of English spellings (grapheme types, such as short vowels)

- English sounds (phonemes)

- English letter(s) (the most common grapheme(s) used to represent the sound)

- Examples of English sounds in various positions in words (initial, medial, and final position)

- Whether that sound exists in each of the nine languages

- Whether the letter(s) that represent that sound exist in each language

The Value of Contrastive Analysis

by Silvia Dorta-Duque de Reyes and Jill Kerper-Mora, Ph.D.

Contrastive analysis is the systematic study of two languages to identify their similarities and differences. Contrastive analysis charts help educators recognize distinctions between a student's primary language and English. The *Benchmark Advance* Contrastive Analysis Charts address the similarities and differences between English and nine of the most common world languages spoken by English Learners.

For both students and teachers, using a language construction process that recognizes the similarities and differences between a primary and secondary language, rather than an error correction procedure, builds students' awareness of how English works. In every contrastive analysis lesson, students benefit when their primary language is respected and tapped as a resource for learning English through an additive approach that honors their primary language.

All oral languages consist of phonemes, and each of those sounds is articulated in a particular position in the mouth. As teachers are helping students to recognize and pronounce the sounds of English (phonology), they need to know whether the students' primary language utilizes particular sounds. If the target sound is found in the student's primary language, it will be fairly easy for the student to articulate and use that sound in English. If, however, the sound is not found in the student's primary language, teachers will need to provide additional instruction and support to ensure that students "hear" (discriminate) and articulate the sound in English.

Students will need instruction in recognizing and distinguishing the sounds of English as compared to or contrasted with sounds in their primary language (e.g., vowels, consonants, consonant blends, syllable structures). An example is the short vowel sounds of English that are not equivalent to vowel sounds in Spanish. In an alphabetic language system, phonology and phonemic awareness are the foundation for reading and writing.

There are many writing systems in the world. Latin-based languages, such as English and Spanish, use a writing system that is based on the letters of the alphabet; words are formed by combining different letters. Other languages, such as Chinese, use a completely different system of writing. It is called the logographic system. Each character represents a meaningful (morphological) unit. Because these two systems are entirely different, there is no basis for comparison of the writing systems. For students who have been taught to use the logographic system, an introduction to the alphabet is necessary, and the instruction needs to include the sound–symbol relationship.

The Structure of the Sound-Spelling Contrastive Analysis Charts

In order to support students who are acquiring new sounds and letters in a new language, it is important to map out which sounds and letters are familiar to students, the extent to which the sounds and letters are familiar, and which sounds and letters are new and unfamiliar. The charts indicate whether the English phonemes and graphemes exist in both languages (positive), are about the same (approximate), or have no equivalency.

Transfer Indicators in the Charts	What They Mean
Yes	There is an equivalent, or positive, transfer relationship between English and the student's primary language.
Approximate	This term is used when referring to phoneme variants that are considered close enough to the corresponding English language sound not to cause confusion for English Learners.
No	There is no equivalent or transfer relationship between English and the student's primary language.

Although some world languages use an alphabetic system for writing (e.g., Spanish, Vietnamese), they each vary in both sounds and symbols used to encode those sounds. Some sounds and spellings are fully transferable (e.g., sound /b/ can be encoded with letter *b* in both Spanish and English, as in [botón/button]). Some sounds that are transferable can be encoded in English using spelling patterns *not* found in the primary language (e.g., /k/ spelled *ck* in English, as in *duck*).

The Structure of the Grammar-Syntax Charts

The Grammar-Syntax charts compare the grammatical differences between English and each of the nine world languages. The charts are divided into the conventions of standard English grammar: verbs; nouns; word order; adverbs and adjectives; pronouns; and prepositions, conjunctions, and articles.

These charts provide teachers with information relating to potential error patterns that may result as students generalize what they know and use in their home language to English. Once teachers know which grammatical structures transfer to academic English conventions, and which do not, they can adjust instruction accordingly. For example, English is an inflectional language. In an inflectional language, verbs change forms. For example, the verb "see" can appear as "see," "sees," "saw," "seen," or "seeing." Other languages, such as Chinese, are noninflectional. Words/verbs do not change shapes. The word "see" 看 is always written as 看, and there is no change. In addition, the word "to" in front of an English "verb" such as "to go" is nonexistent.

When teachers learn to identify and capitalize on students' existing language skills, they are able to use positive transfer to support students in gaining English language proficiency and biliteracy. Instructional approaches that promote students' awareness and understanding of language variety are particularly useful for supporting students' metalinguistic knowledge and positive language identity.

We extend our appreciation to the language consultants, educators, and linguists who reviewed these charts for accuracy and completeness, and we extend special recognition to Sandra Ceja, who compiled these charts.

Using Contrastive Analysis to Inform Instruction

The Contrastive Analysis charts give teachers information about students' native language usages, structures, and grammar to enable them to accomplish the following:

1. Support students' overall understanding of how English works in ways that are similar to or different from usages in their native language.

2. Identify specific teaching points where metalinguistic knowledge of linguistic similarities and differences will enable students to self-monitor and correct errors and error patterns in English in both oral and written production. This includes teachers' use of phonological differences between students' primary language and English that impact their pronunciation and spelling.

3. Scaffold and support students' developing strategies in gaining word-level meaning of English forms, such as nominalization (converting a verb to a noun) and noting the way English words are formed (morphology), such as prefixes, root words, and suffixes that support students in deciphering new vocabulary based on their knowledge of their native language. This is especially helpful in learning cognates.

4. Scaffold and support students in developing language learning strategies for increasing their ability in sentence- and clause-level meaning-making strategies of sentence deconstruction ("unpacking sentences") and for understanding phrase-level meaning conveyed through English grammar and syntax in informational and literary text.

Sound-Spelling: Consonants

	English						Spanish		Vietnamese		Hmong	
	Sound (phoneme)	Most Common Spelling Patterns (graphemes)	Notes	Word Examples			Sound (phoneme) transfer?	Spelling pattern (grapheme) transfer?	Sound (phoneme) transfer?	Spelling pattern (grapheme) transfer?	Sound (phoneme) transfer?	Spelling pattern (grapheme) transfer?
Consonants				initial	medial	final						
The sound /b/ is used or approximated in all of these languages, but the spelling used to communicate /b/ varies.	/b/	b	Subject to medial consonant doubling. Consonant blends include bl and br. Spelling b(e) in long vowel syllables	button	cabin (bubble)	lab (cube)	yes	yes	yes	yes	approx.	no
The sound /k/ is used in all of these languages, but the spelling used to communicate /k/ varies.	/k/	c	Primarily followed by another consonant, or short/long a, o, u vowel sound. Consonant blends include cl and cr.	castle	act	music	yes	yes	yes	yes	yes	no
		k	Primarily followed by short/long e, i vowel sound	karate	monkey	mask		yes		yes		yes
		_ck	Following short vowel sound at the end of a syllable or word	(n/a)	blacksmith	duck		no		no		no
		-lk	Low frequency when preceded by o or a	(n/a)	chalky, yolks	talk, folk		no		no		no
		ch	Greek words	chorus,	echo	stomach, ache		no		no		no
		qu, que	French	quay	conquer	antique		yes (qu but not que)		no		no
The sound /d/ is used or approximated in most of these languages, but the spelling used to communicate /d/ varies.	/d/	d	Subject to medial consonant doubling. Consonant blends include dr and dw.	dice	maiden (paddle)	mad (add)	approx.	yes	yes	yes	yes	yes
The sound /f/ is used or approximated in many of these languages, but the spelling used to communicate /f/ varies.	/f/	f	Subject to medial consonant doubling. Consonant blends include fr and fl.	family	after (baffle)	self, knife, muff	yes	yes	yes	no	yes	yes
		gh	-ough and -augh patterns	(n/a)	laughter	enough		no		no		no
		ph		photo	aphid	graph		no		yes		no
The sound /g/ is used or approximated in many of these languages, but the spelling used to communicate /g/ varies.	/g/	g	"Hard g" sound, mainly when followed by a, o, u. There are exceptions (girl, get and others). Subject to medial consonant doubling. Consonant blends include gr and gl. /gw/ sound spelled with gu (language, penguin)	goal	drags (baggage)	tag, (egg)	yes	yes	yes	yes	approx.	no
		gu ("silent u")	"Hard g" sound spelled gu when followed by e, I, or y to prevent "soft g" sound	guide	intrigued	(gue) league, plague		yes		no		
		gh		ghost	aghast			no		yes		no

Sound (phoneme)	Most Common Spelling Patterns (graphemes)	Tagalog Sound (phoneme) transfer?	Tagalog Spelling pattern (grapheme) transfer?	Korean Sound (phoneme) transfer?	Korean Spelling pattern (grapheme) transfer?	Cantonese Sound (phoneme) transfer?	Cantonese Spelling pattern (grapheme) transfer?	Mandarin Sound (phoneme) transfer?	Mandarin Spelling pattern (grapheme) transfer?	Farsi Sound (phoneme) transfer?	Farsi Spelling pattern (grapheme) transfer?	Arabic Sound (phoneme) transfer?	Arabic Spelling pattern (grapheme) transfer?
/b/	b	yes	yes	approx.	no	approx.	no	no	no	yes		yes	
/k/	c	yes	no	yes	no	yes	no	yes	no	yes	no	yes	no
	k		yes		no		no		no		no		no
	_ck		no		no		no		no		no		no
	-lk		no		no		no		no		no		no
	ch		no		no		no		no		no		no
	qu, que		no		no		no		no		no		no
/d/	d	yes	no	approx.	no	approx.	no	no	no	yes	no	yes	no
/f/	f	no	no	no	no	yes	no	yes	no	yes	no	yes	no
	gh		no		no		no		no		no		no
	ph		no		no		no		no		no		no
/0/	g	yes	yes	approx.	no	approx.	no	no	no	yes	no	no	no
	gu ('silent u')		no				no	no	no		no		no
	gh		no		no		no	no	no		no		no

Sound-Spelling: Consonants

		English				Spanish		Vietnamese		Hmong	
	Sound (phoneme)	Most Common Spelling Patterns (graphemes)	Notes	Word Examples		Sound (phoneme) transfer?	Spelling pattern (grapheme) transfer?	Sound (phoneme) transfer?	Spelling pattern (grapheme) transfer?	Sound (phoneme) transfer?	Spelling pattern (grapheme) transfer?
The sound /h/ is used or approximated in many of these languages, but the spelling used to communicate /h/ varies.	/h/	h_	/h/ sound in English occurs only at the beginning of a syllable and never as the final sound in a word. When not in the first syllable, it is paired with a consonant ch, gh, rh, ph, sh, th, or wh.	hip	enhance	approx.	no	yes	yes	yes	yes
The sound /j/ is used or approximated in some of these languages, but the spelling used to communicate /j/ varies.	/j/	j	j used at the beginning of a syllable. ge or dge used for /j/ at the end of a word or syllable. Few exceptions (algae, margarine)	jam	inject	no	no	approx.	no	no	no
		ge	"Soft g" when followed by e. Final /j/ sound when part of a long vowel/final e pattern.	gems	angel / page		no		no		no
		gi_	"Soft g" when followed by i	gist	margin		no		no		no
		gy	"Soft g" when followed by y	gym	biology		no		no		no
		_dge	Used as /j/ spelling at the end of a syllable when following a short vowel sound	badger	wedge		no		no		no
		du	More complex Latin words	gradual, educate			no		no		no
		di	Lower frequency, more complex words	soldier			no		no		no
The sound /l/ is used or approximated in all of these languages, and the common spelling used to communicate /l/ is l among the alphabetic languages.	/l/	l	Used as spelling for initial sound of a syllable and the last sound of a consonant blend (bl, cl, chl, fl, gl, pl, sl, spl). Doubled when adding suffix -ly (equal --> equally).	lion	melt, (follow) / girl	yes	yes	yes	yes	yes	yes
		ll	More frequently used than l at the end of a syllable after short vowel	yellow	bell		no		no		no
		-el	English suffix		tunnel		no		no		no
		_le	English suffix, used more often than -el. When added to a closed syllable, can influence consonant doubling (i.e., ap-ple, bab-ble).		maple		no		no		no
The sound /m/ is used or approximated in all of these languages, and the common spelling used to communicate /m/ is m among the alphabetic languages.	/m/	m	Most common spelling, can be subject to medial consonant doubling (hammock).	medal	hamper / ham, become	yes	yes	yes	yes	yes	yes
		mn	Low frequency. When adding affixes, can "cause" both letters to be pronounced (i.e., autumn --> autumnal)		condemned / hymn		no		no		no

Sound (phoneme)	Most Common Spelling Patterns (graphemes)	Tagalog		Korean		Cantonese		Mandarin		Farsi		Arabic	
		Sound (phoneme) transfer?	Spelling pattern (grapheme) transfer?	Sound (phoneme) transfer?	Spelling pattern (grapheme) transfer?	Sound (phoneme) transfer?	Spelling pattern (grapheme) transfer?	Sound (phoneme) transfer?	Spelling pattern (grapheme) transfer?	Sound (phoneme) transfer?	Spelling pattern (grapheme) transfer?	Sound (phoneme) transfer?	Spelling pattern (grapheme) transfer?
/h/	h_	yes	no	yes	no	yes	no	no	no	yes	no	yes	no
/j/	j	no	no	approx.	no	approx.	no	no	no	yes	no	yes	no
	ge		no		no		no		no		no		no
	gi_		no		no		no		no		no		no
	gy		no		no		no		no		no		no
	_dge		no		no		no		no		no		no
	du		no		no		no		no		no		no
	di		no		no		no		no		no		no
/l/	l	yes	yes	yes	no	yes	no	yes	no	yes	no	yes	no
	ll		no		no		no		no		no		no
	-el		no		no		no		no		no		no
	_le		no		no		no		no		no		no
/m/	m	yes	yes	yes	no	yes	no	yes	no	yes	no	yes	no
	mn		no		no		no		no		no		no

Sound-Spelling: Consonants

	English						Spanish		Vietnamese		Hmong	
	Sound (phoneme)	Most Common Spelling Patterns (graphemes)	Notes	Word Examples			Sound (phoneme) transfer?	Spelling pattern (grapheme) transfer?	Sound (phoneme) transfer?	Spelling pattern (grapheme) transfer?	Sound (phoneme) transfer?	Spelling pattern (grapheme) transfer?
The sound /m/ is used or approximated in all of these languages, and the common spelling used to communicate /m/ is m among the alphabetic languages. *continued*	/m/	lm	Low frequency. Some regions do pronounce the l separately.		alms	calm		no		no		no
		mb	Low frequency. When adding affixes, can "cause" both letters to be pronounced (i.e., crumb --> crumble)		climber	lamb		no		no		no
The sound /n/ is used or approximated in most of these languages, and the common spelling used to communicate /n/ is n among the alphabetic languages.	/n/	n	Subject to consonant doubling (inn, connect)	nest	pants	fan	yes	yes	yes	yes	yes	yes
		kn_		knee				no		no		no
		gn	Initial Anglo-Saxon consonant blend that lost "g" sound over time, German, Scandinavian, Latin, Greek	gnome	designing	reign, assign, foreign		no		no		
		pn	Consonant blend in Greek words that "lost" /p/ sound across languages	pneumonia				no		no		
The sound /p/ is used or approximated in most of these languages, and the common spelling used to communicate /p/ is p among the alphabetic languages.	/p/	p	subject to medial consonant doubling	paper	steps (happy)	help	yes	yes	yes	yes	approx.	yes
The sound /n/ is used or approximated in few of these languages.	/kw/	qu_		queen	liquid		yes	no	yes	yes	no	no
The sound /r/ is used or approximated in few of these languages. Many of these languages use a trilled version of /r/ that is not used in English (e.g., Spanish carro).	/r/	r	subject to medial consonant doubling	radio	carpet (arrow)	star	approx.	yes	approx.	no	no	no
		wr_		write	unwrap			no		no		no
		re	French, British low frequency			acre, theatre		no		no		no
		er, ur, ir (r-controlled vowels)	Syllables where /r/ is the sound requiring a vowel. Frequently misspelled without the vowel.	ermine, herbal, urgent, irk	interest	wonder, fir, fur				no		no
		rh	Greek words	rhyme	hemorrhage			yes		no		no
		ear (r-controlled)		earth	learn			no		no		no
The sound /s/ is used or approximated in all of these languages, and the common spelling used to communicate /s/ is s among most of the alphabetic languages.	/s/	s		sun	past	gas	yes	yes	yes	yes	yes	no
		ss	Consonant team at the end of a root or last syllable after a short vowel (not a suffix)		lesson	bless, toss, pass		no		no		no
		se	At the end of word or syllable	horse		else, goose		no		no		no
		ce	"Soft c" /s/ when followed by e	cereal	paced	face		yes		yes		no
		ci_	"Soft c" /s/ when followed by i (very rarely at the end of a word, e.g. foci)	circle	incite, incident			yes		yes		no
		cy		cycle, cyst	bicycle	racy		no		no		no

Sound (phoneme)	Most Common Spelling Patterns (graphemes)	Tagalog Sound (phoneme) transfer?	Tagalog Spelling pattern (grapheme) transfer?	Korean Sound (phoneme) transfer?	Korean Spelling pattern (grapheme) transfer?	Cantonese Sound (phoneme) transfer?	Cantonese Spelling pattern (grapheme) transfer?	Mandarin Sound (phoneme) transfer?	Mandarin Spelling pattern (grapheme) transfer?	Farsi Sound (phoneme) transfer?	Farsi Spelling pattern (grapheme) transfer?	Arabic Sound (phoneme) transfer?	Arabic Spelling pattern (grapheme) transfer?
/m/	lm		no		no		no		no		no		no
	mb		no		no		no		no		no		no
/n/	n		yes		no		no		no		no		no
	kn_		no		no		no		no		no		no
	gn	no	no	yes	no	yes	no	yes	no	yes	no	yes	no
	pn		no				no		no		no		no
/p/	p	yes	yes	yes	no	yes	no	yes	no	yes	no	no	no
/kw/	qu_	no	no	yes	no	approx.	no	no	no	no	no	no	no
/r/	r		yes		no		no		no		no		no
	wr_		no		no		no		no		no		no
	re		no		no		no		no		no		no
	er, ur, ir (r-controlled vowels)	yes	no	no	no	no	no	no	no	no	no	no	no
	rh		no		no		no		no		no		no
	ear (r-controlled)		no		no		no		no		no		no
/s/	s		yes		no		no		no		no		no
	ss		no		no		no		no		no		no
	se	yes	no	yes	no	yes	no	yes	no	yes	no	yes	no
	ce		no		no		no		no		no		no
	ci_		no		no		no		no		no		no
	cy		no		no		no		no		no		no

Contrastive Analysis of English and Nine World Languages

Sound-Spelling: Consonants

	English				Spanish		Vietnamese		Hmong	
	Sound (phoneme)	Most Common Spelling Patterns (graphemes)	Notes	Word Examples	Sound (phoneme) transfer?	Spelling pattern (grapheme) transfer?	Sound (phoneme) transfer?	Spelling pattern (grapheme) transfer?	Sound (phoneme) transfer?	Spelling pattern (grapheme) transfer?
The sound /s/ *continued*	/s/	sc		scene, science, descend, disciple		no		no		no
		ss	used at the end of a root or last syllable after a short vowel (not a suffix)	assess, grass, princess		no		no		no
The sound /t/ is used or approximated in all of these languages, and the common spelling used to communicate /t/ is t among most of the alphabetic languages.	/t/	t	initial, medial, and final sounds	telephone, after, just, wheat, late	approx.	yes	yes	yes	approx.	no
		tt		bitten, battle, mitt		no		no		no
		_ed	suffix	raced		no		no		no
		pt	few words of Greek origin	pterodactyl		no		no		no
		te, tte	French origin	suite, gazette		no		no		no
The sound /v/ is used or approximated in few of these languages.	/v/	v		van, flavor	no	no	yes	yes	yes	yes
		ve	Word or syllable endings; never end in solo v.	driven, give, brave		no		no		no
The sound /w/ is used or approximated in some of these languages.	/w/	w	Note that many vowel sounds are changed when following w.	Washington, away, cow	yes	approx.	no	no	no	no
The unvoiced sound /hw/ is not used or approximated in any of these languages.	/hw/	wh	Old English beginning of word or syllable. Many question words or whistling/whining sounds. Modern day /w/	why, whale, nowhere	no	no	no	no	no	no
The sound /ks/ is not used or approximated in a few of these languages.	/ks/	_x	Preceded by vowel. Latin prefix ex-. Distinguish between plurals and words (tax vs. tacks)	extra, fix	yes	yes	no	no	no	no
		-cks	plural	ducks		no		no		no
The sound /y/ is used or approximated in most of these languages, but the spelling used to communicate /y/ varies.	/y/	y_	Y is a consonant letter at the beginning of a word or syllable. Any other placement is a vowel.	yucca, lawyer	yes	yes	no	no	yes	yes
The sound /z/ is used, or approximated in some of these language but the spelling is not the same in the alphabetic languages.	/z/	z	subject to medial consonant doubling	zip, lazy (puzzle)	no	no	yes	no	yes	no
		ze	at the end of a word or syllable	ooze, haze		no		no		no
		_s	sm at the end of syllable or word, between 2 vowels, few HFWs (his, is, was, as, has). Suffix after vowel.	laser, prism, has, lens, bees, days		no		no		no
		_se	long vowel pattern with s (rise). Suffix after s, z, ch, sh	cheese, wise, passes, gazes, coaches, wishes		no		no		no
		s contractions		it's, she's he's		no		no		no
		x	at the beginning of a word	xylophone		no		no		no

Sound (phoneme)	Most Common Spelling Patterns (graphemes)	Tagalog Sound (phoneme) transfer?	Tagalog Spelling pattern (grapheme) transfer?	Korean Sound (phoneme) transfer?	Korean Spelling pattern (grapheme) transfer?	Cantonese Sound (phoneme) transfer?	Cantonese Spelling pattern (grapheme) transfer?	Mandarin Sound (phoneme) transfer?	Mandarin Spelling pattern (grapheme) transfer?	Farsi Sound (phoneme) transfer?	Farsi Spelling pattern (grapheme) transfer?	Arabic Sound (phoneme) transfer?	Arabic Spelling pattern (grapheme) transfer?
/s/	sc		no		no		no		no		no		no
	ss		no		no		no		no		no		no
/t/	t	yes	yes	yes	no	yes	no	yes	no	yes	no	yes	no
	tt		no		no		no		no		no		no
	_ed		no		no		no		no		no		no
	pt		no		no		no		no		no		no
	te, tte		no		no		no		no		no		
/v/	v	no	no	no	no	no	no	no	no	yes	no	no	no
	ve		no		no		no		no		no		no
/w/	w	yes	yes	yes	no	yes	no	no	no	no	no	yes	no
/hw/	wh	no	no	no	no	no	no	no	no	no	no	no	no
/ks/	_x	no	no	yes	no	no	no	no	no	no	no	no	no
	-cks		no		no		no		no		no		no
/y/	y_	yes	yes	yes	no	yes	no	no	no	yes	no	yes	no
/z/	z	no	no	no	no	no	no	no	no	yes	no	yes	no
	ze		no		no		no		no		no		no
	_s		no		no		no		no		no		no
	_se		no		no		no		no		no		no
	s contractions		no		no		no		no		no		no
	x		no		no		no		no		no		no

Sound-Spelling: Consonant Digraphs

English						Spanish		Vietnamese		Hmong	
Sound (phoneme)	Most Common Spelling Patterns (graphemes)	Notes	Word Examples			Sound (phoneme) transfer?	Spelling pattern (grapheme) transfer?	Sound (phoneme) transfer?	Spelling pattern (grapheme) transfer?	Sound (phoneme) transfer?	Spelling pattern (grapheme) transfer?
			initial	**medial**	**final**						
/ch/	ch		chile	satchel	inch	yes	yes	yes	no	no	no
	_tch	Used after short vowel in root.		hatchet	crutch		no		no		no
	tu	Latin origin. Unstressed long u impacts the /t/ sound.		culture, situate, fortunate, mutual			no		no		no
	ci, ce	Small number of foreign words commonly used in English	cello	concerto, ancient, financial			no		no		no
/sh/	sh		sheep	ashes	wish	no	no	yes	no	no	no
	ch	French words	chef, chic	machine	mustache		no		no		no
	ci	Latin (-cial, -scious, -cious)		social, efficient			no		no		no
	ti			nation, patience, initial			no		no		no
	ssi	Latin, unstressed i before a vowel. Adding /shun/ after ss.		passion, (express) expression			no		no		no
	-su-	Usually sh sound, sometimes /zh/	sure	insure, pressure			no		no		no
	si	Latin. Unstressed i before a vowel.		mansion, tension			no		no		no
/hw/	wh_		when	nowhere		no	no	no	no	no	
/th/ (voiced)	th	Native English words, most in beginning reader level words. Often "pointing" words (this, there, thy, thee, theirs)	these	feather	bathe, smooth	approx.	no	no	no	no	

Sound (phoneme)	Most Common Spelling Patterns (graphemes)	Tagalog		Korean		Cantonese		Mandarin		Farsi		Arabic	
		Sound (phoneme) transfer?	Spelling pattern (grapheme) transfer?	Sound (phoneme) transfer?	Spelling pattern (grapheme) transfer?	Sound (phoneme) transfer?	Spelling pattern (grapheme) transfer?	Sound (phoneme) transfer?	Spelling pattern (grapheme) transfer?	Sound (phoneme) transfer?	Spelling pattern (grapheme) transfer?	Sound (phoneme) transfer?	Spelling pattern (grapheme) transfer?
/ch/	ch	yes	no	no	no	no	no	approx.	no	yes	no	no	no
	_tch		no		no		no		no		no		no
	tu		no		no		no		no		no		no
	ci, ce		no		no		no		no		no		no
/sh/	sh	yes	yes	no	no	no	no	approx.	no	no	no	yes	no
	ch		no		no		no		no		no		no
	ci		no		no		no		no		no		no
	ti		no		no		no		no		no		no
	ssi		no		no		no		no		no		no
	-su-		no		no		no		no		no		no
	si		no		no		no		no		no		no
/hw/	wh_	no	no		no	no	no	no	no	no	no	no	no
/th/ (voiced)	th	no	no		no	no	no	no	no	no	no	yes	no

Sound-Spelling: Consonant Digraphs

Sound (phoneme)	English						Spanish		Vietnamese		Hmong	
	Most Common Spelling Patterns (graphemes)	Notes	Word Examples				Sound (phoneme) transfer?	Spelling pattern (grapheme) transfer?	Sound (phoneme) transfer?	Spelling pattern (grapheme) transfer?	Sound (phoneme) transfer?	Spelling pattern (grapheme) transfer?
/th/ (un-voiced)	th	At the beginning of nouns, verbs, adjectives. In Greek words between vowels. Beyond children's book words, most are unvoiced.	think	panther	math		approx.	no	no	no		no
/ng/	ng (a few exceptions such as tongue)			mango	hang		yes	yes	yes	yes		no
	n (followed by /k/)			uncle, conquer, sphinx	thank			no		no		no
/zh/	-si-	/s/ changed to /zh/ when followed by unstressed i before a vowel			vision, division, version		no	no	partial	no		no
	ge, gi	French "soft g" before e, I, y	gendarme	regime	garage			no		no		no
	-su-	Usually sh sound		usual, visual, closure				no		no		no
	z	Unstressed I or long u before vowel		azure, brazier				no		no		no
/gz/	ex	When syllable ending in x is unstressed and the next syllable begins with a vowel or silent h	exhaust, exact	unexampled			no	no	no	no		no

Sound (phoneme)	Most Common Spelling Patterns (graphemes)	Tagalog		Korean		Cantonese		Mandarin		Farsi		Arabic	
		Sound (phoneme) transfer?	Spelling pattern (grapheme) transfer?	Sound (phoneme) transfer?	Spelling pattern (grapheme) transfer?	Sound (phoneme) transfer?	Spelling pattern (grapheme) transfer?	Sound (phoneme) transfer?	Spelling pattern (grapheme) transfer?	Sound (phoneme) transfer?	Spelling pattern (grapheme) transfer?	Sound (phoneme) transfer?	Spelling pattern (grapheme) transfer?
/th/ (unvoiced)	th	no	no		no	no	no	no	no	no	no	yes	no
/ng/	ng (a few exceptions such as <u>tongue</u>)	yes	yes		no	yes	no	yes	no	no	no	no	no
	n (followed by /k/)		no		no		no		no		no		no
/zh/	-si-	no	no		no	no	no	no	no	no	no	no	no
	ge, gi		no		no		no		no		no		no
	-su-		no		no		no		no		no		no
	z		no		no		no		no		no		no
/gz/	ex	no	no		no	no	no	no	no		no		no

Sound-Spelling: Short and Long Vowels

Short Vowels

English						Spanish		Vietnamese		Hmong	
Sound (phoneme)	Most Common Spelling Patterns (graphemes)	Notes	Word Examples			Sound (phoneme) transfer?	Spelling pattern (grapheme) transfer?	Sound (phoneme) transfer?	Spelling pattern (grapheme) transfer?	Sound (phoneme) transfer?	Spelling pattern (grapheme) transfer?
			initial	medial	final						
//	a	closed syllables	apple	cab		no	no	approx.	yes	yes	yes
//	e	closed syllables	egg	pet		yes	yes	approx.	yes	no	no
//	i	closed syllables	igloo	bit		no	no	no	no	no	no
//	o	closed syllables	octopus	rock		no	no	approx.	yes	approx.	yes
//	ough		ought	bought					no		no
	augh		aught	daughter, caught					no		no
//	u	closed syllables	under	munch		no	no	yes	no	no	no

Long Vowels

English						Spanish		Vietnamese		Hmong	
			initial	medial	final						
//	a	open syllable	able	caper		yes	no	approx.	no	approx.	no
	ai_		aim	stair			no		no		no
	_ay				stay		no		no		no
	a_e		ale	baseball	paste		no		no		no
	eigh		eight	neighbor	weigh		no		no		no
//	e	open syllable	ether	defend	me	yes	no	yes	no	yes	no
	ee			seed	knee		no		no		no
	ea		east	wheat			no		no		no
	e_e		*eke		these		no		no		no
	_y				happy		no		no		no
	_ie_						no		no		no
	igh			light	sigh		no		no		no
//	i	open syllable	item	bicycle	*hi	yes	no	yes	no	yes	no
	i_e		ice	tired	bik1		no		no		no
	_y			myself	fly		no		no		no
	igh			bright	high		no		no		no
	_ie				tie		no		no		no
//	o	open syllable	open	motor		yes	yes	approx.	no	no	no
	oa		oath	boat			no		no		no
	_oe				toe		no		no		no
	ow				bow		no		no		no
	o_e		ode		globe		no		no		no
	ough	low frequency			though				no		no
//	u	open syllable	unicorn	cucumber		yes	no	no	no	no	no
	_ue				rescue		no		no		no
	u_e				cube		no		no		no
	_ew				few		no		no		no

Table 1

Sound (phoneme)	Most Common Spelling Patterns (graphemes)	Tagalog Sound (phoneme) transfer?	Tagalog Spelling pattern (grapheme) transfer?	Korean Sound (phoneme) transfer?	Korean Spelling pattern (grapheme) transfer?	Cantonese Sound (phoneme) transfer?	Cantonese Spelling pattern (grapheme) transfer?	Mandarin Sound (phoneme) transfer?	Mandarin Spelling pattern (grapheme) transfer?	Farsi Sound (phoneme) transfer?	Farsi Spelling pattern (grapheme) transfer?	Arabic Sound (phoneme) transfer?	Arabic Spelling pattern (grapheme) transfer?
//	a	no	no	yes	no	no	no	no	no	approx.	no	approx.	no
//	e	yes	no	yes	no	approx.	no	approx.	no	approx.	no	approx.	no
//	i	no	no	yes	no	approx.	no	approx.	no		no	approx.	no
//	o	no	no	approx.	no	approx.	no	approx.	no	approx.	no	approx.	no
	ough		no		no		no		no		no		no
	augh		no		no		no		no		no		no
//	u	yes	no	no	no	approx.	no	approx.	no	no	no	yes	no

Table 2

Sound (phoneme)	Grapheme	Tagalog Sound	Tagalog Spelling	Korean Sound	Korean Spelling	Cantonese Sound	Cantonese Spelling	Mandarin Sound	Mandarin Spelling	Farsi Sound	Farsi Spelling	Arabic Sound	Arabic Spelling
//	a	no	no	yes	no	approx.	no	approx.	no	yes	no	yes	no
	ai_		no		no		no		no		no		no
	_ay		no		no		no		no		no		no
	a_e		no		no		no		no		no		no
	eigh		no		no		no		no		no		no
//	e	yes	no	yes	no	approx.	yes	approx.	no	yes	no	yes	no
	ee		no		no		no		no		no		no
	ea		no		no		no		no		no		no
	e_e		no		no		no		no		no		no
	_y		no		no		no		no		no		no
	_ie_		no		no		no		no		no		no
	igh		no		no		no		no		no		no
//	i	no	no	yes	no	approx.	no	approx.	no	no	no	approx.	no
	i_e		no		no		no		no		no		no
	_y		no		no		no		no		no		no
	igh		no		no		no		no		no		no
	_ie		no		no		no		no		no		no
//	o	yes	no	yes	no	approx.	no	approx.	no	approx.	no	no	no
	oa		no		no		no		no		no		no
	_oe		no		no		no		no		no		no
	ow		no		no		no		no		no		no
	o_e		no		no		no		no		no		no
	ough		no		no		no		no		no		no
//	u	no	no	yes	no	approx.	no	approx.	no	no	no	no	no
	_ue		no		no		no		no		no		no
	u_e		no		no		no		no		no		no
	_ew		no		no		no		no		no		no

Sound-Spelling: R-Controlled Vowels, Other Vowel Patterns

		English			Spanish		Vietnamese		Hmong	
		initial	medial	final						
R-Controlled Vowels	/är/ ar	arm	barn	far	approx.**	yes	no	no	no	no
	/ûr/ er	ernest	fern	teacher	no	no	no	no	no	no
	ir	irk	girl	fir		no		no		no
	ur	urn	curl	fur		no		no		no
	ear	early,	pearl			no		no		no
		initial	medial	final						
Other Vowel Patterns	/oi/ oi	oil	broil		yes	yes	approx.	yes	no	no
	_oy	*oyster		boy		yes		no		no
	/ou/ ow	owl	brown	how	yes	no	yes	no	approx.	no
	ou_	out	cloud			no		no		no
	/ô/ aw	awful	crawl	draw	approx.	no	yes	no	approx.	no
	au_	augment				no		no		no
	/ôl/ al	also			approx.	yes	yes	no	no	no
	all	all		hall		no		no		no
	ol		follow			no		no		no
	awl	crawl				no		no		no
	/ōō/ oo	ooze	moon	boo	yes	no	yes	no	yes	no
	u_e	ruler				no		yes		yes
	_ew	flew				no		no		no
	_ue	blue				no		no		yes
	ui	suit				no		no		yes
	ough			through		no		no		no
	/oo/ oo		book		no	no	approx.	no	no	no

		Tagalog		Korean		Cantonese		Mandarin		Farsi		Arabic	
R-Controlled Vowels	/är/	no	no	no	no	no	no	no	no	no	no	no	no
	/ûr/	no		no	no	approx.		approx.	no	no	no	no	no
					no				no		no		no
			no		no				no		no		no
					no				*no*		*no*		*no*
Other Vowel Patterns	/oi/	yes	no	yes	no	approx.	no	no	no	no	no	no	no
			no		no		no		no		no		no
	/ou/	no		yes	no	approx.	no	approx.	no	yes	no	no	no
			no		no		no		no		no		no
	/ô/	yes	no	approx.	no	yes	no	no	no	no	no	no	no
					no		no		no		no		no
	/ôl/	yes	no	approx.	no	approx.	no	no	no	no	no	no	no
			no		no		no		no		no		no
			no		no		no		no		no		no
			no		no		no		no		no		no
	/ōō/	yes	no	yes	no	approx.	no	yes	no	yes	no	yes	no
			no		no		no		no		no		no
			no		no		no		no		no		no
			no		no		no		no		no		no
			no		no		no		no		no		*no*
			no		no		no		no		no		*no*
	/oo/	no	no	approx.	no	approx.	no	approx.	no	no	no	no	no

Syntax and Grammar: Verbs
Differences and Potential Errors for English Learners

English Grammar	Spanish	Vietnamese	Hmong	Tagalog
VERBS				
Use of **infinitives*** (He wants them *to learn* quickly.)	Clause "that" is used rather than an infinitive (He wants *that they learn* quickly.)		Clause "that" is used rather than an infinitive (He wants *that they learn* quickly.)	
Use of **infinitives to express** purpose (We go out *to have* dinner.)				
Verbs are separated with punctuation or other words (I throw, catch, and kick the ball).		Verbs can be used together without punctuation or other words (I *throw catch kick* the ball.)	Verbs can be used together without punctuation or other words (I throw catch kick the ball.)	
Use of **gerund*** (-ing) /infinitive distinction). (She enjoys cook*ing*.)	No use of gerund (-ing)/ infinitive distinction. (She enjoys to cook.)	No use of gerund (-ing)/ infinitive distinction. *(She enjoys to cook.)*	No use of gerund (-ing)/ infinitive distinction. (She enjoys to cook.)	
Use of the **verb "to be"** (He is walking. They are coming to school.).		Be can be omitted. *(He walking. They coming to school.)*	Be can be omitted. *(He walking. They coming to school.)*	Be can be omitted. *(He walking. They coming to school.)*
Use of the verb "to be" for adjectives or places (The lock is strong. The book is on the desk.)		The verb "to be" is not used for adjectives or places *(The lock strong. The book on the desk.)*	The verb "to be" is not used for adjectives or places *(The lock strong. The book on the desk.)*	The verb "to be" is not used for adjectives or places *(The lock strong. The book on the desk.)*
Use of the **verb "to be" to express states of being** such as hunger or age).	The verb "to have" can be used to express states of being (age, hunger, etc.). She *has* ten years. They *have* hunger.			
Use of **"there is/are,was/were"** (In school, *there are* many students.")	Can use "have" (In school they have many students.) or "there are" (In school, *there are* many students.)	Use of "have" instead of "there is/are,was/were" (In school, *have many* students.")	Use of "have" instead of "there is/are,was/were" (In school, *have* many students.")	
Change in verb "to be" in past perfect form. (They are climbing --> They climbed).				
Use of **verb "to have"** (*I have* one book.)				
Verb inflection for person and number. (*Everyone cooks* food. *She has* a large cat.)		Verbs are not inflected for person and number. (Everyone *cook* food. She *have* a large cat.)	Verbs are not inflected for person and number. (Everyone *cook* food. She *have* a large cat.)	
Verb tenses change within the same sentence. (When we eat, we *will be* full.)			Verb tenses do not change within the same sentence. *(When we eat, we full.)*	
Use of **tense boundaries** (*I will study* here for a year. When she *was* young, *she played* with dolls.)		Tense can be indicated by context or an expression of time rather than through the verb tense. (I study here *for a year. When she* is *young,* she play with dolls.)	Tense indicated by use of infinitive of verb with an expression of time rather than through the verb tense.	
Use of **future tense** (I will go tomorrow) and **present perfect** tense (I have been there many times).	Present tense can replace future tense (*I go* there tomorrow) and can replace present perfect (*I go* there many times).		Present tense can replace future tense (*I go* there tomorrow) and can replace present perfect (*I go* there many times).	
Use of **passive tense** (Their window *was broken.*)		Different limits for use of passive tense (*They were broken* their window.)		

*An infinitive can be considered the "base verb" that can be conjugated into different forms to represent past, present, future (e.g., to run, to sing, to eat, to be).

**A gerund is a verb that functions as a noun in a sentence. Gerunds end in -ing (e.g., Running is great exercise. In this sentence, the verb (in infinitive form) to run is functioning as a noun and the verb is (conjugated from the infinitive to be) functions as the verb.

English Grammar	Korean	Cantonese	Mandarin	Farsi	Arabic
VERBS					
Use of **infinitives*** *(He wants them to learn quickly.)*					
Use of **infinitives to express** purpose *(We go out to have dinner.)*	Infinitives not used to express purpose *(We go out for having dinner.)*				
Verbs are separated with punctuation or other words *(I throw, catch, and kick the ball).*					
Use of **gerund**** (-ing) /infinitive distinction). *(She enjoys cooking.)*	No use of gerund (-ing)/ infinitive distinction. *(She enjoys to cook.)*	No use of gerund (-ing)/ infinitive distinction. *(She enjoys to cook.)*	No use of gerund (-ing)/ infinitive distinction. *(She enjoys to cook.)* Tense is expressed by adding adverbs of time instead of changing the verb form.	No use of gerund (-ing)/ infinitive distinction. *(She enjoys to cook.)*	No use of gerund (-ing)/ infinitive distinction. *(She enjoys to cook.)*
Use of the **verb "to be"** *(He is walking. They are coming to school.)*	Be can be omitted. *(He walking. They coming to school.)*	Be can be omitted. *(He walking. They coming to school.)* Tense is expressed by adding adverbs of time instead of changing the verb form.	Be can be omitted. *(He walking. They coming to school.)* Adjectives an be directly used as verbs.		Be can be omitted. *(He walking. They coming to school.)*
Use of the verb "to be" for adjectives or places *(The lock is strong. The book is on the desk.)*					
Use of the **verb "to be"** to **express states of being** such as hunger or age).				The verb "to have" can be used to express states of being (age, hunger, etc.). She *has* ten years. They *have* hunger.	
Use of **"there is/are, was/ were"** *(In school, there are many students.")*					
Change in verb "to be" in past perfect form. *(They are climbing --> They climbed).*				Past perfect form for "to be" changes differently. *(They are climbing --> They were climbed.)*	Past perfect form for "to be" changes differently. *(They are climbing --> They were climbed.)*
Use of **verb "to have"** *(I have one book.)*	The verb "to have" can be substituted with "to be" *(I am book.)*				
Verb inflection for person and number. *(Everyone cooks food. She has a large cat.)*	Verbs are not inflected for person and number. *(Everyone cook food. She have a large cat.)* In Korean verbs are inflected for age or status.	Verbs are not inflected for person and number. *(Everyone cook food. She have a large cat.)*	Verbs are not inflected for person and number. *(Everyone cook food. She have a large cat.)*		
Verb tenses change within the same sentence. *(When we eat, we will be full.)*					
Use of **tense boundaries** *(I will study here for a year. When she was young, she played with dolls.)*		Tense can be indicated by context or an expression of time rather than through the verb tense. *(I study here for a year. When she is young, she play with dolls.)*	Tense can be indicated by context or an expression of time rather than through the verb tense. *(I study here for a year. When she is young, she play with dolls.)*		Tense can be indicated by context or an expression of time rather than through the verb tense. *(I study here for a year. When she is young, she play with dolls.)*
Use of **future tense** *(I will go tomorrow)* and **present perfect** tense *(I have been there many times).*				Present tense can replace future tense *(I go there tomorrow)* and can replace present perfect *(I go there many times).*	
Use of **passive tense** *(Their window was broken.)*	Different limits for use of passive tense *(They were broken their window.)*				Different limits for use of passive tense (They were broken their window.)

Syntax and Grammar: Nouns
Differences and Potential Errors for English Learners

English Grammar	Spanish	Vietnamese	Hmong	Tagalog
NOUNS				
Nouns and adjectives use different forms (*They felt safe in their home.*)	Suffixes can be added to nouns (e.g. -ito, -oso) to combine description with a noun.		Nouns and adjectives can use the same form (*They felt safety in their home.*)	
Nouns and verbs are distinct.			Nouns and verbs may not be distinct.	Nouns and verbs may not be distinct.
Use of **proper names** in first, middle, last order (*George Lucas Smith*).		Proper names can be ordered in last, first, middle order or last, middle, first. First and last names can be confusing to teachers and students.	Proper names can be ordered in last, first, middle order, or last, middle, first. First and last names can be confusing to teachers and students.	Depends on familiarity.
Use of 's for **possessive nouns** (*This is Holly's box.*)	Possessive nouns are formed with an "of phase" (This is the box of Holly.)	Possessive nouns are formed with an "of phase" (This is the box of Holly.)	Possessive nouns are formed with an "of phase" (This is the box of Holly.)	Possessive nouns are formed with an "of phase" (This is the box of Holly.)
Use of **plural nouns** (*She makes many friends. He has few questions.*)		No use of plural nouns (*She make many friend. He has few question.*) *Plurals can be expressed through an adjective quantifier.*	No use of plural nouns (*He has few question.*) Plurals are used for nouns related to people such as "friends." Plurals can be expressed through an adjective quantifier.	No use of plural nouns (*She make many friend. He has few question.*) Plurals can be expressed through an adjective quantifier.
Use of **plural forms** after a number (We go home in two weeks. They are bringing five shirts.)		Use of plural forms after a number (*We go home in two week. They are bringing five shirt.*)	Use of plural forms after a number (*We go home in two week. They are bringing five shirt.*)	Use of plural forms after a number (*We go home in two week. They are bringing five shirt.*)
Use of -es to make **plural nouns** only used after nouns ending in consonants s, x, ch, sh, and z. (*passes, foxes, catches, wishes, buzzes*) Nouns ending in y change the y to i before adding -es. (*candies*)	Use of -es to make plural nouns for all nouns that end in consonants or y (walls --> walles, pay --> payes)			
Use of **noncount nouns** that do not have plurals such as *weather, homework, money, rain*, etc. (*We have different types of weather. We have a lot of homework.*)		Confusion with noncount nouns that do not have plurals (*We have different types of weathers. We have a lot of homeworks.*)	Confusion with noncount nouns that do not have plurals (*We have different types of weathers. We have a lot of homeworks.*)	Confusion with noncount nouns that do not have plurals (*We have different types of weathers. We have a lot of homeworks.*)

English Grammar	Korean	Cantonese	Mandarin	Farsi	Arabic
NOUNS					
Nouns and adjectives use different forms *(They felt <u>safe</u> in their home.)*		Nouns and adjectives can use the same form *(They felt <u>safety</u> in their home.)*	Nouns and adjectives can use the same form *(They felt <u>safety</u> in their home.)*		
Nouns and verbs are distinct.		Nouns and verbs overlap, may not be distinct.	Nouns and verbs overlap, may not be distinct.	Nouns and verbs may not be distinct.	
Use of **proper names** in first, middle, last order *(George Lucas Smith).*	Proper names can be ordered in last, first, middle order, or last, middle, first. First and last names can be confusing to teachers and students.	Proper names can be ordered in last, first, middle order, or last, middle, first. First and last names can be confusing to teachers and students. (Chinese: Always last name first)	Proper names can be ordered in last, first, middle order, or last, middle, first. First and last names can be confusing to teachers and students. (Chinese: Always last name first)		
Use of 's for **possessive nouns** *(This is <u>Holly's</u> box.)*		Possessive nouns are consistently formed (<u>Holly's</u> box.)			
Use of **plural nouns** *(She makes <u>many friends</u>. He has <u>few</u> <u>questions</u>.)*	No use of plural nouns *(She make <u>many friend</u>. He <u>has</u> few question.)* Plurals can be expressed through an adjective quantifier. In Korean, nouns related to people (e.g., *children*) have plural forms, but not other nouns.	No use of plural nouns *(She make <u>many friend</u>. He has <u>few question.</u>)* Plurals can be expressed through an adjective quantifier.	No use of plural nouns *(She make <u>many friend</u>. He has <u>few question</u>.)* Plurals can be expressed through an adjective quantifier or number word.		
Use of **plural forms** after a number *(We go home in <u>two</u> <u>weeks</u>. They are bringing <u>five</u> <u>shirts</u>.)*	Use of plural forms after a number *(We go home in <u>two</u> <u>week</u>. They are bringing <u>five</u> <u>shirt</u>.)* Students may add a word rather than adding -s to a noun.	Use of plural forms after a number *(We go home in <u>two</u> <u>week</u>. They are bringing <u>five</u> <u>shirt</u>.)*	Use of plural forms after a number *(We go home in <u>two</u> <u>week</u>. They are bringing <u>five</u> <u>shirt</u>.)*	Use of plural forms after a number *(We go home in <u>two</u> <u>week</u>. They are bringing <u>five</u> <u>shirt</u>.)*	
Use of -es to make **plural nouns** only used after nouns ending in consonants s, x, ch, sh, and z. *(pass<u>es</u>, fox<u>es</u>, catch<u>es</u>,wish<u>es</u>, buzz<u>es</u>)* Nouns ending in y change the y to i before adding -es. *(candi<u>es</u>)*					
Use of **noncount nouns** that do not have plurals such as *weather, homework, money, rain,* etc. *(We have different <u>types</u> <u>of weather</u>. We have a lot <u>of homework</u>.)*	Confusion with noncount nouns that do not have plurals *(We have different types of <u>weathers.</u> We have a lot of <u>homeworks</u>.)*	Confusion with noncount nouns that do not have plurals *(We have different types of <u>weathers.</u> We have a lot of <u>homeworks</u>.)*	Confusion with noncount nouns that do not have plurals (We have different types of weathers. We have a lot of homeworks.)	Confusion with noncount nouns that do not have plurals *(We have different types of <u>weathers.</u> We have a lot of <u>homeworks</u>.)*	

Syntax and Grammar: Word Order and Sentence Structure
Differences and Potential Errors for English Learners

English Grammar	Spanish	Vietnamese	Hmong	Tagalog
WORD ORDER				
Subject-Verb-Object and, Object-Verb-Subject order can be used. (*Every student in the class received good grades. Good grades were received by every student in the class.*)	Word order can change and can change the emphasis.	The usual word order is subject-verb-object.	The usual word order is subject-verb-object.	The word order is subject-verb-object, or object-verb-subject.
Use of subject pronouns (*They are coming. He is running.*)	Optional use of subject pronouns when the subject is understood (*They coming. He running*).	Optional use of subject pronouns when the subject is understood (*They coming. He running*).	Optional use of subject pronouns when the subject is understood (*They coming. He running*).	Optional use of subject pronouns when the subject is understood (*They coming. He running*).
Pronouns used as Indirect objects precede the direct object (*He gave her an umbrella.*)			Direct objects precede pronouns used as Indirect objects (*He gave an umbrella her*).	
Verbs precede adverbs and adverbial phrases (*She runs quickly. They travel to work by train.*)				Adverbs and adverbial phrases precede verbs (She quickly runs. They by train travel to work).
Sentences always include a subject. (*Is this your chair? Yes, it is. Is it raining?*)	Sentences do not always include a subject (*Is this your chair? Yes, is. Is raining?*)			
Subjects and verbs can be inverted (*He is cooking and so am I.*)	Verbs can precede subject (Good grades were received by every student in the class).		Subjects and verbs are rarely inverted, so one might be deleted or flipped in English (*He is cooking and so am. He is cooking and so I am*).	
Relative clause or restrictive phrase follows a noun it modifies (*The student enrolled in community college.*)				

English Grammar	Korean	Cantonese	Mandarin	Farsi	Arabic
WORD ORDER					
Subject-Verb-Object and, Object-Verb-Subject order can be used. *(Every student in the class received good grades. Good grades were received by every student in the class.)*	Verbs are placed last in a sentence. The usual word order is subject-object-verb *(Every student in the class good grades received).*	The most common word order is subject-verb-object but object-subject-verb is used to emphasize the object.	The most common word order is subject-verb-object but object-subject-verb is used to emphasize the object.	Verbs are placed last in a sentence. The usual word order is subject-object-verb *(Every student in the class good grades received.)*	Verbs can precede subject and subject can precede verbs in Arabic. When the subject precedes verb, the sentence is nominative. When the verb precedes subject, the sentence is verbal. *(Good grades received every student in the class.)*
Use of subject pronouns *(They are coming. He is running.)*	Optional use of subject pronouns when the subject is understood *(They coming. He running).* Korean: Can omit the subject pronoun "you."	Optional use of subject pronouns when the subject is understood *(They coming. He running).*	Optional use of subject pronouns when the subject is understood *(They coming. He running.)*	Optional use of subject pronouns when the subject is understood *(They coming. He running.)*	
Pronouns used as Indirect objects precede the direct object *(He gave her an umbrella.)*		Direct objects precede pronouns used as Indirect objects *(He gave an umbrella her).*	Direct objects precede pronouns used as Indirect objects *(He gave an umbrella her).*	Direct objects precede pronouns used as Indirect objects *(He gave an umbrella her.)*	
Verbs precede adverbs and adverbial phrases *(She runs quickly. They travel to work by train.)*	Adverbs and adverbial phrases precede verbs *(She quickly runs. They by train travel to work).*	Adverbs and adverbial phrases precede verbs *(She quickly runs. They by train travel to work).*	Adverbs and adverbial phrases precede verbs *(She quickly runs. They by train travel to work).*	Adverbs and adverbial phrases precede verbs *(She quickly runs. They by train travel to work.)*	Some adverbs can precede or follow verbs. *(Sometimes he studies. He studies sometimes. They travel by train. By train they travel.)*
Sentences always include a subject. *(Is this your chair? Yes, it is. Is it raining?)*					*Sentences do not always include a subject (Is this your chair? Yes, is. Is raining?)*
Subjects and verbs can be inverted *(He is cooking and so am I.)*	Subjects and verbs are rarely inverted, so one might be deleted or flipped in English *(He is cooking and so am. He is cooking and so I am).*	Subjects and verbs are rarely inverted, so one might be deleted or flipped in English *(He is cooking and so am. He is cooking and so I am).*	Subjects and verbs are rarely inverted, so one might be deleted or flipped in English *(He is cooking and so am. He is cooking and so I am).*	Subjects and verbs are rarely inverted, so one might be deleted or flipped in English *(He is cooking and so am. He is cooking and so I am).*	
Relative clause or restrictive phrase follows a noun it modifies *(The student enrolled in community college.)*	Relative clause or restrictive phrase precedes a noun it modifies *(The enrolled in community college student).*	Relative clause or restrictive phrase precedes a noun it modifies *(The enrolled in community college student.)*	Relative clause or restrictive phrase precedes a noun it modifies *(The enrolled in community college student.)*		

Syntax and Grammar: Word Order and Sentence Structure
Differences and Potential Errors for English Learners

English Grammar	Spanish	Vietnamese	Hmong	Tagalog
QUESTIONS				
Yes/No questions usually begin with a question word. *(Do you eat broccoli? Is this your sweater?)*	Yes/No questions can be formed by adding an element to the end of a declarative statement. *(You eat broccoli, yes? This is your sweater, no?)*	Yes/No questions can be formed by adding an element to the end of a declarative statement. *(You eat broccoli, yes? This is your sweater, no?)* Vietnamese can also use a statement followed by the phrase: "or not."	Yes/No questions can be formed by adding an element to the end of a declarative statement *(You eat broccoli, yes? This is your sweater, no?)* Yes/No questions can be formed by adding the question word between the pronoun and the verb. (You [question word] take the bus?)	Yes/No questions can be formed by adding an element to the end of a declarative statement *(You eat broccoli, yes? This is your sweater, no?)*
Yes/No questions can be formed by adding a verb followed by its negative at the end of a statement. *(Do you like to go to the beach or not?)*		Yes/No questions can be formed by adding a verb followed by its negative within a statement. *(Do you not like to go to the beach?)*	Yes/No questions can be formed by adding a verb followed by its negative within a statement. *(Do you not like to go to the beach?)*	
Questions words are usually placed at the beginning of the sentence. *(Where is the book? What did my sister tell you?)*		Question words are placed according to the position of the answer. For example, if the answer functions as an object, the question words are placed in the regular object position *(The book is where? My sister told you what?)*	Question words are placed according to the position of the answer. For example, if the answer functions as an object, the question words are placed in the regular object position. *(The book is where? My sister told you what?)*	
Yes and no answers are used in a consistent manner. *(Do you play soccer? Yes. Do you play hockey? No.)*			The answers yes and no vary depending upon the verb used in the question. Students may substitute a verb for a yes-no answer *(Do you play soccer? Soccer. Do you play hockey? No hockey.)*	The answers yes and no vary depending upon the verb used in the question. Students may substitute a verb for a yes-no answer *(Do you play soccer? Soccer. Do you play hockey? No hockey.)*
COMMANDS				
Commands are formed consistently. *(Stop it now!)*		Commands can be formed by adding an adverb after the verbs to be emphasized. *(Stop right now!)* Commands can be formed by adding the verb "go" for emphasis at the end of the sentence. (Get my slippers, go!)	Commands can be formed by adding an adverb after the verbs to be emphasized. *(Stop now!)*	
Commands do not require a time indicator after the verbs to be emphasized *(Take out the trash).*			Commands can be formed by adding a time indicator after the verbs to be emphasized. *(Take out the trash at 9:00.)*	
Commands use consistent verb form (Show it to me).				Commands can be formed by changing the verb ending *(Show[ing] it to me).*
NEGATIVES AND NEGATIVE SENTENCES				
Double negatives are not used (She doesn't eat anything).	Double negatives are routinely used to reinforce the thought *(She doesn't eat nothing).*			
The negative marker goes after the verb phrase *(They have not been there before).*	The negative marker goes before the verb phrase *(They not have been there before.).*		The negative marker goes before the verb phrase *(They not have been there before.)*	The negative marker goes before the verb phrase *(They not have been there before).*

English Grammar	Korean	Cantonese	Mandarin	Farsi	Arabic
QUESTIONS					
Yes/No questions usually begin with a question word. *(Do you eat broccoli? Is this your sweater?)*	Yes/No questions can be formed by adding an element to the end of a declarative statement *(You eat broccoli, yes? This is your sweater, no?)*	Yes/No questions can be formed by adding an element to the end of a declarative statement. *(You eat broccoli, yes? This is your sweater, no?)*	Yes/No questions can be formed by adding an element to the end of a declarative statement. *(You eat broccoli, yes? This is your sweater, no?)*	Yes/No questions can be formed by adding an element to the end of a declarative statement. *(You eat broccoli, yes? This is your sweater, no?)*	Yes/No questions can be formed by adding "or not" to the end of a declarative statement. *(You eat broccoli, or not? This is your sweater, or not?)*
Yes/No questions can be formed by adding a verb followed by its negative at the end of a statement. *(Do you like to go to the beach or not?)*		Yes/No questions can be formed by adding a verb followed by its negative within a statement. *(Do you not like to go to the beach?)*	Yes/No questions can be formed by adding a verb followed by its negative within a statement. *(Do you not like to go to the beach?)*		
Questions words are usually placed at the beginning of the sentence. *(Where is the book? What did my sister tell you?)*	Question words are placed according to the position of the answer. For example, if the answer functions as an object, the question words are placed in the regular object position *(The book is where? My sister told you what?)*	Question words are placed according to the position of the answer. For example, if the answer functions as an object, the question words are placed in the regular object position. *(The book is where? My sister told you what?)*	Question words are placed according to the position of the answer. For example, if the answer functions as an object, the question words are placed in the regular object position. *(The book is where? My sister told you what?)*	Question words are placed according to the position of the answer. For example, if the answer functions as an object, the question words are placed in the regular object position. *(The book is where? My sister told you what?)*	
Yes and no answers are used in a consistent manner. *(Do you play soccer? Yes. Do you play hockey? No.)*				The answers yes and no vary depending upon the verb used in the question. Students may substitute a verb for a yes-no answer *(Do you play soccer? Soccer. Do you play hockey? No hockey.)*	
COMMANDS					
Commands are formed consistently. *(Stop it now!)*			Commands can be formed by adding an adverb after the verbs to be emphasized. *(Stop now!)*		
Commands do not require a time indicator after the verbs to be emphasized *(Take out the trash).*			Commands can be formed by adding a time indicator after the verbs to be emphasized *(Take out the trash at 9:00).*	Commands can be formed by adding a time indicator after the verbs to be emphasized *(Take out the trash at 9:00).*	
Commands use consistent verb form *(Show it to me).*			Commands can be formed by changing the verb ending *(Show[ing] it to me).*	Commands can be formed by changing the verb ending *(Show[ing] it to me).*	
NEGATIVES AND NEGATIVE SENTENCES					
Double negatives are not used *(She doesn't eat anything).*		Double negation is usually used in reverted sentence order with "nothing" and a word of emphasis before the verb *(They nothing have not been there before).*	Double negation is usually used in reverted sentence order with "nothing" and a word of emphasis before the verb *(They nothing have not been there before).*	Double negatives are routinely used *(She doesn't eat nothing).*	Double negatives are sometimes used. *(He doesn't drink coffee never).*
The negative marker goes after the verb phrase *(They have not been there before).*	The negative marker goes before the verb phrase *(They not have been there before)* Korean: used regularly in informal situations.			The negative marker goes before the verb phrase *(They not have been there before).*	

Syntax and Grammar: Adverbs and Adjectives
Differences and Potential Errors for English Learners

English Grammar	Spanish	Vietnamese	Hmong	Tagalog
ADVERBS				
Use of adverbs to describe an adjective or a verb (*I ate _really_ fast. I ran _quickly_ to the store*).			Adverbs are not used. Two adjectives or two verbs can be used to describe an adjective or verb (*I ate _fast fast_. I ran _ran_ to the store*).	
ADJECTIVES				
Adjectives precede nouns they modify (*We live in a _coastal_ city. She has a _yellow_ shirt.*)	Adjectives follow nouns they modify (*We live in a city _coastal_. She has a shirt _yellow_*). The adjective position can also reflect meaning.	Adjectives follow nouns they modify (*We live in a city _coastal_. She has a shirt _yellow_*).	Adjectives follow nouns they modify (*We live in a city coastal. She has a shirt _yellow_*).	
Use of **possessive adjectives** used to indicate ownership (*This is _her_ sweater. She wears _her_ sweater*).		Omission of possessive adjectives when ownership is clear (*She wears sweater*).	Use of another word, article or character used to indicate ownership (*This is _she_ sweater*).	
Comparative adjectives change form (*He is _taller than_ me. They are _slower than_ him*).	Comparative adjectives change form (*He is _more tall_ than me. They are _more slow_ than him*).		Comparative adjectives change form (*He is _more tall_ than me. They are _more slow_ than him*).	Comparative adjectives change form (*He is _more tall_ than me. They are _more slow_ than him*).
Nouns and adjectives have different forms (*They want to be _independent_*).				
Adjectives do not reflect gender or number of nouns they modify (*They have _sharp_ teeth*).	Adjectives reflect gender and number of nouns they modify (*They have _sharps_ teeth*).			Adjectives reflect gender and number of nouns they modify (*They have _sharps_ teeth*).
Use of **possessive adjectives** used for parts of the body (*The boy skinned _his_ knee*).	Use of definite article instead of possessive adjectives used for parts of the body (*The boy skinned _the_ knee*).			
Distinction between personal pronouns and possessive adjectives (*This is _my_ friend*).		Distinction between personal pronouns and possessive adjectives (*This is friend _I_*).		

English Grammar	Korean	Cantonese	Mandarin	Farsi	Arabic
ADVERBS					
Use of adverbs to describe an adjective or a verb *(I ate really fast. I ran quickly to the store).*					
ADJECTIVES					
Adjectives precede nouns they modify *(We live in a coastal city. She has a yellow shirt).*				Adjectives follow nouns they modify *(We live in a city coastal. She has a shirt yellow).* The adjective position can also reflect meaning.	Adjectives follow the nouns they modify.
Use of **possessive adjectives** used to indicate ownership *(This is her sweater. She wears her sweater).*	Omission of possessive adjectives when ownership is clear *(She wears sweater).*	Use of another word, article or character used to indicate ownership *(This is she sweater).*	Use of another word, article or character used to indicate ownership *(This is she sweater).*		
Comparative adjectives change form *(He is taller than me. They are slower than him).*	Comparative adjectives change form *(He is more tall than me. They are more slow than him).*				
Nouns and adjectives have different forms *(They want to be independent).*		Some nouns and adjectives use the same forms *(They want to be independence).*	Some nouns and adjectives use the same forms *(They want to be independence.)*		
Adjectives do not reflect gender or number of nouns they modify *(They have sharp teeth).*					Adjectives agree with the gender and number of nouns they modify.
Use of **possessive adjectives** used for parts of the body *(The boy skinned his knee).*					
Distinction between personal pronouns and possessive adjectives *(This is my friend).*					

Syntax and Grammar: Pronouns
Differences and Potential Errors for English Learners

English Grammar	Spanish	Vietnamese	Hmong	Tagalog
PRONOUNS				
Distinction between **subject and object pronouns** (*He gave it to me. We spent the time with her*).	No distinction between subject and object pronouns (*He gave it to I. We spent the time with she.*)	No distinction between subject and object pronouns (*He gave it to I. We spent the time with she.*)	No distinction between subject and object pronouns (*He gave it to I. We spent the time with she*).	
Distinction between **subject and object** forms of pronouns (*I gave the book to him*).	No distinction between subject and object forms of pronouns (*I gave the book to he*).		No distinction between subject and object forms of pronouns (*I gave the book to he.*)	
Use of **pronoun "it" as a subject** (*It is four o'clock now. What time is it?*)		Optional use of pronoun "it" as a subject (*Four o'clock now. What time?*)	Optional use of pronoun "it" as a subject. (*Four o'clock now. What time?*)	Optional use of pronoun "it" as a subject. (*Four o'clock now. What time?*)
Distinction between **object, subject, simple, compound, and reflexive pronouns** (*He is my cousin. The pencil is mine. I can do it by myself*).		Reflexive pronoun is formed by adding "oneself" to the verb phrase.	No distinction between object, subject, simple, compound, and reflexive pronouns (*He is I cousin. The pencil is I. I can do it I.*)	
Use of **gender specific third person singular pronouns** (*Go talk to the man and ask him for directions*).	No use of gender specific third person singular pronouns (*Go talk to the man and ask it for directions*).	No use of gender specific third person singular pronouns (*Go talk to the man and ask it for directions*). Vietnamese uses familiar form of third person singular.	No use of gender specific third person singular pronouns (*Go talk to the man and ask it for directions*).	No use of gender specific third person singular pronouns (*Go talk to the man and ask it for directions*).
Use of **relative pronouns** (*Go get the book that is on the desk. If you want to drive, there are three ways to get there*).		No use of relative pronouns (*Go get the book is on the desk*).		
Use of **human/nonhuman distinction for relative pronouns** (who/which) (*She is the one who wants to go. The neighbors who just moved in are at the door*).	*Quien* is a relative pronoun used specifically for humans.		No human/nonhuman distinction for relative pronouns (who/which) (*She is the one which wants to go. The neighbors which just moved in are at the door*).	
Use of **possessive pronouns** to indicate ownership (*The shorts are his. These snacks are theirs*).		A separate word or character is used before a pronoun to indicate ownership (*The shorts are (of) him. These snacks are [of] them*). Omission of possessive pronoun when association is clear (He raised his hand).	Use of a possessive character between pronoun and noun to indicate ownership (He [*possessive character*] shorts. Snacks [*possessive character*] them). Possessive pronoun can come after the noun. Omission of possessive pronoun when association is clear (He raised his hand).	
Personal pronouns are not restated (*Your sister wants to go too*).				
No use of **pronoun object at the end of a relative clause** (*The mouse that ran by was small*).				

English Grammar	Korean	Cantonese	Mandarin	Farsi	Arabic
PRONOUNS					
Distinction between **subject and object pronouns** (*He gave it to me. We spent the time with her*).		No distinction between subject and object pronouns (*He gave it to I. We spent the time with she*).	No distinction between subject and object pronouns (*He gave it to I. We spent the time with she*).	No distinction between subject and object pronouns (*He gave it to I. We spent the time with she*).	
Distinction between **subject and object** forms of pronouns (*I gave the book to him*).	No distinction between subject and object forms of pronouns (*I gave the book to he*).		No distinction between subject and object forms of pronouns (*I gave the book to he*).	No distinction between subject and object forms of pronouns (*I gave the book to he*).	
Use of **pronoun "it" as a subject** (*It is four o'clock now. What time is it?*)	Optional use of pronoun "it" as a subject. (Four o'clock now. What time?)	Optional use of pronoun "it" as a subject. (Four o'clock now. What time?)	Optional use of pronoun "it" as a subject. (Four o'clock now. What time?)		
Distinction between **object, subject, simple, compound, and reflexive pronouns** (*He is my cousin. The pencil is mine. I can do it by myself*).		Uses possession words to distinguish.	Uses possession words to distinguish.		
Use of **gender specific third person singular pronouns** (*Go talk to the man and ask him for directions*).		No use of gender specific third person singular pronouns (*Go talk to the man and ask it for directions*).	No use of gender specific third person singular pronouns (*Go talk to the man and ask it for directions*).	No use of gender specific third person singular pronouns (*Go talk to the man and ask it for directions*).	
Use of **relative pronouns** (*Go get the book that is on the desk. If you want to drive, there are three ways to get there*).	No use of relative pronouns (*Go get the book is on the desk. If you want to drive, three ways to get there*). In Korean, a modifying clause can function as a relative clause.				
Use of **human/nonhuman distinction for relative pronouns** (who/which) (*She is the one who wants to go. The neighbors who just moved in are at the door*).				No human/nonhuman distinction for relative pronouns (who/which) (*She is the one which wants to go. The neighbors which just moved in are at the door*).	No human/nonhuman distinction for relative pronouns (who/which) (*She is the one which wants to go. The neighbors which just moved in are at the door*).
Use of **possessive pronouns** to indicate ownership (*The shorts are his. These snacks are theirs*).	Omission of possessive pronoun when association is clear (*He raised his hand*).	Use of a possessive character between pronoun and noun to indicate ownership (*He (possessive character) shorts. Snacks (possessive character) them.*) Character sometimes omitted.	Use of a possessive character between pronoun and noun to indicate ownership (*He [possessive character] shorts. Snacks [possessive character] them*). Omission of possessive character when association is clear or to limit redundancy (*He raised [possessive character] hand*).	No distinction between personal and possessive pronouns (*The shorts are him. These snacks are they*).	
Personal pronouns are not restated (*Your sister wants to go too*).					Personal pronouns are restated (*Your sister she wants to go too*).
No use of **pronoun object at the end of a relative clause** (*The mouse that ran by was small*).					Pronoun object added at the end of a relative clause (*The mouse that ran by it was small*).

Syntax and Grammar: Prepositions, Conjunctions, Articles
Differences and Potential Errors for English Learners

English Grammar	Spanish	Vietnamese	Hmong	Tagalog
PREPOSITIONS				
Use of prepositions (*The movie is on the DVD*).	Use of prepositions may be different than in English (*The movie is in the DVD*).			
CONJUNCTIONS				
Only one conjunction is needed (*Although, I know her, I don't know what she likes. OR I know her but I don't know what she likes*).				
ARTICLES				
Use of articles.			Classifiers take the place of articles in Hmong.	
Use of **indefinite articles** (*I bought an orange. Do they go to a market for groceries?*)		No use of indefinite articles (*I bought one orange. Do they go to market for groceries?*)	Plural form of classifiers take the place of articles. (*I bought one orange. Do they go to market for groceries?*)	
Use of **indefinite articles** before a profession (*She is a brilliant scientist. He is an electrician*).	Use of indefinite articles before a profession is optional (*She is brilliant scientist. He is electrician*).	No use of indefinite articles before a profession (*She is brilliant scientist. He is electrician*).	In Hmong, professions have unique classifiers, although some are shared. (*She is brilliant scientist. He is electrician.*)	
Consistent use of **definite articles** (*I have the piece of paper. She has a pencil*).	Definite articles can be omitted or used (*I have [a] piece of paper. She has [a] pencil*).		Definite articles can be omitted. (*I have piece of paper. She has pencil.*)	Definite articles can be omitted (*I have piece of paper. She has pencil*).
No use of **definite article** for generalization (*Eating vegetables is healthful for people*).	Use of definite article for generalization (*Eating the vegetables is healthful for the people*).		Use of definite article for generalization (*Eating the vegetables is healthful for the people*).	Use of definite article for generalization (*Eating the vegetables is healthful for the people*).
No use of **definite articles** with a profession (*Doctor Sanchez is at the hospital*).	Optional use of definite articles with a profession (*The Doctor Sanchez is at the hospital*).		Optional use of definite articles with a profession (*The Doctor Sanchez is at the hospital*).	Optional use of definite articles with a profession (*The Doctor Sanchez is at the hospital*).
No use of **definite articles** with months, sometimes not used with places (*We will go in May. She is in bed*).	Use of definite article with months, sometimes not used with places. (*We will go in the May. She is in the bed.*)		Use of definite article with months, sometimes not used with places. (*We will go in the May. She is in the bed.*)	

English Grammar	Korean	Cantonese	Mandarin	Farsi	Arabic
PREPOSITIONS					
Use of prepositions (*The movie is on the DVD*).					
CONJUNCTIONS					
Only one conjunction is needed (*Although, I know her, I don't know what she likes. OR I know her but I don't know what she likes*).		Conjunctions occur in pairs (*Although, I know her but I don't know what she likes*).	Conjunctions occur in pairs (*Although, I know her but I don't know what she likes*).		Coordination favored over subordination (frequent use of and and so).
ARTICLES					
Use of articles.		Use of articles to be very clear and definite.	Use of articles to be very clear and definite.	No use of articles.	
Use of **indefinite articles** (*I bought an orange. Do they go to a market for groceries?*)	No use of indefinite articles (*I bought one orange. Do they go to market for groceries?*) Depends on the context.	No use of indefinite articles (*I bought one orange at the store. Do they go to one market for groceries?*)	No use of indefinite articles (*I bought one orange at the store. Do they go to one market for groceries?*)		No use of indefinite articles (*I bought one orange. Do they go to market for groceries?*)
Use of **indefinite articles** before a profession (*She is a brilliant scientist. He is an electrician*).	No use of indefinite articles before a profession (*She is brilliant scientist. He is electrician*).	No use of indefinite articles before a profession (*She is brilliant scientist. He is electrician*).	No use of indefinite articles before a profession (*She is brilliant scientist. He is electrician*).	No use of indefinite articles before a profession (*She is brilliant scientist. He is electrician*).	No use of indefinite articles before a profession (*She is brilliant scientist. He is electrician*).
Consistent use of **definite articles** (*I have the piece of paper. She has a pencil*).		Definite articles can be omitted (*I have piece of paper. She has pencil*).	Definite articles can be omitted (*I have piece of paper. She has pencil*).		
No use of **definite article** for generalization (*Eating vegetables is healthful for people*).					
No use of **definite articles** with a profession (*Doctor Sanchez is at the hospital*).				Optional use of definite articles with a profession (*The Doctor Sanchez is at the hospital*).	The definite article is used with names of professions before a proper noun (*The Doctor Sanchez is at the hospital*).
No use of **definite articles** with months, sometimes not used with places (*We will go in May. She is in bed*).					Use of definite article with days, months, places, idioms (*We will go in the May. She is in the bed*).

Vocabulary with Spanish Cognates or Translations

Unit	Week	Type	Vocabulary Word	Spanish Cognates or Translations
1	1	D	delegates	delegados(as) (los, las)
1	1	D	federal	federal
1	1	D	ordain	decretar
1	1	D	consent	consentimiento (el)
1	1	D	disenfranchisement	inhabilitación (la)
2	2	D	fresh-water fish	pez de agua dulce (el)
2	2	D	channel	canal (el)
2	2	D	quicksilver	azogue (el)
3	1	D	root	raíz (la)
3	1	D	carbon emissions	emisiones de carbono (las)
3	1	D	ethanol	etanol (el)
3	1	D	glucose	glucosa (la)
3	1	D	photosynthesis	fotosíntesis (la)
3	2	D	Three Sisters	Las Tres Siembras Principales (calabaza, maíz y frijoles)
3	2	D	industrialization	industrialización (la)
3	2	D	monoculture	monocultivo (el)
3	3	D	argonomists	agrónomos(as) (los, las)
3	3	D	biodegradeable	biodegradable
3	3	D	fallow	en barbecho
5	1	D	gearing	mecanismo (el)
5	1	D	loom	telar (el)
5	1	D	boll	baga (la)
5	3	D	gin	gin (el)
5	3	D	assembly line	[asssembly] línea (la)
5	3	D	blast furnace	alto horno (el)
5	3	D	power loom	telar mecánico (el)
5	3	D	water wheel	molino de agua (el)

Unit	Week	Type	Vocabulary Word	Spanish Cognates or Translations
7	1	D	erosion	erosión (la)
7	1	D	abolitionists	abolicionistas (los)
7	1	D	revolution	revolución (la)
8	1	D	confederacy	confederación (la)
8	1	D	horticulture	horticultura (la)
8	1	D	xeriscaping	xerojardinería (la)
8	3	D	solar system	sistema solar
8	3	D	acidic	ácido(a)
8	3	D	alkaline	alcalino(a)
9	1	D	tribes	tribus (las)
9	1	D	civilization	civilización (la)
9	1	D	hub	buje (el)
9	1	D	incorporated	incorporado(a) (incorporar)
9	3	D	economic boom	[boom] económico
9	3	D	entrepreneurs	empresarios (los, las)
9	3	D	photo voltaic	fotovoltaico(a)
10	1	D	axle	eje de rueda (el)
10	1	D	inclined plane	plano inclinado (el)
10	1	D	lever	palanca (la)
10	1	D	pulley	polea (la)
10	1	D	screw	tornillo (el)
10	1	D	wedge	cuña (la)
10	2	D	force	fuerza (la)
10	2	D	fulcrum	fulcro (el)
10	2	D	winch	manija (la)
10	3	D	schematic	esquemático(a)
10	3	D	contraption	dispositivo (el)
10	3	D	perpetual motion	[motion] perpetuo

D = Domain-Specific